When the Railroad Leaves Town

WHEN THE Railroad LEAVES TOWN

AMERICAN COMMUNITIES IN THE AGE OF RAIL LINE ABANDONMENT

WESTERN UNITED STATES

JOSEPH P. SCHWIETERMAN

Foreword by John R. Stilgoe

TRUMAN STATE UNIVERSITY PRESS

Published 2004 by Truman State University Press, Kirksville, Missouri 63501
tsup.truman.edu

Front cover photo: Abandonment is only a few years away for the "Slim Princess"—Southern Pacific's narrow-gauge line in eastern California. In this classic 1953 scene, the southbound mixed train heads through the Owens Valley, south of Laws. The snow-capped elevations of the Sierra Nevada loom in the distance (Wendell Mortimer, Jr., courtesy of Mallory Hope Ferrell).

Back cover photo: The tracks are gone and little more than the crumbing abutments of an old water tower remain along the Southern Pacific narrow-gauge. This photograph was taken at nearly the same location as the one appearing on the front cover (James N. Saylor).

Cover design: Teresa Wheeler
Interior design: Winston Vanderhoof
Body type: Centaur; display type: Univers
Printed by: Thomson-Shore, Dexter, Michigan USA

Library of Congress Cataloging-in-Publication Data (applied for)

Schwieterman, Joseph P.
    When the railroad leaves town : American communities in the age of rail line abandon-
  ment, v. 2 / Joseph P. Schwieterman.
       p.   cm.
    Includes bibliographical references and index.
    ISBN 1-931112-13-4 (cloth : alk. paper) — ISBN 1-931112-14-2 (pbk. : alk. paper)
    1. Railroads—United States—History. 2. Railroads—Abandonment—United States. I.
  Title.

    TF23 .S35 2001
    385'.0973—dc21   00-054505

CONTENTS

CONTENTS

FOREWORD

Imagine the interstate highway grown quiet, its broad pavement cracked, buried in weeds, and traversed by one or two vehicles a week. Abandoned by automobiles and buses, the derelict roadway carries only the rare eighteen-wheel truck creeping along at 15 miles an hour. Gleaming green signs, mowed shoulders, and painted bridges shimmer in some distant past almost impossible to discern; these roadside accessories stand rusted, if they stand at all. Hunters and hikers walk in the linear forest that replaced the grassy shoulders long ago. The scenario is difficult to imagine, but decades ago many Americans faced a nearly identical one as railroad abandonment transformed the landscape and culture of many communities.

If the interstate highway system did shrivel, then disappear, what of the interchange businesses once dependent on it? Gas stations, truck stops, fast-food restaurants, and motels all depend on a steady flow of traffic along both the great highway and the state or county road crossing it at right angles. These businesses employ people who live nearby, and the people in turn need services, from doctors and teachers to plumbers and house painters. Do the people move away, abandoning their homes and businesses, or do they adjust and prosper, or at least endure?

In so many communities across the United States, a casual stroll brings the thoughtful observer in contact with remnants of railroad corridors. Here and there, the walker finds parallel steel rails embedded in the asphalt of a rarely used road, an old depot used to shelter grain or law offices, or a ribbon of gravel and crushed-rock ballast winding behind warehouses, feed mills, and the new discount department store at the edge of town.

Long ago passenger and freight trains arrived in clouds of steam and glamour. When rails formed the only regularly used long-distance connection between towns, everyone understood that news and novelty arrived by train. The long-distance luxury express, the local passenger train linking adjacent towns, even the slow-moving freight train, all moved in a corridor shimmering with technological advancement and urbane allure. Electrically illuminated when small towns still burned kerosene, the passenger express swept urban passengers, newspapers, cuisine, and fashion past awestruck townspeople. The disjunction between metropolitan glamour and small-town and rural ordinariness made everyone conscious of the importance and seeming permanence of corridors now scarcely discernible to motorists.

Railroads served towns in many ways. Resort towns attracted railroads that ferried tourists, and mining camps drew railroads that lugged out ore. Logging railroads meandered toward logging camps, but the agricultural railroads tended to run ruler straight, punctuated by depots and grain elevators every 10 miles or so, the distance a farmer might move grain by wagon over poor roads. The railroad often preceded towns, and the railroad companies colonized the grasslands and plains with farm families from the American East and Europe. Some towns became cities, often because intersecting rail routes made them not only easily accessible, but also perfect centers of manufacturing. Long-distance travel meant following specific routes across the nation, moving from one community to another, each with its peculiar understanding of the trains that seemed national or regional in character.

From the 1960s onward, as the interstate highway system was completed, Americans have watched the nationwide mystery of railroad abandonment. Communities saw the disappearance of long-distance, fast passenger trains, then the vanishing of the local passenger trains, then the end of through freight trains. Imperceptibly, the railroad corridor grew seedy and unpainted, then weed-grown and neglected, then rarely visited by the local freight train passing through without stopping or pausing only to shift a car or two at some industry that still used the railroad. Railroad abandonment is a national issue, but its real-world ramifications are fundamentally local and extraordinarily varied.

A peripatetic scholar created the book that follows. Only someone who realizes that open-air research in the backstreets of America must complement the data in government and industry reports produces a book as valuable as this. United States communities, especially those west of the Mississippi River, demand more than a cursory look at how they function today, for their histories are diverse and complex. Such detailed research produces not only a far richer understanding of the past of any community, but also provides glimpses of how any community might prosper in the future.

It is difficult to imagine the interstate highway system so long abandoned as to be difficult to locate in larger landscape—once the railroad seemed as permanent. But the railroad did leave town, and the chapters that follow analyze the impact of its departure, opening larger issues of how Americans view change and permanence, all the while evoking the lingering echo of the locomotive whistle.

John R. Stilgoe
Harvard University

ACKNOWLEDGMENTS

This manuscript would not have been possible without the assistance of those listed below, many of whom reviewed drafts of written materials and provided extensive historical information.

Alaska *Nome* Howard Clifford; Cornelius W. Hauck; Cussy Kauer; Lisa Reddaway; Charles Reader.

Arizona *Prescott* Marc Pearsall; Nancy Burgess; R. L. Knoll; John W. Sayre; Sharlot Hall Museum. *Tombstone* Art Austin, Tombstone Courthouse State Historical Park; Vernon Glover; David F. Myrick; Marc Pearsall.

Arkansas *Booneville* Bill Pollard; Steve Allen Goen; Clifton Hull; Dean Remy; Gary Stanford; Max Carter. *Eureka Springs* Eureka Springs Historical Museum; Bill Pollard; Edward Toole.

California *Beverly Hills* Jim Walker, Los Angeles County Metropolitan Transportation Authority Library; Russ C. Davies; Carol Inge. *Coronado* Page Harrington, Coronado Historical Association; Larry Rose, Pacific Southwest Railroad Museum; Jim Walker. *Folsom* Bill Anderson; Robert L. Minshew; El Dorado and Sacramento Historical Railroad Association; Wendell Huffman. *Glenwood* Martin Rice; Jon Pullman Porter; Steve Fischer, Santa Clara Valley Transportation Authority. *Laws* Jim Saylor, Laws Railroad Museum; Jim Walker; Dudley Westler. *Monterey* James B. Toy; Patrice Goodchild; Dave Hambleton; Monterey County Historical Society; Jon Porter. *Newport Beach* Steven E. Donaldson; Patrick Alford; William Hendricks, Sherman Library and Gardens; Greg Smith. *Placerville* Douglas Noble; E. Keith Berry, El Dorado Western Railway Foundation; Mary Cory, El Dorado County Historical Museum; Wendell Huffman. *San Rafael* Fred Codoni and Allen Tacy, Northwestern Pacific Railroad Historical Society; Joslyn Moss, Marin County Historical Museum; Maurice Palumbo; Steve Petterle. *Santa Monica* Russ C. Davies; Louise Gabriel; Bill Moran; Jim Walker, LAMTA Library. *Sausalito* Fred Codoni, Northwestern Pacific Railroad Historical Society; Phil Frank, Sausalito Historical Society. *Vacaville* Dudley Westler; Ronald H. Limbaugh; Michael R. Palumbo; Vacaville Museum, A Center for Solano County History.

Colorado *Aspen* Stan Clausen; Kenton Forrest; Wheeler/Stallard House Museum. *Cripple Creek* Mel McFarland; Kip Peterson. *Gunnison* Richard L. Dorman; Dwayne Vandenbush, Western State College; Vernon Glover. *Lakewood* Kenton Forrest, Colorado Railroad Museum; Lakewood's Heritage Center.

Hawaii *Honolulu* MacKinnon Simpson; Robert Paoa; Hawaiian Railway Society.

Idaho *Avery* Wade Bilbrey; Kurt E. Armbruster; Rocky Gibbs, MilWest. *Wallace* John Amonson, Wallace Mining Museum; Robert Dunsmore.

Illinois *Carpentersville* William C. Bartels, Dundee Historical and Genealogical Society; Paul L. Behrens; Mark Llanuza; Don MacBean, Fox River Trolley Museum.

Iowa *Decorah* Don Wurtzel; Stan Jeffers; Gilmer J. Seegmiller. *West Branch* Edward Bonner; Bruce Hoffman; Dwight Miller and Timothy Walch, Herbert Hoover Presidential Library; Kenneth "Chief" Thomas.

Kansas *Valley Falls* Clarke Davis; William A. Gibson, Sr.; Tom Ryan; Arthur R. Strawn; I. E. Quastler.

Louisiana *Ferriday* Louis R. Saillard; Judith Bingham, Delta Music Museum; Albert A. Forrester; Amanda Taylor; Michael Palmieri.

Minnesota *Currie* Louis Gervais, David J. Hansen, and Dorothy Rupport, End-O-Line Museum; George W. McKinney. *Ely* Mike Hillman; Steve Glischinski; Leighton Hudson; Missabe Railroad Historical Society; Judy Swenson, Ely-Winton Historical Society.

Montana *Harlowton* Rocky Gibbs, MilWest; Steve McCarter; Jerry Miller. *Red Lodge* William R. Taylor; Jayce M. Taylor; Joel Bertolino and Penny Redli, Peaks to Plains Museum; Warren R. McGee; Shirley Zupan.

Nebraska *Long Pine* Bill Kratville; Rob Coupland; Wardene Roark, Long Pine Heritage Society.

Nevada *Boulder City* Dennis McBride; Boulder City Museum and Historical Association; Greg Corbin,

Boulder City Railroad Museum; Shirl R. Naegle. *Carson City* Kyle Williams Wyatt, California State Railroad Museum; John Ballweber, Nevada State Railroad Museum; Northern Nevada Railroad Foundation. *Virginia City* Kyle Williams Wyatt, California State Railroad Museum; Judie Fischer-Crowley, Northern Nevada Railroad Foundation.

New Mexico *Española* Vernon Glover; John Ashcraft; Frederick S. Friedman. *Farmington* Catherine Davis; Farmington Museum; Frederick S. Friedman; Vernon Glover; Michael Quinn Heavener; Joseph A. Schmitz, City of Farmington.

North Dakota *Watford City* Max Ulver, Great Northern Railway Historical Society; Ron Broderson; John Mielke; Francis Olson; Bill Shemorry; Ray Trumpower.

Oklahoma *Okemah* Keith L. Bryant, Jr.; Virginia Dill; Martha G. Merideth; Kathryn Ward, Okfuskee County Historical Society.

Oregon *Astoria* Kent Dahlgren, Spokane; Portland and Seattle Railway Historical Society; Duane Cramer; Martin Adams, Astoria Railroad Restoration Association; Harold Gjerman; Rosemary Johnson; William R. (Mitch) Mitchum, City of Astoria; Al Simenson. *Burns* Judge Dale White; Jeff Asay; Diana Jackson, Harney County Historical Museum; Thornton Waite. *Seaside* Kent Dahlgren; Phyllis Hamlin, Seaside Museum and Historical Society; Harold Gjerman.

South Dakota *Hot Springs* Rick Mills; Everett T. Gillis; Helen Magee; Bob Chisholm.

Texas *Fredericksburg* Lester Haines; Janet Harris, Fredericksburg Public Library; Mark Wieser. *Kerrville* Lester Haines; Paul Barwick; Carl R. Condney; Hill Country Museum; E. C. Parker, Jr. *Mineral Wells* Lester Haines; Bill Bennett; City of Mineral Wells; Susan O'Neil, Mineral Wells Historical Society; A. F. Weaver.

Utah *Park City* Sandra Morrison, Park City Historical Society; Caine Alder; Don Strack. *Promontory* Wendell Huffman; Rick Wilson, Golden Spike Historical Site; Delone Bradford-Glover and Richard E. Felt, Golden Spike Association; John J. Stewart.

Washington *Bothell* Eric Erickson; Kurt E. Armbruster; Jim Frederickson; M. Sue Kienast and Jeanette Backstrom, Bothell Historical Museum; Barbara J. Grace; Rick Leach; George Werkema. *Issaquah* Eric Erickson and Erica Maniez, Issaquah Historical Society; Thomas P. Strand; Dick Welsh. *Lynnwood* Marie Little, Alderwood Manor Heritage Association; Kathy Johnson; City of Lynnwood; Warren W. Wing; Frederick Bird. *Port Angeles* Dona R. Cloud, Clatham County Historical Society; Scott Brodhun; John Illman.

Wisconsin *Lake Geneva* Paul L. Behrens; Stanley Brandt; Bill Lovell. *Platteville* Gregg Condon; Stephanie Saager-Bourret, Mining Museum and Rollo Jamison Museum; Richard Brockman. *Sturgeon Bay* Stanley Brandt; Ann Jinkins, Door County Museum; Roger Schroader; Paul Spanbauer.

Wyoming *Riverton* Loren Jost, Riverton Museum; Bob Peck; Rick Mills.

I also thank Robert Lange and Renee Michaels for their editorial assistance, Seth Bramson and Stan Brandt for their historical guidance, Richard Longoria and Judy Sharp for their cartographic assistance, many graduate students at DePaul University, and members of various chapters of the National Railway Historical Society and Railway & Locomotive Historical Society not included on the above list. The company heralds for many Class I railroads appearing in this volume are provided courtesy of Benamin Coifman and www.railfonts.com.

Any opinions expressed in this document, or any errors that remain, are solely the responsibility of the author.

INTRODUCTION

The history of the American West is an epic tale richly accompanied by the sounds of the railroads. From the thunderous roar of steam locomotives to the rhythmic churning of wheels on track, these sounds are the background beat to an extraordinary saga of technological innovation and engineering achievement. For shrewd businessmen assembling far-flung transportation systems, they were a cadence of opportunity and enterprise.

Despite all its glory and all the miles it tamed, this saga could not in the end triumph over changing times in many western towns. Thousand of miles of railroad routes steeped in history are now dusty trails bereft of their former significance. Rendered expendable by evolving market forces, these bygone corridors are testaments to the profound changes in the way we travel and conduct business.

Through the use of maps, photographs, and historical perspective, *When the Railroad Leaves Town* tries to illustrate the circumstances surrounding the rise and fall of rail service in places that are distinguished for their illustrious railroad histories or for their unusual experiences with rail line abandonment. The experiences of these towns demonstrate how rail line abandonment can be the culmination of a process dating back many years and can bring unexpected and enduring consequences. What emerges is a portrait of an industrial shift that has left an indelible mark on the region's social, economic, and physical landscape.

Featured in this book are fifty-eight communities on the Pacific side of that imaginary line that divides the eastern and western halves of the American rail network and that stretches from Chicago to Peoria, south to St. Louis, and down the Mississippi River to New Orleans.

A wooden culvert slowly rots along a now-abandoned portion of the country's first transcontinental railroad near Corrine, Utah. (Photo by author.)

These communities vary greatly in population, ranging in size from Honolulu, Hawaii, which has more than 800,000 residents, to Promontory, Utah, which today is home to only a park ranger. Representing great geographical diversity, the communities extend as far north as Nome, Alaska, and as far south as Kerrville, Texas.

Although separated in many instances by thousands of miles, all these places once contributed to the colorful mosaic of western railroading. Some communities were important terminals or division points on steam railroads, while others were thriving hubs for electric interurban railways. Several derived much of their prosperity from logging railways reaching deep into the hinterland. A few towns heard only the whistles of trains operating on obscure branch lines before feeling the effects of abandonment issues germinating many miles away.

The incidents highlighted in this volume illustrate how communities not only grew up around rail lines but also came to depend on them for employment, industrial expansion, and municipal leadership. The essence of the railroad remains part of the fabric of a community many years after the last train departs.

The Abandonment Saga

Readers familiar with the history of rail line abandonment recognize that this volume considers only some of the more noteworthy places that today are separated from the rail system. Since 1916, the nation's railroads have abandoned roughly 125,000 miles of routes—nearly half of the total system. When the lines eliminated by streetcar companies and electric interurban railways are added to the total, there is enough abandoned mileage to build at least forty railroads from the east coast to the west coast of the United States.

Although there has been no definitive estimate made of the number of towns across America that have lost their rail service, the diminishing size of the *Official Guide of the Railways* offers insight on the total. The number of the cities, towns, junctions, and other places listed in the index of this publication, excluding Canadian and Latin American points, declined from about 75,500 in 1916 to about 53,000 in 1957, and then to about 34,000 in 2004.[1] The number of communities losing their rail service appears to have exceeded 25,000.

The bygone transportation corridors that crisscrossed the country hold a deep fascination for many people with an interest in the changing Americana—of

whom I am certainly one. For the past twelve years, I have tried to systematically investigate the withdrawal of railroads from American communities. My efforts began with the collection of data for 1,900 communities that currently do not have any rail freight or rail passenger service. As the project advanced, I found myself in touch with growing numbers of planning officials and historians while making visits—and in most instances repeat visits—to the communities featured in this book.

From the exercise, it became quite clear that, contrary to the prevailing view that abandonment has eliminated predominantly redundant lines, this phenomenon has left many places with large populations bereft of all rail transportation. In fact, a number of the places in question have populations of more than 80,000; some even have economies large enough to support commercial air service.

The collection of this information also showed that the closing of railroads was significant to communities in ways that have not been adequately documented in other works. Although the amount of local traffic handled by the railroad had often dwindled to almost nothing, the abandonment of lines still had a tendency to elicit a sharp municipal response. In some instances, municipal governments, local chambers of commerce, and businesses took extraordinary steps to keep trains running.

To commemorate the departure of the last train, citizens in some communities assembled at the depot and took part in ceremonies extolling the railroad's historical contributions. Railroad enthusiasts came from considerable distances to capture on film the images of the last train working its way down the rails; newspapers often deemed the event worthy of a front-page news article. To mark their final run, locomotives and trolley cars were occasionally festooned with signs and flowers.

In other communities, the scene unrolled in a more prosaic fashion. Freight trains crept over the tracks with a string of empty cars, barely noticed by those living nearby. The railroad era often ended without fanfare, earning little more than a passing glance from residents who happened to be in the track's vicinity. Within a few weeks, a salvage crew would arrive to pull up the rails and draw to a close that chapter of the town's history.

Abandonment, of course, was rarely the end of the story. Some communities soon found their abandoned rights-of-way the source of disagreement—accompanied by either threatened or actual litigation—as various parties sparred over issues related to land ownership and re-use. In many places, the withdrawal of the railroad forced community leaders to come to terms with the

Flowers bloom on a high embankment supporting a steel trestle at Long Pine, Nebraska—a magnificent span once part of the Chicago & North Western "Cowboy Line." (Photo by author.)

industrial or technological changes that threatened to separate their town from the flow of commerce—a phenomenon that made the term "abandonment" applicable to much more than the loss of the train. For other towns, the closing of the railroad was a springboard to municipal improvement. In many such places, it freed up large swaths of land for economic development, highway projects, or new outdoor amenities.

The emotional impact of the closing of rail lines in small communities is a poignant, largely undocumented, part of the American railroad saga. For older residents, the loss can be a sad and unwelcome reminder of the ways in which everyday life has changed. Among both young and old, it can elicit nostalgic sentiment about the excitement and romance associated with travel years ago. Or it can rekindle fond childhood memories of watching trains pass, waving to engineers, and hearing the echoing sounds of locomotive whistles. In some communities, the railroad's withdrawal was the impetus for the creation of historical societies, museums, and tourist railways.

Even for those who do not have a personal connection to trains, the sight of abandoned railroad corridors in the process of being reclaimed by weeds and trees often stirs profound reactions. Evoking images of the powerful market forces that pushed once mighty transportation companies toward oblivion, these routes are reminders of how the work of entire generations can be discarded with the advent of new technology or business practices. Where once these routes hummed with the sounds of steam power and commerce, now they elicit mere whispers of an industrial saga that brought prosperity to past generations but remains little known to many in contemporary times.

The Orientation of This Volume

Like those community sketches in the companion volume devoted to the eastern United States, the descriptions appearing in this book have been prepared with cooperation from many local historians and railroad enthusiasts. Representing collaborative efforts, they draw upon the knowledge and insights of people who have studied or experienced the decline of rail service in various towns; some of these individuals have written extensively on the topic, while others have shared their knowledge through less formal means.

Readers will notice several notable differences between this volume and the companion volume devoted to the eastern United States. The aura of the Wild West, where legend and exaggeration prevail, is clearly felt in these chapters. Generally tending to play larger and more prominent roles in American history, many of the communities featured here are today notable tourist destinations, renowned for their pioneering role on the seemingly limitless frontier.

Great mining booms, the lumber industry, and the challenges posed by rugged terrain become familiar elements to the stories in this volume. Not surprisingly, private industrial railways, such as lumber and mining operators, are more common in the chapters that follow than in the earlier volume. On the other hand, electric interurban railways and streetcar companies, as well as the efforts to serve heavy industry—especially those involving the fabrication of iron, steel, and textile products—receive less attention in these towns.

In all their variety, these communities show why bygone rail lines have had the capacity to inspire historians and railroad enthusiasts to spend years accumulating artifacts, information, and photographs. Several communities are the focus of books that have become classics in the transportation field; others are the focus of excellent technical articles. To draw attention to the most notable of those works, suggested readings are offered at the end of each section with special emphasis given to the publications of railroad historical societies.

For a more general account of the changing railroad scene in the West, readers are encouraged to consult historical works by Gerald M. Best, H. Roger Grant, Donovan L. Hofsommer, George W. Hilton, David Myrick, Fred A. Stindt, and many others listed in the reference section. For an informal perspective of the market forces that led to the abandonment of rail lines through the twentieth century, readers may wish to consult the background chapter of the eastern United States volume.

As a striking manifestation of a phenomenon described by economist Joseph Schumpeter many years ago as "creative destruction," abandoned rail lines underscore the profound effects of new transportation technologies on our communities and our lives. If we stop and view the landscape that has emerged from this transformation, we find trails of ballast, embankments overgrown with weeds, telephone poles marching wireless to the horizon, and viaducts crumbling from erosion. All are poignant reminders of the changing American scene.

ENDNOTE

1. Estimates are derived from reviewing the June 1916, July 1957, and January 2004 editions of the *Official Guide of the Railways*. This approach slightly overstates the number of communities with rail service in 2004 due to the growing propensity for some railroads to list in the index certain places they do not directly serve.

ABANDONED CORRIDORS—
A NATIONAL PERSPECTIVE

In the late nineteeth century, conventional wisdom was that every town needed a train. If a railroad did not come to a town, a town often moved to a railroad. While bringing the benefits of faster and less expensive transportation to the vast continent, railroads built depots, sold off land to entrepreneurs and farmers, and shaped thousands of communities that grew along their rights-of-way. All of this raises the question: In an age when railroads have declined in importance, what happens when the last train leaves town?

This chapter offers an informal analysis of how the reduction of the rail network has affected the access of small- and medium-sized communities to rail transportation in the continental United States.[1] Drawing upon data collected about the loss of rail access to incorporated communities with a population of 3,000 or more in both the eastern and western United States, the chapter offers perspective on the evolving public response to the abandonment of railroads. For a community to be classified as having rail service, it must have an active right-of-way within its incorporated boundaries capable of handling conventional freight or passenger trains on an intercity route.

Historical Perspectives on Abandonment

Abandoned rail lines have been part of the American landscape almost since the industry's earliest days. Even in the middle of the nineteenth century, numerous railroads succumbed to market forces and left behind corridors that slowly withered away. Overall, however, the expansion of new railroads and routes vastly outpaced the number of lines abandoned. Between 1880 and 1900, the number of miles of routes rose from 92,147 to 193,346. In 1916, the railroad system reached its peak of 254,251 route-miles.[2]

When truck transport as well as bus and automobile travel escalated after World War I, the miles of rail line abandoned began to significantly exceed the miles of new rail construction. Thousands of miles of routes that had never been more than marginally profitable were relegated to scrap. By the late 1920s, the spread of paved highways and major improvements in automotive technology brought motor transportation even to remote areas, threatening the survival of railroad companies that had been financially strong only a decade or two before.

Despite the inroads made by more flexible forms of transportation, most towns with more than a handful of businesses could still scarcely imagine life without a railroad. Few communities with more than several hundred residents had lost all of their rail access by the late 1920s. Many towns that lost rail service were worked-out mining and lumber areas or communities on routes that lacked connections to the remainder of the U.S. rail system. When the Colorado Midland Railway ended service in 1918, it was one of the first carriers with several hundred miles of track to meet its demise; nevertheless, it left no on-line community of 500 or more residents without access to the rail system.[3]

The continuing demand for rail service in rural areas encouraged railroads to invest in the upkeep of a vast network of existing branches and even build new ones through certain sparsely populated regions. In other locales, the rulings of the Interstate Commerce Commission (ICC) assured that railroad companies would maintain at least minimal levels of service. The ICC, which had been empowered to oversee the abandonment process through the Transportation Act of 1920, initially adopted a relatively permissive stance toward abandonment. Over time, however, the agency became more assertive in denials of abandonment petitions until, ultimately, it came to be seen as a significant barrier to the elimination of unprofitable routes, especially when shippers lacked access to other rail lines.

Although municipal leaders considered preserving rail service a matter of the utmost importance during the Roaring Twenties, few actually had reason to worry about their railroad connections at the time. With businesses and public officials strongly opposed to the outright removal of track, railroads shied away from the abandonment of lines, instead preferring service cutbacks or the sale of a marginal line to another railroad.

Most communities losing rail service during the 1920s were victims of small railroad bankruptcies and liquidations rather than of large (Class I) carriers shedding unprofitable lines. With few exceptions (such as

Remnants of the Pacific Electric along Santa Monica Boulevard in Los Angeles bear silent testimony to "the largest electric interurban system in the world." (Photo by author.)

Half Moon Bay, California; Perryville, Missouri; and Roswell, Georgia), virtually all of these communities had populations of fewer than 1,000 and possessed decidedly modest railroad facilities. The vast majority of these towns had little heavy industry and were located in close proximity to other routes.

The loss of rail service was nevertheless a traumatic event for communities left without good transportation alternatives. The newspaper in Perryville, Missouri, a town of 3,050 people, warned in 1920 that the loss would lead to "chaos if not ruin."[4] As early as 1926, at least one town with more than 1,000 inhabitants suffered the loss of both its electric interurban and steam railroad routes, dashing its hopes for industrial expansion.[5]

The Great Depression hampered industrial production, reduced consumer spending, and accelerated interest in the construction of hard-surface roads to stimulate economic development. In most small towns, these developments had a profound effect on the dynamics of local transportation. Railroad revenues in rural communities dropped at an alarming rate, delivering a fatal blow to dozens of short lines and rendering some of the branch lines of many larger carriers woefully unproductive. In 1932, the mileage abandoned in a single year exceeded 1,000 for the first time.

A few communities affected by the Depression-era abandonments are deeply etched into railroad lore. In 1934, service ended on the Chicago, Burlington & Quincy Railroad's famed High Line to Spearfish, South Dakota (population: 2,139), leaving this prominent mining town without rail access. On September 2, 1935, Henry Flagler's "oversea railroad" (106 miles) that linked Key West to the mainland was the victim of a Labor Day hurricane that made Key West (13,000 permanent inhabitants) the largest community to lose its link with the national rail system.[6] Also in 1935, the Florida East Coast Railway abandoned its 2-mile spur to Palm Beach, a famous resort town with a permanent population of about 1,800.

With the construction of hard-surface roads, many communities softened their stance on the necessity of having an active rail line, especially when it came to passenger service.

This attitudinal shift was especially pervasive in eastern and midwestern towns served only by electric interurban railways. As passenger boardings on the interurban railways plummeted, hundreds of places in the American heartland lost all their rail connections. By the end of the 1930s, the closing of interurbans and streetcar lines left at least four communities in Ohio (Bexley, Mt. Healthy, North Olmstead, and Reynoldsburg), two in Michigan (St. Clair Shores and Troy), and one in Wisconsin (Whitefish Bay), each with more than 2,000 residents, without any rail service.

From beneath the surface of the Snake River, rails formerly part of the Seward Peninsula Railroad point the way toward the historic gold-mining fields north of Nome, Alaska. (Photo by author.)

The absence of a concerted civic response to the abandonment of interurban rail lines in towns without access to other rail lines spoke volumes about the changing times. In some places, municipal governments were glad to see these railways go—an attitude manifested in the refusal of town councils to renew ordinances allowing these operators to maintain tracks in city streets due to concerns over traffic congestion. In 1939, when the last streetcar rolled out of Miami Beach, Florida—a community with 28,000 inhabitants but little traditional industry—officials heralded the occasion as an important step in modernizing the local transportation system, despite the fact that for the next thirty years this resort town would apparently be the largest community on the American mainland without an active rail route.[7]

Steam railroads, of course, were still vital to the overwhelming majority of communities of this size. In fact, with the exception of communities served exclusively by interurban and streetcar lines, most locales with more than 2,000 or 3,000 people during the late 1930s still had several railroad lines. Remarkably few communities of this size lost their rail connections prior to the start of World War II. In most instances, the abandonment of lines merely left towns with fewer active railroads rather than no railroad at all. The 1939 demise of the 250-mile Fort Smith & Western Railway, for example, left only one community with more than 1,000 residents—Okemah, Oklahoma—with no rail service.

To be sure, the loss of passenger service was pervasive at that time. By the late 1930s, many communities with populations over 5,000 had witnessed the departure of their last passenger train. (Three of these communities, Bristol and Coventry, Rhode Island, and Farmington, New Mexico, are discussed in this volume or the companion volume I of *When the Railroad Leaves Town*). Between 1916 and 1938, the number of locations in the United States with passenger service listed in the *Official Guide of the Railways* dropped from about 75,000 to 61,500.[8]

The spectacular rise in freight and passenger traffic during World War II rejuvenated the nation's railroad sector, but did little to ensure that trains would continue running on the dwindling network of narrow-gauge routes. Although the abandonment of these lines had once left mostly tiny hamlets without rail service, it now began to affect communities with appreciable populations. In 1940, the fondly remembered "Tweetsie," a mixed train steeped in Appalachian narrow-gauge history, made its final arrival into Boone, North Carolina, a community of

With its last run only six days away, the Del Monte—the longest continuously operating "name" train on the Southern Pacific—has just left Monterey, California, and is rolling through Seaside on April 24, 1971. This fondly remembered streamliner typically departed on its 126-mile journey to San Francisco with just three cars, including a parlor-snack-lounge car, but on this sunny morning it boasts five. These tracks have lain dormant since the early 1990s. (Photo by Dudley Westler.)

The strong demand for scrap materials during the war also rendered many communities on standard-gauge routes at risk of losing rail service. In 1940, the Erie Railroad ended service to Geneseo (population: 2,144) in upstate New York. In 1942, Fredericksburg, Texas, with about 3,500 residents, became one of the most populous communities in the central United States without a railroad when the Fredericksburg & Northern Railroad ended service. During that same year, the Northwestern Pacific Railroad abandoned service to San Anselmo (population: 5,790) in California's Marin County.

Although the withdrawal of railroads from these communities foreshadowed abandonment patterns of the future, they would be merely footnotes in the saga of twentieth-century railroading. Remarkably, the elimination of tens of thousands of miles of steam and electric routes through 1949 separated few towns of appreciable size from the rail system. As late as 1950, fewer than 1 percent of all communities with more than 3,000 residents had lost their access to the rail system.

The Age of Abandonment

Robust agricultural harvests, the efficiencies provided by diesel locomotives, and a strong national economy allowed rail service to thousands of small communities to remain financially self-sufficient well into the postwar era. Nevertheless, as the years passed, the foundation for the local railroad network weakened. Revenues dropped due to the construction of interstate expressways, the expansion of trucking, the collapse of the residential anthracite coal business, and other developments, while operating costs—especially labor—continued to climb. By the late 1950s, the nation's railroad mileage was again falling at a brisk rate.

A more turbulent phase of rail line abandonment began with the liquidation of the 541-mile New York, Ontario & Western in 1957. As concerns arose about the loss of rail service to dozens of communities, members of the New York legislature attempted to rescue the debt-ridden mountain road. When these efforts ended unsuccessfully, five communities in New York State with populations of 2,000 or more (Delhi, Ellenville, Hamilton, Liberty, and Monticello), two of which had populations exceeding 5,000 (the largest being Monticello),

1,450 on the Linville River Railway. Española, New Mexico (population: 1,059), lost its service with the abandonment of the Denver & Rio Grande Western's "Chili Line" in 1941. In 1942, the Pacific Coast Railroad ended service to Arroyo Grande (population: 4,000) in southern California. The 21-mile Nevada County Narrow Gauge Railroad pulled up its spikes that same year, leaving Grass Valley (population: 5,701) and Nevada City (population: 2,445) in northeastern California without railroads. This appears to be the first time that the abandonment of a single route outside of a major metropolitan area left two communities, each with several thousand residents, without rail access.

were left without railroads. Never before had a single abandonment left so many communities of such size without rail access.

Concerns about rail line abandonment gradually spread throughout the country as other financially troubled roads, such as the Vermont-based Rutland Railway, petitioned for abandonment. By the late 1960s, numerous communities having populations exceeding 15,000 had lost their service—a phenomenon that would have seemed almost unimaginable forty years earlier. Among them were several towns holding a prominent place in American history, including Marblehead, Massachusetts, which lost its Boston & Maine service in 1962; Newport Beach, California, which lost its Pacific Electric service in 1965; Farmington, New Mexico, which saw its last Denver & Rio Grande Western narrow-gauge train in 1969; and Coronado, California, which bid farewell to the Southern Pacific in 1971. All of these communities had lost passenger service years before. Their experiences are described in this volume and in volume I of *When the Railroad Leaves Town.*

Several more state capitals were also left without active rail lines. Carson City, Nevada, had for many years been the only state capital on the American mainland without a railroad. Although railroad enthusiasts and town leaders lamented the departure of the last Virginia & Truckee Railway train in 1950, Carson City had only about 3,000 residents and little industry at the time. The loss of rail service to Annapolis, Maryland (population: 28,000), triggered a more vigorous governmental response. Local officials fought hard to restore service but ultimately lacked the necessary resources to repair the eastern end of the Baltimore & Annapolis Railroad—a short line badly damaged during Hurricane Agnes in 1972. All rail service in Hawaii ended during the early 1970s, making Honolulu the nation's largest city (and another state capital) without a railroad of any kind.

The cost and unpredictability of the ICC abandonment process was by now the only reason many small towns had direct access to railroads. Although the most populous communities losing rail service years before had been predominately on short lines or interurbans going out

of business, most of the largest communities at risk of losing service during the early 1970s were accessible only on Class I railroads. With the plight of these carriers evoking little sympathy among regulators and on-line communities, railroads found themselves saddled with routes that generated barely enough revenue to cover the costs of labor. Freight trains often crawled over tracks overgrown with grass and weeds until a cataclysmic event, such as a bridge failure, flood, or derailment, provided the justification needed for abandonment.

By 1972, approximately 300 communities that today have populations of 3,000 or more had lost their rail service.[9] In the East and Midwest, a veritable abandonment crisis loomed on the horizon as the Penn Central and other bankrupt roads hemorrhaged red ink, putting thousands of communities at risk of losing freight service. Municipal governments and local chambers of commerce exerted significant pressure on state and federal authorities to take steps to avert the wholesale abandonment of routes. As heavy industry scaled back and motor carrier service improved, the outlook for rail service to many towns appeared grim.

In the midst of rising fears about abandonment, Congress passed the Regional Railroad Reorganization (3-R) Act, in 1973, greatly elevating the federal government's role in railroad infrastructure management, and, in the process, giving the ICC the impetus to quietly

Along the former Southern Pacific Monterey Branch in Seaside, California, geese waddle where the Del Monte Express once rolled. (Photo by author.)

relax its abandonment standards. As plans moved forward to create the federally owned Consolidated Rail System (Conrail) from the holdings of the Penn Central and other bankrupt roads, many states developed far-reaching programs to avert the loss of rail service to communities. The federal effort to preserve lightly used routes reached another milestone upon the passage of the Railroad Revitalization and Regulatory Reform (4-R) Act during America's bicentennial year.[10]

The 4-R Act took effect as falling industrial production, rising property taxes, and a drastic fall in transportation rates (fueled by dramatic improvements in the productivity of trucking companies) pushed concerns about abandonment to the forefront of the transportation policy agenda. It allowed for greater public oversight over the divestment of routes, thus encouraging community leaders to develop contingency plans and, in some cases, marshal the resources to keep local trains running. With multitudes of railroad structures urgently needing replacement, and private investment capital almost nonexistent, an unprecedented number of small towns found themselves at risk of losing service, generating thousands of pages of governmental analysis and ICC testimony in the process. Service to hundreds of communities rested on government financial support, such as the federal Local Rail Service Assistance program (LRSA).

Despite an infusion of state and federal money, the number of municipalities without rail access climbed

sharply during the late 1970s. For some communities, service ended due to the limit imposed on the length of time operators could receive LRSA subsidies; in others, state governments opted to cut their losses and redirect their resources elsewhere. By the time Congress passed the Staggers Rail Act in the fall of 1980, nearly 400 communities with populations of 3,000 or more had lost service.

Impact of the Staggers Act

The federal initiatives of the 1970s, while shifting the parameters of the debate about rail line abandonment, were merely preludes to the changes precipitated by the Staggers Act—a landmark measure enacted in 1980 that freed the industry from a great deal of regulation and precipitated a massive restructuring of the rail system. Carriers developed ambitious plans to reduce their networks in response to mounting competition from trucks and other railroads and to developments unrelated to deregulation, such as a lingering national recession and consolidations and mergers approved in earlier decades. Although Staggers did not formally change the ICC's abandonment procedures, federal officials could plainly see that state governments were now closely monitoring rail infrastructure issues. As a result, the ICC loosened its grip on the abandonment process.

As railroads exercised the freedoms granted through the Staggers Act, abandonment started to strike at the core of the national railroad system. In the lower Great Lakes region, many communities lost their rail access as Conrail divested itself of unwanted parallel and secondary routes inherited from Penn Central. Throughout the Corn Belt and Great Plains, state governments found themselves overwhelmed by the concerns of communities affected by the sale and dismemberment of two bankrupt systems—the Chicago, Milwaukee, St. Paul & Pacific Railroad and the Chicago, Rock Island & Pacific Railroad—as well as by the divestments of more financially stable carriers. In 1982, the number of abandoned miles in one year reached a historic peak, surpassing 5,000 miles for the first time. In some agriculturally productive areas, entire counties were left without rail service.

Ultimately, federal, state, and local agencies had the resources to preserve only

Narrow-gauge tracks along the west coast of Oahu at Ko'Olina appear fit for service despite having lain dormant for many years. This segment, discarded by the U.S. Navy in the 1970s and now inoperable, survives as a National Historic Landmark. (Photo by author.)

a small share of the routes at risk of abandonment. By 1985, several hundred communities that had been served by two or more railroad companies fifteen years earlier had no rail service at all. Seven of these towns—Amherst, New York; Inverness, Florida; Vacaville, California; Crown Point, Indiana; South Haven, Michigan; Xenia, Ohio; and Platteville, Wisconsin—are featured in this volume or volume I of *When the Railroad Leaves Town*. By the early 1990s, at least twenty-three states had acquired railroad routes threatened with abandonment and leased them to short-line operators as a means of preserving service. Six states banked (that is, set aside for future use) disused routes with the tracks intact to facilitate the resumption of service. At least forty-six states developed comprehensive rail plans created in part to monitor the effects of railroad closures.

Former transportation assets relegated to scrap are ironically juxtaposed on a remnant of the Chicago, Rock Island & Pacific "Choctaw Route" in Booneville, Arkansas. (Photo by author.)

By the mid-1990s, railroads had withdrawn from more than 150 communities with populations exceeding 10,000 and from approximately sixty-eight with populations exceeding 20,000; several dozen of these communities are featured in this volume and its companion volume. Although the elimination of freight service in communities with populations approaching or exceeding 50,000 residents would have seemed highly improbable several generations before, it now occurred in many such communities, including Bethesda, Maryland, and Daly City, Vacaville, Santa Monica, and San Rafael, California. (Both Bethesda and Daly City were served by heavy-rail transit systems when local freight service ended.) Illustrative of the changing times, three cities on the American mainland with populations of more than 100,000—Lakewood, Colorado, and Pasadena and Santa Rosa, California—eventually lost their rail service as well. Pasadena had once been a station stop on the Santa Fe's Super Chief and El Capitan, as well as Amtrak's Southwest Chief.[11]

Concern about the adverse consequences of rail line abandonment diminished sharply by the mid-1990s. The tenor of public discourse changed due not only to the gradual decline of heavy industry but also to the growth of the service economy and the high-tech sector that left numerous towns without any apparent need for rail service. It became increasingly rare to hear local officials say that the closing of a railroad would cause a community's economy to dry up—a fear that had been commonly voiced twenty years earlier. The amount of paper generated by government agencies espousing public intervention to prevent abandonment diminished sharply. Class I carriers also helped ameliorate concern by transferring tens of thousands of miles of routes to newly created short line railroads. In some locales, the ability of short lines to provide more reliable service and operate at lower costs allowed for a modest traffic renaissance. In others, these carriers could do little to reverse a decline in tonnage that dated back to the era of steam locomotives.

Even though abandonment still met with stiff opposition in agricultural districts, many grain distribution points had been relocated—or could be relocated—to terminals along viable main lines. The rise in rail-truck intermodal services (including piggyback and containerized freight) also lessened the advantages of having direct access to a rail spur. Attention gradually shifted from abandonment's probable implications for existing shippers—who were often few in number—toward the potential consequences for future economic development, a more hypothetical concern that tended to attract less notice.

A deteriorating billboard promoting rail access in an industrial park in Manteno, Illinois, brings to mind the diminished status of railroads in small towns in the American Midwest. (Photo by author.)

With the highway system increasingly prone to congestion, some government agencies took an interest in preserving abandoned routes as potential paths for light-rail, mass transit, and other passenger services—a phenomenon virtually unheard of just a decade or two before.[12] Several communities that had lost all rail service, including Newburyport, Massachusetts, and Pasadena and Santee, California, saw their abandoned routes rebuilt to support the expansion of commuter-rail or light-rail systems. Old routes to Walnut Creek, California (former Sacramento Northern), and Vienna, Virginia (former Washington & Old Dominion), emerged as rapid-transit corridors.

A growing number of communities looked to abandoned railroads, typically in situations where the tracks were still in place, for their potential to transport tourists. A few, such as Astoria, Oregon, Cape May, New Jersey, and Saranac Lake, New York, reestablished (with considerable fanfare) their connections to the rail system for this purpose. The restoration of freight service to Ashland City, Tennessee, Myrtle Beach, South Carolina, and Wellsville, Pennsylvania, each after a long absence, showed that preserving routes for local commodity shipments could also pay dividends.

Public agencies came to the conclusion that the elimination of certain rail lines had potentially detrimental implications for the flow of freight and passenger traffic between major population centers. By 1996, at least forty corridors linking metropolitan areas with populations of 100,000 or more no longer had active railroad lines. As discussed in the appendix (see especially table 1), governments took steps to protect numerous rights-of-way, thus keeping their options open.

As main lines that had once been icons of efficiency devolved into lengthy trails of weeds and rust, a growing number of communities developed plans to use railroad-occupied land for nonrail purposes. Many towns eyed railroad property for retail strips and malls, industrial parks, residential home building, and recreational trails. Local officials in suburban areas often viewed abandonment as a positive rather than a negative development, especially where rail corridors flanked busy arterial roads. Increasingly, communities turned to a coercive process—adverse abandonment—to compel railroads to vacate land wanted for other forms of development.

The number of communities in the United States with populations of 3,000 or more that had lost rail service rose to about 800 in 1996 (see fig. 1) and to around 1,100 in 2004. By the late 1990s, some of the nation's most successful communities were without rail transportation.[13]

Hundreds of communities also sprouted up and prospered many miles from active rail lines. By 1996, there were more than 1,000 communities with 3,000 or more residents that had never had rail service (see fig. 2)—nearly 15 percent of all communities of this size. Since then, the number of highway-dependent communities of this type appears to have risen to at least 1,300, if not substantially more.[14]

Scottsdale, Arizona, with an estimated 203,000 residents, is at this writing the largest municipality on the American mainland without an active rail line. (Scottsdale historically never had rail service, but has been included in proposals for the construction of a light-rail system serving the metropolitan Phoenix area.) Other places, such as Moreno Valley, California (near Los Angeles), and Cape Coral, Florida (near Fort Myers), also have populations of more than 100,000 and are projected to continue growing. Although these communities have a suburban quality, a few places never served by rail, such as Bullhead City, Arizona, and St. George, Utah, which boast populations well in excess of 40,000, are long distances from major cities and officially classified as metropolitan areas. Like many booming Sun Belt locales, these communities exemplify a new breed of community with minimal demand for direct rail freight service.

The Rise of Rail-Trails

When railroad routes are abandoned in the United States, the original charters that allowed for the creation of the

Figure 1: Communities with estimated populations of 3,000 or more losing rail service by 1996

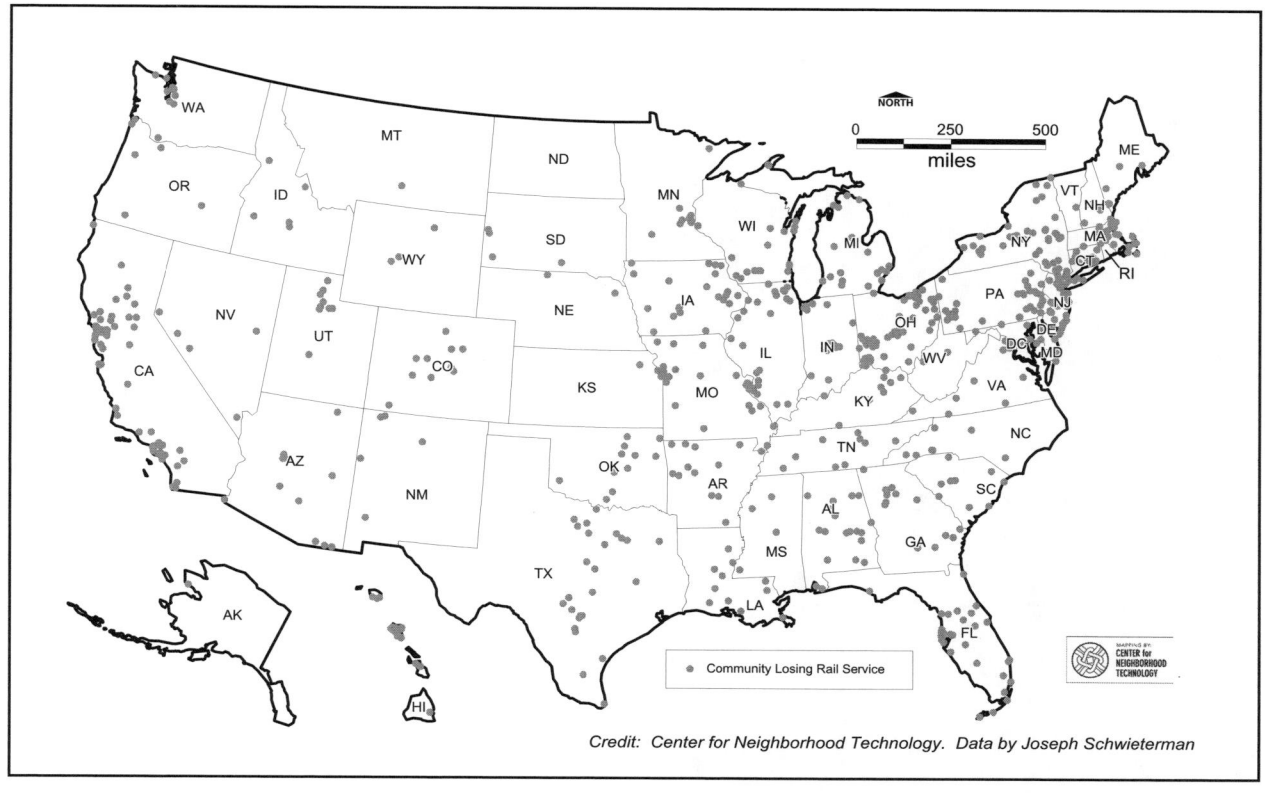

Credit: Center for Neighborhood Technology. Data by Joseph Schwieterman

Figure 2: Communities with estimated populations of 3,000 or more never served by rail as of 1996

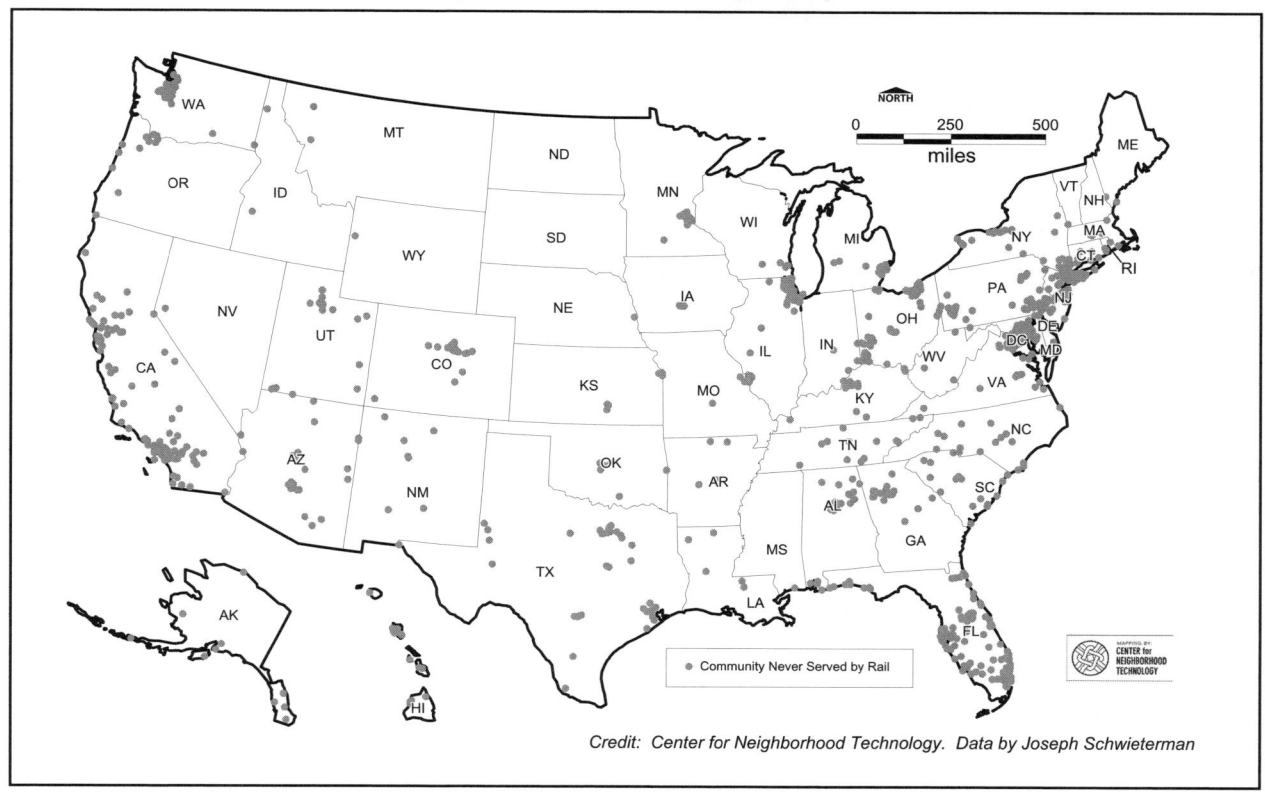

Credit: Center for Neighborhood Technology. Data by Joseph Schwieterman

A lengthy trestle and drawbridge, formerly part of the Northwestern Pacific Railroad's route to Sausalito, lies dormant along Drake Boulevard near San Rafael, California. (Photo by author.)

through the railbanking technique. In a legal sense, rail-trails are railroads, albeit ones where the operator has been awarded a Certificate of Interim Trail Use. The railbanking technique in effect "freezes" the abandonment process, suspending the need to return land held by the railroad companies in easement.

Although there has been no comprehensive assessment of railbanking, opinions are sharply divided about whether this technique has significant potential to facilitate the resumption of rail service. At least three segments have been converted into rail freight routes, but in none of these corridors were the tracks actually removed. Nevertheless, government agencies have a strong interest in exercising their right to rebuild rail lines along several railbanked corridors.

The National Trails System Act has had several unintended consequences and in certain situations can actually be detrimental to efforts to protect rail corridors serving small communities. The funds made available for recreational trails have encouraged carriers to curtail service on marginal routes—even those that might be modestly profitable—in order to allow for the sale of rights-of-way. In some instances, Class I carriers have paid shippers to switch to other modes of transportation to facilitate the sale of the right-of-way to trail-related organizations. In other cases, carriers have acted on incentives to take large tax deductions by curtailing service and donating the right-of-way to nonprofit groups.

Both the tax deductions and cash payments for rights-of-way property turned over to trail-related organizations are raising difficult legal questions. Some argue that railroads have taken tax deductions (or accepted payment) for land that they actually do not own.[15] Another concern is whether nonprofit or government organizations have acquired active railroads for the primary purpose of encouraging the abandonment of service, despite federal law intended to prevent such actions.

This is not to say that rail-trails will not eventually prove to be more instrumental to rail restoration initiatives. The rail-trail movement is still relatively new and has delivered on the promise of keeping tens of thousands of miles of right-of-way free of obstruction. It appears probable that efforts to reinstitute rail service on at least a few railbanked corridors will gather momentum as the demand for transporation capacity escalates. Moreover, there is growing interest in "rails-with-trails" development (that is, creating routes with trails alongside active railroad routes, but separated with fencing). On the other hand, as state officials gain experience in

railroad often dictate to whom the land must then be given. Most railroad right-of-way is held in easement, requiring that it revert to those who hold title to the property once the rails are removed. Although railroad companies can sell the track materials for salvage, they must cede the land held in easement to the proper titleholder (for example, farmers and other neighboring tenants).

Under the provisions of the National Trails System Act (NTSA) of 1983, however, unused rights-of-way held in easement can be preserved through a process called railbanking. This allows them to be set aside for future transportation use by a qualified organization while being used on an interim basis as recreational trails (rail-trails) or other civic amenities.

To date, more than 800 rail-trails encompassing more than 10,000 miles of route have been created corridor preservation, there is a general belief that rail-banking corridors through the National Trails System Act is not the best strategy in situations where there is strong interest in restoring rail service in the not-so-distant future.

Past and Future

History will remember the withdrawal of railroads from many small and medium-size towns as a colorful but ultimately inevitable stage in the evolution of American railroading. In the aggregate, reductions to the industry's physical plant have been a painful but necessary step in enhancing productivity and cutting costs. America's railroads now ship more ton-miles of freight than ever before, despite the fact that they operate only about half the track they had during World War I.

Even after the abandonment of more than 125,000 miles of routes, communities without railroads account for less than 10 percent of the nation's industrial output (measured on the basis of the value added from local manufacturing activity). The 300 most populous and most industrialized metropolitan areas on the mainland continue to have rail freight service. Many customers in towns without railroads today rely extensively on the sophisticated and expanding system of rail-truck intermodal connections.

The Iron Horse will continue its thunderous gallop through thousands of cities, towns, and rural places, but with fewer paths upon which to travel. With an estimated 10,000 miles of routes at risk of abandonment over the next decade, there can be little doubt that the loss of rail service to American communities will remain part of the national transportation discussion. In hundreds of communities, it is unclear whether local carriers will be able to marshal the resources necessary to make improvements allowing them to handle the heavier (286,000 pounds) freight cars that are becoming the industry standard. Many light-density lines (some of which are still equipped with rail laid in the 1930s) are not built to handle such heavy loads.

Gone is the labyrinth of rural branches, interurbans, and narrow-gauge routes that were once such a pervasive part of the fabric of many towns. The swaths of land now left behind slice through communities both large and small and endure as withering reminders of the era when the railroad reigned supreme.

ENDNOTES

1. An expanded version of this analysis appears in Joseph Schwieterman, "Abandoned Corridors," *Railroad History* 185 (Autumn 2001): 20–45.

2. U.S. Bureau of the Census. *Historical Statistics of the United States, Colonial Times to 1970*, Part 2 (Washington D.C.: Bureau of the Census, 1975).

3. This observation is based on population estimates reported in *Rand McNally Commercial Atlas and Marketing Guide*. (Chicago: Rand McNally, 1922).

4. "Perryville is Faced with Alarming Railroad Situation," *Perryville New Republican*, July 1, 1920, 1.

5. Service to West Milton, Ohio, which had about 1,300 residents at the time, ended with the abandonment of a steam railroad, the Dayton, Toledo & Chicago, in 1922, and a traction line, the Covington & Piqua, in 1926.

6. Seth H. Bramson, *Speedway to Sunshine: The Story of the Florida East Coast Railway* (Erin, Ont., Canada: Boston Mills Press, 1984), 30–35, 49–53.

7. For a description of Miami Beach's rail heritage, see Joseph P. Schwieterman, *When the Railroad Leaves Town*. Vol. I, *Eastern United States*. (Kirksville, Mo.: Truman State University Press, 2001), 40–44.

8. This estimate is based on a review of the changing status of rail service in a sample involving approximately 20,000 places listed in the index of this volume.

9. For a description of the data collection process, see Joseph P. Schwieterman and Elaine M. Crowley, "Keeping Track: An Inventory of Rail Service to U.S. Urban Areas," *Transportation Quarterly* 50 (1996): 65–78.

10. See William R. Black, *Railroads for Rent: The Local Rail Service Assistance Program* (Bloomington: Indiana University Press, 1986).

11. The Los Angeles Country Metropolitan Transit Authority was already evaluating plans for light rail service to Pasadena when AT&SF ended service in the early 1990s. The LAMTA inaugurated light rail service—the Gold Line—over the former Santa Fe corridor in 2003.

12. Government agencies acquired former railroad rights-of-way to Aspen, Colorado; Astoria, Oregon; Bethesda, Maryland; Beverly Hills, California; Carmel, Indiana; Coventry, Rhode Island; Ellsworth, Maine; Hellertown, Pennsylvania; Lexington, Massachusetts; Marlboro, New Jersey; Monterey, California; Newtown, Pennsylvania; Prescott, Arizona; and Scituate, Massachusetts.

13. The Grand Trunk Western's Detroit-Pontiac route constitutes the southwestern boundary of Troy for a short distance but does not formally enter the municipality nor does it directly serve any local businesses. See Schwieterman, *When the Railroad Leaves Town*, I:149–53. When measured on the basis of total value-added manufacturing activity, for example, Troy, Michigan, appears to have become the most industrially oriented community without a railroad.

14. This estimate is based on trends observed prior to 1996 and adjusted for subsequent changes in total abandonment mileage. Most of the growth in the number of communities meeting this criteria was attributable to the expansion of small communities that did not meet the population threshold of 3,000 during the

1990 Census but did so in 2000. Most of these communities had lost their rail service years earlier.

15. Harold Welsh, founder of the National Association of Reversionary Property Owners, has been a particularly vocal proponent of this view. See also Emily Drumm, "Addressing the Flaws on the Rails-to-Tails Act," *Kansas Journal of Law and Public Policy* 8, no. 3 (Spring 1979).

COMMUNITY SKETCHES

By drawing on a variety of published and unpublished materials, as well as field visits and correspondence with local historians and historical societies, the community profiles appearing in this volume illustrate the many ways in which rail line abandonment has left its mark on the West. Accompanying the profiles are maps, historical and contemporary photographs, and lists of suggested readings.

Each section includes the herald of the last railroad company to provide passenger service and the approximate population of the community in the year 2000 based on U.S. Census Bureau enumeration. The various sections also include an inventory of carriers providing service at the beginning of the modern era which, for simplicity, is defined as the beginning of 1940. For routes abandoned prior to the modern era, the name of the last carrier to

Communities in the shaded area are included in this volume.

operate the route is listed.

Descriptive symbols accompany each section to indicate the broader dimensions of the community's railroad heritage, such as whether the community was served by a steam, streetcar, or interurban route, or whether it is today home to a historical depot, perhaps one listed on the National Register of Historic Places. The legend summarizes various elements of the symbols and maps.

To simplify the presentation, communities are referred to as towns—even though some are formally incorporated as boroughs, villages, and cities. The abbreviations on the maps have been selected for editorial clarity and do not conform to official railroad markings. In addition, the word "Company" is omitted from the formal names of many corporations mentioned in the text.

Full citations are provided for all suggested readings and references at the end of each section. References of secondary importance, including many government reports as well as notable newspaper and magazine articles, are organized alphabetically by community at the back of the book. In some situations, communities are identified as being the "largest" or "most populous" in a region without rail services. These conclusions are based on the analysis of the database described in the appendix.

Topics Omitted

Among the topics important to the railroad history of many communities but beyond the purview of this volume are the following:
1. Events accompanying the construction of railroad lines
2. Periods of economic downturn, including the depressions of 1890, 1900, and 1930
3. Events taking place during military conflicts, including the federalization of the railroad industry during World War I
4. Corporate histories of individual railroad companies (Only the names of the railroad companies operating lines in the modern era are provided universally.)
5. Physical specifications of local railroad lines, including grades, weights of rails, and the configuration of track
6. The process of dieselization
7. Profiles of major railroad customers in a community
8. Technical aspects of local freight and passenger services or rolling stock
9. The legal debate surrounding ICC abandonment proceedings

As this list suggests, the volume does not attempt to summarize financial, operational, or technical aspects of rail service in the various communities. Although the sections may include a few paragraphs about the history of the community and its railroad lines, no attempt is made at historical completeness. Recent events may have led to important changes in the status of abandoned lines since research for this volume drew to a close. I encourage readers to consult the DePaul University website (www.depaul.edu/~chaddick) for additions or errata, or to bring to my attention any relevant information.

Readers should also bear in mind the following issues relating to the descriptions of abandoned rail lines: I have attempted to distinguish between the dates on which the ICC approved a line's abandonment and the actual date on which abandonment was consummated. Such a distinction, however, could not always be made reliably for each line. Routes preserved (that is, railbanked) through the provisions of the National Trails Act or through other governmental initiatives, popularly called rail-trails, are described as being abandoned despite legal arrangements allowing for their preservation as transportation corridors. To simplify the presentation, only a few pertinent details, such as the name of the organization managing the rail-trail, are provided.

Legends

SYMBOLS

One of the heralds used by last railroad company to provide local passenger service (except as noted in text). Generally excludes streetcar operators and public transit agencies.

Formerly served by a steam/diesel railroad route (never electrified). Standard gauge at time of abandonment.

Formerly served by a steam/diesel railroad route (never electrified). Narrow gauge at time of abandonment.

Formerly served by private logging, quarry, or incline railway, or tramway operation.

Formerly served by an electric railroad route (for example, interurban or electrified mainline).

Formerly served by streetcar company (or mule-car line) with routes confined to a single urbanized area.

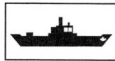 Formerly on the route of ferries, carfloats, or steamships operated by a railroad company or close affiliate.

 Site of a tourist railway operating over abandoned right-of-way or using historical railroad equipment.

 Substantial local, state, or federal funds earmarked for local route prior to abandonment.

 Site of notable preserved depot. Listed on the National Register of Historic Places or preserved by local government/organization.

 Significant portions of abandoned railroad right-of-way preserved as recreation trail.

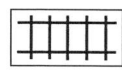 Significant stretch(es) of track were left in place in the community for five or more years after the end of rail service. Intended to facilitate possible resumption of freight or passenger service.

 Formerly along the route of a regularly scheduled Amtrak train. (Not a station stop except in the case of Thalmann, Georgia.)

MAP ABBREVIATIONS

A&NM – Arizona & New Mexico Railroad

A&W – Ahnapee & Western Railway

AE&FR – Aurora, Elgin & Fox River Electric Railway

AT&SF – Atchison, Topeka & Santa Fe Railway

B&B – Bodie & Benton Railway & Commercial Co.

BG – Bullfrog Goldfield Railroad

C&NW – Chicago & North Western Railway

C&S – Colorado & Southern Railway

CB&Q – Chicago, Burlington & Quincy Railroad

CC – California Central Railroad

CC&SR – Council City & Solomon River Railroad

CH&GL – Chicago, Harvard & Geneva Lake Railway

CM – Colorado Midland Railway

CP – Central Pacific Railroad

CP&LT – Camino, Placerville & Lake Tahoe Railroad

CR&IC – Cedar Rapids & Iowa City Railway

CR&N – Coeur d'Alene Railway & Navigation Co.

CRI&P – Chicago, Rock Island & Pacific Railroad ("Rock Island")

CS&CCD – Colorado Springs & Cripple Creek District Railway

D&C – Diamond & Caldor Railway

D&IM – Denver & Intermountain Railroad

D&RGW – Denver & Rio Grande Western Railroad ("Rio Grande")

DSP&P – Denver, South Park & Pacific Railroad ("South Park")

DM&IR – Duluth, Missabe & Iron Range Railway ("Missabe Road")

EJ&E – Elgin, Joliet & Eastern Railway

EP&SW – El Paso & Southwestern Railway

F&CC – Florence & Cripple Creek Railroad

F&N – Fredericksburg & Northern Railroad

Frisco – St. Louis-San Francisco Railway

FS&W – Fort Smith & Western Railway Route

G&BV – Gulf & Brazos Valley Railway

GB&W – Green Bay & Western Railroad

GN – Great Northern Railway

GN/NP – Great Northern Pacific Steamship Co.

GT&W – Gulf, Texas & Western Railway

HRT&LC – Honolulu Rapid Transit & Land Co.

KRy – Koolau Railway

KGB&W – Kewaunee, Green Bay & Western Railroad

KO&G – Kansas, Oklahoma & Gulf Railway

L&A – Louisiana & Arkansas Railway

LA & Independence – Los Angeles & Independence Railroad

LA-P – Los Angeles-Pacific Railway

LM – Louisiana Midland Railway

LV&T – Las Vegas & Tonapah Railroad

M&A – Missouri & Arkansas Railway

M&PG – Monterey & Pacific Grove Street Railway

M&PP – Manitou & Pikes Peak Railway

M&SV – Monterey & Salinas Valley Railroad

MCL – Michigan-California Lumber Co.

Milw – Chicago, Milwaukee, St. Paul & Pacific Railroad ("Milwaukee Road")

MP – Missouri Pacific Railroad ("MoPac")

MT – Midland Terminal Railway

MT&MW – Mount Tamalpais & Muir Woods Railway

MW Elec – Mineral Wells Electric System

MW&LP – Mineral Wells & Lakewood Park Railway

MW&S – Montana, Wyoming & Southern Railroad

NRR&T – Natchez, Red River & Texas Railroad

NMC – New Mexico Central Railroad

NP – Northern Pacific Railway

NWP – Northwestern Pacific Railroad

O&NW – Oregon & Northwestern Railroad

OR&L – Oahu Railway & Land Co.

OWR&N – Oregon-Washington Railroad & Navigation Co.

P&AC – Prescott & Arizona Central Railroad

P&P – Pasadena & Pacific Railroad

Paj V – Pajaro Valley Consolidated Railroad

PAW – Port Angeles Western Railroad

PE – Pacific Electric Railway

PNT – Pacific Northwest Traction Company
PTS – Port Townsend Southern Railroad
SCI – Six Companies, Inc.
SD&AE – San Diego & Arizona Eastern Railway
SD Elec – San Diego Electric Railway Co.
Sew P – Seward Peninsula Railroad
SN – Sacramento Northern Railway
SP – Southern Pacific Railroad
SP&N – Sacramento, Placer & Nevada Railroad
SP&S – Spokane, Portland & Seattle Railway
SR&N – Sabine River & Northern Railroad
T&G – Tonapah & Goldfield Railroad
T&P – Texas & Pacific Railway
T&S – Tombstone & Southern Railroad
Utah East – Utah Eastern Railroad
USG – U.S. Government Railway
UP – Union Pacific Railroad
UV&P – Utah Verde & Pacific Railroad
V&T – Virginia & Truckee Railway
WMW&NW – Weatherford, Mineral Wells &
   Northwestern Railway

ILLUSTRATIONS

————————	Active railroad routes
—·—·—·—·—·—·	Railroad-operated ferry or steamship route
— — — — — —	Abandoned steam or diesel railroad route, except narrow gauge
—··—··—··—··	Abandoned narrow-gauge steam route
··················	Abandoned electric railroad route
— — — — —	Proposed railroad route
————————	Highway
·—··—··—··—	State or international boundary
CRI&P	Name of railroad company operating line in 1940. Last operator shown for lines abandoned before 1940.
★ **TOWN NAME**	Focus town
O TOWN NAME	Other towns
⬭	Body of water

Historic operator: Seward Peninsula Railroad
Last route abandoned: 1955
Notable reuse of right-of-way: Public road

  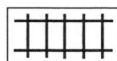

ome might be an international railway center today had investors a century ago fulfilled their dream of establishing a rail or ferry link between Alaska and Siberia. Although these proposals never advanced beyond the planning stage, a rail line of more modest design—the Wild Goose Railroad—made important contributions to this storied community. Carrying merchants, miners, and rollicking day-trippers, its trains supported one of the greatest gold-mining booms in American history.

Historical Perspective

Sustaining themselves primarily through fishing and hunting, the Inuit, or Eskimo, lived harmoniously 150 years ago on the landmass known today as the Seward Peninsula. Few white people ventured into this remote area (the westernmost part of the Alaskan Peninsula) before construction workers for the Western Union Company began stringing a telegraph cable through it in 1865. Although hoping to join Alaska to Siberia, the contingent experienced great difficulty during the winter months, nearly freezing to death while suffering from malnutrition. After learning that a telegraph cable was in operation across the Atlantic in 1867, the demoralized crew, which had strung a mere 23 miles of cable, abandoned the effort and left the area—despite having found evidence of gold.

When U.S. Secretary of State William H. Seward purchased Alaska from Russia for $7.2 million in 1867, skeptics heralded the agreement as "Seward's Folly," believing the price

NOME-ARCTIC RAILWAY

was far too high. But the Klondike gold rush in the neighboring Yukon Territory during 1896 suggested that these northern lands might be laden with precious metals. Two years later, "three lucky Swedes," John Byrnteson, Erik Lindblom, and Jefet Lindeberg, struck gold on Anvil Creek several miles north of present-day Nome, marking the beginning of the Alaskan gold rush.

Within months, thousands of miners, having exhausted most of the "easy" gold in the Klondike, had packed their belongings and moved to the even more frigid climes of the Seward Peninsula. Many miners and merchants accepted primitive living arrangements in a massive tent city along the beach that was reportedly 20 miles long. A map showing this area as "?Name" was inadvertently deciphered by a cartographer as Cape Nome. As a result, the settlement was christened Nome.

Life for the peninsula's gold miners was notoriously difficult. Food was scarce, the wind was bitterly cold during the winter months, and sanitation was woefully inadequate. The soft

Although more used to soft tundra, a dogsled team seems at home journeying on the tracks of the Wild Goose Railroad near Nome, circa 1914. Note the modest standards to which the line was built despite the hazards created by operating trains over permafrost. (Rasmuson Library, University of Alaska Fairbanks.)

tundra often rendered dogsleds the area's only reliable form of transportation. Mining companies desperately wanted a railroad to move workers, equipment, and supplies north into the Seward Peninsula's gold-rich interior.

Many people considered operating trains across the permafrost to be a foolhardy proposition, but the enterprising Charles D. Lane, president of a successful local enterprise known as the Wild Goose Mining and Trading Company, believed a narrow-gauge line could succeed. Lane purchased a steamer and sent it north from Puget Sound loaded with a locomotive, eight flatcars, and building materials. By the autumn of 1900, his company had laid more than 6 miles of track from a coastal location near Nome. This line originated near the mouth of the Snake River, passed through Discovery—the booming mining camp where the Scandinavians had found gold—and terminated at Banner, a thriving settlement up in the mountains that, like Nome, was still composed largely of tents.

By the time Nome became an incorporated city in 1901, its ramshackle neighborhoods reportedly had more than 20,000 inhabitants, including the likes of the legendary adventurer Wyatt Earp, who operated a saloon. Those living in the area considered the Wild Goose Railroad to be far more than an industrial enterprise. They took delight in its special excursions on holidays and chartered trains for various events.

Riding the Wild Goose was a rousing experience, for the only accommodations for most passengers were chairs on flatcars with canvas roofs, leaving them exposed to inclement weather. The tracks had sunk deep into the permafrost from the weight of passing trains, making the roadbed treacherous and uneven and necessitating a speed limit of only 8 mph. Miners sang songs to pass the time and assisted in putting the train back on the tracks after derailments, which were frequent except during the winter months when the railroad lay dormant. Fond of their diminutive short line, many miners called it the Paystreak Express.

In addition to carrying miners, supplies, and ore, the Wild Goose brought day-trippers to saloons and eateries in Banner (a place known by several different names, including Anvil Station). The company's business was so robust in 1902 that it bought its third locomotive and began work on the Golovin Sound Railroad. This new Wild Goose line did not serve Nome, operating instead from Council City, a mining center some 60 miles northeast of Nome.

In 1903, when Charles Lane began selling his interest in both the original Wild Goose Railroad and the mining company, Jafet Lindeberg, one of the prospectors who had discovered gold, emerged as one of the buyers. The legendary Swede reorganized the carrier the following year as the Nome-Arctic Railroad and built two extensions, one along Norton Sound and another along the Nome River north of Banner. His railroad also built a spur to downtown Nome equipped with a terminal on Second Street.

These endeavors, while important to those living in the region, paled in comparison to the investments envisioned by those hoping to create a long-distance railroad route across the Seward Peninsula. As early as 1900, surveyors had evaluated the possibility of building a route from Nome to the vicinity of Fairbanks, a distance of more than 400 miles. In 1902, a Chicago-based company made known its desire to operate trains across the rugged terrain between Nome and Cook Inlet, a port along the Gulf of Alaska near Anchorage.

On an even more grandiose scale, investors contemplated the creation of rail lines between Alaska and Siberia, despite the obvious problem that Russian railways operated with a track gauge different from most of their North American counterparts. Proponents of such plans initially contemplated building to the tip of the peninsula and ferrying railcars in both directions across the Bering Strait's treacherous waters. After a 38-mile trip, the westbound ferries would dock in the eastern extremity of Russia, where the cars would be conveyed on a newly built rail line linked to the trans-Siberian railway, which was then under construction.

These far-flung efforts generated much enthusiasm across the United States. In 1902, the Trans-Alaska Railroad & Navigation Company received its incorporation and aggressively solicited financing for a rail-boat connection. This company proposed building from southern Alaska to the Bering Strait, where railcars would be loaded onto massive steel vessels and conveyed to Siberia. Another venture, the Grand Trunk Pacific Railroad, incorporated in 1903, anticipated creating an interconnected system of routes extending all the way from the Atlantic Ocean to the Strait via Nome. It, too, envisioned ferrying cars across the Strait to and from a railhead in Siberia.

Other companies seriously explored the possibility of operating trains all the way to Russia. The Trans-Alaska Siberian Company actually went so far as to receive concessions from the Russian government and reportedly raised $6 million to build a route with a tunnel under the Bering Strait by way of the Diomede Islands. Even Union Pacific magnate E. H. Harriman, who had traveled through the Seward Peninsula region with an elite crew of scientists and artists in 1899, looked with intrigue at the possibility of one day operating a railroad from New York to Paris.

The movement to build to Russia continued through 1906, when the American Trans-Siberian Company revealed an interest in building a line from the Alaskan interior to Siberia with a tunnel originating at Cape Prince of Wales, a desolate location at the tip of the Seward Peninsula. The company considered two prospective routes, one of which passed through Nome.

Unfortunately for Nome, none of these ambitious projects moved beyond the planning stage, leaving the city's economy to dwindle. By 1903, the gold was largely exhausted and many miners had moved away. The Wild Goose encountered labor problems with longshoremen and was evidently asked to pay a considerable sum in property taxes that it could not afford. In 1905, after only four years of operation, its trains ground to a halt.

Construction crews returned to the region to lay more track, but only to tap into new gold-mining areas in the region. The Seward Peninsula Railroad purchased the dormant Wild Goose in 1906 and extended the line at Lane's Landing (Shelton) on the Kuzitrin River—a location 85 miles from Nome and at the heart of a booming new mining district farther north than the original one. Nome's reconstructed railroad boasted 128 bridges and trestles, including a majestic span over the Kuzitrin River approximately 1,000 feet long.

Changing Times

The reconstituted Seward Peninsula Railroad would ultimately suffer from the same problems as its failed predecessor. In addition to suffering from a downturn in mining output and the high costs of operating over a tortuous route, this carrier had to contend with melting permafrost and frequent derailments. The line was sold to the Maine Northwest Development Company in 1913 and then leased to Lindenberg two years later, but demand was so weak that the railroad could not justify regular operations. As Nome's railroad once again fell onto hard times, the right-of-way evolved into a public thoroughfare regularly used by handcars drawn by teams of dogs.

Remnants of a lengthy trestle along the former Seward Peninsula Railroad march into the distance in Nome, Alaska. Containers and oil tanks can be seen at the wharf, the railroad's point of origin. (Photo by author.)

flights following the Arctic Circle route began making fuel stops at Nome's airport. With air travel between North America and Asia expanding rapidly, civic boosters once again held out hope that their community would become an important international transportation gateway. Nevertheless, Nome's proximity to Asia seemed more a liability than an asset during World War II, when warnings about a possible Japanese invasion necessitated heightened military preparedness. The U.S. Army not only brought additional troops to town, it took over the rail line, made significant improvements, and resumed train operations.

With Leningrad under siege, the idea of building railways on the peninsula rose again. The Army considered building an entirely new route to Norton Sound for the delivery of raw materials and equipment to the Russian government. In 1942, the Army Corps of Engineers surveyed a prospective supply route through Nome from a junction on the Alaska Railroad south of Fairbanks. This proposal was of great interest to the War Department, which anticipated operating up to twenty trains per day over the line and envisioned making Teller (a port northwest of Nome) the route's terminus. Along with this latest round of proposals came serious discussion about linking the federally owned Alaska Railroad with Canada's transcontinental routes, thereby establishing a rail link to the U.S. mainland. Like the many preceding proposals, none of these efforts were to advance beyond the planning stage.

Within a few years of the war's end, trains used Nome's rail line only sporadically. The Wild Goose soared once more, however, when in 1953 an entrepreneur, Charles Reader, began offering excursions as far north as Salmon Lake using a gasoline-powered rail-bus. After Reader sold the so-called Curly Q operation in 1955, the construction of a highway severed a portion of the line south of Banner. Reader donated the right-of-way to the municipal government, and soon all the tracks had been removed except for a few miles near Nome.

The Russian Revolution in 1917 rendered moot the very idea of a rail link to Siberia. By 1920, mining had fallen dramatically and Nome had dwindled to fewer than 900 inhabitants, less than 5 percent of its population of nineteen years earlier. Lindeberg purchased the railroad that year and sold it to the territorial government. By early 1921, public officials had turned the line over to the Alaska Road Commission.

The commission rehabilitated the line and installed wooden planks between the rails on bridges and trestles to make them suitable for draft animals pulling various types of railcars. It established regulations to ensure that the public would use the line safely, creating a shared right-of-way that would become deeply rooted in Alaskan railroad lore. Automobiles with flanged wheels and other motor vehicles were allowed to travel on the line provided they had been equipped with a siren, a sander, and workable brakes. With automobiles relatively scarce, carts pulled by teams of dogs remained the preferred means of travel.

Then in 1934 a fire swept through the old mining town. The blaze reduced much of Nome's downtown and surrounding neighborhoods to ruins. As citizens rebuilt the city, Nome lost some of its haphazard qualities and assumed a more conventional and permanent character. Illustrative of the changing times, several airlines with

Abandonment's Legacy

Considering the number of times that rail service to Nome stopped and started over the years, it was not surprising that one more attempt was made to revive the community's rail service. Reader's plan to restore his fondly remembered Curly Q service over the municipally owned track during the 1960s was not to be, however, and nearly all of the track was eventually removed.

As Nome moved toward an uncertain future bereft of a significant mining industry, Carrie M. McLain, the daughter of a prospector, assembled in her home a collection of artifacts devoted to local history. In 1969, the municipal government integrated this collection into a historical museum (housed in the same building as the community library) and named it in McLain's honor.

With the local economy in a slump, Nome's population slipped to less than 4,000 during the 1970s. In recent decades, its business conditions have improved modestly due to the strength of tourism and commercial shipping. Each March, many curious travelers come to witness the spectacle of the dogsled teams competing in the annual Iditarod race. Although Nome is no longer a fuel stop for international flights, it benefits from frequent air service to Anchorage and a rubble-mound seawall that protects vessels entering its port.

railroad was built to modest standards and abandoned so many years ago. Within city limits, ruins of the carrier's trestle over the Snake River and two railcars along Third Street memorialize the railroad that gave Nome, if only briefly, the reputation of being a place economically as well as geographically on top of the world. At the Carrie M. McLain Memorial Museum, exhibits and displays take visitors on a journey through the Seward Peninsula's past.

Many tourists might come and go completely unaware of the Seward Peninsula's railroad history were it not for the desolate remains of the "Last Train to Nowhere." These rusting steam locomotives and railcars were once part of the Council City & Solomon Railroad, a standard-gauge mining road farther east on the Seward Peninsula. Visitors regularly make a side trip from Nome to see this equipment, which has languished on the tundra since the railroad ceased operations in 1907.

Today Nome is the northernmost community of its size in the United States that lacks rail service. Although much has changed since the first grandiose schemes to tunnel beneath the Bering Strait more than a century ago, a few determined souls, including those affiliated with the Bering Strait Tunnel & Railroad Group, still champion this idea, hoping to finally overcome the financial obstacles that doomed so many like-minded initiatives of the past.

Epilogue

Visitors to Nome will find that it still possesses many of the qualities of a frontier town. More than a third of its population is of Inuit descent. Fairbanks, the nearest town of appreciable size, is more than 300 miles away and inaccessible by car, making Nome's airport and harbor vital to mobility. Many residents oppose the idea of building a road from their community to eastern Alaska, preferring instead to live in relative solitude with a continuing dependence on airlines and the sea.

Travelers searching for remnants of the original Wild Goose along Kougarak Road will not be disappointed. The right-of-way is easy to discern as it winds its way across the rocky and rolling terrain. Several culverts and wooden trestles seem remarkably well preserved considering that the

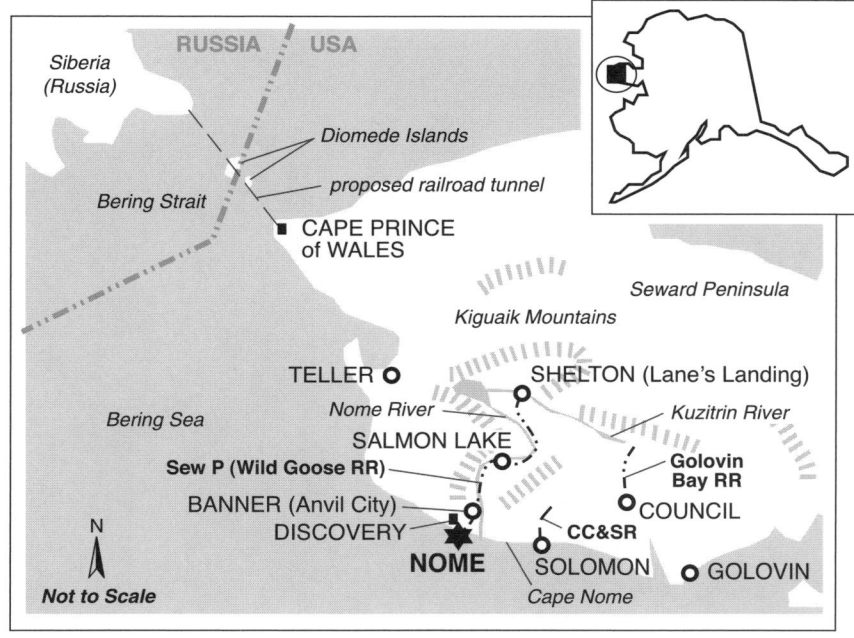

For Further Study

SUGGESTED READINGS:

Clifford, Howard. *Rails North: The Railroads of Alaska and the Yukon.* Seattle: Superior Publishing, 1981, 163–81.

Hauck, Cornelius W. "Narrow Gauge in the Arctic," In *The Collected Colorado Rail Annual.* Golden: Colorado Railroad Museum, 1974, 124–35.

OTHER PRINCIPAL REFERENCES:

Cole, Terrance, ed. *Nome: City of Golden Beaches.* Anchorage: Alaska Historical Society, 1984, 11–175.

Hilton, George W. *American Narrow Gauge Railroads.* Stanford: Stanford University Press, 1990, 305.

Kennan, George. *E. H. Harriman: A Biography.* Boston: Riverside Press Cambridge, 1922, 2:1–29, 185–231.

While, John H., Jr. "Ice Bound." *Railroad History* 183 (Aug. 2000): 103–5.

PRESCOTT, ARIZONA (33,938)

Historic operators: Atchison, Topeka & Santa Fe Railway; Prescott & Arizona Central Railroad
Last route abandoned: 1984
Notable reuses of right-of-way: Privately and municipally owned corridor; Peavine Trail

  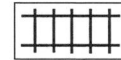 

*B*usiness leaders in Prescott adamantly opposed the Atchison, Topeka & Santa Fe Railway's plans to divert trains away from their community onto a newly built bypass more than forty years ago. Their testimonials failed to persuade federal officials to block the Santa Fe's effort to create a more efficient route through that part of Arizona. After the completion of the bypass, rail service to Prescott gradually diminished and eventually drew to a close.

Historical Perspective

The vast territory formerly known as Nuevo Mexico came under the jurisdiction of the United States with the signing of the Treaty of Guadalupe Hidalgo in 1848. When the federal government designated a portion of this region as the Arizona Territory in 1863, President Abraham Lincoln requested that officials establish a relatively northern capital in order to minimize the influences of Confederate sympathizers.

Lincoln's directive was fortuitous for those living along Granite Creek, including the many miners and prospectors who had migrated there following the discovery of gold only a short time before. On this site in 1864, officials built a governor's mansion and platted a new town named after author William Hickling Prescott, whose essays, including "History of the Conquest of Mexico," were popular at the time. The community would also become the seat of Yavapai County.

Surrounded by plentiful timber and game, and situated around a large plaza, Prescott grew rapidly over the next several years. Although the community relinquished its role as the territorial capital to Tucson in 1867, it regained this role ten years later while in the midst of another mining boom. As merchants and miners poured into the region, elevating the county's population to more than 5,000 by 1880, Prescott grew so rapidly that some anticipated the city would someday become one of the greatest cities of the West.

After such a promising beginning, Prescott's fortunes began to diminish, especially after the uncharitable events of 1884. That year, the territorial government moved its capital to Phoenix, and fire reduced a portion of Prescott to ruins. A community that had seemed poised for lasting prominence now appeared destined for relative obscurity—especially if its separation from the West's expanding railroad system continued.

The outlook for the region improved as the city quickly rebuilt its neighborhoods and the Prescott & Arizona Central Railroad laid its tracks south from the main line of the Atlantic & Pacific Railroad (an Atchison, Topeka & Santa Fe Railway predecessor). Although this carrier operated its first train in 1887 from Prescott Junction (Seligman), Arizona, to Prescott, a distance

A string of F-units (locomotives at left-center), several GP7s (center), and four cabooses at the Prescott yard await their next assignment. The Santa Fe used the extra power to move freight over the Sierra Prieta summit. (Photo by R. L. Knoll, Tucson, Arizona.)

of 73 miles, the town's rail connections remained poor until another rail line, the Santa Fe, Prescott & Phoenix Railway (SFP&P), arrived six years later. Popularly known as the Peavine due to its many curves and bridges, SFP&P provided a direct route from the Santa Fe's main line at Ash Fork, Arizona, and had the ultimate goal of operating trains all the way to Phoenix.

The Prescott & Arizona Central fared poorly against the upstart Peavine and suffered inordinately from the severe downturn in silver mining following the panic of 1893. After less than a decade of service, this older carrier abandoned its entire route in 1896. Fortunately for Prescott, its demise had few lasting implications. The SFP&P extended its route to Phoenix in 1895 and gradually expanded the scale of its operations. In 1898, it gained a new interchange partner, the Prescott & Eastern Railway, which commenced service over a route originating on the Peavine northeast of town and eventually stretched 31 miles to Mayer, a thriving mining center. This short line derived much of its business from

still another ore-hauling line, the Bradshaw Mountain Railroad, which by 1900 operated a pair of routes in the region, including one to Crown King, another booming mining town.

The SFP&P and its feeder railroads nurtured the development of silver and gold mining as well as small industry and ranching in central Arizona. The ensuing prosperity allowed Prescott to quickly emerge from the rubble of another devastating fire in 1900 as an even more impressive city, with dignified downtown storefronts similar to those commonly found in the Midwest.

In the midst of great optimism about its future, the SFP&P invested heavily in improvements. It relocated a lengthy stretch of track near Drake, Arizona, built a magnificent steel bridge through Hell Canyon, and made other improvements north of Prescott to lessen the severity of its grades. Even so, portions of the Peavine remained poorly suited for high-density operations. Between Prescott and Skull Valley, trainmen had to contend with the excruciating 3 percent grades over Ramsgate Hill and the Sierra Prieta Mountains. On this segment, locomotives toiled to climb more than 700 feet to reach Prieta, the highest point on the Peavine (9 miles west of Prescott), before beginning a meandering and dangerous descent into the Skull Valley. Due to the steep grades, the Santa Fe maintained numerous helper locomotives in Prescott.

Despite the obvious limitations of the Peavine, the Santa Fe purchased the SFP&P in 1901, propelling Prescott's railroad era to its pinnacle. The Santa Fe built a two-story depot in town in 1907 and within a decade had expanded its facilities to include a freight yard with two turntables, several roundhouses, a large freight house, a boiler machine shop, and a paint shop. The Santa Fe's intricate system of branch lines grew to encompass both the former Prescott & Eastern Railway and Bradshaw Mountain Railroad—feeder routes generating large shipments of ore.

By the mid-1920s, Prescott boasted more than 6,000 inhabitants and one of the largest downtown districts in the state. Its magnificent performance hall, the Elks Theater and Opera House, had seating for 900 guests, while the legendary Whiskey Row, an area with many bars and saloons, was one of its most talked-about neighborhoods. Many travelers arrived by train to stay at the community's hotels, including the Vendome, the Hotel St. Michael, and the elegant Hassayampa Inn. The eating house adjacent to the station was also a bustling place when passenger trains made meal stops in town. Around this time, Prescott embraced its still-famous motto, "Arizona's Mile High City."

Before the end of the 1920s, the Santa Fe formally absorbed the SFP&P into its system and introduced café-lounge cars to its passenger trains, ending the need to make meal stops in Prescott. The quality of its local passenger services further improved in 1928, when the carrier rerouted two Chicago–Los Angeles trains, the westbound Navajo and the eastbound Missionary, off its main line west of Ash Fork. By putting these trains on a more circuitous route through its junction at Matthie (near Wickenburg), the Santa Fe provided Prescott travelers with more options for reaching the Midwest and through service to southern California.

Changing Times

As highways improved and the Great Depression crisis deepened, much of the traffic that had sustained the Peavine began to dry up. In 1935, the Navajo and Missionary trains were put back onto the main line, ending Prescott's through service to Los Angeles. With the copper and silver markets slumping during the late 1930s, the Santa Fe abandoned the last portion of the former Bradshaw Mountain and substantial parts of the

former Prescott & Eastern.

Not all the changes in regional transportation were detrimental to the Santa Fe. Growing numbers of long-distance travelers used the Peavine to reach dude ranches in the vicinity of Wickenburg. In 1939, the carrier introduced streamlined sleeping cars to the Phoenix section of the Chief, a train providing through service to Chicago via the junction at Ash Fork. During World War II, its freight and passenger business surged.

After the war, however, many travelers destined for central Arizona turned their loyalties to the Golden State, a faster train jointly operated between the Windy City and Phoenix by the Chicago, Rock Island & Pacific and the Southern Pacific. In 1955, the Santa Fe reduced passenger service on the Peavine to a single daily Phoenix–Ash Fork train in each direction, which was unofficially called both the Hassayampa Chief and Hassayampa Flyer, names derived from the route's proximity to the Hassayampa River. This "pocket streamliner" offered "chair car" and sleeping-car service between the Arizona capital and Chicago through connections with the westbound San Francisco Chief and eastbound Chief at Ash Fork.

Santa Fe officials began to seriously consider a bypass around the 6,100-foot elevations of the Sierra Prieta in 1955. Their evaluation soon culminated in a formal plan for a new line between Paulden (Abra), a small town 28 miles north of Prescott, and Skull Valley. This route would shave 14 miles from trip distances, reduce the line's maximum elevation by more than 400 feet, and

More than forty years after the departure of its last passenger train, the former Santa Fe depot appears to await the arrival of the Hassayampa Chief. Behind this restored landmark, all evidence of the track-bed is gone. (Photo by author.)

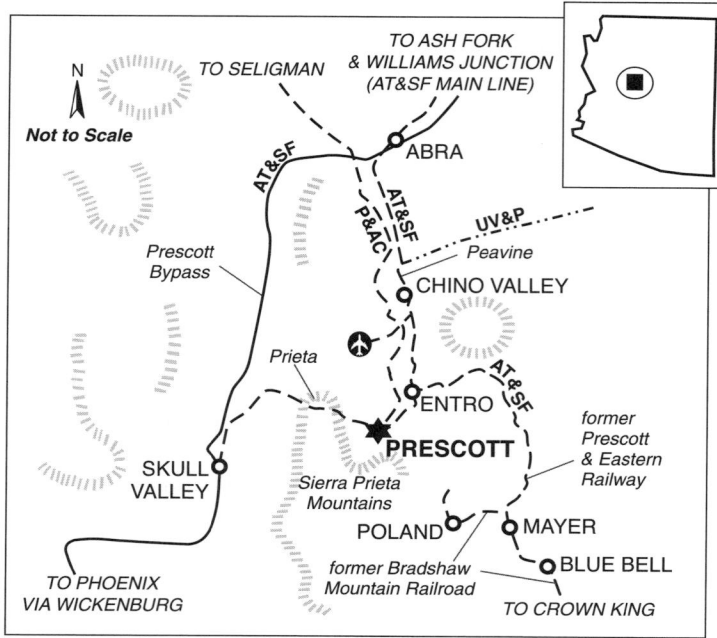

allow for the abandonment of the tortuous Prescott–Skull Valley segment. The proposal generated vigorous opposition from local business leaders, who recognized that it would greatly diminish freight operations in their community and doom local passenger service. Despite the fact that the Hassayampa Flyer passed through Prescott at inconvenient hours (the southbound run stopped in the middle of the night), officials had a strong psychological attachment to this train. More significantly, the new line would also end Prescott's role as a station for helper locomotives, thereby eliminating numerous railroad jobs.

The company formally announced its plans to move forward with the bypass project in 1959. When the matter was brought before the ICC, representatives of the city demanded during six days of contentious hearings that, at a minimum, the existing alignment be preserved as a secondary route. Their emotional pleas were to no avail. After receiving approval to build the Skull Valley Cutoff/Prescott Bypass, the carrier wasted little time. It began construction in early 1961 and completed the project at a cost of $3.5 million the following year. In April 1962, the Santa Fe rerouted trains, including the Hassayampa Flyer, onto the bypass. That same year, it abandoned the segment between Prescott and Skull Valley, leaving Arizona's Mile High City at the end of a lengthy branch.

The elimination of Prescott as a stop on the Hassayampa Flyer reduced ridership and heightened the carrier's interest in eliminating the train. In 1967, the Santa Fe terminated through Pullman service between Chicago

and Phoenix, removed the diner-lounge, and lost its contract to carry first-class mail. All travelers bound for out-of-state destinations now had to make cross-the-platform transfers at inconvenient times at Williams Junction (which had replaced Ash Fork as the junction between the Peavine and the Main Line seven years before).

The Santa Fe abruptly dropped the Hassayampa Flyer in October 1967 without ICC permission, only to be ordered to reinstate it several months later. Service resumed, but the train lost its connection to Chicago upon the discontinuation of the Chief in April 1968. Only a handful of customers were generally now onboard, putting the train once again on the path to oblivion, and, in April 1969, the Hassayampa Flyer made its last run.

Disappointing as this departure was, the potential loss of freight service to Prescott was an even more troubling proposition. Concerns about the loss of industrial jobs escalated as another mining downturn pushed the region's economy into a recession. In 1974, the last remnant of the former Prescott & Eastern was abandoned, leaving the 28-mile branch from Abra to Prescott with little traffic potential. In 1979, the Santa Fe stopped staffing its Prescott depot with an agent. The following year, it eliminated the community's role as a base for the train crew working the branch. Instead, it dispatched local trains on an as-needed basis from Ash Fork. By 1982, the future of the branch appeared bleak. In only two years, shipments to and from Prescott had dropped from 306 carloads to barely more than 100.

After a flood washed out the tracks in six locations between Chino Valley and Prescott in the autumn of 1983, the Santa Fe made clear that it could not justify spending $170,000 for repairs. Local businesses that had used the railroad, including an aluminum company, had a strong interest in saving the branch, but without new sources of revenue, it was obvious that freight service would no longer be viable. In August 1984, the carrier received ICC approval to abandon the 28-mile segment from the vicinity of Abra to Prescott.

Abandonment's Legacy

The Santa Fe left the tracks in place for several years, generating discussion about transforming the route into a short-line or tourist railway. When the railroad offered to sell the branch, including locomotives and cars, to the city of Prescott, reportedly for $700,000, municipal officials expressed their interest in having scenic excursions operate from Prescott to the Grand Canyon or Clarkdale. Between 1986 and 1989, private developers attempted to raise capital to create such a railroad while also evaluating the potential for providing freight service, but their negotiations with the city of Prescott, the Santa Fe, and the Yavapai Tribe eventually broke down. In the end, the municipal government voted against spending $200,000 to support the effort to purchase the line.

The success of the newly reopened Grand Canyon Railway, a tourist line operating over another former Santa Fe branch, encouraged the Prescott city government to reconsider its position. During the early 1990s, the government persuaded the Santa Fe to temporarily suspend its plans to salvage the tracks and hired Kyle Railways to analyze the market potential of the route. The short line's assessment was discouraging, however. It showed that more than $1 million would be needed to rehabilitate the line and provide freight and excursion service, an amount the municipal government deemed prohibitive. By early 1992, the Santa Fe had lost its patience over the lingering efforts to find a buyer for the route. The carrier hired a salvage company to remove the remaining tracks, except for a 1-mile storage spur near Abra.

Over this same period, the pleasing climate, spectacular scenery, and affordable housing of Chino Valley and Prescott Valley—towns northeast and east of Prescott—attracted thousands of new residents. The Hotel Vendome and the Hassayampa Inn underwent major restoration and reemerged as prominent tourist destinations. The Santa Fe Depot, a mission revival structure, was added to the National Register of Historic Places and refurbished. Several hundred feet west of the depot, a streamlined passenger car was placed on an abandoned railroad bridge and fashioned into a dining room for a newly built restaurant.

Although a small part of the abandoned route in the Chino Valley was converted into the Peavine Trail, a popular recreational path, the debate about the future of the right-of-way resumed after the municipal government purchased approximately 6 miles of the abandoned corridor in 1997. The municipality later expanded its holdings by purchasing 7 more miles of the right-of-way in hopes of creating a continuous rail-trail between Prescott and the Peavine Trail or a regional light-rail system to meet the needs of the county's expanding population.

Epilogue

Visitors to Prescott find more than 700 buildings in historic districts listed on the National Register. At the heart of town, the Courthouse Plaza and Whiskey Row are beautifully preserved and among the most significant of these districts. Several blocks north of the plaza, the former Santa Fe station and the adjacent baggage room anchor a modern commercial development called the Depot Marketplace. Although a shopping mall has altered the old rail-yard area beyond recognition, the 1972 movie *Junior Bonner*, a "modern western" starring Steve McQueen and Robert Preston, has a timeless scene depicting this bygone facility as well as the adjacent depot. The motion picture even has a segment involving a pair of Santa Fe GP-35 locomotives.

Those following the former Peavine right-of-way between Skull Valley and Prescott will notice that its deep cuts and sharp curves have been preserved by Arizona's arid climate. On State Route 89 north of town, large embankments along the abandoned portion near Abra are easily identifiable by motorists. Prescott's Sharlot Hall Museum displays a standard-gauge Porter locomotive that dates back to 1887.

Sixty years ago, it would have been difficult to imagine Prescott without a railroad. The bypass that bears the community's name remains instrumental to Arizona transportation as part of the Burlington Northern Santa Fe Railway. In the Prescott vicinity, however, the Peavine is now mostly just a dusty trail barely noticed by those passing by.

For Further Study

SUGGESTED READINGS:

Myrick, David F. *Railroads of Arizona.* Vol. 5, *Santa Fe to Phoenix.* Winton, Calif.: Signature Press, 2000, 11–134.

Pace, Richard. "The Abra-Skull Valley Line Change." *The Warbonnet: The Official Magazine of the Santa Fe Railway Historical Society* 3, no. 4 (1997): 17–21.

Sayre, John W. *The Santa Fe, Prescott & Phoenix Railway: The Scenic Line of Arizona.* Boulder, Colo.: Pruett Publishing, 1986, 173.

OTHER PRINCIPAL REFERENCES:

August, Jack, Jr. *We Call It "Preskit": A Guide to Prescott and Central Arizona High Country.* Phoenix: Arizona Department of Transportation, 1996, 1–41.

Sayre, John. W. *Ghost Railroads and Ghost Towns of Central Arizona.* Boulder, Colo.: Pruett Publishing, 1985, 28–32.

TOMBSTONE, ARIZONA (1,504)

Historic operators: Southern Pacific Railroad; Tombstone & Southern Railroad
Last route abandoned: 1960
Notable remnant of railroad era: Tombstone Depot

The gunfight at the O.K. Corral and the first great mining boom were only distant memories by the time the first train steamed into Tombstone in the early twentieth century. The El Paso & South-western Railroad laid the groundwork for an industrial renaissance that allowed this legendary community to reclaim the title of Arizona's leading silver-mining center. Today, little more than old embankments, a preserved depot, a boxcar, and a caboose survive to memorialize the town's bygone rail lines.

Historical Perspective

Following the discovery of gold and silver in northern Nevada in 1859, many prospectors combed the vast, arid expanse east of California in the hope of making the next big strike. However, the lucrative deposits of ore east of the San Pedro River eluded them for years. Most gold-seekers considered the dangers posed by Apache Indian tribes to be too great to justify exploratory incursions along the San Pedro, but one rugged individualist named Edward Schieffelin was willing to take such risks. He left Nevada's Comstock region for the Arizona Territory during the mid-1870s and lived briefly with a company of soldiers at Fort Huachuca. Then, in 1877, as Schieffelin embarked on his own to examine rock formations 16 miles away that looked promising, a soldier reportedly uttered the soon-to-be-famous phrase: "All you'll find out there is your tombstone and your graveyard."

Schieffelin ignored this warning, discovered what appeared to be a lucrative vein of silver ore, and brought his sample to Tucson. After being turned away by skeptical businessmen, he traveled another 300 miles north to Signal to solicit the assistance of his brother, whose opinion he trusted. Shortly after their return to "Tomb Stone," the enormity of Schieffelin's discovery attracted thousands to the region.

At the site of Schieffelin's claim, in an area called Goose Flats, a shantytown came into being. Platted in 1879, the community was renamed Tombstone and became infamous for its swashbuckling and renegade character—a place notorious for brothels, saloons, and opium dens. Access to the mining camp improved when Southern Pacific built its transcontinental main line as far west as Benson in 1880, bringing rail service to within 20 miles of the community. By

12

the end of the year, Tombstone was the hub of one of the most productive mining districts in the West and had a population of 10,000, rivaling Prescott (the territorial capital) and Tucson (the county seat). In 1881, it was designated the seat of newly formed Cochise County.

Although fire raged through the community in 1881, the townspeople quickly rebuilt their devastated businesses, allowing prosperity to start anew. Later that year, the gunfight at the O.K. Corral (which pitted Doc Holliday, Wyatt Earp, and Earp's brothers Morgan and Virgil against the cattle-rustling Clanton family and Tom and Frank McLowery) epitomized the rough-and-ready conditions that made Tombstone famous.

A variety of businesses, including the Oriental Saloon, the Grand Hotel, and a popular vaudeville playhouse called the Bird Cage Theater, flourished as the mines enjoyed great success. A magnificent county courthouse and the towering St. Paul's Episcopal Church, both built in 1882, testified to the community's rising wealth and sophistication. Only a few years after its creation, Tombstone was the center of the largest silver-producing area in Arizona—a place reportedly having fifty mines and seven quartz mills (which processed ore) in its vicinity.

The community benefited greatly from a 21-mile pipeline, which supplied water from the Huachuca Mountains, but it lacked and desperately wanted efficient rail transportation. Leaders searching for a solution considered both a streetcar line and steam railroad to be priorities. Although plans for a streetcar line never advanced beyond the discussion stage, the Arizona & New Mexico Railroad, an entity affiliated with the Atchison, Topeka & Santa Fe Railway, envisioned running steam trains from Nogales, Arizona, to Deming, New Mexico, over a route passing through Tombstone. To support the construction of this new east–west route, the company, in 1882, built south from Southern Pacific's main line at Benson along the San Pedro River to Fairbank (9 miles west of Tombstone). From this rural location, it built west to Nogales but never finished the portion east to Tombstone, much less to New Mexico, despite having prepared some of the grading.

The promoters of several other railroads also sought to profit from the mining district's expansion. The most ambitious venture was the San Diego Bee Line, a corridor intended to link southern California and Deming via northern Mexico and southern Arizona. Unfortunately for local businesses, none of the proposed railroads came to fruition. Consequently, travelers bound for Tombstone continued to endure the inconvenience of stagecoach travel from Benson, Fairbank, and other railroad towns.

Over the next several years, water accumulation in some of the larger mines and decreasing output from several smaller ones dashed all hope for uninterrupted prosperity. Two of the largest companies, Grand Central Mine and Contention Works, worked frantically to pump out the water, only to realize that it was a losing proposition. In 1884, a financial panic spread throughout Tombstone and two years later, a fire severely damaged the Contention Works pumping facility. Bowing to the inevitable, the struggling operator chose not to reopen its mine. In response, the Grand Central mine abandoned its pumping effort as well.

A passenger train on the Tombstone Branch is heading west and about to pass the impressive Cochise County Court House in 1905. The junction at Fairbank is just 9 miles away. (Arizona State Library.)

Tombstone's future appeared to be as dismal as its name, as virtually all of its silver mines closed and both men and investment capital gravitated towards copper excavation sites in the south of the county. To serve these emerging copper mines, the Arizona & Southeastern Railroad, a carrier owned by Phelps Dodge Company, built north from Bisbee during the late 1880s to an interchange with the Arizona & New Mexico at Fairbank. In 1894, the carrier constructed its own route along the opposite side of the San Pedro River from Fairbank to the Southern Pacific main line at Benson.

Tombstone, however, still lacked a railroad of any kind. By the time the legendary Edward Schieffelin died in Oregon in 1897, almost penniless but still searching for gold and silver, the famed mining center that he had helped establish was a veritable ghost town. Schieffelin's discovery eighteen years before would be the last major silver strike in the United States. He was buried in his prospector's clothes a few miles east of town.

The local mining district slumped until the Tombstone Consolidated Mines Company succeeded in pumping water from one of its mines in 1901. Using massive machinery, the company continued this effort until it had removed hundreds of millions of gallons of water, allowing it to resume excavating large quanities of ore. At approximately the same time, railroad construction crews returned to the region to lay more track. In 1902, Phelps Dodge turned over the Arizona & Southeastern to the newly created El Paso & Southwestern

Railroad. The new owner (working through a subsidiary) soon finished an extension of its route from Douglas (near Bisbee) across the vast and desolate expanse to El Paso, Texas. In 1903, this company built a branch from Fairbank to Tombstone using a portion of the rail grade prepared more than twenty years earlier.

Tombstone residents were jubilant when the first train arrived and came to depend on the Tombstone & Fairbank Limited (an impressive name for a train that traveled a mere 9 miles), as well as the carrier's growing shipments of commodities, silver bullion, foodstuffs, and supplies. Town leaders nevertheless welcomed the possibility of additional rail service. In 1905, with local mines expanding at a rate reminiscent of twenty years before, the Tombstone & Southern Railroad constructed several miles of track extending southeast from near town. Negotiating the mineral-rich Tombstone Hill to reach the Contention Mine and several other underground facilities, this short line's trains conveyed vast shipments of ore to the Southern Pacific interchange for shipment to processing mills in El Paso.

Changing Times

Although the synergy between Tombstone's railroads helped the mining district to reestablish itself as Arizona's largest silver-producing area, the duration of the second mining boom was shorter than that of the first. By 1909, flooding in the mines was again significantly inhibiting production. In 1910, Tombstone & Southern discontinued operations and turned portions of its route over to El Paso & Southwestern. In 1911, the last pumping efforts in the district ceased. With Tombstone in the throes of another catastrophic downturn, citizens began to look back fondly on the glory years that had passed.

From this point until the end of service, the branch to Tombstone was never more than a lightly used freight-oriented corridor. The El Paso & Southwestern did, however, improve its services in the region with the opening of the Tucson Extension in 1912. Originating near Fairbank at a location named Benson Junction, this line gave the carrier its own route to Tucson—one that virtually paralleled the rival Southern Pacific east of Mescal, Arizona.

More than forty years after the abandonment of service, Tombstone's depot seems frozen in time, flanked by an ex-Southern Pacific caboose. (Photo by author.)

The El Paso & Southwestern competed vigorously with Southern Pacific for long-distance freight and passenger traffic during the late 1910s, but by the middle of the 1920s, this rivalry had ended. Dwarfed by its powerful rival, the El Paso & Southwestern merged with the Arizona & New Mexico before ultimately being acquired by the San Francisco-based Southern Pacific in 1924. Unwilling to maintain two rail lines between Benson and Fairbank, Southern Pacific abandoned the original Arizona & New Mexico route between those towns in 1926.

Tombstone and its rail line faded into virtual obscurity as the local economy slumped yet again. Passenger service dwindled from three trains in each direction daily to a single daily round trip. By the time the townspeople held the first Helldorado Day celebration to attract tourists in 1929, the community had diminished to about 300 inhabitants. Although residents staged the event annually—and gave the town its now-familiar nickname, The Town Too Tough To Die—the legendary mining camp's future appeared bleak when, in 1931, the last county offices were moved out of the courthouse to Bisbee, the new county seat. By then, more of the former Tombstone & Southern had been pulled up, and passenger traffic had dropped to the point that Southern Pacific operated only a twice-weekly mixed train from Benson to Tombstone. Fourteen years later, when the El Paso & Southwestern was formally absorbed into Southern Pacific (and thus lost its identity as a distinct company), the future of the branch was in doubt.

As Tombstone languished, films such as *My Darling Clementine*, starring Henry Fonda, and *Gunfight at the O.K. Corral*, starring Burt Lancaster, dramatized its spirited past—in some instances with little attention to historical accuracy. With the public's fascination with the community—and especially the legendary shootout—on the rise, a resident rebuilt the famed corral to the dimensions recollected by old timers. The state government took occupancy of the former courthouse in 1959 and converted it into a historical museum.

When Tombstone's last mine ceased operations that year, the end of its railroad service seemed almost inevitable. Freight shipments between the community and Benson yard (hauled using a diesel locomotive) dropped to an average of less than one carload of freight per month. Southern Pacific closed the Tombstone depot in the spring of 1960. It discontinued local service and abandoned the branch in August of that year.

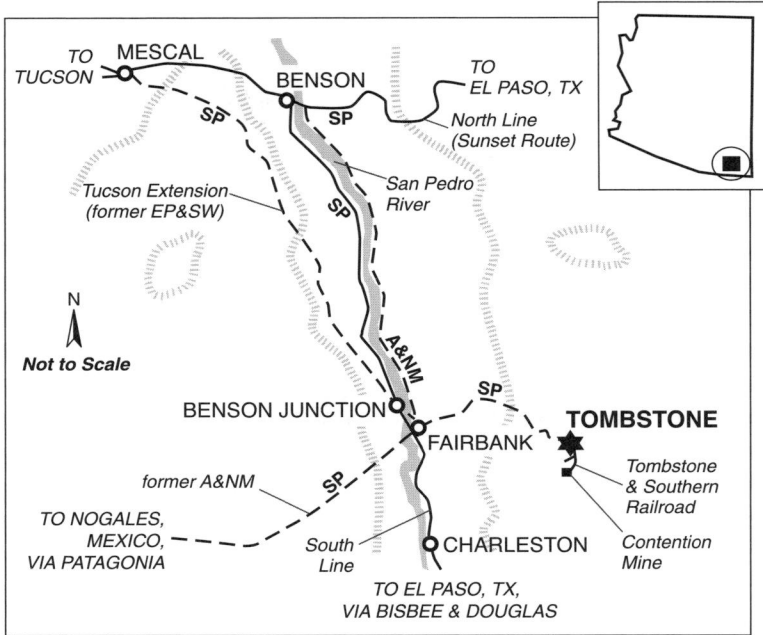

Abandonment's Legacy

Within a few years, much of the former El Paso & Southwestern had been relegated to scrap. By the end of 1960, Southern Pacific had rerouted the passenger trains operating over the Tucson Extension and the rest of the more southerly route to El Paso (a long-distance corridor it called the South Line) onto its original line (the North Line) through Benson. No longer would the Sunset Limited, Golden State, and other passenger trains grace the South Line's rail through Douglas and Fairbank. In 1961, Southern Pacific received approval to abandon the portion of the Tucson Extension between Benson Junction and Mescal as well as the South Line east of Douglas. In 1962, it abandoned its branch to Patagonia, part of the old route to Nogales.

Southern Pacific donated a boxcar, caboose, and its depot to Tombstone's municipal government, which transformed the station into the local library in 1961. The following year, the entire town of Tombstone was declared a National Historic Landmark, protecting its aging streetscape for future generations to see. Southern Pacific's remaining freight service between Benson and Douglas, a lightly used route called the Douglas Branch, seemed destined for abandonment after Bisbee's last major mining operation closed in 1974.

A recession hampered the region's economy for several more years, but automobile traffic on Interstate 10 through Benson and on other roads continued to grow.

By the end of the decade, many motorists were making side trips to Tombstone, hoping to see the legendary O.K. Corral, only to find that nothing of the place had survived. As tourism grew, new restaurants and shops began to sprout up on Allen Street, Tombstone's main thoroughfare.

By the late 1980s, Southern Pacific had formally expressed interest in divesting itself of the Douglas Branch. Recognizing the area's tourism potential, an investor publicized his interest in acquiring the branch for a steam-powered excursion railway around 1990. As part of this plan, he envisioned rebuilding the tracks and trestles of the old Tombstone Branch despite the opposition this action would likely generate from advocates of the San Pedro Riparian National Conservation Area, a popular birdwatching area along the river. When this bold proposal, which also called for constructing a new station and a hotel-resort complex in Tombstone, garnered little municipal support and failed to advance beyond preliminary discussions (largely due to the investor's limited financial resources), Southern Pacific reassessed its options and leased the Douglas Branch to the newly created San Pedro & Southwestern Railway in 1992. The rebuffed investor objected to this transaction and took the matter to court without success.

In early 1995, the San Pedro & Southwestern purchased the route and pleased railroad enthusiasts by inaugurating its own excursion service. These trains, operating between Benson and Charleston, skirted the western edge of the mining district and appeared to be a great success. Nevertheless, the short line stopped operating the trains in 1999 while undergoing a change in management. Although the company scrapped the tracks to Douglas and removed the line to Bisbee from service, this railroad came under new ownership in 2003, raising hope for a revival in the freight business, including cross-border interchange traffic with rail lines serving Mexico.

Epilogue

With covered sidewalks, old storefronts, and wide streets, Tombstone retains the semblance of a late-nineteenth-century town. The absence of casinos, fast-food restaurants, and motels differentiates the community from many former mining towns and has helped preserve its distinctive western character. The Episcopal Church, the City Hall, and the Court House, landmarks listed on the National Register of Historic Places since the early 1970s, survive as timeworn reminders of the boom times that ended years ago.

Much like their counterparts from a bygone era, many contemporary travelers visit the Bird Cage Theater, Oriental Saloon, and the replica of the O.K. Corral. Those visitors ambling south of Allen Street will see the boxcar and caboose still painted in the Southern Pacific color scheme but will find little evidence of the Tombsone & Southern's route.

Railroad passengers can follow part of the path of nineteenth-century Tombstone-bound travelers when they ride Amtrak's Sunset Limited, which uses a portion of the former Tucson Extension that has become part of Union Pacific's California–New Orleans main line. Virtually nothing remains of Fairbank, however, where the once-intricate network of lines is now reduced to a single track. The bygone branch to Tombstone, encroached upon by several private homes on the western edge of town, is today difficult to discern on the rugged desert terrain.

For Further Study

SUGGESTED READING:
Myrick, David F. *Railroads of Arizona.* Vol. 2, *Phoenix and the Central Roads.* Berkeley, Calif.: Howell-North Books, 1975), 226–31, 443–63.

OTHER PRINCIPAL REFERENCES:
Dollar, Tom. *Tucson to Tombstone: A Guide to Southeastern Arizona.* Phoenix: Arizona Highways, 2001, 60–68.
Lewis, Edward A. *American Shortline Railway Guide.* 5th ed. Waukesha, Wis.: Kalmbach Publishing, 1996, 277.
Myers, John. *Tombstone's Early Years.* Lincoln: University of Nebraska Press, 1995, 46, 81, 188.
Spude, Robert L. *Tombstone: Arizona Silver Camp.* Las Vegas: Nevada Publications, 1979, 15–16.

BOONEVILLE, ARKANSAS (4,117)

Historic operator: Chicago, Rock Island & Pacific Railway
Last route abandoned: 1980
Notable reuse of right-of-way: None

Many railroaders remember Booneville as a division point on the Chicago, Rock Island & Pacific's "Choctaw Route," a corridor that saw passage of notable long-distance trains, including the Memphis section of the Californian. This community is also significant for being one of the largest communities left without rail service when the Rock Island suspended operations in 1980. Twenty-one years later, fire obliterated Booneville's historic railroad eating house, the last salient reminder of its rail-oriented past.

Historical Perspective

Many wagon teams departing Little Rock traveled west through the Ouachita Mountains on their way to the Petit Jean River Valley in the 1820s. On one of these journeys, a friendship developed between pioneer Walter Cauthron and U.S. Army Captain Benjamin Bonneville. While Bonneville continued on to Fort Smith, Cauthron stopped in the valley and established a trading post there around 1828. Cauthron christened the emerging settlement Bonneville to honor his friend the captain. For reasons that remain poorly understood but may relate to public sentiment for frontiersman Daniel Boone, the townspeople soon changed the community's name to Booneville.

The difficulty of reaching the valley did not stop leaders from clinging to the notion that their isolated settlement would some-day become an important trading center.

Local officials platted the town in 1836, the same year that Arkansas attained statehood. Nevertheless, relatively few newcomers arrived over the next several decades, when tens of thousands poured into other communities in the state. At the start of the Civil War, Booneville still had only about 400 inhabitants.

On two occasions, community leaders moved the center of town short distances in the hope of fostering development. As late as 1878, when Booneville became an incorporated town, some still firmly believed that it had the potential to become a prominent city. Railroad companies evidently did not share this dream; their absence from the community gave another generation of townspeople little choice but to rely on wagon travel.

Booneville's isolation finally ended in 1899, when the Choctaw, Oklahoma & Gulf Railroad, which was building eastward from Howe in Indian Territory, operated its

17

In a scene almost frozen in time, a trainman looks on as the westbound Choctaw Rockette pauses at Booneville, circa 1960. This Budd rail diesel car will travel another 511 miles to Amarillo, Texas. (Photo by Ed Wojtas, Rock Island Technical Society Collection.)

first train through the valley. Shortly after rail service began, community leaders once again relocated portions of Booneville by moving downtown buildings from the south side to the north side of the tracks. Almost overnight, the community's ramshackle downtown gave way to a well-planned business district.

The railroad rose greatly in status as the construction crew worked eastward and met another crew building westward from Little Rock. In late 1899, the carrier inaugurated through service on the new Choctaw Route from Memphis, Tennessee, to Weatherford, Indian Territory—a corridor stretching 563 miles and providing direct service between Little Rock, Oklahoma City, and other important business centers.

The next several years were exciting times for Booneville. When the state divided Logan County into two districts in 1901, the community became the seat of the southern district. The following year, its residents dedicated a fine brick courthouse at the center of town. Although Booneville had missed the opportunity to share in the spectacular population growth that brought great prosperity to other Arkansas towns, its transportation role grew larger after the Chicago, Rock Island & Pacific gained control of the Choctaw in 1902. Gradually, the Rock Island transformed the route into one of the state's most prominent transportation corridors. Lengthy trains now rolled across the vast and open expanse to Tucumcari, New Mexico, a junction with the El Paso & Northwestern Railroad (a Southern Pacific predecessor). A trackage-rights agreement between the two carriers allowed them to maintain their interchange 59 miles farther east on the Choctaw Route at Santa Rosa, New Mexico.

As a division point on the Rock Island, Booneville had all the qualities of a successful railroad town, including a depot, engine house, railroad offices, freight yard, and several hotels near the tracks. One of the largest of the hotels, situated on railroad property, was operated by the highly reputable John J. Grier Hotel Company. This company secured the franchise to operate eating houses along the Rock Island in 1907 and opened one of its Grier Houses next to the hotel in 1910. The Grier eating house boasted a dining room with an attractive arched ceiling that seated fifty and a lunchroom that seated thirty-four. Patrons relaxed in comfort with varnished white maple floors and fine tables and chairs made of Arkansas gum.

Booneville also enjoyed a degree of commercial diversification, especially after the Arkansas State Tuberculosis Sanatorium opened south of town in 1910. Both the healthy and the afflicted traveled long distances to reach this renowned facility. At the corner of Main and Broadway, meanwhile, two prominent financial institutions, the Bank of Booneville and the Farmers and Merchants Bank, emerged as symbols of Booneville's prosperity and vitality. Even so, the Rock Island was still Booneville's foremost business enterprise. When the town observed its fiftieth anniversary in 1928, eight daily passenger trains served its depot. A pair of long-distance passenger trains operated in each direction over the Choctaw Line (one of which ran the entire distance from Memphis to Tucumcari), while local trains worked the route in opposite directions from Booneville to Little Rock and El Reno, Oklahoma (a junction with the carrier's Twin Cities–Fort Worth main line). Although the dining room in Grier House had served its last customer (improvements in railroad dining-car service led to its closing in 1925), the lunch counter and depot remained vibrant and attractive places.

By 1929, Booneville had obviously triumphed over its earlier economic woes. The county dedicated a three-story masonry courthouse that year, and a large cotton yard adjacent to the depot shipped carloads of cotton bales to Memphis and other major cities. The Rock Island provided stable employment to a large number of men, and the eating house bustled at certain times of the day.

Unfortunately, such prosperity could not be sustained. The Great Depression pushed the Rock Island into bankruptcy in 1933 and necessitated the elimination of many local jobs and certain services, including the lunch counter, which saw its last customer in 1936. The railroad gradually reduced Booneville's role primarily to that of a crew-change point bereft of major service facilities.

Despite the suffering that ensued, the townspeople's spirits were momentarily lifted in 1938 when President Franklin D. Roosevelt made a campaign speech at the depot from his private railcar—the only such stop he made in Arkansas. Two years later, the Rock Island introduced the Choctaw Rocket—the first diesel-powered streamliner to operate in Arkansas—giving residents faster and more comfortable passenger service. It equipped this train, which operated between Memphis and Amarillo, with lightweight coaches, a sleeping car, and a combination parlor-dining-observation car. As the nation deepened its involvement in World War II, increasing numbers of residents rode the Choctaw Rocket and the Memphis section of the Californian, a heavyweight Pullman-equipped train providing direct service to Los Angeles through the Southern Pacific interchange at Santa Rosa.

Changing Times

Life in Booneville continued to center on the Rock Island after the war, but the glamour of the railroad faded. In 1945, the carrier transformed Grier House into its Booneville depot (equipped with an office and telegraph station), allowing the old station to be demolished. In 1959, it dropped the Memphis section of the Californian, replacing it with the Cherokee. In 1953, it replaced the Rocket with the more economical Choctaw Rockette, a daylight service consisting of two Budd rail diesel cars (RDCs). For a brief time, the RDCs operated in tandem between Oklahoma City and Little Rock; later they were used as single-car trains between Memphis and Oklahoma City.

Booneville had an especially strong connection to the Rockette due to its continuing role as a crew-change point. On its eastbound run, the conductor took orders for box lunches from passengers in Oklahoma and gave this information to the agent in Howe. The agent telegraphed a message to Booneville, where the meals were prepared and brought onboard. The RDC traveled at speeds of up to 79 mph and traversed diverse scenery,

Eighteen years after the departure of its last train, Booneville's former Grier eating house and railroad station crumbles from neglect. In 2001, the structure went up in flames. (Photo by author.)

ranging from the vast Oklahoma plains to the heavily forested slopes of Magazine Mountain (the highest point in Arkansas), east of Booneville.

The future of both the Rockette and local freight service appeared bright in 1954, when the railroad acquired a third RDC and extended the Rockette's service west to Amarillo, lengthening its run to 762 miles. The following year, the Ace Comb Company opened a new production plant in Booneville, a factory that became an important local freight customer. In 1960, the Western Pacific Railroad discontinued its Zephyrette (RDC) service between Oakland and Salt Lake City, giving the Rockette the distinction of being the country's longest RDC route.

From this point forward, though, nearly all of the major developments affecting rail service in Booneville were negative. The Rockette disappeared from company timetables during the summer of 1964, reducing passenger service to the train formerly known as the Cherokee. The company later stripped three of the RDCs of their motors, refurbished their interiors, and relegated them to the rear of this unnamed Memphis–Tucumcari mail train until the route became freight-only in late 1967.

As the Rock Island scaled back, it reduced the number of crews based in Booneville to only a few. By the late 1960s, the outlook for Booneville turned sharply for the worse. Many small businesses closed, the community experienced a precipitous drop in population, and the completion of Interstate 40, which bypassed Booneville

by more than 25 miles, separated it from the flow of commerce.

As its physical plant declined and its losses escalated, Rock Island declared bankruptcy for a third and final time in 1975. Although the carrier continued to provide freight service, a devastating labor strike during the summer of 1979 disrupted operations over its entire system. Fearing that the work stoppage would cripple the regional economy, the ICC ordered the Kansas City Terminal Railway to temporarily provide rail service over the Choctaw Route and several other routes in the region.

By this time, only two businesses in Booneville—an Ace Comb plant and Wolverine Toys—shipped by rail. Not only were the tracks in poor condition, limiting speeds in certain areas to around 20 mph, but a fire had damaged a bridge in western Arkansas, severing the route between Booneville and the Oklahoma state line for almost a month. Local officials rallied to save the Choctaw Route, warning that Booneville would "dry up" without continued access to a railroad. Their task became more difficult when Rock Island formally suspended service on the line and other parts of its system in March 1980.

Abandonment's Legacy

Influential public officials felt strongly that the Choctaw Route, now more commonly called the Sunbelt Line, had the potential to reemerge as a viable freight corridor. The most direct route available between Little Rock, Oklahoma City, Amarillo, and northeastern New Mexico, it appeared to be a high priority for preservation.

A committee organized through the Booneville Chamber of Commerce joined representatives of Native American groups, shippers, and state officials on a trip to Chicago to discuss with trustees of Rock Island the possibility of acquiring a portion of the line. The group supported the state government's effort to apply for a low-interest federal loan and urged the Arkansas legislature to allocate funds to acquire the portion of the Rock Island east of the Oklahoma line, a segment with a value placed as high as $36 million. The legislature rejected their proposal by a narrow margin in late 1981.

Despite this, hope for the Sunbelt Line was high in early 1982, when Oklahoma officials reported that the Atchison, Topeka & Santa Fe Railroad (Santa Fe) had an interest in the entire Memphis–Amarillo portion. Santa Fe officials entered negotiations, met with prospective shippers, and traveled with public officials on an inspection trip aboard a motorized car. Their interest waned, however, due in part to the formidable costs of rebuilding the line.

The governors of Arkansas, Kansas, and Oklahoma sponsored a meeting during March of that year to discuss the sluggish pace of Rock Island's liquidation. The company's trustees agreed to leave the Sunbelt Line (that is, the Choctaw Route) in place until early 1983, making possible several more legislative attempts to preserve the corridor. Budgetary problems and opposition from two Santa Fe competitors, the Missouri Pacific Railroad and the St. Louis Southwestern (Cotton Belt) Railway, each with much to lose from its rival's expansion, hampered these last-minute initiatives. Although they gathered considerable support, the proposed legislation was ultimately to no avail.

The historic Rock Island emblem vanished from the American transportation scene in 1984 when the trustees transferred the company's assets to the newly created Chicago Pacific Corporation. Deeply involved in real estate and other nontransportation activities, Chicago Pacific sold a portion of the Sunbelt Line to a salvage company, which, in 1985, removed most of the track between Danville, Arkansas, and Howe (including the track in Booneville), severing the most direct route between the state capitals of Arkansas and Oklahoma.

Various institutions intervened to save other portions of the Choctaw Route. A grain company bought the 35-mile segment from Perry to Danville in 1986, allowing the Little Rock & Western Railroad, which had already resurrected part of the route, to resume freight service over this segment. In Oklahoma, the state government took steps to preserve a lengthy segment threatened with abandonment. In Booneville, however, the Choctaw Route had been relegated to the past. Much of the former railroad property, including Grier House and the rest of the depot area, was now in the possession of a scrap metal company.

Notwithstanding the financial issues facing their community, townspeople had an interest in showcasing their proud heritage. The Grier House joined the Bank of Booneville on the National Register of Historic Places in 1992. Farmers and Merchants Bank Building and the Courthouse—a fine structure in the Italian Renaissance revival style—received the same designation in 1993 and 1997, respectively. The community also studied the possibility of converting Grier House into a restaurant, museum, or city hall, but these efforts eventually stalled. Tragically, the landmark went up in flames in 2001, saddening those who had hoped that it would once again become a prominent civic facility.

Epilogue

Visitors to Booneville will find strips of track embedded in the pavement at the former Grant Street crossing east of the depot. On the salvage company's property, several hundred yards of track are partially obscured by rusting automobiles—an ironic fate for a once-important passenger route. Near the toy factory, which now ships entirely by truck, the right-of-way remains plainly visible.

Today Booneville continues to be one of Arkansas' largest communities that is inaccessible by rail and lacking convenient access to an interstate highway or a major airport. Businesses in the community, like those awaiting the railroad's construction more than a century ago, suffer from comparatively poor transportation options. Although concerns that Booneville would dry up without rail service have proved unfounded, this community clearly would be much different today had the Choctaw Line been able to sustain its role as a major route though the heart of the Sunbelt.

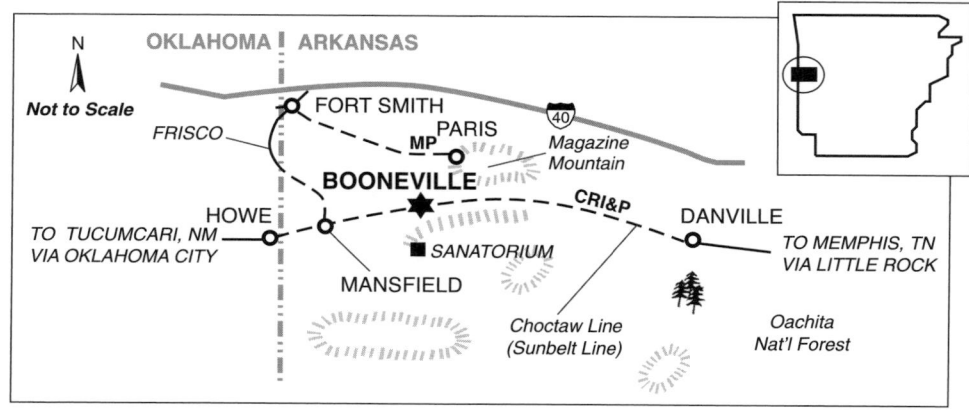

For Further Study

SUGGESTED READINGS:

Goen, Steve Allen. *Down South on the Rock Island: 1940–1969.* La Miranda, Calif.: Four Ways West publications, 2002, 55–59, 75, 96–102.

Hull, Clifton E. *Railroad Stations and Trains though Arkansas and the Southwest.* Little Rock: Arkansas Railroad Club, 1997, 11, 16–35.

Lane, Richard L. "Liquidating the Rock." *Railroad History* 181 (Autumn 1999): 103–12.

Logan County, Arkansas: Its History and Its People. Booneville, Ark.: Logan County Historical Society, 1987, 35–45.

Pollard, Bill. "Railroad Eating Houses Along the Rock Island." *Rock Island-Technical Society Digest* 11 (1993): 66–101.

OTHER PRINCIPAL REFERENCES:

Back on Track: A Guide for New Uses for Old Depots. Little Rock: Arkansas Historic Preservation Program, 1993.

Duke, Donald, and Edmund Keilty. *RDC: The Budd Rail Diesel Car.* San Marino, Calif.: Golden West Books, 1990, 217–20.

Maiken, Peter T. *Night Trains: The Pullman System in the Golden Years of American Rail Travel.* Baltimore: Johns Hopkins Press, 1989, 244.

Pollard, Bill. "Booneville's Rock Island Depot—An Obituary," *Booneville [Arkansas] Democrat,* 27 June 2001.

Wojtas, Ed. "Vest-Pocket Rockets." *Passenger Train Journal* 13, no. 12 (1982): 34–41.

EUREKA SPRINGS, ARKANSAS (2,278)

Historic operator: Missouri & Arkansas Railway
Last route abandoned: 1961
Notable reuse of right-of-way: Tourist railway

The short line serving Eureka Springs rose to its zenith during an era of Victorian elegance and commercial extravagance. This line supported a small community's transformation into an internationally renowned resort acclaimed for its fine hotels, luxurious spas, and breathtaking mountain views. After many years of prosperity, both the rail line and the celebrated city it served fell on hard times, causing many colorful Ozark traditions to disappear.

Historical Perspective

In the middle of the nineteenth century, the Osage Indian chief White Hair informed J. M. Richardson, a settler who made the Ozarks his home, that the substance emanating from a nearby limestone fissure had mysterious healing powers. Shortly after Richardson visited the spring and reported his discovery, a primitive settlement emerged adjacent to the waters. This community, consisting mostly of transients, became known as Indian Healing Springs and Big Spring.

When medical workers used the water to treat wounded soldiers during the Civil War, its therapeutic qualities captivated the general public. The townspeople christened the village Eureka Springs in 1879 for reasons that are unclear, but the name undoubtedly added to the town's mystique. After a yellow fever epidemic raged through Memphis that same year, thousands of disease sufferers arrived to "take the cure" in the village's waters. Word of miraculous healing quickly spread throughout the country. By the time Eureka Springs became an incorporated city in 1880, its sprawling environs reportedly included several thousand homes and more than 10,000 inhabitants.

For Eureka Springs to distance itself from its humble origins, however, it needed a railroad. To the disappointment of business leaders, several heavily publicized efforts to build rail lines through town failed to move beyond the planning stage. Within a few years, though, it appeared only a matter of time before the town's railroad problem would be resolved. In 1882, the St. Louis-San Francisco (Frisco) Railway created the Missouri & Arkansas Railway, which built a 13-mile line from Seligman, Missouri, to Beaver, Arkansas, a small town within a few miles of the resort. Early the following year, the Frisco consolidated the short line's operations into the newly created Eureka Springs Railway, which laid the final 6 miles of track to the booming spa town.

The townspeople's convictions about the importance of rail service proved to be correct.

23

The Missouri & North Arkansas' Blue Goose shows signs of age as it picks up cans of cream but apparently few passengers in Eureka Springs during the 1940s. (Photo by Clifton Hull, William Pollard Collection.)

Soon, multitudes of travelers arrived at the depot, many in the comfort of palace cars built by the Pullman Company. A turntable, roundhouse, freight depot, and shop facilities on the depot grounds generated many well-paying jobs. Freight trains hauled coal and general merchandise, as well as stone used to construct new downtown buildings—the most magnificent being the five-story Crescent Hotel. Completed in 1886, the Crescent earned accolades for its one hundred oversized rooms and spacious dining facilities. Built atop a hill, it came to be affectionately called the Grand Old Lady of the Ozarks, a title befitting its status as the region's most recognizable structure.

For decades, Eureka Springs basked in the spotlight as a center for the "healing arts." Likened to Switzerland on account of its narrow and angular streets, it became a prototype for successful community planning and attracted travelers from around the world. Passengers arriving by train relished the beautiful mountain views, the scenic ride along Leatherwood Creek, and a brief stop at the Narrows, a 100-foot cut through a ridge along the White River featured in the railroad's advertisements. Beginning in 1891, passengers could make transfers at the Eureka Springs depot to mule-drawn streetcars that took them up a steep hill to reach the center of town. One of the few streetcar companies in Arkansas, the line enjoyed significant increases in patronage following its electrification in 1898.

The Eureka Springs Railway's passenger service put the community's fine hotels, restaurants, and spas within reach of millions of prospective visitors. By interchanging passenger cars with the Frisco at Seligman, it allowed travelers to arrive from Kansas City and St. Louis without changing trains. The railway reorganized as the St. Louis & North Arkansas Railroad in 1899 and extended its route two years later from a rural location north of town to Harrison, a thriving business center to the southeast.

As Eureka Springs blossomed, the Frisco leased the Crescent Hotel for five years beginning in 1902. The community's social standing rose further in 1905 when the townspeople celebrated the opening of the palatial seven-story Basin Park Hotel, a facility equipped with electric elevators and a dining room large enough to seat 200 guests. The community soon grew to more than 4,000 permanent inhabitants and was among the few towns in the region with a sewage system, electricity, gas, and waterworks.

The railroad era entered its most illustrious phase after the St. Louis & North Arkansas reorganized as the Missouri & North Arkansas Railroad (M&NA) in 1906. Popularly called the North Arkansas Line, the M&NA extended its northern terminus from Seligman to Joplin, Missouri, by laying more than 30 miles of new track and negotiating trackage rights agreements with the Frisco and Kansas City Southern. In 1909, it completed an eastward extension from Harrison to Helena, Arkansas, a port on the Mississippi River.

Travelers benefited from these projects when, in 1910, the carrier introduced an experimental Pullman service over the entire length of its system—a distance of more than 370 miles. While this particular travel accommodation lasted less than a year, the company continued to offer a diverse array of services. Some of the carrier's freight trains operating over the main line bypassed the community, but passenger trains and local freights used a 2-mile stretch of the original Eureka Springs Railway to reach the town's depot and rail yard. In 1913, the M&NA built a fine gabled passenger station in Eureka Springs made from locally quarried stone.

Changing Times

Relatively few major travel destinations of this era experienced a more precipitous fall in popularity than Eureka Springs. The luster of its resorts and spas faded as medical practices evolved and travelers turned to other warm-weather destinations. Extensive promotional efforts during World War I failed to rekindle enthusiasm for its fabled waters.

The community's diminishing appeal to travelers was only the beginning of the railroad's problems. An accident in Joplin during 1914 involving a gas-electric car headed for the spa town killed several dozen passengers and left the company in a greatly weakened financial state. That same year, Powell Clayton, one of the carrier's most faithful supporters, passed away. Making matters worse, labor costs rose sharply after the nation's railroads were put under federal management for several years beginning in 1917.

The Eureka Traction Company's termination of streetcar service in 1920 foreshadowed further losses. Seven years later, the M&NA fell into receivership. By the early 1930s, only three of fifty hotels in the community remained in business, and those few hotels still open, including the Crescent, were on the brink of insolvency. As the Great Depression devastated the tourism businesses, the community's population sank to only 1,700—less than half the number of a quarter century before.

The newly formed Missouri & Arkansas Railway acquired the former M&NA at foreclosure in 1935. The new operator tried to reinvigorate the passenger business three years later by placing the "Blue Goose," a

At the heart of the Ozarks, the Eureka Springs depot stands as a reminder of a bygone transportation era. Today the stone structure is home to an excursion railway. (Photo by author.)

streamlined and air-conditioned rail motorcar, into service. Despite the initial popularity of this self-propelled unit, the prospects for all the railway's services, as well as for Eureka Springs, were decidedly poor. In 1940, the controversial owner of the Crescent, who had been converting the structure into a hospital, was convicted of fraud for purporting to cure cancer. Soon the massive Victorian-Gothic edifice stood vacant, casting an ominous shadow over the community. While experiencing its own financial problems as well as employee unrest, the Missouri & Arkansas suspended operations in 1946.

After a group of investors from the East Coast purchased the moribund railway, there was speculation that the M&NA would be scrapped. Despite the line's poor financial history, the newly created Arkansas & Ozarks Railway reactivated the portion between Seligman and Harrison as well as the branch to Eureka Springs for freight service in 1950. At approximately the same time, other developments signaled a modest economic turnaround. The Crescent reopened under new management, catering to honeymooners and others seeking brief romantic getaways. During the 1950s, many first-time visitors arrived to attend the Ozark Folk Festival, which gradually emerged as a widely anticipated annual event. Although travelers could no longer arrive in Eureka Springs by rail, many rode the Meteor, Will Rogers, and other Frisco trains to Monett (or rode the Meteor to Seligman) and finished their journey by bus.

The tourism revival, unfortunately, lasted only a few years. By the early 1960s, abandoned buildings and crumbling streets once again marred Eureka Springs' image, and still more businesses closed, leaving the town

with a population of only about 1,400. The demise of its railway seemed all but inevitable when the federal government condemned a portion of its route near Beaver for the construction of the Table Rock Dam reservoir.

Ironically, it was water—in this case a flood—that finally ended service on the railroad so widely associated with Eureka Springs' famed spas. In the spring of 1960, high water along the Leatherwood Creek washed out some of the tracks between Beaver and Junction, stranding more than fifty freight cars. After suspending operations and removing the stranded cars, the Arkansas & Ozark abandoned its route in March 1961. Most of the rails had been removed by the spring of 1962.

Abandonment's Legacy

The rising waters of the Table Rock Dam reservoir soon submerged some of the right-of-way, and the Eureka Springs depot fell into poor condition while being used as storage space for a beverage company and a furniture manufacturer. Railroads distanced themselves farther from this part of the Ozarks when the Frisco ended all scheduled passenger service, including the Oklahoman—the lone remaining train through Monett—in 1967. A fire swept through the Crescent Hotel that same year, forcing this fabled institution to close once again.

Eureka Springs might never again have become a prominent tourist destination were it not for the persistence of its leaders. In 1971, a group of residents founded the Eureka Springs Historical Museum in a nineteenth-century stone building on Main Street. By the end of the decade, they had successfully listed the entire community on the National Register of Historic Places and supported efforts to lavishly restore the Crescent. In 1980, the hotel reopened for business. That same year, the townspeople organized the Eureka Springs Historical Society to manage the museum and embark on other commemorative activities.

In the midst of this latest revival, during 1981, the privately owned Eureka Springs & North Arkansas Railway received its papers of incorporation. This private operator acquired several miles of reconstructed former right-of-way bridges and bought several steam locomotives and

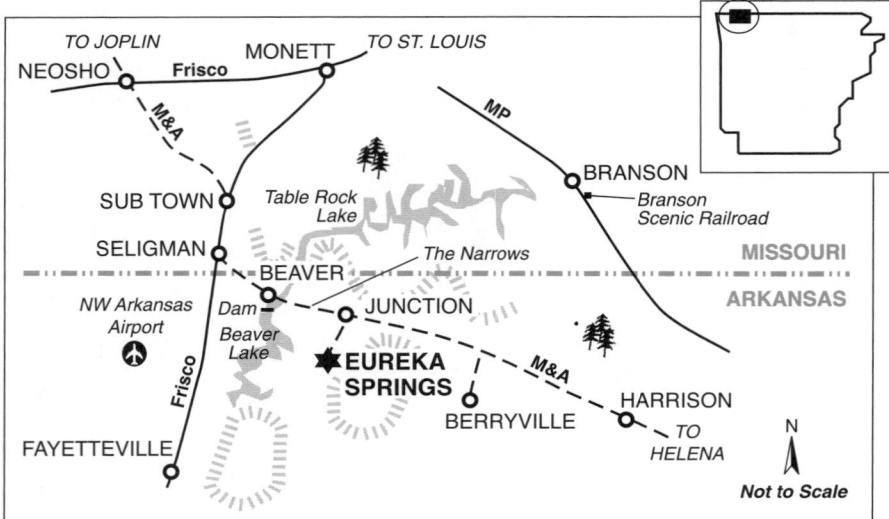

passenger cars before inaugurating excursion service over 2 miles of rebuilt track between the depot and the former junction. It also generously restored the Eureka Springs depot, which was used as a backdrop for the television miniseries *The Blue and the Gray* in 1982. Although disconnected from the national rail system, the excursion line allowed a new generation of visitors to experience the splendors of traveling through the Ozarks by rail.

The community's economy rebounded to such an extent by the mid-1990s that an entrepreneur developed an ambitious proposal to provide excursion service between Eureka Springs and Branson, Missouri, a thriving country-music resort. This proposal not only called for acquiring lengthy portions of the abandoned route but also envisioned building an entirely new route through difficult terrain north from Harrison. The newly laid track would terminate, ironically, at a location along a short line railway calling itself the Missouri and North Arkansas Railroad, a name honoring the legacy of the bygone railway to Eureka Springs. Over the short line's tracks (which were formerly part of the Missouri Pacific Railroad), the Branson Scenic Railway had a successful excursion business that annually carried thousands of tourists on trips through the Ozarks, much like the bygone North Arkansas line had done generations before. Financial considerations and landowner opposition, however, prevented the plan to link Branson and Eureka Springs by rail from moving beyond the discussion stage.

Epilogue

Eureka Springs is once again recognized for its elegant hotels, restaurants, and stores. The Basin Park has rejoined the Crescent as a first-class hotel regularly filled to capacity. Thousands of visitors arrive annually to attend the community's celebrated Passion Play, said to be the world's most heavily attended outdoor drama, and the Ozark Folk Festival, a continuing annual event.

Much like their predecessors 130 years ago, leaders in Eureka Springs struggle with concerns about inadequate transportation. In addition to lacking a connection to the rail system, the community has lost its intercity bus service and has neither commercial air service nor convenient access to an expressway. It did become more accessible to tourists, however, when the Northwest Arkansas Regional Airport—one of the few large-scale commercial airports built in the United States in recent decades—opened near Bentonville in 1998.

During the summer season, the municipal government operates motor coaches whose appearance and function are reminiscent of the bygone streetcars. These decorative buses—popularly called trolleys—carry many travelers to the depot where, just as a century ago, a steam locomotive and a string of coaches await. Gone, though, are the finely upholstered Pullman sleeping cars that once provided passengers with a luxurious and memorable journey home.

For Further Study

SUGGESTED READINGS:
Fair, James R. *The North Arkansas Line: The Story of the Missouri and North Arkansas Railroad.* Berkeley, Calif.: Howell-North Books, 1969, 29–31.
Toole, Edwin R. *The Eureka Springs Railway: A Short Line to a Little Town.* Eureka Springs, Ark.: Edwin R. Toole, 1992, 1–27.

OTHER PRINCIPAL REFERENCES:
Eureka Springs, Arkansas. Eureka Springs, Ark.: Eureka Springs Commercial Club, 1916, 1–20.
Hull, Clifton E. *Railroad Stations and Trains though Arkansas and the Southwest.* Hart, Mo.: Whiteriver Publications, 1997, 72, 100.
Potter, Janet Greenstein. *Great American Railroad Stations.* New York: Wiley & Sons, 1996, 231–32.
Wollery, D. R. *The Grand Old Lady of the Ozarks.* Hominy, Okla.: Eagle's Nest Press, 1986, 3–111.

BEVERLY HILLS, CALIFORNIA (33,784)

Historic operator: Pacific Electric Railway
Last route abandoned: 1986
Notable reuses of right-of-way: Walking trail; public right-of-way

It has been more than a half century since the Pacific Electric Railway's Red Cars regularly traveled along Santa Monica Boulevard, yet Beverly Hills retains the aura of a premier streetcar suburb. Fine homes, luxurious hotels, and strong commercial ties to Hollywood testify to the prosperity engendered by "the largest electric interurban railway system in the world." With the exception of a few strips of rail just beyond the city's western boundary, few physical remnants of this once-extensive traction system survive.

Historical Perspective

European explorers first set foot on the lush landscape east of Santa Monica Bay in 1769, during the expedition of conquistador Gaspar de Portola, the Spanish governor of California. After admiring the plentiful springs, abundant wildlife, and fertile meadows, Portola's expedition resumed its northward voyage. The Spanish later established a permanent presence in the area in the form of several large missions and, in 1821, turned the territory over to Mexico.

When jurisdiction of California passed to the United States in 1848, El Rancho Rodeo de las Aquas (The Ranch of the Gathering of the Waters), dominated commercial affairs east of the bay. Streams flowing through Coldwater and Benedict Canyons formed a *cienega*, or swamp, filled with luxuriant vegetation. The temperate climate and abundant water made this fertile land amenable to agriculture, and by the 1880s much of it was used to cultivate lima beans.

The boom in southern California's real estate market beginning in 1887 brought hope for economic development on a much larger scale. Amid a burst of commercial expansion, railroad companies hurriedly laid track through the region, but it was not until 1896 that the Pasadena & Pacific Railroad inaugurated service over a narrow gauge (3 feet 6 inches) route between Los Angeles and Santa Monica. This electric railway served local residents from a station known as Morocco (later Beverly Hills) and passed through the legendary Rancho Rodeo on the same route that Santa Monica Boulevard would follow later.

With Santa Monica poised for rapid growth, the Pasadena & Pacific built two more routes through the area in 1897. The first route, called the Santa Monica via Sawtelle Line, followed West 16th Street in Los Angeles and

28

traversed private right-of-way to reach the Morocco depot. The second route, opening only weeks after the first, extended from the Santa Monica via Sawtelle Line to the carrier's newly created shops at Sherman. This line was likened to a "back door" to the shops; it joined the original line east of the Morocco depot and—like the shops—was named in honor of the company's visionary leader, "General" Moses Sherman.

The Pasadena & Pacific's routes formed a triangle in the area that would later become Beverly Hills. This system was consolidated into the Los Angeles-Pacific Railway (LA-P) in 1898 and resembled the shape of a balloon affixed to a string, generating the new operator's official moniker of the Balloon Route. Passengers used one line between Santa Monica and Morocco but could travel in either direction over its circular system between Morocco and Los Angeles.

As investment poured into southern California, LA-P greatly improved its services. The carrier opened a new line through the Hollywood business district, expanded its shop facility at Sherman, and added a second track between Sherman Junction and Santa Monica. Never-

theless, the pace of development near the Morocco depot did not satisfy area businessman Burton E. Green and his associates. Their frustrations escalated after drilling for oil on their property only to "discover" water instead. Seeking to make the best of the situation, they formed the Rodeo Land and Water Company in 1907 to promote real estate development.

The investments made in the Rodeo Company came at an opportune time. The company's newly platted Beverly Hills subdivision—a development named after Beverly Farms, Massachusetts, where Green once lived—proved to be a great success. Green envisioned this subdivision as an integral part of a larger planned community called Beverly, with large lots and curved tree-lined streets. To stimulate the sale of property, he

A Pacific Electric Red Car, bound for Santa Monica, pauses in April 1939 at the Beverly Hills Station with the magnificent City Hall—a structure built partially on former railroad land—visible in the distance. (Photo by Ivan Baker, collection of Craig A. Rasmussen.)

worked with the railway to build an attractive stucco station along the boulevard.

Green was not content to see Beverly become a mere residential community. He and his associates also planned to build a magnificent three-story resort, the Beverly Hills Hotel, several blocks north of the depot. Progress on the resort moved slowly, even with the construction of a railway spur to the property in 1907. As hotel construction dragged on, the railway converted its tracks through Beverly to standard gauge in 1909; two years later, with the Great Merger of 1911, the LA-P became part of the Pacific Electric Railway (a subdivision of parent Southern

Just a short distance west of Beverly Hills, old Pacific Electric rails are embedded in pavement next to Santa Monica Boulevard, with a sea of modern development visible in the distance. (Photo by author.)

Pacific at the time).

When Green's hotel finally opened in 1912, word quickly spread of its spacious rooms, manicured lawns, attractive gardens, and striking Spanish architecture. As people flocked to the new community and its new hotel, officials showcased the town's busiest street by planting lines of trees along Santa Monica Boulevard and erecting a large arch above it emblazoned with the words "Beverly Hills." By the time Green moved into a palatial home in town in 1914, Beverly Hills had been incorporated as a city and had grown to more than 500 residents.

For the next thirty years, both the Pacific Electric and the Beverly Hills Hotel were among the community's most prominent institutions. The hotel attracted luminaries and other well-heeled travelers from great distances, while the interurban's car yards and shop buildings in Sherman grew to encompass more than 6 miles of track. With more than a 1,000 miles of routes in the Los Angeles area, the company could credibly claim to be "the largest electric interurban system in the world."

The interurban's Red Cars operated at 10-minute intervals on the Hollywood Line from Beverly Hills throughout much of the day, passing through the intersection of Hollywood and Vine, a renowned location in the motion picture business, and reaching the Hill Street Subway Terminal (one of the Pacific Electric's two terminals in downtown Los Angeles) in about 55 minutes. On the Santa Monica via the Sawtelle Line and the Westgate (or Brentwood) Line, Red Cars operated at similar frequencies but on these less-congested routes offered substantially faster service to downtown Los Angeles. By the early 1920s, Beverly Hills was a cosmopolitan city of more than 12,000.

As the motion picture industry grew, Beverly Hills became a prominent celebrity haunt, known especially for humorist Will Rogers. With the openings in 1925 of the Beverly Theater, a cinema with striking Moorish architecture, and, three years later, the Beverly Wilshire Hotel, a majestic $3 million "apartment hotel," the community's standing rose among the cultural elite. Boasting more than 300 luxury rooms, the nine-story Beverly Wilshire earned accolades as one of California's finest hotels. With Beverly Hills' economy in full bloom, the Triangle—the famed area bounded by Wilshire and Santa Monica Boulevards on the west and Crescent Drive on the east (substantially smaller than the triangle formed by the community's rail lines)—attracted shoppers with discerning tastes.

Changing Times

Despite the community's buoyant economy, ridership on the Pacific Electric's rail lines waned as private automobiles and motor coaches grew more widespread. Worsening congestion on local streets greatly reduced the speed of travel. The number of people riding the Red Cars fell precipitously before the Pacific Electric sold some of its local property during the early 1930s to support the construction of a new city hall.

Beverly Hills' fine residential properties and its strong commercial links to Hollywood spared the community from some of the devastation that crippled other cities during the Great Depression. The city dedicated a magnificent new post office adjacent to the depot in 1934 and continued to depend on the Pacific Electric's Red Car service as well as the "box motor" to transport express shipments and other goods to Los Angeles. Originating in downtown Beverly Hills, this freight-hauling electric car operated via West Los Angeles, Home Junction, and the Santa Monica Air Line.

By the end of the 1930s, the Pacific Electric's local passenger service was generating large deficits. In 1941, the interurban abandoned both the Santa Monica via Sawtelle Line and the Westgate Line and replaced its rail passenger service with buses between Beverly Hills and Santa Monica.

The Red Cars operating between Beverly Hills and Los Angeles via Hollywood served a vital role during World War II, only to see business plummet once again when peacetime resumed. In 1951, the beleaguered interurban, desperate to cut costs, implemented one-man operations on this route, which increased running times by about 10 minutes. In 1953, the carrier replaced two-car trains with more frequent one-car trains operating approximately every 8 minutes. This service appeared to have a bleak future, at least when compared to the region's newest streamliner, the Atchison, Topeka & Santa Fe Railway's Chief, which made a special publicity trip to Beverly Hills on the Pacific Electric that year to showcase a new era in rail travel.

Unlike the Santa Fe Chief, which became an instant success, the one-car trains serving Beverly Hills had disappointing results. The Pacific Electric's successor in the passenger business, Metropolitan Coach Lines, eliminated the last of Beverly Hills' passenger service in the autumn of 1954. To comply with a municipal ordinance, the freight trains serving customers west of West Hollywood (Sherman) yard along Santa Monica Boulevard

operated with electric locomotives. In 1958, trains on this remnant of the Hollywood–Santa Monica route were converted to diesel power. Six years later, the Pacific Electric lost its distinct identity upon being merged into its parent, Southern Pacific.

These developments seemed of little consequence to a community experiencing momentous change. By the mid-1960s, hundreds of accountants, financiers, and other professionals had established offices in Beverly Hills, rendering its downtown area a premier business location. In 1964, the immense Beverly Hilton Hotel opened along Santa Monica Boulevard. In 1971, the newly enlarged Beverly Wilshire Hotel earned distinction as Los Angeles County's first hotel to receive *grand luxe* status. During America's bicentennial year, the opening of the Museum of Television and Radio attracted still more visitors to the community.

The growth was so dramatic that motorists began to suffer from serious traffic congestion. The "big" Santa Monica Boulevard (that is, the main road from Hollywood to the coast) and "little" Santa Monica (a parallel street immediately to the south) saw a particularly large rise in the number of vehicles—a problem compounded by Southern Pacific freights using the old Pacific Electric tracks situated between these streets. These trains occasionally created awkward and dangerous situations for motorists, who were surprised to see a train in such close proximity to busy lanes of traffic. Although Southern Pacific abandoned the portion of the route from West Los Angeles to Santa Monica in 1972, its trains continued to run between Beverly Hills and Home Junction on their way to the central part of Los Angeles. Resembling the shape of the letter J (and called the West Los Angeles Branch), this remnant of past transportation glory eventually served only one regular customer in Beverly Hills, the Continental Bakery. Southern Pacific received approval to abandon the branch in 1983 and ended regular service to the community, operating its last train from Beverly Hills in 1986.

Abandonment's Legacy

By the early 1990s, employment in Beverly Hills had grown to 200,000, and municipal concerns about housing shortages and inadequate transportation were escalating. To keep its options open, Los Angeles County Transportation Commission in 1992 purchased 2.5 miles of the former West Los Angeles Branch from

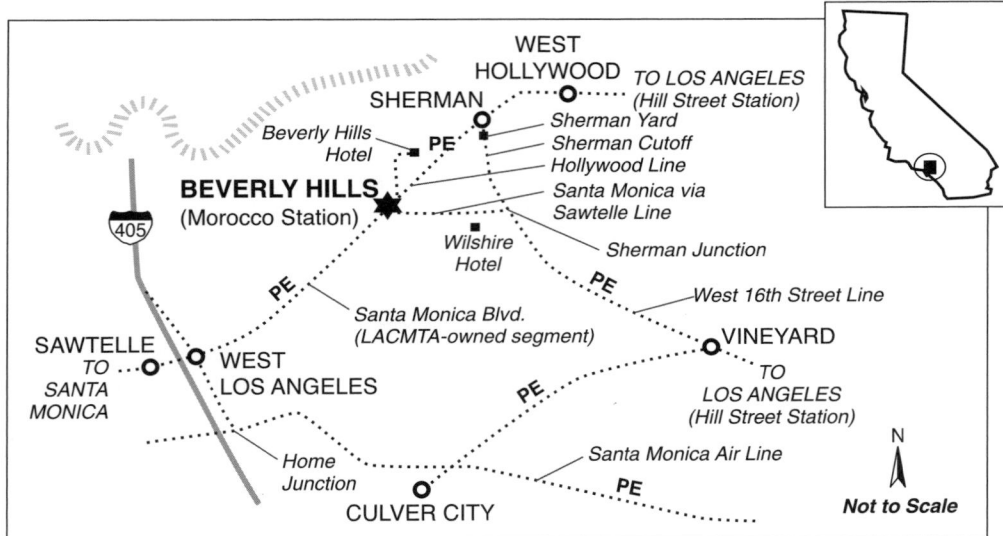

Southern Pacific. The agency's successor, the Los Angeles County Metropolitan Transportation Authority (LAC-MTA), explored the possibility of transforming this segment (which follows the median of the twin Santa Monica Boulevards between the western limits of Beverly Hills and Sepulveda Boulevard) into a rail transit line or busway—the so-called Multimodal Transit Parkway.

With an eye to the future, transit officials also considered installing an aerial people-mover system along this segment and other local streets. Despite relatively strong community support, the absence of funding and lukewarm political endorsements nullified this plan. Attention then turned to a proposed extension of the LACMTA's Red Line, which the agency envisioned following Vermont Avenue from Los Angeles to Hollywood. Although this route would pass a considerable distance from Beverly Hills, the agency sought to build a branch along Wilshire Avenue to the center of town.

The subway proposal fared little better than the people-mover had. As concern grew about the aesthetic implications of subway service, Beverly Hills officials indicated that they would consider allowing a local station to be built only if approved by referendum. Of even greater concern were methane gas fissures at risk of exploding during the construction process. Wary of these and other problems, planners eventually chose a different Red Line alignment and scuttled plans to build the branch to Beverly Hills.

Another controversial proposal moved forward in 2001, when the LACMTA adopted a plan for "bus rapid transit" on dedicated bus lanes through Beverly Hills, linking the Wilshire/Western subway station to

Santa Monica. Once again, staunch opposition forced the agency to reconsider its plan. LACMTA instead instituted "rapid bus" service using the existing traffic lane configuration.

Today, the legacy of the Pacific Electric's abandonment can still be felt in the local planning process. There is uncertainty, for example, surrounding the legal ownership of some of its former right-of-way due to ambiguity in deeds, some dating back to the nineteenth century. Officials have concerns that the right-of-way could be occupied by structures built by individuals or corporations who do not have proper title to the land.

Epilogue

Widely known for its tree-lined boulevards and curved residential streets, Beverly Hills is, in the opinion of some observers, one of the country's most exclusive and desirable communities. Many tourists congregate in its restaurants, shops, and immaculately maintained hotels, including the Beverly Hills and the Beverly Wilshire.

Travelers with an interest in the early development of Beverly Hills will find only limited evidence of its bygone interurban railways. The Beverly Hills depot was razed years ago. The land formerly occupied by the interurban's shop facility at Sherman (just east of the municipal boundary) is today an LACMTA bus service facility. On the east side of town, some of the old right-of-way lying in the median of the twin Santa Monica Boulevards is a walking trail—a path flanked by mature eucalyptus trees giving a cathedral-like appearance.

The City of Los Angeles began work in 2003 on the reconstruction and realignment of Santa Monica Boulevard from the western boundary of Beverly Hills to the Interstate 405 expressway, greatly changing the character of the old interurban route. Near the former junction in West Los Angeles, though, several sections of encrusted rail survive in the pavement, offering sad and rusting reminders of the "largest electric interurban system in the world."

For Further Study

SUGGESTED READINGS:

Basten, Fred E. *Beverly Hills: Portrait of a Fabled Lady.* Los Angeles: Douglas-West Publishers, 1975, 8–61, 154–94.

Swett, Ira L., and William A. Myers. *Trolleys to the Surf: Interurbans Special 63.* Glendale, Calif.: Interurbans Publications, 1976, 17–26, 37.

OTHER PRINCIPAL REFERENCES:

Crump, Spencer. *Ride the Big Red Cars: How Trolleys Helped Build Southern California.* Glendale, Calif.: Trans-Anglo Books, 1988, 43–46.

Hilton, George W., and John F. Due. *The Electric Interurban Railways in America.* Stanford: Stanford University Press, 1964, 412.

"Metro Rail Station Plans." *Timepoints: The Southern California Traction Review* 79, no. 5 (1992): 5–6.

Swett, Ira L. *Lines of Pacific Electric: Western District: Interurbans Special 16.* Glendale Calif.: Interurbans Publications, 1965, 43–71.

CORONADO, CALIFORNIA (24,100)

Historic operators: San Diego & Arizona Eastern Railway; San Diego Electric Railway
Last route dismantled: 1969
Notable reuses of right-of-way: Silver Strand Bikeway; access roads for San Diego–Coronado Bay Bridge

Coronado rose to the forefront of southern California's commercial affairs through the visionary leadership of towering figures such as Elisha S. Babcock Jr. and John D. Spreckels. Considering the lofty role of trains and trolleys in Coronado's past, it seems ironic that its local government pushed for the abandonment of the community's last rail line in order to support improvements to the highway system. Nevertheless, the town's renowned Hotel del Coronado survives as a majestic symbol of its rail-oriented past.

Historical Perspective

The first European to sail the waters along southern California's coast was navigator Juan Rodriguez Cabrillo, who anchored at the port that later became San Diego in 1542. Sixty years later, another explorer sailing for Spain, Sebastian Vizcaíno, christened a small group of islands along these shores Las Yslas Coronadas, meaning "the crowned islands." This name honored his four brothers, who had been canonized as saints in Rome.

Jurisdiction over these islands and the rest of Alta California passed from Spain to Mexico in 1821, and ultimately to the United States in 1848. Gradually, businessmen working in the area cleared the brush-covered North and South Islands to grow crops and sell wood, whale, and other products. By the middle 1880s, two of the proprietors who owned this property, Elisha Babcock and Hampton L. Story, had devised a plan to transform the most

southerly island into a great city and commercial port.

Babcock and Story moved forward with their grand scheme in 1886 by laying out the streets for this city—a place they called Coronado. That same year, their newly constructed Coronado Beach Railway began carrying passengers in horse-drawn cars between the island's eastern shore and a location along the coast where they envisioned building a spacious resort complex. The entrepreneurs also founded a ferry company to link the island to the wharf in San Diego and soon upgraded the streetcar's motive power from horses to steam.

By the end of 1887, excitement about the impending completion of Babcock and Story's resort, the Hotel del Coronado, was building. Early the following year, dignitaries from around the country gathered to celebrate the opening of this palatial institution—a milestone in the development of southern California. One of the largest wooden buildings in the United States, the hotel attracted patrons from distant cities and raised hopes that Coronado was on the road to commercial greatness.

Recognizing the need for the community to have direct rail service from San Diego, the streetcar company changed its name to the Coronado Railroad and laid tracks around the head of the bay and across several miles of marshland. This horseshoe-shaped route from San Diego, built to standard gauge in 1888, became universally known as the Belt Line.

Unfortunately, the optimism of this era turned to despair when an economic downturn crippled the entire region. Babcock's companies fell onto hard times, leading him to sell shares of the business to John D. Spreckels. The irrepressible Spreckels, who had amassed a fortune from his sugar holdings and real estate projects, purchased Story's shares as well. By 1893, Spreckels was the sole owner of the hotel and other valuable Coronado properties. Spreckels and his brother, Adolph, also held a considerable stake in the San Diego Electric Railway, one of the state's largest street railways.

Under John D. Spreckels's leadership, the Hotel del Coronado achieved a level of success that had eluded Babcock. Affectionately called the Grand Lady by the Sea, the hotel benefited from its close proximity to San Diego and earned accolades for elegantly furnished

rooms, superb cuisine, and fine Victorian architecture. Guests reveled in its many amenities, including a bathhouse, saltwater plunge, and private beach. Travelers unable to afford the hotel's lavish accommodations could find more modest, but still elegant, lodging at a neighboring encampment known as Tent City, which could be reached on an extension of the streetcar line.

The Coronado Railroad benefited greatly from the hotel's rising popularity. It operated excursions on the Belt Line from San Diego, conveyed the private cars of dignitaries, and, in 1893, electrified the streetcar line. With prolific ferry and streetcar service now available, the carrier discontinued regular passenger service on the Belt Line in 1896.

Less favorable to Coronado's development was its susceptibility to inclement weather. A fierce storm in 1905 was particularly devastating, ravaging the hotel and other parts of the community, including the Belt Line and streetcar routes. The forward-looking Spreckels

Reminiscent of a fairgrounds, the ambience is festive in Tent City in 1903. The San Diego & Arizona's Belt Line passes through its center, while the magnificent Hotel del Coronado towers in the distance. (Ticor Collection, San Diego Historical Society.)

All evidence of the Belt Line is gone from the former grounds of Tent City just south of Coronado's famous hotel. (Photo by author.)

responded by marshaling the resources to repair these rail lines and building a protective seawall. After the San Francisco earthquake of 1906, he moved to Coronado and built a stately mansion next to the hotel.

In addition to investing in Coronado, Spreckels worked tirelessly to promote the entire San Diego area and championed the construction of the San Diego & Arizona Railway—an extraordinarily ambitious project at the time. The proposed rail line—called "the Impossible Railroad" by some—would challenge the Atchison, Topeka & Santa Fe Railway by providing San Diego with a more direct route to major trunk lines serving the central United States. This route (which would not directly serve Coronado) was to pass through northern Mexico and tortuous mountain terrain, including the Carrizo Gorge, to its terminus in eastern California's Imperial Valley, where the carrier could maintain an interchange with Southern Pacific.

Although this railway was years away from completion, Coronado had all the qualities it needed to flourish, including a large downtown, an expanding tourism sector, and frequent streetcar service. The operators of its rail lines shouldered the burden of heavy traffic while experiencing a series of ownership changes. In 1908, the streetcar division of the Coronado Railroad became part of the San Diego Electric Railway. The remainder of its system (principally the Belt Line) became part of the San Diego Southern Railway in 1908 and San Diego & South Eastern in 1912 before being turned over five

years later to Spreckel's San Diego & Arizona.

Coronado had much to celebrate during these prosperous years. The completion of the Spreckels Securities Company Building in 1914—boasting fourteen stores, a dozen office suites, a large theater, and a bank—bolstered its image as an up-and-coming business center. That same year, the U.S. Naval Air Station opened on the North Island, allowing the Navy to expand considerably the scale of its operations.

The optimism that these developments created paled in comparison to the excitement generated by the completion of San Diego & Arizona's route to eastern California in 1919. Spreckels and other dignitaries gathered for a banquet at the Hotel del Coronado to celebrate this momentous occasion, which finally provided San Diego a direct route to the East. Over the new route, the San Diego & Arizona inaugurated through passenger service to places as far away as Chicago through its newly established connection with Southern Pacific at El Centro, California.

Nurtured by astute civic leadership and blessed with an advantageous location, Coronado grew to more than 3,000 permanent residents by 1920. By the time Spreckels died in 1926, Coronado had a firmly established reputation as a major Army and Navy base. Known as the birthplace of naval aviation—the first amphibious flight ascended from the bay in 1911—it guaranteed its place in American transportation history in early 1927 when Charles Lindbergh departed on the first leg of his historic transatlantic trip from the U.S. Naval Air Station.

Changing Times

Coronado's dependence on tourism rendered it highly vulnerable to the effects of the Great Depression, which interrupted the community's holiday spirit and raised difficult questions about the future of its hotel. As revenues diminished, Spreckel's heirs struggled to keep the streetcar system solvent and divested themselves of the financially disappointing San Diego & Arizona in 1932. The following year, the new owner—Southern Pacific—renamed the carrier the San Diego & Arizona Eastern Railway. The army vacated the North Island in 1937, and Tent City closed soon thereafter.

The community's economy took a more fortuitous turn as the country made massive investments in military facilities during World War II. As the home of the U.S.

Pacific Fleet, the community rose to the forefront of the nation's naval affairs. With the naval base busy around the clock, streetcars operating down Orange Avenue were regularly filled to capacity. Massive freight trains looped around the South Bay on the Belt Line (a route by now commonly called the Coronado Branch) to bring coal, fuel oil, and supplies to a freight yard on the North Island.

The dramatic rise in military activity during the war created significant logistical challenges in Coronado. Dredging crews deposited sand from the bay to fill the Spanish Bight, the waterway separating the North and South Islands. Farther south, the crews also filled the boggy terrain between the hotel and Imperial Beach to form a narrow strip of land that became known as the Silver Strand, improving the right-of-way available to trains and motor vehicles.

After the war, the navy remained an important freight customer, but the gradual diversion of traffic to more flexible forms of transportation necessitated that the region's railroad system be downsized. Buses replaced the trolley cars on Orange Avenue in 1947, ending Coronado's streetcar service. In 1948, the Spreckels Company sold all of its interest in the hotel and streetcar company. The following year, the last streetcars operated in the San Diego area, and the final excursion train on the Coronado Branch departed from the hotel. San Diego & Arizona Eastern's last passenger train—an overnight run between San Diego and Phoenix (operated jointly with Southern Pacific)—made its final trip in 1961.

By the time the naval station commemorated a half century of naval aviation in 1961, the Coronado Branch was nearing the end of its useful life. Although Coronado's population had grown to more than 25,000, the railroad now handled so little tonnage that it generally limited local service to one train per week. In late 1966, as plans moved ahead to build a highway bridge across the bay, officials expressed interest in using portions of the right-of-way near the area that would become the western base of the bridge for a series of toll-collection booths. Officials also targeted railroad property for use in reconfiguring streets as part of improvements to State Route 75—a highway slated for expansion to facilitate traffic flow on the bridge.

The state highway department encountered little resistance from the municipal government when it announced its interest in severing the line. With military cutbacks threatening to derail the community's economy, local leaders voiced unconditional support for the bridge project. The demise of the Coronado Branch seemed

imminent when local officials representing various naval bases wrote letters in 1968 indicating they would not oppose the line's abandonment. As the bridge and highway projects moved ahead, a small group of residents gathered near the Coronado Boat House to watch the departure of a train that was reportedly the community's last. After the last car had passed by, the mayor and a local beauty queen, Miss Coronado, embarked in a handcar down the tracks to commemorate this ending.

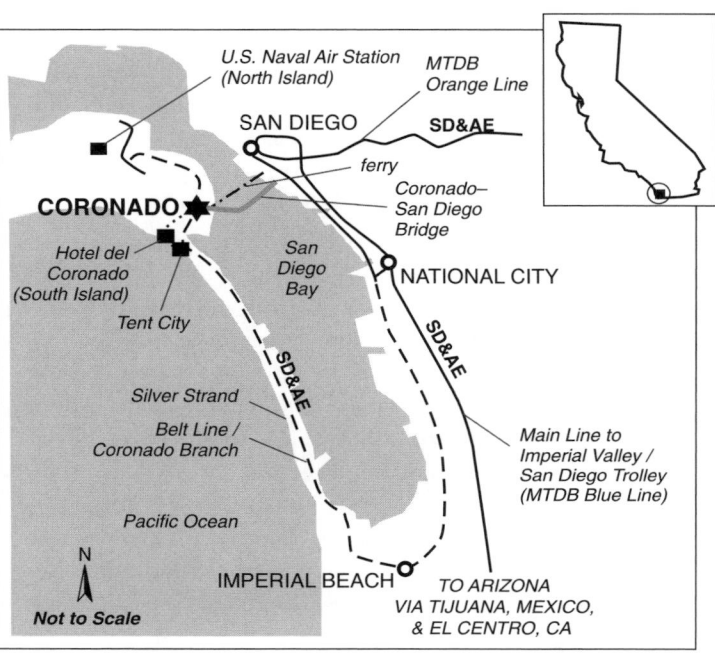

Abandonment's Legacy

Workers soon removed the track near the base of the bridge and altered this segment beyond recognition. In the summer of 1969, Governor Ronald Reagan arrived with other dignitaries to dedicate a magnificent 2-mile highway span to San Diego. Recognizing that their community was at a crossroads, residents formed the Coronado Historical Association that same year.

Along with the bridge came the demise of the ferry service to Coronado, which dated back to the community's earliest days, and the addition of thousands of motor vehicles on its streets. A salvage company purchased the Southern Pacific tracks between Coronado and Imperial Beach for a nominal price in 1971, removed them, and restored the abandoned corridor to its natural contour as stipulated in the purchase agreement.

As another development boom gathered momentum, Coronado gradually evolved into a relatively densely populated community with significant traffic problems. In due time, support grew for using the abandoned right-of-way south of the hotel for a recreational trail. After the state provided funds for the Bayshore Bikeway in 1975, a portion of the 7-mile trail was opened to the public.

Over the next fifteen years, Coronado took several ambitious steps to memorialize the past. In 1988, tour buses reminiscent of the bygone streetcars began operating over the city's streets in conjunction with the hotel's centennial celebration. That same year, the city passed an ordinance limiting the development of fast-food restaurants to protect its historic streetscape, and the owners of the hotel embarked upon a $50 million rehabilitation project. In 1989, the historical association opened a museum in a venerable three-story home—an attraction later replaced by the much larger Museum of Art and History in a historic bank building.

The saga of the Coronado Branch would ultimately become just a small part of the well-documented history of Spreckel's transportation empire. Even this legendary businessman's "impossible railroad" to eastern California would eventually be targeted for abandonment. After a severe storm damaged the line in Carrizo Gorge, officials expressed concern about the impending loss of the region's only direct railroad route to eastern California. In response, San Diego's Metropolitan Transit Development Board (MTDB) acquired most of the former San Diego & Arizona property from Southern Pacific in 1979 and arranged for the Kyle Railways to provide freight service over it.

After extensive debate, the MTDB rebuilt and electrified the portion between San Diego and the border town of Tijuana for the San Diego Trolley (today's Blue Line), which carried its first passenger in 1981, thus rekindling the legacy of Spreckel's vast electric railway system. In 1984, the MTDB turned freight operations (and the inactive portion of the old Coronado Branch to Imperial Beach) over to the newly created San Diego & Imperial Valley Railroad, a short line that still operates most of the former main line today. Planning is currently under way to reopen the old main line through Carrizo Gorge.

Epilogue

Those searching for remnants of the Coronado Branch line near the hotel will find little more than unusual property lines in the Coronado Beach Island subdivision to reveal its historical alignment. On the military grounds, tracks that once served massive naval ships are today buried beneath several layers of asphalt—not a surprise ending for a rail line offered in trade for improved motor transportation.

History enthusiasts should also enjoy visiting the Historic Railcar Plaza in National City, which showcases a National City & Otay passenger car dating back to the 1880s—the oldest known surviving piece of rolling stock that once served the South Bay. Over the years, there has been discussion about using the long-dormant and overgrown segment between National City and Imperial Beach for an excursion railway or trolley line.

The Grand Lady by the Sea is indisputably the most notable reminder of the community's impressive past. On the hotel's interior walls, photographs offer visitors a glimpse of an earlier time, when travelers arrived by rail from faraway places to enjoy the attractions of one of America's most celebrated resorts.

For Further Study

SUGGESTED READINGS:

Carlin, Katherine Eitzen, and Ray Brandes. *Coronado: The Enchanted Land.* Coronado, Calif.: Coronado Historical Association, 1998, 47–276.

Dodge, Richard. *Rails to the Silver Gate: The Spreckels San Diego Empire.* San Marino, Calif.: Pacific Railway Journal, 1960, 1–89.

Hanft, Robert M. *San Diego & Arizona: The Impossible Railroad.* Glendale, Calif.: Trans-Anglo Books, 1984, 20–25, 40–42, 54, 114, 148, 157, 182.

OTHER PRINCIPAL REFERENCES:

Fickewirth, Alvin. A. *California Railroads.* San Marino, Calif.: Golden West Books, 1992, 32–33.

San Diego Metropolitan Transit Development Board. *San Diego & Arizona Eastern Railway—Chronology.* April 1992, 1–2.

Wolinsky, Julian. "San Diego's LRT: Trying to Stay Lean." In *Light Rail Annual and Users Guide.* Pasedena, Calif.: Pentrex, 1994, 15–19.

FOLSOM, CALIFORNIA (51,884)

Historic operators: Sacramento Valley Railroad; California Central Railroad Co.;
Sacramento, Placer & Nevada Railroad; Southern Pacific
Last route abandoned: 1987
Notable reuses of right-of-way: Light-rail corridor; Folsom's Railroad Block; dormant rail line

 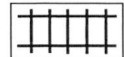 

In the nineteenth century, miners and merchants who were eager to find fortune arrived in Folsom on the first conventional passenger railroad west of the Rocky Mountains. To reach the booming gold-mining towns of the Sierra Nevada, many of them continued east on foot, by stagecoach, or by any means available. More than a century later, after the route of the Sacramento Valley Railroad had lain dormant in Folsom for more than fifteen years, railroad workers returned to this historic corridor to build a light-rail line.

Historical Perspective

The first American explorer to spend time in the vicinity of present-day Folsom is believed to have been the legendary Jedediah Smith. This frontiersman, perhaps the most famous of all mountain men, camped in the area in 1827 to evaluate its potential for beaver trapping. Although Smith issued a favorable assessment of its potential, few people migrated to this remote area in the years that followed.

The situation dramatically changed after the discovery of gold along the American River's South Fork in 1848. This chance occurrence at Sutter's Mill, approximately 20 miles northeast of present-day Folsom, set into motion the California gold rush and immeasurably changed the American West. Thousands of men soon traveled up the American River to Mormon Island, Negro Bar, and other booming mining camps. By 1853, more than 2,000 people lived at Mormon Island alone.

Believing that profits could be made from mining-related commerce, Sacramento businessmen and community leaders organized the Sacramento Valley Railroad in August 1852 to connect navigable tidewater with the foothill mining region. The railroad was to follow the American River from Sacramento to a crossing point at Negro Bar, and then turn northward to the Bear River. The company's chief engineer, the young Theodore D. Judah, found the work easy enough to allow him to join several partners and lay out a town site above Negro Bar, where the railroad was to cross the American River. The town site was named Granite City—a testament to the seams of granite that the river had exposed at that point.

39

With its crew having "gone to beans" (that is, lunch), a Southern Pacific train awaits its next assignment at the Folsom depot in July 1956—just a few weeks before an excursion honoring the centennial of California railroading made its celebratory arrival. The boxcar and caboose are today on display in the town. (Photo by Alan R. Aske.)

Unfortunately for Judah and his partners, the site of Granite City turned out to be part of the extensive holdings of Joseph Libby Folsom, a West Point graduate and former U.S. Army captain. Indeed, over half the land the railroad was to cross between Sacramento and Negro Bar belonged to Folsom, who was just as anxious to have the railroad built, because it would increase the value of his real estate. Therefore, Folsom was a natural partner in the railroad and was made company president in early 1855. Recognizing the value of the Granite City town site, Folsom paid Judah and his partners for their survey and improvements.

Property in the newly platted community sold quickly in anticipation of the railroad, but Folsom, the company's president, never lived to see the first train. He died in July 1855, only weeks before the first sections of rail were laid. In the following year, the Sacramento Valley Railroad inaugurated service over its 23-mile route from Sacramento to Granite City (which was by this time commonly called Folsom), making it the first North American steam-powered railroad operating conventional passenger cars on iron rail anywhere west of the Great Plains. Its tracks were built to five-foot gauge.

As it happened, 1855 was an exceptionally dry year. Without water in the streams, gold could not be washed from placer deposits, and without new gold in circulation, San Francisco's real estate market collapsed, marking the end of the gold rush boom. As a result, the railroad canceled plans to extend its route north of Folsom. This setback actually worked to Folsom's advantage: by remaining the end of the line, the community became the home of many railroad jobs and large shop facilities.

Fortuitously, the little Sacramento Valley Railroad turned out to be in exactly the right location to prosper from the Comstock mining boom, which began in 1860 in what is now western Nevada. Its route was along the corridor linking San Francisco to Virginia City, the hub of the flourishing Comstock Lode region. The demand for the railroad's services grew spectacularly, pushing employment at its Folsom shops to more than 1,500 jobs. When the Pony Express established its western terminus in the community during 1861, Folsom indeed appeared destined for greatness.

The fervor of this era made it inevitable that other railroads would soon proffer their services. The California Central Railroad Company inaugurated service over a 5-foot-gauge line from Folsom northward to Lincoln in 1861. The following year, a third carrier, the Sacramento, Placer & Nevada Railroad (SP&N), commenced broad-gauge service to Auburn Station, 13 miles from Folsom in the direction of Auburn.

Passengers arriving on any of these rail lines had only a short walk to bustling hotels, restaurants, and stores along Sutter Street, as well as the renowned Folsom Institute, one of the first institutions of higher learning in California. Elegant Victorian homes on Nob Hill, one of Folsom's most desirable neighborhoods, showcased the affluence of its business leaders, while working-class neighborhoods attracted throngs of men relocating from Negro Bar or other mining towns where gold sources had been depleted.

The impending construction of the Pacific Transcontinental Railroad generated further optimism about the community's future. In 1860, Judah prepared a profile for the Sacramento–Donner Pass portion of this line with the assumption that it would pass through Folsom. Hope turned to frustration, however, when Central Pacific decided to build its own line directly from Sacramento, bypassing the Sacramento Valley Railroad and its feeder railroads. When the Central Pacific reached a point closer to Auburn than the SP&N in 1864, the latter carrier became the first California railroad to be abandoned. The California Central fared little better; it soon became the property of the principal directors of the Central Pacific, which abandoned the Folsom–Roseville portion in 1865.

The Sacramento Valley Railroad, on the other hand, did not give up to the Central Pacific without a fight. The superintendent of the Sacramento Valley bought the SP&N's rails at a sheriff's sale and sold them to the newly created Placerville & Sacramento Valley Railroad (P&SV). This railroad was opened for business in the summer of 1864 over track it had laid eastward from Folsom to Latrobe. Some envisioned that this route would be extended all the way to Virginia City, but the P&SV made it only to Shingle Springs, 25 miles from Folsom. The Southern Pacific eventually extended the line another 12 miles to Placerville.

The high expectations during this phase of Folsom's development soon faded. The decision to build the country's first transcontinental rail line on a more northerly alignment through Roseville and the Donner Pass essentially stripped Folsom of its role as an important railroad town. When the principal directors of the Central Pacific gained control of the Sacramento Valley Railroad in August 1865, the railroad's days as an independent carrier ended. The Sacramento Valley was soon converted to standard gauge, and the Folsom shops were used for the construction of rolling stock for the transcontinental line. With the opening of new shops in Sacramento in 1869,

however, most of the Folsom facilities were rendered superfluous. In 1877, the carrier closed the last of this once-sprawling local shop complex.

Folsom weathered these transitional years better than might have been anticipated. Its two railroads, the Sacramento Valley and the Placerville & Sacramento Valley, consolidated in 1877 to form the Sacramento & Placerville Railroad, which linked the towns after which it had been named. The opening of a major state penitentiary, Folsom Prison, along the river in 1880 generated many jobs. The penal institution depended heavily on a newly built spur, the Folsom State Prison Railroad, which originated at the former Sacramento Valley terminus near the center of town. Traffic on these routes remained relatively strong in 1888, when the Sacramento & Placerville consolidated with several lines to create the Northern Railway, an entity that the Southern Pacific controlled and eventually absorbed.

Although Folsom would never again vie to be a major railroad center, it remained an important station on the Southern Pacific that was now situated, in effect, at the end of a short branch that trains reached by diverting from the Sacramento–Placerville route at Folsom Junction. In 1913, Southern Pacific built a wye (a track arrangement used to reverse the direction of trains) at Folsom Junction, which allowed for the retirement of the Folsom turntable and facilitated the operation of gasoline-powered McKeen cars between Sacramento and Placerville, a service popular among local travelers. After fire destroyed the Folsom depot in 1913, Southern Pacific replaced the station (itself a replacement structure) with another wooden edifice.

Changing Times

Folsom residents needed only to drive over the magnificent Rainbow Bridge—a motor route across the American River completed in 1918—to understand the changes that would forever alter transportation in their community. Although Southern Pacific enlarged its Folsom station in 1925, passenger counts dropped sharply as a result of investments in hard-surface roads and, later, the onset of the Great Depression. In 1939, Southern Pacific canceled the McKeen-car service, thus reducing the branch to freight-only status.

Although the freight business remained strong through the end of World War II, the shipments of lumber and fresh fruit originating in Placerville and the other points east of Folsom sharply diminished after the war. The Prison Railroad, meanwhile, saw its role dwindle to little more than hauling steel coils used to manufacture license plates at the penitentiary.

As Folsom modernized, residents looked back upon the community's past with a sense of pride. In the early 1950s, the Folsom Powerhouse—a historic facility dating back to 1895—was retired but preserved as a local landmark. In the summer of 1955, hundreds of railroad enthusiasts, including many eminent historians, visited Folsom to commemorate a century of California railroading. Their arrival on a special steam-powered train from San Francisco sponsored by the Pacific Coast Chapter of the Railway & Locomotive Historical Society rekindled memories of past transportation glory.

An important opportunity to memorialize the past slipped away in 1959 when a developer razed one of

Ironically, a sign welcoming motorists to Folsom, complete with a drawing of the depot, was placed on the right-of-way formerly used by the Sacramento Valley Railroad (bottom center). Several years later, however, a light-rail line was built over this corridor. (Photo by author.)

Folsom's most notable historical structures, the Wells Fargo building, to make room for a service station. Recognizing that other century-old structures were at risk of demolition, the community formed the Folsom Historical Society the following year and preserved pieces of granite salvaged from the rubble, eventually reconstructing the fallen landmark as part of their museum building. The process of historical preservation took another important step in 1970 when the city moved the former SP&N Ashland station, the oldest standing depot west of the Mississippi River, to a site near Sutter Street.

By the mid-1970s, the prognosis for continued rail service was decidely poor. The Prison Railroad had been abandoned, and traffic on the Southern Pacific branch consisted primarily of lumber received from the Camino, Placerville & Lake Tahoe Railroad in Placerville, a source of revenue expected to decline.

The Southern Pacific route generated little tonnage in spite of a population boom on a scale not seen since the famous gold rush of more than a century before. In the early 1980s, professionals attracted by easy commutes to Sacramento flocked to the community, pushing Folsom's population to more than 18,000 in 1985, a level over 200 percent higher than only fifteen years before. Several massive subdivisions and stores sprouted adjacent to the little-used tracks between Folsom Junction and Placerville, offering a stark contrast between old and new.

As Folsom acquired a distinctly suburban quality, few considered the railroad's freight service to be economically important. When lumber shipments ended in 1987, Southern Pacific filed with the ICC to abandon its branches to Placerville and downtown Folsom. Although the petition was denied, the carrier imposed a surcharge on each car handled, a policy the ICC upheld, delivering a blow to those clinging to the hope that freight service would continue. By the end of 1987, the last Southern Pacific had departed for Sacramento, ending service over one of the oldest rail lines west of the Rockies.

Abandonment's Legacy

Recognizing the historical significance of the railroad, the municipal government designated much of the land along Sutter Street as the Railroad Block. Within this historical area were the former SP&N and Southern Pacific stations as well as the crumbling remnants of the Sacramento Valley turntable. Although the municipal government removed some of the tracks along Folsom Boulevard to allow for highway improvements and residential development, officials sought to preserve the remainder of the Southern Pacific's local system. In the summer of 1996, the Sacramento–Placerville Transportation Corridor Joint Powers Authority, a government entity, composed of the city of Folsom, the counties of El Dorado and Sacramento, and the Sacramento Regional Transit District (RTD), reached an agreement to purchase 56 miles of this track, between the state capital and Placerville, including the historic segment to downtown Folsom. RTD then announced its interest in establishing light-rail service between Sacramento and Folsom.

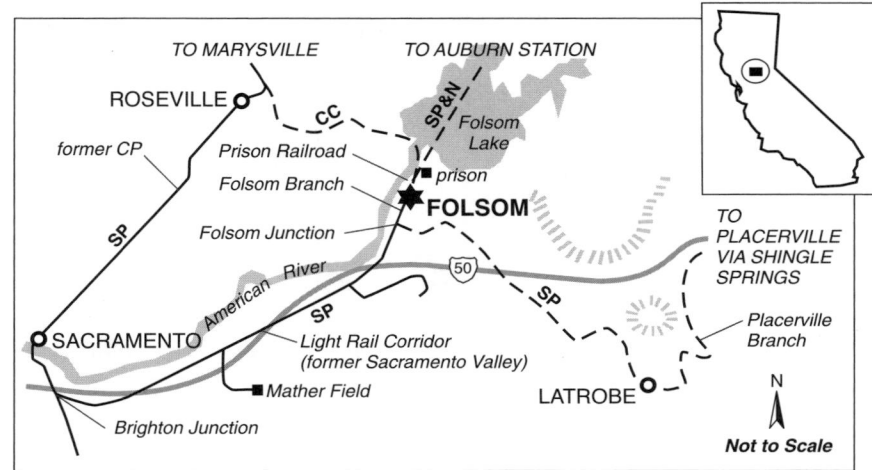

Fueling the debate about the benefits of rail transit service was growing congestion on local roads, including U.S. Route 50, an east–west arterial road passing several miles south of downtown. This debate took an unexpected turn when the municipal government proposed using self-propelled diesel railcars over the single-track corridor from its downtown (Old Town) district, thereby eliminating the need for installing electric catenary and making other costly right-of-way improvements. The RTD, however, reaffirmed its interest in creating a light-rail corridor in 1997, which, it maintained, could better meet the area's mobility needs. The agency proposed building an 11-mile extension equipped with parallel tracks from Sacramento's Mather Road to Folsom's Old Town.

As business leaders voiced support for RTD's ambitious proposal, an investigation revealed that much of the granite pivot stone that had been part of Folsom's gallows-style turntable—remnants dating back to the early years of rail service—had survived. A comprehensive restoration effort ensued, requiring extensive fund-raising and the relocation to another site of several old boxcars on display in the Railroad Block. The completion of the project in 1999 enhanced the Block's reputation as a historically significant site and was the impetus for further improvement. A proposal emerged to operate excursion trains over portions of the dormant branch from Folsom Junction to Latrobe—tracks that follow East Bidwell Street (one of Folsom's busiest roads) to the edge of town and slip through a Route 50 underpass before reaching the rolling countryside. This idea attracted attention for several years but remains only in the discussion stage.

The legacy of the Sacramento Valley Railroad could be felt in 2001 as work crews embarked on the construction of the light-rail line east from Sacramento. The project fell behind schedule, however, necessitating that officials revise the projected completion date to 2005. The revised timetable, coincidentally, gave railroad enthusiasts the opportunity to plan for a joint celebration of the introduction of light-rail service and the sesquicentennial of California railroading.

Epilogue

Visitors will find the false-front buildings on Sutter Street evocative of Folsom's spirited past. The preserved Southern Pacific depot, restored turntable, and historical museum built with materials salvaged from the Wells Fargo Building are testaments to its storied role in the development of the West. An elementary school named after Theodore Judah, the historic powerhouse, and the Rainbow Bridge bring to mind the railroad's historic place in American transportation. A miniature railroad operates in Folsom City Park.

Like Folsom's legendary prison, the city's Railroad Block attracts historically minded tourists from throughout the country. Many make stops at the Folsom Railroad Museum, an institution created by the Folsom, El Dorado & Sacramento Historical Railroad Association in 2003 and housed in a restored passenger car. Inside, exhibits describe the thunderous origins of railroading in the Golden State. The deteriorating remnants of the wye and the Placerville Branch east of Folsom are less conspicuous but, to many railroad enthusiasts, offer a somber reminder of how a railroad once so widely associated with gold could eventually become little more than a lengthy trail of rust.

For Further Study

SUGGESTED READINGS :

Briggs, Robert. "Building the Sacramento Valley Railroad," *Western Railroader* 20, no. 2 (Oct. 1957): 3–9.

Folsom Historical Society. *Folsom, California.* Charleston, S.C.: Arcadia, 1999, 1–50, 91–108.

Huffman, Wendell, "Railroads of Sacramento 1855–1870." Collection of the California State Railroad Museum, 30 November 1983.

Noble, Douglas. "The Sacramento Valley Railroad," *Western Railroader: A Publication of the Pacific Coast Chapter of the Railway & Locomotive Historical Society* (Winter 1990): 1–9.

OTHER PRINCIPAL REFERENCES:

Baker, Cindy. *First in the West: The Sacramento Valley Railroad.* Folsom, Calif.: City of Folsom, 1996, 1–22.

"Folsom, El Dorado, & Sacramento Historical Railroad Association," *FEDS Newsletter* 1 (1995): 4.

Folsom: Hub of the Mother Lode. Folsom Historical Society, 1992, 1–31.

Huffman, Wendell, "Rival Rails: A History of the Early Sacramento Area Railroads and the Placerville Branch of the Southern Pacific." Unpublished manuscript, November 1997.

Lewis, Oscar. *The Big Four.* New York: Alfred A. Knopf, 1938, 10–16.

GLENWOOD, CALIFORNIA (100)

Historic operator: Southern Pacific
Last route abandoned: 1940
Notable reuse of right-of-way: None

 undreds of vacationers once arrived on the "Picnic Line" each summer to stay at the Glenwood Hotel, where they enjoyed a pleasant small-town ambience and the fabled Magnetic Springs. The hotel, town, and trains these vacationers used eventually passed into oblivion. Nevertheless, the uncertanties of war, the need to protect documents from nuclear fallout, and the desire to alleviate highway congestion eventually brought attention back to the railroad tunnels that had been left behind.

Historical Perspective

Charles Christopher Martin, a young man of Scottish descent, planned to follow his father's example of a life at sea when he left the comforts of his Maine home in 1847. Martin soon found that he strongly disliked his new vocation. After a difficult voyage around Cape Horn, he jumped ship in northern California, where he fended for himself in the Santa Cruz Mountains, earning a living cutting logs and supplying livestock to gold miners working in the area—even, legend has it, repelling grizzly bears on occasion.

Soon after California received its statehood in 1850, Martin established a homestead in a valley near Los Gatos and created a toll station on a turnpike through his property. Although Martin moved to Santa Cruz in 1866, where he ran a livery stable, he later returned to the mountains to satisfy his yearning for life in the hinterland. He established a general store and a vineyard around 1873 on a clearing in this new locale.

Soon, his businesses and a one-room schoolhouse became the nucleus of the newly created village of Martinsville. When a friend visiting from Scotland expressed dislike for the community's name, Martin had it changed to Glenwood.

An astute businessman, Martin authorized the construction of a railroad through his property and assisted in the creation of a depot. When the narrow-gauge South Pacific Coast Railroad began service to Santa Cruz in 1880, he established himself as the postmaster of a new fourth-class post office. The route originated at Newark on the east side of San Francisco Bay, passed through San Jose, and took trains through six tunnels in the Santa Cruz Mountains that cumulatively stretched 2.6 miles before reaching Santa Cruz proper. The product of tens of thousands of hours of arduous labor, the route included a lengthy tunnel near Glenwood and offered passengers views of spectacular scenery, including giant redwoods, the San Lorenzo River, and Zayante Creek.

Martin's store and vineyard, as well as his

45

Three men on a handcar pose for a photograph in front of Glenwood's modest but attractive wooden depot (date unknown). The handle of the town's manual turntable is visible at the right. (Roy D. Graves Collection, Bancroft Library, University of California.)

newly established sawmill, came to depend heavily on the railroad. His most prized possession was the two-story Glenwood Hotel, a popular destination for vacationers. Martin gradually expanded his complex to include eight cottages along Bean Creek, a swimming "tank," a dance floor, and a building for theater performances. Many arriving guests made side trips to the Magnetic Springs to indulge in waters reported to have curative qualities. Having flowed past a field of magnetic iron ore, these mineral-laden waters were reported to be so potent that they could magnetize metallic objects.

When the railroad consolidated with several other lines to form the South Pacific Coast Railway in 1887, it put the entire corridor from the Bay Area to Santa Cruz into the hands of one company, which Southern Pacific leased that same year. Much of the lumber hauled on this route originated on a branch to the town of Boulder Creek that joined the main line south of Glenwood at Felton. Southern Pacific typically divided northbound trains carrying lumber at Felton and reassembled them at Glenwood, rendering Martin's community, which boasted a small yard, wooden depot, and turntable, the equivalent of a division point.

From its earliest days, the narrow-gauge railroad supplemented its freight and lumber business by carrying vacationers destined for both mountain resorts and the

beaches of Santa Cruz. Travelers visiting Glenwood customarily spent time at local wineries as well as Martin's resort and vineyard, which some claimed produced the finest table grapes in the world. Others detrained at Wrights to visit the rustic Hotel de Redwood or enjoyed the serene atmosphere of guesthouses in Alma, Laurel, and other small communities along the line. This mountainous route also saw the passage of dignitaries, including President Benjamin Harrison, who traveled by private train in 1891, and President Theodore Roosevelt, who did the same in 1903. Due to the festive ambience of its trains and stations, the route came to be affectionately called the Picnic Line by both travelers and railroaders.

Changing Times

The Picnic Line's tortuous grades and sharp curves—as well as seismic activity along the Zayante and San Andreas faults, which the tracks crossed—had been serious, though manageable, problems for years. In 1906, however, the San Francisco earthquake wreaked such havoc that the tracks lay dormant for several years before Southern Pacific rebuilt them to standard gauge. The railroad equipped the Glenwood turntable with dual-gauge track to support this reconstruction effort before retiring the aging piece of equipment.

Many businesses of this era failed to recognize that major advances in automobile travel and truck transport loomed on the horizon. Martin had a keen sense of the future, however, and had his property surveyed for a road—a move that paid off handsomely when a public agency established a motor route through Glenwood in 1916. When the agency paved a portion of this road three years later, the legendary proprietor commemorated the occasion by inscribing his name and imprinting his foot in the concrete. Nevertheless, Martin died in 1919 without seeing the highway's completion. The Glenwood Highway—reputedly the finest road in the state—opened the following year and soon attracted large numbers of motorists traveling from San Francisco to Monterey and Santa Cruz. Many of these motorists dined or refueled their cars in Glenwood.

Southern Pacific received approval to close its Glenwood station in 1927, but the Picnic Line was still an important component of the local economy. That same year, the carrier introduced a seasonal excursion train operating from San Jose (and later from San Francisco) to Santa Cruz. Christened the Suntan Special in 1929, the train attracted surprisingly large numbers of beachgoers, many of whom had grown tired of massive weekend traffic backups on the Glenwood Highway.

The Suntan Special continued to operate into the 1930s, resurrecting the Picnic Line's festive ambience. This train and the passenger trains oriented toward nonvacationers attracted fewer riders, however, as the Great Depression deepened. Anticipation grew about construction of a major new highway that would link San Jose to Santa Cruz while bypassing Glenwood, Wrights, and other historic vacation spots. After the state opened parts of the road, the number of cars passing through Glenwood diminished to such an extent that the store and gas station formerly operated by Martin went out of business in 1934.

Prospects for the Picnic Line were far from promising in 1939, when Southern Pacific rerouted its freight trains over a less direct but also less mountainous route through Watsonville. After several March rainstorms severely damaged the line the following year, Southern Pacific rerouted the Suntan Special over the Watsonville route and abandoned the 15-mile stretch from Los Gatos to Olympia Pits (a quarry location near Felton), bringing Glenwood's railroad era to a close.

Abandonment's Legacy

Only months after the last train operated over the 15-mile segment, residents of the area gathered in Los Gatos for a three-day celebration marking the opening of Highway 17. The new road, crossing the abandoned

rail line above the mile-long Glenwood Tunnel (tunnel No. 2) and again near Alma, provided a more direct route between San Jose and Santa Cruz than the old Glenwood Highway. Motorists no longer needed to stop (or slow down) in small towns along the way.

Martin's hotel, the general store, the school, and all but one of the cottages were eventually torn down. By the end of 1941, almost all the tracks on the abandoned Los Gatos–Olympia Pits segment were removed. Without the resort, a major highway, or a railroad, Glenwood essentially lost its reason to exist.

The country's involvement in World War II brought

The east portal of the Glenwood Tunnel crumbles from neglect more than sixty years after the last train emerged from its dark interior. (Photo by author.)

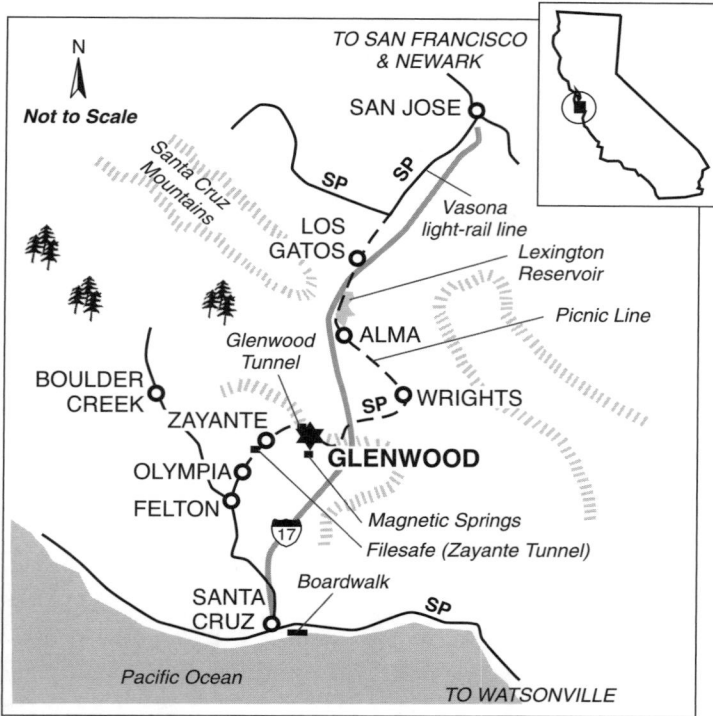

renewed attention to the abandoned corridor. In 1942, military personnel reportedly guarded several tunnels on the abandoned segment, including the Wrights and Glenwood tunnels, due to concerns about Japanese espionage. As fears mounted about a possible invasion of California, Southern Pacific reportedly sealed several other tunnels to make them unusable to Axis forces.

The right-of-way was covered with plant growth by 1950 when officials gathered along the old Glenwood Highway to dedicate a plaque honoring a community slowly passing into oblivion. After Glenwood's post office closed four years later, the community devolved into a thinly populated residential area without a distinct identity. One of the old railroad tunnels, however, once again attracted attention due to renewed concerns related to national security. In 1954, the Western States Atomic Vault Company modified the 240-foot curved Zayante Tunnel, which had been retained by Southern Pacific for storage use, to become a storage facility. In the midst of the escalating tensions and nuclear proliferation of the Cold War, many governments, citizens, and corporations used the concrete-lined passage, located about 5 miles from the Glenwood depot site, to store documents.

Over the next several years, many reminders of the glory years of rail service were, quite literally, washed away. The Lexington Reservoir, created in 1956, submerged 2 miles of the old railroad grade, including the

former town site of Alma. Two years later, Southern Pacific abandoned the segment between downtown Los Gatos and Vasona Junction in San Jose. The Suntan Special continued to operate over the longer route through Watsonville, but the completion of a Highway 17 bypass linking Los Gatos to San Jose in 1959 further eroded its commercial viability. The Special made its final run as a regularly scheduled seasonal train later that year.

As San Jose grew at a spectacular rate, concerns about roadway congestion escalated in intensity. Highway 17 attracted notoriety for its poor safety record and came to be called derisively Bloody Alley or Killer 17. During the 1960s, officials discussed the possibility of upgrading the road to freeway standards and building an interchange near Glenwood. With an eye toward the future, others called for building a monorail along the corridor. Neither proposal came to fruition, nor did an ambitious plan developed by a Lockheed Missile and Space Company engineer in 1971 to use much of the old rail grade for an electrified transit line between San Jose and Santa Cruz.

Few motorists on the Glenwood Highway had more than a vague awareness of Charlie Martin's legacy when a highway crew poured fresh asphalt on this road in 1972, covering his name and footprints. As the region modernized, more proposals emerged to rebuild the rail line that once passed through his property. In 1978, the state transportation agency, Caltrans, evaluated at length the idea of building a rail transit line to Santa Cruz. The agency's proposal garnered little support among Santa Cruz County residents, including its board of supervisors, who feared its transit service would create excessive noise and congestion.

Southern Pacific continued to haul freight over the remnant of the Picnic Line linking Felton to Santa Cruz and categorically opposed all proposals to reuse this surviving portion for transit service. In 1985, however, the company sold the segment to the Santa Cruz, Big Trees & Pacific Railway, which introduced excursion service over these rails. The train, appropriately called the Suntan Special, proved commercially popular and brought a new generation of visitors to the boardwalk, albeit without the thunderous steam locomotives of a half century before.

The debate about restoring rail service over the right-of-way through Glenwood resumed in 1988. In response to concerns about the region's rapid population growth, a private enterprise launched another effort to build an electrified transit line from San Jose to Santa Cruz—with assurances that any profits would go to historical societies and other civic groups. Support for this unconventional idea rose as Silicon Valley professionals living in Santa Cruz grew tired of highway congestion, especially after the Loma Prieta earthquake severely damaged Highway 17 in 1989. In the end, the enormous costs of rebuilding the railroad, reconstructing bridges, and reopening tunnels (several of which had collapsed) prevented this latest initiative from moving beyond the discussion stage.

Although these efforts to rebuild the railroad generated significant grassroots support, none were as comprehensive as a subsequent effort led by the Santa Clara County Transit District. In 1993, the agency assessed its budgetary options and hired a consulting company to evaluate the viability of both commuter-rail and light-rail service between San Jose and Santa Cruz. The company dispatched engineers to survey the right-of-way and estimated the following year that approximately $400 million would be needed to repair tunnels, purchase equipment and materials, relocate the document storage facility, and create a rail-line alignment that skirted the reservoir. The outcome was again dispiriting to transit supporters. On balance, the agency did not consider the estimated 4,000 daily riders as sufficient justification for the capital outlay.

Attention gradually turned to less costly congestion-mitigation strategies, such as creating high-occupancy lanes on Highway 17. In 2001, the transit district began constructing the Vasona light-rail line on the former Picnic Line right-of-way between San Jose and the eastern edge of Los Gatos. In the process, it quietly dropped from discussion the possibility of extending the line to Santa Cruz. The state, meanwhile, focused on reestablishing regularly scheduled passenger service to Santa Cruz over the longer—but gentler—railroad route through Watsonville.

Epilogue

Visitors to Glenwood will find little more than the tarnished historical plaque and the former station agent's home, which is today the upper floor of a two-story house, informing them of the community's colorful past. Nothing appears to be left of Martin's hotel, and decades of plant growth have rendered much of the abandoned rail line barely visible. The south portal of the Glenwood Tunnel and one cottage from Martin's resort both survive but are in severe disrepair.

Signs on Highway 17 informing motorists of the Glenwood Cutoff, a secondary road, offer travelers a more conspicuous reminder of the community established by Martin many years ago. Those following the old Glenwood Highway (which is today Glenwood Drive) will notice that Laurel and Wrights have also lost their identities. Only nearby Zayante retains the semblance of a distinct community, in part due to the jobs created by Filesafe (successor to the Western States Atomic Vault Company), which still uses the curved tunnel to store both microfiche and printed materials.

Unlike other railroad corridors that were abandoned at the end of the age of steam, the Picnic Line will likely remain part of the debate about mobility for years to come. Had the rail line survived to bear witness to the region's rising population, it seems likely that passenger trains would once again be rolling past the site of Martin's rustic resort.

For Further Study

SUGGESTED READINGS:

Hamman, Rick. *California Central Coast Railways.* Boulder, Colo.: Pruett Publishing, 1980, 82–167.

Koch, Margaret. "Glenwood: Charlie Martin's Town," *Santa Cruz County History Journal* 1, no. 1 (1994): 107–12.

MacGregor, Bruce A. *South Pacific Coast.* Berkeley, Calif.: Howell-North Books, 1968, 126–28, 136–37, 151–52, 228, 248.

OTHER PRINCIPAL REFERENCES:

Beal, Richard. *Highway 17: The Road to Santa Cruz.* Aptos, Calif.: Pacific Group, 1990, 44–48, 85–88, 117–28.

Cather De Leuw and Company. "Santa Cruz–Los Gatos Rail Corridor Feasibility Study" (Feb. 1995): 7.

Stindt, Fred. "To Santa Cruz on Southern Pacific's Sun-Tan Special." *Railroad History* 152 (1988): 111.

Wullenjohn, Chuck. "SP's Suntan Special." *Passenger Train Journal* 25, no. 4 (April 1994): 26–31.

Historic operator: Southern Pacific
Last route abandoned: 1960
Notable reuse of right-of-way: Laws Railroad Museum

The closing of the narrow-gauge route through Laws saddened railroad enthusiasts who were fond of its rustic and rural character. Trains on this route passed near snow-covered peaks and crossed miles of desolate terrain—and for many years provided the only reliable transportation available to remote towns in eastern California. Today, historically minded travelers drive hundreds of miles to visit Laws and see the remnants of a railroad universally called the Slim Princess.

Historical Perspective

The origin and evolution of Laws is closely linked with that of Bishop, an older and much larger community only 3 miles away. This neighboring community's origin can be traced to the 1859 arrival of Samuel A. Bishop, a native of Virginia who drove more than 500 head of cattle and 50 horses along the Owens River. Bishop's contingent built two log cabins and established the San Francis Ranch along a small stream later named Bishop Creek.

After the discovery of silver in the Owens Valley, a small village, Bishop Creek, emerged roughly halfway between the existing communities of Little Pine and Oak Creek. The inhabitants of this village found themselves embroiled in hostilities with the Paiute and other Indian tribes over the next several years, but they firmly established their dominance over the area after the Battle of Bishop in 1862. Four years later, the state created Inyo County out of several existing counties and designated Independence, a settlement farther south along the river, as the county seat.

By the mid-1870s, a growing number of mule-drawn wagons laden with bullion were passing through the area from the booming mining towns of the Sierra Nevada. In 1878, the completion of a large irrigation project allowed for bountiful agricultural harvests in the valley. While looking ahead to an apparently prosperous future, residents built wooden homes, established a Baptist church, and shortened their community's name to Bishop.

Leaders expressed hope that a rail line—possibly even a trancontinental railroad—would be built through the valley. Rail service seemed on its way to becoming a reality when the Carson & Colorado Railroad announced its ambitious plan to build a narrow-gauge (3-foot) line from Mound House, Nevada (an interchange point with the standard-gauge Virginia & Truckee Railroad) to the Colorado River, a distance of more than 400 miles. In early 1883, this railroad completed the 200-mile segment south from

Mound House to Benton, California (just west of the Nevada boundary). Several months later, it finished an extension through the Bishop Creek area to Hawley (Keeler), a desolate location along Owens Lake.

The completion of the railroad was no panacea for the hardworking citizens of the valley. After riding an inspection train, Darius O. Mills, one of the line's officers, made the famous and prophetic comment: "Gentlemen, either we built this line 300 miles too long, or 300 years too soon." Not only did the Carson & Colorado prove to be a financial weakling, but it laid its tracks east of the Owens River, bypassing Bishop by several miles. This made it necessary for local residents to shuttle back and forth from a depot area—a place the railroad called Bishop Station—on a mule-powered taxi.

Despite the limitations of this arrangement, Bishop Station (later renamed Laws) evolved into a bustling railroad town and division point with a large depot, agent's house, section boss's house, small freight yard, water tank, and turntable. Bishop, too, experienced significant growth, fostered by the construction of an elaborate series of irrigation ditches that further expanded agricultural production. Growing livestock herds, meanwhile, made possible the opening of a creamery that established the community as a noted dairy center.

Local business leaders eagerly awaited the day that the railroad would widen its tracks to standard gauge and make them part of a more significant transportation route, preferably one linking the Central Pacific's main line in northern Nevada with Los Angeles. Notwithstanding the railroad's poor financial performance and a sharp downturn during the 1890s, there were continuing hopes for such a project, especially after Southern Pacific purchased the line in 1900.

By the early twentieth century, the depot and the small town of Bishop Station became known as Laws in honor of R. J. Laws, the railroad's superintendent. The community continued to derive considerable prosperity from its expansive railroad facilities as well as its two general stores, an eating house, a hotel, a post office, and many homes. Its rail yard was particularly busy following the discovery of gold near Tonapah, Nevada, in 1904, which made Laws an important staging area for

Three children and an adult watch as crewmen turn locomotive No. 18 on the gallows-type turntable in Laws, California, in April 1952. Laws was by now the northern end of this narrow-gauge route. (Photo by Wendell Mortimer Jr., collection of Hope Mallory Ferrell.)

In August 2002 (fifty years after the previous photo was taken) the Slim Princess stands next to the Laws depot, seemingly poised for a northbound departure. This is the same locomotive (No. 9) that appears on the cover of this volume. (Photo by author.)

the shipment of fruit, grain, livestock, water, and dairy products destined for the mining camps.

Southern Pacific continued to operate the line as the Carson & Colorado before renaming it the Nevada & California Railway in 1905, the same year it equipped the route with a long-anticipated southern outlet in the form of a connecting route from Mojave, California. Established primarily to haul materials for the construction of the Los Angeles Aqueduct—a massive undertaking that employed more than 5,000 workers at the height of its construction—this new route terminated at a location near the southern end of the narrow-gauge

called Owenyo. Although the new line (called the Jaw Bone) eliminated the need to send all long-distance shipments via Nevada, it did little to elevate the status of the former Carson & Colorado, partially because it had been built to standard gauge. Consequently, most shipments originating on the older route still had a break of gauge before reaching their final destination.

A final opportunity for major improvements to rail service in the valley presented itself in 1911 when the Owens River Valley Electric Railway Company surveyed two prospective trolley routes, the longer of which extended 16 miles from Bishop to Laws and Big Pine. As this interurban—the so-called Red Apple—graded the segment between Bishop and Laws, it appeared that Bishop proper would finally have a railroad.

Changing Times

The anticipation that the Red Apple would soon whisk passengers through the valley proved to be misplaced. Operating an interurban railway through such a sparsely populated region was a questionable financial proposition from the start, and the company abandoned the project in 1912.

The steam railroad also fell onto hard times. After Southern Pacific absorbed the struggling Nevada & California into its system in 1912, a lengthy recession buffeted the valley's economy. Making matters worse, the city of Los Angeles purchased ranches in the valley to acquire water rights, resulting in severe water shortages following the opening of its 233-mile aqueduct in 1913. Water for irrigation suddenly became less readily available, devastating the dairy and livestock operations.

Although trains handled expanding shipments of sheep during the late 1910s, the railroad's best years were now relegated to the past. With automobiles and trucks widely available by the mid-1920s, both Laws and the rail line gradually surrendered their transportation role. Although Laws continued to be a division point and a terminus for the helper locomotives used to assist trains negotiating the difficult Nevada grades, the number of railroad jobs diminished.

By 1930, Laws's official population had dropped to about 75, more than a third less than a generation before. The number of passengers using the Southern Pacific's daily mixed train operating between Keeler and Mina, Nevada, plummeted as the county invested in improved roads. The carrier eliminated the train in 1932—the same year, coincidentally, that the community's first street was paved.

With the abandonment of the 31-mile stretch from Laws to Benton in 1942, Laws became the northern terminus of one of the last narrow-gauge lines operated by a common carrier west of the Rocky Mountains. By then, the country's narrow-gauge systems had dwindled to approximately 1,200 miles, only about 10 percent of the mileage that was in place sixty years before. The survival of the route through Laws now seemed doubtful.

The resurgence in freight shipments during World War II dissipated after the conflict ended, giving Southern Pacific little choice but to lower costs. When the carrier put a diesel locomotive into service on the branch in 1953, most railroad enthusiasts reserved their fond sentiments for the Slim Princess, a name applied to all the aging steam engines still working the route. A few went so far as to call the dieselized imposter the "Skinny Bitch."

Some nostalgic observers sought to preserve the 71-mile branch to Keeler, only to reluctantly conclude that such an endeavor was not economically feasible. Hopes also faded that Walt Disney, who had a personal interest in the line, would assist with its preservation. Nevertheless, hundreds participated in steam-powered excursions sponsored by various organizations, including the Bishop Chamber of Commerce, that rekindled memories of train rides from years before. On certain occasions, the carrier accommodated excursiongoers simply by adding a car to its regularly scheduled train.

By the time the railroad closed the Laws depot in 1959, abandonment seemed inevitable. The symbolic importance of the Southern Pacific in Owens Valley could be plainly seen as the end drew near. In early 1960, public hearings drew widespread attention to the line's impending abandonment, a move Southern Pacific conceded was "regrettable from a sentimental point of view." The carrier received permission to abandon the Keeler–Laws segment in April 1960 and immediately pulled up some of the tracks.

Abandonment's Legacy

Laws seemed to be on the verge of becoming a ghost town when its post office closed in 1963. The outlook for the community, however, improved as officials made plans to reuse 11 acres of property Southern Pacific had donated to the county and the city of Bishop several years before. This gift and the carrier's subsequent

contribution of rolling stock, 1,100 feet of track, and former railroad buildings, provided the nucleus for a popular tourist attraction. Government officials made arrangements to have a newly formed group, the Bishop Museum and Historical Society, establish a museum in Laws devoted to the area's history.

Paramount Studios erected several buildings in Laws to serve as props for the 1964 movie *Nevada Smith*. As the cameras rolled, the old railroad town bustled with activity once again. In 1966, the historical society converted the largest of the studio's buildings into a reception area for the Laws Railroad Museum. The society gradually expanded the institution's collection to encompass more than thirty historic structures, including the Laws agent house, turntable, oil and water tanks, and depot (which dated to 1883). On the donated stretch of original track, the society displayed Southern Pacific steam locomotive No. 9 as well as its tender and six pieces of rolling stock.

The museum attracted diverse groups of patrons over the next several years and, in 1981, became the first property in the Bishop area listed on the National Register of Historic Places. As the number of customers increased over the next fifteen years, the museum's leaders contemplated creating a recreational railway between Laws and Bishop. In 1998, it received funds from Caltrans, a state

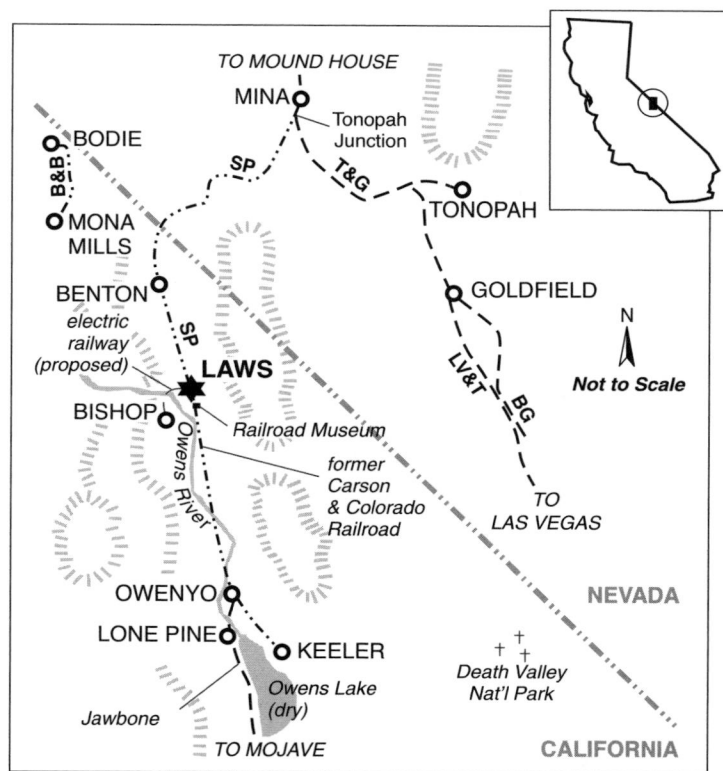

transportation agency, to rebuild a historic gasoline-powered Brill railcar for this purpose.

After evaluating two possible alignments, the museum selected the corridor originally envisioned as the Red Apple trolley line for its excursion railway. With assistance from the Owens Valley Railway Company, a volunteer organization committed to honoring the line's heritage, it diligently worked to restore the railcar. The museum, however, scaled back its plans for the excursion railway to 2 miles of track due to concerns about interference with a local airport. In 2004, the restored Brill car made its inaugural run.

Epilogue

The Owens Valley today welcomes many travelers on their way to the Inyo National Forest and the eastern slopes of the Sierra Nevada. Planners in the area, however, grapple with environmental issues created by the growing demand for water and the changing ecology of the river. Owens Lake and the lower portion of the river are now dry, and dust blowing from the lake bed has heightened concerns about air pollution. This problem is especially severe in Keeler, the railroad's former terminus, which is suffering from decay and neglect. Plans to "rewater" the lake and river are in preliminary stages.

Travelers unaware of the legacy of the Carson & Colorado may consider Laws, separated by hundreds of miles from a major city, an unlikely place for a popular railroad museum. The valley is difficult to reach from the Bay Area and the nearest railroad line is more than 100 miles away. Its scheduled bus service has gone the way of the mixed train, leaving the entire region without a passenger-hauling common carrier. Nevertheless, railroad enthusiasts routinely drive hundreds of miles to see the Slim Princess and other historical displays at the Laws Railroad Museum.

On their arrival, many are surprised to find that Laws has largely surrendered its role as an autonomous community. It lacks a post office, municipal government, or retail store. However, as a result of its museum and several industrial concerns (including the Atlantic Richfield warehouse, a former railroad customer), Laws has avoided the fate of other station towns along the Carson & Colorado, which have passed into antiquity.

Perhaps the most notable aspect of Laws's saga is not that its rail service ended, but that it lasted for so long despite the small population and dearth of large-scale industrial activity along its route. Today, visitors following this route outside of town may have trouble discerning the right-of-way, largely due to the modest construction standards to which the line was built. Without the aid of a good historical map, it can be difficult to find even a trace of the narrow gauge railroad built "either 300 miles too long, or 300 years too soon."

For Further Study

SUGGESTED READINGS:
Hungerford, John. *The Slim Princess: The Story of the Southern Pacific Narrow Gauge.* Reseda, Calif.: Hungerford Press, 1961, special supplement.
Myrick, David. F. *Railroads of Nevada and Eastern California.* 2 vols. Berkeley, Calif.: Howell-North Books, 1962–63, 166–210, 313–15.
Turner, George. *Slim Rails Through the Sand.* Long Beach, Calif.: Johnston & Howe, 1963, 440.

OTHER PRINCIPAL REFERENCES:
Chalfant, W. A. *The Story of Inyo.* Bishop, Calif.: Community Printing and Publishing, 1933, 142–43, 209, 233, 326-29.
Ferrell, Hope Mallory. *Southern Pacific Narrow Gauge.* Edmonds, Wash.: Pacific Fast Mail, 1962, 100–101, 174–85, 192, 259.
Hawkins, Clarabelle E. *The Story of Laws.* Bishop, Calif.: Chalfant Press, 1975, 1–28.
Hilton, George W. *American Narrow Gauge Railroads.* Stanford: Stanford University Press, 1990, 439– 40.

MONTEREY, CALIFORNIA (29,674)

Historic operators: Monterey & Del Monte Heights Railway Co.; Monterey & Pacific Grove Street
Railway & Electric Power Co.; Southern Pacific Railroad
Last route abandoned: 1979
Notable reuses of right-of-way: Proposed rail passenger route; Monterey Peninsula Recreational Trail

   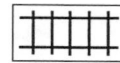 

Affluent travelers from faraway places once arrived at Monterey's Southern Pacific depot on the elegantly furnished Del Monte Express, the premier train from San Francisco. During their stay, they savored the atmosphere of a beautiful and bustling community widely known for its Cannery Row, Fisherman's Wharf, and palatial Hotel Del Monte. Although the last train departed Monterey years ago, an ambitious planning initiative might restore passenger service to its legendary route.

Historical Perspective

Sailing under the Spanish flag in 1542, the Portuguese explorer Juan Rodriguez Cabrillo encountered a beautiful peninsula resplendent with pristine beaches, dramatic cliffs, and lovely cypress trees. This unspoiled land similarly impressed Spanish navigator Sebastian Vizcaíno, who in 1602 named this peninsula after Count de Monte-Rey, a viceroy of New Spain. Recognizing the value of the placid harbor on the peninsula's northern shore, settlers established a mission and the Presidio of Monterey, a stockade made of earth and pine logs, on this site in 1740.

Monterey emerged as the capital of Alta California during the mid-1770s and remained the center of government when the territory became part of the newly formed Republic of Mexico in 1823. Five years later, it became home to a large custom house that processed cargo and immigrants arriving by sea. The influence of Americans, most notably merchant Thomas O.

Larkin, who became consul in 1835, could be felt especially in a local architectural tradition noted for hipped roofs and symmetrical design. Many attractive two-story adobe dwellings, including a stately home built for Larkin, emerged in the "Monterey style."

Historical circumstances later pushed Monterey to the forefront of American-Mexican political affairs. In 1846, American forces under the command of Commodore John D. Sloat captured Monterey and raised the American flag over the custom house. In 1849, the newly established territorial government completed an assembly building popularly called Colton Hall, where it drafted a constitution for California. The community remained the capital until the territory achieved statehood, when the seat of government was moved to San Jose.

Monterey received its incorporation as a city in 1850, but its importance to the region gradually ebbed. The migration of business to northern California, where a gold rush was under way, hindered its commercial development.

A Caltrans demonstration train travels west on the out-of-service Monterey Branch near Seaside on July 22, 1995. The state agency sponsored this run— the first passenger train to operate over the branch since the last run of the Del Monte in 1971—and several others to build public support for restoring passenger service. Today, the switch connecting the branch to the main line has been removed and the tracks remain dormant, but the effrort to restore service continues, in part due to worsening traffic on U.S. Route 1 (background). (Collection of John Pullman Porter.)

Monterey lost its legal status as a city in 1853 and was unable to regain this standing for many years. Although the expansion of fishing and agriculture, as well as the arrival of many Chinese and Japanese immigrants, helped stabilize its population, hopes that Monterey would someday become one of California's great cities slowly dissipated. Some considered it the "Sleepy Hollow of California."

The opportunity for an economic recovery slipped away in 1872, when Southern Pacific worked its way south along an inland route through a rival community, Salinas, instead of following the peninsula's shores as local leaders had hoped. Making matters worse, political deal-making allowed Salinas to wrest from Monterey its role as the seat of Monterey County that same year. Unfortunately, the construction of the Monterey & Salinas Valley Railroad—California's first narrow-gauge carrier—in 1874 did relatively little to offset the peninsula's economic woes. This carrier, operating a 19-mile route from Salinas to Monterey, struggled from its earliest days and

suffered from a fire at its local roundhouse in 1877. It was sold at a foreclosure sale in 1880 and conveyed to the Monterey Railroad, a unit of the Pacific Improvement Company (an arm of Southern Pacific).

A more auspicious railroad era began when the Monterey Railroad converted the western end of the line to standard gauge and built a new route from Castroville (a location along the Southern Pacific coastal main line) to Bardin (present-day Marina). With travelers now able to arrive from San Francisco over a more direct route, the Pacific Improvement Company moved forward with the construction of a splendid resort—the Hotel Del Monte. It envisioned this hotel, located about a mile east of the Monterey depot, as having 500 guestrooms, a nature area, a bathing pavilion, four saltwater swimming pools, and a bowling alley. There was a great celebration when this palatial institution opened in the spring of 1880. Many dignitaries arrived on a special train from San Francisco to participate in the festivities and stay at the hotel. After a fire destroyed it in 1887, an even more impressive Hotel Del Monte rose from the ashes of its predecessor, replete with its own railroad station and a dining hall that could accommodate more than 700 people.

Recognizing that Monterey had the potential to become an important passenger destination, Southern Pacific merged the Monterey Railroad (which had abandoned the narrow-gauge segment between Bardin and Salinas) into its system in 1888. The following year, it christened one of its trains the Del Monte Express and built an extension of its line through Pacific Grove to a sand and silt facility at Lake Majella, several miles west of Monterey. This train, making a daily round-trip between Pacific Grove and San Francisco, delighted passengers with scenic vistas of the waterfront as well as fine dining and parlor-car service. Presidents William McKinley and Theodore Roosevelt were among the most famous travelers who came to Monterey by train to stay at its renowed hotel.

Monterey's emerging reputation as an up-and-coming community attracted a great deal of investment. In 1891, the Monterey & Pacific Grove Street Railway inaugurated service using horse-drawn cars over narrow-gauge tracks linking the Hotel Del Monte to Pacific Grove. This company (reorganized and renamed on several occasions) turned to electric power in 1902 and two years later built a 1-mile extension to the Ord Barracks, part of a newly created military cantonment at the historic Presidio of Monterey.

As many tourists, midshipmen, and residents took to the rails, the streetcar company widened its tracks to standard gauge in 1905 and planned to build a 7-mile extension from Pacific Grove to Carmel. The extension never materialized, but another local provider, the Monterey & Del Monte Heights Railway, opened a route in 1912 to a subdivision now part of present-day Seaside (a community several miles east of Monterey). Although this subdivision proved relatively unsuccessful, leading to the permanent cessation of its trolley service in 1914, the other rail lines proved to be more resilient and benefitted from the dramatic expansion of the sardine-canning industry during World War I. By the end of the war, twenty-seven plants lined the streets of the Cannery Row neighborhood, making Monterey the world's leading supplier of this seafood mainstay.

Changing Times

The peninsula's economy moved in a new direction in 1919, when the Pacific Improvement Company sold the Hotel Del Monte and other properties on the peninsula to a consortium affiliated with one of its former managers, Samuel F. B. Morse, a distant cousin of the celebrated inventor of the telegraph, Samuel Morse. The philanthropic-minded financier oversaw the liquidation of the Pacific Improvement Company, invested in the hotel's rehabilitation, and set aside vast acreage along the coast for conservation areas

and the Pebble Beach Golf Links.

Although the construction of a new wood-frame depot in Monterey in 1921 suggested otherwise, Southern Pacific's passenger business—like the streetcar company—suffered greatly as automotive technology improved. In 1922, a bus company received a franchise to operate over a route parallel to the streetcar line, contributing to the cessation of the last of Monterey's trolley service the following year. In 1924, another fire destroyed the central portion of the Hotel Del Monte. Although rebuilt once again, the institution's most illustrious years had passed.

Recognizing that their community was changing, the citizens of Monterey sought to cultivate an appreciation for its rich heritage. The Monterey History and Art Association was formed in 1931 and took steps to showcase the town's famed waterfront, which had inspired Jack London, Robert Louis Stevenson, and other literary figures. This same shoreline also touched the imagination of Salinas native John Steinbeck, who delighted millions with his descriptive accounts of Monterey in several notable works of fiction, including *Cannery Row*, a novel published in 1944.

Visitors to the waterfront during the final years of World War II found the Southern Pacific tracks once again teeming with activity. Both Monterey and Fort Ord—a major military base near Seaside equipped with a balloon track and several spurs—generated extensive freight and passenger traffic. After the war, however, the railroad business rapidly deteriorated. Production at the canneries dropped in a particularly disturbing fashion,

The absence of tracks notwithstanding, the Monterey depot, shown circa 2003, appears virtually unchanged since the final days of operation of the Del Monte. (Photo by author.)

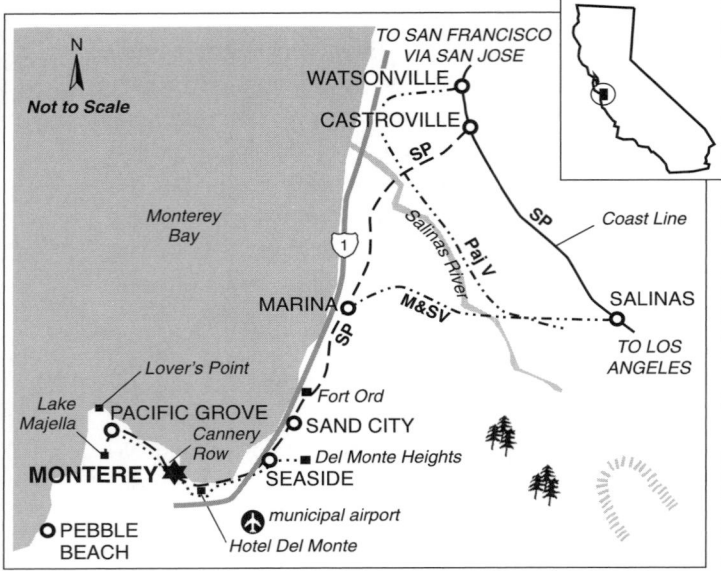

partially because the sardine companies had ignored warnings about overfishing.

The hardship created by the decline of traditional industries was gradually offset by the arrival of thousands of new residents attracted by the peninsula's amenities. During the 1950s, Monterey's population doubled, tourism rebounded, and the peninsula established its claim as one of the world's premier golfing areas. Southern Pacific increasingly relied on hauling sand from local mines to support its freight service on the peninsula.

The resurgence in tourism helped sustain the operation of Southern Pacific's daily passenger train, the Del Monte, the diesel-powered successor of the Del Monte Express. Nevertheless, as passenger revenues ebbed, Southern Pacific sought to eliminate this train. State regulators approved the carrier's petition to discontinue the Del Monte's operation west of Monterey and to close its station in Pacific Grove in 1957, but the train continued its 126-mile run between Monterey and San Francisco.

Southern Pacific then made a valiant attempt to stimulate the remaining passenger business by introducing streamlined equipment to the Del Monte in 1959. Among its attractive new cars was a parlor-snack-lounge that, for some travelers, evoked memories of the train's glorious past; however, the public's response to this modern equipment was disappointing. In 1961, Southern Pacific consolidated the Del Monte with a commuter run operating between San Francisco and San Jose; from this point forward, the train operated with extra cars north of San Jose.

By 1970, Monterey was a cosmopolitan community with more than 48,000 residents and extensive commercial air service to Los Angeles and San Francisco. With the inception of Amtrak in 1971, the Del Monte—the oldest "name train" on the Southern Pacific—made its last run, ending local rail passenger service. Three years later, Southern Pacific received approval to discontinue staffing the local station with an agent.

As tourists flocked to the peninsula, a plan emerged to transform the little-used Monterey–Pacific Grove segment into an excursion railway linking such prominent local attractions as Fisherman's Wharf and Cannery Row to Lover's Point in Pacific Grove. The Monterey Peninsula Railroad Company's proposal attracted considerable attention in 1977 but its plans never came to fruition.

Investments in State Route 1, on the other hand, moved forward without delay. Southern Pacific realigned portions of the local branch to aid in the widening of this highway near Fort Ord, notwithstanding the fact that these tracks were by now only lightly used. In 1979, the carrier abandoned the western end of the branch from Seaside (a community sharing a common boundary with Monterey) to Pacific Grove (Lake Majella), ending service through Monterey. The carrier sold the Monterey–Seaside portion to the municipal government for $4.3 million, allowing officials to preserve it, albeit without approximately 2 miles of track that the carrier had previously removed.

Abandonment's Legacy

The restoration of rail-passenger service on the Monterey Peninsula has been a topic of discussion almost since the last train left town. With more than 70,000 residents living there by 1980, passenger trains were seen as a solution to the growing congestion on Route 1. An ambitious plan to rebuild the municipally owned stretch for streetcar service between Fisherman's Wharf and Cannery Row gathered momentum in 1984, but this idea suffered from inadequate financing and a competing interest in creating a recreational trail. By 1987, the municipal streetcar plan had been scuttled, and the western end of the branch from Monterey to Pacific Grove was fashioned into the Monterey Peninsula Recreational trail.

Although Southern Pacific continued to serve customers between Castroville and Seaside (a segment called the Seaside Industrial Lead), the outlook for continued operations was poor, especially after the Loma Prieta earthquake damaged the Salinas River Bridge in 1989.

Repairs allowed service to resume, but the disruption of operations and the closing of Fort Ord in 1993 reduced traffic to a negligible level. Soon thereafter, Southern Pacific discontinued the last of its freight operations on the Seaside Industrial Lead, leaving the entire peninsula without an active railroad.

These developments did not dampen the enthusiasm for bringing rail passenger service back to the Monterey Peninsula. To build support for this idea, the county's transportation agency operated a demonstration train in 1995 over the dormant tracks between Castroville and Seaside. Planners proposed passenger service as far as Seaside and hoped to eventually add a westward extension over the municipally owned corridor to downtown Monterey.

Encouraged by the success of other efforts to restore rail passenger service in California, officials looked for ways to generate the $12 million necessary to purchase equipment and rehabilitate the inactive branch. Nevertheless, with funding in doubt and a vocal minority in Marina staunchly opposed to the idea, planners scaled back their plans and considered the possibility of initially operating only two or three round-trips each day. This plan gathered momentum in late 2003, when the county's transportation agency purchased the Seaside Industrial Lead from Union Pacific (successor to the Southern Pacific).

If trains eventually return, they will serve a city vastly different from what it was during the glory years of the Del Monte Express. Caltrans provides bus service to the depot in San Jose, and several dozen flights arrive daily at the Monterey Peninsula Airport, principally from points within the state. The railroad industry's presence is currently limited to an Amtrak Thruway Bus providing connections to the Coast Starlight at Salinas.

Epilogue

Travelers tracing the route of the Del Monte Express will find the dormant branch partially covered by drifting sand. The switch at Castroville has been removed, leaving the branch, at least temporarily, without an outside connection. Weeds and debris obscure some of the rail that survives between Monterey and Seaside. Other portions of this segment are used as a walking trail.

The beautiful shoreline and nature areas on the Monterey Peninsula are legacies of Morse's conservation efforts more than sixty years ago. Monterey's waterfront remains a vibrant place, although today it stands bereft of the famed sardine industry that John Steinbeck so vividly described in his novels. The former Hotel Del Monte now serves naval officers as part of the Naval Postgraduate School. The Monterey depot is today owned by the municipal government but stands in relatively poor condition, having been relegated to use as a storage facility for many years. Relieved of its military role, Fort Ord has been partially fashioned into the California State University–Monterey Bay campus.

In the heart of Old Monterey, Monterey State Historic Park encompasses several notable buildings, including the custom house. Today Colton Hall and the Larkin House are museums, while the nearby Royal Presidio Chapel stands in silent tribute to the era of Spanish rule. The tracks at Cannery Row are mostly gone, but old grade-crossing equipment that is still in place fosters a sense of continuity between the past and present. Resting on a short strip of track rebuilt by area merchants, a caboose and a baggage car serve to remind passersby of a branch once graced by the legendary Del Monte Express.

For Further Study

SUGGESTED READINGS:
Fink, Augusta. *Monterey County: The Dramatic Story of its Past.* San Francisco: Chronicle Books, 1972, 122–35.
Hanson, Erle. C. *Monterey & Pacific Grove Street Car Era.* Glendale, Calif.: Interurban Press, 1990, 6–66.
"Travels Aboard Del Monte." *Santa Clara Block: Quarterly Publication of the South Bay Historical Railroad Society* 10, no. 3 (Summer 2001): 1–11.

OTHER PRINCIPAL REFERENCES:
Dorin, Patrick. *Commuter Railroads: A Pictorial Review of the Most Traveled Railroads.* Seattle, Wash.: Superior Publishing, 1970, 159–60.
Fickewirth, Alvin A. *California Railroads.* San Marino, Calif.: Golden West Books, 1992, 83.
Hilton, George W. *American Narrow Gauge Railroads.* Stanford: Stanford University Press, 1990, 326.
Lewis, Oscar. *The Big Four.* New York: Alfred A. Knopf, 1938, 121–23.
Planer, Edward T., Jr. "The Monterey and Salinas Valley Railroad: California's First Operating Narrow Gauge." *Railway and Locomotive Historical Society Bulletin* 66 (1945): 7–27.
"SP Monterey Branch." *The Ferroequinologist* (Dec. 1994): 3–9.

NEWPORT BEACH, CALIFORNIA (70,032)

Historic operators: Pacific Electric Railway; Southern Pacific Railroad
Last route abandoned: 1962
Notable reuses of right-of-way: Balboa Boulevard; Newport Boulevard; Costa Mesa Freeway; West Newport Park

 Travelers once arrived in Newport Beach on the trains and gasoline-powered motorcars of the Southern Pacific Railroad and the well-known Red Cars of the Pacific Electric Railway. During the summer season they came to enjoy the community's ocean wharf, beach, and popular bayside attractions, including the famed Balboa Pavilion. Today, Newport Beach lacks a railroad of any kind and has been excluded from plans for rail transit service largely due to the absence of a preserved route as well as long-standing political indifference.

Historical Perspective

Situated along a beautiful stretch of shoreline, the present-day Newport Beach area had yet to be settled by Europeans when Spanish soldiers and missionaries passed through the hinterland in 1769 intent upon selecting sites for southern California's first churches and towns. The lush landscape proved to be amenable for raising livestock and foodstuffs and eventually attracted a small population of permanent settlers. In 1810, Spain awarded a land grant for the creation of large ranches in the area. Thirty-two years later, a similar grant by the Mexican government put a large swath of land under the stewardship of the legendary cattleman José Sepulveda.

By the time California passed to the United States in 1848, Sepulveda, a Mexican, had created a massive ranching operation in the area, but several devastating droughts eventually killed much of his herd. After Sepulveda disposed of his holdings in 1864, his property and adjacent parcels came into the possession of James Irvine and his partners, astute businessmen who sought to raise sheep rather than cattle with hopes of eventually planting crops.

Irvine's vast holdings included a long tidal inlet divided into upper and lower sections. Government surveyors and the operators of large commercial vessels had long considered these waters impassable—until Captain Samuel Dunnells successfully navigated his shallow-draft steamer *Vaquero* across both bays in 1870. When Irvine learned of Dunnells's achievement, he returned from San Francisco to oversee the creation of a commercial port. Wasting little time, Irvine and his successors, including James and Robert McFadden, worked to develop the upper bay. While Irvine platted a village called Newport in this area, Dunnells built a wharf on the narrow neck between the upper and lower bays that became known as Newport Landing.

Unfortunately for these entrepreneurs, the outside world showed little interest in either Newport or a subdivision near Dunnells's wharf, partially due to a lack of promotion. Furthermore, before Irvine's death in 1886 it had become apparent that the bay's waters were indeed too shallow to support the expansion of commercial shipping. The McFaddens pursued federal support to deepen the inlet but could not secure the necessary funds. This disappointment, coupled with several fatal boating accidents and continuing navigational problems, led to a shift of local commerce to a new oceanfront landing bearing the McFaddens' name.

The next phase of Newport's development had a more favorable outcome. The McFadden Wharf, equipped with a lengthy pier in 1888 and adjacent to a new town site, handled rising tonnage and and saw the arrival of the Santa Ana & Newport Railroad in 1891. This 12-mile carrier, built with the support of the McFaddens, hauled substantial shipments of lumber and merchandise between the wharf and Santa Ana (the seat of Orange County) and grain from the region's fertile interior to the coast. In 1893, the carrier was reincorporated as the Santa Ana & Newport Railway to support the construction of new routes, including a northwesterly extension—called the Smeltzer Branch—from Newport to Huntington Beach.

In 1899, Southern Pacific acquired this company "lock, stock, and locomotive," giving it a third route to the coast in the greater Los Angeles area. Its other routes to the coast served wharves in Santa Monica and San Pedro Bays.

Despite these investments, there was little to suggest that this coastal region would one day become a prominent leisure destination. Other than several cottages, a hotel, and a small pavilion, the wharf area had few man-made amenities. The situation changed, however, after the McFaddens sold the town site to W. S. Collins in 1902. Collins had a flair for marketing and sought to transform the lower bay into a prominent leisure and residential area—efforts aided by major expansions to the electric railway system then under way in the Los Angeles area. In 1905, the Los Angeles Inter-Urban Railway completed an extension of its Huntington Beach route to the Newport Wharf, allowing it to offer direct service from Los Angeles. The following year the interurban extended its track to Balboa, the home of the newly completed Balboa Pavilion, a new pleasure pier, and a two-story hotel.

With convenient and inexpensive transportation now widely available, an appreciable number of Los Angeles

A Pacific Electric train heads south along the coast near Huntington Beach, only a few miles from its final destination of Newport and Balboa, on June 12, 1947—three years before the end of regularly scheduled passenger service. Note the drilling equipment at right. (Collection of Craig A. Rasmussen.)

residents bought or built homes in the area. In 1906, the consolidation of Balboa, Newport, and several other communities into the newly created city of Newport Beach appeared to mark the beginning of a new era of rapid residential expansion. The nature of the development that followed, however, proved disappointing; instead of attracting a larger permanent population, Newport Beach became known principally as a haunt for holiday-goers and day-trippers arriving on the interurban.

The community and its railroads nonetheless prospered from the expansion of tourism and agriculture. In 1907, Southern Pacific (which had absorbed the Santa Ana & Newport into its system at the turn of the century) built an extension off its Anaheim–Los Alamitos Branch to Smeltzer, where it joined the Smeltzer Branch from Newport, thus forming the Orange County Loop Line. On this system of freight-oriented routes, circumscribed by Newport Beach, Santa Ana, Tustin, West Anaheim, Stanton, and Huntington Beach, Southern Pacific operated a mixed train—aptly called the Merry-Go-Round—in clockwise fashion, with occasional service in the opposite direction.

More significant to the tourism industry was the assimilation of the Los Angeles Inter-Urban into the Pacific Electric Railway in 1908. The latter carrier's Red Cars set a high standard for service and operated at considerable speeds along its scenic shoreline route, despite the need to funnel traffic over a single track south of Huntington Beach. The carrier's Newport–Balboa Line grew in popularity among commuters and shoppers, as well as socialites and beachgoers from Los Angeles. Many arriving passengers strolled along the ocean piers and enjoyed the Pavilion and other attractions along the bay.

At the height of the railroad era in 1913, travelers could reach Newport Beach on three different routes from Los Angeles. Although the overwhelming majority arrived along the coast on the Pacific Electric's Red Cars, passengers could also book passage on Southern Pacific's daily gasoline-powered McKeen motorcar as well as the carrier's mixed trains operating via Santa Ana and Stanton.

Ridership on the Pacific Electric's Newport–Balboa Line reached its peak in 1914 and remained strong for another ten years. Following the discovery of a major oil field in Huntington Beach and a smaller field near Newport in the 1920s, both Pacific Electric and Southern Pacific (by then the interurban's parent company) derived significant revenues from the shipment of petroleum as well as drilling and production supplies.

Changing Times

The profound implications of improved automobile and bus travel were readily apparent by 1923, when Southern Pacific discontinued the last of its passenger service to Newport Beach. Although the completion in 1927 of a new Greek revival depot (jointly operated with the Pacific Electric) suggested otherwise, the community had little place in the carrier's long-range plans. After Southern Pacific secured the right to use the Pacific Electric (which it owned but allowed to operate with its own management organization) between Huntington Beach and Newport Beach, the carrier abandoned its Huntington Beach–Newport Beach–Santa Ana lines in 1933. That same year, the carrier relinquished the remaining freight service between Huntington Beach and Stanton to Pacific Electric (which was already a joint operator of the route).

Despite the disappointments of the past, Newport Beach officials clung to the notion that their community would one day become an important commercial port. When the federal government completed an effort to deepen and improve the harbor in 1936 (including the construction of twin jetties at the harbor mouth with rock brought in by rail), some believed that the opportunity for major marine-oriented industrial development was finally at hand. The pace of

Although Newport Pier is still a popular summer destination for day-trippers from Los Angeles, a historical monument is the only sign of the community's former rail lines near the pleasure pier. (Photo by author.)

NEWPORT BEACH, CALIFORNIA

development remained sluggish, however, and the community retained a principally residential and leisure area.

Even as droves of passengers abandoned the Red Cars in favor of other modes of transportation (including buses operated by Pacific Electric itself), the interurban continued to shoulder the burden of heavy seasonal traffic. During the summer of 1936, the company introduced parlor-car service between Balboa and Los Angeles. The following year it enhanced this service with the Special Club Car Commodore, a parlor car that served many executive commuters, including local resident Oscar Smith, the Pacific Electric company president.

Unfortunately for the Red Car faithful, the Commodore was no match for the newly completed Pacific Coast Highway and other roads. The demand for the parlor service fell to such an extent that the railway discontinued this offering after the 1939 summer season. That same year, a storm knocked down the ocean wharf, which was replaced with a much smaller pleasure pier. In 1940, Pacific Electric eliminated all remaining passenger service except for a daily run it had to operate to maintain its franchise. The carrier abandoned the Newport–Balboa segment that year and removed the tracks in 1941, thereby limiting its services to the northern part of town. The municipal government quickly transformed the abandoned segment into an extension of Balboa Boulevard, the peninsula's primary road.

The Pacific Electric experienced a revival during the thunderous years of World War II, when its services were instrumental to several major military bases in the area. With the local economy blossoming once again, Pacific Electric restored seasonal passenger service, including its Commodore service, on the Newport Line in 1942. For the next several years, the interurban continued to offer regular freight serice as well as parlor-car service on an intermittent basis.

Such diverse offerings were more difficult for the company to justify after the war. The carrier permanently dropped the parlor accommodation in 1949 and ended the remaining local passenger service in 1950. Although Pacific Electric freight trains continued to serve boat distributors and a handful of other local businesses, the carrier closed its depot. In 1958, it dismantled its bridge between Seal Beach and Long Beach, severing the route to Los Angeles. Its diesel-powered freight trains now reached Newport Beach via Stanton.

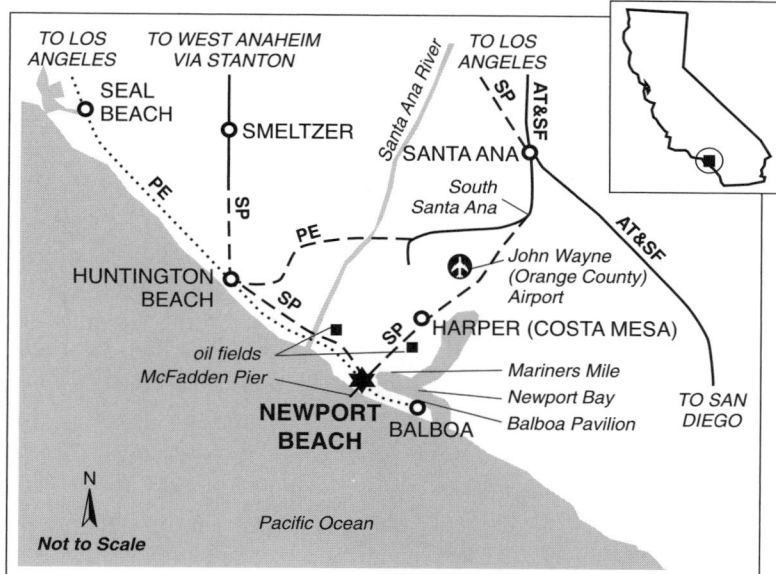

As residential construction and rising high-tech employment brought great prosperity to Newport Beach, the Pacific Electric tracks devolved into little more than an eyesore. After the opening of the town's first major hotel, the Newporter Inn, in 1959, and the Newport Harbor Art Museum two years later, the community showcased its growing affluence and its shift towards exclusivity. By 1960, there was apparently little demand for the carrier's freight service, allowing the Pacific Electric to abandon the Newport Beach–Huntington Beach segment without significant opposition in 1962.

Abandonment's Legacy

The absence of heavy industry along the harbor had preserved Newport Beach's natural beauty and made it a desirable location for corporate offices and luxury homes. Soon, the creation of upscale residential buildings, a shopping center, and West Newport Park altered parts of the old Pacific Electric right-of-way beyond recognition. In 1963, county officials lengthened a runway at the old Santa Ana army base to create a commercial airfield, which later became John Wayne (Orange County) Airport.

With Newport Beach in the midst of yet another transformation, still more remnants of the past slipped into oblivion. In 1966, fire reduced to ruins the Rendezvous Ballroom, historic entertainment venue adjacent to the Pavilion, obliterating a cherished reminder of simpler and slower-paced times. In 1975, another fire destroyed many buildings along the Mariners' Mile, a commercial area on the bay waterfront. Two years later, a work crew removed 2 additional miles of former Pacific Electric track in Huntington Beach.

Much as the McFaddens had supported the construction of a railroad ninety years before, regional business leaders pushed for the expansion of the nearby John Wayne–Orange County Airport. Despite fierce opposition, an agreement between airport and municipal officials in 1981 cleared the way for this ambitious project. The enlarged airport sparked a construction boom that pushed property values to spectacular levels.

Seeking to improve mobility in the midst of the real estate boom, the Southern California Association of Governments conducted a study of potential rail corridors in 1989 and evaluated the possibility of restoring rail transit service between Los Angeles and Huntington Beach. This organization, however, did not formally explore scenarios for rebuilding a corridor to Newport Beach due to the absence of an unobstructed right-of-way and the disinterest, if not outright hostility, of municipal leaders to the idea of rail transit. Proponents of rail transit over the years have nevertheless criticized the planners who allowed former Pacific Electric rights-of-way to fall prey to real estate development many years ago. As in other prosperous southern California communities, traffic in Newport Beach has become a serious problem, especially during the summer months.

As the process of modernization continued, individuals and organizations took a variety of steps to recognize the community's past. Officials had the Balboa Hotel and Pavilion listed on the National Register of Historic Places and supported the latter structure's conversion into a seafood restaurant. In 1992, a group of residents designated the Red Cars as a significant part of the city's heritage. The following year, the Pacific Railroad Society organized a bus excursion through the community that rekindled fond memories of its Red Car specials.

Epilogue

Newport Beach is perhaps the quintessential example of a town that has expanded rapidly in recent decades in part due to its inability to achieve its economic goals at the height of the railroad era. The community's population has risen to more than 70,000 and its harbor is currently home to one of the world's largest fleets of small recreational boats. Its waterfront is superbly suited for commercial and residential development.

Travelers with an interest in railroad history will find little left of the former Newport & Santa Ana except the Costa Mesa Industrial Lead, a remnant used by Union Pacific branch to serve a *Los Angeles Times* printing plant. Farther north, the Metro Blue Line, a light-rail corridor linking Los Angeles and Long Beach, follows part of the former Red Car route to Newport Beach.

Visitors will find that older parts of Newport Beach are a colorful agglomeration of communities, each with a distinct character and business district. In Newport, tourists stroll along the pier on the site of the old McFadden Wharf. In Balboa, shoppers enjoy the ambience of a retail district steeped in local history. In this neighborhood, a short strip of the track, once part of a Pacific Electric spur, is embedded in pavement. This remnant, preserved for reasons that are not entirely clear, disappears into the side of a luxury condominium complex—an interesting visual connection between the different phases of this coastal community's past.

For Further Study

SUGGESTED READINGS:

Donaldson, Stephen E., and William A. Myers. *Rails Through the Orange Groves: A Centennial Look at the Railroads of Orange County, California.* Glendale, Calif.: Trans-Anglo Books, 1989–90. 1:69–133, 2:221, 224, 275–76.

Felton, James P. , ed. *Newport Beach: The First Century, 1888–1988.* Newport Beach, Calif.: City of Newport Beach, 1988, 19–110.

Lee, Ellen K. *Newport Bay: A Pioneer History.* Newport Beach, Calif.: Newport Beach Historical Society, 1973.

Swett, Ira L. *Lines of Pacific Electric: Southern District: Interurbans Special* 17. Glendale, Calif.: Interurbans Publications, 1959. 104–6.

OTHER PRINCIPAL REFERENCES:

Crump, Spencer. *Ride the Big Red Cars.* Glendale, Calif.: Trans-Anglo Books, 1988.

Donaldson, Stephen. "Santa Ana & Newport Railway." *Western Railroader* 36, no. 395 (March 1973): 2– 11.

———. "Southern Pacific Railroad: Newport and Smeltzer Branches." *Western Railroader* 36, no. 396 (April 1973): 5–14.

PLACERVILLE, CALIFORNIA (9,610)

Historic operators: Camino, Placerville & Lake Tahoe Railroad; Diamond & Caldor Railway; Southern Pacific
Last route abandoned: 1990
Notable reuses of right-of-way: El Dorado Trail; potential trail and demonstration railway

  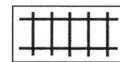 

Reaching vast groves of virgin timber and a mining district etched into American history, the railroad lines of Placerville were once vital arteries into the heart of the Mother Lode. These lines, supporting a historical gold-mining area and a vast system of private logging railways, nurtured the development of the northern Sierra Nevada. Today, the trains are gone, but Placerville recognizes its bountiful railroad heritage in a variety of ways.

Historical Perspective

In 1844, legendary guide Kit Carson hurried his fellow frontiersman John C. Frémont through the forests along the south fork of the American River. Weary after a long journey and on the verge of starvation, Frémont and his party spent little time assessing the area's potential and ended their travels at Sutter's Fort, a compound belonging to John A. Sutter and situated within present-day Sacramento.

Several years later, the commercially minded Sutter made the fateful decision to hire James Marshall to construct a sawmill along the fork. On January 24, 1848, while testing a millrace (a channel of water to drive a mill wheel), Marshall noticed shining objects in the sediment that he collected for evaluation—objects he confirmed to be gold. Marshall and Sutter tried to keep the finding a secret, fearful that an influx of prospectors would destroy Sutter's commercial fiefdom. As word of the discovery spread, however, gold seekers swarmed into this mountainous region. Within months, they had overrun Sutter's crops, disrupted his live-stock herds, and squatted on the land that he claimed to have leased from a Native American tribe.

With the California gold rush in full swing, miners panned elbow-to-elbow in rivers and streams along a lucrative vein of gold widely known as the Mother Lode, carefully examining the placer deposits (gravel and other sediment often containing particles of gold). Although Sutter sold the mill site in late 1848, he was embittered by the expansion of mining that he felt violated his property rights. He tried for years to obtain compensation for damages, but with no avail.

As newcomers hastily erected tents and shanties on the hillsides, numerous towns, including Coloma, grew at a spectacular rate. Several months after Marshall's discovery, a gold strike farther south spurred the creation of Old Dry Diggings, a community along the Carson Trail (part of the Central Overland Route) between Carson City and Sacramento. Later that year, three men accused of thievery were put to death in Old Dry Diggings, giving the community the nickname Hangtown.

Coloma and Hangtown were fierce rivals and vied to become the seat of newly created El

65

A Southern Pacific freight begins its undulating descent from downtown Placer-ville toward Sacramento, its final destination, in 1982. Rail service to the historic mining camp ended four years later. (El Dorado Historic Museum.)

Dorado County. Although Coloma prevailed, Hangtown had an upper hand in the battle for commercial supremacy. After being incorporated in 1854 and formally renamed Placerville (a name derived from the Spanish word *placer*, which means "sand bank"), the community became the county's principal business center and honed the skills of merchants destined for industrial greatness. John Studebaker made wheelbarrows for gold miners in a local shop many years before becoming a leader in the automobile industry. Philip Armour supposedly owned a local butchery on his way to becoming America's "pork baron." Mark Hopkins managed a store in a nearby town before emerging as a founder of the Central Pacific—one of the indomitable "Big Four."

As several other communities in the Mother Lode district faded into obscurity, Placerville adjusted well to a southward shift in mining. It reportedly grew to approximately 20,000 residents in 1854, making it California's third largest city, behind only San Francisco and Sacramento. Placerville replaced Coloma as the county seat in 1857 and seemed destined for lasting prosperity in 1860

as countless wagons made their way through town en route to Virginia City, where a new mining boom was under way. Its good fortunes continued after it became a stop on the Pony Express in 1861 and the originating point for a series of toll roads to Virginia City the following year.

Even more promising was the prospect that the first transcontinental railroad would be built through town. Placerville's political clout allowed it to become an influential participant in the debate about the route of this railroad. Nevertheless, many years passed without the arrival of even a short-line railroad. Not only was the transcontinental line built along a more northerly alignment bypassing the county, but the more modest Placerville & Sacramento Valley Railroad laid its tracks only as far as Shingle Springs when it extended its line (which originated at Folsom, the terminus of the Sacramento Valley Railroad) in 1865. As a result, another generation of miners and businessmen were left dependent on non-motorized travel.

When the Shingle Springs & Placerville Railroad finally closed the 11-mile gap from Shingle Springs in early 1888, thousands gathered in Placerville to commemorate the occasion. This company and numerous others were consolidated into the newly formed Northern Railway that same year, which put the entire route from Sacramento to Placerville in the hands of this Southern Pacific-controlled entity.

Although the railroad arrived too late for Placerville to sustain its position as an important commercial hub, it did mark the beginning of a logging era prominent in California industrial lore. In 1892, Michigan businessmen organized the American River Land and Lumber Company, which built a narrow-gauge railway from the vicinity of Pino Grande (a settlement east of where James Marshall discovered gold) deep into the hinterland. The railway shipped logs on flatcars to the edge of the river valley and then sent them down a chute for flotation to a sawmill in Folsom.

The logging era reached its climax in 1901 when D. H. McEwen, the leader of the Eldorado Lumber Company (successor to American River Land and Lumber) built a mill at Pino Grande and a steam-operated cable tramway across the American River valley. Nearly a half mile long, the aerial tramway was one of the most remarkable systems of its kind in the country. It allowed loaded railcars to be conveyed by cable to a newly constructed narrow-gauge line linking the northern side of the valley to Camino, an outpost 8 miles outside Placerville that had a large drying yard.

As impressive as this tramway-equipped system may have been, massive steam traction engines still had to be used to haul lumber over dirt roads from the Camino drying yard to the Southern Pacific (formerly Northern Railway) branch in Placerville. This primitive arrangement held sway until the Placerville & Lake Tahoe Railroad finally closed the 8-mile gap in 1904—a banner year in El Dorado railroading. The completion of this railroad and the narrow-gauge Diamond & Caldor Railway—a 34-mile line from Diamond Springs to Caldor—the same year established Southern Pacific's Placerville Branch as one of the most productive lumber-hauling branches in the region. As its name implied, the Diamond & Caldor served a sawmill operated by the California Door Company.

Although the passenger business was less robust, Southern Pacific's daily passenger train to Sacramento was interwoven in Placerville life. After crossing miles of rolling terrain as well as a beautiful grassy plain, this train (which was later replaced by a McKeen car) backed up a short branch from Folsom Junction to the depot in Folsom. It then finished its journey to the state capital over one of the oldest railroad routes in the West. Travelers could also ride the Placerville & Lake Tahoe, which began providing accommodations in a combination car

in 1905 and reached the Southern Pacific depot through a trackage-rights agreement.

The enormity of the region's timber operations and its increasingly bountiful harvests of fresh fruit allowed Placerville to weather the changing times better than most other towns in the area of the Mother Lode. Although the Placerville & Lake Tahoe discontinued operations in 1909, services on its line resumed three years later through the auspices of the newly incorporated Camino, Placerville & Lake Tahoe Railroad. Vast amounts of lumber still moved through Placerville when the Eldorado Lumber Company entered the fold of the Michigan-California Company in 1917. The new owner rebuilt much of the logging railway and expanded it to more than 50 miles of routes.

Changing Times

The gradual depletion of the region's gold and timber made it only a matter of time before Placerville fell into a severe economic slump. Although Michigan-California improved the efficiency of its aerial tramway by switching

Vegetation begins to encroach upon the dormant Placerville Branch in 1999, more than a decade after its last train. The debate about reinstituting rail service continues today. (Photo by author.)

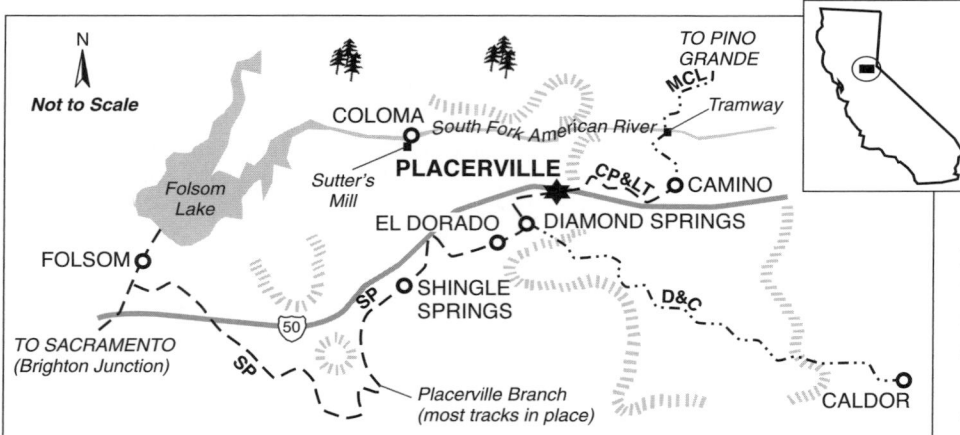

Railroads receded further from public view when the Camino, Placerville & Lake Tahoe operated its final train and abandoned its route in 1986. A horseback rider who noticed the short line's rails being removed proposed that the right-of-way be converted to a recreational path—an idea that the county formally studied and eventually embraced.

The Southern Pacific was left without a significant source of local revenue and operated its last train from Placerville in 1987. Eager to make additional improvements to Route 50, Caltrans, the state transportation agency, purchased the 4-mile portion of this line between the center of Placerville and Diamond Springs. After the railroad abandoned service over this segment in 1990, Placerville's railroad era formally drew to a close.

to electric motive power in 1928, it suffered from the dwindling supply of high-grade timber. Making matters worse, unemployment rose as the county's fresh-fruit industry declined and Placerville's Pacific Mine, an underground facility within municipal boundaries, greatly scaled back its production. By 1930, Placerville's population had plummeted to a mere 6,400.

As the years passed, Placerville evolved into a substantially different community than the bustling mining and lumber center that many older residents remembered. A modest revival in gold mining ended prematurely when the federal government ordered the remaining mines closed during World War II. A fire destroyed the tramway in 1949, contributing to the abandonment of the entire Michigan-California Company rail system in 1951. The last of the county's narrow-gauge operators, the Diamond & Caldor line, was dismantled two years later.

A growing number of commercial trucks traveling down U.S. Route 50, the main road through Placerville, signaled the region's changing transportation practices. Although many residents strongly supported upgrading this road into a freeway, they feared that it would lead to the destruction of several of the town's fine historic homes. The completion of the project in the 1950s altered Placerville's character precisely as some had feared but also stimulated tourism development.

A decade later, Southern Pacific's local revenues were so weak that the carrier could no longer justify major outlays for track maintenance and rehabilitation. In 1974, it received approval to discontinue staffing an agent at its local depot. In 1985, the most conspicuous reminder of the glory years of rail travel—a former Southern Pacific steam locomotive (a 2-6-0) on display at a highway intersection in Placerville—was donated to the California State Railroad Museum in exchange for a retired caboose.

Abandonment's Legacy

Government agencies took numerous steps to bring the railroad rights-of-way into the public realm over the next several years. After one work crew removed the Southern Pacific tracks within Placerville, another began work on the Route 50 improvements. In 1992, the county and municipal government converted the abandoned Camino, Placerville & Lake Tahoe into the El Dorado Trail recreational path. Anticipating that Southern Pacific would soon abandon the remainder of its line between Diamond Springs and Sacramento, various local government agencies created the Sacramento–Placerville Transportation Corridor Joint Powers Authority. This intergovernmental agency spent $15 million to purchase the 53-mile segment in 1996.

A consultant working for the authority then explored the possibility of restoring rail freight and passenger service or creating a bikeway or recreational path on this preserved route. Planners also left open the possibility of allowing a short-line railroad to operate steam-powered excursion trains over these rails, an idea of special interest to the Folsom, El Dorado, and Sacramento Historical Railroad Association (FEDS). Officials later contemplated making the corridor available to the Union Pacific Railroad for honing the track-repairing skills of its employees.

Bringing rail service back to downtown Placerville, however, was understood to be an exceedingly difficult endeavor. Running trains in such close proximity to the highway could not be done without resolving challenging engineering and safety issues. Nevertheless, the county government acquired most of the Placerville–Diamond Springs segment (which was by this time bereft of tracks) from the state to keep its options open.

By the century's end, the dormant tracks from Sacramento to Diamond Springs were covered with weeds and small trees, even though this segment had never been officially abandoned. Recognizing the line's historical significance, FEDS cleared some of the track near Folsom for annual handcar races. Another group affiliated with the El Dorado Museum, meanwhile, worked to restore a former Diamond & Caldor Shay steam locomotive (No. 1) with an eye toward one day creating a demonstration railway operating between Diamond Springs and Shingle Springs, notwithstanding the fact that this would require equipping this segment with a third rail or converting the track to narrow gauge. After years of work, a formal plan emerged in 2003 to create the demonstration railway as well as a parallel equestrian trail. At this writing, there is hope of commencing operations using the historic Shay locomotive by 2006.

Epilogue

More than 150 years after James Marshall discovered gold at Sutter's Mill, the northern Sierra Nevada is once again in the midst of a development boom. As metropolitan Sacramento expands outward, new housing developments encroach on portions of the famed mining district.

Thousands of travelers stop in Placerville annually on their way to the Marshall Gold Discovery Historic Park in Coloma. Those who visit will find several dozen preserved nineteenth-century structures evocative of the community's storied past. One of the mines within city limits, the Gold Bug, having ended production decades ago, is currently a municipally owned attraction listed on the National Register of Historic Places.

Although the railroad has largely faded from modern recollection, many residents commuting to the state capital ride buses from the transit center, which appropriately

enough is situated on the former Placerville depot grounds and resembles a railroad station. The caboose acquired years ago, long a tourist information center, now awaits an uncertain fate along Route 50.

Travelers following the former Southern Pacific right-of-way east of Diamond Springs will find a large trestle vaulting over Weber Creek, a graceful 1906 viaduct over Hangtown Creek, and rail encrusted in concrete near downtown Placerville. The tracks are still in place between Diamond Springs and Folsom, but they are now covered with weeds and may never again be used by a common-carrier railroad. Regardless, it is clear that the intergovernmental effort to preserve this corridor has given planners a variety of alternatives to support transportation and tourism development that would otherwise be unavailable. After thousands of hours of volunteer labor, trains are poised to steam through this part of the Mother Lode district for the first time in many years.

For Further Study

SUGGESTED READINGS:
"Camino, Placerville & Lake Tahoe R.R.: Michigan-California Lumber Co." *Western Railroader* 21, no. 2 (Dec. 1957): 3–13.
Ferguson, Marilyn, and Jane Schlappi. *A Walking Tour of Historic Placerville: 1848–1874.* Placerville, Calif.: Heritage Association of El Dorado, 1973, 1–41.
McAffee, Ward. *California's Railroad Era: 1850–1911.* San Marino, Calif.: Golden West Books, 1973, 35–69.

OTHER PRINCIPAL REFERENCES:
Crosley-Griffin, Mary. *Hangtown: Tales of Old Placerville.* Universal City, Calif.: Crosley Books, 1994, 1–53.
Fickewirth, Alvin. A. *California Railroads.* San Marino, Calif.: Golden West Books, 1992, 26, 36.
Hilton, George W. *American Narrow Gauge Railroads.* Stanford: Stanford University Press, 1990, 324.
Huffman, Wendell, "Rival Rails: A History of the Early Sacramento Area Railroads and the Placerville Branch of the Southern Pacific." Photocopy, unpublished manuscript, November 1997.

SAN RAFAEL, CALIFORNIA (58,063)

Historic operator: Northwestern Pacific Railroad
Last route abandoned: 1985
Notable reuse of right-of-way: Proposed rail passenger corridor

    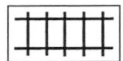

The saga of San Rafael's last rail line illustrates the vicissitudes of corridor preservation in affluent and expanding suburban areas. Those tracks, once part of an electrified system that was vital to thousands of commuters residing north of San Francisco Bay, are today largely overgrown with vegetation. The debate about reusing them to relieve traffic congestion has continued unabated for more than a decade.

Historical Perspective

Spanish settlers under the supervision of Father Junipero Serra, the president of California's missions, established the Misión San Francisco de Asis, commonly called Mission Dolores, near San Francisco Bay in 1776. The brothers of this enclave tended their livestock for many years while focusing their spiritual endeavors on spreading the Christian faith. Another settlement, the Mission San Rafael Arcángel, emerged on the rolling terrain farther north in 1817 and prospered to such an extent that it obtained independence from the older mission in 1823.

The inhabitants of the new mission built large adobe structures, expanded their herds of cattle and sheep, and overcame a Native American uprising in 1824. In the early 1830s, the Republic of Mexico secularized the San Rafael mission and other settlements on the Marin Peninsula, transforming them into pueblos, or towns.

The commercial potential of the area rose markedly when jurisdiction over California passed to the United States in 1848. After California attained statehood two years later, officials designated San Rafael the seat of Marin County, believing that rapid expansion would soon follow. To their disappointment, however, the county grew only sluggishly and was largely bypassed by the California gold rush, when untold numbers of miners and prospectors swarmed across northern California.

The opening of a post office and a general store in 1851 appeared to be a turning point for San Rafael. A federal prison in nearby San Quentin opened in 1854, and the community emerged as a stop for steamers working their way from San Francisco to Petaluma. Commerce did not expand, however, as rapidly as hoped. By 1860, other Marin cities were vying to replace San Rafael as the county seat—a concern the townspeople eventually put to rest by building a grand Greek revival courthouse.

San Rafael remained of little consequence in the region's commercial affairs until several railroad lines arrived on the scene. In 1871, the San Rafael & San Quentin Railroad opened a 3-mile route to Point San Quentin, where it provided ferry service to San Francisco. In 1874, a second railroad, the North Pacific Coast

(NPC), built a narrow-gauge line to town from Sausalito, a port in the southern part of the peninsula. The same railroad then built a lengthy extension from the nearby community of San Anselmo to Tomales in northern California and leased the San Rafael & San Quentin, which it converted to narrow gauge.

Travelers soon flocked to the NPC's trains as well as connecting boat services from Point San Quentin and Sausalito to San Francisco. Still more took to the rails when the Sonoma & Marin Railroad linked Petaluma to San Rafael in 1876, thereby establishing the community as an important interchange point. By the time the Sonoma & Marin consolidated in 1877 with several other companies to form the San Francisco & North Pacific Railroad, San Rafael had become a booming town barely resembling the sleepy hamlet it had been only a decade before.

For San Rafael to enjoy the benefits of vigorous railroad competition, however, it had to wait until the San Francisco & North Pacific extended its line south from San Rafael to Tiburon in 1884, thus establishing a new transfer point for passengers bound for San Francisco. The battle for market share between the NPC and this newly expanded rival grew to legendary proportions. In 1884, to protect its business, NPC built a more direct and more westerly line from the vicinity of Corte Madera (several miles south of San Rafael) to Sausalito.

With attractive neighborhoods and ample rail service, San Rafael evolved into a popular weekend and holiday destination for affluent San Franciscans. By the early 1890s, several fine guesthouses—including the luxurious five-story Hotel Rafael—as well as many stores, office buildings, and lovely homes lined its streets. San Rafael's economy remained strong after NPC reorganized as the North Shore Railroad in 1902. The new operator widened some tracks to standard gauge and equipped others with three rails to allow for joint standard-gauge/narrow-gauge operation.

The crowning achievement in the development of the peninsula's railroad system took place in 1903, when the North Shore installed an energized fourth rail to allow for electrified operations from San Rafael to both San Anselmo and Sausalito—an improvement that greatly enhanced the ability of suburban passenger trains to negotiate the difficult grades. After the San Francisco earthquake in 1906, multitudes of refugees arrived over this well-engineered system.

Several thousand passengers boarded trains each

On October 19, 1940, a Northwestern Pacific passenger train, drawing its power from an electrified third rail, passes an interlocking tower on its way to the San Rafael depot, which is visible in the distance. A few months later, this service ended. (Photo by Charles Savage, collection of Ted Wurm.)

The former Northwestern Pacific station in San Rafael appears ready for trains to return. The effort to restore passenger service over the adjacent rail lines, however, has lingered for more than a decade. (Photo by author.)

week in San Rafael in 1907, when all of the Marin Peninsula's rail lines, along with numerous others, were assimilated into the Northwestern Pacific Railroad, an entity jointly owned by Southern Pacific and the Atchison, Topeka & Santa Fe. For the next thirty years, the carrier's electrically propelled trains operated over two routes from San Rafael to Sausalito (via San Anselmo and Detour), where ferries destined for San Francisco awaited their arrival. Timetables published in 1908 show fifty-five daily electric trains and twenty-four steam trains (including long distance trains operating north to Santa Rosa and Eureka) departing San Rafael daily, with added service on Sunday.

By the end of World War I, Northwestern Pacific, calling itself the Redwood Empire Route, had electrified the route from San Anselmo to Manor. The carrier eliminated its narrow-gauge service on the Marin Peninsula in 1920 and built a spacious new mission-style station at the heart of San Rafael several years later. It provided freight service to the region principally from the wharf in Tiburon, where outbound freight cars were loaded onto large marine vessels, but also served this area through its interchanges with the Southern Pacific at Santa Rosa and Shellville (near Sonoma).

Changing Times

Such an extensive system could not be sustained as more flexible forms of transportation grew in popularity after

World War I. The railroad's tourist business diminished gradually as Bay Area residents grew accustomed to traveling longer distances to reach more exotic destinations. In addition, the Hotel San Rafael was destroyed by an arsonist's fire in 1928.

The Great Depression had truly catastrophic effects on the railroad and necessitated dramatic reductions in both freight and passenger service. Already suffering from the rise in motor-vehicle travel and expanding auto-ferry service across the bay, Northwestern Pacific (by now solely owned by Southern Pacific) saw its remaining passenger business devastated in 1937 by the opening of the Golden Gate Bridge and an adjoining segment of Highway 101. In 1941, the carrier suspended all of its suburban passenger service, ended electric operations, and stopped operating long-distance passenger trains south of San Rafael.

The railroad promptly abandoned its Fairfax–San Rafael route and eliminated its Eureka–San Rafael day train in 1942, reducing its once-vast passenger system to a single overnight train between these cities. In only a few years, the number of weekday passenger trains departing San Rafael dropped from more than thirty to only one.

Freight service to San Rafael fared better, especially during World War II. The Northwestern Pacific hauled enormous commodity shipments to Sausalito's bustling shipyard and moved its company offices to San Rafael in 1944. Unfortunately, the postwar years brought more retrenchment, including the abandonment of the little-used route to San Quentin in 1946.

Much as the old San Rafael mission had gradually evolved into a railroad town many years before, the community now made the transition into a thriving residential community with a distinctly suburban orientation. Major improvements to highways, including the Richmond–San Rafael Bridge, which opened in 1956, accelerated this process and fostered a boom in housing construction that helped sustain the Northwestern Pacific's local freight operations from the wharf in Tiburon.

The housing boom did little to assure the continued operation of the overnight train to Eureka, which was put on a daylight schedule in 1956. Ridership on the tri-weekly train, christened the Redwood, improved only marginally, leading to its replacement in 1958 with a rail-diesel car operating only between Willits and Eureka, leaving the entire Marin Peninsula without any rail passenger service.

The opportunity for a rail passenger revival slipped away several years later, when the San Francisco Bay Area Rapid Transit (BART) District withdrew plans to build a rapid-transit route—the so-called Marin Line—through San Rafael.

Slated to follow near Highway 101 and use portions of the Northwestern Pacific right-of-way, this proposed service had generated strong opposition from residents of the county. Echoing the public's sentiment about building the BART route, the Golden Gate Bridge District refused to allow the transit district access to the bridge. BART eventually droppd the line from consideration.

The freight business was also experiencing problems, highlighted by a fire started by several adolescents in 1961 that caused the collapse of the Puerto Suello tunnel (Tunnel No. 4) north of San Rafael. The carrier continued freight service over the community's newly "orphaned" line using a switch engine—the oldest diesel in Southern Pacific's fleet—stationed at the ferry dock in Tiburon. Nevertheless, the state's Public Utilities Commission ordered Southern Pacific to repair the 1,350-foot Puerto Suello passage. In 1967, the carrier grudgingly restored service to the north but abandoned the branch to Tiburon.

As the railroad receded to the margins of the peninsula's economy, San Rafael stengthened its reputation as a desirable Bay Area suburb. A magnificent civic center designed by Frank Lloyd Wright (completed in 1962) exemplified its growing wealth and exclusivity.

As the county's population rose dramatically (San Rafael grew from less than 21,000 in 1970 to more than 38,000 in 1980), residents began to consider the railroad to be a potential solution to the problem of rising traffic congestion. Freight trains operating over deteriorating tracks between Ignacio (a junction 11 miles north of the county seat) and San Rafael, however, could no longer be sustained by the handful of businesses being served. When Northwestern Pacific's parent company, Southern Pacific, abandoned this route in 1985, San Rafael's railroad era quietly came to a close.

Abandonment's Legacy

Transportation planners devoted a tremendous amount of time and energy to exploring potential reuses of the former Northwestern Pacific rail lines on the Marin Peninsula over the next fifteen years. By 1990, the Golden Gate Bridge, Highway, and Transportation District (GGBHTD) and the county jointly had purchased the entire route from Detour (a junction on the line to Sausalito) to Ignacio while keeping nearly all the tracks in place, including those through San Rafael. GGBHTD had a strong interest in rail transit but was also attentive to proposals to use the corridor for a recreational trail, provided that such a trail would be compatible with the eventual restoration of rail service. As highway congestion worsened, the agency built a transit station adjacent to the depot in San Rafael to serve local buses, with the possibility of rail passenger service in mind.

The saga of San Rafael's dormant rail line ultimately became only part of a much larger story about the future of the Northwestern Pacific system. Railroad advocates pushed hard to avert the abandonment of the rest of this system and felt a tremendous sense of relief when the North Coast Railroad Authority, an intergovernmental agency, purchased 139 miles of route from Ignacio to Willits during the mid-1990s, thus putting the entire railroad from the Marin Peninsula to northern California under public control. Over the next

several years, as virtually all of this track lay dormant, GGBHTD formally explored scenarios for operating commuter trains from Cloverdale, a growing community north of Santa Rosa, to the Larkspur Ferry Terminal, a facility south of San Rafael where passengers could transfer to ferries destined for San Francisco. Support for the project escalated as traffic delays grew to seemingly intolerable levels on the Golden Gate Bridge and at other choke points on area freeways

Consultants estimated that diesel-powered trains over this route would carry thousands of daily riders. Despite this relatively favorable assessment, the necessity for prospective passengers to make transfers between trains, ferries, and in some instances buses, raised concern about the project's viability. Moreover, GGBHTD estimated that the combined capital costs of rehabilitating the rail line, together with other transportation improvements to alleviate congestion on Highway 101, approached $1 billion, adding a considerable element of risk to the initiative. The absence of public support for tax increases became evident in 1998 when voters overwhelmingly defeated a referendum to increase the sales tax to fund these transportation improvements. In addition, the relationship between transit advocates and a no-growth faction in the region became strained, and the plan seemed incompatible with interest in San Rafael to extend Andersen Drive across the right-of-way.

To the disappointment of those who had pushed hard to bring passenger trains back to the peninsula, the debate about restoring rail service lingered for many years. In response to the entrenched opposition in Larkspur, some proposed rebuilding the abandoned line to a rail-ferry terminal in San Quentin. Although this option was feasible only if the prison closed, it rose in visibility after a wayward truck damaged a lengthy railroad trestle over Drake Boulevard in Larkspur (a span immortalized in motion picture history as a prop in the Clint Eastwood movie *Dirty Harry*), culminating in the partial removal of the trestle in 2003. California's budgetary situation, meanwhile, greatly deteriorated, giving planners reason to contemplate providing service with diesel multiunit railcars, thus lowering the project's cost. Even as the state's fiscal crisis worsened, officials held firm to their commitment to restoring rail service and insisted in 2003 that the state government relocate a lengthy portion of track within San Rafael as part of a project to widen Highway 101. Such a mandate necessitated the condemnation of several homes.

Epilogue

Visitors to San Rafael will find an attractive downtown and a variety of historical landmarks, including a replica of its historic mission. The gatehouse formerly belonging to nineteenth-century industrialist Ira Cook is now a historical museum that, along with the Marin Country Civic Center, is listed on the National Register of Historic Places. A more direct legacy of the railroad era is China Camp, a tranquil waterfront area outside of town (now a state park) that was once inhabited by Asian immigrants, many of whom endured great hardship building the county's rail lines.

High property values and attractive tree-lined streets underscore San Rafael's reputation as a premier residential suburb. The San Rafael depot, now partially occupied by a county paratransit provider, survives as a symbol of a time when electric trains reigned supreme in communities north of the Golden Gate. Members of Northwestern Pacific's historical society regularly gather inside for slide presentations rekindling the legacy of the Redwood Empire Route. Whatever the future holds for railroading in this community, its weed-covered former main line offers a poignant reminder of the difficulty of restoring service in densely populated and affluent suburban areas.

For Further Study

SUGGESTED READINGS:

Keegan, Frank L. *San Rafael, Marin's Mission City: An Illustrated History.* Northridge, Calif.: Windsor Publications, 1987, 1–136.

Stindt, Fred A. *The Northwestern Pacific Railroad.* Redwood City, Calif.: Fred A. Stindt, 1964, 11–34, 54–58, 83.

OTHER PRINCIPAL REFERENCES:

Demoro, Harre W., and Vernon J. Sappers. *Rails to San Francisco Bay.* New York: Quadrant Press, 1992, 80–85.

Sievers, Walt. "Electric Interurban Service of Marin County." *Western Railroader* 17, no. 10 (Aug. 1954): 3–12.

Tacy, Allen. "San Rafael Commutes By Steam." *The Northwesterner: Quarterly Publication of the Northwestern Pacific Railroad Historical Society* 14, no. 2 (Fall-Winter 2000): 18–22.

SANTA MONICA, CALIFORNIA (84,084)

Historic operator: Pacific Electric Railway
Last route abandoned: 1986
Notable reuses of right-of-way: Prospective light-rail route; city streets

The familiar Red Cars of the Pacific Electric Railway were once ubiquitous in Santa Monica. These cars brought passengers to the community's popular coastal attractions on a variety of routes from neighboring Los Angeles and directly from dozens of other points, fostering tremendous development. Although rail service ended years ago, the persistence of a group of concerned citizens has helped keep the oldest route largely free of obstruction so that it might see trains again.

Historical Perspective

When Portuguese navigator Juan Cabrillo and his Spanish crew explored the California coast in 1542, they were the first Europeans to sail Santa Monica Bay. Spanish authorities later created a series of missions in the area and gradually expanded their livestock herds. The strikingly beautiful shoreline that would later become part of Santa Monica, however, had yet to be formally claimed when the California territory passed to Mexico in 1821.

Ranching in the area rose to new heights after Francisco Sepulveda acquired coastal property in 1828 for a massive cattle operation. Unfortunately, Sepulveda and his rivals, the Reyes and Martinez families, argued over his claim to the land. Their disagreement lasted for decades, even after California became part of the United States in 1848. When a land commission finally settled the matter in 1851, it divided the property among the disputants,

awarding Sepulveda the largest share.

Blessed with attractive beaches, a pleasant climate, and the striking Santa Monica Canyon, the area gradually evolved into a popular leisure and camping destination for Los Angeles residents. Nevertheless, the economy still revolved around ranching when Colonel R. S. Baker acquired the Sepulveda property to raise sheep in 1872.

The shrewd Baker gradually enlarged his estate and formed a partnership with Senator John Percival Jones, who had amassed considerable wealth in silver mining in Nevada. This legendary pair organized the Los Angeles & Independence Railroad to link a proposed wharf in Santa Monica with Independence, a thriving mining camp in eastern California. With visions of creating a great city, Baker and Jones founded the town of Santa Monica, commenced work on the wharf, and completed the railroad between their emerging community and Los Angeles (well short of Independence) in 1875. As residential lots in Santa Monica sold quickly, many merchants arrived to sell their wares and services.

Hopes that Santa Monica would become the maritime center envisioned by its founders would soon be abandoned. Vigorous competition from Southern Pacific's port in San Pedro was a particularly devastating problem, leaving the wharf greatly underutilized. Unable to justify the cost of extending the railroad east of Los Angeles, Jones leased the Los Angeles & Independence to the Central Pacific. In 1877, Southern Pacific took control of Central Pacific and increased rates to discourage use of Santa Monica's port. By 1879, the carrier had removed the wharf, leaving Santa Monica with a seemingly dismal future.

The growing numbers of tourists visiting the beach and canyon offset some of the hardship that ensued. After Santa Monica incorporated as a city in 1886, its population began to dramatically expand once again.

A Red Car working the Hollywood–Venice route follows Santa Monica Boulevard at 5th Street in March 1941. Passenger service on this Pacific Electric route ended less than six months later. (Photo by Ivan Baker, collection of Craig Rasmussen.)

During the "Great Real Estate Boom of 1887," which stimulated the economy of the entire Los Angeles area, throngs of travelers came to stay at local inns. Many guests enjoyed the splendor of the Santa Monica Hotel, the community's first resort, and the stately Arcadia Hotel, which delighted guests with a curious "gravity" railroad taking patrons down a steep cliff to the beach.

By the end of 1888, the Central Pacific had been formally consolidated into Southern Pacific, and Santa Monica was a leisure destination of considerable renown. Answering the community's pleas for more efficient ways to move people along the streets, the Santa Monica & Soldiers Home Railroad in 1891 opened a 6-mile line, using cars pulled by horses, from the downtown district to Soldiers Home near Sawtelle. The following year, the Atchison, Topeka & Santa Fe Railway—Southern Pacific's rival—opened a branch from Los Angeles to Inglewood and the southern part of Santa Monica.

The community's fervor during these formative years was attributable in no small measure to an ambitious Southern Pacific plan to establish a major wharf along Santa Monica Bay. In 1893, Southern Pacific, under the leadership of Collis P. Huntington, finished

building Port Los Angeles, a massive pier several miles northwest of town in what is now the Pacific Palisades section of Los Angeles. The ocean wharf extended 4,700 feet, had two tracks, and was accessible on an extension of the former Los Angeles & Independence route. Huntington envisioned Port Los Angeles becoming a major transfer point for freight and passengers moving between northern and southern California.

When residents congregated at the pier—the venerable Long Wharf—to celebrate the arrival of the first steamer, Santa Monica appeared on the verge of becoming one of southern California's greatest cities. Expectations remained high in 1896, when the Pasadena & Pacific Railway transformed the western end of the Soldiers Home horsecar line into part of an electrified route linking Santa Monica to Hollywood and Los Angeles. These tracks followed a route through town that later became Santa Monica Boulevard.

The assumptions behind the creation of Long Wharf, unfortunately, proved to be seriously flawed. The massive facility could not begin to fulfill the lofty expectations of Southern Pacific's leaders and gradually faded in importance. Even so, Santa Monica's most illustrious years of rail service were yet come. In 1900, the Pasadena & Pacific's successor, the Los Angeles-Pacific Railway (LA-P), built a streetcar line through the center of town called the North Loop. The carrier soon operated a more southerly downtown loop as well. In 1902, LA-P built the Venice Short Line (which linked both Santa Monica and Venice to Los Angeles) and acquired the Santa Fe route, which it promptly electrified.

On an even larger scale, Southern Pacific developed plans for a new line along the coast between Los Angeles and Santa Barbara—a route that, if built, would give Santa Monica access to a major long-distance route. However, even the well-financed Southern Pacific could not overcome the cunning and machinations of an isolationist Malibu rancher who, before dying in 1905, instructed his wife to create a railroad over a portion of this same route. This narrow-gauge carrier, christened the Hueneme, Malibu & Port Los Angeles Railway, thwarted Southern Pacific's plan, thus denying Santa Monica a railroad outlet to the north.

This setback and the sharply diminished role of Long Wharf did not stop Santa Monica's railway system from continuing to expand. In 1906, LA-P opened the Westgate Line, a 6-mile electric route looping through Sawtelle and passing near the edge of the canyon. The carrier's Ocean Park car barn and yard in nearby Venice

emerged as important sources of local jobs.

LA-P operated all of the community's routes after it leased the former Los Angeles & Independence west of Sentous (midway between Santa Monica and Los Angeles) from Southern Pacific in 1908. The interurban soon electrified this line (which was popularly called the Santa Monica Air Line) and made other improvements that enhanced the speed and reliability of its services. As Santa Monica enjoyed more robust expansion, the LA-P's green cars operated frequently on both Santa Monica's streets and over private rights-of-way to dozens of prominent destinations, including Beverly Hills, Redondo Beach, and Venice. During these illustrious years, cars departed for Los Angeles every few minutes, carrying passengers directly to downtown terminals on four routes: the Santa Monica Air Line and Venice Short Line as well as the Westgate (Brentwood) and Sawtelle (Santa Monica Boulevard) routes.

Few events affecting San Monica during this period, therefore, could match the significance of the "Great Merger" in 1911. LA-P and several major traction lines were consolidated that year into an enlarged Pacific Electric Railway under the ownership of Southern Pacific. The familiar LA-P green soon gave way to PE red.

Pacific Electric's services encouraged the construction of luxury cottages and single-family homes while facilitating the expansion of tourism. Many arriving passengers reveled in the ambience of the Municipal Pier, completed in 1909, and the adjacent Pleasure Pier, which opened in 1917. Pacific Electric's freight services were also important to both small businesses and heavy industry, which grew dramatically after 1920, when Donald Douglas founded the Douglas Aircraft Company in Santa Monica to produce commercial airplanes. The Long Wharf was eventually dismantled, but Santa Monica's fine buildings in the Spanish colonial revival style, especially the Bay Cities Guaranty Building, an eleven-story "skyscraper" built in 1929, heralded its growing wealth and sophistication.

Changing Times

As residents turned to automobiles and buses during the late 1920s, the glimmer of the Red Cars began to fade. More traffic on the streets led to progressively longer schedules, reducing the convenience of the interurban's services. In 1929, the Pacific Electric abandoned the North Loop, the last of its two streetcar loops, and accelerated its

A large tree encroaches on the Santa Monica Air Line, a corridor being preserved by the county transportation agency. Note the mound covering the tracks at the grade crossing ahead. (Photo by author.)

efforts to replace its Red Cars with motor coaches.

The demand for the railway's services diminished further during the Great Depression, when Santa Monica's most significant contributions to American transportation revolved increasingly around aviation. In 1934, a court ruling supported the expansion of a local airfield and set a precedent for airport development nationwide. Two years later, the Douglas Aircraft Company began producing the workhorse DC-3 airplane at its Santa Monica plant, a milestone in commercial aviation.

Most residents had already made the switch to other forms of transportation when the Pacific Electric abandoned the secondary route from Los Angeles to Santa Monica via Sawtelle and Westgate (Brentwood) in 1940. The remaining rail passenger service down Santa Monica Boulevard to Beverly Hills ended the following year. Although ridership on the Venice Short Line surged

after America's entry into World War II, it dwindled after peace resumed, even though many new homes and apartment towers sprouted near the tracks. The carrier abandoned the Venice route in 1950 and tore down its Ocean Park car barn the following year. Its passenger service dropped to only one train per day, a little-used run operated just to hold the franchise on the Air Line between Los Angeles and Santa Monica.

Upon the 1953 elimination of this franchise run— the last regularly scheduled rail passenger service on the Pacific Electric system—an important chapter in the history of American electric railroading drew to a close. The carrier removed the electric wires on the Air Line route and transformed this route to diesel motive power that same year. A local ordinance required that the Santa Monica Boulevard line to Hollywood remain electrified, but by 1958 this requirement had been lifted.

By the time Southern Pacific formally absorbed Pacific Electric into its system in 1965, the remnants of both the Hollywood Line down Santa Monica Boulevard and the Air Line (by now part of a single route called the West Los Angeles Branch) were only lightly used. Memories of the Red Cars were fading when the Santa Monica Freeway opened the following year, allowing cars and trucks to travel to downtown Los Angeles at unprecedented speed. In 1972, freight service on Santa Monica Boulevard west of Sepulveda Boulevard in West Los Angeles drew to a close, removing what had become a traffic obstacle in the middle of this busy street.

Santa Monica's railroads were not the only historic institutions undergoing profound change. Amid a flurry of development, residents voiced their concerns about the need for more comprehensive historical preservation and more rigorous urban planning strategies, especially after a proposal emerged during the early 1970s to demolish the Santa Monica Pier (formerly the Municipal Pier). Officials responded with a large-scale effort in 1973 that ultimately saved the landmark. The closing of the Douglas Aircraft Company plant the following year spurred further debate about the community's changing character.

In the midst of this debate, few officials voiced concern about the uncertain fate of Santa Monica's oldest— and last—rail line. By the early 1980s, the West Los Angeles Branch had only one regular customer in Santa Monica, a local lumberyard. After the branch saw the passage of its last regular freight train in 1986, however, local residents recognized that a potential transit corridor was about to be lost. In response, a group of volunteers formed the Committee to Preserve the Right-of-Way for the sole purpose of saving the Los Angeles–Santa Monica portion of this route (the former Air Line).

In 1990, the Los Angeles County Transportation Commission, acting on the recommendation of the citizens' committee, acquired the Air Line corridor as far west as 17th Street in Santa Monica. The citizens' committee dubbed the corridor the Exposition Right-of-Way because of its proximity to Exposition Boulevard.

Abandonment's Legacy

As the Exposition Right-of-Way lay dormant, the transportation committee leased some of the right-of-way west of the underpass at Interstate 405 to local businesses. Much of the track east of this bridge was

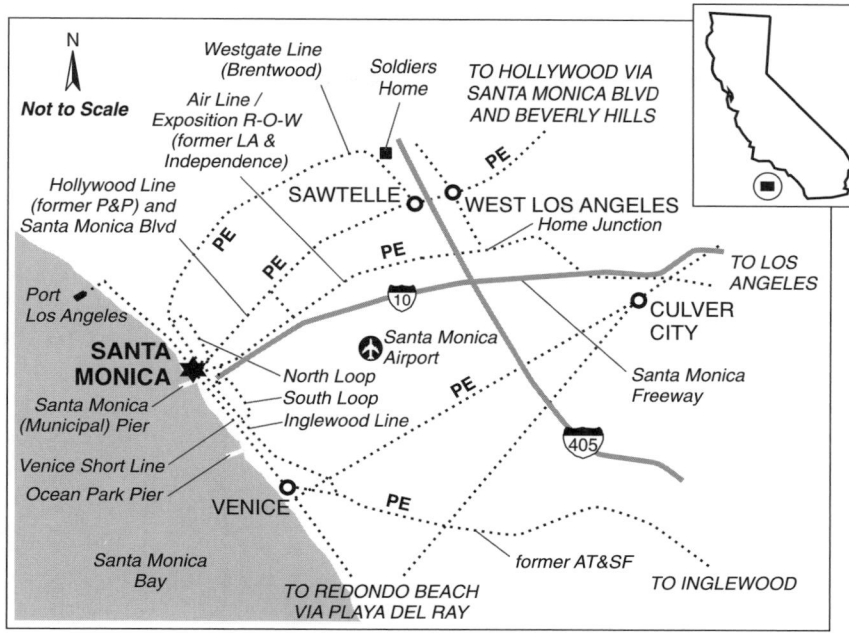

removed, and some businesses erected temporary structures on the corridor with the understanding that these obstructions might eventually have to be removed. Even though the remaining track was inoperable, it kept hopes alive that rail passenger service would eventually resume, possibly linking downtown Santa Monica, Culver City, and central Los Angeles.

The worsening problem of traffic congestion and the Northridge earthquake in 1994, which caused substantial damage in Santa Monica and disrupted freeway travel, galvanized interest in restoring passenger service on this route. Proponents of rail transit recommended that the right-of-way be converted into a light-rail line—an idea greeted with ambivalence by public officials and one that generated outright opposition in the Los Angeles neighborhood of Rancho Park. Moreover, Culver City officials voiced their aesthetic concerns about an aerial railroad line but indicated they would accept a surface-level line only if highway overpasses were built to minimize noise and traffic disruptions.

The Los Angeles County Metropolitan Transportation Authority, which had assumed stewardship of the line from the transportation commission, estimated the cost of building a double-track line for light-rail service to be more than $800 million. In deference to budgetary realities, some rail proponents called for the operation of multiple-unit rail diesel cars over a single-track route without investments in highway/rail grade separation. The transit authority and Santa Monica officials, meanwhile, explored

the potential conversion of the corridor into a busway.

Momentum began to build for passenger rail in 2001, when the transit authority adopted the Exposition Boulevard Light Rail Line as its "preferred alternative." Its plan called for a light-rail line from the Blue Line Metro Station near 7th Street in Los Angeles to Culver City's Robertson Boulevard—a 10-mile corridor that would include a short tunnel near the University of Southern California campus. The agency left open the possibility of eventually extending the light-rail line to downtown Santa Monica—and possibly to the ocean shore—an improvement that would likely require laying track in local streets due to obstructions on the former Air Line near Olympic Boulevard. Still, officials conceded that this was at least a decade away due to funding uncertainties, the project's complexity, and continuing opposition by certain area homeowners.

Epilogue

With nearly 90,000 residents, Santa Monica is today one of the largest communities in the United States that has lost all rail service. Those following former Pacific Electric routes in the area will find that little more than the withering Exposition Right-of-Way and a preserved station on the grounds of the Soldiers Home (in neighboring Los Angeles) survive from the railroad era. Virtually nothing remains of the complex network of lines through Santa

Monica's downtown and the legendary Long Wharf.

As the home to a major convention center and a popular state beach, Santa Monica is firmly established as a major tourist destination. The former streetcar route, Third Street, is today devoid of all vehicular traffic, having become a successful promenade widely known for its nightlife, restaurants, and stores. On Main Street, the California Heritage Museum, housed in a stately nineteenth-century home, tells the story of the community's spirited past through exhibits and displays.

The weed-covered tracks on the Exposition Right-of-Way east of Interstate 405 might seem to be merely a sad reminder of the fate of one of the world's greatest electric railway systems, but this preserved corridor still arouses hopes in many that rail passenger service might some day resume, even after a hiatus of more than fifty years.

For Further Study

SUGGESTED READINGS:

Basten, Fred E. *Santa Monica Bay: The First 100 Years.* Los Angeles: Douglas-West Publishers, 1974, 1–192.

Swett, Ira L. *Lines of Pacific Electric: Western District: Interurbans Special* 16. Glendale, Calif.: Interurbans Publications, 1968, 43–71.

Swett, Ira. L., and William A. Myers. *Trolleys to the Surf: Interurbans Special* 63. Glendale, Calif.: Interurbans Publications, 1976, 9–140.

OTHER PRINCIPAL REFERENCES:

Crump, Spencer. *Ride the Big Red Cars: How Trolleys Helped Build Southern California.* Los Angeles: Crest Publications, 1962, 43–44.

Electric Railway Historical Association of Southern California. "A Guide to the Electric Traction Heritage of the Los Angeles Region." http://www.erha.org (accessed 26 July 2003).

Hilton, George W., and John F. Due. *The Electric Interurban Railways in America.* Stanford: Stanford University Press, 1964, 412.

SAUSALITO, CALIFORNIA (7,330)

Historic operator: Northwestern Pacific Railroad
Last route abandoned: 1971
Notable reuses of right-of-way: Mill Valley–Sausalito Path; municipal parking facility

  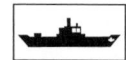  

Hundreds of thousands of passengers once rode ferries each year to Sausalito, the southern terminus of the Northwestern Pacific Railroad. Some transferred to electric trains operating to points throughout the Marin Peninsula; others boarded steam-powered trains for the far reaches of northern California. With the opening of the Golden Gate Bridge, however, travel patterns in the region changed dramatically, hastening the demise of this once vibrant multimodal transportation system.

Historical Perspective

During the early nineteenth century, the rolling hills north of California's Golden Gate were under the stewardship of Misión San Francisco de Asis, a Spanish-Mexican outpost with a large livestock operation. Most of the shoreline was still uninhabited in 1838 when William Richardson obtained a sizable parcel of this land as part of a Mexican land grant. The enterprising Englishman, who had strong loyalties to Mexico, used this land to supply fresh water to whaling vessels entering San Francisco Bay.

Richardson was not content with the earnings he derived from this modest business as well as his cattle operation on El Rancho del Sausalito (the Ranch of the Little Willow Grove). Believing that this property had vast potential, Richardson developed an ambitious plan to create a commercial port that would allow him, in effect, to control access to the bay.

The enterprising businessman had little hope of implementing this plan under the turbulent conditions that existed following the discovery of gold in the Sierra Nevada in 1848. His dream of finding great fortune faded during the California gold rush as newcomers poured into the region and other businessmen opened new wharves on the bay. Richardson felt a great sense of injustice as newcomers squatted on his land and rustled his cattle, and reluctantly abandoned his far-flung scheme. The unlucky Richardson became disillusioned and sold his land to Charles Botts, another businessman with visions of grandeur. Botts attempted to establish a great city and naval shipyard on the property, but ultimately fared no better than Richardson. This entrepreneur, in turn, sold his land to the newly formed Sausalito Land & Ferry Company in 1868.

The new owner of the waterfront property harnessed the commercial skills of noted San Francisco businessmen to promote development. Nevertheless, Sausalito remained a sleepy hamlet with only a few modest dwellings as late as 1870. Around this time, it became an accepted practice to spell the name of the community "Saucelito," despite the inconsistency of this

The stub-end terminal along Sausalito's waterfront bustles with activity in October 1914. The special trains on the right of this photograph will travel to Cain Rock, California, where the Northwestern Pacific will drive the golden spike to complete its route to Eureka. (Collection of Fred Codoni.)

practice with the Spanish language.

The tide began to turn in favor of Sausalito when the Land & Ferry Company negotiated with the North Pacific Coast Railroad (NPC) to build a line from the community north to San Rafael, the seat of Marin County. This railroad then set out to establish a route across difficult terrain, build a lengthy trestle near the west shore of Richardson's Bay, and open a 1,250-foot tunnel through White's Hill. When the NPC completed these projects in 1874, Sausalito emerged as a busy freight and passenger gateway to the peninsula. Many wealthy San Franciscans built homes in town and throughout the surrounding hills while relying on ferries to reach their jobs.

The railroad crossed another milestone in 1877 when the NPC extended its tracks through the vast redwood forests of northern California and crossed the Russian River. Although this extension generated significant lumber revenues, the carrier faced vigorous competition from the San Francisco & North Pacific Railroad, which opened a line to neighboring Tiburon in 1884. To meet the challenges posed by this rival, the NPC opened a faster and more westerly route between Corte Madera (a community several miles south of San Rafael) and Sausalito that same year. Approaching Sausalito on the western shore of Richardson's Bay, this corridor allowed the railroad to retire its trestle across the bay.

Sausalito was now poised to become a transportation center of considerable importance. Within a few years, the NPC had discontinued its marine operations at San Quentin, consolidated its operations into Sausalito, and built a branch to Mill Valley (Eastland). By the time Sausalito received its incorporation in 1893, thousands of passengers regularly made connections between trains and ferries at its wharf.

More good fortune arrived when the railroad put a massive double-ended ferry named *Sausalito* (the second ferry of this name) into service in 1894 and opened a new office building and terminal on the community's wharf. The railroad expanded its services to handle the growing number of passengers, including leisure travelers arriving by boat on their way to the Mill Valley & Mt. Tamalpais Scenic Railway. Opening in 1896, this scenic line, affectionately called "the crookedest railroad in the world," took passengers from Mill Valley to the resort area around Tamalpais Tavern at an elevation of 2,400 feet.

The dramatic rise in freight and passenger traffic was not without its problems. At the turn of the century, Sausalito struggled to shed its image of being a gritty railroad town, a place notorious for its noxious odors, noise, and filthy streets. Relief from these problems, however, was only a few years away. After the North Shore Railroad purchased the NPC in 1902, this operator redesigned the wharf area, tore down its aging train shed, and built an attractive two-story terminal adjacent to a plaza known as Depot Park. As the North Shore made improvements to Sausalito's waterfront, this area—once a municipal embarassment—evolved into the object of civic pride.

The North Shore also laid a third rail to allow for dual standard-gauge/narrow-gauge operation on much of the southern part of its system. In 1903, it installed an elevated fourth rail on the lines from Sausalito to Mill Valley, San Anselmo, and San Rafael to allow for electric operations, thus helping trains accelerate quickly and overcome severe grades. These improvements, as well as the addition of a second track to several segments and the eventual electrification of the route from San Anselmo to Manor, transformed the carrier into a veritable showpiece of modern engineering.

The railroad era in Sausalito rose to its pinnacle after the unification of the North Shore, the San Francisco & North Pacific, and several other railroads serving the region into the Northwestern Pacific Railroad in 1907. This carrier established Sausalito as its primary transfer point for passengers and designated Tiburon as its principal transfer point for the peninsula's freight. By 1910, Sausalito had grown to support a population of more than 2,300 and seemed poised to occupy a position of lasting transportation importance. According to company timetables, travelers in 1914 could depart on any of eighty multiunit electric trains and eleven steam trains (which operated to points as far north as Eureka) from Sausalito daily, with additional Sunday service to some communities. Electric trains, departing at regular intervals over four routes, operated to Mill Valley, Manor (near Fairfax), and San Rafael, which trains reached via both Detour and San Anselmo.

The installation of an Italianate fountain and two flagpoles mounted on elephant statues in Depot Park amplified Sausalito's image as a successful and progressive community. These works of art, notable for having been created for San Francisco's Panama Pacific Exposition, seemed to portend a prosperous future.

Changing Times

Although Sausalito derived great benefit from Northwestern Pacific, the city had an unhealthy reliance on the carrier for jobs, revenue, and municipal leadership. By the late 1910s, rail travel between inland points was falling at an alarming rate. In 1920, the carrier ended narrow-gauge service from Sausalito to Point Reyes (part of the old route to the Russian River). Standard gauge service to both communities continued, but travelers needed only to observe the growing motor-vehicle congestion on local streets to understand the enormity of the changes under way. When a rival ferry company specializing in carrying automobiles across the bay began service from the wharf in 1922, Northwestern Pacific responded by placing into service three massive new ferries designed to carry automobiles. The railroad company's parent, Southern Pacific (which became its sole owner in 1929) eventually bought the rival auto-ferry company in an effort to protect its share of the market.

By 1930, the outlook for Sausalito's railroad operations had taken an abrupt turn for the worse. That year, Mill Valley's "crooked" railway ceased operating and Northwestern Pacific instituted significant cutbacks in service. Even as the Great Depression crisis deepened, local residents were sharply divided on issues related to the impending construction of the Golden Gate Bridge, a highway bridge slated to link San Francisco to the peninsula. Some citizens hoped that the superhighway leading

With nothing left of the Northwestern Pacific wharf and terminal complex, Sausalito's waterfront is now uncluttered, giving the onlooker a panoramic view of the San Francisco skyline. (Photo by author.)

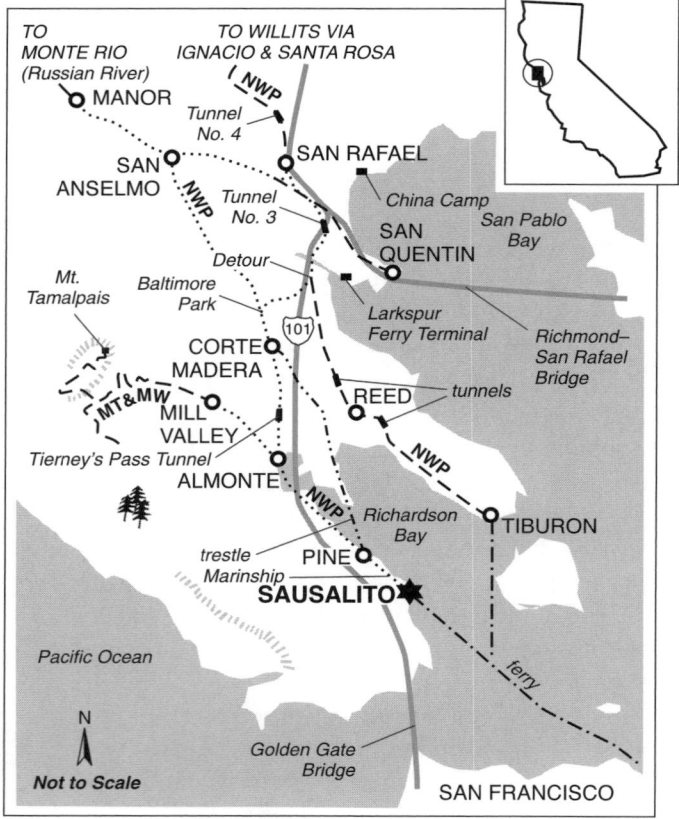

great railroad terminal to a community bereft of rail passenger service. Its transportation capacity diminished further when Northwestern Pacific dismantled its electrified third rails in 1941. Concern that the economy would never recover, however, proved overly pessimistic. As the country retooled to fight a global war, the federal government identified property north of Sausalito's downtown for a massive shipyard. Within months, the government commissioned W. A. Bechtel Company to raze neighborhoods, fill in portions of the bay, and build the sprawling Marinship complex. The project necessitated relocating several miles of Northwestern Pacific's main line and building new railroad spurs as well as a new ferry slip.

The Marinship complex brought a level of vitality to Sausalito reminiscent of a quarter century before. The complex grew to employ more than 70,000 workers and relied extensively on Northwestern Pacific for shipments of coal, wood, steel, bronze propellers, and other materials. Officials pleaded with Northwestern Pacific to provide passenger service but were refused due to a severe shortage of locomotives and rolling stock.

Marinship remained a busy place for the duration of World War II, but the Allied victory rendered the entire facility surplus. It was conveyed to the U.S. Army Corps of Engineers in 1946 and summarily dismantled. The old ferry slips deteriorated, the former depot site became overgrown with weeds, and Sausalito once again faced hard economic times.

The community's once superbly maintained route gradually devolved into a lightly used set of freight-only tracks called the Sausalito Branch. The railroad abandoned service to the local pier as well as its line to Mill Valley in 1955 and handled most of its subsequent business from the wharf in Tiburon. Much as the gold rush had bypassed Sausalito a century before, the real estate boom that transformed other older communities on the peninsula into thriving suburbs largely eluded the town.

Hope for the community was gradually restored during the late 1960s, when ferryboats once again brought travelers attracted to its downtown shopping district and panoramic views of the bay. A portion of the former shipyard took the unlikely turn of becoming an enclave for artists. With little industry remaining, the Sausalito Branch became expendable. Few expressed concern when the railroad abandoned the deteriorating portion between Sausalito and Detour (near Corte Madera) in 1971, ending the last of the community's rail service. The carrier sold some of the land to a local developer, who brought several boxcars to town prior to the removal of the tracks.

up to the bridge would be built through the center of town. Others pushed for a bridge and highway alignment farther west, thus averting the demolition of many homes and businesses. Southern Pacific, understandably, opposed the entire bridge project.

Supporters of building the bridge had the upper hand when the municipal government renamed Water Street (one of its principal thoroughfares) Bridgeway Boulevard. The Northwestern Pacific freight station was moved in 1933 to facilitate construction. In the end, planners chose an alignment for the Golden Gate Bridge and U.S. Route 101 over an aligment bypassing Sausalito.

After the bridge and highway opened in 1937, local officials expected ferry and rail passenger services to continue indefinitely, albeit on a smaller scale, despite credible claims by Northwestern Pacific that these services had long been unprofitable. The grim reality could no longer be denied, however, when Northwestern Pacific eliminated all of its remaining commuter service and discontinued long-distance passenger service south of San Rafael in 1941. Its last ferry to Sausalito, the *Eureka*, sailed from the wharf for a final time that same year.

In just a few years, Sausalito had gone from being a

Abandonment's Legacy

Rumors of a railroad rebirth circulated in 1974 when the city approved a proposal for a steam-powered recreational railroad operating over rebuilt narrow-gauge track between downtown Sausalito and the northern city limits. Although this proposal did not advance beyond the planning stage, the railroad's withdrawal came at an opportune time: it freed up land along the waterfront that aided efforts to promote tourism and historical preservation.

The city dedicated Marinship Park on a portion of the old shipbuilding area during America's bicentennial year and bestowed monument status on the freight depot in 1978. Near the wharf, improvements to a parking lot on former railroad land enhanced the downtown's appeal to out-of-town guests. By the time officials certified the Sausalito Historic District in 1980, a municipal renaissance was under way. Once again, affluent residents made Sausalito their home and commuted to San Francisco by ferry. In 1981, officials opened the first portions of the Mill Valley–Sausalito Path on the abandoned right-of-way, one of the first rail-trail conversions in the West.

The community that had suffered so greatly from the demise of passenger trains forty years before now had little interest in any form of rail transportation—a fact evident to the planners in the early 1980s who explored alternatives to relieve congestion on the Golden Gate Bridge and Highway 101. Public officials rejected the idea of rebuilding the local railroad due to probable conflicts with an expanding residential population and the advantages of establishing a terminal farther north on the peninsula.

Whispers of the railroad era could be heard again in 1996 when a local construction company acquired the former freight depot and restored it with assistance from the California State Railroad Museum. Local historical officials also sought to preserve the wooden pilings from the former rail-ferry terminal. These remnants, however, were removed that same year to allow for the expansion of the modern ferry terminal nearby.

Epilogue

Sausalito is today widely recognized as one of California's most attractive communities—an unlikely ending to its thunderous industrial saga. Many visitors amble along its waterfront and narrow streets totally unaware of the electric and steam railroad systems that once were so dominant in community life.

At a downtown museum operated by the Sausalito Historica Society, patrons are told of the many different phases of the community's past. Travelers with an interest in railroad history will find that few remnants of its once-sprawling railroad facilities near the old ferry terminal survive except for the figurines and fountain in Depot Park. Those venturing farther north, however, are rewarded with views of many buildings once part of the Marinship complex, a beautifully restored station in Mill Valley, and old station platforms and a well-preserved electrical substation in a peaceful Baltimore Park neighborhood. A short strip of track has held out against the forces of modernization along Bridgeway Boulevard near the historic shipyard site.

It seems fitting that many commuters use the recreational trail to reach the Sausalito wharf, following the same path used by generations of railroad passengers. The contemporary vessels taking them across the bay, though, are modest compared to the venerable *Eureka*, which is permanently moored at the National Maritime Museum in San Francisco.

For Further Study

SUGGESTED READINGS:

Stindt, Fred A. *The Northwestern Pacific Railroad.* Redwood City, Calif.: Fred A. Stindt, 1964, 30–35, 52–58.

Tracy, Jack. *Sausalito: Moments in Time.* Sausalito, Calif.: Wingate Press, 1983, 2–50.

OTHER PRINCIPAL REFERENCES:

Codoni, Fred. "The NWP Goes to War." *The Northwesterner: Quarterly Publication of the Northwestern Pacific Historical Society* 15, no. 2 (Fall-Winter 2001): 7–15.

Demoro, Harre W., and Vernon J. Sappers. *Rails to San Francisco Bay.* New York: Quadrant Press, 1992, 80–85.

Sievers, Walt. "Electric Interurban Service of Marin County." *Western Railroader* 17, no. 10 (Aug. 1954): 3–12.

Wurm, Ted, and Al Graves. *California's Mt. Tamalpais & Muir Woods Railroad: The Crookedest Railroad in the World.* Glendale, Calif.: Interurban Press, 1983, 10–16.

VACAVILLE, CALIFORNIA (88,625)

Historic operators: Sacramento Northern Railway; Southern Pacific
Last route abandoned: 1985
Notable reuses of right-of-way: Municipal recreational trail; Intermodal Transportation Center

he harvest season once saw more than 3,000 freight cars laden with apricots, grapes, plums, and other fresh fruit departing from Vacaville on Southern Pacific trains. Such massive shipments established the Vaca Valley as one of the country's leading suppliers of produce. By the time the Northern Electric Railway answered the community's appeals for the services of a second railroad, however, fruit production in this part of California had already begun its sharp decline.

Historical Perspective

During the eighteenth century, the valley surrounding Ulatis Creek in the Spanish province of Alta California was inhabited mainly by the Patwin Indians. The presence of these indigenous people had greatly diminished by the early 1840s, when Juan Manuel Vaca acquired this grassy plain from the Mexican government for the creation of the Rancho de los Putos. When Vaca sold his cattle ranch to William McDaniel in 1850, he stipulated that McDaniel plat a town bearing the Vaca name. The developer faithfully adhered to the deal and created a plat for Vacaville—a town within view of a beautiful mountain range also named after the pioneering Mexican rancher.

The expansion of wheat and livestock production brought considerable prosperity to the community during the early 1850s, as did the earnings from services provided to travelers on their way to the gold-mining areas of the Sierra Nevada. The town's hotels and stores bustled with activity as travelers made rest stops in Vacaville on trips between Benicia and Sacramento. Nevertheless, Vacaville's importance in overland transportation did little to dampen its leaders' enthusiasm for rail service after the Civil War. In 1869, the townspeople were elated when the Vaca Valley Railroad completed a line to the community from Elmira, a junction on the Central Pacific Railroad.

Less than two weeks after the line's opening, the Central Pacific met the Union Pacific at Promontory, Utah, thus completing the nation's first transcontinental railroad. This historic occasion marked the beginning of a promising new era in freight and passenger travel between California and the rest of the country. Although fresh fruit and other perishables could now be shipped efficiently to large cities in the East, neither the Vacaville area nor other agricultural areas would achieve their potential for many years. Consequently, the 4-mile Vaca Valley Railroad struggled before reorganizing under new ownership in 1870.

When the railroad's financial performance improved, it was due in no small part to the commercial acumen of Leonard W. Buck, who arrived in Vacaville in 1871. This astute businessman, together with his oldest son, Frank, and their associates, invested in a vast system of orchards that proved enormously productive. The rail carrier expanded its fruit-hauling potential by extending its route 13 miles to Winters (a small town near Esparto) in 1875. It was turned over to the newly created Vaca Valley & Clear Lake Railroad in 1877, extended another 24 miles from Madison to Rumsey in 1888, and consolidated into the Southern Pacific-controlled Northern Railway that same year.

Vacaville gradually earned its reputation as a major component of California's "fruit belt" while contending with significant economic and social problems. The nature of the fruit business exposed it to an up-and-down annual business cycle, and a fire raged through town in 1888, destroying dozens of businesses in its path. There was inadequate housing and sanitation for Chinese laborers who worked in the orchards and lived in overcrowded and poorly planned neighborhoods. Nevertheless, the community's influential business leaders remained optimistic about the town's future. Frank Buck, for example, built a large home near the center of town in 1890. Although an earthquake in 1892 damaged much of Vacaville, it also provided the impetus for its incorporation as a city.

Leonard Buck emerged as a dominant figure in the state's fresh-fruit industry and joined other prominent growers in 1894 to form the California Fruit Union, an organization that pushed hard to improve transportation and to negotiate favorable rates for its members. By the mid-1890s, the valley was supplying nearly one-fourth of the fruit marketed within California. The valley's fruit growers depended heavily on the Northern Railway, which hauled more than a thousand carloads of apricots, grapes, and other fresh fruit to eastern markets from Vacaville each harvest season.

Many businessmen of this era were frequent visitors to the community's wooden depot, where trains departed for Elmira, allowing them to transfer to Southern Pacific's (former Central Pacific) main line between Oakland and Sacramento. Those arriving from out of town often stayed at the Hotel Raleigh, a prominent local guesthouse within walking distance of the depot.

On October 10, 1965, excursion-goers of the Bay Area Electric Railroad Association, having reached the end of the line at Vacaville, walk along the Sacramento Northern tracks. A diesel locomotive, GE 70-tonner No. 202, is at the head of this special train. Several of the cars, built for the Bay Area's Key System (note the pantographs), today belong to the Western Railway Museum. The impressive Vacaville Town Hall can be seen in the background. (Photo by Addison Laflin, Bay Area Electric Railroad Association Archives.)

Despite another ruinous downtown fire in 1895, the local economy prospered as growing numbers of Japanese immigrants arrived to work in the Buck Company's orchards and warehouses. In the late 1890s, the California Fruit Union's shipments rose to their peak, with an estimated 3,000 carloads of produce from the community annually—much of it originating from warehouses along the south bank of the creek.

After the Northern Railway was consolidated into the Southern Pacific Company in 1898, city leaders and the Fruit Union became increasingly vocal in their complaints about the carrier's rates and service. Vacaville grew to more than 1,200 residents by the turn of the century, making the effort to attract a second railroad an almost overriding local priority. The municipal government made the best of the less-than-superb rail connections while conducting its business from a splendid 1907 Town Hall known for its distinctive masonry tower.

A grassy berm along Elmira Road bears testimony to the fate of Vacaville's oldest railroad. The sign in the distance, next to the I-80 underpass, points the way, ironically, to Depot Street. (Photo by author.)

Changing Times

The outlook for Vacaville took a turn for the worse as natural disasters and increased competition from other fruit-growing areas weakened its economy. Another major fire swept through Vacaville's downtown in 1909, destroying the Hotel Raleigh and leaving the community without any public accommodations. Four years later, still another blaze reduced a portion of the Japanese district to ruin. Although many hoped that the newly incorporated Vallejo & Northern would break Southern Pacific's monopoly, the railroad experienced delays as it attempted to build north from Woodland in 1911.

The parent company of the Vallejo & Northern, the Northern Electric Railway, finally completed Vacaville's long-desired second rail line the following year. This 11-mile route from Suisun, while equipped with a powered third rail, was isolated from the rest of its system and opened at a time when truck transport had already begun to diminish the demand for local rail service. In 1915, the state completed a highway from Sacramento to San Francisco through the valley.

The freight business declined further as fruit production shifted to the San Joaquin Valley and other more southerly locales. This problem had grown appreciably by the time Northern Electric was renamed the Sacramento Northern Railroad in 1918. Three years later, ownership of the latter railroad passed to the newly incorporated Sacramento Northern Railway, which terminated passenger service to Vacaville in 1926. By the time Sacramento Northern completed a connecting route from Vacaville Junction to Creed (thus linking the branch to its main line) in 1930, it was evident that the railroad industry's best years in the community had passed.

Southern Pacific's route to Vacaville fared little better during the Great Depression. Ridership on the carrier's daily train between Elmira and Winters as well as its daily run between Elmira and Rumsey fell to such an extent that the carrier discontinued both runs in 1934, thus ending all passenger service to Vacaville. That same year, the carrier abandoned the northern end of the route (or eastern end, in railroad terms) beyond Capay, a small town near Esparto.

Fresh-fruit production, meanwhile, continued to fall. By 1940, this industry generated fewer than 250 railroad carloads of fruit annually—less than 10 percent of the shipment fifty years before. Freight traffic recovered during World War II, largely due to expanded output at the Basic Vegetable Products Company, one of the nation's leading producers of dehydrated onions—a product used to feed tens of thousands of Allied troops, but the postwar years were far less favorable to the valley's railroads. Sacramento Northern gradually scaled back freight service and ended electric operations on its branch to Vacaville in 1947. Vacaville shipped its last railcar of fruit in 1956.

As Vacaville's passenger train era slipped from modern recollection, railroad enthusiasts gathered on several occasions for excursions commemorating the past. The Railway & Locomotive Historical Society operated an excursion train over the Southern Pacific branch in 1950. In 1952, the Bay Area Electric Railroad Association operated a three-car electric train over the Sacramento Northern to Vacaville Junction while having a diesel pull the cars the rest of the way to town. Members of this group returned thirteen years later to ride a diesel train over these same rails.

Travelers returning to Vacaville after the construction of Interstate 80 during the 1960s (which required the removal of some of Sacramento Northern's track) found the historic fruit-shipping center undergoing a metamorphasis. Commuters were arriving in droves to take advantage of the community's close proximity to Sacramento. Many of these newcomers built homes in newly platted subdivisions outside of town, giving Vacaville an increasingly residential orientation. Vacaville's centralized location and abundant transportation links also attracted new businesses, including American Home Products, which established a local storage-in-transit warehouse along the Southern Pacific route.

Recognizing that the old fruit-growing town was acquiring a more suburban orientation, citizens formed the Vacaville Heritage Council in 1969. This organization took steps to encourage the preservation of the community's historic structures and landmarks, such as the Old Town Hall, which earned distinction in 1978 as Vacaville's first property listed on the National Register of Historic Places. Another growth spurt pushed Vacaville's population from less than 22,000 in 1980 to more than 43,000 a decade later. In 1984, as the real estate boom gathered momentum, the Buck family donated land and money for the creation of the Vacaville Museum to assure that the past would not be forgotten.

The end of rail service, meanwhile, attracted little attention. By 1984, Sacramento Northern had removed

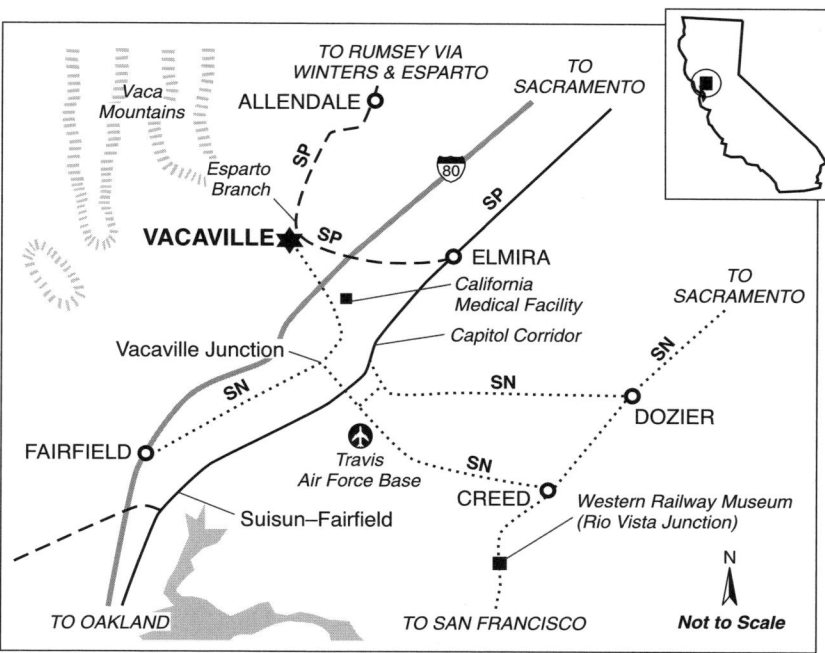

a portion of its local branch from service and surrendered most of its identity as a separate company, having been largely absorbed into its parent, the Western Pacific Railroad. Western Pacific, in turn, had been assimilated into the still-larger Union Pacific, which abandoned its 4-mile segment from Vacaville to Vacaville Junction early in 1985.

The Southern Pacific line, now commonly called the Esparto Branch, also was nearing the end of its useful life. The transit-in-storage warehouse had ceased shipping by rail, and the carrier's remaining local traffic had dwindled to little more than sporadic freight shipments for the Basic Vegetable Products Company. Southern Pacific abandoned the line during the summer of 1985, ending more than a century of local railroading.

Abandonment's Legacy

In only months, Vacaville had gone from having a pair of railroads to having none. The Basic Vegetable Products Company soon exited the scene as well, suspending operations at its onion-dehydration plant. The plant's demise eliminated yet another reminder of the community's agriculturally oriented past.

The Sacramento Northern left a deep imprint on Vacaville and other communities it served. Its successor, Union Pacific, sold the right-of-way in Vacaville to the municipal government and 21 miles of its former main line through Rio Vista Junction (near Fairfield) to the Bay Area Electric Railroad Association. At the former junction—the home of the association's Western Electric Railroad Museum—work commenced in 1996 on an interurban railway display and large visitors' center devoted to the Sacramento Northern's heritage.

The city of Vacaville converted the former Sacramento Northern right-of-way into a recreational trail and drafted plans to extend the trail over rural portions of the abandoned route to another trail in Fairfield. Next to the abandoned right-of-way, the Regional Transportation Center opened in 1997 to serve commuters traveling by bus.

Much of the former Southern Pacific route was altered beyond recognition. The municipality used a portion of the right-of-way, including its underpass beneath Interstate 80, for additional traffic lanes on Elmira Road, one of the community's busiest streets. Southern Pacific offered to sell other portions of its right-of-way through northern Vacaville to the local government in 1996. Although the city had an interest in this property for further recreational trail development, the carrier's asking price was reportedly too high. Southern Pacific consequently sold the property in piecemeal fashion to various private parties.

Epilogue

The absence of rail service may have prevented Vacaville from vying for certain forms of heavy industry, but it did not prevent the town from gradually expanding its tax base. Today the municipality supports a population of more than 100,000 and prospers from its role as a bedroom community for those working in Sacramento and San Francisco, and at Travis Air Force Base in Fairfield. Like many communities once oriented toward railroads, much of Vacaville's commercial activity has today shifted to the vicinity of its expressway interchanges.

Visual reminders of Vacaville's railroads are becoming harder to find each year. Diesel trucks now roll through both of the local Interstate 80 underpasses that once saw diesel locomotives. Only a few parcels of land formerly occupied by fresh-fruit warehouses today lie vacant. The former station site along Depot Street is poised for redevelopment, and there are little more than crumbling remnants of the old Southern Pacific bridge over Ulatis Creek. Even so, travelers will find that the older parts of Vacaville, including the Buck Mansion, continue to embody elements of its proud agricultural past. A few miles away, the town of Elmira retains some of the small-town qualities that its prosperous neighbor has lost.

Vacaville is one of several communities in the West that have restored their connections to the national rail system; in its case, however, this is only because the municipal government has annexed a thin sliver of rural land that reaches but does not cross the Union Pacific (former Southern Pacific) main line through Elmira. Although this land is not suitable for development, it does put Vacaville nominally along the Capitol Corridor—a busy passenger route with more than ten Amtrak trains operating in each direction between Sacramento and San Jose. The state's transportation provider, Caltrans, has considered building a station farther east along this route to jointly serve Fairfield and Vacaville.

For Further Study

SUGGESTED READINGS:
Limbaugh, Ronald H., and Walter A. Paine. *Vacaville: The Heritage of a California City.* Vacaville, Calif.: Vacaville City Council, 1978, 142–51.
Limbaugh, Ronald H. "Vacaville's Railroad Era: 1870–1930." *National Railway Historical Society Bulletin* 43, no. 5 (1978): 4–47.
Swett, Ira L. *Sacramento Northern.* Glendale, Calif., Interurban Press, 1981, 199, 206.

OTHER PRINCIPAL REFERENCES:
Hilton, George W., and John F. Due. *The Electric Interurban Railways in America.* Stanford: Stanford University Press, 1964, 400.
Stephens, Meredith. "The Vaca Valley and Clear Lake Railroad." Photocopy, unpublished manuscript, University of California at Davis, 1971, 1–15.

ASPEN, COLORADO (5,914)

Historic operators: Aspen City Railway; Colorado Midland Railway; Denver & Rio Grande Western Railroad
Last route abandoned: 1969
Notable reuses of right-of-way: Rio Grande Trail; State Route 82 (Maroon Creek Bridge); proposed transit route

 spen's experiences illustrate the difficulties of transportation planning where challenging terrain limits the possibilities for cost-effective highway expansion. Officials have envisioned using rail-passenger service to make this community a pioneer in modern "resort-rail development," a phenomenon pervasive in contemporary Europe but long ago abandoned in the United States. None of the ambitious efforts to rebuild a railroad through the Roaring Fork Valley, however, has advanced beyond the planning stage.

Historical Perspective

Few people considered the valley of the Roaring Fork River amenable to settlement through the end of the Civil War. Bounded by the Elk Mountains on the south and west and the Wasatch Mountains on the east, this remote area near the center of Colorado Territory was difficult to reach and its weather tended to be severe. Inhospitable Ute Indian hunting parties further discouraged migration to the region.

By the late 1870s, however, a silver boom was under way in Leadville and the valley seemed so promising that its problems were ignored. Eager to make the next big strike, prospectors intensified their search in the vicinity of the Roaring Fork River. After four prospectors from Leadville struck gold during the summer of 1879, entrepreneurs, miners, and merchants poured into this remote area. The enterprising Henry B.

Gillespie arrived early the following year and immediately recognized the valley's enormous potential. Gillespie purchased several properties suitable for mining and enough land for the creation of a community. He christened the settlement Ute City and arranged for the establishment of a post office.

Before the snow had melted, Clark Wheeler, another pioneering figure, arrived and announced plans for establishing an even larger city than the one envisioned by Gillespie. Wheeler, backed by out-of-town investors, began by having the town surveyed and renamed Aspen. Through his leadership, Aspen soon evolved into a well-planned gold- and silver-mining center boasting a hotel, sawmill, and numerous small businesses.

In 1881, the community became the temporary seat of newly created Pitkin County. Surrounded by vast deposits of gold and silver, Aspen now appeared to be on the verge of commercial greatness. It became home to a smelter (a

91

A three-car Colorado Midland train, probably destined for the carrier's main line, negotiates the magnificent Maroon Creek bridge near Aspen, circa 1900. The bridge, a historic landmark, has has been retrofitted to accommodate motor vehicles traveling down State Route 82. (Photo by Frank Buckwalter, courtesy of Colorado Historical Society.)

mill used to process silver ore) in 1884 and the country's first privately operated hydroelectric plant the following year. As mining companies dug deep into the mountainsides, tapping rich veins of silver ore, Aspen's population grew to 3,500.

The reality of inadequate transportation tempered the spreading optimism of this era. Without rail transportation, businesses and citizens had no choice but to rely on more costly and time consuming forms of transportation. Relief appeared in the form of the Denver & Rio Grande (Rio Grande) and the Colorado Midland railways, which vied to operate the first trains to the booming mining camp. This saga, deeply etched in western railroad history, rose to its climax as these bitter competitors worked furiously to lay track along the Roaring Fork.

Colorado Midland had invested an enormous sum in building a main line from Colorado Springs west of Leadville across Hagerman Pass and seemed destined to prevail over its larger rival. Construction delays and the need to build the Maroon Creek viaduct, an enormous iron trestle near the edge of Aspen that stretched 650

feet, prevented this, and the narrow-gauge Rio Grande caught up and eventually arrived in Aspen first. The townspeople celebrated the arrival of the first Rio Grande train from Glenwood Springs in 1887 and the first Colorado Midland train from Basalt (a junction on its main line) several weeks later.

Many fine Victorian buildings showcased the wealth created by Aspen's flourishing industrial sector. In 1889, the community celebrated the openings of the Wheeler Opera House, one of the finest theaters in the state, and the Hotel Jerome, an attractive three-story institution. These edifices, while magnificent for their time, were soon dwarfed by the towering Pitkin County Court House, completed two years later.

The Rio Grande widened its Aspen Branch to standard gauge in 1890 and offered passengers sleeping-car service to Denver by way of the Tennessee Pass and Pueblo. Its vigorous competition with the Colorado Midland contributed to a surge in development that pushed the community's population to more than 12,000 in 1892, making Aspen the third largest city in Colorado and one of the most famous mining centers in the West. In the midst of the continuing boom, silver-mining companies built large networks of industrial railways through cavernous underground passages. Above ground, the Aspen City Railway, a mule-powered streetcar operator, inaugurated service over a route linking Aspen's railroad depots. Newly built tramways scaled the rugged slopes of the Elk Range, hauling silver ore excavated from the mines to Aspen's southern periphery.

Rail service in central Colorado crossed yet another milestone in 1893 with the opening of the Busk-Ivanhoe Tunnel, a 7-mile passage through the Continental Divide. Built at a staggering cost, this tunnel allowed Colorado Midland to greatly improve the quality of its services to Aspen and other cities on the western end of its system.

Changing Times

Typical of mining boomtowns of this era, Aspen's fortunes would soon take an abrupt turn for the worse. The panic of 1893 depressed silver prices, forced mines to close, and left thousands in the community unemployed. Aspen's economy deteriorated to such an extent that the Opera House suspended performances, dozens of businesses closed, and thousands of miners relocated to Cripple Creek, where a gold-mining boom was under way. In 1899, the city authorized the removal of the streetcar railway's sporadically used tracks.

By the end of the nineteenth century, Aspen's population had dropped by two-thirds to little more than 3,300 people. The new century initially brought little hope that Aspen's economy would soon markedly improve. The Opera House closed after a devastating fire in 1912, and by 1920 Aspen was reduced to a mere 700 residents.

The region's transportation practices also changed with the times. The financially troubled Colorado Midland ended service in 1919 and then abandoned its route in 1920, leaving Aspen with only one railroad. Workers retrofitted the massive Maroon Creek Bridge to accommodate cars and trucks. More favorable to railroad passengers, the Rio Grande (which changed its name to the Denver & Rio Grande Western Railroad) opened the Dotsero Cutoff in 1921—a route that included the 6-mile Moffatt Tunnel and shaved 175 miles off the trip to Denver. Trains using the carrier's main line through Glenwood Springs could now reach Colorado's largest city with unprecedented speed.

These investments, unfortunately, did little to stimulate the economy of the Roaring Fork Valley. By the late 1920s, the Rio Grande branch through the valley was only lightly used and supported heavily by revenues derived from serving local sheep and cattle ranchers. Even before the Great Depression, Aspen was languishing.

The outlook for the community did not significantly improve until after a small skiing area known as Roch Run opened on Aspen Mountain in 1936. Five years later, Aspen hosted the U.S. World Alpine Championships, an event attracting the attention of Walter Paepcke, a visionary Chicago investor.

Paepcke soon developed an ambitious plan to establish Aspen as a major cultural and winter sports center. In 1946, his company installed a single-chair ski lift—the longest of its kind in the world—and purchased a block of downtown property from the Rio Grande and the Hotel Jerome. To the townspeople's delight, Paepcke also rehabilitated the Opera House and founded the Aspen Institute and the Aspen Music Festival, which opened the community's Goethe Bicentennial celebration in 1947.

While the Rio Grande operated occasional ski trains to town and continued to regularly operate a mixed train on its branch, its trains on the main line would prove to be far more important to this phase of Aspen's development. Beginning in 1949, the Rio Grande brought travelers to nearby Glenwood Springs (41 miles from Aspen) in the comfort and elegance of

Although much of the former Denver & Rio Grande's Roaring Fork Branch (shown here near Woody Creek, circa 1998) is enshrouded in vegetation, it is nonetheless preserved for possible transit service. (Photo by author.)

the California Zephyr. Operating daily between Chicago and Oakland in conjunction with the Chicago, Burlington & Quincy and the Western Pacific railroads, this streamlined train (which used the Moffatt Tunnel route through central Colorado) was sufficiently popular during the winter months that it occasionally operated in multiple sections. Aspen-bound passengers on the Zephyr customarily detrained in Glenwood Springs at convenient midday hours and finished their journey on Glenwood-Aspen Stages, a bus service promoted in the Rio Grande's timetables.

With the appearance of many skiers, a revival in silver mining, and an increase in coal shipments from Woody Creek by the early 1950s, Aspen once again gave every indication of being a prosperous community. In 1953, Aspen Airways launched a shuttle service to Denver, which, along with better highways, reduced the community's reliance on passenger trains operating through Glenwood Springs. As roads improved and ranchers thinned their herds, the south end of the Aspen Branch surrendered most of its transportation importance.

The Rio Grande targeted the segment south of Woody Creek for elimination in the mid-1960s. The opening of the Snowmass ski area in 1967 reinforced views held by many community leaders that mining and other forms of heavy industry had little place in Aspen's long-range plans. With tourism projected to grow, a proposal emerged to acquire the branch for a steam-powered excursion railway. Although endorsed by Pitkin County commissioners, this idea did not advance beyond the planning stage.

Unlike the heavily anticipated race to operate the first train to Aspen, the departure of its last train in early 1969 was a low-key event that went largely unnoticed. The Aspen Times nevertheless commemorated the occasion with a front-page photograph.

Abandonment's Legacy

When the Rio Grande abandoned the 8-mile segment from Aspen to Woody Creek that same year, it ceded much of the right-of-way to the county and sold property near the depot to the developer of a new shopping center. Meanwhile, despite staunch opposition from environmentalists, the state government had crews working around the clock to complete Interstate 70. This highway, built roughly parallel to the Rio Grande main line through Glenwood Canyon, would prove to be one of the most expensive stretches of rural interstate ever built. To link Aspen to the expressway, the state paved part of the long-abandoned Midland right-of-way for the creation of State Route 82 and fitted outriggers on the Maroon Creek Bridge trestle to allow it to accommodate additional highway traffic.

Such investments diminished the role of the California Zephyr, which suffered a slump in ridership and ceased operating west of Salt Lake City, Utah, in 1970. The famed "Silver Lady" made its final trip the following year. Nevertheless, the Rio Grande opted to remain independent of Amtrak and continued to operate the Denver–Salt Lake City portion of this train. It christened this triweekly run the Rio Grande Zephyr and assigned to it streamlined equipment formerly used by the famed predecessor.

Railroad enthusiasts had a strong interest in this vestige of past transportation glory, but in 1983, Rio Grande finally turned its deficit-ridden intercity passenger operations over to Amtrak. Although the quasi-governmental carrier dropped the Rio Grande Zephyr, it rerouted its Chicago–Oakland train, which had been operating via Wyoming, over the Moffat Tunnel route and renamed this run, appropriately, the California Zephyr.

In Aspen, rail service would continue to be relegated to the distant past. The demolition of the Rio Grande depot eliminated a reminder of railroad preeminence in the community, leaving the Maroon Creek Bridge as a relic of the era of train travel. The bridge was added to the National Register of Historic Places in 1985—the same year, ironically, that Aspen Airways introduced jet service to the Aspen-Pitkin Airport, marking the beginning of a new chapter in local transportation. As Aspen grew at a rate reminiscent of a century before, mostly due to the expansion of winter recreation, the county fashioned the abandoned Rio Grande rail segment from Aspen to Woody Creek into the Rio Grande Trail.

The Rio Grande continued operating freight trains over a remnant of the Aspen Branch between Glenwood Springs and Carbondale to serve the last remnant of the valley's mining industry. In 1988, the Rio Grande's parent company acquired the much larger Southern Pacific, leading to the gradual loss of the Rio Grande's distinct identify. In 1994, coal shipments from Carbondale's Mid-Continent Mining Company ceased, ending all rail service along the Roaring Fork.

Despite the rather modest heritage of the Rio Grande's branch as a passenger route, there was strong grassroots support for rebuilding this corridor to support the valley's expanding population and outdoor recreation sectors. As early as the mid-1970s, officials had submitted proposals to establish rail transit service on this route. The movement did not gather a great deal of momentum, however, until after county governments in the area purchased the remainder of the former Rio Grande corridor, between Woody Creek and Glenwood Springs in 1997. Soon, a plan reemerged to build a light-rail line linking Aspen to its airport, with the hope of eventually extending the route to Glenwood Springs.

The obvious financial risks associated with building the first entirely "rural" light-rail line in the country did not dissuade local residents from enthusiastically supporting its construction. Many considered rail service a solution to mounting traffic congestion and severe shortfalls of moderately priced housing. Nevertheless, county planners recognized that the southern end of the abandoned Rio Grande route was not ideal for modern passenger use, due to its difficult grades and distance from lodging facilities and the airport. A plan emerged, therefore, to build the route to the airport adjacent to Route 82 along the more westerly Colorado Midland route.

By the end of 1997, a federal agency had recommended construction of the Aspen-to-Airport portion, and the county had received federal funds for a "corridor investment study" to evaluate an eventual extension to Glenwood Springs following the old Rio Grande route. Illustrative of the optimism of this era, an even more ambitious proposal simultaneously moved forward, one that would provide rail passenger service between Aspen, Vail, and Steamboat Springs. In 1997, consultants working for the state estimated that the nearly 200-mile system, with connecting service to Denver, would generate more than two million passenger trips annually and cost $447 million to build. Contemplating the possibilities, officials envisioned using rail passenger service to make Aspen a pioneer in modern "resort-rail development," a phenomenon pervasive in contemporary Europe but long ago abandoned in the United States.

Events would soon converge to doom both the local and statewide rail initiatives. A referendum that would have generated funds for the construction of the Aspen-to-Airport transit line failed in 1999. Meanwhile, the corridor investment study generated both controversy and concerns over cost escalation. As a result, politicians in Aspen increasingly considered the rail issue as something

to be debated only in the future and redirected their support to improved bus service.

The statewide effort to build new rail passenger systems also stalled, hampered by the results of a 2001 referendum about funding a monorail to link the resorts along the heavily used Interstate 70 corridor with Denver. The prospects for all the above projects now seem remote—at least until new sources of funding emerge.

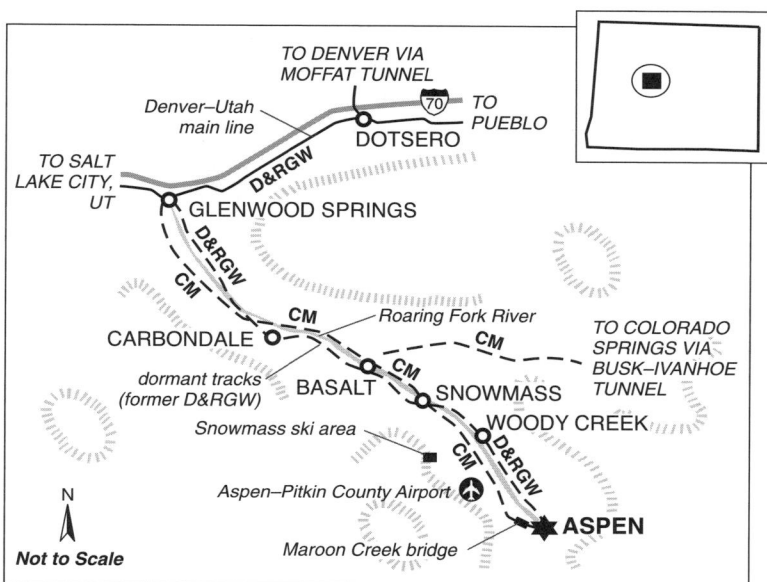

Epilogue

Aspen is perhaps the most famous community in the Rocky Mountains to have lost its rail service. This community is widely known for its fine boutiques, restaurants, and well-groomed ski slopes and has substantially more resources for preserving historical buildings than most other former mining centers. The Opera House, Hotel Jerome, and Maroon Creek Bridge, all in excellent condition and listed on the National Register of Historic Places, remain prominent community landmarks. Nearby, the Aspen Historical Society's Wheeler-Stallard Museum offers visitors dramatic images of the valley's industrial past.

A significant number of travelers destined for Aspen continue to ride the California Zephyr to Glenwood Springs. Those who travel along the former Rio Grande branch to Aspen will find portions of the long-dormant tracks, especially between Carbondale and Woody Creek, now in ruins as they lie covered with brush and other vegetation. Some of these tracks have been paved over, at least temporarily, for a recreational trail extension. While the future of this rail is uncertain, the battle to build railroads along the Roaring Fork appears destined to continue in the years to come.

For Further Study

SUGGESTED READING:

Danneman, Herbert. "A Ticket to Ride the Narrow Gauge." In *Colorado Rail Annual 24*. Golden: Colorado Railroad Museum, 2000, 70–83.

Ormes, Robert M. *Tracking Ghost Railroads in Colorado*. Colorado Springs, Colo.: Green Light Graphics, 1992, 110–11.

Pearce, Sarah J., and Roxanne Eflin. *Aspen and the Roaring Fork Valley*. Aspen Historic Trust, 1990, 29–32.

OTHER PRINCIPAL REFERENCES:

DeGolyer, Everett L. *The Track Going Back*. Fort Worth, Tex.: Amon Carter Museum, 1969, 92.

Fletcher, Ken. *Centennial State Trolleys: The Life and Times of Colorado's Streetcars*. Golden: Colorado State Railroad Museum, 1995, 11–12.

LeMassena, Robert L. *Rio Grande. . . . To the Pacific!* Denver: Sundance Limited, 1974, 51–58, 87, 202.

MacGregor, Bruce A., and Ted Benson. *Portrait of a Silver Lady: The Train They Called the California Zephyr*. Boulder, Colo.: Pruett Publishing, 1977, 207–38.

Ohlrich, Warren H. *Take the Train to Aspen*. Aspen, Colo.: Who Press, 1992, 51–55.

Shoemaker, Len. *Roaring Fork Valley: An Illustrated Chronicle*. Denver: Sundance Limited, 1958, 105–21, 188–97.

Historic operators: Colorado Springs & Cripple Creek District Railway;
Florence & Cripple Creek; Midland Terminal Railway
Last route abandoned: 1949
Notable reuse of right-of-way: Narrow-gauge tourist railway

ittle remains of the labyrinth of railroad routes once serving Cripple Creek, a community that long ago stood at the forefront of one of the country's greatest gold-mining booms. Over this intricate system of steam and electric routes, trains hauled enormous quantities of high-grade ore and delighted passengers with breathtaking mountain views. By the middle of the twentieth century, however, all of these routes had disappeared and the outlook for Cripple Creek was grim.

Historical Perspective

Conditions were far from ideal for the ranchers who grazed livestock on the open range southwest of Pikes Peak during the 1870s. Nevertheless, a few of these ranchers gradually expanded their herds and established homesteads in the shadow of Mount Pisgah, a towering peak some 20 miles from Colorado Springs. Several lived along the fast-flowing waters of Cripple Creek, a small stream whose name, according to local legend, arose from a long-ago injury—though whether it was due to a man or a beast is now unclear.

By the mid-1880s, several ranchers had moved their herds elsewhere and a Denver investment company belonging to Horace Bennett and Julias Myers held title to much of the land. Bennett and Myers renamed the area Broken Box Ranch, established an office along the creek, and worked to attract newcomers. An employee of the company,

THE MIDLAND TERMINAL RAILWAY

Bob Womack, tried to convince those who would listen that the area held lucrative deposits of gold ore. In late 1890, Womack struck gold near the head of Poverty Gulch, only a short distance from the ranch's headquarters, and brought samples to Colorado Springs for evaluation. Initially, those living in the area were skeptical of his enthusiastic report about the region's mining potential. Many were aware of Womack's drinking problem; others remembered an earlier hoax. The hapless prospector soon sold his claim for a trifling sum.

Despite Womack's misfortune, his discovery was a turning point in the entire region's economy. By the time officials created the Cripple Creek Gold Mining District in 1891, Colorado's last great mining boom was rapidly gathering momentum. To serve the mining companies and other businesses as well as laborers pouring into the region, Bennett and Myers laid out a town site for Cripple Creek and incorporated the community in 1892. By the end of the year,

Rounding the bend over Poverty Gulch in 1911, a CS&CCD passenger train approaches Cripple Creek, where it will terminate at the two-story station (center of the photo) which the Short Line shared with the Midland Terminal Railway. (Photo by H. E. High, collection of Mel McFarland.)

newly incorporated Cripple Creek had dozens of businesses, an estimated fifty mines, and strong ties to Victor, a neighboring town approximately 5 miles southeast. The influx reached staggering proportions in 1893, when more than 10,000 people arrived in the district, causing severe overcrowding of its ramshackle communities.

Notorious for its brothels, saloons, opium dens, and rows of unkempt shanties, Cripple Creek suffered greatly from poor planning and inadequate sanitation. Although stagecoaches departing the two-story Palace Hotel carried passengers to the Colorado Midland's depot in Divide as well as to the Denver & Rio Grande's station in Florence, the community desperately wanted a railroad of its own. Both the Florence & Cripple Creek Railroad and the Midland Terminal Railway vied to be the first to serve the district. The Florence & Cripple Creek had the advantage of building its route to narrow gauge and arrived earlier than its rival. In the summer of 1894, it

completed a 40-mile line to Florence, over which it established Pullman service to Denver in conjunction with the Rio Grande.

Although the Florence & Cripple Creek greatly improved the mining district's accessibility, its route had unfortunate shortcomings. Excruciating curves and tortuous grades, which took trains to an elevation of nearly 10,000 feet through the Eight Mile (Phantom) Canyon, hampered speeds and added to operating costs. Trips to Colorado Springs and Denver through the company's interchange with the Rio Grande were also highly circuitous.

The Midland Terminal's arrival in late 1895, therefore, was a momentous occasion. Created by the Colorado Midland Railway (a company owned by the Atchison, Topeka & Santa Fe at the time), this standard-gauge line provided a much more direct route to Colorado Springs. Its trains began their run at a fine three-story depot near the foot of Bennett Avenue, ran nearly parallel to the narrow-gauge line to Victor, and then proceeded north through the Victor Pass to Divide, a junction on the Colorado Midland.

The advantages of relatively low-cost rail transportation helped establish Cripple Creek as the country's premier gold-mining center and one of Colorado's largest cities. Massive shipments of silver ore moved over its rail lines to processing mills in Colorado Springs. Even disaster hardly slowed the community's growth. In early 1896, two fires in four days destroyed nearly the entire community. Within months new masonry buildings emerged from the rubble, including the five-story National Hotel and the stately Imperial Hotel. Gambling houses, hotels, and the offices of mining companies soon lined both sides of Bennett Avenue, the city's principal commercial thoroughfare. Myers Avenue, a street parallel to Bennett, became home to the Grand Opera House, various theaters, and a booming red-light district.

The enormous investments flowing into the mining district created an urgent need for more efficient ways to carry workers to and from its many underground mines. The Cripple Creek District Railway helped solve this problem by opening an electric line through Poverty Gulch, linking Cripple Creek and Victor in 1898. Its route provided the equivalent of streetcar service down Bennett Avenue and offered tourists awe-inspiring vistas of the snow-capped Rocky Mountains.

Cripple Creek was awash in prosperity in 1899 when it became the seat of newly created Teller County. Its businesses provided vital services to the several hundred mines in the district and the approximately 8,000 men the mines employed. By the turn of the century, Cripple Creek boasted an official population of about 10,000. Some have speculated that its actual population might have been several times higher.

The development of the city's transportation system crossed another milestone in 1901 when the Colorado Springs & Cripple Creek District Railway (CS&CCD) inaugurated service. Supported by local investors, the "Short Line" afforded passengers a more direct, albeit still tortuous, route to Colorado Springs. CS&CCD also operated the original electrified line between Cripple Creek and Victor and completed a second such line between these communities that same year. Travelers could now choose from hourly departures on the new route (known locally as the Low Line due to its lower elevation) as well as its original route (known as the High Line), which the company realigned on several occasions to improve service.

As the local railroad era entered its most illustrious phase, many long-distance travelers rode the Cripple Creek Flyer, a Pullman-equipped train to Denver jointly operated by the Midland Terminal, the Colorado Midland, and the Rio Grande. The Florence & Cripple Creek also had daily passenger service and used a subsidiary

called the Golden Circle Railroad to provide suburban-style passenger service between Cripple Creek and Victor. It was the CS&CCD's Short Line, however, that welcomed large numbers of leisure travelers during the summer months and earned accolades for its festive ambience and panoramic vistas. The railroad's patrons during the first year of operation included Vice President Theodore Roosevelt.

Changing Times

Cripple Creek had long been susceptible to up-and-down business cycles, but the strikes and labor violence of 1903 were devastating, putting more than 3,500 miners out of work. The accumulation of water in underground mines was also a serious problem that, unfortunately, was only partially solved by the completion of a 3-mile drainage

The former Midland Terminal depot, now a museum, survives as a striking reminder of Cripple Creek's days as a premier mining center. (Photo by author.)

tunnel in 1911. As companies consolidated and turned to new technologies, the number of jobs in the mines diminished significantly.

Hopes for a major economic recovery had already faded when a flash flood damaged the Florence & Cripple Creek line south of Victor in 1912, severing its mountainous corridor. A small portion of this route, including the Cripple Creek–Victor segment (part of the Golden Circle Railroad), was converted to standard gauge and remained in service. The rest of the company was dissolved in 1915, with much of its right-of-way transformed into the Phantom Canyon Highway.

CS&CCD responded to its mounting deficits by reducing the frequency of trains traveling on the High Line. In 1917, the Colorado Midland was sold at foreclosure to Albert A. Carlton, an investor who briefly united all of the rail lines under the name of Cripple Creek & Colorado Springs Railroad. Carlton's company abandoned the former narrow-gauge route between Cripple Creek and Victor that same year and experienced the trauma of another Cripple Creek fire, which disrupted the CS&CCD's operations in late 1919. The following year, his beleaguered carrier terminated the last of its electric-car service between Cripple Creek and Victor as well as operations on the Short Line. The Short Line was then dismantled and sold to businessman W. E. Corley, who converted it into a toll road.

In only ten years, Cripple Creek had gone from being the hub of a great steam- and electric-rail system to a dying town with only a single route, the freight-only Midland Terminal. The number of mines dropped to forty in the early 1920s. By the end of the decade, many of these mining companies had further consolidated and Cripple Creek had shriveled to fewer than 1,000 permanent residents.

The Midland Terminal carried on the practice of hauling ore to the Gold Cycle Mill in Colorado Springs and benefited from a modest revival in traffic that was facilitated by the 1931 completion of the Carlton Tunnel, a 6-mile underground passage that helped drain some of the deepest mines. A sharp rise in gold prices in 1934 further stimulated the mining sector, which remained relatively strong through the early years of World War II. When the federal government ordered the mines closed in 1942, however, it pushed the mining district into another long and difficult economic slump.

After Charles and Dorothy Mackin restored the Imperial Hotel and began staging melodramas there in 1947, officials began to recognize that tourism could help improve business conditions. The need to bring greater diversification to the economy had become imperative by 1949, when the Carlton Mill, a modern processing facility located between Cripple Creek and Victor, replaced the aging mill in Colorado Springs and ushered in a more modern mining era. No longer needed to haul ore, the Midland Terminal operated its last freight train that same year, ending Cripple Creek's rail service.

Abandonment's Legacy

After abandonment, portions of the Midland Terminal route were transformed into state Route 67, a paved road that quickly emerged as the most heavily used highway in the central part of the county. The accessibility provided by this road and the conversion of the carrier's depot into a historical museum in 1963 provided a much needed stimulus to local tourism. By the time Cripple Creek earned a spot on the National Register of Historic Places in 1966, the number of visitors had risen sharply. Optimism was building the following year, when a short stretch of 2-foot-gauge track was laid over the former Midland Terminal route for the newly created Cripple Creek & Victor Narrow Gauge Railroad, an excursion operator using steam locomotives reminiscent of those of the Florence & Cripple Creek.

To the disappointment of community leaders, many of the visitors who took trips through the Rockies made

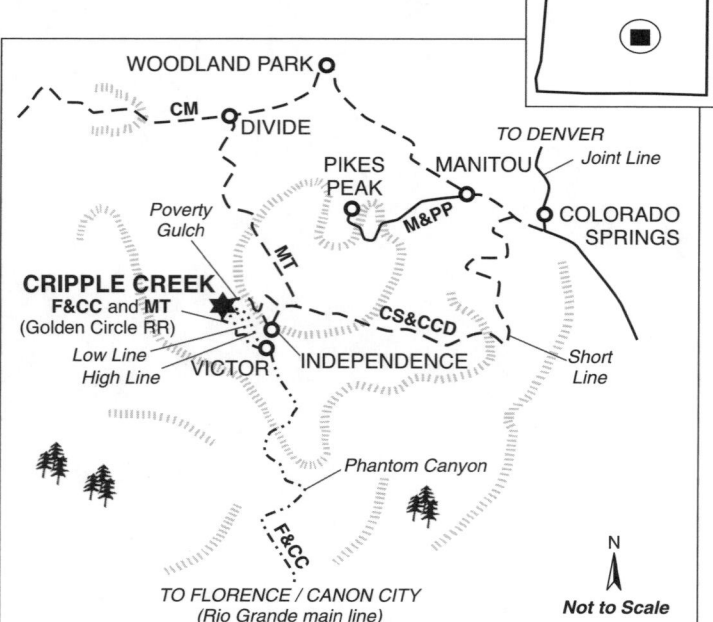

only cursory stops in Cripple Creek. As tourism waned and the area's remaining mining operations adopted more modern production methods, further diminishing their manpower needs, the town's population dropped once again to fewer than 1,000. By the mid-1980s, an alarming drop in tourism had pushed the community's economy to the brink of collapse.

The state government responded to calls for assistance by passing a historic piece of legislation in 1991, legalizing casino gambling in Cripple Creek and several other communities. Much like during the gold rush a century before, investment began to pour into the community. Soon new casinos, hotels, restaurants, and souvenir shops lined Bennett Street and catered to busloads of tourists. In only a few years, Cripple Creek had made the transition into a bustling entertainment center and began to again experience traffic problems and housing shortages similar to those from the height of its mining era.

Unable to build new roads or large housing facilities, civic boosters once again looked to the benefits of rail service. In the mid-1990s, a private developer, supported by the local government, announced his intention to rebuild the Short Line for passenger service to Colorado Springs. With relatively little traffic on the Corley Mountain Highway (formerly Gold Camp Road) and most of the 51-mile corridor free of man-made obstructions, the developer prepared an environmental impact statement. His ambitious proposal called for a railway providing frequent service from Colorado Springs to cater to tourists and employees. This railway would also carry inbound shipments of supplies and freight and would serve mines in the region, which by now were all open-pit operations belonging to one company.

Despite unresolved financial issues and opposition from residents along the route near Colorado Springs, the project gathered a considerable amount of political momentum. Three different groups made known their interest in building and operating the line. To the disappointment of those involved, however, all of these efforts eventually stalled.

Further discussion about rail service took place in 1997 when the state government released a study about reestablishing rail service to Cripple Creek by using portions of the former Midland Terminal grade. The study determined that building a 43-mile route from Cripple Creek would be technically challenging due to steep grades, real estate development, and the obstructions created by Route 67. Although rail service would potentially generate more than 300,000 passengers per year, the state considered the $420 million cost to be prohibitive.

County and city officials then turned their attention to more modest alternatives, such as a 4-mile extension of the excursion railroad to Victor, a proposal that some hoped would help this struggling community share in Cripple Creek's commercial boom. This option was soon rendered infeasible due to excavation by mining companies and the creation of leaching pits (that is, mines that extract precious metal by dissolving deposits embedded in crushed ore). Even the Carlton Mill was torn down to make way for a leaching excavation.

Epilogue

Many other gold rush towns steeped in American history have experienced the loss of all rail service, but none of these towns had a system of steam and electric routes as extensive as Cripple Creek's. The scale of Cripple Creek's rail operations exemplified both the enormity of its mining district and the timing of the community's creation, which took place only a few years before another wave of railroad construction gathered momentum across the West.

Today, the abandoned railroad grades, mounds of dirt, and sealed entrances of underground mines serve as sober reminders of the environmental consequences of the quest for gold. A series of tunnels once traversed by the Short Line's trains are now part of Gold Camp Highway, a scenic motor route. The Midland Terminal depot, adjacent to the legendary Poverty Gulch, remains a treasured brick-and-stone landmark, home to the Cripple Creek District Museum.

Visitors often leave Cripple Creek with a sense of ambivalence about the effect of casino gambling on the town's character. Positive changes include a rejuvenated economy and new resources for historic preservation, especially along Bennett Avenue, where numerous casinos and restaurants serve their customers in attractively restored Victorian buildings. However, some lament the extent to which gaming has changed the essence and feel of one of the county's most historic mining towns. Gone forever are the gritty saloons, homegrown businesses, and working-class qualities that were a part of Cripple Creek life long after the last train left town.

For Further Study

SUGGESTED READINGS:

Feitz, Leland. *Cripple Creek Railroads: A Quick History.* Colorado Springs, Colo.: Little London Press, 1968, 9–15.

McFarland, Edward M. *The Cripple Creek Road: A Midland Terminal Guide and Data Book.* Boulder, Colo.: Pruett Publishing, 1984, 81–110.

Wilkins, Tivis E. "Short Line to Cripple Creek: The Story of the Colorado Springs & Cripple Creek District Railway." In *Colorado Rail Annual* 16. Golden: Colorado Railroad Museum, 1993, 9–133.

OTHER PRINCIPAL REFERENCES:

Danneman, Herbert. "A Ticket to Ride the Narrow Gauge." In *Colorado Rail Annual* 24. Golden: Colorado Railroad Museum, 2000, 91, 112, 129.

Feitz, Leland. *Cripple Creek: A Quick History of the World's Greatest Gold Camp.* Colorado Springs, Colo.: Little London Press, 1967, 9–68.

Ormes, Robert M. *Tracking Ghost Railroads in Colorado.* Colorado Springs, Colo.: Green Light Graphics, 1992, 93–96.

Potter, Janet Greenstein. *Great American Railroad Stations.* New York: Wiley & Sons, 1996, 485.

Wilkins, Tivis E. "The Florence & Cripple Creek and Golden Circle Railroads." In *Colorado Rail Annual* 13. Golden: Colorado Railroad Museum, 1976, 9–161.

GUNNISON, COLORADO (5,409)

Historic operators: Colorado & Southern Railway; Denver & Rio Grande Western Railroad
Last route abandoned: 1954
Notable reuses of right-of-way: Gunnison Pioneer Museum; Blue Mesa and Morrow Point reservoirs

When the indomitable General William Jackson Palmer pushed his Denver & Rio Grande Railway across the Rocky Mountains in 1881, Gunnison emerged as one of central Colorado's leading railroad towns. With the arrival of the Denver, South Park & Pacific Railroad the following year, the town seemed on the verge of becoming a great industrial center as well. Although Gunnison never became the "Pittsburgh of the West" as some had anticipated, its story marks the fervor that once surrounded the region's narrow-gauge routes.

Historical Perspective

In 1853, Captain John W. Gunnison surveyed the corridor along the river that would later bear his name, hoping to find a route suitable for a transcontinental railroad. His expedition came upon a magnificent gorge, which the party christened the Black Canyon, but they concluded that the treacherous terrain and severe weather would make the gorge impassible by rail. Gunnison's party also encountered problems with the Ute tribe, which had controlled this land for generations.

The region's commercial potential impressed frontiersman John C. Frémont as he followed the river on his way to California later that year, but several decades passed without significant settlement in the area. In 1873, Sylvester Richardson arrived in the river valley with the dream of creating a large agricultural colony. Richardson's hopes were still high in 1876 when

Colorado became the country's thirty-eighth state and the settlement he founded, Gunnison, was named the seat of a newly created county of the same name. The expectations that the community would rapidly grow, however, were at odds with its difficult-to-reach location.

As in so many other western towns, the situation changed when prospectors found lucrative deposits of silver. A great strike north of town in 1879 attracted thousands of newcomers, culminating in an intense rivalry between East Gunnison, the original town, and its upstart neighbor, West Gunnison. Each community had a flourishing downtown district and vied for commercial supremacy. West Gunnison was incorporated in 1880 and benefited greatly from the leadership of Louden Mullin, a prominent businessman who built the Mullin House, a first-class hotel at the center of town. Nevertheless, the community had trouble matching the success of East Gunnison,

A worker lightens the load of a Denver & Rio Grande train on the loop track through downtown Gunnison on 28 May 1923. The building at the left is the La Veta Hotel, a fine guest house. (Photo by Otto Perry, Denver Public Library.)

which warmly greeted visiting former President Ulysses S. Grant in 1880.

The two communities realized the advantages of putting their differences aside when the time came to attract a railroad. Their mutual efforts took a dramatic turn when legendary capitalist Jay Gould's Denver & Rio Grande Railway (Rio Grande) struck a deal in 1880 with the Atchison, Topeka & Santa Fe Railway. These railroad companies had been such fierce competitors that they resorted to acts of sabotage as they vied to lay tracks through the Royal Gorge. The historic agreement stipuated that the two carriers build in different directions across the West.

As part of the so-called Treaty of Boston, the Rio Grande resolved to build across central Colorado and, through the leadership of General Palmer, pushed its rails from Salida to Gunnison County by way of the Marshall

Pass in 1881. Palmer's narrow-gauge railroad flanked the southern periphery of East Gunnison and West Gunnison and maintained a depot midway between the towns. It also built a branch to Crested Butte that was soon considered to be the boundary between the rival communities. In 1882, the Rio Grande pushed its line west along the river through the Black Canyon and reached Montrose.

The railroad era was in full bloom by the time a second carrier, the Denver, South Park & Pacific (South Park), arrived in the river valley in 1882. The South Park offered a more direct route to Denver and crossed the Continental Divide through the famed Alpine Tunnel, which stretched more than 1,700 feet, making it the longest narrow-gauge tunnel ever built in Colorado. Inside the tunnel, trains climbed to an elevation of 11,612 feet—the highest point reached by a railroad in the United States at the time. After descending several thousand feet, trains passed through East Gunnison in the middle of San Juan Avenue (several blocks north of the Rio Grande tracks) and terminated in West Gunnison.

With an extensive rail system now in place, there was a surge of investment in Crested Butte and the two Gunnisons. Large deposits of coal, limestone, and iron ore were available for exploitation, raising hope among local business leaders that the Gunnison area would become a major iron- and steel-making center—the so-called Pittsburgh of the West. In the enthusiasm of the moment, proponents of local streetcar service announced plans to establish the East and West Gunnison Railway Company in 1882.

Gunnison's depots teamed with activities the following year, when the South Park completed a branch from Gunnison to Baldwin, and the Rio Grande inaugurated through service over its newly completed narrow-gauge line between Denver and Salt Lake City. Although the South Park never built west to Gunnison as originally planned (thus never reaching the Pacific as suggested by its grandiose name), passengers riding the Rio Grande could now make the 771-mile trip between Denver and Salt Lake City on the Atlantic Express and Pacific Express. With Gunnison an important station and division point along this busy main line—and located at the heart of a region endowed with plentiful raw materials—the creation of major iron and steel mills in the community seemed within the realm of possibility. Optimism certainly prevailed as hundreds gathered in West Gunnison to celebrate the opening of the magnificent La Veta Hotel in 1884, an event that appeared to raise the town's status above that of its rival.

Changing Times

The vitality of the Gunnisons diminished when the mining industry fell on hard times, dooming plans for the streetcar line and for construction of major iron and steel mills. The struggling communities merged in 1886 to create Gunnison City, but local leaders soon dropped the "City"—an appropriate move considering that Gunnison clung rather precariously to its role as a major railroad center over the next ten years. Although the Rio Grande's facilities—a roundhouse, car shops, a small freight yard, and separate freight and passenger stations—remained busy places, their role in trans-Colorado transportation gradually diminished.

Gunnison ceased having the benefit of through passenger service to Salt Lake City when the Rio Grande converted the portion of its main line west of Grand Junction to standard gauge in 1890. Three years later, Rio

Grande trains between the Colorado capital and Salt Lake City began using a completely standard-gauge route through the Tennessee Pass. This new route ended Gunnison's role as a stop along a major long-distance corridor and meant the loss of through passenger service to Denver.

These unfavorable developments notwithstanding, the Rio Grande remained Gunnison's most important commercial enterprise. The carrier supported the expansion of gold mining and ranching in the area and handled growing shipments of coal on its Crested Butte Branch after the turn of the century. The carrier operated a loop track through the western half of the town that served, among other businesses, the La Veta Hotel. In 1910, travelers could reach town on the carrier's daily Salida–Grand Junction passenger express as well as mixed trains from Crested Butte, Montrose, and Sargent. Thousands of travelers of this era experienced the splendor of traveling through the awe-inspiring Black Canyon at nearly 8,000 feet while making their way around the Rio Grande's famed Narrow Gauge Circle, a scenic loop through southern Colorado and northern New Mexico that is indelibly etched into railroad lore.

The cost of maintaining such mountainous routes, however, placed a heavy burden on Gunnison's railroads. After the Alpine Tunnel partially collapsed in 1910, the South Park's successor, the Colorado & Southern Railroad permanently discontinued operations through it and abandoned the segment from Gunnison to Parlin. The carrier completely withdrew from the area by leasing its branch to Baldwin and the segment from Parlin to Quartz (10 miles from the tunnel) to the Rio Grande. By

Former Rio Grande equipment shines in the light of the late afternoon sun at Gunnison's Pioneer Museum adjacent to the old main line to Salida, circa 1998. (Photo by author.)

1915, mixed trains to Montrose and Sargent had been discontinued, leaving only the express train and the mixed train to Crested Butte. By the time the carrier was renamed the Denver & Rio Grande Western Railroad in 1921, much of the region's freight traffic was moving by truck.

These problems were partially ameliorated by the expansion of other segments of Gunnison's economy. Enrollment growth at the Colorado State Normal School (an institution of higher learning) and the inaugural Cattleman's Days festival in 1921 signaled the community's changing orientation. As the quality of Gunnison's roads improved, the Rio Grande replaced its mixed train to Crested Butte with a bus in 1932 and abandoned the former South Park segment between Parin and Quartz two years later. The carrier substituted buses for the passenger train between Gunnison and Montrose in 1936.

In 1937, the Rio Grande rekindled memories of the glory years of rail transportation when it replaced its conventional passenger trains between Salida and Gunnison with the Shavano, a train equipped with finely refurbished cars, including a parlor car. This train and its counterpart, the San Juan (which operated between Alamosa and Durango), offered electric lights, vestibules, and other amenities previously unavailable on the narrow-gauge line. The following year, labor problems ended the practice of shipping less-than-carload freight on these trains, thus hampering their financial performance. The cancellation of the Shavano in 1940 ended all rail passenger service to Gunnison and saddened railroad enthusiasts. Although the carrier operated an emergency passenger service between Gunnison and Montrose (due to a mud slide blocking Highway 50) in 1944, this lasted only a few months.

After World War II, major improvements to Highway 50, declining coal shipments, and the diminishing viability of narrow-gauge railroading in general eliminated virtually all hope that Gunnison's rail lines could be operated profitably. The local stockyard's livestock was now moved by truck and the Colorado Fuel and Iron Company closed its coal mine in Crested Butte in 1952, leaving the Rio Grande without a significant source of local revenue. The company abandoned all of its route through Gunnison in 1954, leaving the town of about 2,700 people Colorado's largest community inaccessible by rail. By the end of 1955, the tracks had been scrapped.

Abandonment's Legacy

Many of Gunnison's businesses struggled to survive during these transitional years, giving its downtown an increasingly shabby appearance. The owners of the La Veta Hotel, who had allowed the once magnificent edifice to fall into deplorable condition, removed its upper floors and transformed the ground floor into apartments. Gunnison's economic slump continued until another mining boom—one revolving around uranium in the late 1950s—ushered in another period of significant expansion. The 1961 opening of a ski area several miles to the north in Crested Butte attracted still more residents and businesses. Although uranium production eventually faded, further expansions of Western State College (formerly the Colorado State Normal School) helped sustain Gunnison's economy.

Tourism in the county took a tentative step forward with the opening of the Gunnison Pioneer Museum in a modest aluminum building during 1964. The following year, the completion of the Blue Mesa Dam created an attractive reservoir along the Gunnison River that submerged many miles of abandoned right-of-way as well as much of the Black Canyon. By the end of the decade, the Pioneer Museum had established itself as a notable repository of Rio Grande artifacts and put on display the last caboose that traveled through the community. In 1971, it moved the water tank at Mears Junction (a rural location near Alamosa) to its grounds. The museum later expanded its collection to include the former depot at Sargent, the last steam locomotive to serve Gunnison (No. 268), and several freight cars.

Simultaneously, major investments in wintertime sports facilities at Crested Butte enhanced the county's popularity among skiers. By the late 1970s, large numbers of seasonal visitors arrived by air on the Gunnison County Airport's only runway, which was parallel to the abandoned Rio Grande main line and even, ironically, within a few hundred feet of the carrier's masonry depot—a structure used at the time as a terminal for Rio Grande Motorways, the railroad's trucking subsidiary.

Amid a flurry of development, some people lamented that the county's distinctive western lifestyle was vanishing. Traffic on Highway 50 continued to grow, while a resurgence in uranium mining threatened to spoil the beautiful natural areas just outside of town. With tourism projected to expand rapidly, a group of community leaders explored scenarios for rebuilding the abandoned Crested Butte Branch. Proponents of this idea hoped to emulate the success of the Durango & Silverton Narrow Gauge Railroad, a popular excursion operator using former Rio Grande rail less than 100 miles away. They envisioned that this tourist attraction would relieve congestion on State Route 135, but in the end they could not overcome financial obstacles and opposition from local ranchers.

Discussion about restoring rail service was briefly heard again in 1995, when the state's Department of Transportation considered including the Crested Butte Branch in its comprehensive review of potential rail passenger markets. Due to an apparent lack of local interest, the department did not move forward with a formal evaluation of service between Gunnison and the popular ski center to the north.

Epilogue

Whether the Rio Grande could have recouped its investments from converting its routes to Gunnison to standard gauge will never be known, but the decision not to do so almost certainly assured that its services to the community would end by the 1960s. Today, a bus traveling daily on Route 50 between Pueblo and Grand Junction brings to mind the legacy of a rail corridor once known for the Atlantic Express and Pacific Express.

Visitors may notice that Gunnison still has two downtown areas, a carryover of the rival towns that merged more than a century ago. The former Rio Grande depot is in relatively good condition considering that it has been used only for storage for more than twenty years. A large area of land nearby now lies fallow, rendered superfluous by the abandonment of this carrier's yard. On the South Park, the portals of the Alpine Tunnel are difficult to reach but accessible to railroad enthusiasts willing to negotiate the rugged topography for a glimpse of the legendary passage that once took trains through miles of darkness. Little else remains of the railroad system near the town that vied to be the "Pittsburgh of the West."

For Further Study

SUGGESTED READINGS:

Dorman, Richard L. *Gunnison: From Marshall Pass, Lake City and Crested Butte through to Ouray.* Santa Fe, N.Mex.: R.D. Publications, 1993, 43–60.

Vandenbusche, Duane. *The Gunnison Country.* Gunnison, Colo.: B&B Printers, 1980, 83–123.

OTHER PRINCIPAL REFERENCES:

Danneman, Herbert. "A Ticket to Ride the Narrow Gauge." In *Colorado Rail Annual 24.* Golden: Colorado Railroad Museum, 2000, 57, 162–75, 188–89.

Day, Jerry B. *The Gunnison Train.* Gunnison, Colo.: Gunnison County Pioneer and Historical Museum, 1992, 13, 19–34.

Hilton, George W. *American Narrow Gauge Railroads.* Stanford: Stanford University Press, 1990, 344–53.

LeMassena, Robert L. *Rio Grande. . . . To the Pacific!* Denver: Sundance Limited, 1974, 27–30, 38, 41, 85, 125, 151, 330–32, 349.

Norwood, John B. *Rio Grande Narrow Gauge: From Birth to Abandonment.* River Forest, Ill.: Heimburger House, 1983, 90–97.

Ormes, Robert M. *Tracking Ghost Railroads in Colorado.* Colorado Springs, Colo.: Green Light Graphics, 1992, 63–72.

LAKEWOOD, COLORADO (144,146)

Historic operators: Associated Railways; Colorado & Southern Railway; Denver & Intermountain Railroad;
U.S. Government Railway; West End Street Railway Co.
Last route abandoned: 1989
Notable reuse of right-of-way: Proposed transit corridor

When freight service to Lakewood ended in 1989, the evolution of American railroads reached an ignominious, if unnoticed, milepost. For the first time in modern history, the railroad industry had ended all service to a city on the U.S. mainland with more than 100,000 inhabitants. Although virtually nothing remains of Lakewood's narrow-gauge railway and streetcar line, its former interurban route is still largely intact and could welcome trains once again.

Historical Perspective

Prospectors, merchants, and miners streamed into the western part of Kansas Territory after John Gregory discovered gold in a gulch near Central City in 1859. Within months, more than 10,000 had ascended the mountainous slopes to reach Central City, making it the territory's largest and most famous mining camp. Many others settled near the eastern slopes of the Rockies, spurring the creation of Denver, Golden, and other cities.

Despite the booming mining district nearby, few of the so-called '59ers opted to reside in the Bear Creek Valley, a somewhat flat area southwest of Denver in the foothills of the mountains. Among those few who did were Joseph and William Hodgson, attracted by the area's agricultural potential. After assessing the area's suitability for irrigation, these pioneering brothers built a fine stone home and tilled the soil. Over the next ten years, they worked with other settlers to create an extensive series of ditches from Bear Creek that allowed for more productive harvests.

Both coal mining and agriculture were poised for expansion when the Denver, South Park & Pacific Railway built through the valley in 1874. Over a narrow-gauge route linking Denver to Morrison, the South Park handled local freight and passengers as well as bituminous coal from the Mount Carbon Mine, a facility its trains reached on a spur near present-day Alameda Avenue. Despite the grandiose visions of its creators, this line remained a distinctly local operation. A proposed extension along the Bear Creek west of Morrison never materialized, and the South Park eventually turned its attention to building a more southerly route from the Denver area.

A more illustrious era of economic development began when noted businessman William Austin Loveland, his wife Miranda, and Charles Clark Welch platted a large subdivision several miles north of the rail line in

1889. These prominent Denver figures, deeply involved in Colorado mining and railroading, named the subdivision Lakewood for reasons that are not entirely clear to historians.

The success of their subdivision stimulated interest in building more rail lines. In 1891, the West End Street Railway Company established streetcar service along Sheridan Boulevard, the present-day boundary between Denver and Lakewood. That same year the Denver, Lakewood & Golden Railroad inaugurated service between the communities after which it had been named. In 1893, this standard-gauge operator extended its route beyond Golden to Tinsdale.

As it happened, all of these rail operators struggled with chronic financial adversity. The Denver, Lakewood & Golden suffered greatly from the panic of 1893, strong competition from other railroads, and from a severe flood in 1896 that damaged the extension to Tinsdale. The Sheridan Boulevard streetcar line had such little potential that it was abandoned after the Denver Tramway Company acquired the West End Street Railway in 1899. The South Park, meanwhile, came to be seen as a corporate weakling. Its operations were turned over to Denver, Leadville & Gunnison Railway

in 1889, which in turn was sold to the Colorado & Southern Railway in 1899.

In contrast, the market for real estate around the Lakewood subdivision performed well during the late 1890s and into the early twentieth century. Many fine homes, including one belonging to legendary westerner Molly Brown, emerged in spacious residential neighborhoods. The Jewish Consumptive Relief Society opened a large tuberculosis treatment center near the Denver, Lakewood & Golden that attracted both the afflicted and the healthy from great distances.

Such developments helped lay the groundwork for major improvements in rail service. The newly formed Denver & Intermountain Railway acquired the beleaguered Denver, Lakewood & Golden in 1904 and, after operating under steam power using several different names, finished electrifying its route in 1909. Renamed the Denver & Intermountain Railroad (D&IM) in 1910,

On a sunny day at Lakewood's Devinny Station, date unknown, passengers peer out the window of a Denver & Intermountain car headed for Denver (left), which had met a car destined for Golden. (Colorado Railroad Museum, courtesy of Kenton Forrest.)

At a highway crossing in Lakewood, rails partially covered with pavement reveal the status of the former Denver & Intermountain route, a dormant corridor preserved for potential light-rail service. (Photo by author.)

of the Moffat Filter Plant in Lakewood. The filter plant, vital to the expansion of metropolitan Denver, was supplied with water piped to the area through the Moffat Tunnel, owned by the Denver & Salt Lake Railroad (later Denver & Rio Grande Western). The Colorado & Southern line, however, benefitted little from the region's population growth and was abandoned in 1933.

Changing Times

All communities in the region felt the effects of World War II, but few were as profoundly changed by the global conflict as Lakewood, where the federal government began construction of a massive munitions and testing facility, the Denver Ordnance Plant, in early 1941.

By autumn of that same year, a carrier jointly owned by five railroad companies serving the Denver area—the Associated Railways—began operating a 1.6-mile branch, known as the Remaco Spur, to the armament complex. This nonelectrified line, built by the federal government, originated at the D&IM's Morningside shelter and was operated through a contract with the Remington Arms Company.

The Denver Ordnance Plant soon boasted nearly 200 structures and its own government-operated industrial railway. It expanded its employment to 6,000 and emerged as a critical supplier of armaments during the war. The sprawling complex generated a large amount of freight and passenger traffic, accelerated economic development, and was the unannounced destination of President Franklin D. Roosevelt, whose special train arrived for an inspection visit in 1943. The plant created so much automobile and truck traffic that Lakewood's Sixth Avenue was transformed into U.S. Highway 6. It was also the destination of a Tramway bus route operating from one of the D&IM passenger shelters.

As quickly as the Denver Ordnance Plant rose to become Lakewood's most dominant industrial institution, it fell into disuse after the war. The facility's closing dealt a severe blow to both Lakewood and the D&IM. In 1948, the former munitions plant became Denver Federal Center, a government office and storage facility. Two years later, Denver Tramway replaced its trolley cars operating down West Colfax Avenue with buses. Bereft of the passenger business and having a greatly diminished freight-hauling role, D&IM greatly scaled back, ending electric operations, abandoning its segment from Golden to Lakewood, and selling the surviving 6.5 miles

the carrier established itself as part of the Denver Tramway Corporation's regional system of trolley and interurban lines. Operating between Golden and the Interurban Loop in Denver—a service known as Tramway Route 84—the D&IM made frequent stops at Devinny, Morningside, Wide Acres, and several other passenger shelters near the Lakewood subdivison. By 1923, the carrier relied exclusively on electric motive power for both freight and passenger service.

The D&IM remained an important Tramway route during the Great Depression, providing hourly service at certain times of the day and serving a variety of freight customers, including the Works Progress Administration, which made a large investment in the construction of route between Denver and the Federal Center to the Associated Railways in 1953.

The arrival of throngs of professionals attracted by the prospect of easy commutes to Denver then accelerated Lakewood's transition into a residential- and service-oriented suburb. In the 1950s, many stores and restaurants opened along West Colfax Avenue and a large shopping center was built on the grounds of the former tuberculosis sanatorium. While the community had long been called Lakewood, it formally adopted this name in 1959.

By the mid-1960s, area residents were voicing concern that Denver would annex the area—an issue that ultimately spurred the incorporation of the City of Lakewood in 1969. Despite its status as Colorado's fourth largest city (Lakewood had nearly 90,000 inhabitants at its inception), freight shipments on its rail line dwindled to the point that trains generally ran only on Sundays, with the Federal Center being the most notable customer. Indicative of the economy's changing orientation, a local architect refurbished and lavishly redecorated the shopping center on the former sanatorium grounds in the early 1970s, calling it Casa Bonita and establishing it as a restaurant and tourist attraction.

The expansion of Lakewood over the next fifteen years provided few revenue opportunities for Associated Railways, which operated its last train from the Federal Center in October 1988. By the end of the following year, the handful of businesses that had used a team track on the eastern edge of town had ceased shipping by rail. When the Associated Railways abandoned the route in 1989, Lakewood had a population of more than 126,000, making it the largest city on an American rail line to lose all of its rail service. This event also apparently marked the first instance in modern times that the railroad industry terminated all service to an incorporated community on the mainland with a population of more than a hundred thousand.

Abandonment's Legacy

The local Daughters of the American Revolution chapter placed a commemorative plaque along the abandoned South Park line in 1989 to honor that railway's role in Lakewood's past. Other organizations focused on the more ambitious goal of bringing rail service back to

the community. Denver's Regional Transportation District (RTD) acquired the dormant Associated Railways (D&IM) route following its abandonment in 1989 and preserved it, with the tracks intact, as a prospective transit route. The agency then expanded its holdings by purchasing an additional 2 miles of track at the Federal Center.

Interest in using these tracks for transit service grew in 1994 when RTD opened the first light-rail route in the Denver area. This route, the Central Corridor Light Rail Line, operated along a north–south corridor several miles east of Lakewood. By the time Lakewood celebrated its twenty-fifth anniversary, planners were pushing for the construction of a light-rail branch to their community.

Impressed by the potential of such a branch, RTD selected Lakewood for its next rail extension in 1997. The agency envisioned Lakewood-bound trains operating along the Central Corridor line from Denver's Union Station to the Auraria Campus light-rail station, where the West Corridor would branch along the former D&IM. The RTD hoped to eventually extend the route (also called the Thirteenth Avenue Corridor due to its proximity to Lakewood's Thirteenth Avenue) to the Federal Center as well as the Cold Springs bus stop and parking facility. The RTD also left open the possibility of building a branch to the Jefferson County Government Building and downtown Golden.

Proponents soon learned that bringing an electrified transit line back to the community would require considerable persistence. Opposition by residents along the corridor, especially homeowners worried about noise, and parents whose children attended two nearby elementary schools, gradually stiffened. A further challenge arose as planners estimated the

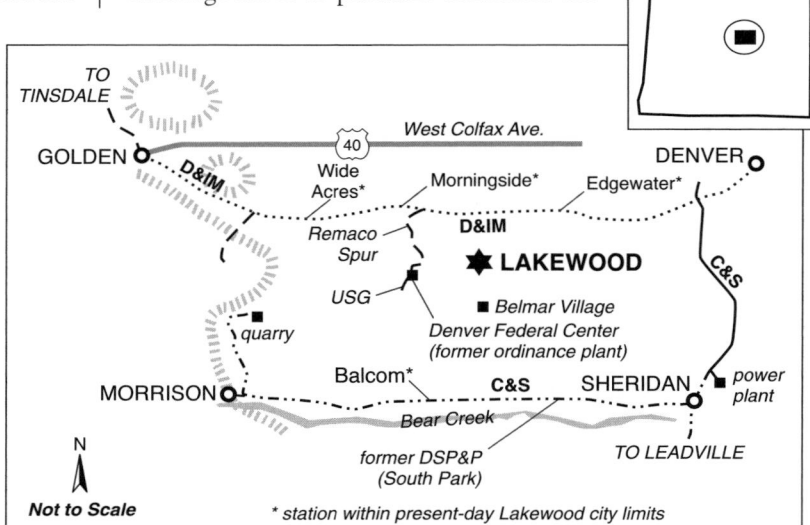

project's costs to be more than $250 million, a greater expenditure than initially anticipated. In 1997, voters in the region rejected a referendum to allow RTD to substantially increase its level of debt, greatly limiting its ability to create new routes.

The municipal government and a group of citizens called Transit West continued to push for construction through the turn of the century. Supported by a study showing that the corridor could generate 25,000 rides daily by 2020, these parties rejected suggestions that a new line should instead be built along West Colfax Avenue. As of this writing, the proposal to build the line is still part of a long-range agenda, but budget issues remain unresolved. The warning equipment at grade crossings throughout Lakewood has been left to deteriorate, and the rails at several of the street crossings have been removed or covered with pavement.

For several years after Lakewood's rail service ended, it was exceedingly rare for incorporated communities of more than 100,000 residents to lack an active railroad line. As the country underwent rapid deindustrialization and experienced migration to warm-weather areas, communities of similar size, such as Pasadena and Santa Rosa, California, also lost their service. Like many large suburbs without active railroads, Lakewood has considerably less manufacturing activity than cities typical of its size. Its relatively small industrial sector tends to focus on time-sensitive and high-value products amenable to shipment by truck.

Epilogue

Visitors will find Lakewood experimenting with new forms of urban development to compensate for the absence of a pedestrian-oriented downtown district. Adjacent to Lakewood's Civic Center, which has been the community's ceremonial center since 2000, is Belmar, a massive development with extensive residential and commercial components that now provide the equivalent of a traditional central business district. Some envision that residents of the neighborhoods created by the Belmar project will one day ride both the proposed RTD light-rail line and trolleys operating along Alameda Boulevard.

Lakewood's commitment to historic preservation is unusually strong for a community less than forty years old. The stone home of Hodgon brothers, portions of the former sanatorium grounds, and Casa Bonita are all listed on the National Register of Historic Places. Since America's bicentennial year, the Lakewood Heritage Center (formerly the Belmar Museum) has been a window to the community's past, boasting a diverse collection of edifices and artifacts, including the restored D&IM Wide Acres passenger shelter.

Travelers with an interest in railroad history will find that virtually nothing remains of the community's oldest rail line. Portions of this right-of-way (formerly the South Park) near U.S. Route 285 have been completely submerged under the reservoir created by the Mount Carbon Dam. The former D&IM tracks, on the other hand, seem conspicuous because of their survival. Although these tracks are covered with plant growth, debris, and other accretions of time, their presence fosters hope that electric trains will return to a corridor that some residents will always remember as Tramway Route 84.

For Further Study

SUGGESTED READINGS:

Forrest, Kenton, and Charles Albi. *Denver's Railroads: The Story of Union Station and Railroads of Denver.* Golden: Colorado Railroad Museum, 1981, 218–22.

Wilcox, P. K., ed. *Lakewood, Colorado: An Illustrated Biography.* Lakewood, Colo.: Lakewood 25th Birthday Commission, 1994, 11–23, 48–151.

OTHER PRINCIPAL REFERENCES:

Fletcher, Ken. *Centennial State Trolleys: The Life and Times of Colorado's Streetcars.* Golden: Colorado State Railroad Museum, 1995, 68, 82–83.

Hilton, George W., and John F. Due. *The Electric Interurban Railways in America.* Stanford: Stanford University Press, 1964, 380.

Ormes, Robert M. *Tracking Ghost Railroads in Colorado.* Colorado Springs, Colo.: Green Light Graphics, 1992, 14, 16.

HONOLULU, HAWAII (876,146)

Historic operators: Hawaiian Tramways; Honolulu Rapid Transit Company; Oahu Railway
and Land Co.; Pacific Heights Electric Railway
Last route abandoned: 1972
Notable reuse of right-of-way: Arterial highway

World War II brought with it a spectacular display of rail activity on the island of Oahu. Passenger trains departed Honolulu for Pearl Harbor as often as every 5 minutes, while freight trains assembled from a fleet of more than two dozen steam locomotives and a thousand cars operated nearly around the clock. In stark contrast, Honolulu today lacks rail service of any kind and is the largest city in the fifty states without an active route. Planners there have considered ambitious proposals for bringing back both trains and trolleys.

Historical Perspective

Honolulu, which means "sheltered harbor" in Hawaiian, was only a small village when Captain James Cook arrived on the neighboring island of Kauai in 1778. The community's inhabitants adhered to traditional Polynesian customs and remained largely separated from western influence until another British explorer, Captain William Brown, sailed into its harbor—the only natural one in the Hawaiian Islands—in 1794.

Brown's historic visit accelerated a process of cultural assimilation. After centuries of local rule by chiefs, the Hawaiian Islands were unified during the early nineteenth century under King Kamehameha, ruler of the island of Hawaii, who established a home in Honolulu in 1809. Over the next fifty years, the gradual expansion of trade, a flourishing whaling industry, and the

**OAHU
RAILWAY**

arrival of missionaries strengthened the community's ties to other countries. After King Kalakaua signed a reciprocity treaty with the United States in 1875, granting sugar duty-free status, the cultivation of sugar in the Hawaiian Islands grew spectacularly.

Oahu lagged behind the islands of Maui, Kauai, and Hawaii in the production of sugar cane until 1879, when the discovery of an artesian well brought abundant irrigation to the arid Ewa plain. Unfortunately, it was not possible to haul sugar efficiently from the plantation mills to docks in Honolulu without the construction of a rail line, which was an enormously capital-intensive proposition.

In 1886, businessman Benjamin Franklin Dillingham received a charter from King Kalakaua to build such a railroad. Dillingham was originally a ship's officer from New England who had been left behind many

113

A special OR&L train, destined for the navy yard at Pearl Harbor, prepares to depart the Honolulu station in 1945. Equipment shortages at the time necessitated placing self-propelled motorcars behind the train's locomotive. (Photo by Kent Cochrane, Bishop Museum.)

years earlier to recuperate from a fall from a horse. Now Dillingham set out to build a narrow-gauge line from Honolulu to Ewa. As his Oahu Railway & Land Company (OR&L) laid 3-foot-gauge track west from Honolulu, a more modest rail line, the London-owned Hawaiian Tramways, initiated transit service within the city. The Hawaiian Tramways' mule-drawn cars made their first trips down the city's streets in 1889.

Although Dillingham's OR&L had 20 miles of tracks in service by early the following year, political unrest in Hawaii delayed his efforts to expand the system. It was not until after Honolulu became the capital of the newly formed Hawaiian Republic in 1894 that construction resumed. Dillingham's steam railway finally reached Waianae, a community on the island's western coast, in 1895.

Dillingham built the OR&L amid a flurry of agricultural and industrial development that continued after the United States annexed the Hawaiian Islands in 1898. An extension of his railway to Kahuku that same year gave Dillingham a 71-mile line around the southern, western, and northern coastline of the island. Over these tracks, the Haleiwa Limited—the island's best-known excursion train—carried passengers to and from Dillingham's Haleiwa Hotel, a popular guesthouse near the end of the line.

The resources of Dillingham and his railway were no match for the bubonic plague, which broke out in Honolulu in 1899. Portions of the city were quarantined and operations were suspended on the easternmost 3 miles of the Oahu Railway until the disease was contained.

By 1900, Honolulu had a population of more than 39,000 and was in the midst of another development boom, creating a tremendous need for more housing and an improved streetcar system. With these dual objectives in mind, developer Charles Desky built the Pacific Heights Electric Railway that year to support a new housing complex he had created near downtown Honolulu. His line climbed to a breathtaking elevation of more than 900 feet and thrilled travelers on their way to a dance pavilion and scenic overlook at Pacific Heights. The following year, a more conventional streetcar operator, the

Honolulu Rapid Transit & Land Company, inaugurated service over city streets. By using electric power, this company soon captured much of the traffic that had previously moved on the mule-powered Hawaiian Tramways system.

Streetcar service remained important to Honolulu for decades, but the number of operators soon diminished to one. In 1903, the Rapid Transit Company acquired the struggling Tramways system and suspended the smaller company's operations. Before the end of the following year, the Pacific Heights Electric had also ended service, largely due to the failure of Desky's housing complex.

The circumstances facing Dillingham's OR&L were much more favorable. As tonnage rose, the carrier evolved into a more modern and industrial enterprise. Primarily a freight hauler, it moved vast amounts of refined sugar from six plantation mills along its coastal route. The railroad also generated substantial revenue serving an entirely new industry—the large-scale production of pineapples—developed by James D. Dole at the turn of the century high on Oahu's central plain. In 1906, OR&L ran a branch from Waipahu to Wahiawa principally to transport pineapples from the Dole (and later Del Monte) plantations to the canneries in Honolulu. This branch also hauled considerable tonnage for the U.S. Army, which operated its own military railroad on the island.

In 1908, as Oahu's economy blossomed, OR&L embarked upon a modernization program that included the construction of a fifteen-stall roundhouse near the Honolulu depot. The Rapid Transit Company also expanded to meet the rising demand. By 1913, the company had enlarged its system to nearly 20 miles of routes and reached almost all of the city's most prominent destinations, including Diamond Head and Kaimuki. Its Waikiki-bound cars brought residents and tourists to a resplendent beach, an aquarium, and a 1-mile horse racing track at Kapiolani Park. Its frequent service also opened up new residential areas, such as Manoa, for development.

At the same time, the dramatic expansion of trans-Pacific trade rendered Pearl Harbor (a port less than 10 miles west of Honolulu) of enormous strategic value to the United States. The port had only one major problem: a coral reef across the mouth limited access to shallow-draft vessels, such as native canoes. To eliminate this obstacle, the U.S. Navy blasted the reef and invested heavily in capital improvements. Soon, Pearl Harbor was a base for extensive naval activity—and vital to the protection of oceanic shipping lanes and military operations.

The rail lines of Oahu made enormous contributions to the island's economy well after Dillingham's death in 1918. Business was so strong during the early 1920s that the OR&L installed a second track between Honolulu and Waipahu and built a new station on King Street. The new station soon teemed with activity and allowed for convenient transfers between trains and streetcars. During its peak year of traffic in 1923, the streetcar system carried a staggering twenty-three million riders—the equivalent of more than 130 rides for every resident of Oahu. Trolleys were a popular means of reaching football and baseball games at Honolulu Stadium and contributed to the city's image as an international business and cultural center.

Nothing is left of the platforms and track, but the former OR&L depot in Honolulu stands otherwise little changed from the railroad's glory years. The city's skyline attests to the dramatic increases in population since the last train departed. (Photo by author.)

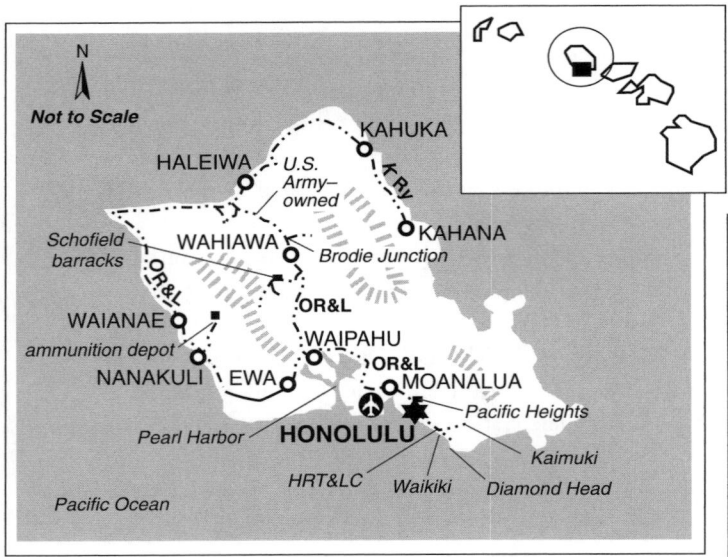

Changing Times

The vast distance separating Honolulu from the U.S. mainland did not shelter its rail service providers from the escalating competition of more flexible modes of transportation. To the contrary, the streetcar operator suffered during the mid-1920s from a profusion of jitneys operating on parallel routes. The OR&L also experienced a sharp decline in ridership and turned to self-propelled motorcars in 1927 to lower the costs of passenger service. Circumstances deteriorated further during the Great Depression, when Dole's Hawaiian Pineapple Company grew more reliant on trucks.

By the close of 1937, the Rapid Transit Company had terminated streetcar service over much of the system, including the once popular route to Diamond Head, over which the company had substituted trolley-bus service. Neither the remaining streetcar service nor the OR&L may have survived the decade were it not for the burgeoning transportation demands of the U.S. military, which stationed ever-rising numbers of troops at Pearl Harbor and Schofield Barracks in Wahiawa.

In the summer of 1941, streetcar service finally ground to a halt. The Rapid Transit Company decorated its last car in commemoration of the occasion. The company replaced its streetcars with trolley coaches and diesel and gasoline buses and by early autumn had pulled up some of its tracks.

The demise of streetcar service took on added significance several months later when Japan bombed Pearl Harbor, killing more than 2,000 men and sinking or

damaging nineteen vessels. As America mobilized for war, OR&L's freight and passenger traffic rose swiftly. The steam railroad instituted around-the-clock operations, and during peak travel times, commuter trains between Honolulu and Pearl Harbor ran every 5 minutes. Thousands of naval personnel relied on these regularly scheduled services as well as troop trains operating between Pearl Harbor and Schofield Barracks. Many also rode special runs to the island's beaches and other leisure destinations.

The U.S. Army considered the threat of another Japanese attack serious enough to warrant the construction of a branch line from an interior point (Brodie Junction) to the island's northern coast near Waialua. This route, completed in 1942, provided the military with greater flexibility in the event of another enemy bombing. Some residents regretted the demise of Honolulu's streetcars, but many of the powerful electric motors that had been salvaged from these cars were used to support the war effort. In 1943, the military employed them to right and stabilize the sunken battleship *Oklahoma* by using a complex system of cables.

By 1944, OR&L owned 26 locomotives, including a pair of diesels, as well as 83 passenger cars and more than 1,000 freight cars. The railway's passenger boardings surged as the war raged over the Pacific but plummeted after Japan's surrender the following year. In the spring of 1946, a tsunami (often erroneously called a tidal wave) destroyed a portion of the main line. Although the railway made repairs, the combined effects of a sharp rise in labor costs and a precipitous drop in military traffic were blows from which it could not recover.

In the autumn of 1946, company president Walter F. Dillingham (son of Benjamin Dillingham) announced that OR&L, along with several plantations, had plans to create a trucking company to haul agricultural products. The following year, the company, by now saddled with deteriorating track and worn-out equipment, applied to abandon all of its system except for a 3-mile segment from Honolulu to Moanalua and various spurs in the Honolulu area, which it planned to use as a terminal railroad. After receiving the necessary approval, the carrier ended service west of Moanalua by the end of the year. It then turned the portion from Pearl Harbor to Nanakuli—tracks serving a major ammunition facility—over to the U.S. Navy.

By the time the Rapid Transit Company phased out trolley coach operations in 1957, Honolulu bore little resemblance to the city once so abundantly served by rail.

Soon after Hawaii became the fiftieth state in 1959, the city grew to more than 250,000 residents, and the introduction of jet service by United Air Lines allowed multitudes of travelers to arrive from the mainland with unprecedented ease. A lawsuit settled in 1961 established that abandoned portions of the OR&L had reverted to the state government, thereby allowing conversion of the right-of-way near the airport into the H-1 highway.

As part of a reorganization in 1961, the surviving portions of the OR&L became the Oahu Railway & Terminal Warehouse Company, a private switching line that conveyed pineapples arriving by barge to canneries operated by Libby, McNeill & Libby Cannery and other California canneries in the Honolulu area. The navy, meanwhile, hauled a considerable amount of freight over the Nanakuli–Pearl Harbor segment to support military operations during the Vietnam War. In 1968, however, its rail operations ended.

The number of tourists visiting Honolulu surpassed a million annually by 1970, but the introduction of jumbo jet service to the city's airport that year pushed Hawaii's travel industry into an entirely new realm. Recognizing that remnants of the state's railroads were being gradually swept away, citizens organized the Hawaiian Railway Society in 1970 to promote railroad preservation. The timing was fortuitous, for the terminal railway suspended its harbor operations (which had been supported by two switch engines) in 1971 and abandoned its entire route the following year, leaving the island without an active railroad.

Abandonment's Legacy

Soon after the terminal railway ceased operating, members of the railway society and other residents of the state intensified their efforts to commemorate OR&L's heritage. In 1975, they succeeded in having the long-dormant Nanakuli–Pearl Harbor segment and several other remnants of the bygone railway listed on the National Register of Historic Places. After these segments were deeded to the state four years later, the railway society built a small yard at Ewa to allow it to refurbish several locomotives and rolling stock for an excursion railway.

As vacationers from Japan and other countries arrived in record numbers, the population of the Honolulu metropolitan area rose to more than 800,000. By the mid-1990s, the construction of many tall buildings, including the thirty-story First Hawaiian Bank and four others at least 400 feet tall, gave the community a distinctly cosmopolitan feel. A century after the first railway opened, the city once again found itself pondering the benefits of a rail transit system.

Unlike the modest efforts to create a mule-car line more than a century earlier, Honolulu now sought to use state-of-the-art technology. Consultants prepared planning and feasibility studies for a fully automated system that would stretch more than 15 miles, equipped with dual lanes and twenty-three stations. However, the city council did not approve the tax initiatives necessary to fund the project.

As the twentieth century drew to a close, policymakers shifted their attention to a proposal to rebuild the OR&L westward from Pearl Harbor to the island's western shoreline. This initiative, intended to serve both commuters and tourists, eventually fell out of favor among planners and has, at least for the present, been dropped from consideration.

Epilogue

Only a fraction of visitors to Honolulu are likely aware of the colorful train and trolley eras that preceded their arrival. It is noteworthy, however, that many tourists use buses resembling streetcars that operate over virtually the same route as trolleys did a hundred years ago. Those following the bygone routes of the OR&L will find several miles of track along the west coast of Oahu, mere vestiges of a narrow-gauge system that once encompassed 160 miles of track. This segment now lies dormant, relieved of its military role and partially shrouded in debris and vegetation. The Honolulu depot (envisioned one day to become a railroad museum) is today used as an office for social service agencies.

At Ewa, the railway society operates excursion trains, powered by two Whitcomb diesels, over approximately half of the 12-mile stretch formerly used by the U.S. Navy. Those searching for evidence of the streetcar system will find little more than a restored streetcar shelter at Kapiolani Park. When highway crews periodically strip away the surface of Kalakaua Avenue in Waikiki to apply a fresh layer of asphalt, the track momentary becomes visible, providing a glimpse of a system that remained in service until only a few months before the bombing of Pearl Harbor pushed the country into the darkness of war.

For Further Study

SUGGESTED READINGS:

Best, Gerald M. *Railroads of Hawaii: Narrow and Standard Gauge Common Carriers.* San Marino, Calif.: Golden West Books, 1978, 53–109.

Simpson, MacKinnon, and John Brizdle. *Streetcar Days in Honolulu: Breezing Through Paradise.* Honolulu: J.L.B. Press, 2000, 9–153.

Simpson, MacKinnon, and James Chiddix. *Steaming Through the Cane: The Story of Oahu Railway.* Honolulu: Sugar Cane Press, 2003.

OTHER PRINCIPAL REFERENCES:

Cochrane, Kent W. "The Oahu Railway & Land Company." *Trains* 7, no. 3 (March 1947): 26–37.

Hilton, George W. *American Narrow Gauge Railroads.* Stanford: Stanford University Press, 1990, 380– 81.

Kyper, Frank. "Hawaii Railroads Today." *Railfan & Railroad* 3, no. 3 (March 2002): 42–47.

Yardley, Paul T. *Millstone and Milestones: The Career of B. F. Dillingham: 1844–1918.* Honolulu: University of Hawaii Press, 1981.

AVERY, IDAHO (125)

Historic operator: Chicago, Milwaukee, St. Paul & Pacific Railroad
Last route abandoned: 1980
Notable reuse of right-of-way: Milwaukee Road Historic District

Of the many towns west of the Continental Divide that lack rail service today, perhaps none was more important to transcontinental movements seventy years ago than Avery, Idaho. At the western end of more than 400 miles of electrified main line, Avery existed almost solely to support the Chicago, Milwaukee, St. Paul & Pacific Railroad ("Milwaukee Road"). Former passengers of the Olympian Hiawatha who now return to northern Idaho will find this community a mere shadow of the sprawling railroad town they remember.

Historical Perspective

Sam "49" Williams was the first to settle in the valley where the North Fork of the St. Joe River flows into the river's main branch. An experienced frontiersman who earned his nickname during the California gold rush, Williams laid claim to a large parcel of land in 1894. After clearing a small portion of his property, he planted a garden, grew hay, and floated freshly cut logs down the river.

The construction of a ranger station in 1905 attracted others to the valley, including forest ranger Ralph Debitt, whose wife, Jessie, established the region's first post office. Although the facility was officially named Pinchot in recognition of Gifford Pinchot, the founder of the U.S. Forest Service, some people still referred to the settlement as 49 City in honor of Williams, or North Fork City due to the proximity of the river branch.

More than 1,000 miles away, the Chicago, Milwaukee & St. Paul Railway, popularly called the St. Paul Road, studied the possibility of building a route to Puget Sound. The Chicago-based carrier was eager to expand its vast system of routes in the upper Great Plains into the Pacific Northwest, a market dominated by the Great Northern and the Northern Pacific at the time. Unfortunately, these entrenched carriers already occupied the most desirable corridors, greatly limiting the St. Paul Road's alternatives. Nevertheless, the company rose to the challenge and reaffirmed its commitment to building a line that would cross several formidable mountain ranges, including the Belts, Rockies, Bitterroots, Saddles, and Cascades, with an ultimate destination of Tacoma, Washington.

After considerable research, the St. Paul settled upon an alignment that would follow the St. Joe River through much of Idaho and thus pass through William's claim at the mouth

Avery's yard along the Little Joe River is bustling on this winter day in 1969. Within six years, however, the Milwaukee Road would de-electrify its route across the Continental Divide and relocate the division point to St. Maries, delivering a severe blow to the local economy. (Courtesy of the Museum of North Idaho.)

of the North Fork. In 1906, various subsidiaries of the railway began working on the new route. The segment between the Idaho-Montana state line and the St. Joe River was an especially ambitious undertaking that would become the most expensive stretch of railroad ever built in the United States up until that time. It required the opening of seventeen tunnels, the most magnificent being the 1.7-mile St. Paul Pass (Taft) Tunnel across the state line. Operating trains across this mountainous region also required large investments in trestles and bridges. East of North Fork City, the Clear Creek and Kelly Creek trestles elevated the tracks more than 200 feet above these streams. This portion of the railway was an awe-inspiring manifestation of the carrier's willingness to spare no expense to reach Puget Sound.

The completion of the route immeasurably changed life along the St. Joe River. In 1908, the same year the

legendary Sam Williams died, the first trains reached the community that had grown around his claim. In 1909, a subsidiary of the St. Paul Road working in Montana drove the final spike to complete the Pacific Coast Extension—the last transcontinental line opened in the United States.

Linking the shores of Lake Michigan to Puget Sound, the St. Paul Road was now among the country's largest railroad companies. The carrier designated North Fork (Pinchot) a division point and thus established it as a base for many well-paying jobs. Railroad men and their families arrived from great distances to supply their labor. The depot, equipped with an eatery and telegraph office, was open around the clock. A mercantile store, the 49 Saloon, and the Mountain Park Hotel were also anchors of Avery's emerging downtown.

A few years earlier, William Rockefeller, a director of the St. Paul Road and a brother of John D. Rockefeller, had celebrated the birth of a grandson, Avery Rockefeller. In 1910, the community, including the post office, was renamed in honor of the child. Establishing major railroad facilities in such a remote area, however, was fraught with problems. The community lacked good roads to neighboring towns and suffered from periodic mud slides. The railway's need for workers quickly outstripped the land available for housing, forcing some residents to live in shanties on the nearby slopes. A forest fire in 1910 forced the evacuation of the townspeople by train and destroyed sixteen of the railway's viaducts.

These problems were not entirely unanticipated by the St. Paul Road, which quickly repaired the damage to its rail line and invested heavily in new services. In 1911, it instituted through passenger service to the West Coast by placing a local train, the Columbian, and a finely appointed express train, the Olympian, into service. Operating between Chicago and Tacoma, these trains brought many travelers through town, some of whom disembarked to stay at the newly built Hotel Idaho. Although the older Mountain Park Hotel burned in 1912, the two-story Hotel Idaho remained a source of great municipal pride.

The difficulty of operating a first-class railroad over the Bitterroots and other mountain ranges, however, was another matter. Although special locomotives with different gears and traction systems were kept on hand, this was hardly an acceptable long-term solution. In 1914, two years after the St. Paul absorbed into its system the Chicago, Milwaukee & Puget Sound Railway, the subsidiary operating the transcontinental line, it embarked on an ambitious effort to electrify the segment between Avery and Harlowton, Montana, a distance of 440 miles.

The completion of this project in late 1916 was another milestone in the company's history and pushed Avery's railroad era into its most illustrious phase. The community became a transfer point between electric locomotives operating over the carrier's Rocky Mountain Division to Harlowton and steam locomotives operating over the Coast Division to Tacoma. The electrification project allowed the carrier to reduce its local workforce, but Avery maintained a population of around 1,000. Encouraged by the success of the project, the St. Paul Road set out to electrify the westernmost 209 miles of the Coast Division from Othello to Tacoma, Washington, a project completed in 1919. One of the most memorable moments in this phase of Avery's history took place in 1924, when President Warren Harding rode into town in the cab of an electric locomotive, describing his trip as "the most delightful ride I have ever known."

Changing Times

Although the Pacific Coast Extension was an engineering marvel, the enormous costs of its construction, electrification, and operation weakened the St. Paul. The carrier entered bankruptcy in 1925 and emerged from reorganization as the Chicago, Milwaukee, St. Paul & Pacific Railroad in 1928. The Milwaukee Road fared poorly in competition with other railroads, declared bankruptcy in 1935, and then successfully reorganized. In spite of its inherent weaknesses, the company deepened its imprint on the communities of the St. Joe valley. The carrier provided stable employment during the Great Depression and supported the creation of the local Civilian Conservation Corps camps. After America was pulled into World War II, it shouldered a substantial expansion of traffic and operated many special trains, including one in 1944 for presidential candidate Harry S. Truman, who made a speech in Avery while waiting for a locomotive change.

The high costs of maintaining the Pacific Coast Extension became increasingly problematic after the war. Even so, the Milwaukee Road boldly entered the modern era two years later by replacing the Olympian with the Olympian Hiawatha, a streamlined train operating between Chicago's Union Station and Tacoma. This sleek train was the pride of the small communities it served and affirmed the company's commitment to serving the Pacific Northwest. Through the late 1940s, the Milwaukee Road continued to employ some 150 workers at its Avery roundhouse and yards. In 1950, it took

As this photograph attests, Avery's character is significantly different now that rail service has ended along the upper St. Joe River. Little more than the depot (center) and a handful of other buildings survive. (Photo by author.)

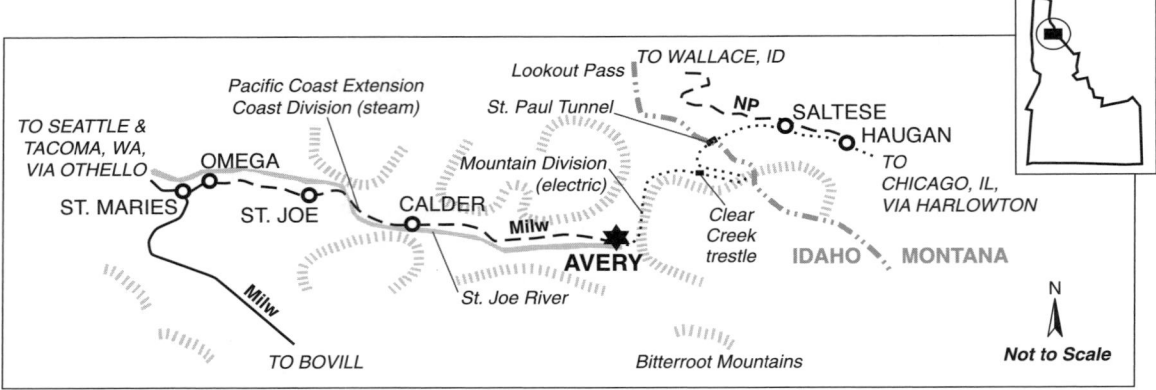

delivery of modern Little Joe electric locomotives and, in 1952, introduced Superdome cars to the Hiawatha.

Like the railroad upon which it depended, however, Avery's economy was starting to crumble. Patronage on passenger trains dwindled as travelers opted for airlines, highways, and faster trains, such as the Great Northern's Empire Builder and the Northern Pacific's North Coast Limited. Several years after the Columbian made its final run in 1955, the Milwaukee Road completed its transition from steam to diesel power on the route, further reducing its needs for local workers. In 1959, Avery's car shop closed, and in 1961, local passenger service ended with the cancellation of the Olympian Hiawatha.

The demise of the Hiawatha foreshadowed further losses. Avery Mercantile, one of the community's best-known historic businesses, subsequently closed, leaving the downtown almost devoid of retail activity. By the late 1960s, the Milwaukee Road operated only a few daily trains in each direction through town. The carrier deferred maintenance on its tracks and facilities, adding to the town's increasingly drab and neglected appearance. By the early 1970s, Avery had dwindled to a few hundred inhabitants, its last store had closed, and the long-vacant Hotel Idaho had collapsed.

When the railroad ended electric operations in 1974 and moved the division point to St. Maries, it stripped Avery of its last significant source of jobs and led to the closing of the depot restaurant, a popular gathering place called "the beanery." Train crews no longer stayed overnight in Avery before returning to Alberton, Montana, or Malden, Washington, the next crew-change points on the line. With the departure of the substation workers, yardmaster, and train crews, the community's economy slumped even further.

Over the next several years, the logging industry was only able to fill a part of the void left by the loss of railroad jobs. Recognizing that Avery was at a crossroads, current and former residents banded together to commemorate its historical role in western railroading. They formed a committee that worked to convert the depot—a large wooden structure that had been listed on the National Register of Historic Places—into the Avery Community Center. In 1978, hundreds of people, including town residents and former railroaders gathered to celebrate the inaugural Avery Day festivities.

As freight trains rolled precariously over the deteriorating tracks, passing through Avery without scheduled stops, railroad enthusiasts arrived to see the forlorn remnants of a legendary corridor. When the bankrupt Milwaukee Road received approval in March 1980 to abandon the portion of the extension west of Miles City, Montana, a storied chapter in American railroading drew to a close.

Abandonment's Legacy

The state government heard emotional pleas to save the route, but with the country then in the midst of a recession, public agencies lacked sufficient resources to embark on such a costly endeavor. In 1981, the Milwaukee Road sold a branch to Bovill and the portion of the main line west from Avery to Plummer Junction, Idaho, to the newly created St. Maries River Railroad, which pulled up the rails east of Omega (near St. Maries). The tracks between Avery and St. Regis, Montana, were sold for salvage in 1982. Avery's electrical substation and roundhouse were summarily demolished.

Not only was Avery left without a railroad, it had little hope of sharing in the state's economic recovery because it still lacked a paved road. Although mobility improved when 9 miles of the abandoned route (including seven tunnels) became part of a gravel road to Wallace, Idaho, the community still did not have a hard-surface road. Hope for new commercial and residential development did not arrive until the 1990s, when another portion of the rail-bed was widened and realigned for a two-lane road linking the town to Marble Creek. This improvement altered the right-of-way west of town beyond recognition but did not stimulate much investment.

As hikers took an interest in the abandoned route, the old Taft Tunnel across the Idaho-Montana state line became an unofficial tourist attraction. On parts of the corridor, motorized all-terrain vehicles trekked where Little Joes once rolled. In 1992, the U.S. Forest Service began exploring the possibility of using the portion of the right-of-way from Avery to western Montana (which it had purchased several years before) as a recreational trail and found support for this idea from an organization devoted to the preservation of the Taft Tunnel. Since many structures and tunnels along this segment had fallen into severe disrepair, the agency had little choice but to close the Taft Tunnel for safety reasons in 1993. The Forest Service closed much of the remaining segment east of the tunnel the following year. In 1996, a flood washed out the fill at Moss Creek.

Despite the corridor's gradual deterioration, the movement to create a trail continued unabated. Using both public and private funds, construction began in 1997, and by the middle of the following year, more than $1 million in federal money had been used to complete the first portions of the route of the Hiawatha Rail-Trail.

Avery benefited from the trail, but the new amenity was no panacea. The town discontinued the annual Avery Day celebration during the late 1990s, partially due to disagreements among its residents. A hotel-resort complex proposed by a developer did not materialize. Today, the opportunity to attract new businesses rests heavily on proposals to lengthen the trail, which will eventually extend 46 miles and encompass eleven tunnels and nine trestles.

Epilogue

Avery is a notable example of a community that has never recovered from its loss of several hundred railroad jobs. Its population has fallen by more than 80 percent since the height of the St. Paul Road's glory. The hardship it has faced is familiar among railroad division points that failed to diversify their economies before experiencing dramatic reductions in employment.

Today the community consists of little more than a tavern, a convenience store, a trail-oriented gift shop, a few dozen homes, and the depot, which serves as both a post office and small museum. The area around the depot—the Avery Milwaukee Road Historical District—and the old ranger station are listed on the National Register of Historic Places. A wayside signal found along the abandoned line adds a decorative element to the depot grounds. A trout pond dating back to the earliest days of the railroad is one of the community's most notable attractions.

Travelers unfamiliar with the heritage of the Pacific Coast Extension may find it surprising that travelers once arrived in this isolated village aboard a streamlined train from Chicago that crossed the mountains on a superbly maintained electrified route. Perhaps no other abandoned route in the West, save for the historic stretch once passing though Promontory, Utah, has generated such voluminous literature. Even though the Olympia Hiawatha made its last run more than forty years ago, the bygone Pacific Coast Extension appears destined to intrigue railroad enthusiasts for decades to come.

For Further Study

SUGGESTED READINGS:

Crowell, Sandra A., and David O. Asleson. *Up the Swiftwater: A Pictorial History of the Colorful Upper St. Joe River Country.* Coeur d'Alene: Museum of North Idaho, 1995, 31–72.

Johnson, Stanley W. *The Milwaukee Road in Idaho: A Guide to Sites and Locations.* Coeur d'Alene: Museum of North Idaho, 1997, 57–83.

OTHER PRINCIPAL REFERENCES:

Drury, George. *Historical Guide to North American Railroads.* Milwaukee, Wis.: Kalmbach Books, 1985, 108–12.

Johnson, Stanley W. *The Milwaukee Road Revised.* Moscow: University of Idaho Press, 1997, 29–49.

Sims, Don. "The Terminal at Avery." *Railroad Modeler* 4, no. 2 (Feb. 1974), 24–27.

Withers, Bob. *The President Travels by Train.* Lynchburg, Va.: TLC Publishing (1996), 100–11.

Wood, Charles R., and Dorothy M. Wood. *Milwaukee Road West.* Seattle: Superior Publishing, 1986, 25– 70

Zimmerman, Karl R. The *Milwaukee Road Under Wire.* New York: Quadrant Press, 1973, 8.

WALLACE, IDAHO (960)

Historic operators: Coeur d'Alene Railway and Navigational Co.; Northern Pacific Railway; Union Pacific Railroad
Last route abandoned: 1994
Notable reuses of right-of-way: Trail of the Coeur d'Alenes; Superfund site

    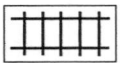

*W*allace offers a vivid illustration of the legal and political forces that can give railroad companies reason to prefer that their tracks be pulled up and replaced with recreational trails rather than preserved for future service—a phenomenon that has manifested itself in unpredictable ways along various lightly used routes. After the last train departed, planners contemplated ambitious proposals to prevent the abandonment of its only surviving route. Environmental issues, however, proved insurmountable.

Historical Perspective

Generations of Coeur d'Alene Indians traveled along the South Fork of the Coeur d'Alene River on their way to hunting grounds in Montana. Recognizing the value of the corridor to the U.S. government, Captain John Mullan prepared a survey for a road along the river in 1859. This road was used by many prospectors and settlers and became an important military route from Fort Walla Walla, Washington, to Fort Benton, Montana.

Miners and merchants took this route in large numbers after prospector Andrew Prichard twice discovered gold, first in 1878 near the village that would become Osburn and again in 1882 north of present-day Wallace. At the rural location along the river fork where several canyons converged, a settlement called Placer Center came into being. The inhabitants of the mining camp came to rely on the leadership of "Colonel"

William R. Wallace, who had not only founded the community but also served as its unofficial mayor. In 1885, the Colonel's wife, Lucy, who assumed the duties of postmistress, was informed that the postal service would not accept the name Placer Center. Over her husband's objections, Lucy submitted the name "Wallace," which the agency accepted.

Within a few years, Wallace had evolved into a community with some 500 residents, numerous businesses, and a strong identity. When the Coeur d'Alene Railway and Navigational Company opened a narrow-gauge route from the Old Mission Landing to Wallace in 1887, the Colonel commemorated the joyous occasion with a rousing speech. Although the carrier built east to the booming mining town of Mullan that year, its line remained disconnected from the rest of the region's rail system. Cargo hauled to the Old Mission Landing, including ore shipped in sacks, had to be transferred by hand onto steamboats and barges operating down the Coeur d'Alene River. After negotiating the river and crossing the lake of the same name, these vessels docked at Coeur d'Alene, where the cargo was conveyed to the Northern Pacific.

Such a complex arrangement, while certainly an improvement over wagon travel, was rendered largely obsolete by the 1889 arrival of Oregon-Washington Railroad and Navigation Company (OWR&N), a subsidiary of Union Pacific. This standard-gauge line, linking Wallace to Farmington, Washington, via Plummer, Idaho, eliminated the need for cumbersome marine transfers. Supported by branches extending north to Burke and Mullan, the route facilitated a dramatic expansion in silver mining. When Idaho achieved statehood in 1890, Wallace was its third largest city.

The arrival of a third railroad, the Northern Pacific, in 1891 raised expectations that Wallace would become a commercial center of considerable renown. This standard-gauge route originating in Desmet, Montana (a junction on its main line near Missoula) was a remarkable piece of engineering. Between Demset and Mullan, the route crossed mountainous terrain and boasted several magnificent trestles, including an S-shaped one near Lookout Pass that spanned 839 feet. West of Mullan, trains used the former narrow-gauge right-of-way, which Northern Pacific leased, widened to standard gauge, and later purchased. Northern Pacific also built branches from Wallace to mines at Burke and Sunset.

Such an extensive rail system allowed the Coeur d'Alene Mining District (part of the so-called Silver Valley) to join the ranks of America's premier mining areas. This system transported vast amounts of silver ore out of the valley and brought foodstuffs, coal, supplies, and materials used to build fine masonry edifices. One such structure, Wallace's Fuller House, came to be regarded as one of the finest hotels in Idaho, while another, the Lux Building, earned an unsavory reputation from the brothel that operated on its second floor.

Wallace sprawls throughout the Silver Valley in 1907. The train (lower right) is at the Union Pacific depot while the Northern Pacific tracks hug the nearby mountain. In later years, a massive Interstate 90 viaduct will partially bridge the railroad corridor and the site of the old Union Pacific roundhouse (visible in distance). (Barnard-Stockridge Collection, University of Idaho Library.)

Typical of silver-mining boomtowns of this era, the optimism gradually faded as unanticipated problems hampered silver production. Disagreements between laborers and mine owners repeatedly ended in violence— a problem compounded by a sharp fall in silver prices in 1893 that precipitated the temporary closing of nearly all of the mines. Worker unrest rose to such an extent that, in 1899, a band of miners hijacked a Northern Pacific train packed with more than a thousand men. Despite the risk of a collision, the hijackers loaded the train with explosives and forced the crew to travel over the OWR&N's route to Kellogg, where they blew up the Bunker Hill Concentrator. Seeking to quell the violence, authorities at one point detained 1,000 miners in "bull-pens"—wooden storehouses and warehouses converted into temporary prisons.

Fortunately for mining companies and their workers, another silver boom was around the corner. By the early 1900s, several new sources of silver ore, most notably the Gold Hunter Mine in Mullan, had proven to be spectacularly productive. Reflecting the valley's rising commercial status, Northern Pacific built a magnificent chateau-style depot near the center of Wallace that welcomed its first train in 1902. With the town's standard-gauge rail lines shouldering a heavy burden, the narrow-gauge route to Mission faded into obsolescence and was

entirely abandoned by the end of 1902.

President Theodore Roosevelt's appearance at the Northern Pacific station in 1903 was perhaps the high point in Wallace's railroad history. Seven years later, Wallace's railroads earned distinction by providing critical logistical support for rebuilding the community after another devastating fire. Even after motor vehicles became common, Northern Pacific's rail yards and roundhouse, as well as the OWR&N's engine house and machine shop, remained important sources of local jobs.

By the late 1920s, the Silver Valley had firmly established its reputation as the country's leader in silver production. In 1931, the Sunshine Mine near Kellogg experienced extraordinary success and, indeed, eventually produced more silver than the entire Comstock Lode district in Nevada. This mine and others relied on rail service to haul ore, machinery, and supplies, while the smelter in Kellogg processed large amounts of ore shipped to it from both inside and outside the region.

Changing Times

The communities of the Silver Valley did not experience devastation as severe as most other silver-mining districts during the Great Depression. Although the downturn did interrupt its prosperity, Wallace remained a major mining center with more than 3,500 permanent inhabitants. With lucrative ore deposits awaiting excavation, the Silver Valley's most productive years were yet to come.

By the mid-1930s, however, more modern methods of silver production and rising competition from trucks were taking a heavy toll on the railroads. Traffic fell to such an extent that Northern Pacific abandoned its branch to Burke in 1938 and ended its passenger service to the valley (provided by a daily train from Missoula) three years later. The remaining passenger train, a daily run on the Union Pacific (former OWR&N) between Spokane and Wallace, was a mainstay of valley life through the end of World War II. Business dropped so sharply after the war, however, that the carrier eliminated the train in 1957.

Railroad enthusiasts rekindled past glory while riding a special Northern Pacific excursion to town the following year. This heavily photographed streamliner was the final passenger train ever to cross the carrier's famed S-curved trestle

The impeccably maintained Northern Pacific depot, built in the chateau style, evokes Wallace's proud past in 1999. Union Pacific's tracks under the Interstate 90 bridge (center) will soon be removed and replaced with a trail. (Photo by author.)

east of Mullan, which was replaced with a switchback in 1963. The devolution of Wallace's railroads seemed destined to continue when attention turned to the impending construction of Interstate 90 through the valley during the mid-1960s.

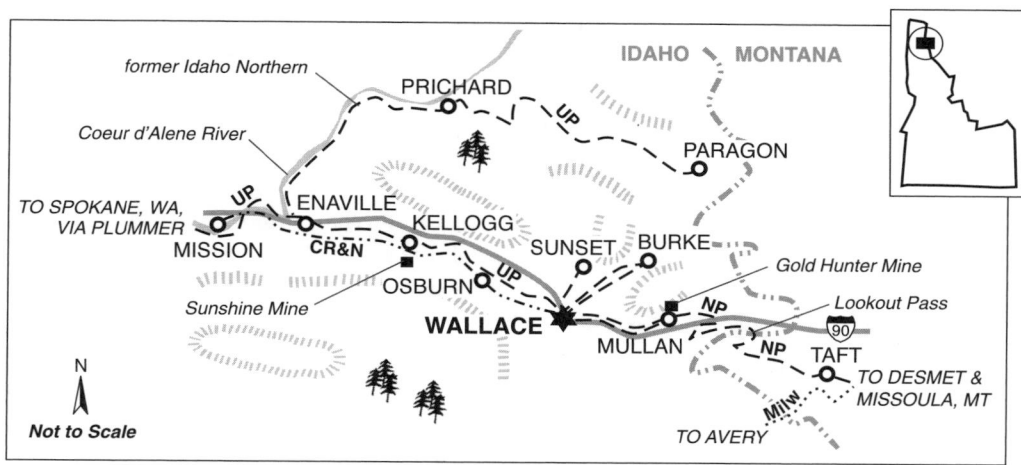

As officials made plans to build this superhighway, the townspeople voiced concerns about the potential loss of the community's historic buildings. Unfortunately, avoiding their destruction would require either building a massive highway bridge above the railroad line, boring a lengthy tunnel, or following an alignment along the hillsides—options that the state government determined to be prohibitively costly. Its solution was simply to have traffic passing through Wallace continue to use local streets, giving Wallace the dubious distinction of having the last stoplight on the entire I-90 corridor between Boston and Seattle.

Despite the bustle in downtown Wallace created by this cumbersome traffic arrangement, the local economy crumbled. In 1972 a fire at the Sunshine Mine killed ninety-one miners, bringing enormous suffering to the town. By 1974, production had once again rebounded, allowing the Sunshine to regain its title as the nation's largest producer of silver, but major cutbacks in mining employment loomed on the horizon.

As Wallace moved toward an uncertain future, the former Northern Pacific depot stood as a salient reminder of the town's proud past. During America's bicentennial year, this station became Wallace's first property listed on the National Register of Historic Places. In 1979, it provided a backdrop in the motion picture *Heaven's Gate*. The title of the movie notwithstanding, the future of Wallace and its rail lines appeared grim. In 1980, the Northern Pacific's successor, Burlington Northern, abandoned the 30-mile segment between Mullan and Haugan, Montana, while ceding the 8-mile segment between Mullan and Wallace to Union Pacific. In 1982, mining companies dramatically scaled back and the smelter in Kellogg closed. Within a few years, the number of mining jobs dropped from 6,000 to a mere 2,200, pushing local unemployment to more than 50 percent.

In response to the sharp decline in production, Union Pacific abandoned its branch from Wallace to Burke in 1985. Local officials faced the prospect of losing all rail service when Union Pacific moved forward with plans to eliminate its route from Mullan to Plummer (a junction in the western part of the state). Officials explored the possibility of purchasing this corridor and leasing it to a short-line railroad or creating an excursion railway offering scenic rides between Kellogg and Mullan. The popularity of the theatrical performances held in the Lux Building instilled optimism that an excursion railway might become a viable tourist attraction.

By the mid-1980s, traffic in downtown Wallace often seemed overwhelming due to the number of cars and trucks using I-90. Even so, a federal plan to eliminate the bottleneck on this divided highway by building the "Wallace Viaduct"—a 1,700-foot concrete expressway bridge—was seen as a mixed blessing. Officials feared that the enormous steel-and-concrete bridge would divert traffic away from local businesses and tourist development.

The state government covered the cost of moving the Northern Pacific depot across the river in 1986 to make way for the viaduct, an event of such historic significance it gave rise to the community's annual Depot Days celebration. Two years later, work on the structure began. Built directly above the Union Pacific tracks, this emerging bridge cast a shadow, both literally and figuratively, over the occasional trains passing below. Creating the structure necessitated the relocation of the Union Pacific yard, a minor realignment of its track, and the demolition of the carrier's depot. In 1991, after several years of work, officials commemorated the completion of the Wallace Viaduct and ceremoniously buried the "last stoplight."

Although the government had gone to considerable expense to make accommodations for rail service, Union Pacific now saw little revenue potential in the Silver Valley. As the carrier disclosed plans to abandon the 72-mile branch from Plummer to Mullan, local leaders joined the governor, two senators, and federal officials in a high-profile effort to preserve the line. A local development corporation conducted a survey showing that most residents supported the idea of creating an excursion railway. Officials could not, however, reach an agreement with Union Pacific, which had serious concerns about the potential financial liability created by environmental contamination along the right-of-way.

Despite their inability to save the railroad, the townspeople extolled the Union Pacific's time-honored place in the valley. Hundreds of citizens, many dressed in tuxedos and historic costumes, gathered in 1993 for a festival and melodrama staged next to the tracks as the last freight train prepared to leave town. Union Pacific abandoned the 72-mile segment the following year.

Abandonment's Legacy

The corridor had been formally abandoned for only a brief period when a work crew covered the tracks at the highway crossings with asphalt. A short time later, a flood rendered another portion of the route inoperable. The push to create an excursion railway continued, but generations of ore shipments had left traces of lead residue in the rail ballast. Although this residue was in a form not normally hazardous to human health, federal officials nonetheless decided (arbitrarily, in the opinion of some in Wallace) to include the rail-bed in a larger Superfund designation. This decision rendered an excursion railway unfeasible unless some of the tracks were temporarily pulled up to clean the ballast. This raised the costs of reactivation to at least $1.75 million.

As officials grappled with these environmental issues, public sentiment about the right-of-way began to change. The Mullan Pass–Lookout Pass Loop, a popular trail fashioned from portions of the former Northern Pacific route east of Mullan, generated interest in building an extension over the dormant Union Pacific line through Wallace. In support of this idea, the state and the Coeur d'Alene Tribe reached an agreement with Union Pacific giving the carrier the responsibility for capping and removing all contaminated materials and converting the railroad embankment from Plummer to Wallace into a recreational path. Planners determined that the carrier could obviate the need for extensive right-of-way cleanup by sealing the lead residue beneath a layer of asphalt. Eager to minimize its liability for environmental mitigation, Union Pacific considered this its best option.

As efforts to create the recreation path moved forward in 2000, salvage workers removed the tracks, saddening those who clung to the notion that the excursion railway might still become a reality. In 2003, officials opened portions of the Trail of the Coeur d'Alene from Mullan to Harrison (near Plummer). An unpaved extension from Harrison to Plummer, administered by the Coeur d'Alene Tribe, will eventually utilize the long railroad bridge and trestle over Coeur d'Alene Lake.

Epilogue

Travelers who visit Wallace will find that a variety of attractions, including the Wallace Mining Museum and depot, celebrate its hardworking past. The station is now the home of the Northern Pacific Depot Railroad Museum and remains the site of the annual Depot Days festival. Inside the museum, a large glass map of the Northern Pacific Railway offers a striking visual perspective of its historic system of routes. The Lux Building still hosts theatrical performances, and the entire city of Wallace is on the National Register of Historic Places.

Longtime residents take considerable pride in the fact that the Silver Valley produced more silver bullion over a century-long period than any other mining area in the world. The legendary Sunshine Mine closed in 2001, but the Lucky Friday and Galena mines carry on some of the industrial traditions of the past. Even today, the Silver Valley remains a major supplier of precious metals. Production at mines in the region is near 70 percent what it had been at its zenith. Gone, however, are the rail lines that supported one of the greatest mining booms in the history of the American West.

For Further Study

SUGGESTED READINGS:
Fahey, John. *Inland Empire: D.C. Corbin and Spokane.* Seattle: University of Washington Press, 1965, 44–47.

Wood, John V. *Railroads Through the Coeur d'Alenes.* Caldwell, Idaho: Caxton Printers, 1983, 13–169.

OTHER PRINCIPAL REFERENCES:
Asay, Jeff. *Union Pacific Northwest: The Oregon-Washington Railroad & Navigation Company.* Edmonds, Wash.: Pacific Fast Mail, 1991, 49, 55, 61–62, 151, 300.

Dunsmore, Robert. *Historic Wallace, Idaho.* Wallace, Idaho: Wallace Chamber of Commerce, 1998, 17–18.

Hilton, George W. *American Narrow Gauge Railroads.* Stanford: Stanford University Press, 1990, 382–83.

Renz, Louis Tuck. *The History of the Northern Pacific Railroad.* Fairfield, Wash.: Ye Galleon Press, 1980, 151–53

Silver Valley Economic Development Corporation. *Gold Strikes and Silver Lining.* Wallace, Idaho: Silver Valley Economic Development Corporation, 1995, 3–7, 46–56.

Wood, Charles R. *The Northern Pacific: Main Street of the Northwest.* Seattle: Superior Publishing, 1996, 120, 132.

Historic operators: Aurora, Elgin & Fox River Electric Railway; Chicago & North Western Railway
Last route abandoned: 1983
Notable reuse of right-of-way: Fox River Trail

A century ago, hundreds of workers traveled along Illinois' Fox River to the factories and foundries of Carpentersville. Arriving on both the Chicago & North Western Railway and one of the nation's first interurbans, these skilled laborers supported a manufacturing complex renowned for its decorative iron and steel products. Eventually, Carpentersville lost its interurban, most of its heavy industry, and its only railroad, rendering it the largest community in Illinois without an active route.

Historical Perspective

Pioneers Charles and Daniel Carpenter were heading west from Massachusetts in 1837 when the flooding waters of the Fox River interrupted their journey. After assessing their options, these resourceful travelers and their families set up camp, built a log cabin, and endured a difficult winter. Although Daniel and his family headed downriver to Aurora a short time later, Charles remained at this remote location, raising his family and helping to establish the community of Carpenters' Grove. Early life in the village revolved around a flour mill and a sawmill built on the river around 1846.

Daniel Carpenter nurtured the leadership skills of his son, Angelo, who developed a strong business acumen. This talented descendant rose to a position of local prominence after opening the first store in Carpenters' Grove at the age of twenty-three. He then established a textile company that manufactured flannel and acquired the local Oatman Dam, giving

him control over the river's water. Angelo also bought the flour mill, built the town's first two-story building, and constructed its first bridge across the river. He and his wife, Mary, generously shared their wealth with the townspeople and contributed to the social and cultural climate of the community, which was renamed Carpentersville in 1851.

When the Fox River Valley Railroad built north from Elgin to Dundee in late 1854, it appeared to be only a matter a time before its trains reached Carpentersville. However, when the carrier built an extension early the following year, it bypassed the community by laying tracks in nearly a straight line to Algonquin. The enterprising Angelo Carpenter made the best of this situation by transporting goods on horse-drawn carts to and from the rail yard in Dundee, approximately a mile away.

Carpenter acquired a small reaper works in town in 1864 and transformed it into the Illinois Iron & Bolt Company. Through his leadership, this local manufacturer rose to the region's industrial forefront as an important producer of flatirons, garden vases, pumps, and decorative ironwork. By the time Carpentersville's first post office opened four years later, the need for rail service had become acute.

A man of deep moral conviction, Carpenter worked to improve the plight of the common man as a member of the Illinois House of Representatives, and he never waivered in his commitment to bring a railroad to town. In the late 1870s, Carpenter finally convinced the Fox River Valley's successor, the Elgin & State Line Railroad, to relocate its main line through the center of the community by offering financial support and donating some of the right-of-way. He also agreed to pay for a railroad bridge across the river for a spur to the Iron & Bolt Company.

The Elgin & State Line completed its line along the east bank of the river (as well as the spur) in 1878, making Carpentersville a latecomer among the region's railroad towns. The carrier built an attractive depot adorned with gingerbread decoration and abandoned most of the original route between Dundee and Algonquin. Absorbed into the Chicago & North Western Railway (North Western) in 1883, the line generated extensive passenger traffic serving growing numbers of city dwellers spending weekends and holidays in Lake Geneva, a popular Wisconsin resort at the end of the line. Still more vacation-going Chicagoans rode these rails after the North Western built an extension from Lake Geneva to Williams Bay in 1888.

The North Western's primary role in Carpentersville was moving freight. Several local businesses, including the Iron & Bolt Company, a door and sash factory, and the Star Manufacturing Company, which produced farm implements, depended heavily on its trains. Nevertheless, by the early 1890s, the need for improved passenger service could no longer be ignored.

One of the nation's first interurban railways partially filled this need by opening a route along the river's west bank in 1896. Operated by the Elgin, Aurora and Southern Traction Company, this rail line crossed the Fox River on Main Street and terminated near the North Western depot. The interurban carried many workers employed at foundries in Carpentersville and Dundee as well as Elgin's famous watch factories. The carrier's services were sufficiently well patronized that there was speculation it would extend its route north to Lake Geneva. Although this extension was not to be, the interurban entered the fold of the Aurora, Elgin & Chicago Railroad in 1906. The new owner—the "Roarin' Elgin"—assimilated the line into a large system of electrified routes extending from Chicago to the Fox River valley.

Several men stand attentively at the Carpentersville station as a Chicago & North Western train approaches in 1908. Note the decorative ironwork on this Victorian-inspired depot, which calls to mind the work of the local Illinois Iron & Bolt Company. (Collection of Arthur Peterson.)

The Old Trestle in Carpentersville, once part of a spur serving industry on the west side of the Fox River, glows in the midday sun in 2000. (Photo by author.)

The interurban and steam railroad remained vital to Carpentersville's economy when the iron and bolt producer consolidated with Star Manufacturing in 1912, creating an industrial complex employing some 2,000 workers. Although the interurban handled a larger number of commuters traveling between the valley's industrial cities, the North Western offered townspeople the benefit of direct service to and from Chicago. Passengers traveling on its steam trains to the Windy City ended their journey at a newly completed terminal on Madison Street heralded as the finest in the city.

Changing Times

Circumstances in Carpentersville changed in unfavorable and unanticipated ways as other metal-fabricating centers expanded during the late 1910s. In only twenty years, the community relinquished most of its industrial importance, its trolley service, and all of its passenger trains.

Several business firms moved elsewhere during the 1920s, and the fortunes of those that remained fell sharply during the Great Depression. Struggling with a precipitous traffic downturn, the North Western eliminated one of the two passenger trains it operated in each direction between West Chicago and Williams Bay in 1931; the remaining train stopped operating south of Crystal Lake early the following year.

The electric railway emerged from receivership as the Fox River Division of the Aurora, Elgin & Fox River Electric Company but continued to suffer from the growing popularity of other forms of transportation. It terminated operations north of Elgin in 1932, rendering Carpentersville one of the first villages of its size in the metropolitan Chicago area to lose its rail passenger service. Any chance that the interurban would resume local service ended the following year when a tornado damaged its dormant route, culminating in this line's abandonment.

Carpentersville surrendered more of its industry during the late 1930s and benefited comparatively little from the revival in manufacturing that rejuvenated other communities during World War II. After the war, municipal attention turned to an immense residential development on the east side of town called Meadowdale. On more than 2,600 acres of newly annexed land, Meadowdale's sprawling environs soon encompassed several thousand prefabricated homes and a large shopping mall.

The new housing development offered low-cost homes to throngs of middle-income residents, including families of returning veterans and city dwellers fleeing Chicago's crowded neighborhoods. The completion of the Northwest Tollway from O'Hare International Airport to Rockford in 1958 stimulated further construction, pushing the number of residents in the community upward from around 1,500 at the beginning of the decade to more than 17,000 in 1960. As Carpentersville's boundaries expanded into the surrounding prairie, it became the most populous community in the metropolitan Chicago area without rail passenger service. Many professionals living in town traveled by private automobile to Elgin to ride the Milwaukee Road commuter trains destined for the Windy City.

Carpentersville's postwar prosperity created few revenue opportunities for the North Western, which ceased staffing its local depot by 1960. To the disappointment of community leaders, the anticipated industrial component of the Meadowdale project never materialized, although the Cargill Company moved a paint factory to town in 1963. Within ten years, Cargill was among the few local businesses still shipping by rail. Unfortunately for the rail carrier, these businesses generated little more than 500 carloads of local freight annually.

Abandonment appeared imminent when Star Manufacturing vacated its historic buildings near the center of town in 1977. Three years later, the Illinois Department of Transportation reported that financial assistance to rehabilite the route could not be justified.

Few were surprised when the North Western petitioned to abandon the segment between Crystal Lake and Elgin, threatening to end Carpentersville's rail service completely. By then, the track was in such poor condition that a speed limit of 10 mph had been imposed. The carrier's interest in eliminating the route was apparently heightened by the state's practice of assessing railroad property for taxation purposes at rates far higher than other land uses. Despite this, the company's petition for abandonment generated substantial opposition from Cargill and other local businesses, which claimed that abandonment would boost their costs by more than $30,000 annually, as well as add to wear and tear on local roads. Even businesses that had not used the railroad in years went on record in opposition.

The Interstate Commerce Commission denied North Western's abandonment application in late 1981, ruling that the carrier had failed to submit the necessary written evidence. The proper documentation eventually followed, leading the agency to approve the application in early 1983. In April of that year, the last revenue train slowly negotiated the weed-covered tracks, ending Carpentersville's railroad era.

Abandonment's Legacy

A revival of rail operations seemed possible when an entrepreneur expressed interest in converting the abandoned stretch into a tourist railway, possibly using equipment leased from the Illinois Railroad Museum (a prominent institution along another North Western branch line in Union, Illinois). This individual made little progress toward this goal, however, and by the end of 1983, the tracks had been removed, except for several miles in Elgin and Crystal Lake. Through the railbanking provisions of the National Trails System Act, the North Western ceded the right-of-way through Carpentersville to the Kane County Forest Preserve District, allowing for the creation of the 33-mile Fox River Trail linking Aurora to Algonquin.

Offering scenic vistas of the river, the trail became a popular component of the region's rail-trail system. By the early 1990s, it was attracting an estimated 700,000 users annually. Between Carpentersville and Algonquin, walkers and bicyclists admired the view of the river from an iron-plate railroad bridge dating back to the late nineteenth century. Upon reaching Algonquin, many continued north on the McHenry County Prairie Trail, another recreational path created on the abandoned branch.

Although the depots in Carpentersville and East Dundee had been razed in 1991, as had the massive North Western terminal building in Chicago, local residents dedicated a wooden "station" in East Dundee that resembled its predecessor. Made possible by funds from the village and various civic organizations, including the Dundee Township Historical Society, this structure serves as a tourist information center and complements the preserved buildings of the East Dundee Historical District.

Some transportation planners lamented the abandonment of the North Western branch as they sought alternatives to a proposed superhighway that would extend from north to south through the region. During the early 1990s, this projected route, the Fox Valley Expressway, generated such strong opposition among residents living in the valley that it was eventually dropped from consideration. Railroad enthusiasts, meanwhile, admired a remnant of the North Western route described as an "alley track" in downtown Elgin. Some were saddened, therefore, when the carrier's successor,

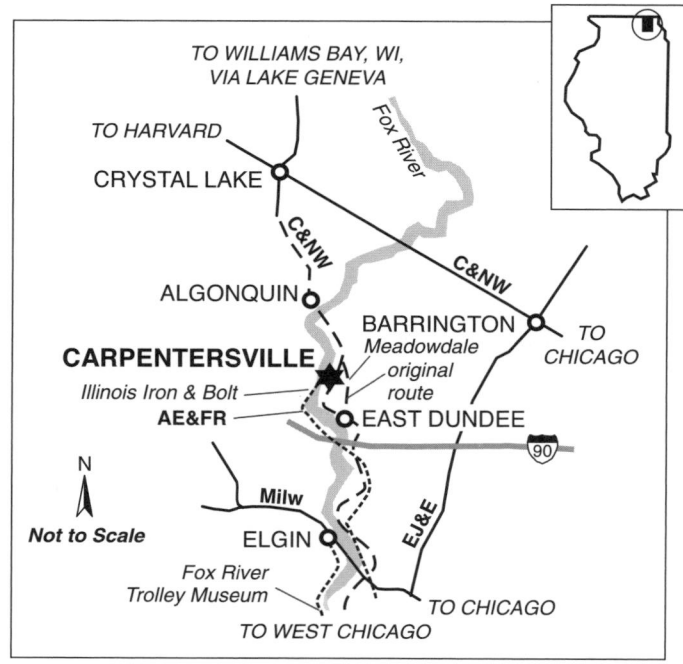

Union Pacific, abandoned this narrow corridor in 1997.

A less favorable legacy of the railroad became apparent that same year, when the local forest preserve district discovered that contaminants dating back many years had permeated a portion of the abandoned route within Carpentersville. Although these contaminants did not threaten the health of residents, in 1998 the agency secured commitments from Union Pacific and several former railroad customers to support a cleanup effort costing several hundred thousand dollars.

As newer suburbs farther west attracted prospective homeowners with larger dwellings and lower taxes, Carpentersville struggled in the late 1990s to promote redevelopment in its older neighborhoods. The community's separation from the region's commuter rail system came to be seen as an obstacle to achieving its long-range planning goals. To encourage development, therefore, the municipal government annexed land west of the river and supported a proposal by Metra, the region's commuter rail operator, to establish suburban service over the Elgin, Joliet & Eastern Railway, a belt line around Chicago passing within 4 miles of Carpentersville's eastern boundary. Officials later modified this proposal to allow for service to O'Hare Airport.

Travelers taking pleasure in the past can make leisurely excursions through the valley on the Fox River Trolley Museum in South Elgin, which operates the only segment of former Aurora, Elgin & Fox River track that survives. Every year, hundreds of people gather at the annual Trolley Fest to celebrate the legacy of one of the country's first interurbans.

Epilogue

The story of Carpentersville's railroad era is typical of industrial communities that have made the transition to residentially oriented suburbs. Its example shows that even communities in regions with the most successful and densely built railroad systems have struggled to attract and retain rail service. The community's separation from the many lines radiating from Chicago virtually assured an early demise to passenger service. Today, this problem prevents Carpentersville from sharing directly in the benefits of the vast commuter rail system serving the Chicago region.

Carpentersville's very name conjures images of its days as a center for the manufacture of fine household products. Visitors will find its Old Town—the area around the intersection of Main and Washington Streets—one the best-preserved industrial districts in the region dating back to the late nineteenth century. Notable among its buildings are the gristmill and the well-maintained Star Manufacturing building, which today belongs to an engineering firm. Nearby is the old Library Hall, a structure of much significance in the lives of the Carpenter family and the community's lone entry on the National Register of Historic Places.

At the center of town is the Old Trestle, a vestige of the spur to the Illinois Iron & Bolt foundry that stands as an unofficial monument to the village's industrial antecedents. In the middle of the span, a riveted truss bridge seems frozen in time, offering a now-ironic reminder of the role of iron and steel in this community's past.

For Further Study

SUGGESTED READINGS:

Behrens, Paul L. *Steam Trains to Geneva Lake*. Hebron, Ill.: Paul Behrens, 1993, 136.

Braden, Beatrice B., and Carolyn J. Bullinger. *Dundee Township: 1885–1985*. Dundee, Ill.: Dundee Township Historical Society, 1986, 46–59, 151–14.

Hopkins, Stolp Peffers. *Aurora-Elgin Area Street Cars and Interurbans*. Vol. 1, *Fox River Division*. Wheaton, Ill.: American Slide-Chart, 1993, 108–15.

OTHER PRINCIPAL REFERENCES:

Bach, Ira J. *A Guide to Chicago's Historic Suburbs*. Athens: Ohio University Press, 1981, 222–28.

Grant, Roger. *The North Western: A History of the Chicago & North Western Railway System*. DeKalb: Northern Illinois University Press, 1996, 66.

Hilton, George W., and John F. Due. *The Electric Interurban Railways in America*. Stanford: Stanford University Press, 1964, 342.

Storm, Roger, Susan Wedzel, Karen-Lee Ryan, and Mike Ulm. *Great Rail-Trails in Michigan, Illinois, and Indiana*. Washington, D.C.: Rails-to-Trails Conservancy, 1994, 134–41.

DECORAH, IOWA (8,172)

Historic operators: Chicago, Milwaukee, St. Paul & Pacific Railroad; Chicago, Rock Island & Pacific Railroad
Last route abandoned: 1979
Notable reuse of right-of-way: Local commercial development

 he railroads of Decorah brought generations of Norwegian immigrants to two fine depots spaced only a few blocks apart. These carriers competed vigorously for the freight and passenger business and helped the community establish its reputation as a center for Nordic-American relations. Although Decorah goes to great lengths to commemorate its heritage as an immigration gateway, the story of its railroads seems relegated to the past.

Historical Perspective

In 1849, three years after Iowa became a state, William Day and his family established a camp next to a spring near the Upper Iowa River. The Days worked with other settlers of English descent, including the enterprising William Painter, to create a viable farming community on the gently sloping terrain. The townspeople chose to name their community after Chief Waukon Decorah, a Native American leader who had come to the aid of settlers during the Black Hawk War.

In its early days, life in the community centered on a two-story mill built by Painter to grind wheat. In 1851, Decorah rose in status by becoming the seat of Winneshiek County. With expansion imminent, community leaders platted the town in 1853 and began work on a county courthouse three years later.

The abundant timber in this part of Iowa and the mechanical power generated by the river encouraged a gradual expansion of industry. Quarries north of town cut slabs of Decorah marble for shipment to distant markets, while

several new sawmills and manufacturers sprouted up along the riverbank, reducing the community's dependence on Painter's mill.

As word of the region's thriving economy spread, many English and Norwegian immigrants traveled long distances over dirt roads to Decorah. Some stayed to work the land while others simply rested before resuming their westward travels. When the Norwegian Lutheran Evangelical Church moved Luther College to the community in 1862, still more Scandinavians established themselves on the area's rolling terrain.

With Decorah's rising economic and cultural status came the need for local rail service, which the Milwaukee & St. Paul Railway partially filled in 1869. By inaugurating service over a 10-mile route from Conover (a junction on the carrier's line from Calmar to Austin, Minnesota), its trains fostered such extensive development that Decorah grew to more than 3,000 inhabitants and became a prominent tourist destination. Formally renamed the Chicago, Milwaukee & St. Paul Railway in 1874, this company—the "St. Paul Road"—emerged as one of northern Iowa's

A classic scene unfolds at the Milwaukee Road depot in Decorah: a train equipped with a baggage and passenger car appears to be departing, probably for Calmar, date unknown. (Collection of Gillmer and Eleanor Seegmiller.)

dominant rail carriers and provided an efficient way to ship goods between nearby business centers, including Calmar.

The completion in 1877 of the Arlington House, an ornate three-story hotel, and the construction of a second rail line, the Chicago, Decorah & Minnesota Railway, seven years later were milestones in the community's expansion. Although never reaching Minnesota as it had planned, this carrier provided a valuable link to a rural junction 3 miles southwest of Postville, where it maintained an interchange with the Burlington, Cedar Rapids & Northern Railway (BCR&N), a carrier popularly called the Cedar Rapids Route.

For the next thirty years, Decorah's railroads competed vigorously for local freight and passengers over tracks on opposite sides of the Dry Run Creek (an estuary of the river). As its name implied, the Cedar Rapids Route (having absorbed the Chicago, Decorah & Minnesota into its system) provided the most direct service to

the largest city in east-central Iowa. Nevertheless, the St. Paul Road ably defended its share of the Decorah market. Apparently to provide its customers with conveniences equal to those of its rival, it built a new passenger station in 1888 that was several blocks closer to downtown than its original depot. This ornate station, complete with separate waiting rooms for men and women, was the source of tremendous municipal pride.

Decorah teemed with activity during the Gilded Age, when its depots saw the arrival of trains filled with immigrants and tourists who stayed at the elegant guesthouses on Water Street. In 1904, residents dedicated a magnificent new county courthouse at the center of town. The following year, they celebrated the opening of the stately Winneshiek Hotel. In the midst of considerable prosperity, the community merged with West Decorah, a village on the opposite side of the river, and benefited from an expansion of its quarries and small industry along with bountiful harvests of corn, soybeans, and wheat.

The BCR&N came under the sole ownership of the Chicago, Rock Island & Pacific Railway (Rock Island) during the early twentieth century and was gradually assimilated into this granger road system (rail lines that carried primarily agricultural products). The Rock Island's daily passenger train between Cedar Rapids and Decorah remained important to the county's mobility for many years, and its large roundhouse generated numerous well-paying jobs. On the other hand, the St. Paul Road offered the widest array of passenger services, providing four weekday departures in 1910 over the 13-mile route to Calmar. At this neighboring junction, passengers could transfer to the long-distance trains operating to Chicago and the other great railroad centers after which the company had been named. Business was sufficiently robust in 1913 that the carrier constructed a baggage building adjacent to its Decorah passenger station.

Changing Times

Throughout most of the 1920s and continuing until their final days of service, the railroad companies serving Decorah were never far from serious financial problems, due in part to intense competition from stronger railroad companies and motor carriers. The St. Paul entered bankruptcy in 1925 and emerged from reorganization three years later as the Chicago, Milwaukee, St. Paul & Pacific Railroad (Milwaukee Road) only to declare bankruptcy once again during the Great Depression. The Rock Island plunged into bankruptcy in 1933 and spent the remainder of the decade working to resolve its lingering financial problems. Even as the passenger business waned, the Rock Island delighted townspeople by occasionally operating excursion trains to a horseracing track at Independence, Iowa.

The Depression accelerated Decorah's shift away from traditional industry toward tourism and educational services. Many visitors came to see the Decorah Ice Cave, a cavern north of the river where columns of ice could be seen throughout the summer months. In 1932, officials transformed Decorah's largest structure, the masonry building that had formerly been the Arlington House, into a new home for the Vesterheim, a museum celebrating the region's Norwegian-American culture. By 1936, Luther College had added several new buildings to its campus and had become a coeducational institution.

Despite the growing number of people arriving to attend school or see the town's tourist attractions, the Milwaukee Road reduced passenger services to a single departure, a self-propelled gas-electric car operating to Calmar. By the early 1940s, passengers arriving

in Decorah on either of its railroads had to settle for the relatively austere accommodations of mixed trains. These trains operated throughout World War II, but ceased running within a few years after hostilities ended.

Although the glory years of railroad passenger travel faded from memory after the war, the Sioux (a train operating over the Milwaukee Road between Chicago and Rapid City), soldiered on, allowing passengers bound for Decorah to detrain in Calmar and complete their journey via private automobiles or the once-popular Noecker's Cab Service. Unfortunately, such passengers had to look elsewhere after the Milwaukee Road stopped operating the Sioux west of Madison, Wisconsin, in 1960, ending the last of Winneshiek County's rail passenger services.

Within a few years, freight service to many small Iowa towns was also nearing its end. The Rock Island generated little tonnage in Decorah, except for commodities moved at the behest of the Winneshiek Cooperative, an agricultural supplier. In 1963, it withdrew from the community by abandoning the Decorah–Postville Junction segment.

By the time community officials transformed the Rock Island's former depot grounds into a municipal park seven years later, the Milwaukee Road route appeared

The former Milwaukee Road depot in Decorah, now a chiropractor's office, stands little changed from the railroad era. (Photo by author.)

headed for the same fate. Track conditions suffered as the carrier struggled to maintain a sprawling system of lightly used branches throughout the northern Great Plains. The railroad's business in Decorah gradually dwindled to little more than sporadic shipments of wood, salt, and grain for a handful of customers, including a pair of feed mills, the cooperative, and a local lumberyard.

Decorah economy adjusted to the changing times relatively well, aided by the expansion of tourism and growing enrollment at Luther College. The Nordic Fest, established in 1967, became a widely anticipated annual event. The Bernatz family, owners of the gristmill, converted the historic limestone structure from water to diesel power before donating it to the museum in 1969. In 1975, King Olav of Norway made a celebrated visit to rededicate the fully restored Vesterheim—by then the country's largest and oldest immigrant museum.

Expansion in the service sector pushed Decorah's population to more than 8,000 but provided few benefits to the struggling Milwaukee Road. The carrier voluntarily entered receivership in 1977 and announced plans to eliminate nearly 70 percent more of its 10,000 miles of routes, including 1,500 miles in Iowa. The state's Department of Transportation found its resources overwhelmed by the number of routes slated for abandonment, including many deteriorating Milwaukee Road and Rock Island branches. Its analysis, however, showed that the costs of operating the Conover–Decorah branch (which served few customers except the Thornton Feed Mill), outweighed the benefits by a ratio of more than three to one, rendering the line a low priority for public support.

The city council was uneasy with the prospect of losing rail service and considered acquiring the branch in

early 1979. It did not take action, however, when the Milwaukee Road received approval to abandon its Decorah Branch during February of that year. In April, the deteriorating tracks gave way, derailing a diesel locomotive pulling empty boxcars. That same month, the carrier formally abandoned the branch. The tracks were soon removed, leaving Decorah the most populous community in Iowa without rail service.

Abandonment's Legacy

The debate about the future of the Milwaukee Road corridor intensified after the departure of the last train. Decorah Railroad Trail, Inc., a nonprofit organization founded by the mayor, explored the possibility of transforming the abandoned branch into a civic amenity, possibly a recreational trail, while making allowances for the eventual restoration of rail service. When the organization finally took steps to acquire the right-of-way from the railroad, nineteen owners of adjacent property, mostly farmers, summoned a prominent lawyer to defend their claim that the abandoned route had legally reverted to them. Milwaukee Road officials rejected these claims, leading to a legal dispute.

In the autumn of 1979, the editors of the *Decorah Journal* announced their support for preserving the corridor, pushing the disagreement to the forefront of civic debate. In the same *Journal* edition, the property owners took out a large advertisement detailing the perceived violation of their property rights.

The following month, area farmers threatened to file lawsuits. A search for title along the right-of-way clearly supported the farmers' position, showing that the Milwaukee Road did not have a deed for title in at least nine quarter-sections (units of land measuring 640 acres). After legal counsel expressed concern about the futility of taking the matter to court, the trail advocacy group dropped its proposal. Had the petition to abandon Decorah's last route taken place several years later, newly approved amendments to the National Trails System Act would likely have allowed the organization to achieve its goals while sidestepping difficult questions about the ownership of the land.

The legal issues surrounding the divestment process proved to be less divisive within the city limits of Decorah, where the Milwaukee

TO ST. PAUL VIA AUSTIN, MN
CRESCO
Luther College
Ice Cave
Upper Iowa River
DECORAH
CONOVER
Milw
Milw
SPILLVILLE
TO MASON CITY
Milw
CALMAR
OSSIAN
CRI&P
POSTVILLE
TO CHICAGO VIA MADISON
CRI&P
Postville Junction
N
TO CEDAR RAPIDS VIA OELWEIN
Not to Scale

Road sold much of its property outright to local businesses, including the feed mill, which had previously leased land from the railroad. Although the railroad's withdrawal opened up large parcels of land for new construction projects, much of the debate revolved around municipal efforts to limit, rather than promote, commercial development along the abandoned right-of-way.

Officials opposed a developer's plans to build a shopping center on a vacant parcel along Decorah's periphery, partially to preserve the vitality of the community's downtown. This zoning dispute led to a lawsuit, which the Iowa Supreme Court decided in favor of the developer, clearing the way for the construction of the Centrum Shopping Center. As Decorah resumed its efforts to curb unwanted development, it found itself embroiled in another zoning dispute involving the construction of a Wal-Mart store. This time, the high court sided with the city, forcing the store to remain empty for an extended period of time.

Epilogue

Many visitors to Decorah are impressed with the fine ornamentation of its Victorian buildings, most notably the Vesterheim, which remains one of Iowa's most notable museums. Eighteen properties or districts in Decorah, including the courthouse—the community's oldest building—are today represented on the National Register of Historic Places. Along Water Street, the site of the Nordic Fest celebration, the municipal government supports the maintenance of a variety of historic edifices. The architecture of these structures contrasts sharply with the simpler, but still elegant, prairie school style of the Luther College campus.

Among the many Iowa communities that have lost rail service due to the abandonment of Milwaukee Road and Rock Island routes, Decorah stands out as one of the largest and most historically significant. Having grown to more than 8,000 residents, it is the most populous of the more than twenty-five county seats in Iowa that have lost rail service.

Observant travelers can still discern ample evidence of Decorah's bygone railroads. The Milwaukee Road passenger depot has been more than adequately restored as a chiropractor's office, and the former Rock Island depot is now a residential home and storage facility. Although the tracks are gone, the continued existence of Railroad Street and Railroad Avenue as well as a former Milwaukee Road freight house (now used by a recycling company) signify the transportation practices of the past. In the countryside outside of town, wooden pilings from the Rock Island's trestle across Trout Run also seem conspicuous for their survival, having been relieved of the burden of supporting trains more than forty years ago.

For Further Study

SUGGESTED READINGS:

Davis, Robert H. *Decorah Visitor's Guide.* Decorah, Iowa: Robert H. Davis, 1996, 1–7, 79.

Grant, H. Roger, ed. *Iowa Railroads: Essays of Frank P. Donovan, Jr.* Iowa City: University of Iowa Press, 2000, 168–231.

Seegmiller, Gillmer and Eleanor. *Decorah: City of Springs.* Decorah, Iowa: Amundsen Publishing, 1998, 1–5.

OTHER PRINCIPAL REFERENCES:

Baumel, C. Phillip, John J. Miller, and Thomas P. Drinka. *An Economic Analysis of Upgrading Branch Lines: A Study of 71 Lines in Iowa.* Washington, D.C.: U.S. Department of Transportation, 1976, 10.

Hofsommer, Donovan L., "A Chronology of Iowa Railroads." *Railroad History* 132 (Sept. 1975): 70–83.

National Register of Historic Places Nomination Form. Milwaukee Road Passenger Depot. Collection of the Office of Historic Preservation, Iowa City, Iowa (1974), 1–6.

Rummery, Chris. "Burlington, Cedar Rapids & Northern." *Midwestern Rails* 84, no. 89 (Feb.–Mar. 1984): 7–14.

WEST BRANCH, IOWA (2,188)

Historic operator: Chicago, Rock Island & Pacific Railroad
Last route abandoned: 1980
Notable reuse of right-of-way: Hoover Nature Trail

The railroad through West Branch left a deep imprint on Herbert Hoover and other natives of this small farming community. Hoover spent hours walking along the tracks during his childhood, and he received a warm ovation when his special train arrived during his first presidential campaign. Despite a spirited effort a half century later to revitalize the route as an excursion railway for tourists visiting Hoover's hometown, little remains of the rail line today.

Historical Perspective

When eight families, including Eli Hoover and his kin, arrived at the west branch of Wapsinonoc Creek in 1853, they chose to end their journey and establish a community devoted to Quaker beliefs. These and other settlers counted their blessings after their abundant harvests and sent their grain to market on the Mississippi & Missouri Rail Road Company, a predecessor of the Chicago, Rock Island & Pacific (Rock Island), which built through Liberty (a nearby community later renamed West Liberty) in 1855. Upholding their beliefs in tolerance and nonviolence, they welcomed noted abolitionist John Brown into their midst during the winter of 1857–58.

The region's hardy settlers platted their town on a rectangular grid in 1869. Although the reasons they named the settlement "West Branch" are unclear, most historians attribute it to either the community's proximity to the local branch of Wapsinonoc Creek or the townspeople's

affiliation with a particular religious sect. Whatever the reason, their community still had only about 200 inhabitants when the Burlington, Cedar Rapids & Northern Railway (BCR&N) reached the eastern part of town in 1870. The community's jubilant leaders commemorated the occasion by arranging for a celebratory dinner that nearly all of the townspeople attended. Building north from Burlington, Iowa, the railway soon reached Cedar Rapids, the region's principal commercial center.

Within a few years, the BCR&N's trains had made possible the expansion of agriculture and small-scale industry in the towns it served. West Branch grew so much that its downtown stretched several blocks. In 1874, Eli Hoover's son Jesse and his wife Hulda celebrated the birth of their second child, whom they named Herbert Clark Hoover. The following year, West Branch became an incorporated community.

The BCR&N expanded its services by negotiating trackage rights over the Iowa Central Railway and building a lengthy track extension, thereby giving it an interchange with the Minneapolis & St. Louis Railway at Albert Lea, Minnesota. These extensions allowed the railway to become part of an important freight and passenger route between southern Iowa and the Twin Cities. With nearly all long-distance shipments in the region moving by rail, BCR&N built new facilities in West Branch, including a depot, tool shed, and water tank. It constructed a 3,000-foot side track near town with a capacity for at least eighty cars.

The carrier's resources, however, could hardly compare to those of Iowa's largest railroads. The BCR&N promoted itself in its marketing literature as "the Burlington," but this moniker was sometimes confused with the much larger Chicago, Burlington & Quincy Railroad, which had adopted the Burlington Route as its official nickname. The local railroad, in turn, later chose a less confusing trade name, the Cedar Rapids Route.

Recognizing that the BCR&N had substantial strategic value, the Burlington Route and the Rock Island jointly acquired it in 1879. These prominent granger roads apportioned the revenues the line generated and designated the 156-mile portion south of Cedar Rapids (which included the segment through West Branch) as Rock Island territory. Nevertheless, the railway retained

its own distinctive character. Its frequent trains and well-maintained right-of-way had a lasting impression on young Herbert Hoover, who lived only four blocks from the route. As a boy, Hoover spent a great deal of time at the depot and occasionally walked along the tracks searching for gems and agate in the ballast—a presage of his distinguished career in the mining industry. In his memoirs, he recalled the railroad line as an "inspiring place."

The Rock Island leased the Burlington Route's share of the BCR&N in 1902 and purchased it the following year. Eventually, the carrier built its own route from Albert Lea to the Twin Cities and terminated its partnership with the Minneapolis & St. Louis. At the southern end of the route, the Rock Island continued to interchange freight cars with the Burlington Route and carried on the practice of jointly operated passenger trains between Minneapolis and St. Louis.

As the Rock Island assimilated the Cedar Rapids Route into its system, an illustrious era of passenger

A lengthy passenger train—possibly a chartered train operated for one of Herbert Hoover's presidential campaigns—faces north at the Rock Island's West Branch depot. The flags decorating the attractively maintained station suggest a special occasion. (State Historical Society of Iowa.)

Grain-storage facilities along the former Rock Island route through West Branch testify to the past role of the railroad in moving agricultural projects. (Photo by author.)

services came to West Branch. In 1910, travelers could board any of ten trains operating daily (except Sunday) in the community, while others trains sped through town without stopping. One of the most notable trains, the Pullman-equipped St. Louis–Twin Cities Express, made an overnight run between the two great railroad centers for which it had been named. The Chicago–Twin Cities Express was also an important train, despite its circuitous route. This train, using the interchange tracks at West Liberty to switch between the Chicago–Des Moines main line and former BCR&N, traveled 82 miles farther than the Burlington Route's trains linking the Windy City and Minneapolis. In West Branch, the trains passed by so closely to the East Side Café, a popular gathering place adjacent to the tracks, that the wooden structure purportedly rattled until the last car had passed.

The Rock Island trains also supported the budding political career of Herbert Hoover. During the summer of

1928, the U.S. Secretary of Commerce rode a chartered train to his hometown while campaigning for the office of the presidency. In anticipation of the train's arrival, the Rock Island painted the community's two-story depot and operated special excursion trains from both the north and south, bringing hundreds of guests to town.

After Hoover won the election by defeating Democrat Alfred E. Smith, the West Branch station became a meeting place for his supporters. In March 1929, hundreds of residents traveled on a chartered train over the Rock Island and the Baltimore & Ohio to Washington, D.C., where they watched the inauguration of the thirty-first president from reserved seats.

Changing Times

The residents of many small towns in Iowa emerged from the Great Depression with diminished expectations about their communities' future. Although some 300 West Branch residents rode another special train during the autumn of 1932 to welcome Hoover's presidential campaign train into West Liberty, the Republican's bid for reelection went poorly. As the specter of high unemployment lingered, Hoover lost to Franklin D. Roosevelt and left office in 1933. While still making Palo Alto, California, his permanent home, Hoover purchased the cottage at the edge of West Branch in which he had been born. With his encouragement, the Herbert Hoover Birthplace Society received its charter in 1939 and assumed stewardship of the aging structure.

Although Hoover spoke out against American involvement in World War II, the country's policies moved in a different direction, and the fateful events that followed put an enormous burden on the nation's railroads. In 1941, the Rock Island and the Burlington Route jointly introduced the first streamlined train operating from north to south across the entire state of Iowa, and in so doing linked Minneapolis and St. Louis with unprecedented speed. In keeping with the Rock Island's practice of naming its streamliners Rockets and the Burlington Route's practice of naming them Zephyrs, the carriers christened the train the Zephyr Rocket. Although the Zephyr Rocket did not initially stop in West Branch, residents needed only to travel 8 miles to West Liberty to board this train and other notable long-distance runs such as the Des Moines Rocket and Corn Belt Rocket, which operated on the Chicago–Iowa main line.

By the time Hoover published his memoirs in the

early 1950s, recalling his childhood along the Burlington Route, motor transport was taking its toll on the rail line he so fondly remembered. In 1955, fire consumed the West Branch depot. By the early 1960s, passenger service on the local route had dwindled to the Zephyr Rocket, which now made local stops but at inconvenient hours.

Although West Branch took considerable pride in the Hoover Birthplace, it benefited little from its association with the Great Humanitarian until 1962, when the federal government dedicated the Herbert Hoover Presidential Library-Museum. After Hoover's death in 1964, the National Park Service began gradually improving the facilities as part of its effort to create a National Historic Site encompassing the cottage, museum, and other properties.

The construction of Interstate 80 near the town's southern periphery during the 1960s enhanced the historical site's accessibility. As the downtowns of other Iowa communities declined in response to the advent of shopping malls, West Branch's business district fared comparatively well—and even enjoyed a modest upsurge—largely due to the growing numbers of tourists visiting the Hoover Birthplace. Few local travelers, however, used the Rock Island's lone remaining passenger train through town, which had become a mere remnant of the Zephyr Rocket. The elimination of this train (which no longer carried sleeping cars) in the spring of 1967, while itself considered a minor event, was emblematic of the changing times. Several years later, leaders in the region braced themselves for the impending cancellation of passenger service on the Rock Island main line through West Liberty. The last train on this route, a vestige of the Des Moines Rocket, made its final run shortly before the inception of Amtrak in 1971.

A state report published six years later concluded that the rail line through West Branch was in good condition. In the mid-1970s, a pair of general merchandise trains, often more than 50 cars long, operated in each direction over these tracks daily. However, a strike by the employees of the financially troubled Rock Island in 1979 raised serious doubt about the entire railroad's future. The labor dispute left the stretch through West Branch, which had served few local businesses except the grain elevator, dormant for an extended period and proved to be a fatal blow to the struggling carrier. In March 1980, freight operations on the Rock Island officially ended. As the carrier once again plunged into bankruptcy, it put more than 1,500 miles of Iowa track at risk of abandonment, overwhelming the resources of

state rail planners. Without fanfare, and almost by default, the railroad era in West Branch drew to a close.

Abandonment's Legacy

Doubtful that the local rail line would be reactivated, the West Branch city council in 1980 expressed its understandable reluctance to allocate funds for the installation of new warning signals at a local highway crossing, which had been planned as part of a state safety program. With tourism in West Branch poised for expansion, however, an effort to bring trains back to town moved forward. In the summer of 1981, a proposal gathered momentum to transform the 8-mile segment from West Branch to West Liberty into an excursion railway and to create a railroad museum at West Liberty. These efforts took place under the auspices of the Des Moines and Raccoon Valley Railroad Museum, a volunteer organization that later changed its name to the Greater Iowa Railway and Museum.

Representatives of the organization worked for months on these proposals and met on several occasions with Rock Island trustees in Chicago. At these meetings, they negotiated possible arrangements for leasing or acquiring the dormant line, the West Liberty depot, and the small freight yard in West Branch. The organization acquired three coaches and brought them to West Liberty for the excursion railway. Supporting their efforts, an entrepreneurial West Branch teenager purchased a small but deteriorating steam locomotive. Volunteers brought

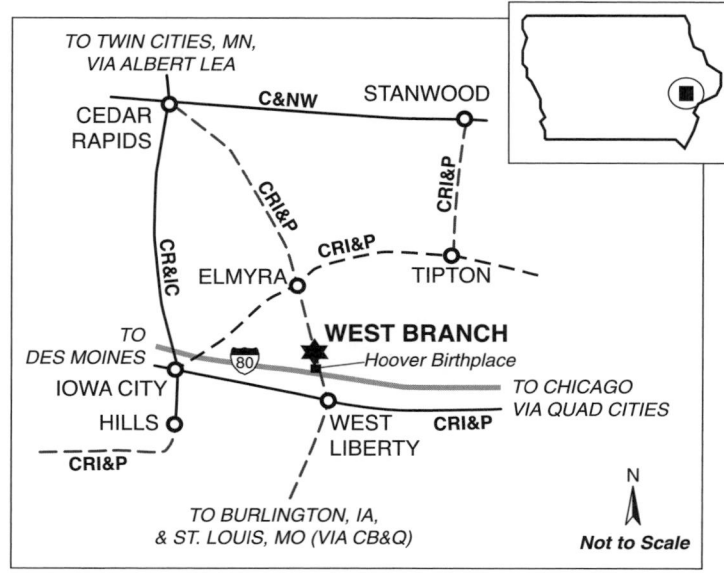

the engine to town for possible rehabilitation and proudly put it on display in a local Fourth of July parade.

The time and money contributed toward this initiative made the revival of West Branch's railroad seem possible, but the organization could not meet the financial demands of the railroad's trustees. One estimate placed the cost of leasing the line at $6,000 per month, an amount that in all probability could not be offset by ticket sales. The initiative stalled after lengthy negotiation with the trustees.

When salvage workers removed the tracks, they extinguished all hope of a railroad revival. Nevertheless, tourism in West Branch continued to blossom. In 1987, the first portions of its downtown district were added to the National Register of Historic Places. During the early 1990s, attention turned to transforming the right-of-way into a recreational trail linking Burlington to Cedar Rapids. Unusually for a proposed trail of this length, the plan moved forward despite the reversion or sale of former railroad property to various property owners. Legendary trail advocate Milly Gregg, a native of West Liberty, worked diligently with others to sustain this complex undertaking. Using more than $900,000 in funds provided from private donors and the state's Department of Transportation, supporters fashioned 27 miles of the former Rock Island right-of-way north of West Branch into the Hoover Nature Trail in the early 1990s.

Efforts to extend the trail south of West Branch through the Interstate 80 underpass and on to West Liberty generated opposition from area landowners and forced this portion of the trail onto country roads. Although Iowa ranked near the top among states in railroad mileage abandoned between 1976 and 1995— 5,500 miles of track were eliminated—a significant share of the rail-trails proposed during this period were blocked by the agricultural community. Despite such resistance, trail advocates strengthened their resolve to complete the trail over the entire 115-mile distance between Cedar Rapids and Burlington, even if it became necessary to deviate from the old rail-bed. In the late 1990s, the unpaved trail became part of the American Discovery Trail, an interconnected system of routes linking the Atlantic and Pacific coasts.

Epilogue

Much has changed since the train once known as the Zephyr Rocket made its final stop in West Branch. Several

new businesses at the southern edge of town cater to motorists exiting Interstate 80. During harvest season, trucks rumble along the abandoned right-of-way as they haul grain to modern storage bins. In West Liberty, the restored depot, a landmark dating back to 1897, has become a museum honoring the Rock Island's historical contributions to eastern Iowa.

The story of West Branch's rail service in many respects typifies the experiences of small communities on branch lines heavily dependent on local agricultural traffic. In other ways, however, its example is extraordinary. A few citizens are even old enough to remember the special trains operated to support the campaigns of Herbert Hoover, whose presidency, like the Rock Island's service, struggled with persistent economic adversity.

For many years, the East Side Café survived as a symbol of this bygone railroad era. In 2000, however, the vacant building went up in flames, saddening those who could remember its creaky walls rattling and rumbling when trains passed by.

For Further Study

SUGGESTED READINGS:

Grant, H. Roger, ed. *Iowa Railroads: Essays of Frank P. Donovan, Jr.* Iowa City: University of Iowa Press, 2000, 168–92, 297.

Hoffman, Bruce. "100 Years of Trains." In *West Branch, the First 100 Years: 1851–2001.* Edited by Dwight E. Jensen. West Branch, Iowa: West Branch Heritage Association, 2001.

OTHER PRINCIPAL REFERENCES:

Bearss, Edwin C. *Historical Base Map and Ground Study: Herbert Hoover National Historic Site, West Branch Iowa.* Washington, D.C.: U.S. Department of Interior, 1968, 56–58.

Iowa Department of Transportation, *Iowa Rail Plan.* 1978, 39.

Overton, Richard C. *Burlington Route: A History of the Burlington Lines.* New York: Knopf, 1965, 165, 174–75.

Stratton, Maud. *Herbert Hoover's Home Town.* West Branch, Iowa: Maud Stratton, 1948.

Withers, Bob. *The President Travels by Train.* Lynchburg, Va.: TLC Publishing, 1996, 124–25.

VALLEY FALLS, KANSAS (1,254)

Historic operators: Atchison, Topeka & Santa Fe Railway; Missouri Pacific Railroad; Union Pacific Railroad
Last route abandoned: 1993
Notable reuse of right-of-way: None

Civic leaders in Valley Falls outlined an ambitious plan to prevent the abandonment of one of the original routes of the Atchison, Topeka & Santa Fe Railway during the mid-1990s. While they succeeded in attracting the attention of influential politicians around the state and preservationists around the country, their resources were insufficient to meet the demands of a company seemingly intent on scrapping the line. Valley Falls' example illustrates the lengths to which some rural communities have gone to try to save their last remaining route.

Historical Perspective

Arriving in early 1854, Henry Zen was the first settler to live next to a small waterfall on the Grasshopper River. Zen lived peacefully among the Kickapoo Indians for several months until, during the autumn of that year, a white man claiming to be an agent for the tribe asked Zen to move elsewhere. Uncertain about his safety, Zen headed west through the Glacial Hills region.

A group of settlers soon established themselves on Zen's abandoned campsite. Before spring arrived, they had constructed several log cabins and christened their new community Grasshopper Falls in recognition of the falls on the river. The townspeople came to depend on the leadership of Isaac Cody, who prepared a survey for their community and built a gristmill. According to community folklore, Cody's son, the celebrated Buffalo Bill, visited the town on at least one occasion.

From these modest beginnings arose a community with a post office, a steam-powered sawmill, and a strong sense of identity. Following the construction of a Lutheran church and a large hotel known as the Cataract House in 1857, Grasshopper Falls appeared poised to be one of the region's leading commercial centers. A recession in the early 1860s followed by deprivation during the Civil War, however, offered a harsh reminder of the hardships of life on the frontier.

The community persevered over these trying times and, after its incorporation in 1869, even prospered on a modest scale. Development was particularly strong after construction crews building in opposite directions for the Atchison, Topeka & Santa Fe Railway (Santa Fe) converged on Grasshopper Falls in 1872. Passing through gently rolling terrain and crossing the river adjacent to the falls, this newly created corridor provided an efficient link between the busy railroad towns of

145

A woman and young girl wait cautiously on the platform of the Santa Fe station in Valley Falls, June 1956. The southbound motorcar, M-117, will stop only momentarily before resuming its trip to Topeka. (Photo by William A. Gibson, Sr.)

Atchison and Topeka. This route—the Santa Fe's only line to the Missouri River for the next several years—provided connections with more "eastern" railroads at Atchison.

Only months after the first Santa Fe train reached town, a second carrier arrived to proffer its services. Hundreds gathered along the tracks later in 1872 to ride excursions on the Kansas Central Railway's newly completed narrow-gauge route between Leavenworth and Holton. In an unusual move for two carriers with different track gauges, the Kansas Central and Santa Fe shared a depot in Grasshopper Falls and operated through town on the same right-of-way, an arrangement made possible by the installation of a third rail. Briefly, the two carriers even offered closely timed connections for passengers traveling between Topeka and Leavenworth.

Both railroad companies contributed greatly to opening up northeastern Kansas for settlement. The region was challenged, however, by the grasshopper plagues that devastated local agricultural production. A particularly severe onslaught occurred in 1874 as grasshoppers destroyed entire fields of crops. Desiring to improve their community's image, the townspeople petitioned the state to rename the town, but they strongly disliked the legislature's choice of Sautrelle Falls. In 1875,

the community was officially renamed Valley Falls and the Grasshopper River renamed the Delaware River.

By 1876, Valley Falls had two banks, a lumberyard, three hotels, six churches, and a population of more than a thousand. Although it already had two rail lines, the community wanted better, cheaper, and more extensive service. This opportunity came in 1881 when the narrow-gauge Kansas Central embarked on a lengthy northward extension to Clay Center (a small community 92 miles from Holton). Then, as railroad fever swept across Kansas again several years later, still another carrier, the Kansas City, Wyandotte & Northwestern Railroad, arrived on the scene. This standard-gauge operator inaugurated service from Kansas City to Seneca via Valley Falls in 1887 and gradually extended its route into southern Nebraska.

Valley Falls now had the benefit of three carriers and direct service to Kansas City. Its railroad era reached another milepost in 1887, when the Santa Fe extended its route to Los Angeles, establishing it as one of the greatest railways in the United States and allowing it to provide through passenger service from Atchison to the West Coast. The Kansas Central's system paled in comparison, but the carrier (controlled by Union Pacific) widened its tracks to standard gauge in 1892 and reorganized as the Leavenworth, Kansas & Western Railway. Service on the former Kansas City, Wyandotte & Northwestern also improved after this line came under the control of Missouri Pacific and was reorganized as the Kansas City Northwestern Railway.

Changing Times

Even before new forms of transportation emerged, the region's sparse population and limited agricultural potential could barely sustain such an extensive railroad system. The Santa Fe's former main line to Atchison diminished in importance as the carrier shifted long-distance traffic to the Kansas City–Chicago route it had completed in 1888. As cars and trucks became more widespread during the early twentieth century, both the freight and passenger business slowed. The Missouri Pacific gave up its route through Valley Falls in 1917, and its independent successor abandoned it two years later. The Union Pacific assimilated the former Leavenworth, Kansas & Western into its vast system and replaced its local passenger trains with gasoline-powered McKeen motorcars ("doodlebugs") in 1921.

Over the next ten years, the options available to local travelers greatly diminished. Union Pacific curtailed its unprofitable doodlebug run between Leavenworth and Garrison in 1933. The Santa Fe became the lone provider of local rail service the following year, when Union Pacific eliminated the remaining mixed-train service through Valley Falls and abandoned its poorly maintained segment between Knox (near Leavenworth) and Clay Center (near Miltonvale). Service continued over the Santa Fe, but the carrier replaced the locomotive-drawn passenger trains on its local route with a gas-electric motorcar. This motorcar, popularly called the Joe, initially made two daily round trips between Topeka and St. Joseph, Missouri, an important regional city east of Atchison.

Freight trains on the Santa Fe were dispatched from Emporia and served a variety of customers in Valley Falls, including the grain elevator and the Meyer Creamery—a processing facility that supplied the military with large quantities of powdered milk during World War II. With gasoline shortages hampering mobility, many passengers relied on Santa Fe's motorcar service, which—despite being reduced to a single daily round trip—allowed for convenient transfers at Topeka to long-distance trains. Although the Santa Fe's extra-fare El Capitan and Super Chief trains bypassed the state capital (these streamliners operated over the Ottawa Cutoff), passengers riding the Joe could reach many major cities with a single change of trains.

The Santa Fe converted the motorcars through Valley Falls from gas-electric to diesel-electric after the war, but ridership diminished until the service was eliminated from the schedule in 1958. Local freight service, conversely, appeared to have a promising future, especially after the carrier made major improvements to the line in conjunction with the creation of the Perry Reservoir during the 1960s. With governmental assistance, the Santa Fe realigned and rebuilt lengthy portions of the route to facilitate the creation of Perry Lake, a reservoir fed by the Delaware River south of Valley Falls.

As part of this track realignment project, construction workers built earthen fills, culverts, and new bridges near Valley Falls on a scale that had not been seen in this part of Kansas since railroad fever had swept through it eighty years before. The grain elevator moved from the center of Valley Falls to a new location near the southeastern edge of town. Trains now crossed the river on the lengthy girder bridge, passed through the community on welded rail, and negotiated a high embankment on part of the abandoned Kansas City Northwestern right-of-way on the east side of town. Altogether, these improvements reportedly cost $3 million and brought the tracks above the flood-pool line (the maximum level) of the new Perry Lake, an elevation of 924 feet.

The completion of this project came only a few years before commerce in this part of Kansas suffered a precipitous fall. A lengthy recession in the farming industry, which began in the 1970s, buffeted the town's economy

Massive concrete abutments, once part of a bridge across the Delaware River, reveal the fate of the oldest line on the Santa Fe system at Valley Falls, circa 2003. (Photo by author.)

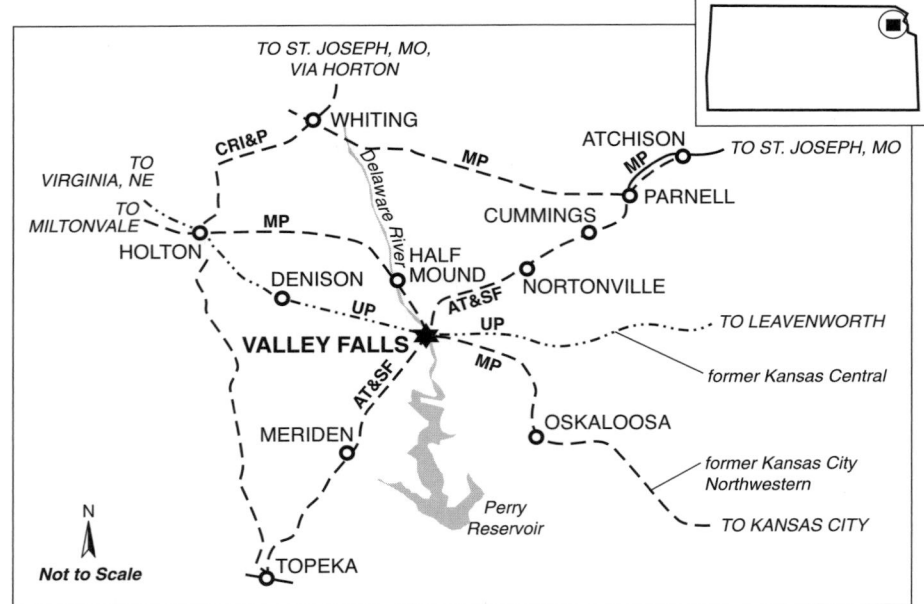

TO ST. JOSEPH, MO,
VIA HORTON

TO VIRGINIA, NE

TO MILTONVALE

CRI&P

WHITING

HOLTON

Delaware River

MP

DENISON

HALF MOUND

AT&SF

UP

VALLEY FALLS

AT&SF

MERIDEN

N

Not to Scale

TOPEKA

ATCHISON

MP

TO ST. JOSEPH, MO

PARNELL

CUMMINGS

NORTONVILLE

UP

MP

TO LEAVENWORTH

former Kansas Central

OSKALOOSA

former Kansas City Northwestern

Perry Reservoir

TO KANSAS CITY

rail service, municipal officials and businesses in Valley Falls joined those in nearby towns to mount a legal challenge to the carrier and to develop a plan for revitalizing the route.

Community leaders exhorted state and federal agencies to act on their behalf. Railroad customers reportedly felt pressure not to oppose the company's abandonment petition due to concerns that T&P could require them to remove buildings encroaching on railroad property. Several elevators had this problem, giving their owners a strong incentive not to oppose the company's plans. As such, in May 1993, the ICC voted by a narrow margin to approve abandonment of the 41-mile stretch linking Parnell to North Topeka, bringing the railroad era in Valley Falls to a close.

and forced several prominent businesses to close. The vacant Santa Fe depot mysteriously burned in 1980, delivering a blow to those committed to its preservation.

The Santa Fe targeted the Atchison–Topeka branch for elimination and in 1991 sold the route to the newly created T&P Railway, a short line named after Topeka and Parnell (a small community on the line near Atchison). This transaction ended more than a century of Santa Fe service both to Valley Falls and, more significantly, to Atchison, one of the communities after which the carrier had been named—an event deemed worthy of coverage in railroad news magazines.

Since the T&P was affiliated with a salvage company and seemed eager to sell the continuously welded rail and other materials, some speculated that the short line had acquired the route merely to tear it up, contrary to regulations against such maneuvers. The company neither owned a locomotive nor employed a train crew. When asked how it would provide service, its owners answered only that they intended to purchase the service from another carrier. The issue was effectively moot, however, since elevator owners complained that they could not afford the carrier's rates.

Only weeks after acquiring this route, T&P dismantled a stretch of track in the nearby town of Cummings—a defiant act considering that abandonment had not yet been approved. Local officials challenged this move before the Kansas Corporation Commission, a state regulatory agency, which ordered that the stretch be rebuilt. Believing that T&P had no intention of providing

Abandonment's Legacy

In response to the ICC ruling, a local advocate, Tom Ryan, spearheaded a large-scale effort to attract a government grant to transform the route into an excursion railway. Using the mailing list from his bed-and-breakfast inn, Ryan organized a committee to solicit donations from around the country and garner support for his plan. The committee wrote letters to preservationists and Santa Fe employees. In response, hundreds of people sent $20 to symbolically buy a crosstie on the route. The group ultimately raised more than $18,000, enough to cover the expenses of a feasibility study for a tourist-oriented service—the Atchison, Topeka & Scenic Railroad—between the historic railroad centers after which it had been named. Due to safety problems created by having excursion trains cross active rail lines, the group envisioned operating from Topeka's northern periphery, near U.S. Route 24.

Several governmental officials lent their support. One congressman wrote more than a dozen letters to influential policymakers in support of the initiative. Governor Joan Finney added to the plan's credibility by joining 300 other people at a 1993 banquet held in town to promote the excursion railway. Committed to seeing the project through to completion, the mayors of several towns joined the governor and symbolically entered Valley Falls on motorized railcars where they ceremoniously drove a silver spike into the dormant tracks.

Despite the relatively favorable assessment provided by the feasibility study, which showed that the tourist line had the potential to be viable if debt were kept to a minimum, the necessary funds were not forthcoming. The state's Department of Transportation rejected the group's request for approximately $4 million in Intermodal Surface Transportation Efficiency Act funds, which were to be partially matched by funds raised by supporters of the excursion railway.

The removal of the tracks came as a profound disappointment to those who had worked long hours to promote the idea of an excursion railway. When Santa Fe merged with Burlington Northern to create the Burlington Northern Santa Fe Railway in 1995, it eliminated the words *Atchison and Topeka* from its corporate name, removing another remnant of the railroad that had once linked these historic towns.

For several years, conservation officials preserved the right-of-way through the National Trails System Act. Plans for fashioning the route into a recreational path, however, met with stiff opposition from adjacent landholders. Several farmers holding title to property remained adamant in their belief that the unused right-of-way had reverted to them. After a banker representing these individuals threatened legal action in 1997, officials quietly dropped the idea of creating a trail.

Epilogue

Today Valley Falls is widely considered to be one of the most attractive small towns in Kansas. Notable for its well-maintained homes, charming downtown, and brick streets, its peaceful ambience belies its energetic past. In an attractive nineteenth-century edifice, the Valley Falls Historical Society's museum recounts the story of the place once called Grasshopper Falls. Several blocks away, Grasshopper Park honors the community's former name and is home to the occasional Grasshopper Days celebration.

Valley Falls illustrates a fundamental paradox in the movement to preserve light-density lines: routes equipped with continuously welded rail, crossties in good condition, and generous allocations of ballast can be the most difficult to save. Their high scrap value provides an added

incentive for their dismemberment, an issue that provided the Surface Transportation Board with the impetus to develop new policies to prevent salvage companies from abusing the abandonment process.

Travelers following the right-of-way farther north will find the Santa Fe corridor near Valley Falls reduced to little more than grassy embankments and piles of rotting crossties. The lengthy steel bridge crossing the river at the edge of Valley Falls, largely hidden from public view, survived for years after the removal of the tracks. For some residents, the bridge's survival had sparked optimism that the ambitious proposals for the Atchison, Topeka & Scenic Railway might someday become a reality, but work crews removed the immense structure in the summer of 1998, extinguishing any remaining hope of a rail service revival.

For Further Study

SUGGESTED READINGS:
Collins, Robert. *Ghost Railroads of Kansas.* David City, Neb.: South Platte Press, 1997, 40, 43.
The First Hundred Years of Jefferson County, Kansas. Valley Falls, Kans.: Wilson-Davis Publishers, 1955, 1–10.
Quastler, I. E. *Kansas Central Narrow Gauge: Slim Rails Across the Midlands.* David City, Neb.: South Platte Press, 1999, 37–45, 56–65, 72.
_____. *Union Pacific West From Leavenworth: A History of the Leavenworth, Kansas & Western Railway.* David City, Neb.: South Platte Press, 1999, 28, 37, 45–49, 59–68.

OTHER PRINCIPAL REFERENCES:
Andreas, A. T. *History of the State of Kansas.* Chicago: W. G. Cutler, 1883, 505–6
Bryant, Keith L., Jr. *History of the Atchison, Topeka & Santa Fe Railway.* Lincoln: University of Nebraska Press, 1974, 23–25.
Crimmins, Harold. "A History of the Kansas Central Railway, 1981–1935." *Emporia State Research Studies* 2, no. 4 (1954): 3–34.
Lewis, Edward A. *American Shortline Railway Guide.* 5th ed. Waukesha, Wis.: Kalmbach Publishing, 1996, 361.
Quastler, I. E. *Missouri Pacific Northwest: A History of the Kansas City Northwestern Railroad.* David City, Neb.: South Platte Press, 1994, 1–136.

FERRIDAY, LOUISIANA (3,723)

Historic operators: Missouri Pacific Railroad; Texas & Pacific Railway; Louisiana & Arkansas Railway
Last route abandoned: 1988
Notable reuse of right-of-way: Municipal park

Ferriday is today a community of modest dwellings and cotton warehouses on the western banks of Lake Concordia, a reservoir along the migrating waters of the Mississippi River. Little now remains of its once-extensive railroad system except for some overgrown embankments and the crumbling foundations of railroad structures. Its current humble appearance notwithstanding, the saga of this small town's trains and the famous personalities who grew up near its tracks has few parallels in the Deep South.

Historical Perspective

When Englishman William Ferriday and his wife, Helen, moved to Concordia Parish in 1840, they established the Helena Plantation near the western banks of the Mississippi. These hard-working settlers accumulated sufficient wealth to send their sons to be educated in Pennsylvania, a privilege enjoyed by few in this rural area. Their youngest son, John, was sent north for schooling in the early 1860s and stayed there after graduation to work for the Pennsylvania Railroad. When John returned to the plantation around 1870, he brought with him insights about the importance of railroads in community development.

The railroad era in Concordia Parish began when the Vidalia & Lake Concordia Railroad & Steamboat Company reached the vicinity of Ferriday's plantation in 1876. This narrow-gauge route, extending from the wharf along the Mississippi River at Vidalia to Concordia (a rural location near the southern tip of the lake), was oriented primarily toward serving agriculture. In 1878, it was sold to the newly created Natchez, Red River & Texas Railroad. The new owner completed a 25-mile extension to Trinity (Black River) in 1886.

Residents of the parish came to depend on both the services of this railroad and the leadership of John Ferriday, whom they elected president of the policy jury, a position giving him considerable power. These proud Southerners looked forward to better transportation connections when a second railroad, the New Orleans & Northwestern Railway, completed a 77-mile route between Natchez, Mississippi, and Rayville, Louisiana, in 1890. This standard-gauge carrier laid its tracks through the heart of Ferriday's plantation and depended on ferries to move freight and passenger cars across the Mississippi River.

With rail service now available on a pair of routes, the economy of Concordia Parish flourished. John Ferriday, however, did not live to see the local railroad industry in full blossom. He died in 1894, the same year the New Orleans & Northwestern Railroad extended its line north to Bastrop, Louisiana, making it part of a new long-distance route. These tracks shouldered an even heavier traffic burden after representatives of the St. Louis, Iron Mountain & Southern Railway (a company popularly called the Iron Mountain) bought the carrier eight years later.

These developments laid the groundwork for an ambitious plan prepared in 1903 by the Iron Mountain in conjunction with the Texas & Pacific Railway to create an entirely new community serving both existing and proposed rail lines. This railroad town, to be built on the Ferriday plantation, would support a system of routes linking both Natchez and New Orleans with Little Rock, Memphis, and other cities. Proponents of the plan believed that such a system would be able to effectively compete with the Illinois Central Railroad and the various steamboat companies—the dominant transportation

providers between the lower Mississippi River Delta and Memphis at the time.

The plan moved forward on an expeditious timetable. By the end of 1903, the Texas & Pacific had laid its tracks north from Addis, Louisiana, to the newly created town of Ferriday. The Memphis, Helena & Louisiana Railroad (an Iron Mountain subsidiary) simultaneously extended its route south from the Arkansas boundary to Clayton, a junction on the Iron Mountain 5 miles north of the town site. For the first time, freight could move by rail over a direct route on the western side of the Mississippi the entire distance from Memphis to New Orleans.

These and other improvements pushed the old narrow-gauge line rapidly toward obsolescence. The Iron

The end of the railroad era is only a few years away as this Missouri Pacific GP-15 pulls a load of lumber in Ferriday on June 3, 1985. The station to the right of the tracks was brought in from Lake Providence, as attested to by fading letters on the side of the building. (Photo by Michael H. Palmieri.)

This large parcel of land adjacent to downtown Ferriday—formerly part of a freight yard—is today part of the community's spacious Depot Park; other property nearby lies fallow. (Photo by author.)

Mountain began operating this line through a subsidiary and converted the tracks west of Concordia Junction (a mile south of Ferriday) to standard gauge in 1906. It abandoned the remaining narrow-gauge segment east to Vidalia the following year (operating trains instead over the parallel Iron Mountain route instead) and then leased the segment west of Concordia Junction to the Louisiana & Arkansas Railway in 1913.

By the time the Iron Mountain became part of the Missouri Pacific (MoPac) system in 1917, Ferriday was a mature community with a downtown several blocks long. The Johnson Hotel, a spacious dry goods store called Pasternack's, and several large sawmills teemed with activity. The opening of the Ferriday Compress & Warehouse Company facility in 1926 established the town as a prominent center for the cotton trade.

MoPac's freight yard was a particularly busy place. The carrier interchanged cars with the Texas & Pacific in Ferriday and with the Louisiana & Arkansas Railway at Concordia Junction. Northbound trains shared a common track to Clayton, where some trains diverged toward Winnsboro and Collinston (on the former New Orleans & Northwestern) while others headed toward Lake Providence (on the former Memphis, Helena & Louisiana). At Vidalia, southbound trains on the MoPac, as well as those of the Louisana & Arkansas, turned freight cars

over to the Natchez & Louisiana Railway Transfer Company, a subsidiary that ferried them across the Mississippi River to Natchez.

The routes through Ferriday apparently never handled a significant amount of Memphis–New Orleans business as originally conceived, but they did become important transportation thoroughfares. In 1928, passengers could depart the Ferriday vicinity on any of eleven trains each day except Sunday. MoPac passenger trains operated to Memphis daily by way of both Helena (via Tallulah) and Little Rock (via Winnsboro). Travelers heading to the Tennessee city via Little Rock had the advantage of Pullman sleeping-car service. Passengers could also book passage from Concordia Junction on the Louisiana & Arkansas, which was by now a prominent route linking eastern Arkansas to the Mississippi River.

By 1930, Ferriday's neighborhoods were home to more than 2,500 inhabitants. In the midst of the Great Depression, three local families celebrated the birth of sons destined for stardom—colorful individuals who would one day establish Ferriday as a noteworthy celebrity cradle. Mickey Gilley, Jerry Lee Lewis, and Jimmy Swaggart were cousins born less than six months apart during the mid-1930s. Gilley would become a noted country singer, Lewis a pop singer, and Swaggert a widely recognized evangelist. Another Ferriday native, Howard K. Smith, Jr., was the son of a former Texas & Pacific conductor. Smith pursued a successful broadcasting career in the late 1930s and eventually earned celebrity status as well.

Changing Times

Operating rail lines in the Mississippi Delta had long been a problem for the railroads of Concordia Parish. Not only was ferrying railcars across the river a heavy financial burden, but chronic flood damage added greatly to maintenance-of-way expenses. In 1940, Texas & Pacific abandoned its flood-prone route to Ferriday, and

MoPac stopped ferrying passenger trains across the river. Instead of loading these trains onto the ferry, MoPac instituted bus service between Natchez and Vidalia over a newly completed highway bridge.

Although railroad traffic rebounded as America deepened its involvement in World War II, MoPac eliminated its lone remaining locomotive-drawn passenger train through Ferriday, ending the community's through service to Little Rock and Memphis. It is ironic that Ferriday native Howard K. Smith, who worked as a CBS correspondent in Germany during the early part of the war, would author a book during this period entitled *The Last Train from Berlin*.

The changes affecting the parish's rail system after the war were not altogether negative. MoPac continued passenger service in the form of a gas-electric motorcar operating between Vidalia and Monroe, as well as several buses operated by its motor-coach subsidiary. In 1945, the Louisiana & Arkansas sold its line between the southern edge of Ferriday (Concordia Junction) and Packton (near Winnfield) to the Louisiana Midland Railway. The new operator joined the Louisiana & Arkansas and the Mississippi Central Railroad to create a prominent east–west freight corridor called the Natchez Route, reinvigorating the ferry operation. In Ferriday, however, the most illustrious years of railroading were relegated to the past. MoPac gradually reduced its employment and suspended its motorcar run in 1950. When Louisiana Midland discontinued its policy of allowing customers to ride in a caboose three years later, local travelers no longer had any rail-passenger service at their disposal.

Despite the loss of many railroad jobs, Ferriday's neighborhoods, while heavily segregated, remained culturally vibrant. Leon "Peewee" Whitaker, a renowned black musician, made Ferriday his home and frequently played at Haney's Big House, a local institution attracting the likes of B. B. King, Muddy Waters, Fats Domino, and the irrepressible Jerry Lee Lewis.

Unfortunately, many of the town's institutions could not be sustained as the number of well-paying jobs diminished. Haney's burned down in 1967, Pasternack's store closed in 1973, and local sawmills scaled back. In 1980,

one of two companies repairing railcars in the Ferriday area closed.

By the time MoPac merged with Union Pacific in 1982, grass and weeds had overwhelmed Ferriday's freight yard. Of the major freight customers in the area, only the International Paper Company in Natchez still used the carrier's services. To serve the paper company, the carrier had to transfer freight cars by way of the *Ste. Genevieve*, an aging barge that was the last railcar-ferry crossing Mississippi.

MoPac discontinued use of the barge and relegated the segment from Clayton to Collinston via Winnsboro for storage of empty railcars before abandoning it in 1983. The Louisiana Midland removed a portion of its route west of Concordia from service in 1984 and received approval to abandon this segment the following year. Consequently, all that remained of the rail network in the Ferriday vicinity was the little-used route linking Vidalia to McGehee, Arkansas (once part of the route to Helena and Memphis via Lake Providence).

A series of derailments on this line exposed an urgent need for track repairs. In early 1987, three empty cement cars from a Union Pacific freight train traveling north from Ferriday derailed near Goldman (a small town northeast of Clayton). After righting the cars, the crew resumed their trip, only to have another car jump the tracks. Several days later, still another derailment interrupted the train's progress. With safe passage obviously no longer possible, the carrier removed the route from

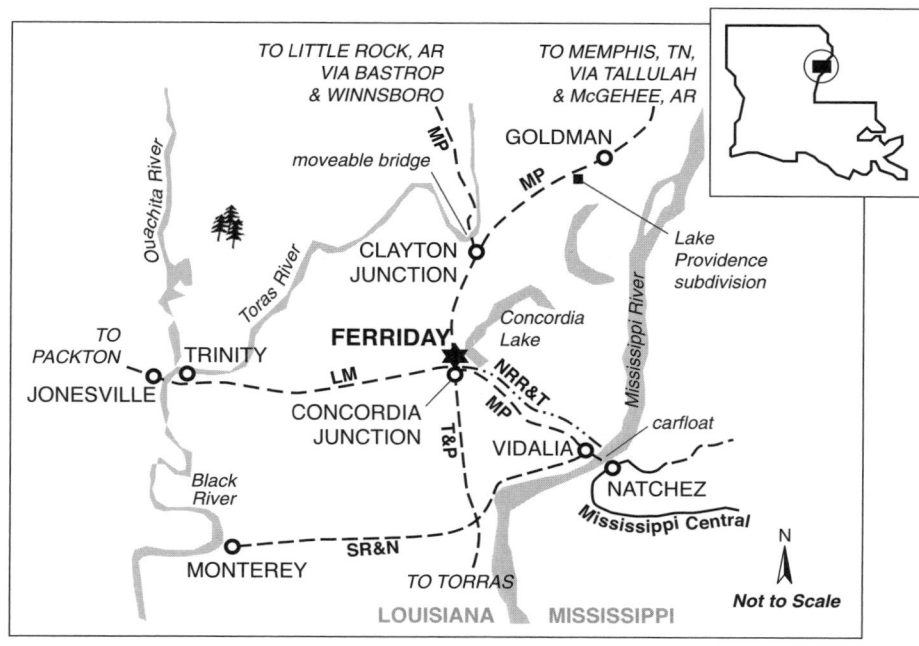

service. During the summer of 1988, MoPac received approval to abandon the entire route between Vidalia and McGehee, a distance of more than 170 miles.

The elimination of rail service came at an inopportune time. Ferriday was struggling with unsafe drinking water, poor trash disposal, municipal corruption, and a series of robberies. Its industrial outlook remained grim. The townspeople felt a sense of loss when their spirited campaign to save the former MoPac depot from demolition ended unsuccessfully.

Abandonment's Legacy

Prospective rail operators considered acquiring portions of both the MoPac and Louisiana Midland lines. The Dixie River Railroad sought to buy the MoPac route from McGehee, Arkansas, to Ferriday and even purchased locomotives, but it could not obtain financing. The Delta Southern Railroad, a short line, purchased and resumed service over the portion of this line north of Quimby, a small town near Tallulah, in 1989. It could not be persuaded, however, to purchase the more southerly portion.

Local railroad customers, including cotton distributors and a lumber company, felt betrayed by the line's abandonment. Louisiana Railcar, a repair shop, had received a letter from Governor Edwin Edwards assuring it that the state government would work to support the continuation of service. With all hope for such service gone, the company reportedly used a trackmobile to pull freight cars stranded at its shop to the interchange at Tallulah.

When salvage workers removed the tracks, they left behind an expanse of unkempt property that physically divided the town. The municipal government worked to rejuvenate the community's sagging economy and successfully had the Ferriday Commercial District listed on the National Register of Historic Places in 1995. However, the area where the freight yard, roundhouse, and other railroad facilities once stood remained vacant.

To draw attention to the community's colorful past, local leaders opened the Ferriday Museum in 1995 and enlisted the help of a garden club to fashion portions of the former freight yard area into Ferriday Depot Park. Another parcel near the center of town became the site of a new post office, but the railroad's withdrawal continued to affect Ferriday in undesirable ways. Officials considered the absence of rail service an obstacle to their efforts to attract industry and expressed concern that, without new employers, further declines in population would be inevitable.

Epilogue

Visitors will find little in Ferriday except vacant property to remind them of the town's heritage as a railroad center. A strip of track encrusted in concrete at the former Louisiana Railcar facility and a dilapidated former MoPac building near the old roundhouse site offer a shadowy reminder of transportation years ago. Pasternack's store burned down in 2001, leaving only its sign, and the Arcade Theater has shut its doors. A thrice-weekly motor coach operating via Ferriday from Natchez to Monroe continues to evoke the travel patterns of the past, and in Clayton, a swing bridge across the Tensas River stands as a silent reminder of the age of steam.

To showcase the past, the municipal government renovated the former post office building in 2002, moved in the collection of the Ferriday Museum, and transformed it into the Delta Music Museum. The institution celebrates the community's musical heritage and holds a festival that attracts crowds to downtown Ferriday, reminiscent of those at the height of the railroad era. Considering the legacy of music in this small town, it seems fitting that Johnny Cash mentions Ferriday in his hit song, "I've Been Everywhere."

For older residents of the community, the horn blasts of diesel locomotives are also familiar sounds of the past. Today, the spirit of the former railroad town lives on in a book by noted author Elaine Dundy and in the motion picture *Great Balls of Fire*, which begins by depicting the youthful Jerry Lee Lewis and Jimmy Swaggart going to "the other side of the tracks" to watch a talented piano player at a black nightclub. In this scene, with a block signal visible in the background, Ferriday's railroad era briefly flashes to life once more.

For Further Study

SUGGESTED READINGS:

Dundy, Elaine. *Ferriday, Louisiana.* New York: Donald I. Fine, 1991, 48–74, 184–216.

Fair, James R. *The Louisiana & Arkansas Railway: The Story of a Regional Line.* DeKalb: Northern Illinois University Press, 1997, 192–93.

Karsen, Bob. "Mo-Pac's Navy: Part II." *Railfan & Railroad* 4, no. 8 (1982): 50–57.

OTHER PRINCIPAL REFERENCES:
Calhoun, Robert Dabney. "A History of Concordia Parish, Louisiana." *Louisiana Historical Quarterly* (Jan. 1932): 175–76.
Hilton, George W. *American Narrow Gauge Railroads.* Stanford: Stanford University Press, 1990, 406.
Missouri Pacific Railway. *The Missouri Pacific Railway Company and the St. Louis & Iron Mountain & Southern Railway Company.* St. Louis: Missouri Pacific Railway, 1915, 85, 99–102.

Smith, Howard K. *Events Leading Up to My Death: The Life of a Twentieth-Century Reporter.* New York: St. Martins Press, 1996, 3–4, 403.
Walker, Dale. "Our Predecessors: The New Orleans and Northwestern Railroad Company." *The Eagle, Quarterly Publication of the Missouri Pacific Historical Society* 19, no. 3 (fall 1994): 11.
Zlatkovich, Charles P. *Texas & Pacific Railway: Operations and Traffic.* El Paso, Tex.: Westerner Press, 1998, 53.

CURRIE, MINNESOTA (303)

Historic operator: Chicago & North Western Railway
Last route abandoned: 1980
Notable reuse of right-of-way: End-O-Line Railroad Museum

*O*f the many Minnesota villages that a half century ago were served only by a lightly used branch line, none has gone to greater lengths to commemorate its railroad heritage than Currie. Although the residents of Currie were unable to save their Chicago & North Western branch, today they honor their railway heritage through their generous support of the End-O-Line Railroad Park and Museum, one of southwestern Minnesota's most notable historical institutions.

Historical Perspective

After arriving at the New Ulm depot in 1872, pioneer Neil Currie and his father, Archibald, set out across the prairie by wagon. Planning to establish a community, these rugged Scots traveled west some 60 miles to a site on the Des Moines River. They established a town site only a short distance from Lake Shetek, the largest lake in southwestern Minnesota, near the spot where a group of Native Americans had taken the lives of fifteen settlers only a decade before.

The Curries, along with the other immigrants from Scotland, dammed the river near its headwaters and built a gristmill. They christened their settlement Shetek and set about providing services to local farmers. The townspeople soon renamed their village Currie, in honor of the pioneers who established it, and looked ahead to a promising future as their town became the seat of Murray County in 1873.

As agriculture spread across the Great Plains, many communities, especially those in Minnesota, voiced outrage over the railroad industry's seemingly monopolistic practices. Their emotional pleas for relief gave rise to the Granger movement, which reached its climax in 1874, when Minnesota passed a law curbing the rate-setting powers of the railroads serving the state. However, a severe depression the following year greatly hurt the railroad industry's financial condition and encouraged legislators to adopt a more conciliatory stance toward the so-called granger roads. Although the Granger movement was short-lived, its legacy would be felt for many years.

Currie was still without a railroad, and this problem discouraged leaders who desperately wanted their community to one day become a prominent city. In 1878, the St. Paul & Sioux City Railroad built a branch from Heron Lake to Woodstock (later extended to Pipestone), but its tracks were laid over a more southerly corridor that did not directly serve Currie. This not only frustrated local development plans but also led to the creation of a new political rival, Slayton, which sought to wrest from Currie its role as the county seat. In 1886, voters authorized the relocation of the seat to Slayton and the outlook for Currie took an abrupt turn for the worse. A bitter dispute about the electoral outcome ensued. The citizens of Currie were jubilant when a court ruled in 1887 that their community should be reinstated as the seat, but had to face more disappointment when a special legislative act two years later reversed that decision.

As Slayton reaped the benefits of being a railroad town and center of government, Currie suffered the loss of at least eight businesses, including the county newspaper, its only remaining hotel, and the Methodist church. The situation did not improve significantly until the Des Moines Valley Railway Company of Minnesota reached Jeffers in 1899 and then closed the 24-mile gap to Currie the following year. By that time, the opportunity for Currie to achieve regional prominence had slipped away.

The line to Currie was assimilated into the Chicago, St. Paul, Minneapolis & Omaha Railway, an entity popularly called the Omaha Road, and stretched 38 miles from Bingham Lake, a junction near Windom on the Omaha Road's main line. Although rumors that the Omaha Road (which the Chicago & North Western controlled) would extend its line to Tyler proved false, the new route brought considerable vitality to the long-suffering community.

Within a few years of the railroad's arrival, Currie grew to have some thirty-three businesses, including a bank and several hotels. In 1907, it became home to a Catholic school staffed by the Sisters of St. Joseph. The townspeople came to depend heavily on the mixed train that departed for Bingham Lake each morning (except Sunday) from the town's spacious four-room depot; this modest service allowed them to make transfers to passenger trains on the main line and arrive in Minneapolis before the end of the business day. In 1918, the carrier built a new depot at the junction in Bingham Lake.

Currie's fortunes took another turn for the worse during the late 1920s when a severe drought crippled its

The crew of a Chicago & North Western train, 38 miles from the junction at Bingham Lake, turns a Fairbanks Morse "Baby Trainmaster" (H16–66) locomotive in Currie in 1955. (Courtesy of the End-O-Line Museum.)

agricultural sector. The community survived the loss of a prominent bank and other local institutions, only to experience more hardship during the Great Depression, when another series of droughts devastated crops. The railroad helped Currie through these difficult times, carrying coal, sand, grain, and carload freight, as well as passengers to Bingham Lake. It also carried many inbound travelers on their way to the spacious hotel and rustic cabins at nearby Lake Shetek.

Changing Times

Currie did not rebound after the Depression to the same extent as many other towns in the area. After the public high school closed in 1939, older students had to be bused to Tracy. The mixed train soldiered on through World War II and into the postwar era, but Currie's population dropped and business conditions remained soft. The North Western still had a variety of local freight customers, with the grain elevator and the Des Moines River Cement Tile Works among the most important. Its trains operated to Currie from the yard in St. James until around 1940, when the carrier began dispatching them instead from Worthington, a division point farther west on the main line. Currie's economy, however, was starting to crumble.

The End-O-Line Museum in Currie, known for its preserved depot and turntable (left), commemorates the colorful heritage of small-town railroading in southwestern Minnesota. (Photo by author.)

By the late 1940s, declining tonnage and competition from trucks had taken their toll on the branch to Currie. In 1951, the tile company went out of business; by the mid-1950s, mixed-train service had ended and an agent no longer staffed the local depot. In 1963, the resort at Lake Shetek closed, putting additional strain on Currie's institutions.

As families moved away, Currie's population began to fall at an alarming rate, prompting the Catholic school to close in 1972. Despite bountiful harvests, the rail line's prospects weakened considerably as the North Western heightened its emphasis on unit trains, which could not be accommodated on the branch without major improvements. Such trains would have allowed grain to be shipped directly to distant destinations in train-size increments.

When the North Western reorganized as the employee-owned Chicago & North Western Transportation Company in 1972, the Omaha Road lost its corporate identity. That same year, Colleen Illg and Roxanne Probst, junior leaders in the local 4-H Club, launched an effort to clean up the badly overgrown railroad yard. After working with fifty-six other volunteers to create an interesting roadside attraction, the teenage girls expressed a desire to find a way to preserve the deteriorating depot and turntable. Inspired by their example, the 4-H Club, led by Louise Gervais, acquired the carrier's wooden depot for a nominal sum in 1972. Lacking the funds to move the depot off railroad property, the club turned to the local government and county board of commissioners for assistance, which they secured the following year. The county acquired 3 acres of railroad land, including the turntable, on the opposite side of County Road 38 and moved the depot to this vacant parcel.

Although these efforts helped commemorate the community's past, they did little to ameliorate concerns about its future. The town was shaken by an armed robbery at the local bank in 1975 and suffered from a continuing loss in population as well as the closing of its public elementary school— its last primary educational institution—during the nation's bicentennial year. Many businesses felt that the loss of rail service would aggravate Currie's economic problems. With the hope of preventing the local route's abandonment, business leaders formed the Currie Branch Transportation Inc. in 1977 and hired an attorney to assess their legal options. It soon became evident that the group lacked the financial capacity either to acquire the line or to offer subsidies large enough to cover the railroad's deficits. Bowing to the inevitable, the organization shifted its attention to ensuring the orderly liquidation of railroad property.

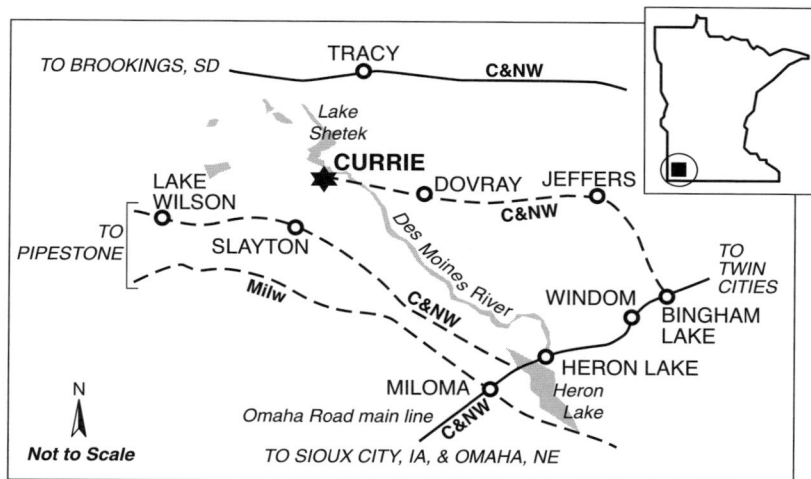

Volunteers in the community, including Gervais and Dorothy Rupport, concurrently worked to transform the properties acquired by the county into the End-O-Line Railroad Museum. The museum received support from a variety of sources, including a state and federal transportation grant program, charitable gambling proceeds from a local Town and Country organization, the American Legion, and the county government. Soon, visitors arrived from considerable distances to see the museum's exhibits, especially its turntable (which was listed on the National Register of Historic Places in 1977), and its depot and engine house.

While businesses in Currie remained deeply troubled about the impending loss of rail service, their concerns were barely perceptible as mergers, bankruptcies, and abandonment reshaped Minnesota's railroad system. With the state's agricultural industry in the midst of a recession, the North Western abandoned its line from Currie to Bingham Lake in January 1980, bringing the local railroad era to a close.

Abandonment's Legacy

After abandonment, the local transportation organization acquired most of the right-of-way in the town's vicinity (which the railroad owned in fee simple) and resold it to area property owners for private use. Currie's grain elevator, already heavily reliant on motor carriers for its shipping needs, used a fleet of private trucks to transport grain to Pipestone and other terminals for transshipment to distant markets. The museum acquired 1,000 feet of preserved track to use for locomotive demonstrations.

By the end of 1980, the North Western had also abandoned its route through Slayton, ending the last of its service to the county as a whole. The carrier's efforts to reduce the size of its system took a more dramatic step forward in 1986, when it sold more than 900 miles of routes—including its lightly used line through Tracy—to the Dakota, Minnesota & Eastern Railroad. Before the decade's end, the carrier had 40 percent fewer route-miles than it had had twenty years earlier.

As the once venerable granger roads, their successors, and other railroad companies moved aggressively to reduce the size of their systems, they abandoned more than 3,000 miles of routes in Minnesota over a two-decade period, pushing the state near the top in total miles abandoned by 1995. In the process, Murray County emerged as one of the nation's most agriculturally productive counties without an active rail line.

The museum, meanwhile, took steps to ensure that the county's railroad heritage would not be forgotten. It enlisted the financial support of the Minnesota Historical Society to acquire historical railroad equipment, including a Fairmont railroad motorcar (popularly called a speeder). In 2004, the institution ceremoniously paraded through town the latest addition to its collection, a narrow-gauge steam locomotive built in 1875, with Gervais ringing the bell. Today, the museum exemplifies the colorful heritage of railroading in the southwestern part of the state.

Epilogue

Visitors to Currie will find the museum an immaculately maintained and popular seasonal attraction. In addition to the depot, engine house, and turntable, its collection includes a local schoolhouse, general store, grist mill, Grand Trunk caboose, North Western water tower from Walnut Grove, and section foreman's home from Comfrey. A former Georgia Northern steam locomotive rests near the old depot platform. Many visitors enjoy the museum's miniature railway, an amusement equipped with its own scale-model depot, coal bunker, and water tower.

A short distance south of the museum, an upscale restaurant established in 2002 occupies a historic structure that originally was the general store owned by the Currie family. At Lake Shetek, portions of the rustic Depresssion-era camp area are today listed on the National Register of Historic Places.

Lacking a major highway or a large retail store, and having lost its railroad and schools and its largest employer (the tile manufacturer), Currie seems destined to remain a substantially smaller community than it was years ago. Although the grain elevator remains in business, its facility is today separated from the old rail grade, having been relocated after a fire damaged the older structure.

The saga of the Currie Branch hardly seems significant against the backdrop of the profound changes that have affected the most prominent rail lines of the upper Great Plains. Considering the problems created by the absence of rail service during the late nineteenth century, however, it seems especially ironic that this community is today home to such a prominent railroad museum while in Slayton, which prospered years ago at Currie's expense, barely a trace of the railroad line remains. The impressive efforts of a 4-H Club to clean up Currie's overgrown railroad yard made the difference, inspiring an entire county to preserve the crumbling remnants of a branch line that few others had considered to have enduring value.

For Further Study

SUGGESTED READINGS:

Currie Town and Country Club. *Currie Yesterday & Today.* Currie, Minn.: Currie Town and Country Club, 1997, 35.

Grant, H. Roger. *The North Western: A History of the Chicago & North Western Railway System.* DeKalb: Northern Illinois University Press, 1996, 69–73.

OTHER PRINCIPAL REFERENCES:

Blaszak, Michael W. "Chicago & North Western: Evolution of a Survivor." *Trains* (April 1994): 32–45.

Grant, H. Roger. "Three Components of the Chicago & North Western: The Omaha Road, the Louie, and the Great Weedy." *Railroad History* 154 (1986): 17–33.

Miller, George H. *Railroads and the Granger Laws.* Madison: University of Wisconsin Press, 1971, 136–38.

ELY, MINNESOTA (3,724)

Historic operator: Duluth, Missabe & Iron Range Railway
Last route abandoned: 1982
Notable reuse of right-of-way: Proposed extension of Missabe Trail

A century ago, at the center of the Vermilion Iron Range, Ely appeared on the verge of becoming one of Minnesota's greatest cities. Today deteriorating shafts, mounds of iron ore, and old railway embankments are nearly all that remain of a mining industry once vital to the community's development. Although Ely is today known mostly as a gathering point for visitors of the Boundary Waters Canoe Area, its industrial heritage is still an important part of its cultural identity.

Historical Perspective

Eighteenth-century trappers working for French trading companies found plentiful wild game near the tree-lined banks of Long Lake, an oblong body of water now known as Lake Shagawa. The British and Americans who later trapped in the area were similarly impressed. Nevertheless, the future of this region's economy rested on a bulkier commodity below the surface: the vast deposits of iron ore.

The Northwest Territory, a region that encompassed much of northern Minnesota, formally became part of the United States in 1814. More than sixty years would pass, however, before the ore deposits near Lake Shagawa would finally be brought to light. In 1880, George Stuntz, a government surveyor, happened upon this iron ore. Stuntz's discovery remained unexploited until 1886, when two pioneering brothers, Martin and William H. Pattison, located this "hill of iron." The Pattisons waited out the winter in Duluth and then returned in

1887 to assist in a formal assessment of the region's ore deposits. These efforts culminated in the opening of the Chandler Mine and, a short time later, the Pioneer Mine, thus launching one of the first great mining booms in the upper Great Lakes region.

The multitudes of men who arrived by stagecoach and sleigh seeking jobs in these mines as well as in the Soudan Mine in neighboring Tower suffered from severe housing shortages. Near the Pioneer, miners crowded into unkempt neighborhoods of tents and shanties. On this 40-acre town site, a ramshackle settlement emerged around a general store, a post office, and the Pioneer Hotel. Initially called Florence, it was soon renamed Ely, after Samuel and George Ely, two brothers who tirelessly championed the mining of, Vermilion iron despite never having visited the region.

When the Duluth & Iron Range Railroad built its main line to Ely in 1888, it gave mining companies the means to ship their products at relatively low cost to various industrial ports on Lake Superior. Immense shipments of

161

An excursion train chartered by a mining company, boasting an assortment of heavyweight cars, makes a rare visit to Ely on September 19, 1981. Powered by two SD-9s, this run was the last passenger train ever to reach the historic mining town. (Photo by Steve Glischinski.)

ore soon arrived at these ports on trains operating from Ely via Allen Junction, a busy railroad hub east of Virginia, Minnesota.

Ely had 600 inhabitants by the end of 1888 and substantially more when it received its city charter three years later. A major beneficiary of the town's prosperity, the Duluth & Iron Range built a 4-mile extension from Ely to Winton, a logging camp, in 1894. This extension generated large shipments of lumber and contributed to the route's reputation as one of the most productive routes in northern Minnesota. Five years later, the Swallow & Hopkins Lumber Company began operating a logging railway at Winton—a narrow-gauge system that hauled pine and spruce to the Winton sawmill and eventually encompassed more than 20 miles of track.

Amid a burst of industrial expansion, scores of Finnish and Slovenian immigrants arrived by train to work in Ely's six underground mines. These hardy laborers accepted notoriously difficult working conditions in the mines, sometimes walking in mud so thick that they had difficulty setting themselves free. Railroad workers and steamship hands also faced significant occupational dangers. In 1896, the *Samuel P. Ely*, an ore-hauling vessel named after the legendary miner, sank near Two Harbors. That same year, a collision between a freight and a passenger train near Ely claimed several lives.

Due to the high oxygen content of Vermilion Range ore, steel producers were more than willing to defray the cost of shipping this raw material to the Great Lakes. Recognizing the quality of the Pioneer's ore, well-known industrialist Andrew Carnegie purchased the property in 1898. Carnegie's company went on to become the largest steel producer in America and merged with the U.S. Steel Company in 1901. Minnesota ore was of such importance to this consolidated entity (which kept the U.S. Steel name) that the company acquired the Duluth & Iron Range that same year.

With the local mines expanding at a spectacular rate, the Vermilion Range and the much larger Mesabi Range to the southwest rose to the top of American iron ore production. In 1910, travelers could arrive in Ely on any of three passenger trains operating in each direction between Duluth and Winton, with two operating on Sundays. Although Winton struggled as the timber supply dwindled, leading to the discontinuation of its private logging railroad before the last sawmill closed in 1923, Ely still had a vibrant economy. The railroad's large roundhouse was the source of many well-paying jobs. The opening of the elegant three-story Forest Hotel in 1927 suggested that further prosperity lay ahead.

The Soudan Mine, one of the country's leading sources of iron ore, emerged as a particularly awe-inspiring manifestation of the region's abundant natural resources, boasting its own large freight yard and sprawling mining railway. The elevator in its shaft took miners 2,400 feet below the surface, a staggering depth for a mine of this era.

Changing Times

Ely's almost total dependence on mining had long raised concerns about its economic future. The true consequences of this dependence became obvious in the late 1920s, when production gradually shifted to the Mesabi Iron Range. Although the completion of a magnificent city hall in 1930 suggested otherwise, Ely's most prosperous years as a mining center had ended.

Mining production sharply diminished after another ore-hauling road, the Duluth, Missabe & Northern Railway, leased the Duluth & Iron Range system in 1930. (The words *Mesabi* and *Missabe* are both derived from the Chippewa word for "giant.") Adversity struck in 1933 when townspeople gathered to dedicate a municipal airport. Expecting to celebrate the beginning of a new transportation era, they were instead burdened with the horrific memory of seeing a flying stuntman plummet to his death. By the time the Duluth, Missabe & Iron Range Railway ("Missabe Road"), the successor to the Duluth, Missabe & Northern, acquired the local railroad's assets in 1938, Ely had fallen on hard times.

Iron ore shipments recovered during World War II, when U.S. Steel and other manufacturers worked around the clock to support the Allied military effort. Many travelers returned to the rails even though the Missabe Road's passenger service had diminished to one train in each direction. The postwar business was less robust, prompting the Missabe Road to replace the steam-locomotive-drawn passenger train with a Budd rail-diesel car in 1953. Despite the initial popularity of these self-propelled cars, which made the 120-mile trip from Duluth to Winton in about three-and-one-half hours, they could not match the convenience of automobiles and buses. When the carrier discontinued the fondly remembered Budd car run during the summer of 1961, the last of its passenger service drew to a close.

The remaining mines approached obsolescence as taconite (a low-grade ore having as little as 20 percent iron content and typically excavated from open pits) replaced iron ore as the region's leading export. Technological improvements allowed oxygen to be blown through liquid steel, greatly reducing the demand for the Vermilion Range's high-oxygen ore. In 1962, the Soudan—the oldest mine in the range—shipped its final carload of ore. In 1967, the Pioneer, the last of Ely's mines, did the same. To mark the end of an era, the train carrying the final shipment of ore headed for Lake Superior was decorated with the American flag. Several months later, with Ely plunging into recession, flames raged through the Forest Hotel, the largest structure in town. The resulting damage left the historic building—including Vertin's café, a popular gathering place on its ground floor—beyond repair. The café later reopened across the street, where it remains today.

The townspeople held out hope that the expansion of tourism would foster a general economic recovery. In 1972, a modern airport opened in Ely, raising expectations that

Ely's depot once again welcomes travelers arriving from distant cities—only now as a sporting goods store. The nearby roundhouse is currently a welding shop. (Photo by author.)

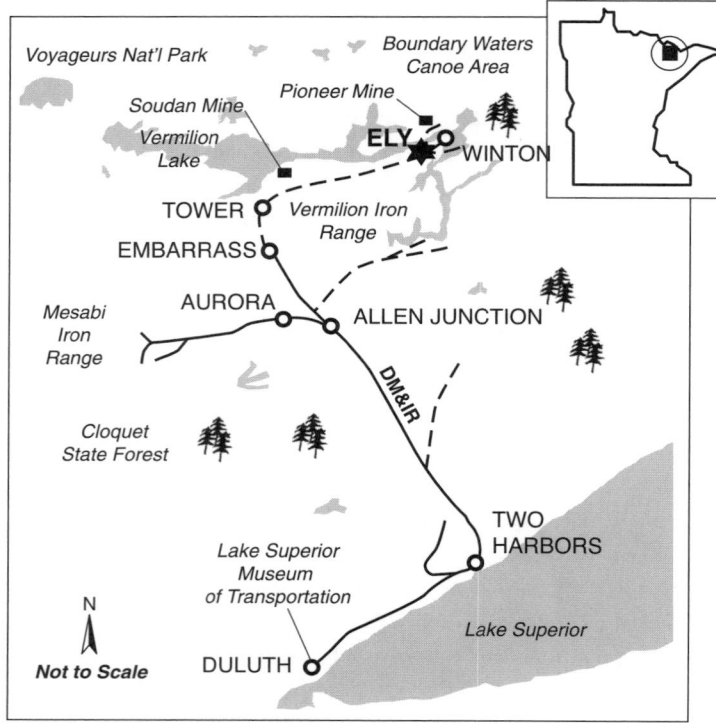

Voyageurs Nat'l Park

Boundary Waters Canoe Area

Pioneer Mine

Soudan Mine

Vermilion Lake

ELY

WINTON

TOWER

Vermilion Iron Range

EMBARRASS

AURORA

Mesabi Iron Range

ALLEN JUNCTION

DM&IR

Cloquet State Forest

TWO HARBORS

Lake Superior Museum of Transportation

N

Lake Superior

Not to Scale

DULUTH

Abandonment's Legacy

In the early 1980s, the state's Department of Natural Resources identified the corridor and other abandoned rail lines in the area as having the potential to serve as recreational trails. Adjacent landholders, concerned about probable snowmobile noise, strongly opposed this idea. By 1983, the effort to acquire the corridor had stalled and the removal of the tracks was under way. Much of the right-of-way reverted to area property owners.

During the mid-1980s, a movement to extend the Mesabi Trail, one of the state's most popular recreational paths, into Ely rekindled the idea of bringing the right-of-way into the public realm. The state sought to create a greenway extending more than 130 miles from Grand Rapids, Minnesota, only to once again suspend these plans due to the continuing opposition of property owners. Recognizing the futility of trying to sway the opinions of landowners, officials instead built the Taconite State Trail, a snowmobile path, into town over another route.

After weathering a long economic slump, Ely began to reap the benefits of the growing popularity of the Canoe Area. To the delight of municipal officials, two hotels emerged at the edge of town, and the commuter partner of Northwest Airlines launched commercial air service to Ely from the Twin Cities.

The difficulty of reaching Ely, however, was a serious impediment to tourism development. For most travelers, airline tickets to the community's small airfield were prohibitively expensive. The nearest major airport was more than 250 miles away, in Minneapolis–St. Paul. In addition, rail passenger service had been unavailable to the county since 1985 when Amtrak discontinued the North Star, a train operating between the Twin Cities and Duluth (over former Great Northern rail), and motorists needed to drive long distances to reach the community.

During the early 1990s, citizens affiliated with the St. Louis and Lake County Regional Railroad Authority considered rebuilding the abandoned route to make Ely more accessible. The authority, which had recently purchased 27 miles of track between the Lake Superior Railroad Museum in Duluth and Two Harbors, believed that tourist trains operating north to Ely would have considerable transportation potential. Despite the popularity of the museum's excursions to Two Harbors and the belief that the resumption of freight service could enhance the viability of the plan, however, the entire initiative stalled due to high costs and uncertain revenues.

commercial air service would soon follow. Not only did the effort to attract an airline initially fail, the federal government began enforcing strict limits on the number of people who could enter the wilderness after the creation of the Boundary Waters Canoe Area in 1978. These regulations, established through the federal Wilderness Act, hampered tourism development and generated strong local opposition.

As Ely struggled to find a solution to its continuing economic problems, officials made an overture to the past by having the headframe of the Pioneer Mine placed on the National Register of Historic Places in 1978. Lumber shipments helped sustain freight service from Allen Junction to Winton, but by the early 1980s, neither the railroad nor the state government considered this route (called Winton Branch) to be viable. With abandonment imminent, a special excursion train operated by the Society for Mining Engineers clipped across the tracks (which remained in relatively good condition), allowing railroad enthusiasts, photographers, and local residents to pay a final tribute to a corridor steeped in regional history. Few officials in Ely or other nearby communities voiced concern when the carrier abandoned the branch in June 1982. By then, most community leaders felt that Ely's growth would depend primarily on expanding tourism, notwithstanding the continuing restrictions on the use of the Canoe Area.

As disappointing as this latest setback was, it did not end public discussion about the abandoned railroad route. Municipal officials used the city's zoning ordinance as a negotiating tool to entice some property owners to grant easements for a recreational trail. In 1998, the federal government earmarked funds to finally extend the Mesabi Trail to Ely. Opposition from landowners remained strong. and at this writing, only a short segment in Ely is complete.

When the Missabe Road phased out steam operations, the company offered a K-I locomotive (a 2–8–0) to the city, only to have local officials decline the donation. The locomotive was instead given to Tower and put on display next to that community's wooden depot. A passenger car coupled to the engine's tender was retrofitted to serve as the Tower Train Museum, an institution honoring the Vermilion Range's railroad heritage.

Epilogue

Visitors to the Vermilion Range will find that the deteriorating structures and earthen mounds left behind after a century of mining activity are now largely concealed by forest regrowth. These half-hidden remnants offer silent testimony to the work of thousands of miners who endured bitter cold and notoriously difficult working conditions to supply a raw material vital to the production of iron and steel. Their contributions are commemorated at the Vermilion Interpretive Center and History Museum, an institution operated by the Ely-Winton Historical Society near the edge of town.

Most travelers today arrive in the area via State Route 169, a road that partially follows the abandoned rail line. On this highway near Tower, many motorists stop for a tour of the famed Soudan Mine, which is now a state-managed historical park widely known for its deep shaft. Farther to the east, motorists ascend the so-called Five Mile Bridge, an overpass across the abandoned rail line that is indeed about 5 miles from the edge of Ely.

The former railroad roundhouse—Ely's oldest brick building—remains in industrial use, providing quarters for a welding shop. A nearby bridge takes motorists who use Shagawa Drive across the old rail grade.

Each year, the old mining town of Ely fades away a little more, and the new tourist town born from it expands. The fine Victorian structures in the downtown district evoke an era when the railroad and mining companies reigned supreme in the region's industrial affairs. Merging past and present, it seems fitting that the depot has been transformed into a sporting goods store, thus enhancing Ely's new role as a jumping-off point for the Minnesota wilderness.

For Further Study

SUGGESTED READINGS:
Ely, Since 1988. Ely, Minn.; Ely Echo, 1988, 15–19.
King, Frank A. The Missabe Road.... The Duluth, Missabe and Iron Range Railway. San Marino, Calif.: Golden West Books, 1990, 33–37, 153–58.

OTHER PRINCIPAL REFERENCES:
Corwin, Chuck. "The Vermilion Range." Ore Extra: A Publication of The Missabe Railroad Historical Society 12, no. 4 (1998): 12–19.
Duke, Donald, and Edmund Keilty. RDC: The Budd Rail Diesel Car. San Marino, Calif.: Golden West Books, 1990, 163.
Ely Miner, Centennial Issue. Ely, Minn.: Ely Shopper, 1988, 1–12.
King, Frank A. Minnesota Logging Railroads. San Marino, Calif.: Golden West Books, 1981, 23, 182–83.
Leopard, John. "Missabe: Duluth, Missabe & Iron Range, Part One." CTC Board Railroads Illustrated 182 (Aug. 1992): 30–33.
Prosser, Richard S. Rails to the North Star. Minneapolis: Dillon Press, 1966, 74.

HARLOWTON, MONTANA (1,062)

Historic operator: Chicago, Milwaukee, St. Paul & Pacific Railroad
Last route abandoned: 1980
Notable reuse of right-of-way: Milwaukee Road Historic District

*T*he serenity currently enjoyed by residents of Harlowton would have been almost inconceivable sixty years ago, when hundreds of workers vigorously supported the Chicago, Milwaukee, St. Paul & Pacific Railroad's operations in the community. As a major terminal, maintenance center, and transfer point for steam and electric locomotives, Harlowton's rail yards were in almost constant motion. Having lost all of its railroad jobs and its most important source of tax revenue, this community is a profoundly different place today.

Historical Perspective

Enthusiasm for building a railroad through the open country along the Upper Musselshell River escalated as businessmen looked for ways to bring central Montana's rich deposits of lead and silver ore to market in the 1880s. Richard A. Harlow, a lawyer from Helena, was among the strongest supporters of building such a railroad, which he believed could efficiently convey raw materials to trunk lines in the region. Such a railroad was on its way to becoming a reality when the Montana Railroad—with Harlow as its financial officer—received its charter in 1894. Six years later, the railroad finally operated its first train from a newly built terminal along the river from Lombard, a junction on the Northern Pacific Railway near Three Forks, Montana.

On a bluff adjacent to the river, the company built a wooden depot and laid out a rectangular community named in honor of Harlow.

By the time the company finished an extension to Lewistown in 1903, Harlowton boasted a small downtown with several businesses and a wooden depot.

Many called the railroad the Jawbone, a humorous reference to the forceful skills that Richard Harlow used to persuade Northern Pacific to support policies important to the carrier's success. Despite Harlow's rhetorical talent, the Montana Railroad proved to be a relatively unsuccessful enterprise. However, its route possessed considerable strategic value to the Chicago, Milwaukee & St. Paul Railway (the "St. Paul Road"), which in 1905 announced an ambitious plan to build a rail line—the Pacific Coast Extension—linking the upper Great Plains to Tacoma, Washington.

The railway formed several subsidiaries to build the line but also recognized that acquiring the Montana Railroad would give it an efficient route across central Montana. Unfortunately, the Great Northern held the carrier's mortgage. Taking advantage of the absence of Great Northern leader James J. Hill, who was in England, the St. Paul Road quietly arranged to pay off the mortgage and acquire the Jawbone through a subsidiary, the Chicago, Milwaukee & Puget Sound Railway. This transaction, etched into western railroad lore, infuriated Hill, but allowed the St. Paul Road's subsidiary to transform the segment from Lombard and Harlowton into its main line at a relatively low cost.

The St. Paul Road's far-flung undertaking required it to make substantial investments in towns along its route, but few communities witnessed as much construction as Harlowton, where Bulgarian and Japanese workers arrived by the hundreds to help build sprawling railroad facilities. Although a fire ravaged Harlowton in 1907 and destroyed twenty-four buildings, the community emerged from reconstruction with a more dignified and enduring character. To comply with a fire-prevention ordinance, many businesses used locally quarried sandstone for their new buildings.

The next several years were exciting times for this newly reconstituted community. As the transcontinental railroad neared completion in early 1908, the St. Paul Road acquired the other subsidiaries that were building the line connecting to the Chicago, Milwaukee & Puget

Sound Railway. That same year, the entrepreneurial A. C. Graves—a legendary figure some called the Father of Harlowton—moved his hotel from Main Street to Robinson Street, midway between the existing downtown area and the depot. As other businesses followed Graves's example, a new business district emerged perpendicular to the original one.

There was great optimism on May 14, 1909, when the Chicago, Milwaukee & Puget Sound drove the final spike near Garrison, finishing its Pacific Coast Extension. With many tunnels, lengthy trestles, and deep cuts, the new transcontinental line was superbly built and engineered. It constituted the shortest route available between the upper Great Plains and Puget Sound in the Pacific Northwest.

As a division point and maintenance center on the railroad, Harlowton prospered from its abundant railroad jobs and soon grew to more than 300 inhabitants.

A pair of Milwaukee Road "boxcabs" work the western end of Harlowton's freight yard—the staging area for trains operating over the carrier's 440-mile electrified district to Avery, Idaho. One of these locomotives (E57b) is today on display in the community, which is visible in this photo on the bluff in the distance. (Larry Zeutschel Collection, courtesy of Rocky Gibbs, MilWest.)

Although Harlowton's depot has changed little since the days of the Olympian Hiawatha, its freight yard is now just a grassy field. The unusual "extension cord" switcher rests on the old track-bed. (Photo by author.)

Its depot—located near the southern edge of the community and equipped with a large waiting area, a beanery, and office space—was open around the clock. Considering the land in the surrounding area to be arable, the St. Paul Road also embarked upon a comprehensive plan to promote agricultural development. In 1909, it purchased more than 13,000 acres of grazing land outside of town and another parcel of land east of the community approximately half that size. These holdings were subdivided into smaller parcels to allow for the creation of farms.

Harlowton flourished during the first six months of 1910, when the carrier operated 284 "immigrant trains" that carried more than 28,000 travelers to the community, many of whom established farms in Wheatland County. By the end of that year, Harlowton's population had risen to more than 900, and Robinson Street had been renamed Central Avenue—a name indicative of the high expectations for the community's future growth.

The enthusiasm for the transcontinental railway, however, was tempered by the harsh realities of operating trains over a route burdened with severe grades and sharp curves. West of "Harlo" (the community's nickname among railroaders), these trains struggled to cross five mountain ranges—the Belts, the Rockies, the Bitterroots, the Saddles, and the Cascades. Overcoming such a tortuous route was inordinately costly and put the carrier at a considerable disadvantage compared to the Northern Pacific and Great Northern.

A solution to this problem appeared to be at hand after the St. Paul Road formally absorbed the Chicago, Milwaukee & Puget Sound into its system in 1912.

Willing to spend large sums to improve the speed and efficiency of its services, it began work to electrify the 440-mile portion between Harlowton and Avery, Idaho, in 1914. Upon finishing the project two years later, the carrier established Harlowton as an important maintenance center for electric locomotives while it continued to use the town as a terminal for steam-powered trains arriving from the east and those working the branches to Lewistown (once part of the Jawbone) and Great Falls. By the end of 1916, the St. Paul had heralded the electrification project a success, enlarged its roundhouse from twelve to seventeen stalls, and constructed other new service facilities in Harlowton.

Harlowton's streets and rail yard bustled with activity as steam and electric trains departed for distant terminals. Residents depended heavily on two passenger trains, the Olympian and the Columbian, which made extended stops on their 2,207-mile runs between Chicago and Tacoma. Many detraining passengers enjoyed the Graves Hotel's well-appointed rooms and its spacious restaurant.

A spirit of camaraderie developed among the many residents working to support the railroad's successful operation. The carrier's continuing demand for workers enabled Harlowton to weather both drought and the effects of falling grain prices after World War I better than many other communities of central Montana. The railroad invested heavily in the community in 1924 by enlarging its freight yard and wiring this expansive facility for electric operations.

Changing Times

The limitations of the Pacific Coast Extension, even with the advantages of electrification, were painfully evident by the mid-1920s. Suffering from intense competition, the carrier fell into receivership in 1925 and emerged from reorganization three years later as the Chicago, Milwaukee, St. Paul & Pacific Railroad (the "Milwaukee Road"). During the Great Depression, Harlowton felt the combined strain of drought, a slump in grain prices, and a downturn in railroad traffic. By the end of the 1930s, the entire county's population had dropped more than 30 percent.

Harlowton's residents felt the energy of a renaissance in railroad freight and passenger traffic during

World War II. After the war, they took particular pride in their town's being an important stop for the Olympian Hiawatha, a modern streamliner introduced between Chicago and Tacoma in 1947. New electric locomotives, called Little Joes, arrived three years later to support the operation of trains between Harlowton and Avery.

Unfortunately, the luster of these postwar investments gradually faded. By the mid-1950s, the outlook for the route had taken a sharp turn for the worse. Saddled with high costs and having few opportunities to enhance revenues, the carrier looked for ways to minimize the deficits the route generated. It eliminated the Columbian in 1955 and demolished some of its facilities in Harlowton, including the machine shop and portions of the roundhouse. In 1961, the carrier replaced the Hiawatha with an unnamed passenger train, referred to sarcastically by some employees as the Limpin' Hiawatha, which operated between Minneapolis–St. Paul and Deer Lodge. This remnant met its demise in 1964, leaving Harlowton without rail passenger service.

The famed Hiawatha name returned to Montana in 1971 when Amtrak introduced the North Coast Hiawatha between Chicago and Seattle, but this train used former Northern Pacific rail through the region and lacked the pedigree of the fine streamliners that had preceded it. Nevertheless, the ghost of the Olympian Hiawatha was awakened in 1977 when Amtrak rerouted its train over a short segment of the Pacific Coast Extension in Washington, giving passengers a rare opportunity to ride a rail line destined for oblivion. This arrangement lasted only a few months, however. By the end of the decade, Amtrak's Hiawatha was gone, too.

As the Milwaukee Road's electrification equipment and locomotives approached obsolescence, rumors spread that the carrier would make the transition to an all-diesel operation. It finally did so in 1974, leaving many workers unemployed and bringing great hardship to Harlowton. By the time the carrier closed the Harlowton depot five years later, it had only one regular customer in the community, a Cargill grain elevator.

A coalition of stakeholders, including railroad workers, shippers, and state agencies, tried unsuccessfully to save the beleaguered route. In March 1980, the carrier ceased operations on its lines west of Miles City, ending rail service to Harlowton and dozens of other communities.

Abandonment's Legacy

Harlowton plunged into an even deeper recession due to the loss of property tax revenues and more than a hundred well-paying railroad jobs. Legislators and local officials attempted to secure funds for retraining laid-off electricians and mechanics, but this effort also ended without success. The Cargill elevator turned to trucks to meet all of its transport needs.

Many railroad workers retired, while others left town to work for other railroads; some of them returned after missing the congeniality of Harlowton life. Others went to work building an overhead power line through the region, a project that helped the community overcome some of the worst effects of the railroad's withdrawal. Stewardship of the 230 acres of land once occupied by the railroad, including the depot and roundhouse, reverted to the local government.

While adjusting to life without the time-honored traditions of the Milwaukee Road, residents looked back with pride at their community's railroader heritage. Only months after the railroad closed, the Graves Hotel earned a spot on the National Register of Historic Places. In the mid-1980s, a preservation committee consisting of both city and county officials began working to restore and convert the depot into a museum. Organizers put a small switch engine (X3800) once assigned to the Deer Lodge yards next to the structure to create an unusual historical

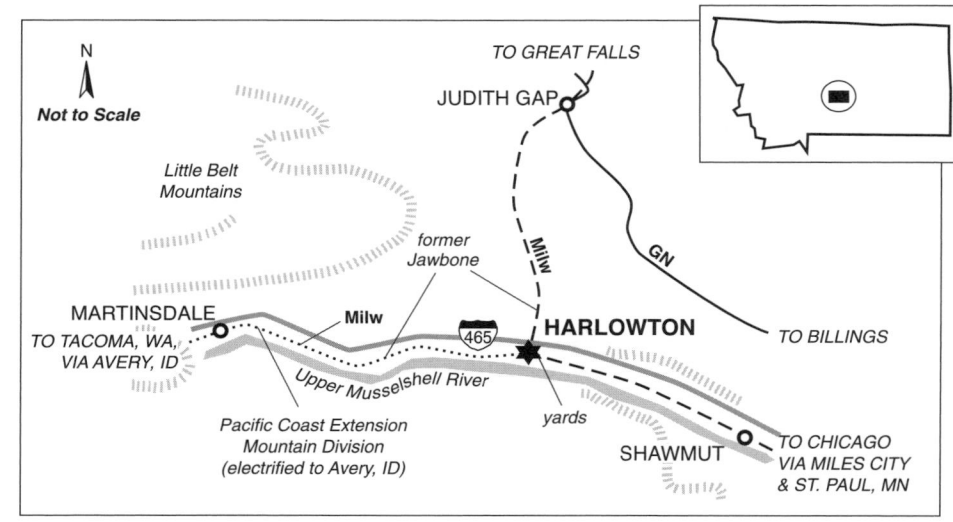

exhibit. The engine received power through a lengthy extension cord. In 1986, the community relocated a much larger locomotive—the electric "boxcab" (U57B) that had for years worked the Harlowton yard—to a prominent roadside location in the community's Fischer Park. The boxcab, donated by Milwaukee Road, previously had been on display near the depot where it was susceptible to vandalism.

Echoes of the past were heard again two years later, when the Montana Preservation Review Board approved creation of the Milwaukee Road Historic District in Harlowton, an area that included both the community's central business district and the depot. The surviving portions of the roundhouse, having been relegated to the storage of fertilizer, and the Graves Hotel, having served its last customer in 1997, today await an uncertain fate.

Epilogue

Visitors will find many miles of open country separating Harlowton from a major city, a commercial airport, or an interstate highway. The intercity buses once serving the community have gone the way of the Olympian Hiawatha. The depot, representative of the Great Plains station architectural style, brings to mind the glorious railroad heritage of the place many old-timers still call Harlo.

Commercial and civic institutions also pay homage to the bygone railroad. The local newspaper, the *Times-Clarion*, prints a sketch of a Milwaukee Road train on its masthead. The high school retains "the Engineers" as its official nickname. Many of the carrier's former employees living in town participate in a railroad retirement club that maintains Fischer Park and holds periodic gatherings. The Graves Hotel, having undergone partial restoration, is once again a prominent local institution.

Many historians agree that no amount of employee diligence or managerial innovation could have saved the Pacific Coast Extension. When this route was completed, railroads generally could no longer spur the creation of large communities with heavy demand for rail service. The line's abandonment, in fact, left only a few communities of more than several hundred residents without a link to the national rail system.

Much of the Hiawatha's route through central Montana has been gradually reduced to an almost unnoticeable footprint on the land. A lengthy bridge on U.S. Route 191 southeast of town takes motorists over the abandoned main line. The old Cargill grain elevator, now owned by a private individual but little changed since the railroad era, seems almost frozen in time.

The remnants of Harlowton's roundhouse today stand out on grassy terrain like ancient ruins, crumbling from neglect. At the community's Upper Musselshell Museum, a large collection of railroad memorabilia is on display. The museum's exhibit tells the improbable story of a small town rising up to become a thriving railroad center before falling back to a position of little significance in western transportation.

For Further Study

SUGGESTED READINGS:

McCarter, Steve. *Guide to the Milwaukee Road in Montana.* Helena: Montana Historical Society Press, 1992, 23–30, 51–53.

Wilkerson, Bill. *The Jawbone Railroad: 100 Years 1984–1994.* Miles City, Mont.: Bill Wilkerson, 1994, 5–7.

OTHER PRINCIPAL REFERENCES:

Derleth, August. *The Milwaukee Road: Its First Hundred Years.* New York: Creative Age Press, 1948, 185–86.

Drury, George. *Historical Guide to North American Railroads.* Milwaukee, Wis.: Kalmbach Books, 1985, 83–84.

Wilkerson, Bill. "Milwaukee's Harlowton Roundhouse." *National Railway Bulletin* 65, no. 2 (2000): 20–27.

Wood, Charles R., and Dorothy M. Wood. *Milwaukee Road West.* Seattle: Superior Publishing, 1986, 162–72.

RED LODGE, MONTANA (2,177)

Historic operator: Northern Pacific Railway
Last route abandoned: 1981
Notable reuse of right-of-way: Carbon County Arts Guild

A wooden depot is nearly all that remains in Red Lodge of one of the Northern Pacific Railway's most productive branch lines. These rails once supported enormous shipments of coal originating at mines owned by the railway and gave passage to prominent figures in American history, including railroad magnate Henry Villard and novelist Ernest Hemingway. Years later, tourists eager to experience the splendors of the Beartooth Highway arrived daily in the comfort of a Pullman sleeping car from Chicago.

Historical Perspective

Legend has it that two clans of the Crow Nation, the Black Lodge and the Kick-in-the-Belly, lived on historic hunting grounds in the foothills of the Bear Mountains. A group of Kick-in-the-Belly separated from their clan and established a camp along a creek with a tepee painted with red clay. Soon thereafter, they found their "red lodge" raided and destroyed by other members of their clan. Whether this incident is indeed the origin of Red Lodge's name is open to debate. Another account attributes the name to a large outcropping of reddish rock resembling a tepee, about which little else is known.

A community took shape in this area after an 1880 agreement with the Crow made land adjacent to Rocky Fork (Rock Creek) available for settlement. By 1884, several large cattle ranches and a post office emerged along

this estuary of the Yellowstone River. In 1885, a group of men interested in developing coalfields established themselves in the area. Soon, miners crowded into shacks and tents in a small village called Red Lodge.

Red Lodge seemed primed for dramatic expansion following the 1887 creation of the Rocky Fork Coal Company, an enterprise seeking to excavate the rich bituminous deposits tucked below the surface, but inadequate transportation was a major problem. After struggling to haul coal to the Northern Pacific's main line in Billings and Park City the company pushed hard for the construction of the Rocky Fork and Cooke City Railway, an entity that sought to link Billings to Cooke City a mining center near the boundaries of Yellowstone.

Unfortunately for the coal company, financial problems prevented the completion of the railway, leaving the company and its development arm (which owned the town site)

In this photograph from September 2, 1939, the daily passenger train has just arrived in Red Lodge, carrying Pullman and coach passengers as well as mail and express freight. The bus for Yellowstone Park waits next to the platform. (Photo by Warren R. McGee.)

desperate for rail service. Relief finally appeared in the form of Henry Villard, president of Northern Pacific. In exchange for stock in the development company, the legendary businessman agreed to have his company finish the line as far south (or west, in railroad terms) as Red Lodge. By early 1889, Northern Pacific's financial backing had allowed construction to resume. Several months later, the track-laying crew completed the Rocky Fork Branch between Laurel (a junction on the main line) and Red Lodge. With vast amounts of coal ready for exploitation, the development company (now a Northern Pacific subsidiary) formally platted Red Lodge that same year and made large investments in local mines.

As the mines expanded and cattle grazers enlarged their herds, the Rocky Fork Branch generated such significant traffic that Villard himself (the company's board chairman at the time) arrived in his private car to visit the town in 1891. Although most of the community's important businesses were initially situated several blocks south of the station, the opening of the three-story Hotel Spofford in 1893 stimulated development in the area adjacent to the depot. This magnificent hostelry (soon renamed the Pollard Hotel) welcomed Buffalo Bill Cody, Martha Jane "Calamity Jane" Burke, and other celebrities among its guests.

Red Lodge was named the seat of newly created Carbon County in 1895, recovered quickly from a devastating downtown fire in 1900, and became the destination of a regularly scheduled Northern Pacific passenger train from Billings in 1903, allowing for substantially faster trips than the carrier's mixed trains. By 1906, the community had 4,000 residents, three hotels, and a business-oriented leadership cultivated by the Red Lodge Board of

Trade. Citizens took great pride in their community's status as the "Coal Metropolis."

The enormous productivity of the county's mines assured an almost continuous flow of investment. The railway-owned Northwestern Improvement Company opened the West Side Mine near the edge of Red Lodge in 1907. Popularly called the Sunset Mine, this facility, like the company's East Side Mine, helped push the county to the top of Montana coal production in 1911. Red Lodge was now at its peak population, with 5,500 people inhabiting its well-planned neighborhoods. The livelihood of more than 1,500 miners depended on Northern Pacific's outbound shipments of coal.

Other railroads also shouldered a heavy burden to keep pace with the county's coal production. The Chicago, Burlington & Quincy Railroad (Burlington Route) inaugurated service to the county in 1911 over a route joining Northern Pacific at Fromberg, a small mining town approximately 15 miles northeast of Red Lodge. Through a trackage rights agreement, its trains operated over Northern Pacific between Fromberg and Billings, including a 10-mile portion of the Rocky Fork Branch between Silesia and Laurel. The Montana, Wyoming & Southern Railroad operated a line from Fromberg to Bearcreek (a town 7 miles east of Red Lodge) that served a mining area unaffiliated with Northern Pacific. Sprawling mining railways, meanwhile, hauled coal to massive tipples used to load cars for shipment on the common-carrier railroads.

In the midst of these prosperous times, the residents of Red Lodge enjoyed leisure time at the Theotorium, a magnificent theater with seating for 600 that opened in 1911. Visits by presidential candidate William Jennings Bryan, who reportedly gave a speech at the depot, and the barnstorming Charles Lindbergh, who stopped in the community on several occasions and frequented the well-known Busy Bee Café, exemplified the dynamism of the town's economy.

Changing Times

Red Lodge's economic dependence on coal mining had long exposed it to a vicious business cycle. The potentially devastating implications of this dependence were revealed in the early 1920s, when the Northwest Improvement Company (still a

Northern Pacific subsidiary) made the unpopular decision to gradually suspend much of its local mining operation in favor of strip mines at Colstrip. While mining in Red Lodge continued, labor strife escalated until the Improvement Company agreed to pay higher wages to its workers. The company then closed the West Side Mine in 1924, leaving hundreds unemployed and dooming many local businesses, including the Theotorium, which ended regular performances that same year.

The suffering intensified during the Great Depression, when the Improvement Company closed the East Side Mine in 1932 and made plans to phase out its remaining coal production. In their search for ways to offset the downturn in mining, community leaders sought to tap the region's tourism potential, an effort that took a fortuitous turn when the federal government completed the Beartooth Highway in 1936. This scenic and winding road extended southeast from Red Lodge to Yellowstone Park, reaching a breathtaking elevation of nearly 11,000 feet and taking motorists through the famed Bear Tooth Pass, which offered striking views of Granite Peak, Montana's tallest mountain. Built largely with federal funds at a cost of $2.5 million, it was the most expensive road in the country at that time.

The opening of the highway, ironically, stimulated the passenger business on the Rocky Fork Branch. Many tourists eager to see the Bear Tooth Pass arrived in a Pullman sleeper from Chicago included as part of a daily passenger train from Billings. At Red Lodge, some travelers made transfers to a bus, operated by one of the carrier's

The depot grounds in Red Lodge, today adorned by a former Northern Pacific caboose, call to mind the final days of Rocky Fork Branch. (Photo by author.)

173

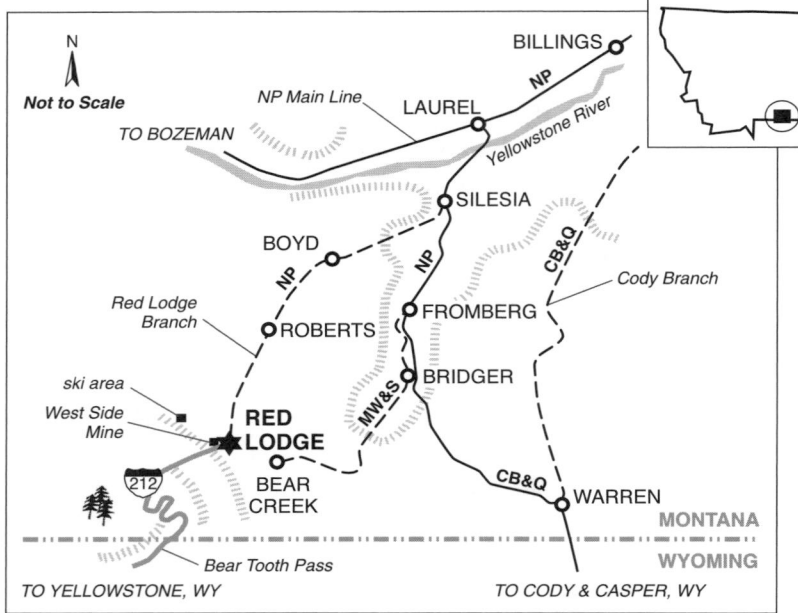

mixed train in 1948 and eventually limited its travel accommodations to bus service. Rail freight tonnage diminished sharply after the Northern Pacific created a trucking company, Northern Pacific Transport, in the 1950s. This subsidiary soon handled the preponderance of nonagricultural shipments from Red Lodge.

Several of the county's most notable businesses disappeared in the years that followed. The last major mines in the region ceased production in the late 1950s. The fabled Busy Bee Café burned to the ground before the decade's end. In 1970, the Burlington, the Northern Pacific, and two other lines merged to form the Burlington Northern Railroad, a carrier dominating rail transportation in the state. Upon the inception of Amtrak the following year, the famed North Coast Limited and the Mainstreeter—trains that for generations had served communities on the former Northern Pacific main line—made their final runs.

By the time area residents formed the Carbon County Historical Society in 1975 to commemorate their local heritage, the Rocky Fork Branch had become largely inconsequential in the region's economy. The Red Lodge Canning Company, a shipper of peas, closed that year, reducing the use of the branch to sporadic shipments of wheat and fertilizer. According to state reports, the branch generated only sixty-eight carloads of freight in 1976 and a mere seventeen the following year, due to stiffening competition from motor vehicles and a federal grain-storage program that postponed the shipment of agricultural products. Although tonnage rose later during that decade, Burlington Northern removed the Silesia–Red Lodge segment from service by late 1980 and abandoned it in 1981, bringing the local railroad era to a close.

Abandonment's Legacy

The city government acquired a portion of the Burlington Northern right-of-way for various municipal purposes. Other portions were sold for development. In 1982, Burlington Northern donated the Red Lodge depot to the Carbon County Arts Guild, allowing the nonprofit organization to fashion the wooden structure into a gallery and office. The carrier also contributed a caboose to lend a decorative element to the depot grounds. The Arts Guild put this car on a track that it

subsidiaries, that took them through the Pass to Yellowstone.

Compared to Northern Pacific's stations in Livingston and Gardiner the depot in Red Lodge remained of minor consequence to Yellowstone tourism. It nevertheless handled an appreciable number of seasonal visitors, including Ernest Hemingway, who had a liking for the community. Hemingway refers to the town in his famous novel *For Whom the Bell Tolls,* in which the hero, Robert Jordan, recollects that he had not "felt so young since he had taken the train at Red Lodge."

Northern Pacific perpetuated its reputation as the "Yellowstone Park Line" for many more years. Although travelers had the option of reaching the park on a variety of other routes (including Union Pacific's branch to West Yellowstone; the Chicago, Milwaukee, St. Paul & Pacific's line to Gallatin Gateway; and the Burlington Route's branch to Cody), it was Northern Pacific's trains that, by far, handled the greatest number of visitors.

Unfortunately, the stimulus provided by the opening of the Beartooth Highway could not possibly offset the problems stemming from the loss of more than a thousand mining jobs. Red Lodge's last business association, the Commerce Club, dissolved in 1940. The Pollard Hotel changed hands three years later, was renamed the Hotel Chief, and gradually fell into disrepair.

As Red Lodge felt the strain of changing times, the railroad retreated to the margins of the economy. Northern Pacific replaced its passenger train from Billings (which carried the sleeping car until the end) with a had rebuilt using rails and crossties acquired from the salvage company.

Over the next several years, the number of motorists making summer trips to Yellowstone once again rose sharply. The Red Lodge Mountain ski resort also grew in popularity, laying the groundwork for a modest economic revival. The first portions of the downtown district, an area called Old Town, were added to the National Register of Historic Places in 1983. Attention then turned to rehabilitating several of the town's most magnificent buildings, including the Hotel Pollard building, the Labor Temple (a three-story hall), and the Theotorium, which had been used as a distillery for many years before becoming a warehouse. The condition of the building that had formerly housed the Hotel Pollard deteriorated as its ownership changed, leaving this once proud institution closed for extended periods.

By the early 1990s, Red Lodge marshaled its resources to support an ambitious historical preservation program. The historical society received the Labor Temple as a donation in 1990 and converted it into the Carbon County Museum eight years later. In the mid-1990s, the owners of the Hotel Pollard meticulously refurbished this structure, making it once again a destination of choice for travelers.

The saga of the Rocky Fork Branch would ultimately become a mere footnote in the larger story about the rail lines serving tourists on their way to Yellowstone Park. By late 1996, travelers could get no closer than within 200 miles of the national park on a regularly scheduled Amtrak train. That same year, however, Montana Rockies Rail Tours began operating special trains over the former Northern Pacific main line, which had been turned over to Montana Rail Link, a regional freight-oriented railroad. These special trains, which now operate weekly during summer months from Sandpoint, Idaho, to Livingston and occasionally to Billings, have restored some of the bygone traditions of the North Coast Limited and other trains steeped in the history of the park. The tour company's buses even periodically stop in Red Lodge on their way to the Bear Tooth Pass.

Epilogue

Travelers with an interest in Red Lodge's railroad history will find that its abandoned right-of-way remains largely free of obstruction. The local elevator, despite having exited the grain business many years ago, looks much the same today as it did when the last train left town. Along U.S. Route 212 to Silesia, the old rail grade is still plainly visible. The portion of the route between Silesia and Laurel survives as an active railway, having been assimilated along with the rest of the Burlington Northern system into the Burlington Northern Santa Fe Railway in 1995.

Without a commercial airline, bus service, interstate highway, or railroad, Red Lodge has a small-town feel that belies its bustling mining heritage. As a prominent gateway to Bear Tooth Pass and Yellowstone, its economy increasingly marches to tourism's drumbeat. Many of the summertime tourists undoubtedly amble through the Old Town district of Red Lodge and admire its striking Victorian facades, all the while unaware of the remarkable story of the Coal Metropolis.

For Further Study

SUGGESTED READINGS:

Renz, Louis Tuck. *The History of the Northern Pacific Railroad.* Fairfield, Wash.: Ye Galleon Press, 1990, 157–58.

Zupan, Shirley. *Red Lodge: Saga of a Western Area.* Red Lodge, Mont.: Carbon County Historical Society, 1979, 47–53, 135–36.

OTHER PRINCIPAL REFERENCES:

Maiken, Peter T. *Night Trains: The Pullman System in the Golden Years of American Rail Travel.* Baltimore: Johns Hopkins University Press, 1989, 285–89.

Overton, Richard C. *Burlington Route: A History of the Burlington Lines.* New York: Knopf, 1965, 233, 276.

Potter, Janet Greenstein. *Great American Railroad Stations.* New York: Wiley & Sons, 1996, 507.

Runte, Alfred. *Trains of Discovery: Western Railroads and the National Parks.* Niwot, Colo.: Roberts Rinehart Publishers, 1994, 1–89.

LONG PINE, NEBRASKA (350)

Historic operator: Chicago & North Western Railway
Last route abandoned: 1994
Notable reuse of right-of-way: Cowboy Trail

mall communities across northern Nebraska pleaded with state officials to prevent the abandonment of the Chicago & North Western's "Cowboy Line" during the early 1990s. By a single vote, however, the legislature rejected a bill that would have provided funds for the route's acquisition and continued operation. Having lost two-thirds of its population since its most notable years as a division point on the railroad, Long Pine has become a much smaller and quieter place than it was years ago.

Historical Perspective

For many generations, the Sioux roamed freely through the grass-covered sandhills south of the Niobrara River. By the time Nebraska achieved statehood in 1867, however, ranchers were gradually expanding their herds in the region and the Sioux presence had greatly diminished. In time, some of the ranches were replaced by homesteads.

In the late 1870s, the small community of Long Pine came into being in the sandy region near beautiful Pine Creek Canyon, a ravine covered with tall stands of pine and cedar. Its townspeople initially drew their livelihood primarily from a steam-powered sawmill supplied by timber from the canyon. Later, they came to depend on the services of the Berry Brothers Stage and Freight Lines, which used animal power to carry goods and passengers across the vast expanse of northern Nebraska.

Expectations about the region's commercial potential rose markedly as railroad fever swept across the Great Plains.

In 1881, the Fremont, Elkhorn & Missouri Valley (Fremont) Railroad extended its route 97 miles from Neligh (a small town west of Norfolk) to Long Pine. As the carrier pushed its tracks farther west, it constructed a large bridge across the canyon—a wooden span of 280 feet that carried trains high above the creek below. The magnificence of this structure was soon surpassed by an even longer bridge across the Niobrara River completed in 1883 at a location about 50 miles from Long Pine, allowing its trains to reach the emerging community of Valentine.

As a division point on the carrier, Long Pine benefited from the creation of many railroad jobs and prospered greatly from the Fremont's freight and passenger services. By the time the community received its incorporation in 1884, it had become a railroad town of considerable regional importance and a popular destination of the Chautauqua, which held events in the canyon annually. Many of Long Pine's men worked at a three-stall roundhouse and machine shop in the south part of town.

The community's significance in trans-Nebraska transportation grew sharply over the next several years. The North Western assimilated the Fremont into its system in 1884 and completed an extension to Chadron in northwestern Nebraska in 1885. By the end of the decade, it had extended its tracks to Fort Casper in the Wyoming Territory and built a branch north from the vicinity of Chadron to the mineral-rich Black Hills in the Dakota Territory. These extensions transformed the rail line into an important long-distance corridor linking Fremont (a busy North Western junction in eastern Nebraska) to thriving lumber and mining towns farther west on the frontier.

By the early 1890s, Long Pine gave every indication of being a successful community, boasting a stockyard, a large icehouse, and a population of more than 250. It was also home to several guesthouses, including the Miller House, the Upstill Hotel, and a combination hotel/eating house attached to the depot, all of which served a steady flow of visitors and railroad employees.

As the years passed, growing numbers of leisure travelers booked passage on the North Western's trains between Chicago and the Black Hills. Considering the stretch through Long Pine to be among the most scenic in all of Nebraska, many travelers admired the Pine Creek Canyon as well as the world's largest grass-stabilized sandhill region, where they could see cranes, deer, and herons. In 1905, the North Western (which formally merged the Fremont into its system) realigned its route over the canyon, putting its trains over a magnificent new

steel bridge about a mile north of the original structure.

Long Pine was much more than a typical division point for railroad crews: it was the point at which the North Western changed between oil-burning locomotives (which operated west to Chadron at the time) and coal-burning locomotives (which operated east to Norfolk). It was also the location at which the carrier adjusted its clocks from Central to Mountain Time. Additionally, Long Pine functioned as a meal stop for passenger trains and as an equipment maintenance center. As the volume of traffic grew, the North Western built a new turntable and a second roundhouse in 1907. The new roundhouse brought the number of locomotive stalls to a dozen.

For the next twenty years, nearly the entire community depended one way or another on the successful operation of the railway. When passenger trains made station stops, the eating house in the depot hotel bustled with activity. Many travelers on extended visits enjoyed the comforts of the Upstill Hotel, which completed a major expansion in 1910, and the rustic ambience of Hidden Paradise Park, a resort that opened in the canyon the following year.

At the beginning of World War I, the North Western employed more than 100 local workers and served a large

A general merchandise freight train, led by a pair of Chicago & North Western SD-40 cars, heads across a culvert near Long Pine in June 1982. This westbound train will end its run in Chadron. (Photo by William W. Kratville.)

Tall grass grows in the old freight yard area in Long Pine. The former railroad dormitory and Cowboy Trail can be seen in the distance. (Author's collection.)

quarry north of town equipped with its own lengthy railroad spur. In 1923, the railway built a new baggage and express building adjacent to its depot. Amid continuing prosperity, Long Pine's population surpassed 1,200 for the first time.

Changing Times

As in many towns on the Great Plains, the buoyant economic conditions of the middle 1920s could not be sustained as farmers and ranchers struggled with insufficient rain and falling commodity prices. Property values fell precipitously and another series of droughts during the Great Depression weakened livestock herds and bankrupted farmers who had survived earlier downturns. Swarms of grasshoppers reportedly became so thick that on occasion they almost blocked the sun.

As the North Western scaled back its operations, a process accelerated by major advances in motor travel, the foundation of Long Pine's economy began to crumble. The closing and demolition of the station hotel in 1935 foreshadowed further losses. By the early 1940s, the North Western had reduced the number of local roundhouse stalls to six and cut back local passenger service to a single train in each direction daily.

The country's deepening involvement in World War II pumped new life into the railroad. Cattle ranching mounted a comeback, and the rail line shouldered a heavy burden by transporting grain, livestock, and coal through the region as well as troops to Fort Robinson, an army base near Crawford. Extra trains were regularly dispatched to and from Long Pine to handle cattle and other types of freight.

The circumstances that had rejuvenated the railway disappeared shortly after the war. By the early 1950s, the North Western had ended through passenger service to Chicago and expressed a desire to eliminate the daily passenger train operating between Chadron and Omaha. In 1958, it discontinued the train (which by now carried a sleeper only on alternate days), demolished the roundhouse, and razed the maintenance shop. After relocating its freight office and station to the former express building in 1965, it tore down the depot.

With further reductions in railroad employment on the horizon, Long Pine's future now appeared bleak. The closing of several businesses, the demolition of the Upstill Hotel, and the closing of the local high school during the 1960s severely hurt its economy. After the railway became the employee-owned Chicago & North Western Transportation Company in 1972, all of its local jobs were eliminated, except for that of the station agent. Although the railroad still dispatched trains to the community from Chadron and Norfolk, the tracks fell into such disrepair that crews could no longer make a round-trip between these communities and Long Pine on the same day. To give these employees a place to sleep, the railroad built a modest dormitory in Long Pine.

Ironically, as the rail line's physical condition deteriorated, growing numbers of railroad enthusiasts expressed their fondness for it. These admirers christened the route the Cowboy Line and traveled long distances to take photographs of trains slowly crossing the rolling terrain.

During the early 1980s, there was room for hope about the line's future. The North Western, supported by funds from the federal Local Rail Service Assistance Program (LRSA), made improvements to the tracks and structures while developing new sources of revenue. The carrier used the line to haul bentonite from Wyoming and South Dakota, as well as coal shipments from the Powder River Basin in Wyoming to an Iowa utility company. It also studied the possibility of transforming the corridor into a major route from the booming Powder River mining district to the Midwest.

The optimism of this era dissipated when the North Western established a new connection with the Union Pacific Railroad in Wyoming during 1984, creating an alternate coal-hauling route to the Powder River Basin. Within a few years, the carrier had made known that it wanted to abandon the Cowboy Line. Alarmed at this possibility, shippers, towns, and the state government embarked on one of the most comprehensive rail service preservation efforts ever to emerge in the Great Plains states. A volunteer group, the Northern Nebraska Rail Preservation Association, opposed the railroad's closing and sent representatives to hearings throughout the state. The association sought to arrange for a deal with Colorado-based Great Western Railway, which expressed an interest in acquiring the corridor.

Policy analysts warned that the Cowboy Line's demise would have broad implications for the region and would negatively affect roadway conditions, especially those on U.S. Route 20, which runs nearly parallel to the route for several hundred miles. A study by the Upper Great Plains Transportation Institute, published in 1991, concluded that abandonment would substantially increase the number of trucks and could add nearly $100 million to highway costs over a twenty-five year period. Momentum built for saving the line as Union Pacific, which owned a majority stake in the North Western, experienced serious congestion on its main line passing about 120 miles south of Long Pine. In 1992, the carrier reconsidered its plans to abandon the Cowboy Line and determined that the bridges on the route, including the Long Pine Trestle, could handle empty coal trains without major work.

The effort to save the corridor then became mired in unexpected problems; however, the weakening economy sharply reduced the demand for rail service and anticipated revenues from an expansion of the region's potato crop never materialized. The North Western diverted bentonite shipments over a line through Pierre, South Dakota, that it had sold to the Dakota, Minnesota & Eastern Railroad. Its parent, Union Pacific, determined it would be preferable to equip the main line with triple track rather than operate empty coal trains

over the Cowboy Line. Making matters worse, the company insisted in negotiations that severe restrictions be placed on any new operator's ability to ship Wyoming coal over the line in order to prevent the route from falling into the hands of potential competitors.

After service on the local portion of the route drew to a close in 1992, the future of the Cowboy Line rested in the hands of the Nebraska legislature. By a single vote, the governing body rejected a proposal to appropriate $5 million for purchasing the line. Some people claimed that this outcome was influenced by the corporate presence of Omaha-based Union Pacific. The legislature's reluctance to invest in an enterprise apparently prone to operating at a deficit, however, also appeared to be an important factor. In 1994, Union Pacific abandoned the 248-mile portion of track between Merriman and Norfolk, one of the longest stretches ever eliminated at one time by the carrier. With that abandonment, Long Pine's railroad era drew to a close.

Abandonment's Legacy

Although trains never returned to Long Pine, the Cowboy Line remained a prominent part of the regional landscape. In 1991, the North Western conveyed a 74-mile portion of the line from Merriman to Chadron (which was not part of the earlier abandonment application) to the Nebkota Railway, an entity operated by shippers along this segment. The Nebraska Game & Parks Commission acquired the balance of the route through the National Trails System Act. Once the track had been removed, the agency moved with dispatch to create the Cowboy Trail—one of the country's longest rail-trails. In 1997, it redecked the enormous bridges over the canyon and Niobrara River for pedestrian use.

Within a few years, an appreciable number of people

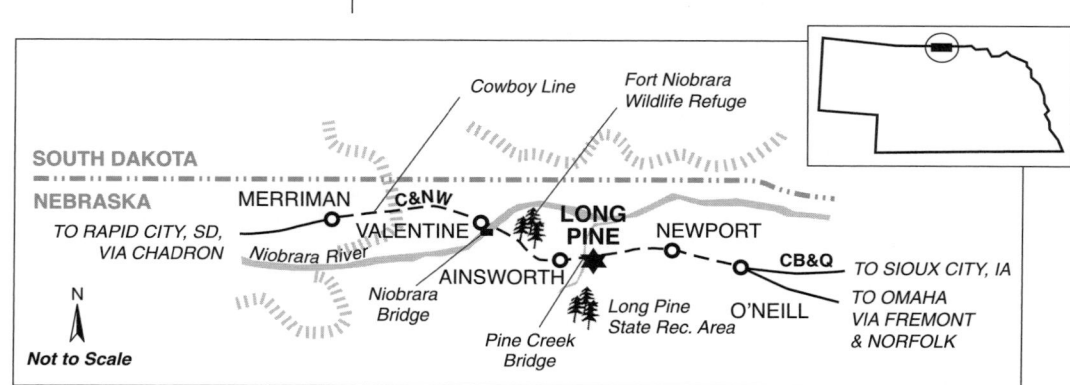

were using the trail during the summer months. Recreational advocates considered the trail to be a success and published estimates that it added upwards of $20 million to the state's economy. The dismantling of the Cowboy Line was, however, a source of concern to the Federal Railroad Administration, which had invested LRSA funds to rehabilitate the line years earlier. Invoking a federal statute, the agency demanded that the North Western and state government reimburse these funds. After a lengthy contractual discussion, the parties reached a repayment agreement in 1997.

Bringing trains back to the abandoned portions of the Cowboy Line received brief consideration in the late 1990s, when the Dakota, Minnesota & Eastern evaluated ways to establish its own route to the Powder River Basin. The company ultimately settled on using the route through Pierre, South Dakota, that it had acquired without restrictions on shipping coal. Nevertheless, rebuilding the Cowboy Line is one of Union Pacific's options as it struggles to expand its freight-hauling capacity across Nebraska. Most expect the carrier to instead shoulder the expense of equipping its main line with a fourth track.

For a retrospective look at the trains running through Nebraska's sand hills, travelers can visit the Long Pine Heritage House Museum, which is open only in summertime. A scale model of the community's once-sprawling railroad facilities, created by railroad historian Bill Kratville, is on display inside the museum (the former Miller House). Outside of town, Hidden Paradise Park remains an attractive leisure area but is now dominated by private homes. The newer of the two railroad bridges built over the Long Pine Canyon still towers above the canyon. The older bridge is gone, but the grassy embankments leading up to it survive.

Epilogue

Without the deafening horns of North Western locomotives, Long Pine is today a much quieter place than it was years ago. The town's population has diminished by more than two-thirds to a mere 350. Families with schoolchildren no longer enjoy the conveniences of a local school.

The rail yard currently lies empty. Only a few remnants of its roundhouse and the concrete abutments from the old railroad water tower can be found. The depot (that is, the express building) is today the most salient reminder of the railroad era and has been converted into a rest stop for trail users.

Some Nebraska officials still question the wisdom of the state legislature's decision not to preserve the Cowboy Line. No other line's abandonment left such a large geographic area in the central United States more than 100 miles from an active railroad. Today, stacks of crossties retrieved after abandonment rest along the right-of-way, providing a vivid reminder of the fate of a line that many wanted desperately to save.

For Further Study

SUGGESTED READINGS:

Bartles, Mike, Bill Kratville, Rick Mills, and Jerry Penry. *The Chicago & North Western Cowboy Line: A History of the Longest Rail-to-Trail Project in America.* David City, Neb.: South Platte Press, 1998, 5–64.

Grant, H. Roger. *The North Western: A History of the Chicago & North Western Railway System.* DeKalb: Northern Illinois University Press, 1996, 49–59, 227–31.

OTHER PRINCIPAL REFERENCES:

Beal, Marianne Brinda. *A Sandhill Century.* Book I, *The Land.* Valentine, Neb.: Cherry County Centennial Committee, 1997, 107–31, 255–59.

Casey, Robert J., and W. A. S. Douglas. *Pioneer Railroad: The Story of the Chicago & North Western System.* New York: McGraw-Hill, 1948, 168–70, 224–25.

Lewis, Edward A. *American Shortline Railway Guide.* 5th ed. Waukesha, Wis.: Kalmbach Publishing, 1996, 213–14.

Tolliver, Denver. *Preliminary Analysis of CNW's Nebraska Rail Line: Impacts of Abandonment.* Fargo, N.Dak.: Upper Great Plains Transportation Institute, 1991, 1–50.

Wright, Danaya C., and Jeffery H. Hester. "Pipes, Wires, and Bicycles: Rails-to-Trails, Utility Licenses, and the Shifting Scope of Railroad Easements from the Nineteenth to the Twenty-First Century." *Environmental Law Quarterly* 27, no. 2 (2002): 351–466.

BOULDER CITY, NEVADA (14,966)

Historic operators: Union Pacific Railroad; Six Companies, Inc.
Last route abandoned: 1985
Notable reuses of right-of-way: Historic Railroad Hiking Trail; tourist railway

   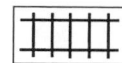

Steam- and diesel-powered trains once hauled concrete, stone, and other materials around the clock at the site of the Boulder (Hoover) Dam. These trains were vital to the work of thousands of laborers, many of whom lived in Boulder City, the first community in the country to be fully planned and developed by the federal government. Some of the tracks, preserved for an excursion railway, survive from this storied chapter in Nevada railroading.

Historical Perspective

For many years after Nevada achieved statehood in 1864, the rolling terrain west of the Colorado River's Black Canyon had few permanent inhabitants. Although a Mormon contingent did establish a presence north of the canyon, the region's separation from the West's principal transportation routes and its inhospitable climate kept most prospective settlers away.

The situation changed when the San Pedro, Los Angeles & Salt Lake Railroad completed a standard gauge rail line between Los Angeles and Salt Lake City in 1905. Its trains crossed hundreds of miles of desolate territory and fostered the creation of new communities, the most notable being Las Vegas. Located some 25 miles west of the Colorado River, Las Vegas prospered both from its role as a supplier of railroad services and from the spectacular expansion of silver mining in west-central Nevada. The community emerged as the seat of newly created Clark County in 1909 and

joined the ranks of Nevada's incorporated communities two years later.

The fervor surrounding Las Vegas' early expansion gradually dissipated as labor-management disputes involving its railroad intensified. The carrier (which shortened its name to the Los Angeles & Salt Lake in 1916) came under the exclusive ownership of Union Pacific in 1921. Union Pacific first reduced the size of and then closed its Las Vegas shops, pushing the community's economy to the brink of collapse.

Meanwhile, with people and industry pouring into other parts of the West, the nearby Colorado River became increasingly significant in regional planning. State officials found themselves inundated with issues about sharing the river's water, controlling flooding, and expanding electrical production. To support all of these objectives, in 1928 Congress passed the Boulder Canyon Project Act, the first major reclamation effort involving the river. Many hoped that the future dam would be Las Vegas' economic savior.

A freight train en route to the Boulder (Hoover) Dam construction site crosses a magnificent trestle on the Six Companies Railroad circa 1932. A few years later, Lake Mead's rising waters submerged this area. (McBride Collection; Boulder City Museum and Historical Association.)

The ambitious plans for creating both the dam and a large reservoir on the river rested on the assumption that extensive investments in infrastructure would first be made. These investments would include not only rail lines but also a new community capable of providing housing, health care, and other necessities for thousands of workers.

Union Pacific was geographically positioned to profit from these developments. In cooperation with federal officials, it drafted plans for a 23-mile branch line to the area. This branch would originate on the Union Pacific main line southwest of Las Vegas, negotiate a crevasse known as the Railroad Pass (to this day, the only named pass in Nevada ever traversed by a rail line), and terminate at the site of the proposed town. In late 1930,

Herbert Hoover's Secretary of the Interior, Ray Lyman Wilbur, ceremoniously drove the first spike to launch its construction. By early the following year, the railroad had reached the town site and had built a large wooden depot. The federal government had bold plans for the community, which it named Boulder City and established as a "reservation" administered through the Bureau of Reclamation. To assist in the city's design, it commissioned a noted city planner, Saco Reink DeBoer, who envisioned various government buildings on a hill near the center of town overlooking a large park. The main streets in town would bear the names of the seven states drained by the Colorado River, all of which had a large stake in the project's success.

Due to the enormity of the Boulder Dam project, the federal government selected a consortium to undertake its construction. Called Six Companies, Inc., the consortium combined the resources of the Henry Kaiser Company, the W. S. Bechtel Company, the MacDonald and Kahn Company, the Utah Construction Company, the Morrison-Knudson Company, and J. F. Shea and

Company. In supporting the consortium's work, the Bureau of Reclamation built a 10-mile rail line from the end of the Union Pacific line branch to the construction site. These tracks, while leased to the U.S. Construction Railway, were operated by Six Companies, which also had 19 miles of its own track. Six Companies' routes originated at Lawler, a rural location east of Boulder City and one of several division points named after the consortium's executives, and consisted of two branches. One branch extended to a gravel pit 7 miles upstream from Black Canyon on the Arizona side of the river. Another branch, the Canyon Railroad, took trains to the upriver face of the dam.

Boulder City flourished as workers arrived from throughout the country to work for Six Companies and its many suppliers. The community, fully planned and developed by the federal government, soon had more than a thousand houses, numerous dormitories, a 700-seat movie theater, a hospital, and a recreational hall. By 1933, more than 5,000 lived in its well-designed neighborhoods. The Boulder Dam Hotel and the Boulder City Company Store were pillars of the community. So, too, was the Union Pacific depot—a large wooden structure near the edge of town, just 7 miles from the dam site— and the Railroad Pass Casino, a popular gathering place located west of the reservation limits and equipped with a walk-in safe to serve the railroad's payroll office.

Most Union Pacific trains dispatched from Las Vegas rumbled through Boulder City without stops on their way to the construction site. At the height of construction, these trains handled more than 300 carloads of materials daily and supported a workforce of more than 4,000 men. A gasoline-powered McKeen car shuttling between Boulder City and Las Vegas, meanwhile, carried commuters as well as travelers making connections with Union Pacific's long-distance trains, including the Challenger, an express run between Los Angeles and Chicago. The McKeen car's accommodations were decidedly modest compared to those offered on many of the special trains that traversed the branch.

In 1934, the railroad brought officials over the Canyon Railroad to the face of the dam in the comfort of the country's first streamlined train, the M-1000 (later called the City of Salina). Later that year, the railroad operated eight special trains from Los Angeles to Boulder City—each equipped with a diner, observation lounge, and at least nine Pullman sleeping cars. These trains and several more chartered runs from Utah brought some 2,000 members of the Shriners to their

organization's annual convention—an event highlighted by a stirring midnight ceremony at the construction site. For many Americans, however, it was the famed Pioneer Zephyr that evoked vivid images of the Boulder Dam. Although the Zephyr never rode Boulder City's rails, this famous Chicago, Burlington & Quincy streamliner was a featured attraction in the 1935 movie *Silver Streak*, which had a story line involving a high-speed trip between Chicago and the Boulder Dam to deliver an iron lung to an ailing worker.

All of these events paled in comparison to the ceremony held in the autumn of that year, when President Franklin D. Roosevelt and other dignitaries arrived on the Union Pacific to dedicate the dam—a moment of tremendous pride for the workers who had contributed to its completion.

A long-dormant segment of track ends near the western edge of Boulder City—well short of its historic terminus at the face of the Hoover Dam. (Photo by author.)

Changing Times

With the mighty Colorado now tamed, a work crew removed the Six Companies' track, and Union Pacific reduced freight operations on its Boulder City Branch to a minimum. Union Pacific turned passenger service from Las Vegas over to a motor-coach subsidiary, the Union Pacific Stage Company. The canyon and its abandoned rail-bed were gradually submerged by the rising waters of Lake Mead. Although Boulder City remained a functioning community, many of its dwellings and stores were vacated as workers and their families moved away.

When the federal government and Basic Magnesium Inc. selected a location between Boulder City and Las Vegas to process magnesium for aircraft parts in 1941, it infused new life into a branch that was fading into obscurity. Union Pacific built a 2-mile spur northwest of the Railroad Pass to serve this facility, which, like other manufacturers, used the inexpensive power harnessed by the dam. The plant flourished during World War II and supported the creation of an entirely new town named after former Nevada senator Charles B. Henderson.

The future of the branch appeared bright when the magnesium facility was converted into an industrial park after the war. Although the immense dam (renamed the Hoover Dam in 1947 in honor of former President Hoover) continued to provide low-cost electricity, however, there was little industrial development in Boulder City, even after Congress ceded much of the bureau's property in the area to other units of government, which allowed for the community's incorporation in 1959. By the early 1960s, the tracks between Henderson and the line's terminus near Lawler were only lightly used, principally to haul generator parts for use at the dam. After the last shipment arrived at Lawler in 1961, the bureau removed its track, making Boulder City the end of the line.

Union Pacific continued to move freight to and from Henderson and occasionally shipped specialized equipment east to Boulder City, where this equipment was loaded onto trucks and hauled to the dam. The carrier also continued to publish in company timetables and the *Official Guide of the Railways* the schedules of motor coaches operated by the Las Vegas–Tonopah–Reno Stage Line between Boulder City and Las Vegas.

The motor-coach schedules vanished from the *Official Guide* with the inception of Amtrak in 1971, when all rail passenger service to Las Vegas ended. However, Union Pacific made a gift to posterity by donating the Boulder City depot to the Southern Nevada Museum (later renamed the Clark County Museum) in 1975. The museum transformed the depot into an exhibit hall at a new museum site near the edge of Henderson.

The spectacular rise in tourism and residential construction rejuvenated Las Vegas beginning in the mid-1970s and gradually spilled over into Boulder City. To showcase the well-preserved downtown, local leaders founded the Boulder City Museum and Historical Association in 1980 and successfully had the Boulder Dam Hotel and the original city hospital added to the National Register of Historic Places in 1982. The Boulder City Historic District, an area encompassing much more of the downtown, earned representation on the register in 1983.

Municipal planners also sought to attract more traditional industry, an attempt some feared would be compromised if Union Pacific moved ahead with its plans to abandon the 12-mile segment between Boulder City and Henderson. In an attempt to preserve local rail freight service, officials tried to attract shippers to nearby undeveloped property. Although this effort ended unsuccessfully, representatives from Boulder City, Henderson, and the state's Department of Museums and History made known their interest in using these tracks for an excursion railway. In support of this idea, Union Pacific donated the entire Boulder City Branch to the state—a gift valued at more than $11 million—after filing its abandonment application in 1985. Recognition of this donation occurred at a ceremony in Las Vegas held in November that same year. The following month, the carrier officially ended service to Boulder City by delivering one last load of generator parts.

Abandonment's Legacy

The dramatic scenery along the dormant corridor and its proximity to Las Vegas and Lake Mead gave many community leaders hope that the route would one day become a tourist railway. A state report supported the notion that the eastern end of the branch had qualities suitable for excursion service, but planners reluctantly conceded that it would be unreasonably difficult to operate trains to and from downtown Las Vegas due to potential interference with freight trains on the Union Pacific main line. Consequently, attention turned to less ambitious proposals.

The movement to create a tourist railway seemed on the verge of succeeding in 1989 when the state's legislature funded an engineering study to investigate the creation of a southern branch of the Nevada State Railroad Museum in Boulder City. The Department of Museums and History then developed a blueprint for an excursion railway equipped with a newly built loop track with a circumference of more than 2 miles on land that remained under the jurisdiction of the Bureau of Reclamation. Having dropped plans to operate excursion trains over the portion of the branch west of Henderson—tracks still used by Union Pacific freight trains—the state transferred control of this segment to the Henderson government.

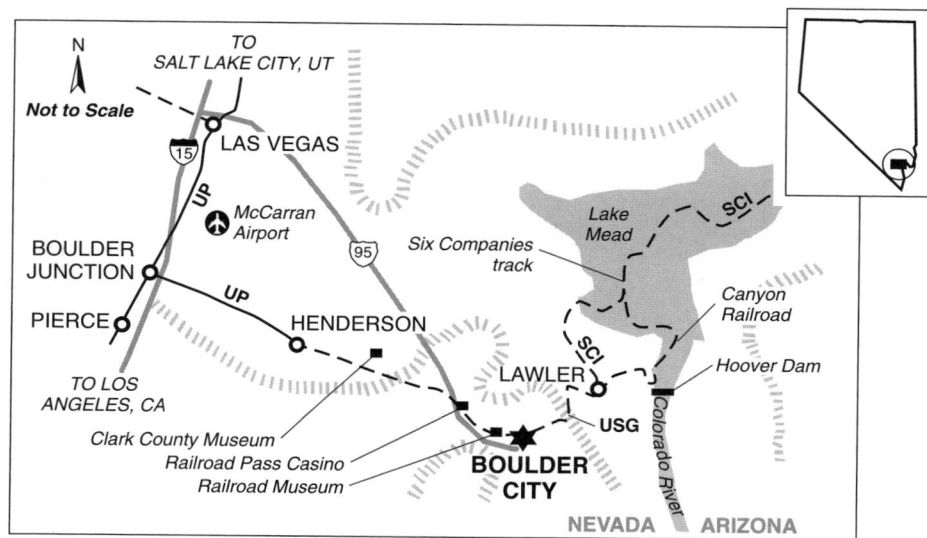

As momentum built for the creation of the railroad museum in the early 1990s, trains returned to Boulder City after a hiatus of several years. These trains brought to the emerging museum more than fifty freight and passenger cars, including rolling stock purchased from Utah's Heber Creeper Railway. However, when the state made improvements to U.S. Route 93/95, the major arterial road extending southeast from Las Vegas in 1993, it covered the grade crossing adjacent to the Railroad Pass Casino with pavement, severing the eastern end of the branch. From this point, rolling stock brought to the museum arrived by truck.

Planning for the excursion railway passed another milestone in 1996, when the state museum completed work on a locomotive maintenance shop in Boulder City. Unlike the effort to build the rail line decades before, however, progress on the tourist railway merely inched forward due to the state's precarious financial situation. In deference to budgetary realities, the museum eventually embraced a less ambitious plan to operate diesel-powered excursions (without the loop track) as far west as the Railroad Pass, a 7-mile round-trip.

After the turn of the century, the museum was the beneficiary of significant financial support. By 2003, it had made improvements to its route, refurbished several historic cars, and built a passenger shelter and parking lot, allowing it to begin offering scenic excursions. In 2004, it completed restoration work on a third diesel locomotive, No. 844, a GP-30 built in 1963. Future plans call for operating excursions all the way to Henderson, which will require equipping U.S. 93/95 with an overpass at the Railroad Pass to eliminate a potentially dangerous railroad crossing.

Epilogue

Visitors to Boulder City will find that the community takes pride in preserving the streetscape created by Saco Reink DeBoer, its famed architect. The downtown area retains an art deco style from the 1930s, with government buildings still overlooking residential neighborhoods. The refurbished Boulder Dam Hotel once again serves overnight guests and is the new home of the Boulder City/Hoover Dam Museum.

Travelers following the historic railroad route to the dam will find Union Pacific freight trains still operating between the junction and Henderson. Along the dormant tracks farther east, the Railroad Pass Casino—one of the nation's oldest gaming establishments—remains a notable entertainment destination. Inside this building, the contents of the former Union Pacific vault, which has been sealed for decades, remain a mystery. Near Lake Mead, some of the right-of-way that was formerly part of the Bureau of Reclamation's rail line has become the Historic Railroad Hiking Trail, a recreational path.

The Hoover Dam, of course, stands as an enduring symbol of American ingenuity, but most of the locomotives and railcars that supported its construction have been relegated to scrap. Boulder City's railroad museum, however, showcases an impressive collection of historic rolling stock and the venerable No. 1000, an LW2 locomotive built in 1939—the first diesel-electric switch engine on the Union Pacific. It seems fitting that such a workhorse locomotive now rumbles over a branch that was once vital to the work of tens of thousands of men.

For Further Study

SUGGESTED READINGS:

Myrick, David F. *Railroads of Nevada and Eastern California.* Berkeley, Calif.: Howell-North Books, 1962, 2:734–52.

Rodden, Mimi Garat. *Boulder City, Nevada.* Chicago: Arcadia Publishing, 2000, 7–12.

Signor, John. *The Los Angeles & Salt Lake Railroad: Union Pacific's Historic Salt Lake Route.* San Marino, Calif.: Golden West Books, 1988, 114–15, 125, 208.

OTHER PRINCIPAL REFERENCES:

Best, Gerald M. "A Very Special Special." *Rail Classics* 6, no. 5 (Sept. 1977): 22–25.

State of Nevada. *Developmental History of the Nevada State Railroad Museum, Boulder City.* 15 July 1996, 1–5.

Toll, David W. *The Compleat Nevada Traveler.* Virginia City, Nev.: Gold Hill Publishing, 1999, 233–39.

U.S. Department of Interior. *Construction of Hoover Dam.* Las Vegas: KC Publications, 1976.

CARSON CITY, NEVADA (52,457)

Historic operator: Virginia & Truckee Railroad
Last route abandoned: 1950
Notable reuse of right-of-way: None

On May 31, 1950, the last Virginia & Truckee train departed Carson City, ending rail service to a community deeply rooted in the history of the American West. Although never operating more than 67 miles of routes, the legacy of the "Queen of the Short Lines" far outstripped its size. Today, the Nevada State Railroad Museum in Carson City honors the carrier's heritage through exhibits, displays, and rides on the Washoe Zephyr as well as a demonstration train powered on special occasions by one of the oldest operating steam locomotives in the United States.

Historical Perspective

When frontiersman John C. Frémont explored the eastern slopes of the Sierra Nevada during the early 1840s, he named a river flowing through the area after his scout, Christopher "Kit" Carson. Within a few years, thousands of wagons were passing through this arid region along the branch of the California Emigrant Trail originating near present-day Reno. Along this route in 1851, a trading post known as Eagle Station opened to attend to the needs of travelers.

In addition to serving the California Emigrant Trail, the Eagle Station trading post emerged as an important stop on the Central Overland Route, a trail well trodden by wagon teams traveling east–west through the region. The location's potential was not lost on the enterprising Abraham Curry, who aspired to establish a city at the intersection of the two trails. He created a town site adjacent to the trading post in 1852 and, believing that the community would one day be a center of government, set aside 10 acres for the construction of a capitol and county courthouse. Curry named the settlement after the Carson River and built a fine sandstone guesthouse, the Warm Springs Hotel, east of town.

The discovery of rich veins of gold and silver in 1859—the "Great Strike"—marked the beginning of a spectacular mining era in the nearby Comstock Lode district. Within a few years, more than twenty ore-processing mills sprawled along the Carson River south of the mines. As newcomers flocked to the region, Carson City became a stop on the Overland Mail route, a station on the Pony Express, and the eastern terminus of a telegraph line from

The Sierra Nevada rises in the distance as Virginia & Truckee locomotive No. 27 billows smoke in front of the Carson City depot in May 1950. The locomotive was placed back in service less than three weeks before the railway's operations officially ended. (Nevada State Railroad Museum at Carson City.)

San Francisco. As Curry had hoped, the community became a regional center of government upon the creation of the Nevada Territory in 1861. The legislature even held its first meeting in his Warm Springs Hotel.

Less favorable to the community were the provisions in the Pacific Railroad Act that called for the first transcontinental railroad to follow a more northerly alignment through Reno and the Donner Pass. Some demanded in 1862 that the federal government amend the act to require that the rail line be constructed through Carson City. Although this effort was unsuccessful, the community continued to have strong growth potential. Carson City became the capital—fulfilling Curry's dream—when Nevada achieved statehood in 1864 while prospering from the sensational rise of Comstock

mining. It also became a regional site of the U.S. Mint and the seat of Ormsby County.

More good fortune arrived with the 1870 completion of the Virginia & Truckee Railroad (V&T) between Carson City and Virginia City, the largest community in the mining district. These tracks negotiated the Brunswick Canyon, crossed several trestles, and passed through seven tunnels to reach the heart of the mining district. Despite lacking a connection to the rest of the state's rail system, the railroad proved to be a great success. Its trains transported passengers, lumber, and supplies to Virginia City, as well as enormous ore shipments from the mines to the mills.

Carson City soon left behind its humble origins, a process highlighted by the completion of a magnificent statehouse built of sandstone in 1871. The community prospered as a center of state government and the home of the Carson & Tahoe Lumber and Fluming Company—an enterprise equipped with a flume stretching 12 miles from Spooner Summit (a location on the eastern slopes of the Sierra Nevada) to a flume yard south of town.

Businessmen could arrive from afar with greater ease in 1872 when the V&T extended its route north between Carson City and Reno—a route traversing Washoe Canyon and providing an interchange with the powerful Central Pacific Railroad. Within a few years, more than forty-five trains rolled through town daily, including a train equipped with a Pullman Palace sleeping car operating to Vallejo (with a ferry connection to San Francisco) via the Reno interchange. Arriving passengers had only a short walk to several fine hotels, including the Ormsby House and the St. Charles Hotel. In 1874, lumber magnate Duane L. Bliss built a stately mansion near the center of town.

Although weakened by a sharp mining downturn during the late 1870s, which led to the elimination of the passenger service to Vallejo, the V&T remained one of northern Nevada's most prominent transportation providers for many more years. As a bridge route between the Carson & Colorado Railroad (which established an interchange at Mound House in 1880) and the Southern Pacific (successor to the Central Pacific) at Reno, it assumed the aura of a main-line railroad. Separate freight and passenger stations, as well as a 55-foot turntable and an engine house built of sandstone, heralded the carrier's vital role in the community's economic affairs. Thousands of passengers crowded onto V&T trains in 1897 on their way to see the much-publicized heavyweight fight between "Gentleman Jim" Corbett and Robert Fitzsimmons in Carson City.

By the turn of the century, however, the carrier was involved in a desperate fight of its own—with its survival at stake. In 1900, the struggling carrier moved its company offices from Virginia City to Carson City and sold the Carson & Colorado to the Southern Pacific. Reincorporated as the Virginia & Truckee Railway in 1904, the carrier faced the dual problems of a precipitous decline in mining and the completion of the Hazen Cutoff in 1905. The cutoff, originating on the Southern Pacific main line east of Reno at Hazen, abruptly ended the V&T's role as a bridge to the Carson & Colorado. Although the V&T survived—it even built a branch south from the state capital to Minden in 1906—its revenue potential gradually diminished.

Carson City weathered the downturns in silver mining and logging substantially better than its hometown railway. It prospered as a center of state government and celebrated several more transportation achievements, including Nevada's first airplane flight in 1910 and the first authenticated flight across the Sierra Nevada nine years later.

Changing Times

The decline of the V&T followed a pattern common among short lines heavily dependent on mining districts undergoing a transition. The company discontinued its last conventional passenger train in 1924 and limited subsequent passenger service to mixed trains and gas-powered motorcars. It struggled as new silver-production facilities reduced the demand for ore shipments and as improvements to roads, such as the paving of U.S. Route 50 through Carson City in 1933, accelerated the shift to trucks for freight transport. In the depths of the Great Depression, the closing of numerous businesses only made matters worse.

As the once-celebrated short line fell on more hard times, company management began selling rolling stock to Paramount Pictures in 1937—a move met with dismay by many in Nevada, who felt that it was disposing of

Despite numerous alterations to the former Virginia & Truckee depot in Carson City, the wooden structure retains the aura of a historic railroad station. (Photo by author.)

treasured parts of the state's past. The carrier fell into receivership that same year and abandoned the Carson City–Virginia City segment in 1939. The funds that the carrier generated by scrapping this historic corridor two years later and selling additional rolling stock helped it to survive through World War II and into the postwar period.

Many railroad enthusiasts and Hollywood producers expressed their fondness for the short line as its struggle for survival intensified. In 1947, MGM Studios used the carrier for the movie *Whispering Smith.*

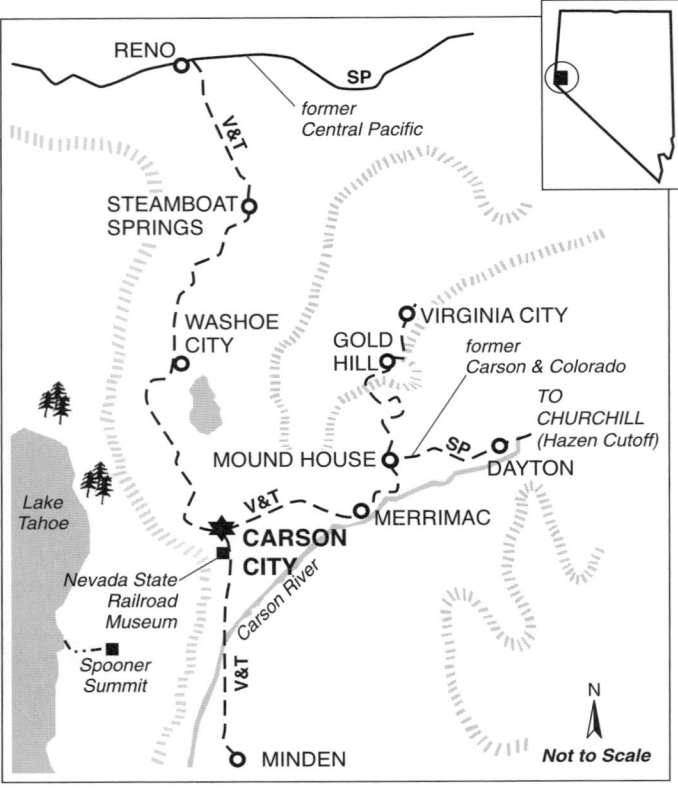

Over the next several years, motion picture companies returned to the V&T four more times for filming. Still operating a triweekly mixed train and relying on steam power, the carrier seemed almost frozen in time, intriguing those interested in the vanishing traditions of Comstock mining.

Some believed the V&T had a future in motion pictures; others felt it had a future as a short line. The company's owners, however, seemed intent on abandoning the line without more than a cursory look at the alternatives. The carrier applied to abandon the remaining route from Minden to Reno in 1949. After more than eighty years of operation, the V&T ran its last train, after a short ceremony at the Carson City depot, in May 1950.

Abandonment's Legacy

The demise of the V&T marked the first time in modern history that an American state capital had been left without an active rail line. Although having only about 3,000 inhabitants at the time, making it the nation's smallest capital, Carson City was poised for expansion.

As subdivisions sprang up along the community's periphery, the community gradually relinquished some

of its Old West qualities. Anticipating further growth, Carson City and the Ormsby County governments consolidated under the Carson City name in 1969. The opening of Interstate 80 through Reno, however, diverted motorists away from the community's hotels and casinos. Much like their predecessors more than a century before, officials vigorously lobbied the federal government with hopes of seeing a new east–west transportation corridor built through their community. At local hearings in 1969, civic leaders delivered passionate testimonials in favor of transforming U.S. Route 50 into a new interstate highway extension. This effort, however, was to no avail.

Motion picture studios experienced problems with the aging V&T equipment and eventually relegated much of it to a Union Pacific yard in Los Angeles. The fleet was further dispersed when the National Park Service leased a pair of locomotives and put them on display in Promontory, Utah. After the Union Pacific asked that the rolling stock in its yard be moved elsewhere during 1971, the state government acquired many of these time-worn cars, including the locomotives leased to the National Park Service.

By the mid-1970s, the state had amassed a substantial collection of historic rolling stock and assumed stewardship over the two locomotives at Promontory. After putting these acquisitions in local storage, it identified a site for a museum near the southern edge of Carson City in 1977. Upon completing a great deal of restoration work, the state's Department of Museums and History opened the collection to the public in 1980. At this location in 1986, the newly created Nevada State Railroad Museum celebrated the opening of an enlarged facility replete with an interpretive center and a 1-mile loop track.

The museum gradually expanded its holdings to

more than thirty pieces of former V&T rolling stock, including several locomotives, giving it the distinction of having the country's largest collection of nineteenth-century railroad cars. Visitors could take rides over the museum grounds on the Washoe Zephyr, once a Tucson, Cornelia & Gila motorcar, and admire the former Southern Pacific depot that had been relocated from Wabuska. On special occasions, visitors climbed aboard trains powered by the venerable Inyo, a former V&T steam locomotive built in 1875—one of the oldest operating steam locomotives in the United States and the pride of the museum.

By the early 1990s, Carson City had grown to more than 40,000 inhabitants, and the museum had become a major tourist attraction. In the midst of such expansion, significant portions of the railroad's abandoned route through town were blocked by real estate development, including a newly built post office. Nevertheless, local officials, with an eye toward creating another V&T attraction and further stimulating development, began to explore the possibility of rebuilding the railroad from the city's eastern periphery to the terminus of the "new" Virginia & Truckee Railroad, a steam-powered operator providing excursions over 3 miles of rebuilt track between Virginia City and Gold Hill. This extension would allow tourists to travel by train all the way from Carson City to the famed historic district in Virginia City.

The proponents of such a plan worked for years to overcome its financial and physical obstacles. In cooperation with the state legislature, the newly created Tri-County Railroad Commission received a state grant in 1993 to create a route across a gold-mining pit created during the 1970s. The commission also informally considered the possibility of reestablishing freight service to Carson City by operating trains over a portion of the excursion railway and some newly laid track to Churchill (a community on the Hazen Cutoff), thereby giving the community a new connection to the national rail system.

The effort to rebuilt the V&T then ran into several obstacles. A sales tax increase that would have financed the construction of the excursion railway and other transportation enhancements was defeated by Carson City voters. The need to find safe ways to cross abandoned mining tunnels in the region delayed work on the project financed through the state grant. Nevertheless, the idea of operating passenger trains from a rural location outside of town to Virginia City continued to garner support. (See page 197 for a summary of this project's status.)

On an even more ambitious scale, the state's rapid population growth spurred interest in high-speed rail service between San Francisco and Las Vegas by way of Reno and Carson City. The California–Nevada Super Speed Train Commission received its charter during the mid-1990s and developed proposals for creating this state-of-the-art intercity corridor. As with so many high-speed initiatives of this era, however, the commission was unable to attract private capital or advance the project beyond the discussion stage.

Epilogue

Carson City would undoubtedly be a larger city today had it succeeded in attracting either a transcontinental railroad or an interstate highway. Considering the town's role in western settlement, it is significant that this historic crossroads currently lacks an intercity railroad line, a limited-access expressway, and commercial air service. Even so, the city's proximity to both Reno International Airport and U.S. Route 395 (a divided highway) has helped it generate thousands of jobs in the service industry and light manufacturing.

Many visitors are struck by the magnificence of the state capitol—the focal point of Carson City's historic district. Now more than 130 years old, this edifice is widely known for its sandstone walls and fine interior. Nearby, sculptures of the legendary Kit Carson and Abraham Curry decorate the grounds of the state's Legislative Building. The former U.S. Mint has become the Nevada State Museum, while the casinos nearby, certainly smaller and less lavish than those in Las Vegas and Reno, bring to mind a slower-paced era in Nevada gaming.

More than a half century after abandonment, much of the V&T can be discerned easily on the arid terrain. The carrier's single-story wooden passenger depot, a local landmark listed on the National Register in 1998, is now used as a Masonic Lodge, which is unusual because most lodges have second-floor meeting rooms and are made of brick or stone. Although significantly modified since the days of its final trains, this historic station, along with the railroad museum to the south, pay homage to the Queen of the Short Lines.

For Further Study

SUGGESTED READINGS:
Beebe, Lucius, and Charles Clegg. *Virginia & Truckee: A Story*

of Virginia City and Comstock Times. Oakland, Calif.: Grahame H. Hardy, 1949, 7–59.

Myrick, David F. *Railroads of Nevada and Eastern California.* Berkeley, Calif.: Howell-North Books, 1962, 1:136–62.

Wurm, Ted, and Harry Demoro. *The Silver Short Line: History of the Virginia & Truckee Railroad.* Glendale, Calif.: Trans-Anglo Books, 1983, 109–209.

OTHER PRINCIPAL REFERENCES:

Drury, George. *Historical Guide to North American Railroads.* Milwaukee, Wis.: Kalmbach Books, 1985, 337–38.

Jensen, Larry. *The Movie Railroads.* Burbank, Calif.: Darwin Publications, 1981, 132–35.

McAfee, Ward. *California's Railroad. Era: 1850–1911.* San Marino, Calif.: Golden West Books, 1973, 58.

Tool, David W. *The Complete Nevada Traveler.* Virginia City, Nev.: Gold Hill Publishing, 1999, 81–87.

Wurm, Ted. *Rebirth of the Virginia & Truckee Railroad.* Virginia City, Nev.: Virginia & Truckee Railroad. 1992, 39.

VIRGINIA CITY, NEVADA (930)

Historic operator: Virginia & Truckee Railway
Last route abandoned: 1939
Notable reuse of right-of-way: Tourist railway

Virginia City was purportedly the greatest city between Denver and San Francisco when its first train arrived in 1870. Admired by Samuel Clemens and other nineteenth-century journalists, it boasted more than 20,000 inhabitants, luxurious hotels, and one of the finest newspapers in the West. Today an excursion railway operates over several miles of Virginia City's abandoned route and rekindles the spirit of this community's legendary past.

Historical Perspective

In the late 1850s, the land along the Carson River in present-day Storey County teemed with activity. As men feverishly panned for gold in the river's fast-flowing waters, wagons destined for California struggled to cross the sandy terrain nearby. Prospectors Pat McLaughlin and Peter O'Reilly clearly chose well when they conducted their search for precious metal on higher ground. Their "Great Strike" near the head of Six Mile Canyon in 1859 attracted throngs of other gold seekers to the region. Seizing the opportunity to profit from the ambiguity in ownership of this land, William "Pancake" Comstock successfully established his claim to the property.

Word of the immense riches of the Comstock Lode spread quickly, resulting in notoriously crowded conditions in a community of tents and shanties known as Mount Pleasant. The inhabitants of this ramshackle settlement soon renamed their community in honor of

James "Old Virginny" Finney, another property owner living in the area. Virginia City received its incorporation through an act of the Utah Legislature in early 1861 and became part of the newly created Nevada Territory several months later.

A more favorable script for Virginia City's expansion could hardly have been written. The completion of a system of toll roads in 1862 created a direct route from California's famed Mother Lode mining area to the new mining district. With the Comstock Lode mining district enjoying extraordinary success, merchants used camels and any other animal power that was available to haul supplies and equipment on these roads. Only a few years after Nevada achieved statehood in 1864, Virginia City was home to about a hundred saloons, six churches, and an immense mining industry. Growing to an estimated 30,000 inhabitants, it became the largest—and in many respects the greatest—city between Denver and San Francisco.

A talented young writer with a gift for

Only a few miles from Virginia City—the heart of the famed Comstock Lode mining district—a passenger train pauses on the Crown Point Trestle in Gold Hill, circa 1889. This enormous wooden span was a notable landmark on the Virginia & Truckee Railroad—the so-called Queen of the Short Lines. (Photo by J. H. Crockwell, Nevada Historical Society.)

humor, Samuel Clemens contributed to the city's spirited character as a reporter for the *Territorial Enterprise*, a local newspaper. While living in the community, he adopted the pseudonym Mark Twain, earned a reputation for exaggeration, and demonstrated a penchant for journalistic hoaxes. Clemens left town several years before the Virginia & Truckee Railroad (V&T) made its celebratory arrival in 1870, which marked the beginning of another period of fantastic expansion that, at times, seemed as exaggerated as some of Clemens's works of fiction.

The railroad was an impressive piece of engineering, with many trestles and seven tunnels, including two within the municipal limits of Virginia City. Its trains passed through the Brunswick Canyon and crossed an awe-inspiring trestle over the Crown Point Ravine near neighboring Gold Hill. Its preponderance of sharp curves led some to call the carrier "the crookedest short line in America." The route nonetheless proved to be an

effective means of transporting passengers, lumber, and supplies from Carson City to the mining district. Massive shipments of ore soon moved by rail from the mines to mills along the river.

The same year that the railroad inaugurated service, businessman Adolph Sutro began work on a 4-mile tunnel from Virginia City to a location he immodestly named Sutro City. The entrepreneur envisioned the tunnel draining scalding water from the mines even as it accommodated the twin tracks of an industrial railroad for shipping ore to the mills. Sensing the possibilities, he imagined Sutro City one day becoming a great commercial center.

The V&T also invested heavily in new facilities and extended its route north between Carson City and Reno in 1872, thereby establishing a connection with the Central Pacific Railroad. Following the discovery of a huge body of high-grade silver ore (the "Big Bonanza") the following year, rail traffic grew at an astonishing rate. Establishing itself as a tourist attraction of considerable renown, the "Queen of the Short Lines" became a source of great municipal pride. Its boasted separate freight and passenger depots as well as a large local roundhouse.

The enormous riches of the Comstock Lode allowed Virginia City to overcome periodic mining downturns and disasters. The Great Fire of 1875 reduced to ruins the famed International House, the county courthouse, and many other prominent structures. Out of the rubble emerged an even more impressive city dignified by a new International House, a hotel standing six stories tall and equipped with the first "moving room" (elevator) in Nevada. A new courthouse, reputed to be the finest in the state, and the ornate Fourth Ward School—both readied for occupancy in 1877— portended an auspicious future.

Changing Times

Virginia City remained a notable mining center for many more years, but it struggled as the Big Bonanza drew to a close. Although the completion of the Sutro Tunnel in 1878 was a remarkable technical achievement that fostered optimism for growth, it came at a time when mining in the Comstock region was in retreat. The tunnel ultimately proved to be a financial disappointment.

The railroad's services helped Virginia City weather the hardship associated with a substantial drop in mining employment. Its trains brought former President Ulysses S. Grant to town in 1879 and President Rutherford B. Hayes the following year. The owners of the carrier, however, recognized that they needed to develop new sources of revenue. With this objective in mind, they commenced construction of the narrow-gauge Carson & Colorado Railroad in 1880 from an interchange point along the V&T at Mound House. Extending through desolate terrain to Hawthorne and on to the Owens Valley in eastern California, this line generated considerable revenue and established the V&T as a bridge route to the Southern Pacific (former Central Pacific) main line through Reno. Unfortunately, however, the Carson & Colorado did not live up to the high expectations of its founders.

As both the V&T and mining district felt the strain of changing times, many prominent Virginia City businesses closed, including the famed *Territorial Enterprise,* which suspended publication in 1893. Virginia City's economy did not substantially

improve until the early twentieth century, when another mining boom rejuvenated many local businesses, including the legendary Piper's Opera House, which attracted such luminaries as band director John Philip Sousa and singer-entertainer Al Jolson. For the owners of the V&T, however, the outlook remained poor. The company moved its offices out of Virginia City in 1900, reorganized as the Virginia & Truckee Railway four years later, and ceased being a bridge route to the former Carson & Colorado (which had been sold to the Southern Pacific) in 1905.

By the end of the decade, both the V&T and the legendary mining camp at the end of its line were fading into obscurity. In 1914, a fire once again destroyed the International House, but this time the wooden structure was not rebuilt. In the 1920s, mining activity fell so precipitously that the community's population dropped to a mere 600. After V&T operated its last straight passenger train in 1924, the carrier limited its passenger operations to mixed trains and gas-powered railcars.

Another mining revival took place in the mid-1930s, but by this time, Virginia City had its own mills, greatly limiting the need to ship ore on the railway. Gradually, strip mining replaced underground mining as

Long retired from regular service, this former Northwestern Pacific postal car (V&T No. 25) now serves as an excursion railway ticket office and gift shop. (Photo by author.)

195

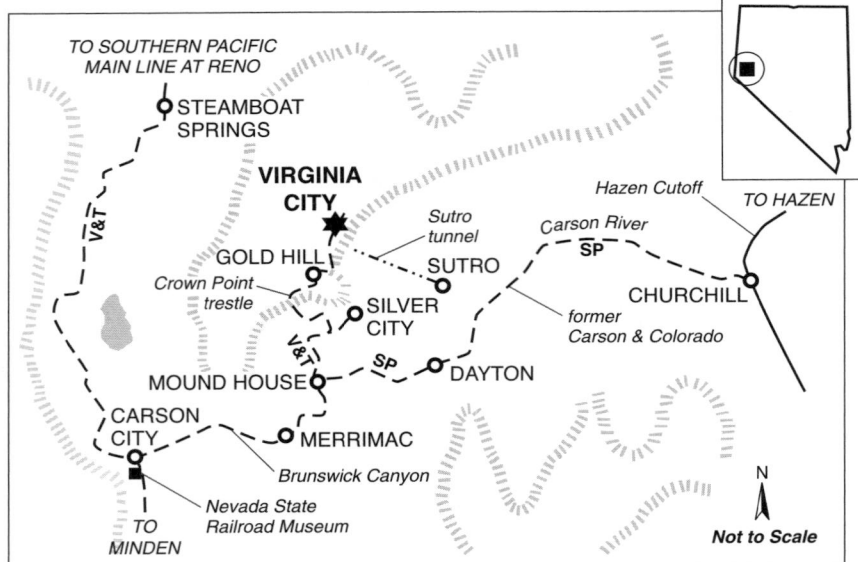

TO SOUTHERN PACIFIC
MAIN LINE AT RENO

STEAMBOAT
SPRINGS

**VIRGINIA
CITY**

Hazen Cutoff

Sutro
tunnel

Carson River

TO HAZEN

SP

GOLD HILL

SUTRO

*Crown Point
trestle*

SILVER
CITY

CHURCHILL

*former
Carson & Colorado*

MOUND HOUSE

SP

DAYTON

CARSON
CITY

MERRIMAC

Brunswick Canyon

N

*Nevada State
Railroad Museum*

Not to Scale

TO
MINDEN

V&T

Humphrey Bogart, Errol Flynn, and Randolph Scott, which was premiering at a local theater. When Beebe returned in 1948 with companion Charles Clegg, the famous pair parked their classic wooden private railroad car, the Gold Coast, in Carson City and made Virginia City one of their homes. Although their deluxe private car had to be moved prior to the abandonment of the remainder of the V&T in 1950, the newcomers planted their roots and revived the *Territorial Enterprise* newspaper in 1952.

During the mid-1950s, artists, writers, and romantics having a similar desire to experience life in the Comstock region moved to Virginia City. The revived *Enterprise* earned considerable critical acclaim and added to the community's mystique. In 1959, the townspeople welcomed then-Vice President Richard Nixon to a centennial celebration of the famous gold strike. Reminiscent of the mischievous ways of Mark Twain, Beebe published a fictional article about wild camel races in Virginia City that year. Mistakenly believing the article was authentic, the *San Francisco Chronicle* published an account of the races. After learning of its embarrassing error, the *Chronicle* sponsored an actual camel race in 1960.

The long-running television series *Bonanza* brought considerable publicity to the community's heritage, but the show's lack of attention to historical accuracy angered Beebe and Clegg, who became disenchanted with the community's changing character. They sold the *Enterprise* in 1960 and increasingly spent their time traveling in their new steel railcar, which they had named the Virginia City.

Another prominent figure with a fondness for the V&T was Robert C. Gray, who had ridden the last excursion to Virginia City. Gray observed in 1965 that much of the bygone carrier's right-of-way near town remained unobstructed. He consulted with area railroad enthusiasts and visited the courthouse numerous times over a three-year period to assess the ownership status of this land. Then he launched an ambitious initiative to rebuild portions of the railway for excursion service.

While Gray worked tirelessly toward his objective, Virginia City was designated a National Historic Landmark and evolved into a nationally known tourist destination. After the county commissioners approved the reconstruction of a small portion of the route in 1972, the

the preferred method of extraction, marring much of the county's landscape. In 1935, the V&T relocated a short segment of track to allow for the demolition of the famed trestle over Crown Point Ravine, thereby allowing a mining company to begin excavation on the site.

V&T suffered sizeable losses during the Great Depression; it fell into receivership in 1937 and petitioned to abandon its local service the following year, arguing that its Ward Tunnel near Virginia City had serious structural defects. After suspending regular service from Carson City to Virginia City in 1938, the carrier bowed to the wishes of hundreds of admirers by operating excursion trains arranged by railroad historical groups. In May 1939, the carrier formally abandoned the Carson City–Virginia City segment.

Abandonment's Legacy

Within the lifetime of some of the region's residents, Virginia City had gone from one of the greatest cities in the West to a dying community with an economy too meager to support even a short-line railroad. The tracks on the abandoned segment were removed in 1941, and Virginia City's main depot was salvaged for firewood. A federal order issued during 1942 required the mines to close, delivering a severe blow to a community already struggling from chronic unemployment.

Several years earlier, newspaper columnist and railroad enthusiast Lucius Beebe had visited the community to review the newly released film *Virginia City*, starring newly formed excursion railway purchased land and acquired rights to the historic V&T corporate name from a railroad collector. The railway built a steel engine house on the original site of the V&T round-house and train shops, and it took delivery of used crossties donated by the Western Pacific Railroad. By 1974, it had begun laying rail and acquired three (non-V&T) wooden coaches from Desilu Studios in Holly-wood, one of which would become the railroad's ticket office and gift shop.

Using leased equipment, the reconstituted Virginia & Truckee Railroad began carrying tourists over a 2-mile route in 1976. The carrier later acquired its own steam locomotive and rolling stock (none of it from the old V&T) for these excursions. It seems ironic that in 1979 Lucius Beebe died, just as the reincarnation of the railway he so passionately admired was reestablishing its place in the Comstock region.

The excursion railway extended its route through old Tunnel No. 4 in 1987 and leased a second steam locomotive two years later. It relocated portions of its route along a scenic ridge after the Ward Tunnel (No. 3) repeatedly collapsed during reconstruction, and extended its tracks to Gold Hill in 1991. The latter improvement took trains onto a massive fill on the former site of the Crown Point trestle and gave riders an opportunity to visit the Gold Hill depot—an attractive landmark dating back to 1872.

These projects, while significant, were modest in scope compared to a proposal to extend the railway to Carson City. An early supporter of this proposal, the Virginia & Truckee Railroad Society, worked to enhance public awareness of the initiative, while the Tri-County Railroad Commission (a government entity representing Carson, Lyon, and Storey counties) formally evaluated the alternatives. The commission determined that deviating from the original route through Mound House would lower construction costs and avoid disrupting a residential area on the original route. Such an alignment would also facilitate the construction of an overpass across U.S. Route 50—an improvement considered necessary for safety reasons—and provide a scenic overview of Carson City.

Storey County voters overwhelming approved a sales tax increase in 1994 that would pay for the reconstruction effort, but a similar tax initiative failed in neighboring Carson City and Lyon County. The project's formidable

costs, estimated to exceed $20 million, spurred the creation of the Northern Nevada Railway Foundation in 1996. That same year, the state legislature expanded the Tri-County Railroad Commission to include several more counties and renamed the entity the Commission for the Reconstruction of the V&T Railway.

Despite the optimism generated by these initiatives, the effort to rebuild the V&T has moved ahead very slowly, partly due to continuing financial and engineering concerns, such as the prevalence of mines at risk of collapse beneath the right-of-way. Nevertheless, as of this writing, there is considerable momentum behind a scaled-back proposal to build a 17-mile extension of the excursion railway to a location east of Carson City.

Epilogue

A beautifully preserved downtown, the tourist railway, and the eloquent prose of Lucius Beebe and Samuel Clemens are enduring reminders of Virginia City's place in western history. Recently, Piper's Opera House was restored and is once again a popular entertainment venue. The courthouse, which is still used by the county, and the historic school, which is now the Fourth Ward School Museum, stand as icons of the community's nineteenth-century prosperity.

The camel races held each autumn and the Bonanza Days festival are widely anticipated annual events. Beebe and Clegg's private car, the Gold Coast, is a featured exhibit at the California Railroad Museum in Sacramento; their beloved Virginia City still rides the rails and is available for charter on Amtrak trains. Along C Street, Virginia City's primary thoroughfare, a former V&T Railway post-office car houses an excursion railway ticket office.

Unfortunately, only a few of the historic buildings that once served the community's mining and railroad industries have survived. One is the original V&T passenger depot; another is the former freight station, both now privately owned. The most dramatic evidence of the region's industrial heritage is hidden below the surface. More than 700 miles of underground mining passages and the enormous Sutro Tunnel bear silent testimony to the partnership between man and machine that once made Virginia City one of the greatest cities in the West.

For Further Study

SUGGESTED READINGS:

James, Ronald M. *The Roar and the Silence: A History of Virginia City and the Comstock Lode.* Reno: University of Nevada Press, 1998, 80–84, 235–57.

Myrick, David F. *Railroads of Nevada and Eastern California.* Vol. I, *The Northern Roads.* Berkeley, Calif.: Howell-North Books, 1963, 136–62.

Wurm, Ted, and Harry Demoro. *The Silver Short Line: History of the Virginia & Truckee Railroad.* Glendale, Calif.: Trans-Anglo Books, 1983, 23–108.

OTHER PRINCIPAL REFERENCES:

Beebe, Lucius, and Charles Clegg. *Virginia & Truckee: A Story of Virginia City and Comstock Times.* Oakland, Calif.: Grahame H. Hardy, 1949, 7–59.

Beebe, Lucius. *Steamcars to the Comstock.* Berkeley, Calif.: Howell-North Books, 1957.

Ferrell, Hope Mallory. *Virginia & Truckee: Bonanza Road.* Mukilteo, Wash.: Hundman Publishing, 1999, 10–42.

Wurm, Ted. *Rebirth of the Virginia & Truckee Railroad.* Virginia City, Nev.: Virginia & Truckee Railroad, 1992, 32.

ESPAÑOLA, NEW MEXICO (9,688)

Historic operator: Denver & Rio Grande Western Railroad
Last route abandoned: 1941
Notable reuses of right-of-way: Railroad Avenue; U.S. Bureau of Land Management property

Businesses in Española vigorously opposed the abandonment of the Denver & Rio Grande Western Railroad's narrow-gauge route to Santa Fe during the early 1940s. Their calls for continued rail service were at odds with the grim realities of the marketplace, which had for years rendered the "Chili Line" woefully unprofitable. Although Española was an integral part of the saga of railroad construction in the West, it was destined to become one of the region's first notable communities bereft of its trains.

Historical Perspective

The valley of the upper Rio Grande, nestled between the Jemez Mountains and Sangre De Cristo Range, has for centuries been an important cultural crossroads. More than a thousand years ago, it was the province of the Anasazi, an indigenous people who constructed strikingly beautiful cliff dwellings in Puye, a settlement west of the river. The valley later became home to the Pueblo Indians, who built many magnificent villages, including Santa Clara Pueblo located in mountainous outcroppings along the the river near present-day Española. In 1598, Spaniard Juan de Onate traveled north from Mexico and claimed most of the Southwest for his country. He established the first Spanish settlement in the Southwest, several miles north of the Santa Clara Pueblo, calling it San Juan.

Spain expanded its dominance over the area in 1695, when the territorial governor founded Santa Cruz de la Canada. For generations, Santa Cruz remained a commercial and political center that attracted people from many countries and cultures.

Mexico gained independence from Spain in 1821 and in 1835, after years of political unrest, General Antonio López de Santa Anna seized control of the government in Mexico City, declaring his intention to tighten control over the northern provinces. A year later, Texas declared independence, and the following year, Santa Cruz revolted against Mexican rule, not attempting to gain independence but arguing for more autonomy from the central government. The United States annexed Texas in 1845, leading to war in 1846–47 as the U.S. asserted claim to the area in the name of Manifest Destiny. The Treaty of Guadalupe Hidalgo ended the war and transferred control of the Southwest to the United States.

On July 2, 1941, with the abandonment of the Denver & Rio Grande's Chili Line less than two months away, the daily mixed train prepares to depart Española on its southbound run to Santa Fe. (Photo by Bob Richardson, collection of Richard L. Dorman.)

After the war ended, American trappers, miners, and settlers streamed into this vast area on the Santa Fe Trail. Many then turned north and followed the upper Rio Grande through Santa Cruz and the other towns, some headed for Taos, a prominent trading center northwest of Santa Cruz. A privately operated "pony express" linking Denver to Santa Fe traversed portions of the valley in 1861.

Large-scale livestock grazing and lumber production became more feasible when the Denver & Rio Grande Railway ("Rio Grande") built a narrow-gauge line through the valley in 1881. Crossing the desolate terrain south of Antonito, Colorado, the line terminated near Santa Cruz at a station called Española. Some historians consider the station's name a legacy of San Gabriel de los Españoles, a pueblo that was in the area several hundred years earlier.

The railroad's construction was constrained by an unusual agreement with the Atchison, Topeka & Santa Fe Railway (AT&SF), which prevented the Rio Grande from extending its line south of Española. This agreement—the so-called Treaty of Boston—specified how these companies would compete in the West and denied the Rio Grande access to Albuquerque, El Paso, Santa Fe, and other notable towns of the Southwest. As a result of this agreement, Española emerged as the end of the line.

The Rio Grande apparently believed that Española would evolve into a railroad center of considerable importance. The carrier hauled increasingly larger shipments of livestock and lumber from the valley, as well as a steady flow of inbound freight. It began work on a second line through the area that was to follow the Chama River northwest from Chamita (a settlement several miles north of Española)—a project intended to discourage the AT&SF and Santa Fe Northern from building north to Colorado's Silverton County.

Although the Rio Grande never finished its route along the Chama, other developments signaled a prosperous future for Española. Small businesses, including a large apple grove established by a former Rio Grande conductor, sprouted up near the tracks. Española's depot attracted growing crowds; in addition to serving its railroad customers, it functioned as a church for Protestant services and a classroom for schoolchildren. Civil War veteran S. S. McBride, Española's agent for more than forty years, personified the Rio Grande's commitment to serving the valley. Legendary for his kindness, McBride was described as a "jewel of a man" in *Harper's Magazine* in 1885.

Merchants in Santa Fe understandably had bitter feelings about the Treaty of Boston. Their community had frequent service over an AT&SF branch to Lamy, a junction on that carrier's main line between Kansas City and Los Angeles, but lacked direct rail service to the north. To improve the community's rail connections, local businessmen created the Texas, Santa Fe & Northern Railroad, which they envisioned would bridge the 33-mile gap with the Rio Grande and build more than 1,000 miles of routes to Mexico, Texas, and Utah. Unfortunately, such a sprawling system proved beyond their grasp. The carrier experienced financial problems and an ownership change before operating its first trains between Santa Fe and Española—the only segment it ever built—in 1887.

The new route established Española as a railroad interchange point and was a boon to local merchants, including Frank Bond, who commenced work on a spacious new home near the depot. By the early 1890s, the Rio Grande was no longer a significant threat to the AT&SF, diminishing the relevance of the Treaty of Boston. Consequently, in 1895, the Rio Grande created a subsidiary, the Rio Grande & Santa Fe, to acquire the former Texas, Santa Fe & Northern (which had by now been reorganized as the Santa Fe Southern Railway). Through its subsidiary, it created an integrated route from Antonito and Santa Fe that came to be popularly called the Chili Line due to the chili peppers grown along the corridor. Although Española lost its role as an interchange when the Rio Grande acquired the route to Santa Fe, it remained an important source of freight revenue and a station stop on the mixed train that traveled the entire length of the 126-mile line.

Changing Times

The absence of significant sources of new revenue and the preponderance of steep grades and sharp curves had long hindered the Chili Line's performance. After World War I, improvements to motor transportation had particularly devastating effects. By the early 1920s, freight and passenger revenues had fallen precipitously and S. S. McBride—the epitome of Española railroading—had died.

Revenues further slipped as lumber companies depleted the supply of quality lumber, necessitating that the carrier (which was formally renamed the Denver & Rio Grande Western Railroad in 1921) accelerate its efforts to reduce costs. In 1931, the carrier abandoned its La Madera Branch, a once-productive lumber spur originating north of town at a location called Taos Junction. Although Española by then had about 900 residents, making it easily the largest community on the line without access to another carrier, the outlook for rail service took a sharp turn for the worse.

During the Great Depression, dwindling traffic and the cost of transferring freight between routes of different gauges rendered the profitable operation of the Chili Line almost hopeless. The number of annual carloads of freight—mostly cement, oil, gasoline, and wheat—shipped to and from Española plummeted by 30 percent

A local business displays a colorful mural along Railroad Avenue, which was once the track-bed of the Chili Line in Española. (Photo by author.)

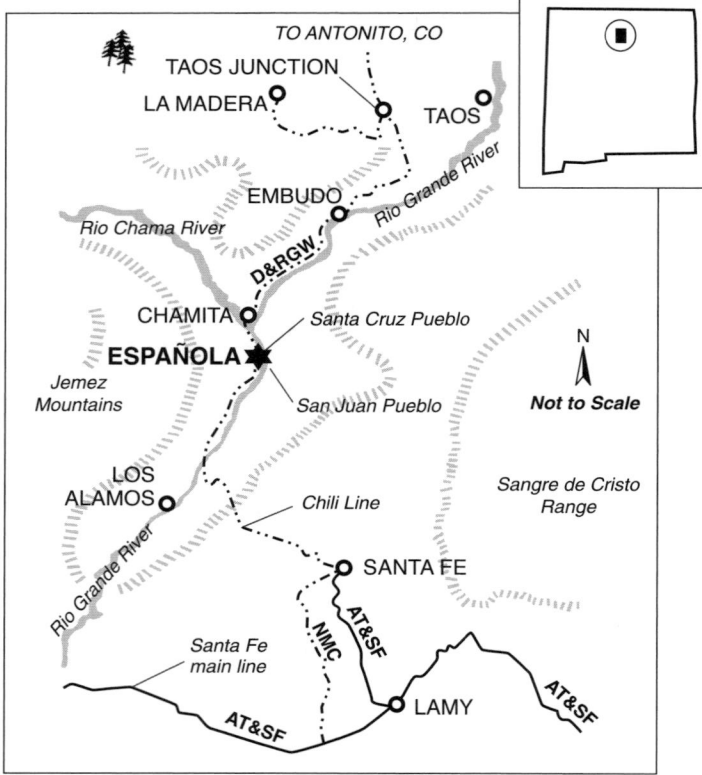

between 1936 and 1939, contributing to the line's dubious distinction of having the lowest traffic density of any route on the entire Rio Grande system. Although Española accounted for more than a third of all freight shipments on the line, this actually amounted to little more than one carload per day on average by 1938—a figure made even more disturbing by the fact that these were undersize narrow-gauge carloads.

Even as its transportation role diminished, the Chili Line remained a defining feature of the communities it served. The mixed train continued to operate, seemingly impervious to the changing times, and carried on the practice of making meal stops in Embudo, a small community 19 miles north of Española. Hollywood producers took a liking to the corridor, using it to film the motion pictures *The Texas Ranger* and *The Light that Failed*.

The Chili Line's survival may have been aided by the Rio Grande's lingering concerns about competition with the AT&SF. In an internal report of 1938, company officials warned of the need to reach an agreement with the AT&SF to ensure that this historic rival would not extend its tracks to Colorado's San Luis Valley if the Chili Line were to be abandoned. This concern seems more in keeping with railroad thinking during the thunderous 1880s than during the Great Depression, when

branch line construction was largely nonexistent. By the end of the 1930s, however, such an agreement must have been recognized as unnecessary.

When the Interstate Commerce Commission authorized the route's abandonment in early 1941, public officials and business leaders vigorously protested the decision. Their complaints resonated with elected officials in Washington, D.C., who arranged for a subcommittee of the U.S. Congress to schedule a public hearing in Alamosa. This hearing, held during April of that year, brought national publicity to the Chili Line and revealed the depth of public concern about its impending demise. A Colorado senator urged that the line remain in service at least until the end of the war. Española merchants complained that poor service and high prices were responsible for the decline in rail traffic. Apparently, their testimonials did not convince the ICC, which stood behind its abandonment decision.

After a life of sixty years, the Chili Line passed into history in the autumn of 1941. Española's last train—carrying the safe that had been housed in the community's depot—departed with a small group of onlookers. The salvaging process began almost immediately, and by 1942 the community's rails had been removed. Some of the right-of-way in town was transformed into Railroad Avenue, while much of the rural corridor between Alcalde (a small town north of Española) and the Colorado border fell under the jurisdiction of the federal Bureau of Land Management. The trestles and culverts along this lengthy segment were left to deteriorate.

Abandonment's Legacy

Only three months after the Chili Line closed, World War II pulled America into battle. The economy of the river valley changed immeasurably in 1942, when the federal government created a laboratory for the Manhattan Engineering District near Los Alamos, a small community southwest of Española, located high on a mesa overlooking the Rio Grande valley. Trucks filled with concrete were soon departing freight yards in Santa Fe and struggling up steep slopes on unpaved roads to the laboratory grounds. Although Robert Oppenheimer, the leader of the Manhattan Project who helped select the site, drove from California in his private automobile, other scientists rode El Capitan, the Super Chief, and other passenger trains to the AT&SF station in Lamy.

By 1945, the laboratory at Los Alamos had grown

to employ several thousand people. Its expanding need for workers contributed greatly to the demand for housing in Española and other parts of the valley. Employees and their families routinely drove to Española to buy groceries and supplies, giving the community a new commercial niche. The laboratory remained the nation's principal center for nuclear research after producing the atomic bombs dropped over Japan. Winter tourism, too, supported the valley's economy, especially after the Taos Ski Valley, a major winter resort, opened in 1956.

Local officials made an overture to the past in 1957 when they purchased the Bond house for the creation of a museum. In 1966, the Anasazi ruins at Puye earned distinction as the first property in the area listed on the National Register of Historic Places. The Santa Clara Pueblo and the plaza at Santa Cruz—a historic location now within the city limits of Española—were later added to the register as well, but these and other historical attractions did little to sustain Española's economy.

As commerce shifted to Santa Fe during the 1980s, the community desperately needed improved housing and jobs for unskilled workers. Another growth spurt pushed its largely Hispanic population to more than 8,000 by 1990 and magnified its social and economic woes. In the process, the 38-mile stretch of U.S. Route 285 between Española and Santa Fe—the so-called Rio Grande Corridor—became the state's busiest stretch of arterial highway and was increasingly prone to congestion during peak periods. Once again, leaders in Santa Fe pondered the benefits of a rail line to Española. During the mid-1990s, the Middle Rio Grande Council of Governments, the regional planning agency, formally proposed relaying track between these communities. The agency envisioned using portions of the abandoned right-of-way to establish both freight and commuter service, a proposal that would have made the communities along the route the first in New Mexico to be served by modern rail transit.

Others identified the old railroad right-of-way north of Española as an attractive candidate for a recreational trail. A study published in 1996 concluded that the corridor's diverse vegetation and dramatic topography would enhance the value of a trail. Although the Bureau of Land Management supported this idea, it was unable to overcome opposition from property owners in the Embudo Canyon region.

Epilogue

Visitors to the Upper Rio Grande Valley will find pueblo settlements, historic churches, and Spanish-American architecture as reminders of Española's rich cultural heritage.

The town's economic and social problems stubbornly persist in spite of Los Alamos' continuing presence as a center of well-paying jobs. Inadequate resources for community planning, persistent crime, and wildfires have hampered commercial development. An uncontrollable blaze in 1999 necessitated the community's evacuation and prompted President Bill Clinton to declare the county a disaster area.

Those following Española's bygone route along Railroad Avenue will find a colorful mural depicting the glory years of railroad service. Farther north along the line, St. Steven's Episcopal Church offers a reminder of the past through its membership in the aptly named Chili Line Team Ministry. Although Española's depot no longer stands, the station in Embudo and an adjacent water tower are listed on the National Register, flanked by a popular restaurant that recalls this locale's heritage as a meal stop.

South of Española, the scene is profoundly different. Thousands of motorists converge daily on the casinos (one of which resembles a shining pueblo) and shopping malls near the periphery of Santa Fe along Route 285, which the state began widening in 2003. As business migrates north, some expect Española to eventually become a bedroom community of this nearby city.

Railroad historical groups recognize the legacy of the Chili Line in a variety of ways. The Cumbres & Toltec Scenic Railway in northern New Mexico has a coach (built in 1987) named Española. At the Colorado Railroad Museum, passenger car No. 284, once assigned to the Chili Line and dating back to 1881, is a prized possession. However, institutions in Española itself do little to commemorate the colorful heritage of the rail line that is so deeply rooted in western railroad lore.

For Further Study

SUGGESTED READINGS:

Chappell, Gordon. "To Santa Fe by Narrow Gauge: The D&RG's 'Chili Line.'" In *Colorado Rail Annual 7*. Golden: Colorado Railroad Museum, 1969, 3–53.

Myrick, David F. *New Mexico's Railroads: A Historical Survey.* Albuquerque: University of New Mexico, 1990, 122–30.

OTHER PRINCIPAL REFERENCES:

Danneman, Herbert. "A Ticket to Ride the Narrow Gauge." In *Colorado Rail Annual* 24. Golden: Colorado Railroad Museum, 2000, 31, 70, 94, 149, 178, 184.

Dorman, Richard L. *The Chili Line: Santa Fe and the City Different.* Santa Fe, N.Mex.: R.D. Publications, 1996, 73–98.

Gjevre, John. *Chili Line, the Narrow Rail to Santa Fe.* Española, N.Mex.: Rio Grande Sun Press, 1969.

Jensen, Larry. *The Movie Railroads.* Burbank, Calif.: Darwin Publications, 1981, 70.

LeMassena, Robert L. *Rio Grande ... To the Pacific!* Denver: Sundance Limited, 1974, 156.

Simons, Marc. *The Last Conquistador, Juan de Oñate.* Norman: University of Oklahoma Press, 1993, 108–9.

U.S. Congress. Senate. Committee on Interstate Commerce. *Abandonment of the Denver and Rio Grande Western Railroad Between Antonito, Colorado, and Santa Fe, New Mexico.* Washington, D.C.: Government Printing Office, 1941, 133, 300, 327, 359–62.

FARMINGTON, NEW MEXICO (37,844)

Historic operator: Denver & Rio Grande Western Railroad
Last route abandoned: 1969
Notable reuse of right-of-way: Municipal park

For several decades, Farmington was the southernmost and westernmost point on the Denver & Rio Grande Western Railroad's narrow-gauge system. This community's fondly remembered route remained in service long after commercial airlines, modern truck transport, and pipelines had arrived on the municipal scene. As one of the most populous cities on the American mainland located more than 100 miles from an intercity route, Farmington has considered scenarios for restoring rail service on several different occasions.

Historical Perspective

More than a thousand years ago, the Anasazi (often called Ancient Puebloans) lived in "pit houses" near the northwest corner of present-day New Mexico. Using sandstone excavated from the surrounding hills, these possible ancestors of the modern Pueblo tribes created strikingly beautiful villages, or pueblos, built on the rugged outcroppings of the Carrizo Mountains. Although the Anasazi disappeared for reasons that are unclear to historians, the rolling terrain they inhabited became the dominion of other tribes, including the Apache, Jicarilla Apache, Navajo, and Ute. The Navajo and Jicarilla Apache considered this land a buffer and referred to the sacred ground near the confluence of the Animas, La Plata, and San Juan rivers as Totah, meaning "where three rivers meet."

By the early nineteenth century, Spanish settlers had established a presence along the Animas River, but there was little migration to their pueblo for many years, even after the United States assumed jurisdiction over the region in 1848. The situation did not dramatically change until after William Hendrickson and his brother Simeon visited the region in 1875. When the New Mexico Territory was opened up for settlement in 1876, the Hendricksons returned with other men from Colorado to choose sites suitable for farming.

At first, these pioneers tilled the soil with mixed results, but after pioneer William Locke brought seeds from Colorado in 1879, they were able to create large orchards of apples, peaches, and walnuts, resulting in bountiful harvests. In the midst of this budding agricultural area, a settlement called Junction City emerged. Founded in 1880 and named for its location at the convergence of the rivers, it prospered as a center of fresh-fruit production.

The townspeople aspired to have Junction City become both a railroad town and the county

Nostalgically called the Red Apple Flyer, this excursion train sponsored by the Rocky Mountain Railroad Club has reached the end of the line at Farmington on May 31, 1958. Two men, quite possibly photographers, look down from above. (Photo by Otto Perry, Denver Public Library.)

seat. The community failed to attract a railroad, but they did celebrate winning a referendum to establish their community as the county seat in 1890. The celebration was short-lived, however, as a judge ruled that they had lost the referendum to the nearby town of Aztec because many of the votes were invalid.

Junction City eventually merged with Farmington (formerly Farming Town), a newer settlement on the opposite side of the river, creating a community that assumed the Farmington name and soon boasted a hotel, boarding house, and several stores and saloons. When the town was incorporated in 1901, community boosters remained hopeful that at least one railroad would eventually link their town to railroad systems in the Arizona Territory or Colorado. Optimism certainly abounded as two prospective operators, the Arizona & Colorado Railroad Company (affiliated with Southern Pacific) and the Denver & Rio Grande Railway (Rio Grande) vied to be first to reach Farmington. Another contender, Phelps Dodge, a major copper producer, sought to build a line from Gallup to Farmington to haul coal to its smelters.

Destiny sided with the Rio Grande when it completed its route from Carbon Junction, Colorado (near

Durango), in 1905. Evidently to thwart Arizona & Colorado's access to the region, the carrier built its tracks to standard gauge. The ensuing court battle would become deeply etched in New Mexico railroad lore. Objecting to the Rio Grande's tactics, the Arizona & Colorado, which sought to gain access to lucrative coal fields near Durango, argued that the Rio Grande had stolen its right-of-way. A judge agreed, but the Arizona & Colorado lost interest in the project and never completed its route.

Despite the exuberance of this era, the Rio Grande would be the only carrier ever to reach Farmington. Its route, stretching 48 miles, mostly along the Animas River, emerged as a profitable appendage to the carrier's sprawling system of narrow-gauge lines through the Colorado Rockies. By the time New Mexico achieved statehood in 1912, the line hauled extensive shipments of fruit, beans, hay, and livestock. Citizens familiar with the line's fruit-hauling role called the mixed train arriving and departing daily (except Sunday) the Red Apple Flyer.

Unfortunately, the Red Apple Flyer had serious limitations. The need to transfer locally generated freight to and from narrow-gauge cars at Carbon Junction was time-consuming and expensive. Freight shipped to Farmington from most major cities had a break of gauge at two locations. Some expected Rio Grande to eliminate this problem either by widening its Alamosa–Durango route to standard gauge or building a new route to the region. Although such costly endeavors never materialized, the carrier (renamed the Denver & Rio Grande

Western Railroad in 1921) converted the Farmington Branch to narrow gauge in 1923—an unusual occurrence in twentieth-century railroad history. The carrier could now haul railcars from town all the way to Alamosa and other interchange points in Colorado, but to reach any city of appreciable size, shipments still had to be transferred between routes of differing gauges.

Changing Times

The logistical challenges facing the Rio Grande did not prevent Farmington from flourishing during the late 1920s. As the expansion in oil and natural gas production stimulated the local economy, lengthy trains regularly left town, and other railroads contemplated laying track to the Four Corners region (the area where Arizona, Colorado, New Mexico, and Utah meet at a common point). Two carriers even received Interstate Commerce Commission approval to begin construction.

The optimism of these boom years faded during the Great Depression. With oil and gas production in retreat, the proposals for new railroads were scrapped, and the viability of the Rio Grande's service took a sharp turn for the worse. By the early 1930s, hard-surface roads had become available, and the railroad's passenger business weakened. The Rio Grande rescheduled its mixed train to arrive and depart Farmington during the middle of the night as a way to create well-timed connections with trains operating between Durango and Alamosa. This schedule was hardly conducive to attracting travelers who were accustomed to the flexibility of motor travel; it lasted only until 1936, when mixed-train service ended.

A resurgence in natural gas production during World War II stimulated the Four Corners' economy. In 1946, Monarch Airlines received approval to establish scheduled air service from Farmington to Denver, Albuquerque, and other cities. As the tempo of life in the community quickened, the Farmington Branch and its trains—still called the Red Apple Flyer—seemed almost frozen in time, to the delight of Hollywood, which used the line to depict an old-time railroad in the 1949 film *Colorado Territory*, starring Joel McCrea.

The Red Apple Flyer soared one last time during the 1950s, when the construction of a major pipeline to transport natural gas from the county to southern California

pushed it back to the economic forefront. Notwithstanding the concerns of the Atomic Energy Commission, which feared the pipeline would be incompatible with atomic experiments at Los Alamos, the El Paso Natural Gas Company completed the controversial project in 1951, setting into motion a great surge in natural gas production. By the middle of the decade, the natural gas industry was enjoying spectacular success, necessitating large shipments of pipeline equipment on the branch. At one point, Farmington received more than 500 carloads each month, causing significant congestion on a rail line that had not been built to handle such intensive operations. Within a few years, Farmington's population rose to more than 23,000, making it New Mexico's seventh largest city.

Unfortunately for the railroad, the renaissance in freight traffic lasted only a few years. By the early 1960s, the natural gas boom was over; Farmington's rail line was used only sporadically and was routinely dormant during the winter months. It seems a cruel irony that a gas explosion in 1962 damaged the Farmington depot and injured the clerk working inside. Although the Rio Grande replaced the wooden structure with an austere metal shed, its occasional trains were by now largely irrelevant to the region's economy. When a major electrical-generation facility, the Four Corners Generating Plant, commenced operations west of Farmington in 1963, it used coal delivered by truck from the nearby Navajo Mines.

More than thirty years after abandonment, little more than the sheet metal building visible in the previous photograph survives in the old depot area of Farmington. (Photo by author.)

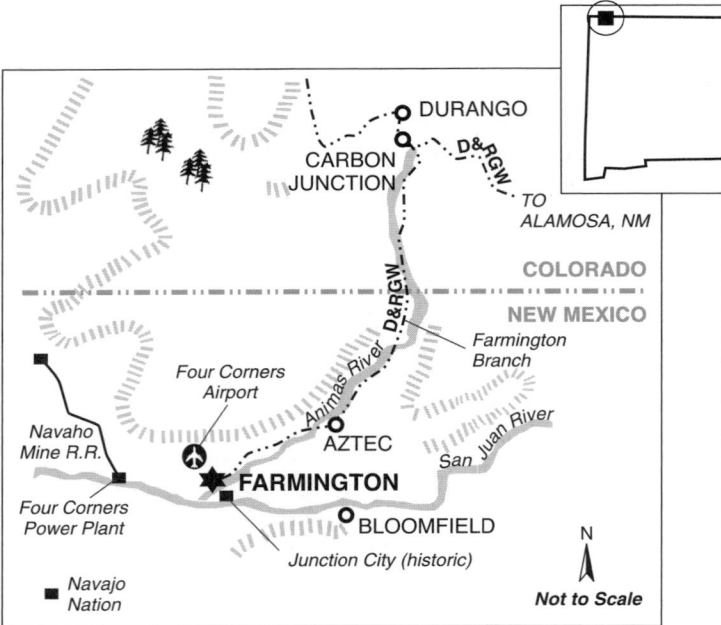

Abandonment's Legacy

Within a few years, portions of the Farmington Branch had been altered beyond recognition. State workers bulldozed some of the old rail grade while making improvements to U.S. Route 550 in southern Colorado. In 1971, Rio Grande deeded approximately 8 miles of the right-of-way west of Flora Vista to Farmington's municipal government. Lengthy portions of the right-of-way reverted to property owners, leaving the municipality with a fragmented corridor. The community used a small segment of the right-of-way to create Gateway Park and then leased, sold, and traded some the remaining property to acquire land closer to the Animas River.

The legacy of the Rio Grande's narrow-gauge trains could be felt in 1971, when the newly created Cumbres & Toltec initiated excursion service from Chama. This tourist operator (about 110 miles east of Farmington) soon won the hearts of nostalgic travelers, who reveled in the historical authenticity of its equipment and the breathtaking vistas of the Cumbres Pass and San Juan Mountains. By the time the Cumbres & Toltec Scenic Railroad was added to the National Register of Historic Places in 1973, the carrier had become a nationally known tourist attraction.

Closer to Farmington, electrical generation at the Four Corners Generating Plant gradually rose to such an extent that its owners made plans to build the "Navajo Railroad" through desolate terrain west of town. Linking the electrical plant with the nearby Navajo Mines, this private industrial railroad commenced operations over a 7-mile route in 1974. Although the carrier eventually doubled the length of its system (which remains in service today) and turned to electric motive power in 1983, it made no plans to build toward Farmington or establish itself as a common carrier.

By the early 1990s, Farmington had grown to more 33,000 inhabitants, making it the largest urbanized area on the mainland situated more than 100 miles (via highway) from the national rail system. Much like their predecessors a century before, officials contemplated the benefits of a railroad. In 1995, the San Juan Basin Transportation Development District (SJBTTD) and the Northwest New Mexico Council of Governments explored various options to move raw materials more efficiently to and from the region. Although SJBTTD concluded that rebuilding the abandoned Farmington Branch would be impractical, it joined the state government to evaluate a potential 115-mile rail line extending

Making matters worse for the railroad, Farmington's population declined significantly during the 1960s. The local Chamber of Commerce sought to preserve the infrequently used rail line, but freight service to Farmington ended in 1967. The following year, the Rio Grande petitioned to abandon nearly all of its remaining narrow-gauge system, including the Farmington Branch.

The outcry from communities sparked by this abandonment petition set into motion one of the country's first large-scale efforts to preserve railroad assets for their historical rather than commercial value. The National Park Service considered buying all or part of the lines slated for abandonment, with an eye toward the creation of a national monument. Although it conducted a highly publicized inspection trip over the narrow-gauge line in 1968, it ultimately chose not to purchase the threatened routes. Nevertheless, the legislatures of Colorado and New Mexico enacted legislation the following year authorizing the creation of public authorities to facilitate the acquisition of railroad corridors to foster economic development.

Rio Grande received permission to abandon its branch to Farmington along with most other surviving portions of its dwindling narrow-gauge system in July 1969. It quickly dismantled the branch but left the abandoned main line between Durango and Alamosa in place. The newly passed legislation made possible the 1970 sale of 64 miles of the main line (from Antonito, Colorado, to Chama, New Mexico) to the Cumbres & Toltec Scenic Railroad, a publicly supported nonprofit organization.

south to the Burlington Northern Santa Fe Railway (former Santa Fe) main line through Gallup.

Such a massive undertaking was motivated largely by a desire to provide access to significant coal reserves and improve transportation to the Navajo Nation, which operated several mines as well as industrial and agricultural facilities in the region. After encountering problems with the proposed $90 million "Navajo Alignment" in 1996, the SJBTDD considered another route farther east that would link Bloomfield with the former Santa Fe main line. This proposed route, projected to follow a natural gas pipeline corridor near State Route 44 (now U.S. 550), was understood to be viable only if the market for high-sulfur coal remained strong. To create this 43-mile route, officials sought to enlist the cooperation of the Lake Star Railroad, a short line projected to build to the vicinity of Lee Ranch from the Burlington Northern Santa Fe at Baca, New Mexico. Negotiations stalled in 1999, however, as the market for high-sulfur coal softened and environmentalists raised concerns.

Other planners during this period considered transforming the abandoned Rio Grande branch into a recreational trail linking Farmington to the Aztec Ruins National Monument. This idea too dropped in priority as attention turned to the advantages of a trail closer to the Animas River.

Epilogue

Much has changed in Farmington since the last Red Apple Flyer rolled toward southern Colorado. Many travelers today arrive at the municipal airport on flights from Albuquerque, Denver, and Phoenix. Large numbers of trucks rumble over U.S. Route 550, which is now a four-lane road. A sophisticated system of pipelines transports vast amounts of natural gas to faraway markets.

Distant echoes of the railroad era still resonate in the Four Corners region. The intercity buses that operate from Durango to Farmington follow nearly the same route as the mixed train did years ago. The municipal government moved the Farmington Museum into a new building (located in Gateway Park on the east side of town) on the abandoned Rio Grande right-of-way in 1999. Near downtown, the right-of-way flanks old industrial structures, including the metal shed "station" and several deteriorating boxcars. In other places, the old rail embankment protrudes from the nearby landscape like an ancient ruin.

This community may well have been able to support rail service to the present day had the vagaries of railroading not relegated it to being the endpoint of a lengthy narrow-gauge branch. For the foreseeable future, though, it appears that Farmington will remain one of the most populous metropolitan areas on the American mainland without an intercity railroad route—an ironic distinction for a community that merged with a town called Junction City.

For Further Study

SUGGESTED READINGS:
Myrick, David F. *New Mexico's Railroads: A Historical Survey.* Albuquerque: University of New Mexico, 1990, 57, 95, 109, 181.
Norwood, John B. *Rio Grande Narrow Gauge: From Birth to Abandonment.* River Forest, Ill.: Heimburger House, 1983, 19, 26, 34, 96, 106–8, 143, 149, 205.

OTHER PRINCIPAL REFERENCES:
Clark, Hartsill Lloyd. "A History of San Juan County, New Mexico." Master's thesis, University of Tulsa, 1963, 102–6.
Dorman, Richard L. *Durango: Always A Railroad Town.* Santa Fe, N.Mex.: R.D. Publications, 1996, 121–33.
Dugan, Tom, and Emery Arnold. *Gas: Adventures into the History of One of the World's Largest Gas Fields: The San Juan Basin of New Mexico.* Farmington, N.Mex.: Dugan Productions, 2002, 33–34.
LeMassena, Robert L. *Rio Grande. . . . To the Pacific!* Denver: Sundance Limited, 1974, 80, 135, 202, 354.
MacDonald, Eleanor D., and John B. Arrington. *The San Juan Basin.* Denver: Mido Printing, 1970, 166, 173–74, 188–91.
Myrick, David F. *Railroads of Arizona.* Vol. 3, *Clifton, Morenci, and Metcalf Rails and Copper Mines, Arizona Locomotive Rosters.* Glendale, Calif.: Trans-Anglo Books, 1984, 615–32.
Waybourn, Marilu. *Homesteads to Boomtown: A Pictorial History of Farmington, New Mexico, and Surrounding Areas.* Marceline, Mo.: Walsworth Publishing, 2001, 40–41, 77–85.
Wilson, Spencer, and Vernon J. Glover. *The Cumbres & Toltec Scenic Railroad: The Historic Preservation Study.* Albuquerque: University of New Mexico Press, 1980, 2–11.

WATFORD CITY, NORTH DAKOTA (1,435)

Historic operators: Great Northern Railway; Wild Cow Railroad
Last route abandoned: 1992
Notable remnants of railroad era: Grain elevator access road; Madson Fill (embankment)

When Burlington Northern petitioned to abandon its branch to Watford City, the state invoked a controversial amendment, the only such legislation ever passed by the U.S. Congress, that set strict limits on the carrier's ability to eliminate track in North Dakota. Nevertheless, that exceptional measure did little more than postpone the demise of one of the most extraordinary branch lines ever built on the upper Great Plains.

Historical Perspective

Attracted by the wild game in the area, E. E Chase and George Frye established a hunting camp near the confluence of Cherry Creek and the Little Missouri River in 1883. These enterprising outdoorsmen built the first log cabin in present-day McKenzie County to provide shelter for sportsmen pursuing antelope, bear, elk, deer, and wolf. Among those who lodged at this primitive dwelling was Theodore Roosevelt, whose legacy would be imprinted in this region for generations to come.

This largely uninhabited part of the Dakota Territory was also suited to ranching, especially after the St. Paul, Minneapolis & Manitoba Railway, a predecessor of the Great Northern Railway, built its main line through Williston in 1887. The conveniences afforded by the railway allowed cattlemen to dramatically expand their herds, which on some properties grew to more than 40,000 head. After North Dakota's admission to the Union in 1889, farming grew more prevalent and in time replaced ranching throughout much of the area. The perseverance of homesteaders in the face of great adversity allowed for a modest economic expansion, exemplified by the opening of the county's first bank in the village of Arengard in 1910.

The Great Northern conducted a survey the following year for a projected rail line that would serve established towns in the county as well as Watford, a community platted by one of its subsidiaries. The carrier's primary reason for building the railroad was to create a second main line across the Great Plains—a route that would support an anticipated rise in freight and passenger traffic to the northern Rocky Mountain states and the Pacific Northwest. The proposed line would extend nearly 550 miles from New Rockford, a community along its Surrey Cutoff (a direct route between Fargo and Minot that opened in 1912) to Lewistown, Montana (the endpoint of an existing branch). Despite the anticipated costs of building such a lengthy route, company president Louis W. Hill and his legendary father, James J. Hill, appeared committed to seeing it through to completion.

The subsidiary created to construct the line, the Montana Eastern Railway, laid tracks south from the Great Northern main line at

Snowden, Montana, installed a massive movable bridge over the Missouri, and reached Fairview, Montana in 1913. From there the Montana Eastern began the laborious task of building both eastward and westward. Crews working from Fairview toward the east installed an even longer lift bridge across the Yellowstone River—a massive 1,320-foot structure that would be the only movable bridge ever built in North Dakota. Construction workers also bored the 1,400-foot Yellowstone Tunnel, the only railroad tunnel in the state.

The effort to build the new main line was sufficiently complex that the contractor built a supply route, the "Wild Cow Railroad," from an estuary of the Missouri River to a rural location west of Watford. This private railway, constructed to standard gauge, operated 20 miles of track and used a system of steam hoists to lift railroad cars and supplies from river vessels. The Wild Cow proved especially important to the construction of the Madson Fill, an enormous embankment near Watford that required the movement of more than 1 million cubic feet of earth. When completed, the fill elevated trains high above the surrounding countryside and provided the Montana Eastern with a gentle route across the Madson Flat.

The Montana Eastern's entry into Watford in late 1914 seemed only the beginning of its long eastward march toward New Rockford. With the rail line expected to become an important long-distance corridor, local officials envisioned great prosperity when Watford received its incorporation in 1915. Indicative of their optimism, they

Soon after this photograph was taken, a salvage crew removed the tracks from one of the most extraordinary branch lines ever built in North Dakota—the former Great Northern branch to Watford City, which had the state's only railroad tunnel. Freight service had ended several years before. (Photo by Faye Carlson.)

Grain elevators flank the abandoned right-of-way in Watford City. Much of the county's grain is now trucked to Williston. (Photo by author.)

added the word "City" to the community's name the following year. By 1916, Montana Eastern crews had laid 108 miles of track on its new main line, including the segment from Richey, Montana (west of Fairview) to Watford City, and had finished grading some of the route farther east. It appeared in early 1917 that the Great Northern was committed to completing the route.

Economic and political circumstances then derailed one of the Great Northern's last major corridor-building initiatives. As American involvement in World War I escalated, the nation's railroads came under federal management, and the Montana Eastern came to be seen as an avoidable expense. By the end of 1918, Great Northern had scuttled the effort to complete the Watford City–New Rockford and Richey–Lewistown segments.

The completed portions of the Montana Eastern were nevertheless important to the communities they served and supported the expansion of both ranching and agriculture. In Watford City, trains departed from a wooden station near the southern edge of town (replaced in 1918 after a fire) and moved enough wheat to justify enlarging the local elevator during the 1920s.

The Great Northern resurrected a plan to build the second main line during the late 1920s. To help reduce the necessary capital outlay, it devised a complex plan to share a significant portion of the track in Montana with the Northern Pacific, which also sought to expand in the region. Nevertheless, Great Northern ultimately came to the same conclusion as before—that the benefits of such a line were insufficient to justify the costs.

In 1929, Great Northern formally acquired all the properties of its moribund Montana Eastern subsidiary. The quality of local passenger service greatly improved that same year when Great Northern replaced the mixed train serving Watford City with a gasoline-powered motorcar. This self-propelled unit, popularly called the Galloping Goose, made a daily (except Sunday) round-trip from Fairview and reduced running times by as much as 90 minutes each way.

Although the Great Depression and a series of devastating droughts weakened the Great Northern, Watford City weathered these difficult times in part due to the carrier's continuing services. The opening of a new Gambles hardware store in 1933, the relocation of a bank from Arnegard to Watford City in 1934, and a new waterworks system completed by the Works Progress Administration (WPA) in 1937, along with a controversial referendum in 1940 establishing Watford City as the new county seat, appeared to signal a bright future.

Changing Times

After World War II, the branch to Watford City faced many of the same problems as other lightly used agricultural routes in North Dakota. Revenue opportunities dwindled as hard-surface roads became more widely available and small shippers turned their loyalties to trucks. Although travelers using the motorcar could still transfer at Fairview to a local train bound for Snowden, allowing them to make connections to several long-distance trains, many undoubtedly found it simpler to drive to their final destination or board trains in Williston, another stop on the carrier's main line.

The advantages of driving to Williston to ride the Great Northern grew stronger after the carrier updated its flagship train, the Empire Builder, with streamlined passenger cars in 1947. Operated jointly with the Chicago, Burlington & Quincy Railroad, the train linked Chicago to Seattle in 45 hours and stopped in Williston at convenient times. With the renewed optimism of this era, an association representing both Montana and North Dakota interests attempted that same year to revive the idea of building a new main line across the Great Plains. This effort did not advance beyond the discussion stage.

Only freight trains served Watford City after Great Northern eliminated the Galloping Goose in 1959. The railroad's role further diminished during the 1960s, when the county's population dropped by a disturbing 16 percent. By the time Great Northern merged with Northern Pacific and several other lines to create the Burlington Northern Railroad in 1970, the Watford City Branch had few regular customers other than a small number of grain elevators and farm-implement dealers. Making matters worse, railcar shortages and other operational problems hampered the quality of rail service, encouraging Watford City's Farmers Cooperative Elevator Company to rely increasingly on truck transportation.

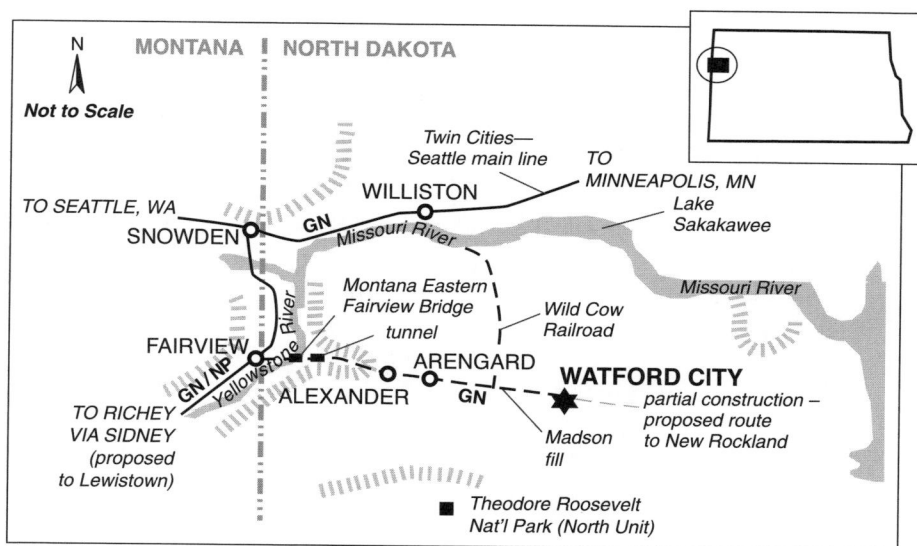

In 1972, Burlington Northern retired the Watford City depot, the last station on the branch east of Fairview to be staffed by an agent. The carrier then sold the depot to a plumbing company, which moved the wooden structure to a location east of its original site. An oil boom reinvigorated the county's economy in the early 1980s, but did little to improve the viability of the local rail branch. By then, only two trains per week used the deteriorating tracks, rendering the route a candidate for abandonment.

An analysis prepared by the state government revealed that the loss of the railroad would increase the costs of shipping grain by as much as twenty cents per bushel. The report also warned that abandonment would boost expenses by several hundred thousand dollars annually and put more than 2,000 additional truck trips on area roads each year. Business and civic leaders joined state and federal officials in Watford City during 1981 to discuss their concerns about the line's future. That year, U.S. Senator Mark Andrews and other elected state officials placed an advertisement in the *McKenzie County Farmer*, the local newspaper, protesting Burlington Northern's plans to eliminate more than 1,000 miles of routes in the state. The advertisement, "Give the Burlington Northern an inch…they'll take a mile," sponsored by the Save Our Towns and Farms Committee, was reminiscent of the antirailroad rhetoric of the nineteenth-century Granger movement.

To reduce the costs of transporting grain over the branch, grain elevator officials made arrangements to ship 26-car trains of wheat. In preparation for these unit trains, the carrier made modest repairs to the tracks. Unable to bear the immense weight of even the first trains, the lightweight rails gave way on several occasions, resulting in derailments. With reportedly $4 million necessary for rehabilitation, the prognosis for continued rail service appeared poor.

Burlington Northern's effort to eliminate the line brought into sharp focus the vagaries of federal transportation policy at a time when abandonment was rapidly changing the structure of the national rail system. In December 1981, the U.S. Senate approved a spending bill with an amendment sponsored by Senator Andrews. The amendment set a 350-mile limit on the Interstate Commerce Commission's ability to process abandonment applications filed by Burlington Northern pertaining to North Dakota. Apparently, this amendment was the only legislative measure ever enacted by the U.S. Senate that specifically addressed abandonment concerns in a particular state.

The agricultural cooperative shipped its last carload of rail freight in 1986, leaving the branch without a regular customer. When the cooperative consolidated with the Williston-based Northwest Grain Cooperative Terminal (a shipper of 52-car unit trains), the new owner expressed its desire to preserve the option of shipping grain by train from its Watford City facility.

As it happened, the so-called Andrews Amendment had little bearing on abandonment proceedings from its enactment in 1981 until the time Burlington Northern petitioned to eliminate the branch to Watford City in

1990. During this interval, Burlington Northern abandoned seventeen segments in North Dakota. The Watford City application, however, put the carrier over the prescribed 350-mile limit. The state's Public Service Commission, in turn, invoked the Andrews Amendment to block the initiative, a move upheld by the ICC.

Questioning the legality of this maneuver, Burlington Northern made plans to deploy legal counsel. The U.S. Senate decided that it would be prudent to avoid a legal battle and modified the amendment to exclude the Watford City line and other routes that had been out of service for more than two years. These lines qualified for an exemption in ICC proceedings (and thus were eligible for an expedited abandonment process). This modification cleared the way for the line's formal abandonment in February 1992.

Abandonment's Legacy

Salvage workers removed the tracks on the branch in 1994 and much of the railroad property reverted to adjacent property owners under the oversight of an association of local stakeholders. Burlington Northern sold several parcels it owned directly to governments in the area as well as to the agricultural cooperative, which used some of the property for an access road. At the time, the cooperative dispatched more than a hundred trucks annually to Duluth, Minnesota, and other points.

Watford City benefited from rising numbers of tourists visiting the North Unit of Theodore Roosevelt National Park (a reserve established by the federal government in 1978); nevertheless, its economic problems seemed to grow worse each year. A downturn in the price of wheat and the emigration of younger residents hampered local business conditions. The region's struggle for improved transportation gradually shifted toward gaining political support for the continued operation of the Empire Builder, which had long been operated by Amtrak, and fostering more competitive air service from Williston, a market dominated by a commuter subsidiary of Northwest Airlines.

Although Watford City has an attractive downtown and welcomes visitors on their way to the national park, it has had difficulty attracting new industry. Its depot is used for storage, and the cooperative (the only grain elevator still open for business in the county) is today operated by Prairie State Co-op, which considers the absence of rail service to be an impediment to expansion.

Epilogue

Visitors will find the abandoned Watford City Branch still visible on the rolling landscape west of town. Deep cuts and large fills as well as the Fairview Lift Bridge and Yellowstone Tunnel—landmarks listed on the National Register of Historic Places since 1997—offer silent testimony to Great Northern's effort to build a second main line across the Plains.

A few miles from the route's terminus, the Madson Fill, now covered with grass, survives as one of most notable embankments along an abandoned rail line anywhere in the Dakotas. Many motorists on Highway 85 traveling west of Watford City undoubtedly mistake this imposing man-made mound for natural terrain.

The U.S. Congress today devotes far less time and energy to concerns related to rail abandonment than it did when Watford City struggled to save its dormant branch. Senator Andrews left office years ago, and Burlington Northern is today the Burlington Northern Santa Fe Railway. The Andrews Amendment, however, remains in effect, albeit greatly diminished in significance due to the exemptions that allow for the abandonment of out-of-service routes.

For Further Study

SUGGESTED READING:

Johnson, Richard E. "The Montana Eastern Railway Company 1912–1935: Great Northern's Second Main Line." *Great Northern Railway Historical Society Reference Sheet* 207 (Sept. 1993): 1–16.

Watford City Diamond Jubilee: 1914–1989. Watford City, N.Dak.: Diamond Jubilee Book Committee, 1989, 24, 60.

OTHER PRINCIPAL REFERENCES:

Hidy, Raphy W., Muriel E. Hidy, and Roy V. Scott, with Don L. Hofsommer. *The Great Northern Railway: A History.* Boston: Harvard Business School Press, 1988, 84–85, 114–15, 183–84.

North Dakota Highway Department. *North Dakota 1981 State Rail Plan Update, Appendices.* A-122–A-124.

OKEMAH, OKLAHOMA (3,038)

Historic operator: Fort Smith & Western Railway
Last route abandoned: 1939
Notable reuse of right-of-way: None

The saga of rail line abandonment in Okemah recounts the hardships of the Great Depression, the vigorous railroad competition once prevalent on the Oklahoma plains, and the legacy of one of America's most beloved songwriters, Woody Guthrie. From the porch of his family's home, the young Guthrie watched the Fort Smith & Western's trains pass through Okemah. Later in life, he immortalized the glory of railroad travel in song.

Historical Perspective

Okemah did not exist during the latter half of the nineteenth century, when the future town site was part of a vast tract in Indian Territory known as the Creek Nation. After the infamous land rush of 1889, tens of thousands of settlers poured into the western half of Indian Territory, leading to the creation of a separate jurisdiction called the Oklahoma Territory. As the years passed, federal officials also sought to open for settlement the more easterly portions of Indian Territory, including the land that would later become Okfuskee County in the state of Oklahoma.

Settlement in this region was occuring on a relatively large scale by the time several pioneers, including H. B. Dexter, created the Okemah town site in 1902. These pioneers named the community in honor of Chief Okemah, an amicable member of the Kickapoo tribe, and hoped that this community would become a railroad junction. It is said that the presence of the chief, who lived in a hut made of bark, contributed to Okemah's reputation as a peaceful and stable place to live.

FORT SMITH & WESTERN RAILROAD

Okemah soon evolved from an agglomeration of tents into a well-planned community with a variety of permanent structures, including a post office, several stores, and the Dexter House, a fine hotel built of stone. The community's hopes of becoming an important rail junction remained very much alive when the Fort Smith & Western Railroad laid its tracks through town in 1903 over a route that extended from Coal Creek (near the Arkansas border) westward to the city of Guthrie. East of Coal Creek, the carrier exercised trackage rights over the Kansas City Southern to Fort Smith, Arkansas, where it interchanged with several larger carriers.

Unfortunately for local businesses, the vagaries of railroad construction in Indian Territory kept other prospective service providers—including a railroad widely anticipated to link Shawnee and Muskogee—from reaching town. To some extent, the community triumphed over its smaller-than-expected transportation role. In 1904 Okemah became an incorporated community, the county seat, and home to a Masonic Lodge. In 1906, it dedicated a three-story brick school. By 1907, when the federal government combined the

Well-wishers stand elbow-to-elbow as a Fort Smith & Western troop train pre-pares to depart the Okemah station in 1917. Note the station sign in the back-ground. (Okemah Historical Society.)

Oklahoma and Indian Territories into the state of Okla-homa (America's forty-sixth state), property in the community was selling briskly.

As the years passed, the Fort Smith & Western had only limited success in its struggle to become a viable east–west transportation route. Intense competition from larger railroads and the relocation of the state capital from Guthrie to Oklahoma City in 1910 hurt it immensely. Hoping to become a major "bridge route," the carrier obtained trackage rights over the Missouri, Kansas & Texas ("Katy") Railway from Fallis (a junction 22 miles east of Guthrie) to Oklahoma City in 1915, enabling it to offer through service from the state capital to Fort Smith.

As the Fort Smith & Western worked to improve its operations and strengthen its financial performance, it

moved its division point from Dustin to Weleetka (a junction with the Frisco 14 miles southeast of Okemah). In 1916, it introduced through sleeping-car service from Oklahoma City to Joplin, Missouri, made possible by interchanging cars with the Missouri, Oklahoma & Gulf Railway at Dustin. After only a few months of service, the carrier transferred the sleepers to one of its Fort Smith–Oklahoma City trains.

These efforts would ultimately prove no match for the powerful competitive forces that gradually pushed the Fort Smith & Western toward insolvency. By the end of 1920, the carrier had reduced passenger service through Okemah to one train in each direction. In 1921, it emerged from reorganization as the Fort Smith & Western Railway, only to face more financial adversity.

The carrier's problems did not prevent it from leav-ing a profound imprint on the many communities it served. It expanded Okemah's depot in 1922 and periodi-cally operated special excursion trains. It supported a spectacular rise in oil production during the early 1920s, which elevated Okemah's population to more than 4,000 and generated much-needed revenue. As wells sprouted up throughout town—even on residential land—Okemah evolved into a prominent oil center and an important source of freight and passenger revenue for the carrier. During these prosperous times, the youthful Woody Guthrie watched from his boyhood home, a wooden two-story structure known as London House, as trains rumbled through town. He later described Okemah as "one of the singingest, square dancingest, drinkingest, yellingest" towns in Oklahoma.

The community's railroad era reached its zenith in the autumn of 1923, when a flood disrupted service on other lines in central Oklahoma. The Atchison, Topeka & Santa Fe, along with the Frisco, the Katy, and other lines, diverted trains over the Fort Smith & Western, giving the townspeople a glimpse of transportation glory that had long eluded them. Even as automobile travel grew more common, some passengers rode the Frisco to Weleetka and transferred to the Fort Smith & Western to reach the Okfuskee County Fair, an event held at spacious fairgrounds adjacent to the tracks in Okemah.

Changing Times

Okemah's reliance on oil production and the inherent weakness of its railroad rendered it vulnerable during economic downturns. By the end of 1931, the flow of petroleum had sharply diminished, and Fort Smith & Western had fallen into receivership. With the Great Depression deepening and a series of devastating droughts ravaging agricultural production, the carrier's revenues dropped to alarmingly low levels. Crop failures throughout the Great Plains' dust bowl, aggravated by the long-standing problem of wind erosion, further weakened the state's economy.

Adding to the railway's plight was the sparse population of the communities that it served. The largest town on the entire railway, Guthrie, had only about 9,500 residents. Intense competition from stronger railroad companies, meanwhile, limited the revenues available to it from overhead freight shipments. Although the Fort Smith & Western trains operated only a few more years, they remained both symbolically and commercially important to the communities they served. Many citizens enjoyed gathering at the Okemah depot on Sunday afternoons to greet the arrival of the eastbound and westbound passenger trains, which at one time were both scheduled to depart at one o'clock.

By the time Chief Okemah died in 1936, many wondered how much longer the carrier could survive. The Katy and the Kansas City Southern rescinded Fort Smith & Western's trackage rights because the carrier was unable to pay its bills. In February 1939, after thirty-six years of service, the carrier suspended operations. Later that year, the carrier abandoned its route of 250 miles, making it one of the country's first interstate steam railroads of its size to be scrapped.

Among the dozens of communities along the line left without rail service, Okemah was easily the most populous. With about 3,800 inhabitants at the time, it emerged as one of the largest communities in the United States to be stripped of all rail transportation before the nation formally entered World War II. The outcome was more favorable in McCurtain, the largest community

A building that once housed a cotton gin stands in isolation along the route Okemah's only railroad once followed. (Photo by author.)

served exclusively by the Fort Smith & Western. Service to this town continued after a subsidiary of the Kansas City Southern acquired 21 miles of track linking that community to Coal Creek.

Abandonment's Legacy

Over the next three decades, Okemah dwindled in commercial significance and lost nearly a third of its population. Separated from the flow of commerce, the community struggled unsuccessfully to attract industrial development. Local residents who preferred to travel by rail customarily drove to Bristow, a community about 30 miles north, where they could board the Will Rogers or the Meteor, trains on the Frisco main line between Oklahoma City and St. Louis.

Travelers inspired by Woody Guthrie's songs and sharing his penchant for riding the rails felt a sense of loss in 1967 when the songwriter died and the Frisco discontinued its remaining passenger trains. That same year, Interstate 40 opened along the community's southern periphery, marking the beginning of a more modern transportation era. The interstate crossed the abandoned railroad right-of-way east of town and emerged as a far more viable link between Fort Smith and the Oklahoma capital than the railroad that had preceded it. The opening of the expressway contributed to a brief economic revival that allowed Okemah's population to rise once again, albeit without many well-paying industrial jobs.

Woody Guthrie's colorful personality, his early days in Okemah, and his connection to railroads were showcased in the 1975 motion picture *Bound For Glory*, which was based on the songwriter's autobiographical novel of the same name. The motion picture starred David Carradine and won an Academy Award.

By then, many of Guthrie's songs, such as "This Land is Your Land," "Dust Bowl Ballad," and "Bound for Glory," had become American classics. To Oklahomans, though, Guthrie's musings about railroads were like recollections from a distant age. The demise of Amtrak's Lone Star in 1979 meant that the entire state was without regularly scheduled passenger service for the first time in its history.

While many buildings along Okemah's Main Street deteriorated, residents set aside one historic property for the creation of the Okfuskee County Historical Museum in 1984. To memorialize the railroad era, they preserved in the museum's collection a 2-foot strip of rail from their bygone route and several spikes donated by local residents.

Some Okemah residents of this era were hesitant to embrace Woody Guthrie, whose liberal, often radical, sentiments clashed with their conservative views; however, interest in the man and his musical legacy gradually surpassed any controversy. A local coalition established the Woody Guthrie Festival in 1997 and the following year dedicated a life-size sculpture of the songwriter, created by local artist Dan Brook. Later, a descriptive plaque was added to the monument, drawing attention to the songwriter's connection to railroads.

One of the participants at the first Woody Guthrie Festival was the songwriter's son, Arlo. The younger Guthrie had captured the spotlight a quarter century earlier by rhapsodizing about the "disappearing railroad blues" in Steven Goodman's classic ballad, "The City of New Orleans." While the lyrics referred to an Illlinois Central train rumbling over tracks hundreds of miles away, Arlo's rendition became an anthem lamenting the nation's vanishing railroads—a phenomenon that left its mark on Okemah well before the train he sang about made its inaugural run. As the festival grew in popularity, planners considered bringing a boxcar to the festival site to commemorate Woody Guthrie's lifelong affinity for rail travel. For budgetary reasons, however, this proposal did not move forward.

Oklahoma regained rail passenger service in 1999 when Amtrak introduced the Heartland Flyer between Oklahoma City and Fort Worth on the Santa Fe's rails that the Texas Chief and Amtrak's Lone Star once plied. In Okemah, however, the nearest rail passenger station was still more than 60 miles

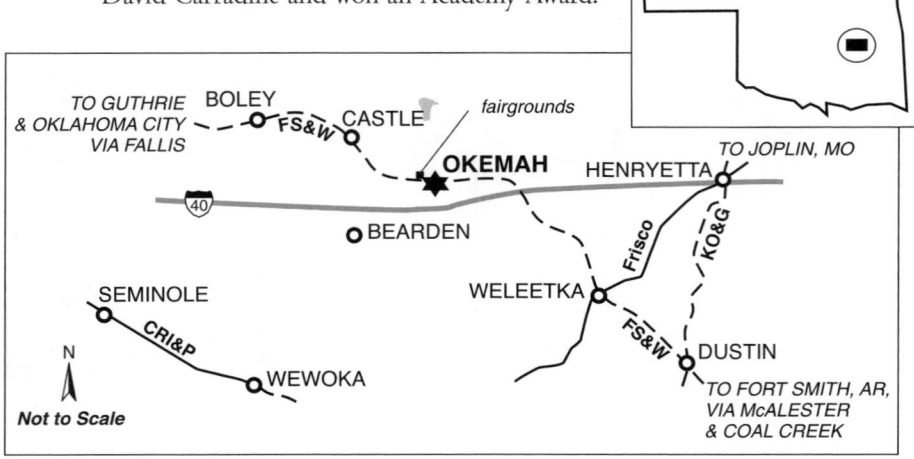

away, and none of the communities along the old Fort Smith & Western line see passenger trains today.

Okemah is only one of many towns along the Fort Smith & Western that diminished significantly in size after the railway's abandonment. Hardly a trace of the bygone carrier remains in Fallis, the former interchange point. Once having twelve trains with passenger accommodations serving its depot daily, except Sunday, Fallis today has a mere 50 residents and no retail businesses.

Epilogue

Observant motorists in Okemah can find several reminders of its bygone steam railroad. On East Broadway Street, a sudden curve marks the location where the tracks once crossed the community's busiest road. On the former depot site, the offices of the Okemah Oil Company recall the link that existed between petroleum companies and the local railroad. Today a portion of the abandoned right-of-way to the west of this parcel of land is occupied by mobile homes and other inexpensive housing. Near the center of town, a tall building used by the local feed company, formerly housing a cotton gin, stands as a testimonial to industries of the past.

The locomotives, depot, and oil wells that inspired Woody Guthrie more than eighty years ago are only memories, as is London House, his childhood home. Nevertheless, the songwriter's ballads of trains, hobos, and the hardships of the Depression—and the railroad song made famous by his son—continue to resonate throughout communities large and small nationwide.

For Further Study

SUGGESTED READINGS:

Bryant, Keith L., Jr. "Railroad Redundant: The Fort Smith & Western Railway." *Railroad History* 174 (1997): 69–89.

Okemah Remembered. Okemah, Okla.: Okfuskee County Historical Board, 1990, 4–24.

Winters, D. "The Fort Smith & Western Railroad: 1900–1923." In *Railroads in Oklahoma,* ed. Donovan L. Hofsommer. Oklahoma City: Oklahoma State Historical Society, 1977, 31–45.

OTHER PRINCIPAL REFERENCES:

Drury, George. *Historical Guide to North American Railroads.* Milwaukee, Wis.: Kalmbach Publications, 1995, 140.

Jensen, Larry. *The Movie Railroads.* Burbank, Calif.: Darwin Publications, 1981, 58–59.

Yurchenco, Henrietta. *A Mighty Hard Road: The Woody Guthrie Story.* New York: McGraw-Hill, 1970, 18–33.

ASTORIA, OREGON (9,318)

Historic operators: Astoria City Railway; Oregon-Washington Railroad & Navigation Co.; Spokane, Portland & Seattle Railway; Great Northern Pacific Steamship Co.
Last route abandoned: 1997
Notable reuses of right-of-way: Astoria River Trail; Astoria Riverfront Trolley; Lewis and Clark Excursion Train

     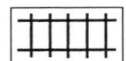

*D*uring the early twentieth century, travelers in Astoria could board trains, streetcars, a railroad-operated ferry, and magnificent ships known as the Twin Palaces of the Pacific. Eventually, all of these services disappeared from the community. To keep its options open, however, the municipal government took the unusual step of acquiring a set of dormant tracks. Only a few years later, it exercised these options by restoring streetcar service and helping launch seasonal rail-diesel-car service from Portland.

Historical Perspective

Meriwether Lewis and William Clark spent the winter of 1805–6 in the heavily forested area that would later become Oregon's Clatsop County. The explorers devoted considerable time to recording their scientific findings in this area while maintaining amicable relations with the Chinook and Clatsop Indians.

When the fur-trading company of John Jacob Astor arrived by sea in 1811, it established a trading post along the Columbia River's southern bank, not far from the former Lewis and Clark encampment. The community around the trading post, named Astoria, was the first English-speaking settlement west of the Rocky Mountains.

The community, principally under British control for the next several decades, struggled as a result of its remote location, but its commercial fortunes improved after it emerged as an important port for the Hudson Bay Company. It became home to the first U.S. Post Office west of the Rockies in 1847, the first customs house in the Pacific Northwest in 1852, and the destination of many settlers heading west on the Oregon Trail, which ended at its waterfront.

Astoria derived considerable prosperity from its sawmills, fishing industry, and salmon canneries, as well as the harborage provided by Young's Bay, an inlet on the Columbia River. Supported by large numbers of Scandinavians and other European immigrants, it became an incorporated city in 1876 and appeared to have all the qualities necessary to become a great port—except for rail service.

By the early 1880s, the absence of a rail line began to generate considerable frustration. Commercial shipping nevertheless remained strong, allowing Astoria's businesses to rebuild quickly after a devastating fire in 1883. When Captain George Flavel, one of Astoria's most prominent

220

citizens, built a magnificent Queen Anne mansion in 1885, he signaled his confidence in the town's future.

Many expected the town's railroad problem to be resolved in 1888, when the Astoria Street Railway began operating horse-drawn cars through the city's streets and the Astoria & South Coast Railway commenced work on a line to Seaside, a popular coastal destination to the south. The Astoria & South Coast also envisioned building a second line from a point near Skipanon, southwest of Astoria to Hillsboro (in the Willamette Valley near Portland), thereby connecting Astoria with the rest of the state's rail system. Unfortunately, the carrier fell far short of its goals: although it laid tracks into Seaside in 1890, it built neither a trestle across Young's Bay to Astoria nor the route to the Willamette Valley.

Other companies attempted to resume construction of the railroad, but several years passed before the steam railroad's successor, the Astoria & Columbia River Railroad, began laying track in earnest. In 1896, it completed a trestle and movable bridge over the bay—a massive structure extending 8,600 feet—allowing for continuous rail trips from Astoria to Seaside. The carrier also worked eastward along the Columbia

from Astoria, installing several more movable bridges across estuaries of the river. In 1898, it created an interchange with the Northern Pacific Railway at Goble, at last completing a direct rail link to Portland.

The synergy of trains and steamboats at Astoria established the town as one of the largest commercial ports of the Pacific Northwest. The railroad built a shop facility in Warrenton and constructed a branch to Flavel, a port on the opposite side of the bay. An extension of the local streetcar system (now using electric power) in 1902 and the construction of a magnificent city hall three years later suggested that more prosperity lay ahead.

Trains could also be seen on the north side of the Columbia River opposite Astoria after the Oregon Railway & Navigation Company built a narrow-gauge line in 1908 from Oysterville, Washington, to a terminal across the river in Megler. Fondly remembered as the "railroad that ran by the tide," this operator's trains

The daily SP&S passenger train between Portland and Seaside negotiates a curve near Fifth Street at the Astoria wharf in 1952, the same year in which passenger service to the community ended. (Walter Grande Collection, courtesy of Duane Cramer.)

could be reached via a railroad-operated ferry sailing from Astoria's wharf. In 1910, this Union Pacific subsidiary was assimilated into the Oregon-Washington Railroad & Navigation Company.

Astoria was clearly at the pinnacle of its railroad era when Great Northern magnate James Hill absorbed the Astoria & Columbia River into his vast holdings during the early twentieth century. When another Hill entity, the Spokane, Portland & Seattle Railway (SP&S), formally acquired the carrier in 1911, trains and trolleys seemed almost omnipresent. The SP&S's turntable, roundhouse, and bustling freight yard were important sources of local jobs, while its daily passenger trains between Holladay (a station near Seaside) and Portland were vital to mobility.

Town leaders sensed the potential for tremendous expansion in 1915, when the Great Northern Pacific Steamship Company, an affiliate of the Great Northern and Northern Pacific railroads, began operating two massive steamships, the SS *Great Northern* and SS *Northern Pacific*, between San Francisco and Astoria. These magnificent vessels, mooring across the bay in Flavel, allowed passengers to make transfers to trains operating on the SP&S. Great Northern Pacific promoted the ships as the "Twin Palaces of the Pacific" in a valiant attempt to compete with Southern Pacific's all-rail route between Portland and San Francisco. These vessels, each capable of carrying more than 800 passengers, were scheduled to

offer convenient connections to the SP&S's "Steamer Express," a train linking Flavel and Portland with a stop in Astoria.

Changing Times

Only a few years after the maiden voyages of the Twin Palaces, the expectation that Astoria would remain a major transportation center diminished. In 1917, the steamship company sold the poorly patronized steamships to the federal government, which used them elsewhere to transport troops as part of the World War I military effort. In 1922, fire destroyed much of Astoria's downtown, including the pilings upon which many buildings and wooden streets rested. Although much of the community was rebuilt on landfills, the trolley line remained on precarious financial footing. Operations were transferred to the Pacific Power & Light Company, which in 1924, replaced its streetcars with buses. Upon the abandonment of the narrow-gauge route to Megler in 1930, only the SP&S remained.

The SP&S weathered the Great Depression comparatively well and benefitted from the expansion of U.S. Navy operations at Astoria during World War II. The postwar economy, however, was less favorable to its business, bringing an erosion of heavy industry, improved roads, and commercial air service to Portland. A sawmill built east of downtown during the 1950s provided SP&S with a new source of revenue. The demolition of the roundhouse to make way for a spur to the sawmill, however, eliminated a prominent reminder of past transportation glory.

Another reminder of the railroad's most prosperous years vanished in early 1952, when the last regularly scheduled passenger train, the Portland–Seaside local, departed, despite municipal effort to prevent its discontinuation. By the end of the decade, the SP&S had reduced local freight service to three trains per week. Although the railroad periodically operated special excursions, its regular businesses suffered from the competition provided by maritime companies and a decline in naval shipments.

Community leaders hoped that the creation of the Columbia River Maritime Museum in the former city hall building during 1962 would mark the beginning of an economic turnaround. The opening in 1966 of the Astoria Bridge—the longest continuous truss span in the world—generated further optimism about the future. This magnificent 4-mile span had replaced the historic state-operated ferry to Megler

The Astoria Branch lies dormant—as the configuration of these warning lights on the wharf attests—on a damp morning in 2000. Today, a municipal trolley operates over this abandoned segment. (Photo by author.)

and greatly improved Astoria's accessibility from southern Washington.

As it happened, these developments, while certainly helpful, were no panacea for a community struggling with a protracted economic downturn. The community lost nearly 10 percent of its population over the course of the decade. A landslide near Wauna disrupted rail service in 1966, and several derailments drew attention to the need for track repairs. By the time SP&S merged into the Burlington Northern system in 1970, the outlook for development was unequivocally grim.

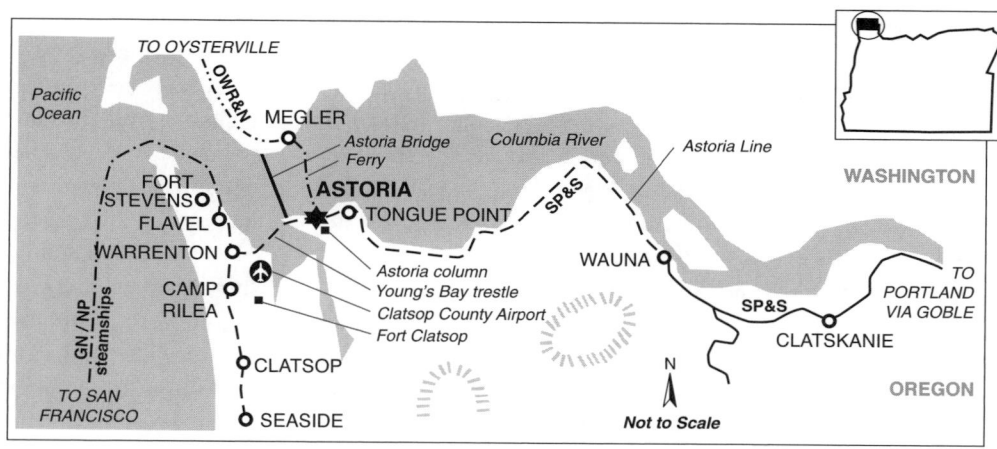

Local officials redoubled their efforts to promote tourism and showcase the community's fine historical buildings. Astoria celebrated its centennial in 1979 and added more than two dozen properties to the National Register of Historic Places over the next ten years. In 1982, the Maritime Museum vacated the old city hall and opened a large new facility along the river adjacent to the tracks. Several years later, the local historical society transformed the old city hall into the Clatsop County Historical Museum. After years of effort, the expansion of tourism began to gather momentum.

With economic development now moving in a promising direction, rail service became expendable. In the autumn of 1982, Burlington Northern, which had already abandoned the portion of the branch between Camp Rilea (southwest of Astoria) and Seaside, condemned the deteriorating Young's Bay trestle. The carrier abandoned its remaining routes west of Astoria in late 1985 and dismantled the trestle the following year. In 1987, it donated its Astoria depot—a landmark dating back to 1915—and a large parcel of nearby land to the Maritime Museum. Sensing that a notable chapter in the community's history was coming to a close, the Astoria Railroad Preservation Association, a volunteer group, acquired a 1925 Baldwin steam locomotive in 1991 with the hope of restoring it for excursion service.

Rumors circulated that Astoria was about to become a major transshipment point for automobiles imported from Asia. This scenario never materialized, nor did other efforts to attract new railroad customers. The plywood mill, one of the railroad's last significant local customers, closed in 1991, further reducing the viability of the so-

called Astoria Line. In late 1995, Burlington Northern removed from service a 5-mile stretch between Astoria and the Tongue Point industrial area east of town, ending the last of community's service.

Abandonment's Legacy

Burlington Northern continued to haul timber and other commodities to Tongue Point until a landslide damaged the tracks about 20 miles east of this location at Aldrich Point (near Wauna) in early 1996. Despite the fact that this landslide and another one nearby at Bradwood necessitated suspending service on the western end of the line, the municipal government moved ahead with plans to railbank the 5-mile segment between Astoria and Tongue Point under the guidelines of the National Trails System Act. Unlike many other efforts to preserve rights-of-way through the act, which were motivated primarily by a desire to create recreational trails, Astoria officials envisioned one day seeing freight and passenger trains return. They moved swiftly, therefore, when Burlington Northern began salvaging the rail and crossties, and persuaded the carrier to deed them to the municipal government in 1997.

The citizens of Astoria strongly supported these efforts. More than 400 residents gathered later that year to help remove debris and brush from the right-of-way. Hoping to find an interim use for the corridor, the city made arrangements to allow tourists to travel on flanged-wheel railbikes along its waterfront. It also created the Astoria River Trail, a pedestrian path along the route within the city limits, while preserving the tracks for eventual rail service.

Burlington Northern had little interest in continuing

service to this part of Oregon and completed its withdrawal from the region in 1997 by conveying the remaining tracks between Portland and Tongue Point to the Portland & Western Railroad and deeding the right-of-way to the state government. Although the short line reopened the route west to Tongue Point, inadequate traffic soon forced it to terminate service over approximately 20 miles of track at the end of the line.

As traditional industry in the region scaled back, it became apparent that Astoria would benefit by redirecting more of its resources to promoting tourism. Thousands of visitors arrived monthly to see the Maritime Museum, the historic waterfront, and the Fort Clatsop National Historic Site. Record numbers of travelers sailed into town on Columbia River tour boats from Portland and Seattle. To provide a new tourist amenity, the municipal government obtained a historic trolley car in 1998 and restored it with the assistance of local volunteers. The streetcar began operation over a 2.5-mile route in 1999 as the Astoria Riverfront Trolley. This popular tourist attraction, powered by an electric generator, soon carried more than 30,000 riders annually.

Several years later, attention turned to operating trains for tourists attending the bicentennial of the Lewis and Clark expedition. After receiving federal funds for this purpose, the state government, in collaboration with Portland & Western, began its work on rehabilitating the entire line from Portland to Astoria and purchased three rail-diesel cars (RDCs) from Rail British Columbia. In 2002, a work crew removed fallen trees and debris from the corridor west of Tongue Point, repaired the tracks, and operated a work train into Astoria—the first train within the city limits in more than six years. Workers also laid new track near the depot to allow for simultaneous trolley and train operations.

These efforts came to a celebratory conclusion in 2003, when the community welcomed the arrival of regularly scheduled excursion trains (that is, the RDCs operated under the auspices of Amtrak) for the bicentennial celebration. At the same time, the local railroad preservation association moved closer to its goal of rebuilding its steam locomotive for scenic excursions along the river.

Epilogue

Visitors to Astoria will immediately recognize that the city remains a notable deep-water port, attuned primarily to fishing, light industry, and tourism. The Maritime Museum and the *Columbia*, a ship permanently moored along its waterfront, honor the city's seafaring past. Day-trippers stroll through the city's well-preserved downtown district. Travelers arriving on the rail-diesel car detrain at the Astoria depot, which is still owned by the museum and listed on the National Register of Historic Places. Officials anticipate the eventual rehabilitation of this timeworn structure.

Astoria's restoration of both railroad and streetcar service is a striking example of the role of corridor preservation in the municipal planning process. The city's efforts illustrate the benefits that can be obtained when creative uses are found for rail lines that have ceased being commercially viable. Although the Twin Palaces of the Pacific no longer sail, the route of the Steamer Express is once again part of the pulse of Astoria life.

For Further Study

SUGGESTED READINGS:

Gaertner, John T. *The North Bank Road.* Pullman: Washington State University Press, 1990, 129–47.

Grande, Walter R. *The Northwest's Own Railway: Spokane, Portland & Seattle Railway and its Subsidiaries.* Vol. 2, *The Subsidaries.* Portland, Ore.: Grande Press, 1992, 29.

Wood, Charles R., and Dorothy Wood. *Spokane, Portland and Seattle Railway: The Northwest's Own Railway.* Seattle: Superior Publishing, 1986, 34–36.

OTHER PRINCIPAL REFERENCES:

Culp, Edwin D. *Stations West: The Story of the Oregon Railways.* Portland, Ore.: Crown, 1976, 98–119.

Currie, Bill. "GNPSS Company." *The Dope Bucket: Magazine of the Spokane, Portland & Seattle Railway* 26, no. 2 (summer 1968): 2–5.

Dennon, Jim. "Astoria's Streetcars." *CUMTUX: Clatsop County Historical Society Quarterly* 9, no. 2 (1989): 24–36.

Hilton, George W. *American Narrow Gauge Railroads.* Stanford: Stanford University Press, 1990, 548.

Miller, Emma Gene. *Clatsop County, Oregon: Its History, Legends and Industries.* Portland, Ore.: Binsford & Mort, 1958, 154–60.

Reagans, Raymond J. *The Railroad That Ran By the Tide: Ilwaco Railroad & Navigation Co. of the State of Washington.* Berkeley, Calif.: Howell-North Books, 1972, 9–14, 58–9, 65, 83–97.

BURNS, OREGON (3,064)

Historic operators: Oregon & Northwestern Railroad; Union Pacific Railroad
Last route abandoned: 1992
Notable reuse of right-of-way: Proposed recreational trail

Public agencies took extraordinary steps to restore rail service to Burns, "the most away-from-it-all town in America." These efforts included building an embankment to elevate 6 miles of track high above the original track-bed and culminated in a well-attended Great Rerailment Celebration. Much to the townspeople's dismay, however, the large expenditure of public funds did not prevent a short-line railroad from exercising its right to dismantle the tracks only a few years later.

Historical Perspective

Fur traders working for a French company were most likely the first white people to venture into the remote area that is known today as the Harney Basin. Harassed by Indians in 1826, these frontiersmen christened a nearby river Malheur, a French word roughly meaning "misfortune." Significant exploration of the basin did not resume until 1859, when a detachment from the U.S. Army passed through the region to assess opportunities for building roads.

The federal government established Fort Harney to facilitate orderly development in the basin during the 1860s and set aside a large parcel of land for the Great Paiute Reservation in 1872. That same year, the pioneering Peter French established a cattle ranch outside of the reservation's boundaries near Lake Malheur, a large body of water at the base of the river. French built a circular barn and gradually expanded his livestock herds.

After a small community with a hotel, saloon, store, and other small businesses emerged near the Silvies River in 1878, storekeeper George McGowan, an admirer of the literary works of Robert Burns, named the post office after this "poet of the people" and established himself as the first postmaster in 1884. Burns was incorporated in 1889 and became the seat of Harney County the following year. By the mid-1890s, French's P Ranch purportedly had become the largest cattle ranch in the United States.

The area around the lake had long been of interest to naturalists and in 1908 was set aside by the federal government as the Malheur National Wildlife Refuge. Increasingly large harvests of wheat and barley, together with the natural beauty of the wildlife refuge, strengthened the basin's reputation as a desirable place to settle. As the years passed, however, the problem of inadequate transportation could not be ignored. The nearest rail line, a 14-mile route operated by the Malheur Valley Railroad (which linked a junction on the Oregon Short Line near Ontario, Idaho, to Vale, Oregon),

UNION PACIFIC

A southbound Oregon & Northwestern freight heads across Fuqua Creek on August 15, 1969, en route to its interchange with the Union Pacific at Burns. (Photo by John C. Illman.)

was more than 100 miles away.

A pair of prospective rail operators, the Boise & Western Railway and the Oregon Eastern Railway, received their incorporation in 1905 and 1909, respectively, to build westward from Vale across south-central Oregon. Neither company had the resources, however, to begin construction. Hopes for rail service then centered on a plan by Union Pacific magnate E. H. Harriman to create a new main line across the area—a line he considered critical to his much larger plan to consolidate Southern Pacific and Union Pacific. He envisioned this route linking the main line of the Oregon Short Line (a Union Pacific subsidiary) in southern Idaho with the Cascade Line of Southern Pacific (another carrier that Harriman controlled) south of Eugene. Harriman's bold plan also called for an extension to Coos Bay on the Oregon coast, where he envisioned creating a great commercial port.

Harriman put his plan into motion by acquiring the Oregon Eastern and having it and the Oregon-Washington Railroad & Navigation Company jointly begin construction westward from Vale in 1911. The project did not go smoothly. The federal government invoked the Sherman Antitrust Act in 1912 to block Harriman's consolidation effort. Although construction continued, progress was slow, and Oregon Eastern did not reach Crane (30 miles east of Burns) until four years later—still more than 180 miles short of its intended destination. Construction then ground to a halt.

The uncertain future of this line and a series of disasters cast a dark shadow over the basin's economy. In 1914, a severe drought and the worst fire in Burns's history pushed the local economy into a recession. The following year, as the townspeople worked to recover from the loss of eighteen businesses, a smaller fire reduced one of the town's hotels to ruins.

Relief from the basin's lengthy economic slump came in the form of a federal plan to harvest timber in the Bear Valley, a sparsely populated region north and west of Burns. After accepting bids from various contractors to bring the pine to market, officials awarded a contract to Fred Herrick in 1920. Herrick had a contractor build an

226

extension from the end of the Oregon Eastern route near Crane to Burns, where he intended to construct an enormous sawmill. The line was to become part of a 157-mile route to southern Idaho operated by the Oregon Short Line Railroad.

When the railway laid its tracks into Burns in 1924, the townspeople were understandably elated. Four thousand gathered to commemorate the arrival of the first train. Due to Herrick's failure to comply with the terms of the federal contract, however, lumber production did not grow as much as anticipated. To resolve this problem, officials had the Edward Hines Western Pine Company take over local woodcutting operations in 1928.

The railway's celebratory arrival into Burns did not end discussion about the need for better transportation in southern Oregon. To the contrary, the state's Public Service Commission had such a strong interest in improving rail connections that it revived the idea of building the route envisioned by Harriman in the late 1920s. It petitioned the Interstate Commerce Commission to order Union Pacific to build the line, arguing that the carrier had already started construction and that improved rail service between Idaho and southern Oregon was critical to economic development. In 1930, the ICC ordered the carrier to build a line from a junction near Crane that would pass south of Burns to the Cascade Line near Eugene. As might be expected, however, this mandate proved to be financially unrealistic as the Great Depression deepened. In 1933, the ICC rescinded its order, a ruling upheld by the U.S. Supreme Court in 1935. Although the state attempted to procure federal funds for the line's construction the following year, trains would never operate over the route originally proposed by Harriman.

By this time, Burns barely resembled the dusty outpost that it had been just twenty years before. In 1930, the Hines Company opened an immense sawmill near the community (at a location referred to as Hines) that generated hundreds of jobs. That same year, a track-laying crew completed a second rail line, extending 51 miles north through Poison Creek Canyon. This route—the Oregon & Northwestern Railroad—terminated in Seneca and made possible an extraordinary expansion of lumber production. Meanwhile, the Union Pacific leased the Oregon

Short Line in 1936 and continued to operate a mixed train that made a round-trip between Ontario and Burns daily except Sunday. Passengers on this train rode in a combination coach-baggage car and could make transfers at Ontario to the Pacific Limited, Portland Rose, and other long-distance trains.

The rising demand for lumber during World War II greatly stimulated traffic on the branch. The Oregon & Northwestern and the Union Pacific shouldered the burden of large shipments of pine, while the lumber company's private logging railway grew to encompass an estimated 40 miles of track. In the late 1940s, the Hines Company facility was believed to be the largest fully enclosed sawmill in the world. Operating twelve months a year, it employed some 240 workers and produced more than 120 million board-feet of lumber annually.

Changing Times

By the time the mixed-train service vanished from Union Pacific timetables in the late 1950s, the valley's economy was once again in transition. Ranching gradually diminished, and many of the prime sources of lumber were being depleted. Even so, the region's economy remained relatively robust. By the late 1960s, Lake Malheur and other parts of the wildlife refuge were attracting thousands of motorists each summer. Tourists increasingly patronized restaurants and small motels in Burns, while

The Union Pacific's Burns Branch is today little more than a gravel path adjacent to the massive sawmill complex formerly operated by the Hines Lumber Company (right), which is largely vacant. (Photo by author.)

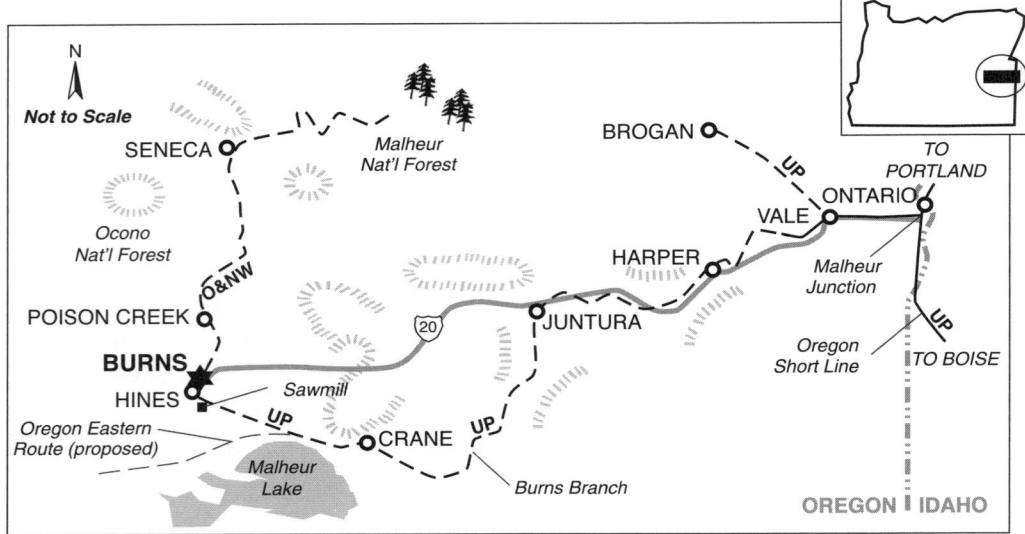

for the music of a Dixieland band, the arrival of a special train, and the participation of the governor and several other dignitaries.

Despite the fanfare, the revenues generated by the railroad were disappointingly low. Some potential customers, having grown accustomed to shipping by truck, hesitated to make the switch back to rail. Cutbacks at the Snow Mountain Lumber Company, the new operator of the former Hines sawmill, also limited the railroad's potential to generate revenue. After the Oregon & Northwestern abandoned its route in 1990, the future of service on the Wyoming Colorado line grew increasingly uncertain. Although local and state agencies, including Oregon's Public Utilities Commission, sought to keep trains running, their efforts were thwarted by a provision in the Wyoming Colorado line's purchase agreement providing it the authority to discontinue service and salvage the route (which it called its Oregon Eastern Division) without ICC oversight. When the short line exercised its option to abandon the 120-mile segment from Burns to Celatom (near Vale) in June 1992, the county's railroad era drew to a close.

the lumber business remained strong enough that Union Pacific interchanged cars Monday through Friday with the Oregon & Northwestern.

Concerns about the future of rail service, however, eventually returned to the municipal agenda. In 1984, the lake's rising waters created hazardous conditions on the Union Pacific route and forced the carrier to place an embargo on the western end of the branch, leaving Burns with no outlet to the national rail system. By 1987, 8 miles of the branch were either badly damaged or had been washed away by the lake's rising waters. Civic leaders in Burns expressed concern about the ramifications of a permanent cessation of rail service. Governmental figures showed that the loss of service was costing the region more than $2 million annually. Local lumber companies made known their willingness to pay a modest surcharge on all freight shipments to support the branch's rehabilitation.

The state's Department of Transportation negotiated for several years with the U.S. Army Corps of Engineers and other entities to find a way to reopen the branch. To lessen its susceptibility to flooding, government agencies invested more than $3 million in improvements that included a 6-mile embankment that elevated the line as much as 15 feet above its original grade—a project reportedly involving the movement of more than 70,000 cubic yards of rock. When Union Pacific sold its Burns Branch to the Wyoming Colorado Railroad Company in late 1989, it cleared the way for the restoration of service on both the western end of this route and on the Oregon & Northwestern. The following June, Burns held the "Great 1990 Rerailment Celebration," remembered

Abandonment's Legacy

To the dismay of those living in the community, the rail carrier began salvaging track almost immediately. County and local agencies reluctantly dropped from consideration the possibility of preserving the branch as a publicly owned corridor, as had been done in the case of Lakeview, Oregon. Attempting to make the best of the situation, some members of the community voiced support for transforming the western end of the Burns Branch into a recreational trail. Although the Wyoming Colorado line donated the short segment from Burns to Hines to a local organization for this purpose, efforts to create a trail over the rest of the route stalled.

The loss of the railroad assumed added significance in 2002, when state transportation officials imposed weight restrictions on State Route 20 between Burns and

Vale. These restrictions forced heavy combination trucks to add 180 miles to their routes and further strained the local economy.

For planners in the region, the saga of the Burns Branch exemplifies how important obtaining meaningful commitments from shippers can be when embarking on projects to rehabilitate lightly used or out-of-service routes. Without such commitments, the large investments made by public agencies in the branch created a high level of financial risk. Although the railroad may have had significant traffic potential in Burns, this amounted to relatively few carloads of freight per mile of track operated, giving agencies little margin for error in implementing their business plans.

Epilogue

Without a rail line or active sawmill, Burns is a much more tranquil place today than it was years ago. The Union Pacific depot is gone, and the old rail grades can be difficult to discern on the basin's rocky terrain. The sawmill has been used for various purposes, including the assembling of recreational vehicles, but is now mostly vacant. Its silhouette provides a constant reminder to the townspeople of the basin's lumber-oriented heritage and the continuing struggle to attract industry to this difficult-to-reach location.

Burns is more than 130 highway miles away from the nearest city with more than 20,000 inhabitants, and is sometimes called the most "away-from-it-all town" in the nation. It is the seat of one of the largest and least densely populated counties in the United States. A state-subsidized bus, which serves a role similar to the mixed train of yesteryear and is the town's only regularly scheduled passenger service, follows the abandoned route much of the way from Ontario. One might reasonably wonder how the completion of the Oregon Eastern years ago would have changed development patterns in this part of the West.

The Harney County Museum in Burns has exhibits and historical displays that vividly describe the community's early days. Outside of town, French's round barn, listed on the National Register of Historic Places, survives as a fading reminder of bygone times. The massive embankment built by the Army Corps of Engineers near Lake Malheur, meanwhile, extends as far as the eye can see. This remnant survives as an unofficial monument to a rail line that public agencies spent millions trying to save.

For Further Study

SUGGESTED READINGS:

Asay, Jeff. *Union Pacific Northwest: The Oregon-Washington Railroad & Navigation Company.* Edmonds, Wash.: Pacific Fast Mail, 1991, 173–79, 313.

Brimlow, George Francis. *Harney County Oregon and Its Range Land.* Burns, Ore.: Harney County Historical Society, 1980, 236–43.

Ehernberger, James L. and Francis G. Gschwind. *Union Pacific Steam.* Callaway, Neb.: EL Publications, 1971, 16.

OTHER PRINCIPAL REFERENCES:

Culp, Edwin D. *Stations West: The Story of the Oregon Railways.* Portland, Ore.: Crown, 1976, 30–40.

Dom, Dick. "Oregon's Last Loggers." *Railfan* I, no. 11 (Aug. 1977): 18–19.

Lewis, Edward A. *American Shortline Railway Guide.* 5th ed. Waukesha: Wis.: Kalmbach Publishing, 1996, 343.

Oregon Department of Transportation. *1994 Oregon Rail Freight Plan,* 34.

Robertson, Donald B. *Encyclopedia of Western Railroad History.* Caldwell, Idaho: Caxton Printers, 1986, 3:102.

SEASIDE, OREGON (5,900)

Historic operator: Spokane, Portland & Seattle Railway.
Last route abandoned: 1979
Notable reuses of right-of-way: Municipally owned corrdor; Seaside Chamber of Commerce

Since the time of Lewis and Clark's famous expedition, travelers from far away destinations have been attracted to Clatsop Beach. Once the site of a magnificent resort belonging to stagecoach and railroad magnate Ben Holladay, this beautiful stretch of Oregon shoreline is deeply etched into the history of the Pacific Northwest and the railroad that called itself the Scenic Sea Coast Route.

Historical Perspective

In early 1805, while the rest of the Lewis and Clark expedition wintered at Fort Clatsop, near the northwestern tip of present-day Oregon, a small detachment traveled south along Clatsop Beach in search of a location where they could establish a primitive salt works. The site they chose near the mouth of the Necanicum River would later become the city of Seaside. There, they boiled more than 1,000 gallons of seawater from which they were able to extract several bushels of salt, something that the expedition urgently needed to cure meat as it prepared for its return trip to St. Louis.

After the expedition departed, the pristine shoreline remained unsettled for several more decades, despite the development of Astoria, a trading center along the Columbia River less than 20 miles away. As Astorians began spending holidays along the beach, two merchants, Helen Lattie and A. J. Cloutrie, opened Summer House, the first hotel near the mouth of the Necanicum, in 1850.

As growing numbers of settlers migrated west on the Oregon Trail, Ben Holladay emerged as a powerful force in the stagecoach business. By the early 1860s, his Overland Mail and Express Company served 2,600 miles of routes, making it one of the industry's largest carriers. In 1866, this legendary "stagecoach king" rose to the forefront of western transportation by acquiring the Butterfield Overland Dispatch. Before the year ended, Holladay consolidated this former rival with his other lines and sold the entire enterprise for a considerable profit to Wells Fargo & Company.

Holladay, one of the state's shrewdest and most respected businessmen, also applied his talents to mining, railroads, real estate, steamships, and other ventures. In the early 1870s, his Oregon & California Railroad, a Southern Pacific predecessor, built in a southerly direction from Portland to the California boundary, greatly accelerating development in the communities it served. Along the coast south of the Necanicum River, Holladay opened the Seaside House, a luxury hotel that won admiration from guests with its well-appointed rooms, fine dining, racetrack, and even wild animals in cages.

Although this fine institution was many miles from the nearest railroad depot, patrons regularly arrived on steamships from distant cities. It is said that passing steamers belonging to Holladay would fire a volley from one of their cannons in honor of their famous leader. In 1873, officials renamed the local post office Seaside House.

Holladay aspired to build rail lines from Seaside to Astoria and Portland, a system having the potential to greatly increase the value of his real estate holdings. However, the panic of 1873 weakened him financially and doomed his railroad building initiative, leaving Seaside heavily dependent on marine vessels. The Tillamook Rock Lighthouse, built in 1881 to warn ships of their proximity to the Columbia River, became a new symbol of the community's continuing connection to the sea.

After Holladay's death in 1887, investment continued to flow into this part of Oregon. In 1888, the Astoria & South Coast Railway was incorporated to build a coastal route from Astoria to Seaside and an inland route from Skipanon (approximately 10 miles north of town) to a junction southwest of Portland near Hillsboro. The carrier finished the portion of the coastal route between Seaside and Warrenton in 1890, but it was unable to span the bay and reach Astoria or to build the inland route to Hillsboro.

Despite these disappointments, the rail line, an isolated and distinctly local operation called the Seashore Railway, proved popular among vacationers traveling between Astoria and Seaside. It spurred the construction of several more hotels and fine shoreline homes in Seaside, including a cottage built in 1893 by businessman Horace Butterfield that today is a local landmark.

The ease of traveling to the community improved a great deal after Andrew B. Hammond bought the railway in 1894. Hammond organized the Astoria & Columbia River Railroad, completed a lengthy trestle across the bay to Astoria in 1896, and reached Goble, the terminus of a Northern Pacific Railway branch, in 1898, thus completing the link to Portland. Adopting the marketing name of Scenic Sea Coast Route, the railroad was now poised to thrive.

The introduction of direct service to Portland was a turning point in Seaside's development. The town received its articles of incorporation in 1899 and came to rely on two local depots, one in downtown Seaside (the primary station) and another at Twelfth Avenue (a depot originally called Necanicum but later renamed Surf). Speculation arose that the railway would extend its route

With the glory years of rail service long over, the atmosphere is decidedly low-key as an SP&S train destined for Portland loads passengers and baggage at Seaside in 1945. (Photo by Al Haig, collection of Duane Cramer.)

south to Yaquina to provide a connection with the Corvallis & Eastern Railroad. Such a link never materialized, but in 1907 the railroad did complete a short extension to Seaside House, which it equipped with a depot called Holladay.

The community's depots were busy all year long as many men commuted to Portland on the so-called daddy trains. These express trains, prominent in community folklore, would typically operate from Seaside each Sunday and return each Friday, allowing workers to spend weekends with their families. The passenger business remained strong well after the Spokane, Portland & Seattle Railway (SP&S) acquired the Astoria & Columbia River in 1911. The freight business was similarly robust, due in part to the expanding output of a sawmill supplied by the narrow-gauge Clatsop Railroad, a privately operated logging carrier reaching deep into the hardwood forests near Seaside.

Seaside merged with West Seaside (a community on the opposite side of the river) in 1912, and over the next ten years became widely known for its fine tourist amenities, including a newly built natatorium. Its lumber industry flourished during World War I, when the War Department commissioned a local sawmill to support the construction of lightweight aircraft. In 1920, Seaside officials replaced the wooden promenade, along the

beach with a concrete structure more than 8,000 feet long. At the foot of the promenade, the community built the now-famous Seaside Turnaround on Broadway Street to reverse the direction of traffic. This widely photographed and deeply symbolic landmark marked the endpoint of the historic Lewis and Clark Trail.

Changing Times

Seaside remained a major vacation destination during the 1920s, but the most glorious years of rail service gradually came to an end. In 1922, the railroad tried to stimulate passenger business by placing a gasoline-powered motorcar into service between Astoria and Seaside, only to withdraw this offering less than two months later. SP&S's regularly scheduled passenger service and special summertime runs for weekend beachgoers continued, but these trains surrendered their place at the forefront of the economy, especially after the carrier created its own motor-coach company in 1924.

The opening of a new Seaside House in 1926 marked the beginning of a more modern phase of local tourism development. Although occupying a different site and unaffiliated with the bygone resort of the same name (which had been razed four years earlier), the hotel attracted a new generation of guests accustomed to traveling by car. With passenger revenues falling at an alarming rate during the Great Depression, SP&S first discontinued its weekend trains to the beach at the end of the 1930 season, then revived them in 1935, only to cancel them once again during the middle of that summer. Improvements to roads, especially the opening of the Sunset Highway in 1937, reduced patronage on the remaining passenger train so severely that SP&S petitioned to eliminate this run in 1942. Residents in both Astoria and Seaside objected strenuously, and the train continued, albeit without parlor-car accommodations after 1946. The carrier converted the train from steam to diesel power two years later, and finally discontinued it in 1952, after handling large crowds eager to take a final ride. By this time,

The Scenic Sea Coast Route is today little more than a dirt path in this part of Seaside. A sporting goods store now obstructs the right-of-way, indicating how times have changed. (Photo by author.)

freight service to Seaside had been reduced to three trains per week.

In the 1950s, SP&S delighted nostalgic travelers by reviving the tradition of operating special summertime beach trains, but by the late 1960s these occasional trains had once again ceased operating, and little remained of the freight business except for sporadic shipments of lumber and building supplies. Municipal planners became interested in acquiring the adjacent railroad right-of-way for various municipal improvements after the opening of the Seaside Convention Center in 1968.

The abandonment of the line soon appeared almost inevitable. SP&S closed its local depot in 1969, suffered from declining production at the Cole Alder Mill, and was merged into the Burlington Northern system in 1970. Despite the deteriorating condition of the track, Burlington Northern operated a series of diesel-powered excursion trains for the Oregon Dixieland Jamboree in Seaside in 1972, bringing a great deal of public attention to the Scenic Sea Coast Route one final time. Never again would the famed line see a passenger excursion. With little opposition, Burlington Northern operated its last train from Seaside in 1978 and abandoned the segment between the community and Camp Rilea in August 1979.

Abandonment's Legacy

Ninety years after local officials celebrated the railroad's completion, many of their successors welcomed its demise, recognizing that abandonment freed up land for new projects. Some of the right-of-way reverted to the local school system, which then leased the property to the city government, allowing for the opening of a new Chamber of Commerce building in 1982. Service over the last remnant of the Scenic Sea Coast Route—the segment between Astoria and Camp Rilea—ended that same year, when Burlington Northern condemned its deteriorating trestle over Young's Bay. The carrier estimated that it would cost $800,000 to repair the span—only a fraction of the projected $13 million replacement cost but nevertheless a prohibitive sum.

As the community moved away from its rail-oriented past, it sought to preserve its rich cultural heritage. In 1983, the lighthouse became the community's first property listed on the National Register of Historic Places, and the newly formed Seaside Museum and Historical Society opened a museum adjacent to the river.

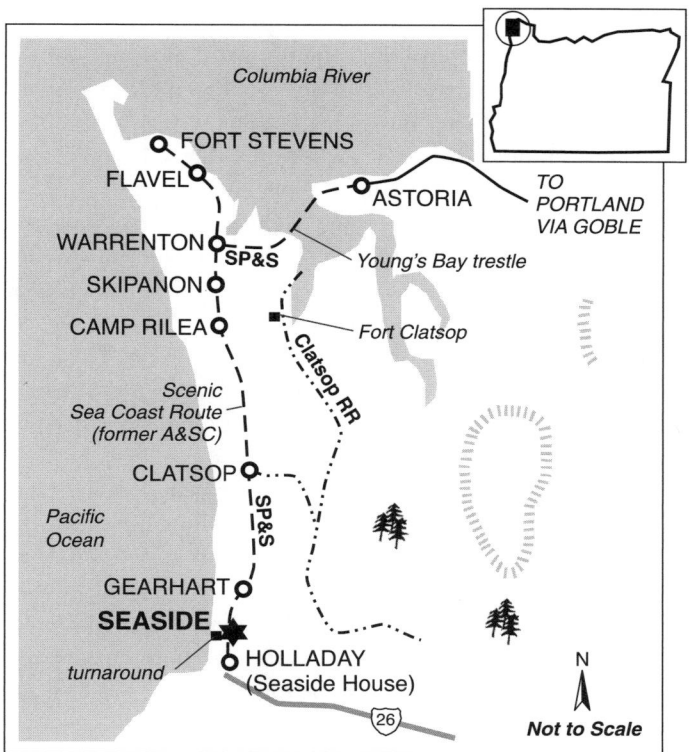

Community leaders restored the former Butterfield cottage the following year and embarked on a project to beautify Seaside's downtown district.

The local government sent a representative to a ceremony in Warrenton during 1989 to commemorate the centennial of the driving of the first spike for the rail line to Seaside. Ironically, the community built a new city hall on the former depot site that same year, altering this property beyond recognition. Another vestige of the railroad era vanished in 1996 when the city razed the alder mill to allow for commercial development. Other reminders were lost shortly thereafter when the state Department of Transportation used some of the former railroad right-of-way along Roosevelt Boulevard (U.S. Route 101) for sidewalks, additional traffic lanes, and other enhancements to mobility.

Epilogue

Visitors to Seaside will find that the downtown district remains a popular place to shop and stroll. The Turnaround on Broadway is a cherished local landmark decorated with a monument that honors the men of the Lewis and Clark expedition. Visitors who are interested in railroad history can find several testimonials to its historic route. Spikes from the local railroad, donated by area residents, are on exhibit at the historical museum. On the museum's exterior walls a large photographic mural with an image of the railroad has been on display since 2001. At the new city hall, a plaque honors the railroad's contribution to the community's development.

Sadly, anyone traveling to the site of Ben Holladay's resort will find nothing to commemorate his many contributions to American transportation. The records kept by his stagecoach line were largely destroyed during the San Francisco earthquake and fire of 1906. The company that acquired his transportation system was reorganized as the Wells Fargo Bank and long ago exited the transportation business.

Holladay's legacy in the development of the West is evident in Seaside and many other communities. During the summer, Seaside's population swells to more than 30,000, and traffic on its roads is then at maximum capacity. The north end of the railroad Holladay built through Oregon passes near his Portland gravesite and survives today as a main line for the Union Pacific Railroad and the route of Amtrak's Coast Starlight.

For Further Study

SUGGESTED READING:
Gaertner, John T. *The North Bank Road.* Pullman: Washington State University Press, 1990, 129–47.

Miller, Emma Gene. *Clatsop County, Oregon: Its History, Legends and Industries.* Portland, Ore.: Binsford & Mort, 1958, 136–64, 251–68.

OTHER PRINCIPAL REFERENCES:
Burkhardt, D. C. *Jesse: Backwoods Railroad.* Pullman: Washington State University, 1994, 134–37.

Frederick, J. V. *Ben Holladay: The Stage Coach King.* Lincoln: University of Nebraska Press, 1940, 71–129, 263–77.

Grande, Walter R. *The Northwest's Own Railway: Spokane, Portland & Seattle Railway and its Subsidiaries.* Vol. 2, *The Subsidiaries.* Portland, Ore.: Grande Press, 1992, 29.

Hobbs, Paul. "Farewell to Passenger Service on the Portland-Seaside Line." *The Northwest's Own Railway: Quarterly Publication of the Spokane, Portland & Seattle Historical Society* (Summer 1989): 1–10.

Labbe, John T., and Vernon Goe. *Railroads in the Woods.* Berkeley, Calif.: Howell-North Books, 1961, 174, 197.

A Pictorial History of Seaside and Gearhart. Portland, Ore.: Pediment Publishing, 2001, 39–44.

Wood, Charles R., and Dorothy Wood. *Spokane, Portland and Seattle Railway: The Northwest's Own Railway.* Seattle: Superior Publishing, 1986, 34–36.

Historic operators: Chicago, Burlington & Quincy Railroad; Chicago & North Western Railway
Last route abandoned: 1978
Notable reuse of right-of-way: City street

Fine sandstone structures testify to Hot Springs' renowned heritage as a resort and medical center. Near the center of town, a graceful structure, once reputed to be the smallest union station in the world, stands almost unchanged from the glory days of local railroad travel. Although the last train departed years ago, the strong market for low-sulfur coal could allow for a dramatic railroad revival in this part of the Black Hills.

Historical Perspective

The first specific English-language reference to the Black Hills is believed to have been made by Meriwether Lewis and William Clark, who reported a conversation with a trapper in the journals of their famous expedition. The government learned a great deal more about these mineral-laden lands when General William Harney intensively explored them in the late 1850s. The prospects for tapping the region's natural resources, however, diminished when the government ceded the Black Hills to the Sioux as part of the Fort Laramie Treaty in 1868. Any hope that the Sioux would amicably surrender this territory ended when chiefs Crazy Horse and Sitting Bull attacked and routed troops under the command of Colonel George Custer during the Battle of Little Bighorn in 1876.

There was less interest in the southern part of the region, but Walter Jenney, an explorer for the Bureau of Indian Affairs, and William Thornby, a newspaper reporter from Deadwood, traveled through this forestland in 1879, always hoping to make the next strike. In the valley of the Little Falls River, these

prospectors encountered a brook emanating from a natural spring, which Thornby immediately claimed as his property. Rumors quickly spread about the possible health-giving qualities of these mineral waters.

With travelers arriving from considerable distances to sample the water, a community interchangeably called Warm Brooks, Warming Springs, and Hot Springs emerged along the river. Recognizing that the valley could support a substantial population, the Hot Springs Town-Site Company platted a community partially on land formerly belonging to Thornby. This settlement became home to a post office in 1881 and was officially christened Hot Springs two years later.

Hot Springs had much to celebrate during these formative years. Access to the town became easier when the Fremont, Elkhorn & Missouri Valley Railroad, a subsidiary of the Chicago & North Western Railway (North Western), reached neighboring Buffalo Gap in late 1885. This carrier built north to Rapid City early the following year, and soon large numbers of travelers were riding stagecoaches to town from the Buffalo Gap depot to "take to the water" at

A train apparently headed for the junction at Buffalo Gap waits at Hot Springs Union Station during the 1890s, with the Gillespie Hotel in the distance. This well-choreographed image was a railroad publicity photograph. (C&NW, Rick Mills Collection.)

local bathhouses and spas. In 1888, a referendum affirmed that the town would remain the seat of Fall River County. The following year, South Dakota achieved statehood and work began on a soldiers' home just west of the river.

The opportunity for Hot Springs to become a major medicinal resort, however, did not arrive until 1890, when two railroads began service to the community. The Fremont, Elkhorn & Missouri Valley built a branch line that year from Buffalo Gap, thereby providing Hot Springs with connections to long-distance trains operating between northern Nebraska and Rapid City. A few months later, the Grand Island & Wyoming Central Railroad, an entity affiliated with the Chicago, Burlington & Quincy Railroad (Burlington Route), completed a branch to town from nearby Minnekahta. The latter route, part of the highly productive system of branches through the Black Hills, approached Hot Springs from the west and was operated under lease by the Burlington

& Missouri River Railroad. Both rail lines made a series of gentle curves along the river and shared lengthy stretches of track near the center of town. All passenger trains terminated at Hot Springs Union Station, an 1891 structure built of locally quarried sandstone.

Arriving passengers relished their stay at the Minne-kahta Hotel, a three-story edifice with the reputation as Hot Springs' premier inn. Although it burned in 1891, an even more impressive structure, the Evans Hotel, opened in 1893, pushing tourism into an entirely new realm. Equipped with spacious rooms, a dining hall, and its own railroad siding for the private cars of dignitaries, this five-story sandstone institution earned accolades as one of finest hotels in the Dakotas. The Evans's magnificence overshadowed the community's smaller but still elegant hotels, such as the Gillespie, Palace, and Plaza.

Over the next decade, travelers arriving from cities as far away as Chicago and St. Louis flocked to Hot Springs. On their stay, many guests enjoyed visiting the Evans Plunge bathhouse, a massive wooden structure with a 200-foot pool filled with soothing mineral water, as well as Wind Cave, a dramatic underground formation north of town. Others shopped at the Minnekahta Block, a fine sandstone edifice in the downtown district which housed numerous stores. The community also enjoyed a degree of commercial diversification. Freight trains working the branches to Hot Springs supported both the expansion of ranching and the sandstone industry while bringing coal and supplies to hotels and the Soldiers' Home.

Hot Springs' rail system was not without its problems. Steep grades and periodic flood damage impaired rail operations. A storm in 1897 washed away lengthy stretches of track, several bridges, and a private railroad car. Even so, Hot Springs seemed poised for further expansion during the early twentieth century. The federal government passed legislation in 1902 making the community the site of a national sanatorium for the treatment of chronic disease, and created the Wind Cave National Park the following year. Passengers could arrive from distant cities with greater ease after the Fremont, Elkhorn & Missouri Valley, the community's predominant passenger carrier, merged into the North Western in 1903.

Changing Times

Serious weaknesses in Hot Springs' economy began to appear during the early 1910s, when medical advances reduced interest in local spas, and improvements to rail service nationwide allowed travelers to reach warm-weather destinations more easily. Although presidential hopeful William Jennings Bryan arrived in 1914 to make a campaign speech, the community gradually faded from the forefront of the region's affairs. The Gillespie Hotel burned the following year, and the Plaza met a similar fate in 1919. As the Evans Plunge deteriorated, the municipal government acquired it for use as a city auditorium. By the early 1920s, Hot Springs had surrendered its role as a prominent spa town and assumed a new identity as a retirement and medical center for veterans—a change that diminished its need for rail passenger service and forced many local businesses to close.

The Great Depression rendered the mere survival of some of the most prominent Black Hills rail lines a questionable proposition. In 1932, the Burlington Route replaced its passenger service between Hot Springs and Minnekahta with buses, and the North Western replaced its passenger train on its mail line through Buffalo Gap with a railroad motor-car operating between Chadron, Nebraska, and Rapid City. Passengers could continue making daily connections to the locomotive-drawn train operating from Buffalo Gap to Hot Springs, but this arrangement ended when a flood washed away a portion of the branch in 1937. Taking a cue from the Burlington, the North Western opted to replace the train with bus service from its depot in Oral and then abandoned its flood-damaged Hot Springs Branch in 1939. The services offered by local railroads diminished further when the Burlington turned its bus service to Hot Springs over to its Burlington Trailways subsidiary in 1944.

By the late 1950s, the once-celebrated resort town was crumbling. During the 1960s, the community's population dropped by more than 10 percent, and the demand for rail service took a precipitous fall. The Burlington Route stopped staffing the local station with an agent in 1967 and allowed its branch to Hot Springs to fall into severe disrepair. When the carrier merged with several other lines to form Burlington Northern in 1970, the branch appeared headed for abandonment.

Although the Burlington Route had deeded the station to the municipal government years before, permitting its partial conversion into a tourist information center, relatively few travelers took an interest in the community's historic structures. Seeking to preserve the

Hot Springs' station possesses a graceful architectural style that is uncommon among small towns bereft of rail service today. The Soldiers' Home is visible on the hill. (Photo by author.)

now-vacant Evans Hotel, the Fall River County Historical Society accepted it as a donation in 1974 and converted it into a senior and low-income housing facility. Although the town took steps to showcase its past (the depot and some three dozen other buildings in the downtown district were added to the National Register of Historic Places in 1974), the prospects for a recovery remained slim. That same year, the community briefly basked in the national spotlight when paleontologists discovered a collection of mammoth skeletons on the southern periphery of Hot Springs. Although few recognized it at the time, this archaeological finding would one day become a critical source of tourism revenue.

With little freight moving on the Burlington Northern branch, its local service appeared destined for the same fate as the mammoths buried nearby. Tonnage dropped to the point where the railroad generally operated only one train per week to the town. After the Veterans Administration Center converted its heating system from coal to heating oil, eliminating an important source of railroad revenue, local freight service diminished to occasional shipments of sand and gravel. In 1975 these shipments amounted to a mere 120 carloads, almost all from a supplier of crushed limestone near Hot Springs. State officials reluctantly concluded in 1978 that the 12-mile branch, whose numerous wooden trestles were deteriorating, had little potential to become financially viable. Later that year, with minimal opposition, the carrier abandoned the route.

Abandonment's Legacy

Following track removal, trees and other vegetation obscured much of the abandoned rail-bed. A short segment along the river became a parking lot for the new Evans Plunge, which catered to a new generation of residents and visitors eager to bathe in the community's fabled waters. County officials transformed another portion of the branch into a road extension.

The decline of railroading in the Black Hills passed another milestone in 1983, when Burlington Northern abandoned more than 60 miles of its famed High Line between Custer and Lead (near Deadwood), saddening area railroad enthusiasts. The carrier operated its final train on the remaining Custer–Edgemont segment in 1986, ending the last of its service on its once-sprawling system of branches in the Black Hills.

Railroading in the region took a more favorable turn during the next several years as Burlington Northern hauled ever-rising amounts of low-sulfur coal from Wyoming's Powder River Basin over its main line through Edgemont. Although the North Western also generated vast tonnage from this strip-mining area, its shipments did not move through South Dakota. In 1996, the carrier sold the Chadron–Rapid City route to the Dakota, Minnesota & Eastern Railroad (DM&E), ending its service to Buffalo Gap and the rest of the Black Hills.

DM&E surprised many observers the following year by announcing a plan to build a new 260-mile line through the Black Hills National Forest to the Powder River Basin. Its plan—the most ambitious proposal for an entirely new rail freight route in the United States in decades—called for an investment of more than $1 billion in order to provide access to this lucrative source of coal. Various alignments that the carrier evaluated through the Black Hills region raised environmental concerns, leading it to eventually settle on a route passing through the vicinity of Oral and Edgemont. This route would pass approximately 9 miles south of Hot Springs and follow an alignment through the Cheyenne River drainage area.

More than eighty residents gathered at the civic center in Hot Springs in 1998 for a public meeting to discuss their concerns about the proposed rail line. As opposition intensified in many communities, the carrier redoubled its efforts to overcome regulatory and environmental issues as well as to alleviate the concerns of landowners and municipal governments. Several years later, DM&E drafted plans to exercise its right, if necessary, to acquire the land through eminent domain, a right affirmed by North Dakota's Supreme Court.

Unlike numerous other communities along the proposed route, leaders in Hot Springs ultimately voiced support for the line's construction. The Chamber of Commerce was a particularly strong proponent, believing that the line's construction would stimulate development and, some hoped, allow local quarries to supply raw materials needed to manufacture concrete crossties. In 2004, DM&E reaffirmed its commitment to building the line.

The historic High Line from Edgemont to Deadwood is today the Mickelson Trail, a recreational path named after the former governor George Mickelson, who championed its creation before his tragic death in an airplane accident. From a depot along the trail in Hill City, the Black Hills Central Railroad operates excursion trains over another former Burlington Route branch. This steam operator, created in 1957, takes passengers to the vicinity of the Mount Rushmore National Memorial.

Epilogue

Hot Springs will likely never again become a prominent spa town. Its fine Romanesque structures, including the immense Evans Hotel building and Minnekahta Block, however, assure that its heritage will not be forgotten. Many visitors on their way to the Mammoth Site, the town's busiest tourist attraction, pause to admire its sandstone edifices.

Vacant storefronts in the downtown district provide a constant remainder of the hardship this community has faced over the years. Many of the community's residents are veterans living in a federal retirement home with little disposable income. A bus operating for many years between Omaha and the Black Hills has gone the way of the North Western, leaving Hot Springs without any regularly scheduled passenger service.

Seventy years ago, few could have imagined that nearly all of the communities west of Rapid City in the Black Hills region, including the towns of Custer, Deadwood, Lead, and Spearfish, would one day be without rail service. Near Hot Springs, large embankments on both the abandoned Burlington Route and North Western branches are vivid reminders of transportation practices of the past. Much like the mammoth skeletons found nearby, the community's Union Station is a mere vestige of a remarkable era that has come to an end, nestled as it is along the river without any evidence of the tracks that once flanked its sandstone walls.

For Further Study

SUGGESTED READING:

Early Hot Springs. Hot Springs, S.Dak.: Hot Springs Star, 1983, 1–117.

Fielder, Mildred. *Railroads of the Black Hills.* Seattle: Superior Publishing, 1960, 93–116.

Mills, Rick. "The Chicago & North Western in Black Hills County." *North Western Lines* 24, no. 1 (1997): 44–79.

OTHER PRINCIPAL REFERENCES:

Mills, Rick. "The Chicago & North Western in Black Hills County–II." *North Western Lines* 24, no. 2 (1997): 35–73.

Overton, Richard C. *Burlington Route: A History of the Burlington Lines.* New York: Knopf, 1965, 227–28, 527.

Potter, Janet Greenstein. *Great American Railroad Stations.* New York: Wiley & Sons, 1996, 401.

FREDERICKSBURG, TEXAS (8,910)

Historic operator: Fredericksburg & Northern Railroad
Last route abandoned: 1942
Notable reuse of right-of-way: Old Tunnel Historic Site

 *At a time when most citizens of Fredericksburg yearned for a railroad, local businessman Charles H. Nimitz was preoccupied with the sea. Legend has it that the spirited hotel owner spoke endlessly about the oceans and once promised, prophetically, to "give to the sea one of my grandsons—as an admiral." Today, longtime residents of the community still recognize the dual legacies of rail and sea that their bygone short line and Nimitz's talented grandson have provided them.*

Historical Perspective

For generations, the Plains Indians used the Pinta Trail to reach the rolling terrain that is today known as the Texas Hill Country. After the Spanish founded San Antonio in 1716, settlers occasionally followed this trail to San Saba Mission, a remote outpost near present-day Menard. One hundred twenty years later, the issue of Texas independence rose to the forefront of Mexican-American affairs. In early 1836, Mexican dictator Santa Anna prevailed over the defenders of the Alamo at San Antonio, but by the end of the year, Sam Houston, shouting "Remember the Alamo!" had led his Texans to victory over Santa Anna's army at San Jacinto.

By 1846, the year after Texas achieved statehood, settlers were arriving in large numbers, and a contingent of more than a hundred people embarked from New Braunfels (a German settlement north of San Antonio) to the site they had selected for a new community. These hardy Germans named their community after Prince Frederick of Prussia. Although they faced almost constant adversity, including a cholera epidemic and a Comanche raid, by 1847 they had succeeded in establishing a permanent town centered around the octagonal Vereins Kirche, a church for all denominations.

Despite chronic hunger and disease, Fredericksburg residents remained deeply committed to religious principles and faithfully adhered to a treaty negotiated with the region's indigenous people. Beginning in 1848, Fort Martin Scott, the first U.S. Army fort on the Texas frontier, offered its protection to the community. This compound played an integral role in the country's Indian affairs.

From these rather trying beginnings, a town with a strong sense of identity emerged. Fredericksburg became the seat of newly formed Gillespie County in 1848. Several of its fine stone buildings, including the Kammlah House (which housed a general store) and a Methodist Church, emerged as stunning testimonials to the skills of local craftsmen. On a less tangible level, the town reaffirmed its strength of character during the Civil War,

Fredericksburg & Northern Ry. Co.

when numerous citizens objected so strenuously to the breakup of the Union that they fled to Mexico or hid in the hills rather than enlist in the Confederate Army.

Although the original town charter contained a provision for a railroad using wooden rails and wheels, the continuing absence of rail line emerged as a serious municipal concern by the 1870s. As the owner of a popular hotel, Charles H. Nimitz had much to gain from the introduction of rail service. His guesthouse, which resembled a steamship, was popular among out-of-town guests. The spirited proprietor, however, instead seemed fixated on the world's oceans. "I turned my back on the sea," he once lamented. "When you do that you can never make another ocean trip. The sea will swallow you up as punishment." According to legend, he asked the heavens for forgiveness and promised that one of his grandsons would become an admiral.

When area residents dedicated a stately new county courthouse in 1881, it seemed only a matter of time before at least one railroad would arrive to serve this community. Over the years, however, the townspeople suffered the disappointment of having at least ten proposals for rail lines come and go without construction. The region's difficult topography and limited population, as well as the vagaries of Texas railroading, repeatedly denied them better transportation options. In 1897, when the townspeople gathered to commemorate Fredericksburg's fiftieth anniversary at the Vereins Kirche (by then converted into a pavilion), the lack of rail service cast a dark shadow over the community's future.

Fredericksburg's separation from the Texas railroad system did not prevent it from expanding and modernizing. By the early 1910s, it boasted a thriving downtown and about 2,000 inhabitants, making it one of the

At a location where visitors often posed for photographs, several well-dressed people watch a Fredericksburg & Northern mixed train cross the Block Creek trestle—a magnificent span more than 700 feet long (date unknown). (Collection of Lester Haines.)

241

The overgrown industrial area behind the Fredericksburg & Northern depot (the rectangular building on the right) evokes the industrial practices of a bygone era. (Photo by author.)

its dismal financial performance. The line was sold to the newly incorporated Fredericksburg & Northern Railroad in 1917, but the flow of red ink continued unmercifully.

Many locals hoped that the railroad would eventually become part of an important long-distance corridor linking San Antonio to San Angelo. This opportunity, however, slipped away when the Gulf & West Texas Railroad (a company receiving its charter in 1929) abandoned its attempt to lease Fredericksburg & Northern, in part due to the latter company's interest in disposing of the property. On several occasions during the 1930s, Fredericksburg & Northern officials tried to persuade Southern Pacific to buy their railroad, but a purchase agreement eluded their grasp. As the Great Depression deepened and roads improved, the short line, adhering to an unusual "daily except Thursday" schedule, saw its commercial niche grow more precarious with each passing year.

Proud of their heritage, area residents formed the Gillespie County Historical Society in 1935 and built a replica of the Vereins Kirche (which had been razed years before) for a community museum. They dedicated a new county courthouse four years later and benefited from a recovering economy until the attack on Pearl Harbor in late 1941 pushed the country into war. On the last day of 1941, Chester W. Nimitz, who had been born in Fredericksburg and spent part of his childhood at the Nimitz Hotel, accepted command of the U.S. Pacific Fleet and thus fulfilled the dreams of his late grandfather.

The drive for scrap materials to support military offensives around the world provided an additional incentive for the Fredericksburg & Northern to end service and dismantle its route. In February 1942, the carrier petitioned the Interstate Commerce Commission for permission to abandon its entire operation. Community leaders pleaded with the ICC to reject the application and claimed that Fredericksburg, if left without rail service, would face "a future of retrogression and deterioration for a quarter of a century." Nevertheless, in May the carrier received the permission it sought and promptly ended freight and passenger service. Fredericksburg, having about 3,500 inhabitants, once again became one of the country's largest communities without an active route.

Considering the loss of rail service to be untenable, the townspeople attempted to buy the carrier and raised $60,000 for this purpose, only to learn that a Chicago

nation's most populous communities without a rail line. The townspeople, nevertheless, felt a tremendous sense of relief when a local railroad committee, chaired by the late hotelier's son, Charles H. Nimitz, Jr., arranged for generous municipal financial contributions in both San Antonio and Fredericksburg that enabled construction to begin. When the San Antonio, Fredericksburg & Northern Railroad operated its first train to town in 1913, the grateful citizenry showed their appreciation for Nimitz and other committeemen by hosting a grand celebration with a parade.

The railroad became widely known for its personal service, rustic charm, and spectacular scenery. Its trains took passengers through one of the few railroad tunnels in Texas, a 920-foot passage bored through almost solid rock, and across an immense trestle stretched more than 700 feet over Block Creek. After a 24-mile trip, southbound trains terminated at a rural location near Comfort, Texas, called Fredericksburg Junction, where passengers could transfer onto the trains of the San Antonio & Aransas Railway (a Southern Pacific predecessor) traveling between Kerrville and San Antonio.

Changing Times

The townspeople's enthusiasm for the railroad notwithstanding, the owners of the company grew impatient with scrapping company had submitted a higher bid. After a work crew dismantled the carrier's route, some of the timbers salvaged from the carrier's trestles were reportedly used to build barns in the area. Other materials are believed to have been dispatched to support the construction of the Alcan Highway, a supply route to Alaska, and to construct railroads at Allied military installations in Australia—improvements critical to Admiral Nimitz's campaign in the Pacific.

Abandonment's Legacy

The absence of rail service remained an item of municipal concern during the war. An enterprising local merchant reportedly tried to have the route rebuilt but was unable to overcome the formidable costs involved. Fredericksburg residents were left further separated from the rail system when Southern Pacific discontinued the motorcar operating on its Kerrville Branch around 1945, ending passenger service to Fredericksburg Junction and the rest of the Texas Hill Country.

As the years passed, nature gradually reclaimed the abandoned railroad grade. The Old Tunnel south of town became a habitat for two species of bats, including the Mexican freetail variety, making it a popular location to observe wildlife. In 1956, the historical society purchased the Kammlah House and converted it into the Pioneer Museum, making the beginning of a period of heightened attention to historical preservation.

When President John F. Kennedy was assassinated in Dallas in 1963, Lyndon B. Johnson, who was born in nearby Stonewall (a town on the eastern edge of the Gillespie County) and had visited Fredericksburg frequently during his childhood, became president. The tourism industry gradually grew as travelers arrived to visit sites commemorating President Johnson and Admiral Nimitz, as well as other area attractions. In 1966, the Nimitz Hotel building (having served its last overnight guest years before) was transformed into the Admiral Nimitz Museum—an institution that opened, coincidentally, the same year the decorated naval hero died. Many visitors learned of the community's bygone railroad on side trips to the Old Tunnel, with its millions of bats and a state historic medallion awarded during America's bicentennial year. In 1980, Fort Martin Scott joined the Fredericksburg Historical District on the National Register

of Historic Places and the late President Johnson's ranch, located 16 miles east of Fredericksburg, was designated a National Historic Park.

As word spread of Fredericksburg's naval museum, antique shops, and pleasing Germanic architecture, the community evolved into one of Texas's leading tourist towns. In 1982, the Nimitz Museum was put under the stewardship of the state government. In 1993, the Old Tunnel came under the management of the state parks and wildlife department, raising its visibility as a "living museum." Another tourist attraction with a connection to a Texas short line emerged when a local businessman purchased a former Quanah, Acme & Pacific Railroad business car and transformed it into a bed-and-breakfast inn.

Expecting tourism to continue to expand, several entrepreneurs explored the possibility of reconstructing both the former Fredericksburg & Northern and the former Southern Pacific route between Camp Stanley and Fredericksburg Junction (which had been abandoned in 1970). Proponents of this project believed passenger trains would be a pleasant and efficient way to move tourists between Fredericksburg and the Fiesta Texas amusement park along the former Southern Pacific route north of San Antonio. In 1996, the group evaluated a plan for operating four daily trips in each direction as well as restoring freight service.

Much like the effort to attract a railroad many years before, however, the rails-to-Fredericksburg initiative faced both financial and physical obstacles. A residential subdivision blocked the former right-of-way at the edge of town. The issue of whether to disrupt the colony of bats living inside the Old Tunnel or reroute the line around the tunnel could not be easily resolved. Without

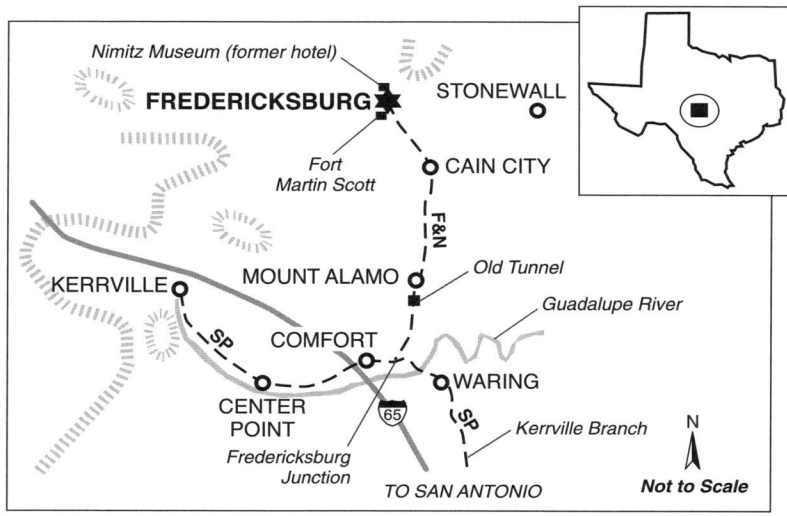

an identifiable funding source, the project failed to advance beyond the discussion stage.

Epilogue

Travelers following the abandoned right-of-way near Old San Antonio Road will find the Old Tunnel and grassy embankments vivid reminders of a short line struggling with almost constant financial adversity. In the town's southern periphery, near Live Oak Road, a variety of aging structures stand as silent monuments to the age of steam. The former depot, however, is barely recognizable, having served as a nut-processing facility before being left to await an uncertain fate.

Upon arriving in downtown Fredericksburg, many visitors are surprised at the scale and grandeur of its historic district. The old courthouse, now the local library, and the replica of the Vereins Kirche stand out among its many prominent structures. The Nimitz Museum is today the cornerstone of the National Museum of the Pacific War, a 9-acre educational complex, while on the well-groomed grounds of the nearby Pioneer Museum, a variety of historical structures honor the early settlers who persevered in the face of adversity. Inside the latter museum's exhibit hall, a ceremonial ribbon that commemorates Fredericksburg's first train is on display.

The absence of a major transportation corridor to Fredericksburg apparently prevented the community from becoming the prominent commercial center envisioned by its early leaders. Instead, its residents came to rely principally on agriculture and tourism to support economic development. The desire of the legendary hotel owner to "give to the sea one of [his] grandsons," however, was gloriously fulfilled. Whether or not trains return to Fredericksburg, Admiral Nimitz and the bygone short line operating "daily except Thursday" will remain treasured parts of this historic community's past.

For Further Study

SUGGESTED READINGS:

Haines, Lester. "Fredericksburg & Northern Railway Company." *Journal of Texas Shortline Railroads and Transportation* 3, no. 3 (Nov. 1998): 3–58.

———. "The San Antonio, Fredericksburg and Northern Railway Company: 1913–1917." *Journal of Texas Shortline Railroads and Transportation* 1, no. 1 (May 1996): 3–50.

Potter, E. B. *Nimitz.* Annapolis: Naval Institute Press, 1976, 22–27.

Schmidt, F. A. *Rails Through the Hill Country.* San Antonio, Tex.: F. A. Schmidt, 1973, 57–63.

OTHER PRINCIPAL REFERENCES:

Bowlin, Michael. "Hill Country Rail History Interesting." *Hill Country* (Jan. 1987): 3.

Reed, G. S. *A History of Texas Railroads.* Houston, Tex.: St. Clair Publishing, 1941, 450–51.

Watt, Don, and Lynn Watt. *Fredericksburg, Texas: Living with the Past.* Fredericksburg, Tex.: Shearer Publishing, 1987.

Zlatkovich, Charles P. *Texas Railroads.* Austin: University of Texas Press, 1981, 69.

KERRVILLE, TEXAS (20,425)

Historic operator: Southern Pacific
Last route abandoned: 1971
Notable reuse of right-of-way: City street

**R**ailroad motorcars and passenger trains carried generations of travelers to Kerrville, a community described as the "mohair capital of the world." Climbing difficult grades and vaulting across the Guadalupe River on a scenic route from San Antonio, these trains supported an economy oriented toward livestock and leisure. When the last Southern Pacific train left town in 1970, a fondly remembered chapter in Texas railroading quietly drew to a close.

Historical Perspective

A group of men led by Kentuckian Joshua David Brown established a camp along the Guadalupe River near present-day Kerrville in 1846. The hardy frontiersmen earned their living by harvesting the area's abundant cypress—a wood that seals itself when moistened, thus making it popular in shingle production. Despite periodic conflicts with Indians in the area, these pioneers saw the profits from the sale of cypress as outweighing the risks associated with bringing the commodity to market.

Their effort to create a viable community along the river took an important step forward after a referendum in 1856, when, by a narrow margin, area residents selected Brown's shingle camp over the more established town of Comfort to be the seat of a newly created county. Brown donated land for a public square and named the community Kerrsville to honor Major James Kerr, a Republic of Texas army officer who had earned distinction during the Texas Revolution.

This locale soon had its own post office, a flourishing shingle industry, and strong commercial ties to San Antonio. In 1866, the community shortened its name to Kerrville.

The townspeople benefited from the astute leadership of "Captain" Charles Armand Schreiner, a native of France, who arrived in Kerrville in 1869. Schreiner, a former private in the Confederate army, opened the Schreiner Store, a purveyor of general merchandise, and in 1873, began cattle drives from the community. Within a few years, his store attracted customers from considerable distances and his Y. O. Ranch grew to encompass more than 50 square miles. Joshua Brown, the original community leader, died in 1874, but Schreiner maintained Kerrville's reputation as an up-and-coming business center. In 1879, he hired skilled masons and stone carvers from Germany to build him a magnificent home. He also worked tirelessly to attract a railroad—an effort that, unfortunately, did not go as smoothly as he had hoped.

245

Having completed what may have been its inaugural westbound run to the "Heart of the Hill Country," a San Antonio & Aransas Pass gas-electric car (No. 300) stands next to the Kerrville depot, circa 1923. (Collection of Lester Haines.)

Schreiner finally succeeded in bringing a railroad to Kerrville in 1887, when the standard-gauge San Antonio & Aransas Pass Railway completed a 70-mile route from San Antonio—an event commemorated with a seven-gun salute and brass band. Its trains crossed the Guadalupe near Comfort, followed the river's north bank into Kerrville, and provided passengers with panoramic views of diverse scenery. Discussion about an extension northwest to the Texas Panhandle or to Colorado raised hope that the route would become an important main line.

Unusual for a branch line in Texas, Kerrville's railway was also notable for its role in carrying vacationers and sportsmen. Visitors from San Antonio, including those hunting waterfowl, enjoyed the temperate climate and cool river water emanating from springs northwest of Kerrville. They congregated at the community's large Masonic Lodge and the Weston Building, attractive structures completed in 1890 in the downtown district.

The Barlemann Saloon in the Weston Building was an especially popular attraction.

Businesses in Kerrville were understandably disappointed when the proposed extension of the rail line never materialized, with the route's tortuous grades partially to blame. The route, consequently, remained oriented primarily toward the convenience of vacationers, local passengers, and ranchers raising cattle, goats, and sheep.

Despite the limitations of its rail connections, Kerrville continued to expand, largely due to Schreiner's acumen in the wool and mohair trade. By the end of the nineteenth century, the Schreiner Wool House was the state's premier institution of its kind and Kerrville's largest employer. The Wool House's success and the expansion of ranching augmented the community's image as a "cowboy town" that delighted travelers from faraway places. As word of Kerrville's offerings spread, growing numbers of passengers arrived by train for extended stays at hotels and cabins along the Guadalupe. During their stay, many enjoyed visits to the Schreiner Store, the Old Bakery, the saloon, and other establishments on Water Street. During the off-season, sportsmen arrived to hunt the abundant waterfowl inhabiting this part of Texas Hill Country.

Business was sufficiently robust that San Antonio & Aransas Pass made numerous improvements to its route.

Following a devastating flood in 1900 that swept away its original wooden bridge over the Guadalupe, the railway built an impressive steel bridge. Three years after Kerrville's freight depot went up in flames in 1912, the carrier finished work on a large new passenger station built of masonry. By 1916, it provided travelers with the convenience of three daily departures from San Antonio, except on Sunday, when it offered two.

Passenger trains brought tourists arriving from great distances as well as local passengers making connections from the newly constructed San Antonio & Fredericksburg Northern Railroad, which established an interchange near Comfort in 1913. The line was important to students enrolled at Schreiner College, a local institution founded by Schreiner in 1921. The railway maintained a manual turntable in Kerrville and greatly improved the efficiency of passenger service by placing Motorcar 300, which resembled a bus, and other self-propelled units into service. On westbound trips, these gas-electric cars proved adept at climbing the steep uphill grades.

This colorful tradition of local passenger service continued despite several changes in the railway's corporate status during the 1920s. Southern Pacific assumed control of the San Antonio & Aransas Pass in 1925 and leased the carrier to a subsidiary, the Galveston, Harrisburg & San Antonio Railroad, which, along with other Southern Pacific-controlled lines east of El Paso, was assimilated into another subsidiary, the Texas & New Orleans Railroad (T&NO). When residents of Kerr County dedicated a large new granite courthouse in 1926, the future of rail service appeared secure.

Changing Times

Even as other forms of travel made inroads in the region, the Southern Pacific still considered the rail line to Kerrville strategically important. In 1930, it revitalized the plan to extend the Kerrville branch (sometimes called the Northwest Branch) to San Angelo and actually prepared some of the grading for this route. The Great Depression prompted the railroad to both scuttle the project and limit passenger service to a single daily arrival and departure.

The outlook for Kerrville and its rail line improved in 1935, when Schreiner's

sons opened a modern warehouse boasting a capacity of four million pounds of wool and mohair. Although the short line to Fredericksburg abandoned its route in 1942, the freight business rose markedly as America deepened its military involvement. Enlisted personnel also arrived to hone their track-laying and maintenance skills at an Army Corps of Engineers railroad training facility in the community. The depot bustled with activity reminiscent of earlier times as travelers returned to the rails, in some instances to visit the Schreiner Store, which was partially integrated into a much larger and more modern structure.

The railroad line, however, fared poorly after the war. Southern Pacific (through its T&NO subsidiary) reduced passenger service on the route to a mixed train before eliminating it altogether around 1945; it then closed the local depot the following year. Although the Schreiner Wool House was rebuilt after a fire in 1948, Kerrville gradually relinquished its role as a major distribution point for sheep and goat products. Aggravating its economic woes, the vacation habits of San Antonians changed as more distant and glamorous destinations beckoned.

Kerrville's economy recovered during the 1960s due to the opening of Interstate 10 through its northern periphery. The superhighway stimulated the expansion of the hospitality sector, encouraged the arrival of many retirees, and pushed Kerrville's population from fewer than 9,000 in 1960 to more than 12,000 in only ten years.

The former Southern Pacific depot in Kerrville, stripped of its transportation role decades ago, now houses a barbecue restaurant. (Photo by author.)

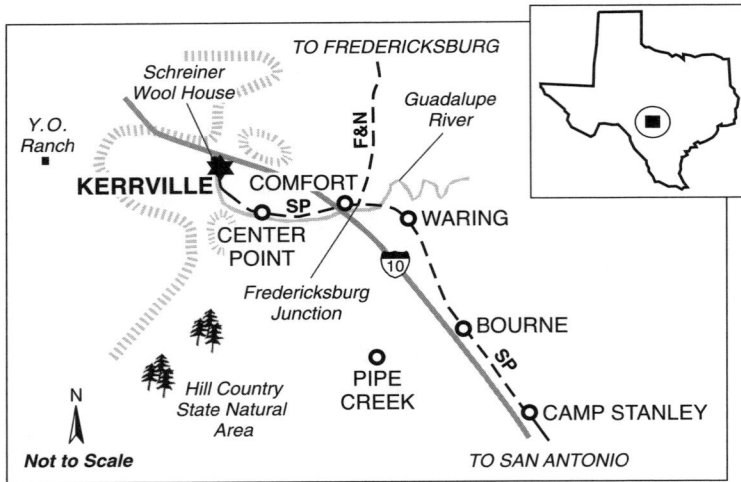

As motor-carrier competition intensified and ranching and other traditional industries declined, Southern Pacific (which merged the T&NO and several other subsidiaries into its system in 1961) deferred maintenance on the branch to such an extent that it became partially overgrown with grass and weeds. When the carrier operated its last train from Kerrville in May 1970, the local newspaper attempted to commemorate the occasion with a front-page photograph. The newspaper inadvertently reversed the image—an oversight that seemed consistent with the apparent lack of municipal concern over the railroad's plight. Without significant opposition, Southern Pacific abandoned the 49-mile portion of the route from Kerrville to Camp Stanley that same year. The removal of the tracks was soon under way.

Abandonment's Legacy

Within ten years of the railroad's abandonment, Kerrville became widely known as a leisure destination catering heavily toward retirees and conventioneers. In 1971, the community staged the first Kerrville Folk Festival, marking the beginning of a highly anticipated annual tradition. In 1975, the Schreiner mansion became the community's first property listed on the National Register of Historic Places, and restoration work began on its conversion into the Hill Country Museum.

The arrival of still more retirees, many of whom had fond memories of childhood train trips to Kerrville, stimulated further expansion during the 1980s. Together with robust convention and tourism businesses, the community's rising population brought renewed vitality to

the downtown district and spurred the opening of the Cowboy Artists of America Museum in 1983, as well as several new hotels near the interstate. The former Masonic Lodge earned a place on the National Register of Historic Places in 1984 and was soon fully restored. A restaurant established in the former Southern Pacific depot initially did poorly but grew in popularity after turning to barbecue cuisine in 1994. The following year, the Weston Building was also remodeled into a restaurant.

By the late 1990s, Kerrville was expanding at a pace comparable to a century before and once again felt the need for improved transportation. To enhance the flow of traffic, the municipal government transformed a small portion of the abandoned route near the depot into a new road (appropriately called Aransas Street). An entrepreneur, meanwhile, revealed an interest in rebuilding the Kerrville Branch between Fredericksburg Junction and Camp Stanley for an excursion railway. His proposal (described in the section devoted to Fredericksburg, Texas) called for reusing the massive steel-truss bridge over the river near Comfort—a towering landmark aptly described as "a bridge to nowhere." The proposal did not advance beyond the discussion stage, but the bridge survives as a vivid reminder of the railroad era.

Within Kerrville, travelers can find a variety of notable remnants of its bygone railroad. Memorabilia are on display on the depot's walls, while crossties unearthed during the construction of a nearby pharmacy are used as bumpers in its parking lot. Along the community's eastern periphery, traces of the old railroad grade can be seen on the campus of Schreiner College. Nothing is left of the Wool House, but strips of rail remain embedded in pavement on McFarland Street adjacent to its former site. At the Hill Country Museum, the safe once used inside the depot is preserved for posterity. Some of the rails retrieved from the abandoned branch now serve as part of the landscaping on the museum grounds.

Epilogue

Kerrville long ago surrendered its image as a cowboy town heavily dependent on the wool and mohair trade. The restoration of the old passenger depot and Barlemann Saloon as well as Schreiner's store and mansion, however, are testaments to its renewed prosperity as a leisure destination. Schreiner's descendents attend to his famous ranches, including the Y. O. Ranch, which is today a game reserve populated with exotic animal species and more than a thousand head of cattle.

Kerrville is a prominent example of a community that was served only by a rail line that might have never been profitable. The decision not to extend the line to San Angelo all but assured that its service would eventually end. Had the Southern Pacific's abandonment application been filed only a few years later, however, it might have precipitated a more vigorous public response. By the mid-1970s, the federal 4-R Act had encouraged Texas and many other states to take a more active stance on branch-line issues.

Today, the community's most visible contribution to transportation is the Kerrville Bus Company, which has operated a large system of routes throughout the state for many years. Several of its buses arrive each day from San Antonio following a highway near the abandoned rail line and bringing to mind the legacy of old Motorcar 300, which, too, once brought travelers to "the heart of the Hill Country."

For Further Study

SUGGESTED READING:

Haines, Lester. "In 1887 the SA&AP Railway Company Builds into the Texas Hill Country." *Journal of Texas Shortline Railroads and Transportation* I, no. I (May 1996): 12–15.

Hedge, John W., and Geoffrey S. Dawson, *The San Antonio and Aransas Pass Railway: The Story of the Famous "SAP" Railway of Texas.* Waco, Tex.: Ama Graphics, 1983, 9–13, 83, 101.

OTHER PRINCIPAL REFERENCES:

Haley, J. Evertts, and Charles Schreiner. *General Merchandise: The Story of a Country Store.* Kerrville, Tex.: Charles Schreiner, 1969, 1–70.

Martinez, Pete. "Daily, Except Sunday." *Trains* (Sept. 1995): 60–61.

Picker, Fred W. *Railroading in Texas: One Man's Memories.* Pittsburgh: Dorrance Publishing, 1996, 1–11.

Watkins, Clara. *Kerr County Texas: 1856–1976.* Kerrville, Tex.: Hill Country Preservation Society, 1975, 18–40.

MINERAL WELLS, TEXAS (16,946)

Historic operators: Weatherford, Mineral Wells & Northwestern Railway; Gulf & Brazos Valley; Gulf, Texas
& Western Railway; Mineral Wells & Lakewood Park Railway; Mineral Wells Electric System
Last route abandoned: 1992
Notable reuse of right-of-way: Lake Mineral Wells State Trailway

Three railroads and two streetcar companies once served Mineral Wells, a destination proclaimed as the South's greatest health resort. The community's mineral-water companies and fine hotels eventually closed, but its municipal government took the unusual step of purchasing and subsidizing the last surviving rail line to keep local trains running. Today, a refurbished masonry depot bears silent testimony to the improbable events surrounding the development and abandonment of Mineral Wells' routes.

Historical Perspective

The rolling countryside north of the Brazos River and west of Fort Worth was only sparsely inhabited at the end of the Civil War. In 1880, however, Judge James Lynch and his family announced that strange-tasting waters extracted from a local well had miraculously cured their ailments. Soon both the sick and the healthy arrived in droves to consume the mysterious solution. In less than a year, as many as a thousand campers lived in a community founded by Lynch adjacent to the "crazy woman well."

As tales of healing spread, the community, called Mineral Wells, became home to several hotels, shops, and purveyors of mineral water. To reach the community, travelers from distant cities customarily rode stagecoaches from the Texas &

Pacific depot in Weatherford. By the end of the 1880s, the expansion of local businesses made rail service a priority.

Community leaders had reason to celebrate when the Weatherford, Mineral Wells & Northwestern Railway (WMW&NW) laid its tracks from this nearby junction to Mineral Wells in 1891. Throngs of travelers soon arrived on its trains, allowing Mineral Wells to join the ranks of middle-America's premier medicinal resorts. In 1899, a prominent resident, D. G. Galbraith, who purportedly invented the paper clip, built a magnificent six-sided rooming house that heralded the community's bright future.

By the early twentieth century, the WMW&NW had proclaimed Mineral Wells to be the greatest health resort in the South. To support the rising demand for its services, it built a large brick depot near the center of town, extended its tracks northwest of Mineral Wells to Salesville and Graford, and provided convenient connections to Fort Worth and Dallas through its interchange with the Texas & Pacific at Weatherford.

The prosperity enjoyed by Mineral Wells at the turn of the century made it only a matter of time before other railroads arrived to proffer their services. In 1900, the 11-mile Gulf & Brazos Valley Railway commenced operations between Mineral Wells and Peck City (near Bennett). Although a proposed extension north to Henrietta never materialized, the carrier provided the town with an alternate route to the Texas & Pacific main line. The short line's presence in Mineral Wells, though, was brief. After the Texas & Pacific acquired control of the WMW&NW in 1902, the Gulf & Brazos Valley had virtually no hope of becoming profitable and, indeed, abandoned its entire route the following year.

The pinnacle of Mineral Wells's railroad era still lay ahead and would not be attained until the construction of a streetcar system with 10 miles of track. In 1905, the Mineral Wells & Lakewood Park Street Railway, known locally as the dinkey, began carrying travelers from the steam railway's depot to Lake Pinto, a recreational area northwest of town. Two years later, a more conventional streetcar provider, the Mineral Wells Electric Railway, initiated trolley service down Hubbard and Oak Streets.

Tourists and residents crowded onto its cars on trips between the depot, stores, and local guesthouses. Many visitors also enjoyed delightful streetcar rides to Elmhurst Park, an entertainment complex on the outskirts of the city.

Although the rise of automobile and bus travel soon pushed the streetcars toward obsolescence—the dinkey met its demise in 1909 and the trolley stopped running four years later—the WMW&NW remained one of the community's most important businesses for many more years. Its freight trains regularly included brightly painted boxcars filled with Crazy Crystals, pellets manufactured by the local Crazy Water Company. These pellets, which created a popular elixir when mixed with tap water, were shipped in large quantities to retailers in distant cities where they were in much demand at the time.

Tourism in Mineral Wells crossed several important milestones in 1912. That year, the Crazy Water Hotel, a stately seven-story institution, welcomed its first guests,

At the pinnacle of the railroad era in 1908, men clad in hats sit comfortably in the Ben Hur, a motorcar belonging to the Mineral Wells & Lakewood Park Street Railway—the smallest of five rail lines that once served the "South's greatest health resort." (Gary Hampton Collection and A. F. Weaver Collection, courtesy of Lester Haines.)

and the WMW&NW purchased a pair of gasoline-powered McKeen motorcars that allowed for substantial improvements in passenger service to Fort Worth and Dallas. The services available to travelers further improved in 1913 when the carrier granted the Gulf, Texas & Western Railway (GT&W) trackage rights over 8 miles of its route from Salesville to Mineral Wells. This allowed the Gulf, Texas & Western to begin its own "doodlebug" service between Seymour and Mineral Wells via Jacksboro. Travelers riding this gas-electric car could make convenient transfers in Mineral Wells to one of the two daily motorcars operating to Weatherford. In 1928, the Frisco acquired the GT&W with hopes of eventually creating a new route to Fort Worth. For the next several years, the railroad regularly ferried equipment through the resort town.

Many considered the Crazy Water Hotel the epitome of elegance and prestige, but the crowning achievement in Mineral Wells' rise to prominence was still ahead. The opening of the enormous fourteen-story Baker Hotel in 1929 proved to be one of the most widely anticipated events in the community's history. Equipped with extravagant hot- and cold-water baths, a bowling alley, restaurants, and other amenities, the hotel, described as "a city within a city," came to be seen as an awe-inspiring manifestation of the community's commercial success. Its 450 rooms posed such a threat to the Crazy Water Hotel that the older institution (which had been rebuilt after a devastating fire several years before) took the unusual step of erecting a large metal sign above the community's main intersection, heralding Mineral Wells as its home. This arched sign immediately became a town landmark.

Mineral Wells' role as a major tourist destination appeared secure as Lawrence Welk and Paul Whiteman brought their big bands to perform at the magnificent Baker Hotel. Although the WMW&NW ended its motorcar runs in 1929, its parent company replaced them with a motor coach (operated by Texas & Pacific Coaches, a railroad subsidiary) from Millsap, a rural station on its main line. More modest accommodations awaited those who rode the mixed train that made a round-trip every day except Sunday from Weatherford. Even as the allure of Mineral Wells' water diminished, the local economy remained buoyant, supported by the Baker Hotel's popularity and the expansion of Fort Wolters, a Texas National Guard facility at the eastern edge of town.

Changing Times

Throughout the country, rail freight and passenger traffic suffered as highways improved and the Great Depression hampered business conditions. In Mineral Wells, these factors manifested themselves through the cancellation of Gulf, Texas & Western's doodlebug service in 1935 and the abandonment of the WMW&NW line from Salesville to Graford the following year. The Frisco abandoned GT&W service south of Jacksboro in 1939 in anticipation of selling the short line to the Rock Island, which prompted the WMW&NW to abandon the Mineral Wells–Salesville segment in 1941.

The railroad's business took a fortuitous turn when Fort Wolters became an Infantry Replacement Training Center for the U.S. Army shortly after America's entry into World War II. The railway even built a 4.5-mile spur to the military installation, helping the camp become one of the country's largest training centers. From 1942 to 1945, Fort Wolters generated more than 400,000 passenger trips, mostly on chartered trains, along with large freight shipments.

The closing of the army base in 1946, however, was a blow that took Mineral Wells years to overcome. In 1947, the beleaguered

The grounds adjacent to the renovated WMW&NW depot and recreational trail (foreground) are today the site of Mineral Wells' annual Crazy Water Festival. (Photo by author.)

Crazy Water Hotel was sold to a religious organization. That same year the railway scrapped its last steam locomotive and began to rely exclusively on its parent company, Texas & Pacific, for its motive power. In the 1950s, the mixed train disappeared from the parent company's timetables. Passengers could still ride the streamlined Texas Eagle and other trains to Millsap and then finish their journey to Mineral Wells by bus, but as automobiles became more widely available, fewer apparently did so.

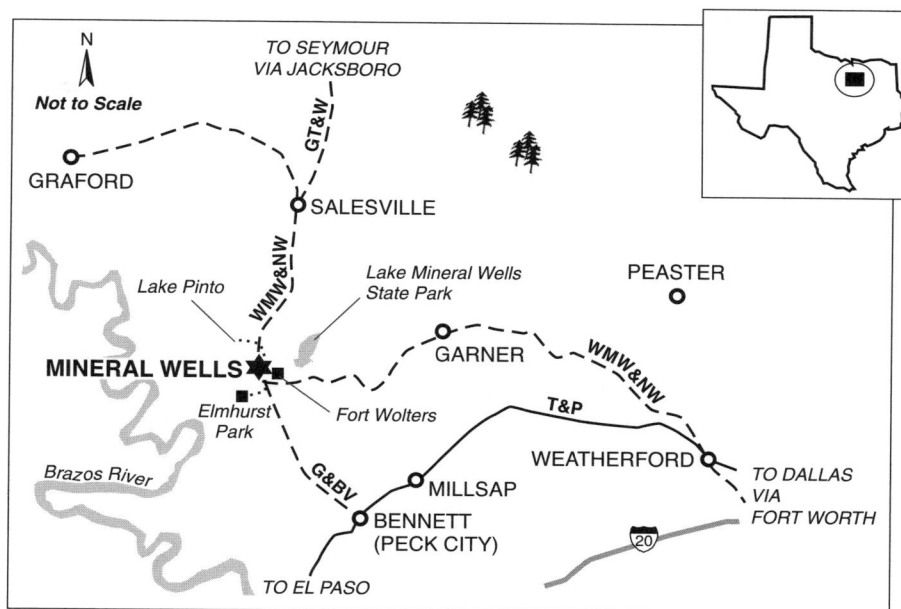

Institutions that were once the pride of Mineral Wells gradually passed into oblivion. The fabled six-sided house built by Galbraith (the Hexagon) was unceremoniously demolished to make room for a service station in 1959. The Texas & Pacific stopped operating buses to Mineral Wells the following year and discontinued its remaining passenger trains on its main line through Weatherford in 1967. Although the community established the Crazy Water Festival in 1970, many vacant buildings spoiled the look of its downtown district. The Baker Hotel shut its doors in 1972.

In an attempt to attract tourists, officials took steps to showcase their community. In 1982, the Baker Hotel earned a spot on the National Register of Historic Places. Two years later, the WMW&NW depot was added to the register, and the newly formed Palo Pinto Historical Foundation embarked on a variety of initiatives to commemorate the past. As retail and commercial activity shifted to the edge of town, however, the condition of the downtown district deteriorated further. With its broken windows and boarded-up doorways, the Baker epitomized the community's plight. Frustrations mounted when efforts by out-of-town investors to transform the hotel into a historical theme park ended unsuccessfully in 1986.

By the time Missouri Pacific (which had assimilated Texas & Pacific into its system more than a decade earlier) formally absorbed the WMW&NW in 1988, the abandonment of Mineral Wells' oldest rail line appeared imminent. Fearful that loss of the railroad would aggravate the community's economic woes, the municipal government purchased the Mineral Wells–Weatherford route for approximately $50,000 in 1989. As part of the

purchase agreement, the government agreed to return the right-of-way to Union Pacific (the parent company of Missouri Pacific) if rail service was discontinued within twenty years.

Community officials arranged to have the newly created Mineral Wells & Eastern Railway provide freight service to the handful of shippers still using the line, including CanTex, a producer of plastic pipe. Unfortunately, instead of the hoped-for railroad renaissance, the officials encountered a host of financial problems. In the spring of 1992, subsidies to the railroad emerged as a budgetary concern, and the leading mayoral candidates spoke out against their continuation. Following the election, at the end of September 1992, the municipality terminated payments to the carrier. Railroad officials asserted that the cancellation of service was illegal due to the absence of federal approval for abandonment. In response, the city agreed to payments that would keep the railroad running, but only through the following month.

Considering the devastating effects of motor carrier competition on local railroads, it seems ironic that during the final week of rail service a train destroyed the trailer of a combination truck. (The driver was not seriously hurt.) Only a few days later, during October 1992, the rail carrier delivered its final freight shipment. To mark the end, the train's engineer ceremoniously blew the locomotive's horn and the local newspaper, the *Mineral Wells Index*, printed a commemorative photograph on its front page.

Abandonment's Legacy

The railroad's demise rendered Mineral Wells, a city with more than 16,000 inhabitants, one of the largest communities in Texas to have lost its rail service. After abandonment, a Louisiana short line acquired the locomotive and freight cars, and a scrap crew removed the tracks.

As local industry slumped, officials turned once again to tourism and recreation to stimulate the economy. In 1993, the historical foundation established the Famous Mineral Water Company, a purveyor of mineral water, in the same buildings once used by the health-drink provider of the same name. When an archaeological evaluation revealed that the former railroad right-of-way between Mineral Wells and Weatherford had few historically significant structures, officials moved forward with a plan to transform the route into a recreational trail. Union Pacific, however, questioned the plan's legality, arguing that the trail's creation violated the original purchase agreement stipulating that the city return the right-of-way after service ceased. To settle the disagreement, the municipal government offered the carrier compensation totaling several hundred thousand dollars.

Public agencies invested another $1.4 million in the Lake Mineral Wells State Trailway in 1996 and made it the cornerstone of a campaign to tap into the community's tourism potential. With an eye to the past, the Lake Mineral Wells State Park, steward of both the trail and a nearby recreation area, put a caboose on display near the Mineral Wells depot.

Epilogue

Perhaps the broadest lesson that can be the learned from Mineral Wells' experience is the necessity for municipalities to develop credible strategic plans for developing new sources of revenue before embarking on investments in light-density lines. Mineral Wells did not have the benefit of such a plan, nor did it put into place an institutional structure that would shield its rail operator from short-term political or budgetary problems facing the city, discouraging this operator from patiently pursuing new revenue opportunities.

Today downtown Mineral Wells is a mere skeleton of the place that welcomed so many visitors years ago. Empty stores and the Crazy Water Hotel's unlikely incarnation as a retirement home bring to mind the market forces that bankrupted many local businesses years ago.

Without the crowds, the streetcars, or the famous metal sign (unceremoniously dismantled and scrapped years ago), one is forced to imagine what this area once was like.

The community has a strong commitment to honoring its past—a commitment exemplified by its refurbished depot, restored mineral-water building, and Little Rock Schoolhouse Museum. In the museum, artifacts and photographs from the railroad era and scale models of both Crazy Crystal boxcars and the Hexagon provide a glimpse of earlier times.

To understand the fervor of a bygone era, however, it is said that one must attend the annual Crazy Water Festival on the former depot grounds. Attracting many visitors who indulge in the town's mineral water and admire the once-magnificent Baker Hotel building in the distance, this festival rekindles, if only momentarily, the spirit of the "South's greatest health resort."

For Further Study

SUGGESTED READING:

Haines, Lester. "The Weatherford, Mineral Wells & Northwestern Railway Company and Other Rail Services in Mineral Wells, Texas." *Journal of Texas Shortline Railroads* 3, no. 4 (March–April 1999): 1–58.

Weaver, A. F. *Time Was in Mineral Wells: A Crazy Story but True.* Mineral Wells, Tex.: A. F. Weaver, 1975, 73–85.

Zlatkovich, Charles P. *Texas & Pacific Railway: Operations and Traffic.* El Paso, Tex.: Westerner Press, 1998, 57, 83–84, 121–25.

OTHER PRINCIPAL REFERENCES:

Fielder, Winnie Beatrice. "A History of Mineral Wells, Texas: 1870–1953." Master's thesis, University of Texas, 1953, 139–41.

Goen, Steve Allen. *Texas & Pacific: Color Pictorial.* La Miranda, Calif.: Four Ways West Publications, 1997, 39–103, 122, 130.

Lewis, Edward. *American Shortline Railway Guide.* 4th ed. Waukesha, Wis.: Kalmbach Books, 1991, 165.

Payne, H. L. *Three Railroads to Mineral Wells.* Mineral Wells, Tex.: H. L. Payne, 1971, 1–21.

Reed, G. S. *A History of Texas Railroads.* Houston, Tex.: St. Clair Publishing, 1914, 366, 453.

Zlatkovich, Charles P. *Texas Railroads.* Austin: University of Texas, 1981, 71, 72, 94.

PARK CITY, UTAH (7,371)

Historic operators: Crescent Tramway; Denver & Rio Grande Western Railroad;
Union Pacific Railroad; Utah Eastern Railway
Last route abandoned: 1989
Notable reuse of right-of-way: Historic Union Pacific Rail Trail

ark City's place in western railroad history extends beyond its days as a great silver-mining center. As the community's economy shifted toward winter recreation, thousands of skiers arrived on "snow trains" from Salt Lake City and rode the fondly remembered "skier subway" through one of Park City's most famous mines on their way to the mountaintop. Had at least one of the community's rail lines survived, it seems likely that passenger trains would once again be a part of contemporary Park City's winter activities.

Historical Perspective

The strikingly beautiful valley on the eastern slopes of the Wasatch Mountains had not yet been explored when mountain man Jedediah Smith traveled through the territory on his way to California in 1823. Twenty-four years later, another legendary figure, Brigham Young, skirted the valley while searching for a new home for his contingent of Mormon faithful. The Mormons founded Salt Lake City that same year and established a viable economy in a region that had long been considered unsuitable for settlement. By 1850, many travelers were using a toll road linking Salt Lake City to Parley's Park, an area in the valley some 30 miles east.

Federal authorities sent troops to the Parley's Park area in 1858 to "restrain the unruly Mormons," but called them back with the out-break of the Civil War. In late 1868, soldiers from Fort Douglas prospecting in the area discovered silver. After marking the spot with a flag, they returned the following spring and created the Flagstaff Mine. This mine and others proved enormously productive, attracting large numbers of men to ramshackle mining camps in the valley. In 1872, pioneers George and Rhoda Snyder named one of the camps Parley's Park City. The word Parley, the name of a Mormon apostle, was soon dropped from the name.

Despite the demonstrated potential of its underground mines, the fledgling community had difficulty attracting a railroad. The townspeople waited until December 1880 for the first Utah Eastern Railroad train to arrive over a narrow-gauge route from Coalville. A second carrier, the standard-gauge Summit County Railroad, which the Union Pacific controlled, was not far behind and completed its own line from Coalville later

255

A Park City Ski Special—the Hootspa Special—works the uphill grade near Coalville in the winter of 1969. The Wasatch Mountains in the background provide spectacular scenery. (Photo by Ralph Gochnour, collection of Don Strack.)

that month. This route originated at Echo, a junction on the nation's first transcontinental railroad, and was almost immediately renamed the Park City & Echo Railroad, another Union Pacific subsidiary.

Park City's railroads competed vigorously for the silver-ore and coal business over the next several years. The tracks of the Park City & Echo and the Utah Eastern were parallel to each other through Silver Creek Canyon, diverged near Atkinson and converged once more at Park City. Although the Park City & Echo had a larger passenger business, the Utah Eastern offered local businesses greater hope for improved mobility because of its plan to build through Parley's Canyon, thereby providing a more direct route to Salt Lake City.

The city did not escape the chronic cycles of boom and bust intrinsic to silver mining in the late nineteenth century—a problem aggravated by water accumulation in the mines. The Ontario Mining Company responded to flooding problems in 1881 by installing a massive Cornish pump, capable of removing more than three million gallons of water per day. By the following year, it had made enough progress to allow a resurgence in production. In the midst of this mining boom, the Crescent Mining Company completed a 5-mile tramway in 1883, consisting of 30-inch-gauge tracks to haul ore from the Thaynes Canyon west of town to the foot of Main Street.

Although the mining industry's recovery was soon complete, the townspeople's desires for major improvements in rail service continued to go unfulfilled. Not only did the Utah Eastern fail to extend its route to Salt Lake City as many had hoped, but it also came under the control of Union Pacific in 1883, giving the latter company a monopoly on local rail service. Although Park City became an incorporated community in 1884 and grew to more than 5,000 inhabitants before the end of the decade, its rail system diminished when Union Pacific dismantled its former rival's route in 1887, disheartening those who hoped that the community's transportation problems would be quickly resolved.

Over the next several years, officials became increasingly desperate to restore rail competition and gain a less circuitous route to Salt Lake City. Relief came in the form of the Utah Central Railway (a successor to the Salt Lake & Eastern Railway), which completed a narrow-gauge line to Park City in 1890. Its trains passed through Parley's Canyon and reached the center of town on the former Utah Eastern right-of-way, providing—at last—direct service to Salt Lake City.

With abundant rail transportation now available, Park City weathered the catastrophic fall in silver mining following the panic of 1893. By the time Utah entered statehood in 1896, its famed Ontario Mine had become one of the most productive sources of silver in the West. Commensurate with the community's rising status, both Park City & Echo and Utah Central built large Queen Anne-style depots. When a fire in 1898 destroyed more than 300 buildings in Park City (but neither of the depots), the community's railroads helped in the task of rebuilding the devastated neighborhoods.

Park City benefited greatly from the investments made by its common-carrier railroads. By 1900, the Utah Central had come under the control of the Denver & Rio Grande Railway (Rio Grande), realigned and regraded portions of its corridor, and widened the tracks to standard gauge. Although the Crescent Tramway ceased operation and was dismantled around the century's end, the Rio Grande (former Utah Central) and Union Pacific (former Park City & Echo) remained engines of municipal prosperity. The construction of many fine buildings, including the Miners Hospital in 1904, suggested that great prosperity lay ahead.

A modest renaissance in mining during the mid-1920s offset some of Park City's woes. In 1926, the townspeople celebrated the opening of the Egyptian Theater, a large performance hall designed for movies and vaudeville shows on the former site of the Dewey Theater. The Union Pacific expanded its system of ore-hauling lines by building a branch line southeast of Park City to a mine in Keetley. It also jointly operated with the Rio Grande a spur southeast of town to the Park City Consolidated Mine (today's Deer Valley area). Although the two railroads replaced their local passenger trains with mixed trains in 1925 and 1927, respectively, each remained pillars of the municipal economy.

During the Great Depression, however, it became imperative that Park City reduce its dependence on mining—a process that began to gather momentum after the community staged the inaugural Winter Carnival in 1936. More than 500 passengers arrived on a special snow train on the Rio Grande (which had been formally renamed the Denver & Rio Grande Western Railroad), bringing renewed hopes for the community's future. This train ran from Salt Lake City to the base of the mountain that is now part of the Deer Valley ski area, and was so popular among skiers and day-trippers that it was operated again the following year.

Although the amenities were undoubtedly less extensive on Park City's mixed trains, these local runs

A large embankment on the former Union Pacific route near the edge of Park City is momentarily deserted on a chilly day in 1998. The right-of-way is now used as a recreational trail. (Photo by author.)

Changing Times

The optimism of this era gradually faded as more flooding at the mines, a sharp decline in silver prices, and the depletion of the most lucrative silver deposits weakened the region's economy. A symbol of the town's illustrious past, the Dewey Theater, collapsed in 1916 due to the weight of accumulating snow. Local rail operations suffered from the mining district's sagging production and a sharp drop in passenger revenues. By the end of World War I, two automobile stage lines were competing for the patronage of those destined for Salt Lake City.

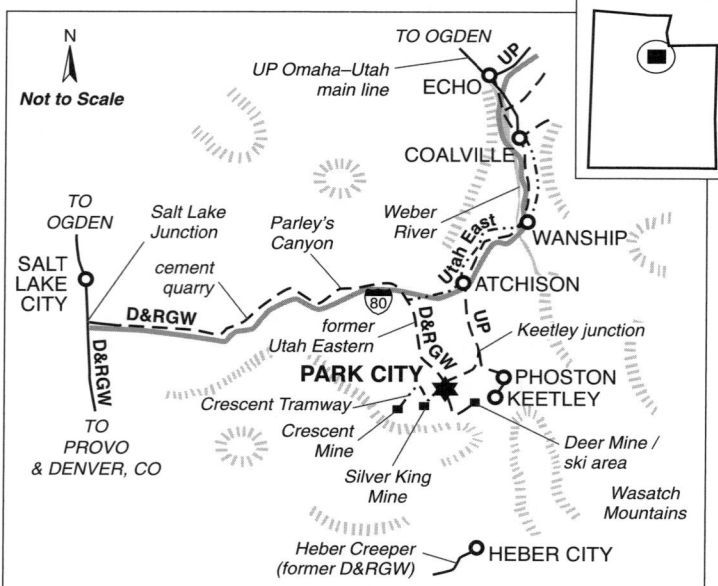

made an investment in another ski area, Treasure Mountain Resort, which opened in 1963. The Silver King Mine in 1965 began the unusual practice of operating a train equipped with specially fabricated cars to carry skiers to Treasure Mountain. After traveling several miles in darkness on the so-called skier subway, passengers rode in the mining company's elevator cage 1,700 feet to a double chair lift and on to the top of Crescent Ridge, where they began a lengthy downhill run. In the same year that the subway opened, the first snow train arrived after a hiatus of fifteen years. These trains, popularly called Hootspa Specials, attracted large numbers of passengers, many of whom took advantage of Union Pacific's ability to serve alcohol onboard.

Such memorable services left a lasting impression on visitors of this era, but neither had a place in the community's future. The subway proved less convenient than conventional chair lifts and ceased operating in 1969. Union Pacific operated its last snow train in 1972 and abandoned a 1-mile stretch of track from the center of Park City in 1978, thereby limiting its service to the community's periphery. By the end of the 1970s, trains on the Park City Branch served only a few freight customers in the region, including a local lumberyard and a Chevron Chemical Corporation plant in Phoston (near Keetley).

The community surrendered more of its industrial way of life when the last mine closed in 1982. Four years later, the Chevron plant closed its loading station (due to the opening of a phosphate-slurry pipeline), prompting Union Pacific to end regular freight service on its branch.

Abandonment's Legacy

As the Union Pacific branch lay dormant, public officials considered ambitious proposals to acquire it and build an extension from Keetley to Heber City. Such investments, they felt, could provide an efficient means of hauling gravel for the construction of the Jordanelle Dam and to forge a connection to the Heber Valley Railroad, an excursion operator popularly called the Heber Creeper. Planners looked with great interest at having this established excursion operator (which operated over a former Rio Grande branch) offer scenic rides from Heber City to Park City and possibly Coalville. Although this ambitious plan had the support of county and state transportation officials, its proponents could not overcome a variety of financial problems, including the railroad's high asking price for the right-of-way.

shouldered a heavy burden when fuel shortages limited highway travel during World War II. Union Pacific's train provided connections to the carrier's famed streamliners at Ogden and trains of lesser status at Echo. The Rio Grande offered connections to the Exposition Flyer, Mountaineer, and other trains at Salt Lake City.

Many of Park City's railroad traditions disappeared after the war. With motor travel on the rise, a government agency condemned a portion of the Rio Grande branch to allow improvements to U.S. Highway 40. In 1946, the carrier abandoned its little-used segment from a quarry deep in Parley's Canyon to Park City—a move necessitating that snow trains use the more circuitous Union Pacific route. In 1949, another difficult round of mine closings left more than a thousand workers unemployed. Although production resumed at several mines in 1953, Park City's population once again fell at a precipitous rate.

By the late 1950s, Park City was in desperate need of new sources of economic development. A new bypass on Route 40 diverted traffic away from its downtown and brought still more economic hardship. As industry retrenched, Union Pacific eliminated its mixed-train service and abandoned the segment south of Keetley (part of a route called the Ontario Branch). As the years passed, the carrier became heavily reliant on phosphate shipments to support local freight operations.

Park City may well have devolved into an obscure mountain village had it not been for its latent potential as a major center for tourism and winter recreation—a potential it began to realize after the federal government

Without opposition from the state, Union Pacific formally abandoned the route and sold the tracks to a salvaging company in early 1989. Within a few months, the tracks were gone and the right-of-way had been deeded to the state government, allowing for the creation of the Historic Union Pacific Rail Trail. Almost from its inception, this trail, extending the entire length of the branch, was one of the state's most heavily used recreation paths.

While condominiums and other modern structures sprouted up on the abandoned right-of-way near the center of town (a segment not used by the trail), rubber-tired vehicles rumbled over roads created on other abandoned routes, including portions of the former Crescent Tramway. The former Rio Grande right-of-way in Parley's Canyon became part of Interstate 80, an expressway partially following old Route 40.

Planners had little reason to reflect upon the loss of rail service until 1995, when the International Olympic Committee chose Salt Lake City to be the site of the 2002 Winter Olympic Games. Much like their counterparts more than a century before, officials bemoaned the absence of a rail line through Parley's Canyon. Passenger trains on this route, they felt, would have offered a welcome respite from automobile congestion and provided a scenic way to bring athletes and visitors from Salt Lake City to skiing venues in Park City. Although there was discussion about using the former Union Pacific rail-bed to create the "Olympic Parkway," a busway linking various athletic areas, such an endeavor never moved beyond the discussion stage. The Heber Creeper, however, earned accolades for operating steam trains that handled large numbers of international visitors to Olympic events in nearby Soldier Hollow.

Epilogue

With more than 300 buildings listed on the National Register of Historic Places, visitors will find ample testimony of Park City's prosperous past. The Egyptian Theater, renovated in 1998, is again a premier venue for live performances and is often filled to capacity during special events, such as the community's annual Sundance Film Festival. The former hospital is today a public meeting venue, while the local historical society operates the Park City Museum in the old city hall.

Some observers lament the changes that contemporary buildings have wrought on Park City's character, especially the loss of many fine edifices in the Queen Anne style. Several historic railroad structures, however, still stand. The former Rio Grande baggage building was converted into a bank (which is now closed), while the former Union Pacific depot, restored after a fire in 1985 and flanked by a historic passenger car, is today a restaurant under the stewardship of actor Robert Redford. The Union Pacific depot at Keetley has been moved to Park City and converted into a senior citizen center.

Proponents of saving Park City's last rail line had to contend with the problem that the route most suitable for passenger transportation had already been abandoned. The Union Pacific route had far less potential than the Rio Grande corridor to serve those traveling to and from Salt Lake City, making large-scale public expenditures difficult to justify. Nevertheless, with thousand of skiers converging on Park City during the winter months, it seems possible—and even probable—that snow trains would be arriving at least occasionally during the community's winter season if either of its rail lines had survived.

For Further Study

SUGGESTED READINGS:

Carr, Stephen L., and Robert W. Edwards. *Utah Ghost Railroads.* Salt Lake City: Western Epics, 1989, 94–106.

Strack, Don. "From Echo to Park City: The Story of Union Pacific's Park City Branch." *The Streamliner: The Official Publication of the Union Pacific Historical Society* 15, no. 2 (2001): 7–25.

Thomson, George A., and Fraser Buck. *Treasure Mountain Home: Park City Revisited.* Salt Lake City: Dream Garden Press, 1981, 113–16.

OTHER PRINCIPAL REFERENCES:

Arrington, Leonard J. "Utah's Coal Road in the Age of Unregulated Competition." *Utah Historical Quarterly* (Jan. 1965): 35–63.

Harop, Doug. "Park City Branch." CTC Board, 265 (Nov. 2000), 48–55.

Hilton, George W. *American Narrow Gauge Railroads.* Stanford: Stanford University Press, 1990, 531– 36.

LeMassena, Robert L. *Rio Grande. . . . To the Pacific!* Denver: Sundance Limited, 1974, 101, 109–11, 117, 161, 249.

PROMONTORY, UTAH (1)

Historic operator: Southern Pacific
Last route abandoned: 1942
Notable reuses of right-of-way: Golden Spike National Historic Site; proposed excursion railway

erhaps more than any other abandoned rail line in the United States, the historic right-of-way across Promontory Summit has come to symbolize the nation's nineteenth-century quest to tame the frontier. Along this desolate segment, officials representing the Central Pacific and Union Pacific railroads drove the final spike to complete America's first transcontinental railroad. Less well known but also historically significant is the story of the small community that existed at this desert location for many years.

Historical Perspective

The arid landscape north of the Great Salt Lake was for centuries the hunting ground for the Shoshone Indians. Due to its remote location, harsh climate, and rugged terrain, few prospective settlers had an interest in inhabiting this land. As late as the 1820s, the Shoshone roamed freely through the area on horses acquired from settlers.

As the country's population migrated west, however, European presence could be increasingly felt. The first wagon train made its way across the elevation that later became Promontory Summit in 1841. Six years later, Brigham Young's contingent of Mormons arrived in what would become the Utah Territory, creating new communities on previously unsettled land. As ranchers arrived to graze cattle, the Shoshone's presence gradually diminished.

While conducting reconnaissance in the area in 1848, Captain Howard Stansbury commented that the mountains rising up from Great Salt Lake resembled a promontory into the sea. He later capitalized the word in his writings and thus was apparently responsible for the range being called the Promontory Mountains. In 1850, this barren land became part of the newly created Utah Territory.

As surveyors examined the area's suitability for a transcontinental railroad during the 1850s, the nation was intrigued by the possibility of operating trains across the West. In 1862, the federal government authorized subsidies for the Union Pacific and Central Pacific railroads to build such a line. Although not specifying where the two railroads would meet, the U.S. Congress stipulated that the line pass over Promontory Summit, the highest point of elevation on the proposed route in the vicinity of the lake. In 1863, a peace treaty with the Shoshone rendered this area safe for construction to begin.

Several developments during the Civil War helped clear the way for the construction of this great railroad. Most importantly, the secession of southern states eliminated from Congress many representatives who strongly opposed building the line over the "central route"—opposition that had almost single-handedly stymied progress for a decade. Additionally, President Abraham Lincoln saw the railroad as a potential inducement to keep California in the Union—and to keep California gold and Nevada silver flowing to Washington. The war also made the cost of building the railroad seem somewhat less daunting to the federal government.

By late 1865, the Confederacy had surrendered, and the two railroad companies were hard at work laying track as quickly as possible, since future revenues would be apportioned by mileage. Union Pacific worked furiously in a westward direction while the Central Pacific rapidly pushed its rails to the east. As the pace of construction quickened, both carriers dispatched men to the Promontory Mountains to begin work in the area. Soon, the carriers completed the grading on parallel routes across the summit.

Recognizing the need for greater coordination between the two companies, the federal government brought representatives of the lines together in April 1869. At this meeting, the railroads agreed to end their race and join their lines at Promontory Summit. On April 28th, as the project neared completion, the Central Pacific crews laid more than 10 miles of track in one day—a record that still stands. With Promontory Summit about to become the junction between the two carriers, several businesses relocated from nearby railroad camps and created a town site.

The events that followed are deeply etched into American transportation lore. Dignitaries, reporters, musicians, photographers, and spectators soon arrived at the "town"—little more than a series of tents adjacent to the railroad tracks—to witness the driving of the last spike. On May 10, 1869, Leland Stanford, the Central Pacific's president, and Thomas Durant, a Union Pacific vice president, gently swung their mauls to tap a pair of golden spikes. As metal met metal, a telegraph signal was activated that transmitted the news around the world. Participants posed for a photograph with Union Pacific locomotive No. 119 and Central Pacific's Jupiter positioned pilot-to-pilot (nose-to-nose), an image soon reprinted across the nation.

After the fanfare ended and most of the participants in the ceremony departed, Promontory Station seemed destined to become little more than a railroad work camp. Most anticipated that the two carriers would quickly agree to move their terminal to Ogden, obviating

Promontory's streets appear desolate but nevertheless were lined with businesses at the time of this photograph, which apparently was taken shortly after the Golden Spike Ceremony. Note the boxcar in the distance. (Photo by A. J. Russell; Oakland Museum.)

the need for making significant investments in facilities at such a desolate location. Until such an agreement could be reached, however, Promontory Station (or simply Promontory) would be the interchange point for the two greatest railroad companies in the West.

Promontory earned a degree of municipal legitimacy by being organized as a precinct within Box Elder County in the autumn of 1869. As a base for railroad crews, an engine terminal, and a rest/meal stop for passengers, the community grew to several hundred people.

History would remember Promontory for the event that linked the East and the West, but many travelers of this era associated the community with gambling, prostitution, and liquor sales. Repulsed by the town's moral depravity, the *Elko Independent* likened Promontory to the biblical city of Sodom. With an economy heavily dependent on the depot, two section houses, a roundhouse, and a combination post office-store-café-school, however, Promontory managed to survive.

The outlook for Promontory turned for the worse when Union Pacific agreed in November 1869 to sell the segment between Ogden and Promontory to Central Pacific. The following month, it moved the interchange and terminal to Ogden, denying Promontory its primary source of livelihood. Although Promontory remained an eating stop and the home of a section crew as well as a helper station for Central Pacific locomotives, the population in the station's vicinity dwindled. By 1880, the precinct was home to only around 130 people.

The events affecting Promontory in subsequent years were not altogether negative. After Southern Pacific

absorbed Central Pacific into its system in 1885, the company expanded the engine house, built a larger turntable, and equipped its helper station with more powerful locomotives. Ranching in the area also grew, especially at the Promontory Stock Ranch Company, an enterprise owned by the family of Charles Crocker, one of Central Pacific's founders. Despite a severe winter during 1887, which greatly thinned the ranch's herd, Promontory retained the semblance of a functional community.

Promontory still clung rather precariously to its role as a railroad town when Utah achieved statehood in 1896. Business ebbed and flowed with the arrival and departure of trains. Eateries fed crowds of varying sizes when passenger trains stopped but otherwise had few customers. The section crews living in the town, once almost entirely Chinese, were now primarily Italian.

Changing Times

Southern Pacific had long struggled with the difficult grades on the line through Promontory, where trains had to overcome the second steepest grade on the entire transcontinental route. Westbound trains climbed nearly 700 feet in a mere 3 miles to reach Promontory Summit. The costs of keeping the workers and helper locomotives available to support the operations on the route were a major financial burden.

Seeking relief from these problems, the railroad moved forward in 1902 with the construction of the Lucin Cutoff, a new route through western Utah. Equipped with an enormous trestle and causeway over the Great Salt Lake, the cutoff would slash travel distances by 40 miles. The completion of this enormously complex project in 1904 was a milestone in western railroad history.

Southern Pacific kept the original route, called the Promontory Branch or the Old Line, as an alternative route in the event that high waters prevented safe passage on the cutoff. Although the railroad continued to operate a mixed train and freight train regularly through Promontory and kept a section crew in town, there was a decided aura of withdrawal about the community. The railroad closed the engine house and depot, leaving local residents without an eating house. The postmaster moved to nearby Corinne, and the ranch company moved its headquarters elsewhere.

Clapboards next to a rebuilt segment of track demarcate the location of what was once a viable community and a notable passenger-train stop. (Photo by author.)

Surprisingly few people expressed regret that a community so deeply rooted in American history was slowly withering away. By 1909, both of the locomotives present at the historic ceremony had been sold for scrap. During the 1910s, Promontory's viability as a community rested tenuously on an agricultural technique known as dry farming. Farmers using this technique brought surrounding acreage into cultivation on an every-other-year cycle, allowing the soil to accumulate moisture. These tillers of the soil depended heavily on the mixed train making a round-trip each week between Brigham City and Montello, Nevada—a local run called the Alkali Flyer due to the salty terrain it crossed.

Promontory's worsening plight after World War I elicited little concern from the outside world. The townspeople anticipated that visitors would arrive into their community in 1919 to celebrate the fiftieth anniversary of the Golden Spike Ceremony, only to experience the humiliation of having no one come. During the 1920s, the viability of dry farming diminished sharply, and many farmers found themselves unable to repay their loans. When Southern Pacific closed the section house in 1930, the outlook for Promontory was unequivocally grim. The Great Depression and severe drought in 1934 further hampered the economy, weakening cattle herds to the point that they had to be removed by rail. In the process, the combination school-store closed and Promontory, for all practical purposes, ceased to exist.

Southern Pacific reduced service on the Old Line to twice weekly before discontinuing all regular service on the route in 1938. Two years later, the last passenger train to operate the entire length of the line—a special carrying the Daughters of Utah Pioneers—passed through the former town site. After the Japanese attack on Pearl Harbor, the national drive for salvage materials raised interest in scrapping the route. In 1942, officials met at Promontory to commemorate the "undriving" of the last spike, an event, ironically, marking the beginning of a period of renewed appreciation for the town site.

Abandonment's Legacy

Soon after the ceremony, the removal of the tracks was under way. Some of the rail was relaid at the Utah Quartermaster Depot in Ogden. Other rail was too worn for military use and had to be scrapped. Southern Pacific retained ownership of the corridor to keep its options open (in case problems prevented use of the Lucin Cutoff) but authorized the construction of a pipeline along the right-of-way.

Few other events of any consequence took place on the piece of land formerly called Promontory until the Golden Spike Association staged the first annual reenactment of the original ceremony in 1951. Five years later, the federal government designated the location a National Historic Site in nonfederal ownership. In 1965, approximately 2,700 acres of land surrounding the old railroad grade, including the historic site, came under the stewardship of the National Park Service.

By then, only a few scattered homes remained in the vicinity of the former town. These structures were moved or razed in 1966 to allow for the creation of the Golden Spike National Historic Site at Promontory Summit. Three years later, the Park Service relaid approximately 1,000 feet of track for the centennial celebration of the Golden Spike Ceremony, which drew 28,000 spectators, including movie star John Wayne, who arrived by helicopter. In 1979, it relaid another stretch, extending about a mile and a half, to accommodate full-size replicas of Jupiter and No. 119—locomotives used by the Park Service during the summer for demonstrations and weekend reenactments of the original ceremony. In 1944, the agency transformed the railroad grade west of the summit into the National Back Country Byway, a 90-mile recreational trail.

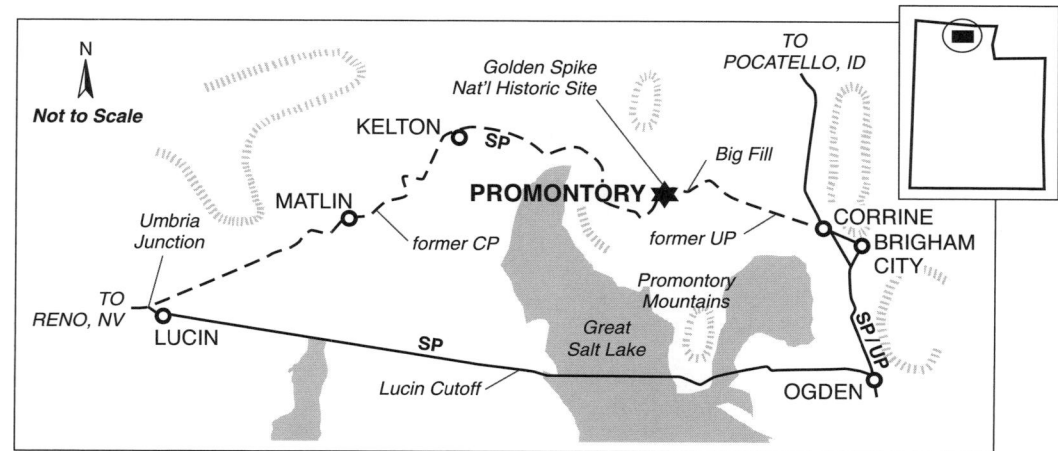

Shortly thereafter, a private group, the Golden Spike Heritage Foundation, announced its interest in rebuilding 26 miles of the historical railroad grade for an excursion railway. The group envisioned this route linking Promontory to Corinne, where the abandoned route meets an active Union Pacific main line, and reported that some of the rails salvaged in 1942 (by this time in storage at the Quartermaster Depot) were available for this effort.

Proponents of the project, however, encountered several notable obstacles. Union Pacific's concerns about the safety of operating trains over its active main line through Corinne precluded from serious consideration the idea of having excursion trains originate in Ogden or Salt Lake City. Planners raised questions about the project's potential impact on significant archaeological structures and on wetlands in a waterfowl sanctuary west of Corinne. The pipeline under the rail grade, maintained by Chevron, added to the complexity of the initiative and, along with other obstacles, pushed the costs of rebuilding the segment from Corinne to Promontory to at least $36 million.

Recognizing the sensitive issues surrounding the proposal, the National Park Service remained officially neutral about the so-called Rails-to-Promontory movement. Although the state appropriated $350,000 for an environmental impact study in 1996, funding issues could not be resolved. Nevertheless, on an intermittent basis, the Golden Spike Heritage Association continues to champion an excursion railway from its headquarters in the former Union Pacific depot at Brigham City.

Epilogue

Unlike other bygone communities that were created to serve the railroad industry, Promontory for all practical purposes ceased being a viable town before its rail line closed. Today, only the park ranger lives at the historic town site. A small group of ranchers tending their herds southeast of the historic site often refer to themselves as the community of Promontory. They live, however, a considerable distance from the former settlement of that name.

Visitors who follow the abandoned railroad grade will find numerous trestles and culverts along the National Back Country Byway and on the unused right-of-way between Promontory and Corinne. East of the renowned location where the final spike was driven, the Big Fill, an immense embankment built by Union Pacific, crosses a shallow canyon. Nearby, portions of the Central Pacific grade destined never to become an active railroad survive as a monument to the race to lay track through the region.

Travelers hoping to find evidence of the former town will have to settle for several images of buildings painted onto large wooden panels at the National Historic Site. These colorful displays recall a settlement that, after rising quickly to the forefront of western railroading, was left to slowly wither away.

For Further Study

SUGGESTED READINGS:

Best, Gerald. *Iron Rails to Promontory*. San Marino, Calif.: Golden West Books, 1969, 52–53.

Carr, Stephen L., and Robert W. Edwards, *Utah Ghost Railroads*. Salt Lake City: Western Epics, 1989, 94–106.

Golden Spike National Historic Site. *The Last Spike Site: History at a Glance*. Promontory, Utah: Golden Spike National Historic Site, n.d., 176.

Stewart, John J. *The Iron Trail to the Golden Spike*. New York: Meadow Lark Press, 1994, 215–79,

OTHER PRINCIPAL REFERENCES:

Raymond, Anan S., and Richard E. Fike. *Rails East to Promontory: The Utah Stations*. Cultural Resource Series. Salt Lake City: Utah State Office, Bureau of Land Management, 1994, 100.

Hofsommer, Donovan L. *The Southern Pacific: 1901–1985*. College Station: Texas A&M University Press, 1986, 3, 15–17, 192, 275.

Rea, John C. "Revival at Promontory." *National Railway Historical Society Bulletin* 44, no. 5 (1979): 11–12, 46.

BOTHELL, WASHINGTON (30,150)

Historic operator: Northern Pacific Railway
Last route abandoned: 1985
Notable reuses of right-of-way: Burke-Gilman Trail; Sammamish River Trail

*B*othell's experiences illustrate the wide range of problems that can hinder the reuse of an abandoned right-of-way. From a landmark court decision that embittered landowners along the route to the incarceration of an adolescent who pushed a companion from an old railroad trestle, this town's saga exemplifies the potential difficulties—and dangers—of bringing disused rail corridors into the public realm.

Historical Perspective

At the end of the Civil War, much of present-day Bothell was part of a large marshland called the Squak Slough. Although seemingly blessed with a favorable location near the northern edge of Lake Washington, it remained separated from the general flow of commerce. Patterns of development began to change after the pioneering George Brackett established a landing on the slough in the early 1870s. Soon thereafter, logging companies were harvesting the area's tall stands of timber and floating thousands of logs down the river. When the logs reached the lake, boomers gathered them for flotation to sawmills.

Businesses around the lake flourished after the Northern Pacific Railroad made its historic entry into Seattle in 1883. George Brackett constructed a large home near the landing in 1884; David Bothell and his wife Mary Ann arrived in the area the following year. The Bothells bought 80 acres of Brackett's property and worked to attract others to the area while offering lodging in their home.

A horse-drawn tramway with tracks consisting of wooden logs 6 inches in diameter allowed logs to be transported to the slough with greater efficiency. Local residents could not, however, fully share in the region's economic boom until a more conventional rail line, the Seattle, Lake Shore & Eastern Railway (Lake Shore), laid track south of the landing in 1887. Following the shores of the lake and slough and equipped with a spur to the landing, this line greatly lowered the cost of transportation between Seattle and Woodinville, an established community east of Bothell. Under the leadership of Thomas Burke and Daniel Gilman, the railroad soon initiated suburban passenger service and, in 1889, extended its route east to North Bend, the foot of the Snoqualmie Pass.

The same year the railway reached North Bend, a great fire destroyed most of the Seattle business district. This event greatly stimulated the demand for forestry products and led to the creation of many shingle and lumber mills along the lake. By late 1889, a small community had been created adjacent to the landing—a place the local postmaster named Bothell after noting that an unusually large portion of its residents had this name. Indeed, David and Mary Ann Bothell—owners

A Northern Pacific W-3 Mikado locomotive pulling a string of cars hugs the shoulder of a road several miles east of Bothell, near Woodinville, circa 1946. With motor travel on the rise, regularly scheduled passenger service on this route had ended years before. (Photo by Douglas S. Leach; courtesy of Rick W. Leach and Northern Pacific Railway Historical Association.)

of the Bothell Hotel—remained prominent townspeople; their son George was the community's first mayor and a partial owner of the George Bothell Lumber Company, one of the village's most successful businesses.

Despite the Lake Shore's importance to the communities it served, the carrier was never far from serious financial difficulty. After abandoning a plan to establish service between Seattle and Spokane—a project that would have required it to cross the mighty Cascades—it turned its attention to the more modest goal of interlining traffic with the Canadian Pacific. To achieve this objective, it built north from Woodinville to Sumas (a small town near the Canadian border) and established an interchange in 1891.

Those hoping that the Canadian Pacific connection would finally allow the Lake Shore to become a consistently profitable railway were left disappointed. Although the Lake Shore interchanged a considerable amount of traffic at Sumas, it was forced into receivership in 1893. The carrier became part of the newly formed Seattle &

International Railway in 1896 and was formally absorbed into the Northern Pacific Railway five years later. Not only did this line never become the major long-distance route many had hoped, it handled a diminishing share of the region's traffic after Northern Pacific opened the Lake Washington Belt Line between Renton and Woodinville in 1904. This new line diverted freight and, later, passenger traffic away from the older route between Seattle and Woodinville.

Despite the diminished role of the former Lake Shore, passengers using the route benefited from gradual improvements in service. In 1905, a new tunnel (jointly owned by Northern Pacific and a subsidiary of the Great Northern Railway) provided trains with a more efficient route into downtown Seattle. The following year, trains began operating into Seattle's King Street Station. In 1907, the Soo-Pacific Train Deluxe, a train originating in St. Paul, Minnesota, and principally using Soo Line and Canadian Pacific rail, began using the route through Bothell. The Seattle section of this superbly furnished train operated over the Northern Pacific south of Sumas and made a station stop in Woodinville.

Upon Bothell's incorporation in 1908, its population stood at 600 and its transportation system was blossoming. Rail service was vitally important to the American Hotel, Bothell Hotel, two shingle mills, and other local businesses. Riverboats worked their way through the slough (which had been dredged and renamed Sammamish River) in competition with Northern Pacific trains. Over the brick-surfaced Pacific Highway, completed in 1913, the Bothell Stage Company (an entity affiliated with the Pacific Northwest Traction Company, a prominent interurban railway) provided bus service to Seattle. A private railway operated by the French & Woodin Logging Company, meanwhile, helped support the lumber industry's expansion by hauling logs to the slough.

Changing Times

Such a colorful array of services remained part of life in Bothell for only a few years. Riverboats made their last trips in 1917, when nearby Lake Washington was lowered for the construction of the Lake Washington Ship Canal—a massive engineering effort that prevented navigation of the Sammamish. Sleeping-car service through the Sumas interchange ended that same year. The Bothell Hotel closed around 1918, and the American Hotel burned in 1926.

Logging companies gradually abandoned the practice of floating logs to sawmills on the lake. Although Northern Pacific freights dispatched from Woodinville served Bothell's lumberyards, its feed mill, and other businesses, the carrier was unable to justify continued passenger service on the line, which ended with the cancellation of a Seattle–Bellingham train in 1938. Four years later, fire destroyed Bothell's last shingle mill, ending the community's role as a major lumber center.

Freight traffic on the line surged during World War II but diminished sharply after hostilities ceased. Even so, the Bothell station remained important to the Northern Pacific, serving customers in a relatively large geographic area. In the 1960s, the carrier equipped this facility with a hip roof and garage door for less-than-carload shipments and delighted local railroad enthusiasts by periodically operating Casey Jones excursion trains through town. Nevertheless, by the end of the decade, the excursions had ended and the local station had closed.

After Northern Pacific merged into the newly created Burlington Northern

system in 1970, the new operator improved its interchange facilities in Sedro Woolley, allowing it to reroute certain Seattle-bound freight trains from the Woodinville/Bothell line to the former Great Northern main line. In 1972, the carrier abandoned the Kenmore–Seattle segment and razed the Bothell depot. Burlington Northern continued service between Woodinville and Kenmore, but its last regular customer in Bothell, the Walters Feed Mill, no longer shipped by rail.

Public agencies grew more interested in using the rail corridor for nonindustrial purposes. In 1978, the King County government converted 12 miles of the abandoned segment between Kenmore and Seattle into the Burke-Gilman Trail, one of America's first rail-trail projects (and named in honor of two of the Lake Shore's legendary promoters). Hoping for an extension of the trail through Bothell, some people looked forward to the day when the railroad discontinued using the remaining Kenmore–Woodinville portion.

By the time the railroad industry was partially deregulated in 1980, Bothell had almost 8,000 residents—a nearly tenfold increase in population since the days of its last passenger train—and little apparent need for rail-freight service. Situated at the intersection of five highway routes, including the Interstate 405 bypass around Seattle, Bothell prospered from its advantageous location

The former Northern Pacific trestle across the Sammamish River in Bothell, photographed in 1996, attracted notoriety before being retrofitted for recreational use. (Photo by author.)

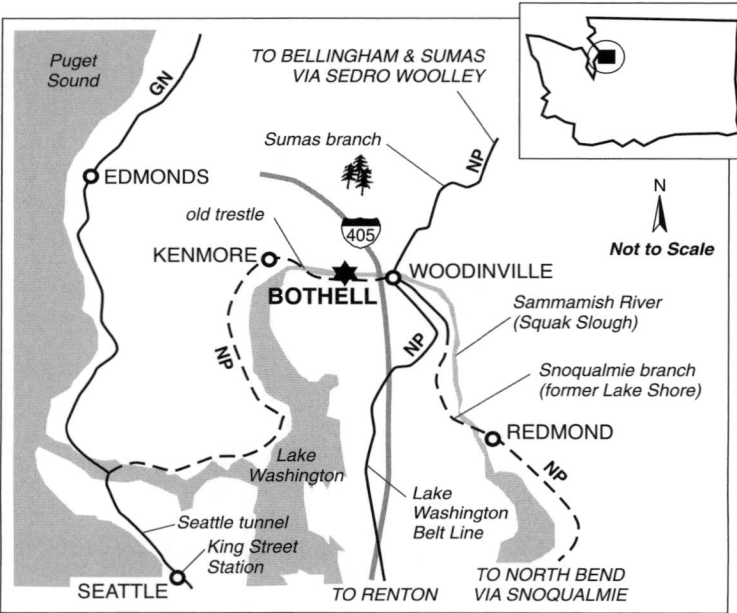

After reviewing the original deeds, however, the court determined that much of the land was owned not by the plaintiffs but by the descendents of the original landowners. Accordingly, the county paid $1.3 million to the newly identified owners, further embittering some residents living along the route who ultimately were left without compensation.

Meanwhile, Bothell continued to grow at a spectacular rate. Its population nearly doubled in 1992 when the municipal government annexed almost 6 square miles of north of the community, including a branch campus of the University of Washington. That same year, the county completed the long-anticipated link between the two recreational trails. This extension of the Burke-Gilman Trail, built partially on the abandoned route (including the entire length of the old spur to the landing) as well as on nonrailroad land at the east end of the town, created a continuous 27-mile greenway between Seattle and Lake Sammamish.

Another emotionally charged situation developed when the municipal government evaluated a plan to transform a portion of the abandoned route into a highway bypass. In response to mounting opposition, local planners opted instead to use this segment, including a trestle over the river (which was not used by the Burke-Gilman Trail), to create a spur linking the recreational trail to the community's Blythe Park. This proved be a fateful decision, for in early 1996, one teenager deliberately pushed another from the trestle into the river as a result of a drug-related bet. A stormy local debate ensued, and the chief instigator was convicted of second-degree murder in 1997.

The incident once again stirred local emotion in 1998 when a judge ordered a new trial that led to a plea bargain resulting in a sentence reduction. Recognizing the need for safety improvements, the county closed the wooden trestle until it could install protective fencing.

Fortunately, other efforts to showcase Bothell's historical landmarks had less contentious outcomes. Several lovely nineteenth-century homes as well as the Pioneer Cemetery, where the city's founders are buried, earned representation on the National Register of Historic Places during the 1990s. The Bothell Historical Society and the municipal government made gradual improvements to the Park at Bothell Landing, which encompassed a log cabin, home, and schoolhouse dating back to the nineteenth century. The Bothell depot sign, donated by a railroad enthusiast, was put on display in the schoolhouse.

but lacked sufficient parks and recreational facilities. Burlington Northern's track, serving only a building supply company in Kenmore, was seen as an obstacle to the creation of these new civic amenities. Although local officials in Kenmore wanted rail service to continue, Burlington Northern abandoned the deteriorating 5-mile segment in December 1985 and brought the local railroad era to a close.

Abandonment's Legacy

The county wasted little time in developing plans to use the abandoned segment for a trail extension. It soon announced that it had acquired the 5-mile stretch from Burlington Northern for several hundred thousand dollars and hailed this segment as the missing link between the Burke-Gilman Trail and Sammamish River Trail, two prominent recreational paths serving the area. Under Washington law, the county's acquisition of the route precluded any need to return the land to those specified in the railroad charter.

This transaction culminated in a legal battle sharply dividing those living along the route. Adjacent property owners questioned the constitutionality of the county's acquisition and pursued legal action that reached the Washington State Supreme Court in 1986. In *Lawson v. State*, the high court ruled that the county's appropriation of the rail-trail was the unconstitutional taking of private property, a decision with broad national implications.

Like many expanding suburbs faced with serious traffic congestion, Bothell struggled to provide alternatives to the automobile in the late twentieth century. Although proposals for commuter-rail lines in the Seattle area did not include Bothell, plans for creating a transit center at the university campus and high-occupancy vehicle lanes on Interstate 405 moved forward in 2001. Some, however, criticized the plans to expand the capacity of Interstate 405, already the state's busiest road, as inadequate for failing to make allowances for light-rail service to Seattle-Tacoma Airport.

Epilogue

Much has changed in Bothell since passenger trains and steamboats vied for customers' loyalties many years ago. Today the community is widely known for its abundance of corporate jobs and high standard of living. Its downtown district is lined with upscale restaurants and boutiques.

Visitors following Bothell's abandoned rights-of-way will find the trail one of the community's most popular amenities. Little else remains of the railroad except a portion of the underpass on 96th Avenue and a few strips of rail on Riverside Drive (part of the former rail line not used by the recreational trail). The depot, feed mill, and shingle mills, however, have gone the way of the Soo-Pacific Train Deluxe.

The saga of the Lake Shore and its predecessors will remain a notable chapter in Washington railroad history. Many residents, however, will remember this corridor mostly for the turbulent legal issues that arose after the last train left town. As their experiences show, reusing the corridors left behind by railroads can have profound and unanticipated ramifications.

For Further Study

SUGGESTED READINGS:

Armbruster, Kurt E. *Orphan Road: The Railroad Comes to Seattle, 1853–1911.* Pullman: Washington State University Press, 1999, 121–41, 201–2.

Evans, Jack. *Little History of Bothell, Washington.* Seattle: WCS Publications, 1988, 122.

Stickney, Amy Eunice, and Lucile McDonald. *Squak Slough: 1870–1920.* Bothell, Wash.: Friends of Bothell Library, 1977, 21–55.

OTHER PRINCIPAL REFERENCES:

Dubin, Arthur D. *More Classic Trains.* Milwaukee, Wis.: Kalmbach Publishing, 1974, 282–88.

Prosser, William Farrand. *A History of the Puget Sound Country.* New York: Lewis Publishers, 1903, 2:163–64.

Renz, Louis Tuck. *The History of the Northern Pacific Railroad.* Fairfield, Wash.: Ye Galleon Press, 1980, 141, 195, 197.

Robertson, Donald B. *Encyclopedia of Western Railroad History.* Caldwell, Idaho.: Caxton Printers, 1995, 3:261, 265–67.

Strand, Thomas. "Snoqualmie Branch '45." *The Mainstreeter: Official Publication of the Northern Pacific Railway Historical Association* 20, no. 4 (2001): 4–13.

Vesper, Stuart, and Walter Grecula. "The King Street Story." *The Great Northern Goat.* Great Northern Railway Historical Society 103, Reference Sheet no. 285 (June 2000).

ISSAQUAH, WASHINGTON (11,212)

Historic operator: Northern Pacific Railway
Last route abandoned: 1998
Notable reuses of right-of-way: Issaquah Valley Trolley; Sammamish Trail

erhaps no other corridor more profoundly illustrates the lengths to which some property owners are willing to go to prevent conversion of rail lines into recreational trails than the former Burlington Northern branch between Redmond and Issaquah. Hundreds of residents along this corridor so strenuously opposed the creation of a trail that they sought to establish their own railroad company to block the initiative. Although this extraordinary effort fell short of its goal, members of the community have taken notable steps to showcase the town's rail-oriented past.

Historical Perspective

Few settlers lived in the Squak Valley when L.B. Andrews purchased 160 acres in this heavily forested area in 1862. Andrews was a surveyor of U.S. government land and had developed good relations with the Duwamish Indians. Legend has it that he listened attentively as they spoke earnestly of "fire rock," a hard substance that could be burned. When he asked these natives where the fire rock "lived," they brought his party to hills that were laden with coal.

By early 1864, the Seattle and Squak Railroad Company had been incorporated—with Andrews among its stockholders—to transport coal to Puget Sound. Financial problems, however, foiled the effort to move forward with construction. For lack of more efficient methods, oxen toiled on dirt paths pulling wagons weighed down with agricultural products and other goods—but little coal—from the area. After reaching Lake Sammamish, this cargo had to be towed along the lake's eastern shore, poled through a marshland called the Squak Slough, and towed once again along Lake Washington and on to Puget Sound.

Many years passed before George Tibbetts, another settler in the valley, opened a combination hotel, store, and stagecoach stop along this busy route. His commercial establishment became the nucleus of the emerging community of Squak, a settlement poised for expansion when Daniel Gilman (a prominent local attorney) and others moved forward with plans to build the Seattle, Lake Shore & Eastern Railroad (Lake Shore) in 1885. After Gilman obtained financing for the route, the Seattle Coal and Iron Company, an entity with close ties to the railroad, invested heavily in new mines in the small town's vicinity.

The residents of Squak celebrated the arrival of the Lake Shore's first train in late 1887 and benefited greatly from the boom in coal mining that soon followed. They depended heavily on the carrier's freight and passenger trains (which reached Seattle over a route passing north of Lake Washington not far from the old wagon trail) and even renamed their community Gilman in honor of the railroad's founder. In 1889, the year Washington achieved statehood, the Lake Shore built a large wooden depot in town and an eastward extension through Snoqualmie to Sallal Prairie, a lumber center near North Bend.

Despite the anticipation surrounding the Lake Shore's construction, this railroad was unable to fulfill the lofty expectations of its founder. The company eventually abandoned an ambitious plan it had developed to provide service all the way to Spokane, but not until it had spent a considerable sum working to prepare a right-of-way west of that city. To the disappointment of many in the region, the route through Gilman would never become more than a local operation. Making matters worse for the community, labor problems at Gilman's mines gradually escalated. In 1890, a strike crippled the local economy, resulting in the creation of a large tent

city filled with members of the Washington state militia.

The tide began to turn in Gilman's favor after it became an incorporated community in 1892. With the coal mining industry on the mend, the Lake Shore shouldered the burden of large outbound shipments of coal. In addition to providing frequent service on its main line, the carrier operated a lengthy spur to the mining company and a loop track through the southern part of town. Below ground, the mining company operated a sprawling network of industrial railways that hauled coal for transfer to the Lake Shore.

The financial problems that had plagued the Lake Shore since its earliest days continued unmercifully. The carrier came under the control of Northern Pacific in 1890, fell into receivership three years later, and was sold to the Seattle & International Railway in 1896. Business leaders held out hope that the Seattle & International

Railroad enthusiasts gather to photograph the Casey Jones Special as it takes excursion-goers across the Issaquah High Trestle in 1956. (Photo by Warren W. Wing.)

271

Grass sprouts up on the tracks in front of the Issaquah depot. This corridor, occasionally traversed by a battery-operated "trolley," now lacks an outside connection. (Photo by author.)

would build an eastward extension to provide one of the granger roads (possibly the Chicago & North Western Railway) access to Puget Sound, but this was not to be.

Even as its railroad struggled, Gilman continued to expand. After the community changed its name in 1899 to Issaquah (a word meaning "sound of water fowl" in the languages of many local tribes), the carrier renamed its depot as such. By the time Northern Pacific regained control of the railroad and absorbed the Seattle & International into its system in 1901, the community had more than 1,000 inhabitants.

Changing Times

The up-and-down business cycles that had long buffeted Issaquah's economy and weakened its social fabric showed little sign of abating during the early twentieth century. Work stoppages and employee unrest—a problem aggravated by a devastating fire in 1904 at one of the mines, reputedly caused by arson—were chronic problems. The blaze damaged many of the community's buildings and forced an important mine to close. Adding to the community's woes, none of the three companies interested in building electric interurban railways through Issaquah arrived, leaving their town with less-

than-superb rail connections.

The community's fortunes took a fortuitous turn in 1912, when Constantine Gustav Alvo von Albensleben, the son of a German ambassador, arrived on the scene. Von Albensleben found Issaquah coal to be a lucrative source of carbon—a material desperately needed by his homeland's industry. By 1914, hundreds of laborers were again working in the mines, apparently supplying large shipments of carbon to German industry. Then, the mysterious Von Albensleben received financing to build a large chemical plant in the community.

Von Albensleben's initiatives proved to be a mixed blessing for the community. As American involvement in World War I escalated, federal authorities arrested von Albensleben on suspicion of being an agent for German industry. The industrialist's arrest forced his Issaquah and Superior Coal Company into receivership. As coal shipments plummeted and competition from motor vehicles intensified, Issaquah's rail line (called the Snoqualmie Branch) surrendered much of its transportation role. With travelers able to reach Seattle over a system of roads and ferry routes in less than half the time required for riding the rails, Northern Pacific suspended the passenger trains operating between North Bend and Seattle (which made stops in Issaquah) on the route in 1922. The mines formerly operated by von Albensleben's company closed permanently in 1923.

The future of Issaquah was not as bleak as many anticipated. The expansion of the Issaquah Creamery and the opening of a new salmon hatchery and other Works Progress Administration projects in 1935 helped the town weather the Great Depression better than many mining towns. Traffic on the railroad recovered during World War II and remained strong into the postwar era.

The railroad's freight business ebbed after U.S Highway 10, a road linking Issaquah with Seattle, was widened to four lanes in 1950, greatly increasing the convenience of truck transport and necessitating significant modifications to one of two railroad trestles east of town. Nevertheless, the tracks remained in good condition and saw pasage of a steam-powered Casey Jones excursion in 1956, taking sightseers from Seattle to Snoqualmie Falls. The ride was so popular that many local residents had to be turned away. Sensing a groundswell of interest, organizer Carol Cornish, a woman of tremendous persistence, arranged for numerous other excursions on this branch and along other Northern Pacific routes, albeit using diesel locomotives after the 1957 season.

The outlook for the rail line deteriorated sharply during the early 1960s, when Issaquah's last coal mines closed and the future of lumber shipments over the branch grew increasingly uncertain. In 1968, the year Cornish died, the final Casey Jones excursion rode Issaquah's rails. By the time Northern Pacific merged with several other railroads to form Burlington Northern in 1970, the condition of the line had markedly deteriorated. The new operator (having negotiated traffic rights on the Chicago, Milwaukee, St. Paul & Pacific Railroad to Snoqualmie) abandoned the Issaquah–Snoqualmie Falls segment in 1974 and announced plans for abandoning the remainder of the branch from Redmond to Issaquah in 1981. Burlington Northern benefited from a modest rise in local traffic during the early 1980s and even built a new siding in Issaquah to deliver buses to the regional transit provider, but the branch had little place in its long-range plans.

When a Woodinville grain company discontinued its rail shipments in 1994, the Darigold Creamery (formerly the Issaquah Creamery) became the only regular railroad customer on the eastern end of the branch, heightening Burlington Northern's interest in abandonment. Against the objections of the municipal government, the carrier discontinued local service in 1996. After the trains stopped running, Darigold reportedly filed a lawsuit, arguing that Burlington Northern was not fulfilling its obligation as a common carrier. Its effort to force the carrier to restore service, however, failed.

Abandonment's Legacy

After the last train left town, an effort to convert the right-of-way into a recreational trail moved forward on an ambitious timetable. In 1997, the Land Conservancy of Seattle and King County paid Burlington Northern $2 million for the dormant 12-mile segment between Issaquah and Redmond for this purpose. Proponents of the idea publicized the benefits of using the right-of-way to provide a connection to the Burke-Gilman Trail, thus

creating a 45-mile recreational link to Seattle. Among those viewing this transaction with considerable skepticism was Dick Welsh, a noted opponent of rail-trail conversions throughout the country who had once lived in East Sammamish.

A central theme in Welsh's legal work was that many rights-of-way used for recreational trails had legally reverted to property owners upon the discontinuance of rail service. As founder of the National Association of Reversionary Property Owners, he maintained that the railbanking process used to create these trails (made possible by the amendments to the National Trail System Act of 1983) constituted a taking of private property and was thus unconstitutional. Establishing a trail as an interim use with the caveat that rail service could someday be restored, he argued, violated the rights of those holding title to the land. Welsh also argued that Burlington Northern, in commanding such a high price for a right-of-way, had effectively sold a corridor it did not own.

These issues were critically important to property owners along the Issaquah branch. The right-of-way's close proximity to homes along Lake Sammamish valued at more than $1 million galvanized opposition to the trail. Welsh and other opponents announced their intention to establish a new railroad in accordance with federal abandonment regulations. They obtained financial support and commitments from a gravel company to ship by train. The Issaquah Historical Society and the

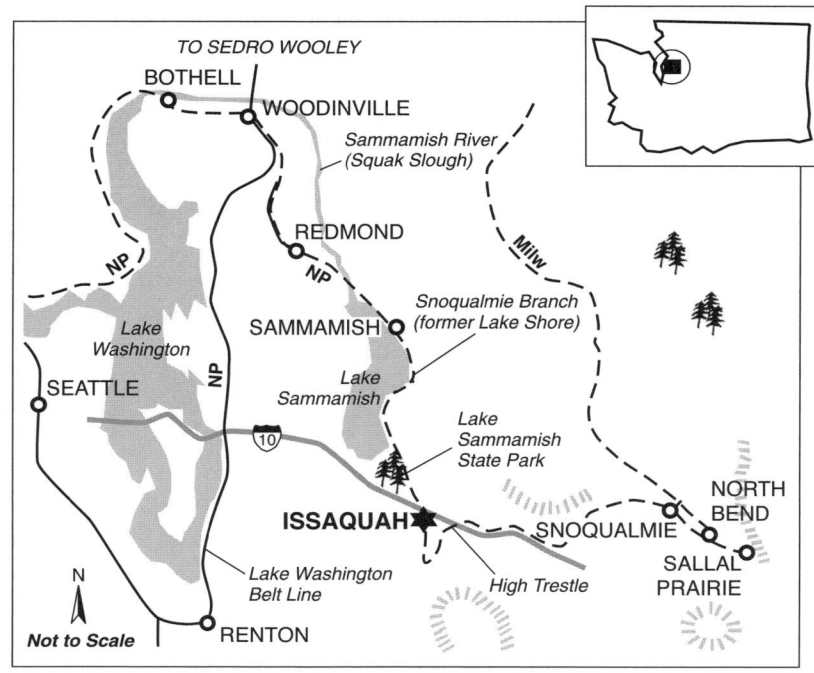

273

municipal government were not formally involved with this proposal but voiced support for saving the railroad, possibly for a tourist-oriented trolley operation between Issaquah and Lake Sammamish State Park. They also had an interest in preserving the route for a commuter-rail line to help alleviate congestion on Interstate 90.

Relations between proponents and opponents of the trail degenerated to such an extent that an East Sammamish couple installed a pair of chain-link fences over the right-of-way in 1997. By refusing to acquiesce to the Land Conservancy's demand for the prompt removal of the fence, the couple attracted significant attention to their cause, receiving coverage in *USA Today* and other newspapers. The county, however, gained the upper hand in the dispute in 1998, when it purchased the property from the Land Conservancy for $2.9 million. The following year, the county had the rails through East Sammamish to Issaquah's Gilman Boulevard removed. Some property owners who had opposed the trail found themselves owing considerable rental fees for encroaching on former railroad property, which now belonged to the county.

Momentum moved even further in favor of trail advocates in 2000, when a federal court concluded that the proposal by area residents to create a railroad would not be viable. Although the decision cleared the way for trail construction, the county recognized the need to demonstrate flexibility and settled upon a compromise measure to divert some (but not all) trail users to an alternate route.

Disappointed that the entire rail line could not be saved, the Issaquah government acquired from the county an isolated stretch of track between Gilman Boulevard and the depot and granted the Historical Society rights for using these facilities. This transaction allowed the society to launch a heritage "trolley" operation (powered by a generator car) through Issaquah in 2001. Taking travelers on scenic excursions between the depot and the town's northwestern periphery, this attraction proved quite popular. Notwithstanding Issaquah's heritage as a steam-railroad town, the trolley was seen as an integral part of the effort to draw attention to the community's rich past.

Epilogue

The economic orientation of Issaquah is much different today than when the controversial Constantine von

Albensleben set into motion its last great mining boom more than eighty years ago. Issaquah is now an affluent and residential suburb of Seattle that is heavily dependent on Interstate 90. Its restored downtown and the Pickering Barn—a registered landmark that played a prominent role in the town's development as a dairy center—add to its rich aesthetic character. The depot is another town landmark, having been purchased by the municipal government and refurbished by the Historical Society for the creation of the Issaquah Depot Railroad Museum, which has put several historical railcars on display.

The events surrounding the Issaquah Branch illustrate the sharp differences of opinion that exist about the railbanking provisions of the National Trails System Act. The simmering dispute that divided residents along the route underscores the sometimes controversial implications of court rulings that uphold recreational trails as interim uses of railroads, which, in a legal sense, have not been formally abandoned.

For Further Study

SUGGESTED READING:
Hjelm, Linda Adai. *Fire Rock: The Story of Issaquah's Coal Mining History.* Isaquah, Wash.: Issaquah Historical Society, 1998, 136.

OTHER PRINCIPAL REFERENCES:
Armbruster, Kurt E. "Seattle's Casey Jones Excursions." *The Mainstreeter: Official Publication of the Northern Pacific Railway Historical Association* 19, no. 1 (2000): 415.
————. *Orphan Road: The Railroad Comes to Seattle, 1853–1911.* Pullman: Washington State University Press, 1999, 121–41, 157, 201–2.
Fish, Edward R. *The Past at Present in Issaquah, Washington.* Issaquah, Wash.: Issaquah Historical Society, 1967, 18–19, 52–53.
Strand, Thomas. "Snoqualmie Branch '45." *The Mainstreeter: Official Publication of the Northern Pacific Railway Historical Association* 20, no. 4 (2001): 4–13.
Renz, Louis Tuck. *The History of the Northern Pacific Railroad.* Fairfield, Wash.: Ye Galleon Press, 1980, 195, 197.

LYNNWOOD, WASHINGTON (33,847)

Historic operator: Pacific Northwest Traction Company
Last route abandoned: 1939
Notable reuse of right-of-way: Interurban Trail

Lynnwood's example illustrates the fervor surrounding real estate development along some interurban routes into the early 1920s. Its railway fostered the creation of a planned community called Alderwood Manor, which enjoyed sustained prosperity and attracted national publicity for its thriving poultry farms many years ago. Today, Lynnwood's restored interurban car and municipal logo—as well as a local brass band and the aptly named Interurban Trail—testify to the days of its trolley.

Historical Perspective

When the federal government created the Washington Territory in 1853, vast forests dominated the shoreline of Puget Sound. This virgin timber became more accessible upon the completion of a military road between Fort Steilacoom (near the present city of Tacoma) and Fort Bellingham (near the Canadian border) in 1859. Within a few years, lumber companies had built sawmills and a system of logging routes deep into the hinterland near present-day Lynnwood. Over these routes, horses and oxen—and, later, a private logging railway—toiled to bring logs to mills along the shore.

By the time Washington became a state in 1889, the entire Puget Sound region was in the midst of a development boom, and Seattle had a population of more than 40,000. The arrival of the Great Northern Railway in 1893 and a gold rush in Canada's Klondike region four years later stimulated still more development in the area and brought great vitality to several ports north of Seattle, including Edmonds and Everett.

Although few newcomers initially established themselves in the landlocked area east of Edmonds, migration accelerated when the Seattle-Everett Traction Company laid tracks through this forestland during the early twentieth century. By 1907 the company (managed by the Stone & Webster Company) operated cars all the way from the Seattle suburb of Ballard to Halls Lake, near the southern edge of present-day Lynnwood. To serve the burgeoning traffic between the cities after which it had been named, the company extended its route to Everett in 1910.

Seattle-Everett Traction greatly expanded the size of its market during the early 1910s by operating trolley cars directly to Seattle on streetcar lines along Greenwood and Phinney Avenues. To promote development, the company established a series of passenger stops in rural areas, including one called Forest Park, approximately 30 miles north of downtown Seattle

The end of an era is near as a North Coast Lines car heads north from the Alderwood Manor shelter in 1939. Visible in the distance are the old Washington Co-op (far left) and the Tudor-style Main Store known today as the Wickers Building. (Photo by Harold Hill, collection of Warren W. Wing.)

near the center of present-day Lynnwood. Popularly called "the interurban" (like many other intercity traction lines of the day), it had become an integral part of the region's transportation mix by 1912, when it merged with the Bellingham & Skagit Railway to create the Pacific Northwest Traction Company.

In 1913, with the demand for its services projected to grow, Pacific Northwest Traction moved forward with an ambitious plan to establish through service from Seattle to Bellingham, a distance of more than 80 miles. Although it laid track south from Bellingham to Mount Vernon, the task of closing the gap between this new route (the carrier's Northern Division) and its older Seattle–Everett route (the Southern Division) proved beyond its grasp.

The lumber industry, meanwhile, gradually depleted the supply of virgin timber near the coast and worked its way deeper into the interior. By 1916, much of the area

near present-day Lynnwood was a desolate wasteland consisting of little more than stumps. The Puget Mill Company, a firm affiliated with the Pope and Talbot Company, owned more than 100,000 acres of property and was eager to find a way to reuse this worked-out land. In 1917, it commenced work on a project to subdivide some 20,000 acres for the creation of homes and poultry farms. The company's investments included a 30-acre demonstration farm created to teach settlers how to make a living from 5 acres of land by raising poultry and growing nuts, fruit, berries, and other crops.

Within months, the company had created a development encompassing more than 700 acres that revolved around a planned community called Alderwood Manor. The interurban renamed its adjacent Forest Park shelter for the community and supported the effort to attract prospective buyers of property by regularly operating special excursion trains from Seattle. Its business at Alderwood Manor had grown considerably by 1919, when the mill company built a brick Tudor-style building that housed the Main Store, a seller of general merchandise next to the tracks.

By the early 1920s, many landowners were raising chickens with considerable success, attracting great publicity to their community. The lumber company proudly reported that "Seattle and the state of Washington have awakened to the fact that here is one of the greatest land settlement projects in the country." As word of Alderwood Manor spread, newcomers did indeed arrive from across the country to enter the poultry business. By 1921, Alderwood Manor's farms were home to more than 200,000 hens, making the community the country's second largest producer of eggs. In only a few years, Alderwood Manor had evolved from a desolate wasteland to a bustling community of nearly 1,500 inhabitants.

Passing through the planned community mostly on private right-of-way, and operating cars as often as every half hour, the interurban handled many commuters, shoppers, and prospective landowners as well as shipments of eggs, feed, mail, and fertilizer. Passengers arriving at the Alderwood Manor shelter, which became one the interurban's most important stops, needed to walk only a short distance to reach the demonstration farm and the Main Store.

Changing Times

The circumstances that had allowed Alderwood Manor and its interurban to prosper soon gave way to a more modern pattern of suburban development centered around the automobile. The 1927 opening of Highway 99 along a route west of town sharply diminished the interurban's passenger revenues and left Alderwood Manor businesses increasingly separated from the flow of commerce. As revenues fell, the traction company formed a motor-coach operation to offer its passengers the conveniences of bus travel. In early 1930, Stone & Webster abandoned the company's entire Northern Division while consolidating the struggling South Division and the bus operation into a newly created entity called North Coast Lines.

The problems facing Alderwood Manor and the railway component of North Coast Lines escalated during the Great Depression. A sharp decline in the price of eggs devastated the community's poultry farms. Its most prominent retailer, the Main Store, struggled before changing hands in 1933 to become Herman Wicker's Grocery. That same year, Puget Mill leased the entire demonstration farm to Norman Collins, who moved his small poultry-breeding and chick-hatching business to this site and established the Washington Breeders hatchery.

As Alderwood Manor fell onto hard times, prospective homeowners took an interest in the rural areas outside of town. In 1937, Seattle realtor Karl O'Beirn subdivided some property into eighteen lots along Highway 99 at an intersection west of Alderwood Manor (called the Crossroads). The name O'Beirn chose for the plat, Lynnwood, honored his wife, Lynn, and was in keeping with the nearby communities of Alderwood and Maplewood. The following year, Lynnwood Lumber emerged as the first commercial establishment to use this name. Soon, the Crossroads was home to a cluster of businesses informally known as Lynnwood.

By the late 1930s, most time-sensitive passengers traveling between Seattle and Everett used cars, buses, and, to a lesser extent, Great Northern trains operating on faster schedules than the interurban. Pacific Northwest Traction seemed to have little hope of winning back

The Interurban Trail—the aptly named recreation path (visible on the right)— abuts Interstate 5 through Lynnwood. The freeway's construction obliterated most of Alderwood Manor. (Photo by author.)

these travelers as rising congestion on Seattle streets and the necessity of making frequent stops in the city reduced the speed of its services. Bowing to the inevitable, it discontinued both rail freight and passenger operations in February 1939.

Abandonment's Legacy

Within a month after the last trolley car had departed, much of the track and catenary had been removed. Some of the scrap metal was dispatched to Japan and presumably used to support that country's military buildup, while the right-of-way, used for electric transmission lines, was turned over to Puget Sound Power & Light Company.

After enduring great hardship during the Depression, many of the residents who had remained in Alderwood Manor suffered through another crisis in 1940, when tainted feed killed much of their livestock. As Alderwood Manor faded into obscurity, the Lynnwood business district welcomed a steady flow of new customers. Homeowners began flocking to the area around O'Beirn's plat, elevating its population to 6,000 by the time Lynnwood incorporated in 1959. The newly created community encompassed the Crossroads, a portion of Alderwood Manor, and several miles of abandoned interurban route.

The opening in 1962 of Interstate 5 over a route nearly parallel to the abandoned interurban route further changed life in the region. Not only did the freeway isolate the 4-acre remnant of the demonstration farm, it also created such heavy traffic conditions on Lynnwood's streets that officials decided to widen 196th Avenue, one of its busiest roads. This project limited the amount of parking available at the Wickers Grocery, prompting the owner of the store to relocate from the historic Main Store building into a

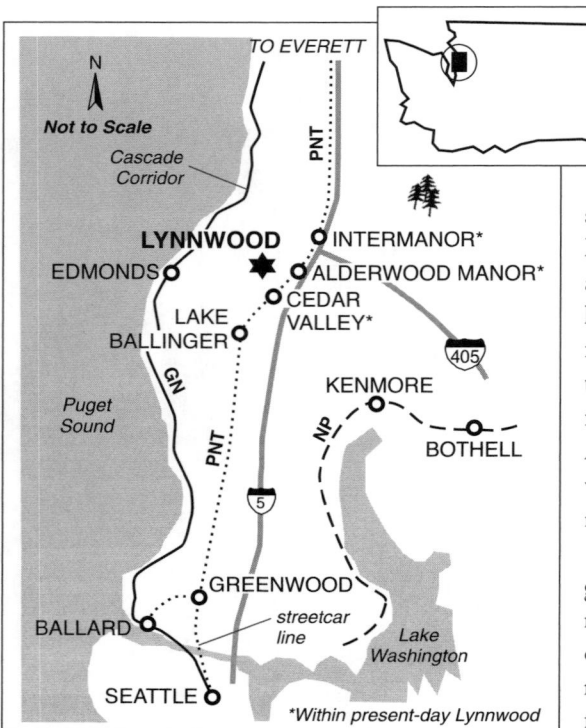

modest strip mall nearby, leaving the former edifice vacant. On a vastly larger scale, developer Edward DeBartolo launched an effort in 1974 to create the Alderwood Mall at the northeastern edge of town. This massive shopping center opened for business in 1979, marking the beginning of a period of spectacular growth in local retail sales.

With tens of thousands of motor vehicles passing through Lynnwood daily on Interstate 5 and Interstate 405 (a newer freeway converging with Interstate 5 near the mall), the community grew to more than 25,000 inhabitants during the mid-1980s. In response to rising congestion, comprehensive proposals emerged for reusing the old interurban right-of-way. A county report issued in 1985 concluded that the abandoned route was wide enough to accommodate multiple uses—a finding that allowed plans to create a local recreational trail and a light-rail line to advance simultaneously. The municipal government obtained a twenty-five-year easement from the utility district in the early 1990s and created the Interurban Trail, a 4-mile recreation path on the former interurban route. The trail's success generated interest in a proposal to make it part of a continuous greenway from south Lynnwood to Everett.

The effort to construct the light-rail line linking Lynnwood to Seattle (the so-called North Corridor Extension Project), however, went less smoothly. Voters rejected the Puget Sound Regional Transit Authority's proposal for expansion in 1995. A scaled-back plan for rail service moved forward the following year, when voters approved a sales tax increase that planners hoped would eventually allow for rail transit service from downtown Seattle to a park-and-ride facility in Lynnwood on 44th Avenue. Still, many years passed without a clear timetable for implementation.

Although the explosive growth of Lynnwood and other northern suburbs added a sense of urgency to the effort to restore rail service, attention increasingly focused on the former Great

Northern route through Edmonds. Not only did Amtrak's Empire Builder use this route, but in 1995, the passenger railroad also launched a daily service linking Seattle to Vancouver—part of the so-called Cascade Corridor—with an Edmonds stop. This service proved sufficiently popular that the state provided support for a second train between Seattle and Bellingham, introduced state-of-the-art Talgo equipment, and also moved forward with plans to establish commuter service between Tacoma and Everett.

The opportunity to ride the rails to Lynnwood, however, was still years away, even under the most favorable assessment. As planners contemplated the benefits of building the line, older citizens took it upon themselves to remind younger residents of the interurban abandoned many years before. To commemorate the carrier, the community inaugurated a Trolley Days Festival in 1997, and the city adopted the trolley as its official logo. A group of local musicians formed the Trolley Days Band in conjunction with the initial festival and found their music in demand throughout the year for community events. With an eye to the past, officials erected informational signs on the trail, displaying the logo of the traction company.

As interest in the community's past grew, the municipal government purchased one of the three surviving Pacific Northwest Traction cars (No. 55) from the Northwest Railway Museum in Snoqualmie in the late 1990s, and received substantial grants for its aquisition and restoration. It also bought the Wickers Building (the former Main Store) and relocated this treasured municipal landmark to the vicinity of the shopping mall to make room for a new freeway interchange. To the disappointment of historically minded residents, though, the interchange obliterated other remnants of Alderwood Manor.

Epilogue

Contemporary Lynnwood derives a great deal of prosperity from its heavily traveled interstate highways. Older residents understand, however, that the cost of abundant freeway access has been the loss of the Alderwood Manor business district, which has left Lynnwood without a traditional pedestrian-oriented downtown. To foster awareness of a past little known to younger residents, the municipal government, with assistance from the Alderwood Manor Heritage Association, recreated the demonstration farm in a 3-acre park in 2003. This site, Heritage Park, displays the Wickers Building, the trolley car, and a preserved water tower along with the original superintendent's cottage from the original demonstration farm, all of which have deep significance to local residents. The Wickers Building is now a popular visitors' center among motorists traveling on Interstate 5.

To those using the Interurban Trail, the legacy of the trolley line may seem modest compared to that of the adjacent Interstate 5, a corridor that currently has ten traffic lanes and is planned to eventually have several more. It is significant, however, that a new freeway exit leads tourists directly to Heritage Park, where the town's appreciation for the electric railway can still be felt many years after the last car rolled toward Seattle.

For Further Study

SUGGESTED READINGS:
Broom, Judith M. *Lynnwood: The Land, the People, the City.* Lynnwood, Wash.: City of Lynnwood, 1990, 49–76.
Wing, Warren. *To Seattle by Trolley.* Edmonds, Wash.: Pacific Fast Mail, 1988, 100–103.

OTHER PRINCIPAL REFERENCES:
City of Lynnwood. *Lynnwood Legacy: Making the Vision a Reality.* June 1993, 73.
Coman, Edwin T., Jr., and Helen M. Gibbs. *Time, Tide and Timber: A Century of Pope & Talbot.* Stanford: Stanford University Press, 1949, 231–42.
Hilton, George W., and John F. Due. *The Electric Interurban Railways in America.* Stanford: Stanford University Press, 1964, 392.
Snohomish County. *South Snohomish County Interurban Trail Implementation Plan.* Everett, Wash.: 1988, 1–4.

Historic operators: Chicago, Milwaukee, St. Paul & Pacific Railroad; Port Angeles Western Railroad
Last route abandoned: 1984
Notable reuse of right-of-way: Port Angeles Urban Waterfront Trail

he struggle to attract a railroad is a momentous chapter in the history of Port Angeles, a prominent harbor town on the Olympic Peninsula. Municipal leaders tried for years to rid their community of its distinction as one of the country's largest towns without a rail line. Although they finally succeeded in 1915, railcars arriving from points beyond the peninsula still had to be floated across Puget Sound. Despite this, the Olympic Branch made an enormous contribution to the region it served.

Historical Perspective

Historians disagree about the identities of the first white settlers to live in the vicinity of Ediz Hook, a narrow body of land extending into the Strait of Juan de Fuca, an estuary of the Pacific Ocean. Most believe, however, that this part of the Olympic Peninsula had a sparse population when a group of men formed the Cherbourg Land Company in 1859 in order to create a town site adjacent to the hook.

Among those providing funds for the company was the opportunistic Victor Smith, who was apparently motivated by the prospect that the new community would divert business away from Port Townsend, a locale he loathed. Blessed with an attractive harbor and located approximately 30 miles to the east, Port Townsend prospered at the time as an official port of entry for the United States.

Smith succeeded in bringing a post office (named Cherbourg) to the town site in 1861 and established his home in the emerging settlement

the following year. The federal government, however, frustrated his attempts to promote development in the area when it established a military reservation there in 1862. Nevertheless, Smith made the best of this situation and persuaded federal lawmakers to both authorize the relocation of the port of entry to this site and make land available for the creation of a model city called Port Angeles. When officials in Port Townsend refused to relinquish the customs records, Smith threatened to bombard the community with cannons mounted on the vessel *Shubrick*. The ploy, firmly etched in the peninsula's folklore, allowed Smith to achieve his intended result.

The residents of Port Angeles took pride in their town's designation as America's second "national city"—a community, like Washington D.C., established on land sold directly by the federal government (rather than on land disbursed by private, state, or territorial entities). Contrary to the admirable intentions behind the creation of the nation's capitol, the rationale for Port Angeles's inception was largely to provide the federal

THE MILWAUKEE ROAD

government with desperately needed funds for its treasury.

Unfortunately, the revenues generated by the sale fell so far short of expectations that the entire project was a fiasco. Although a small community emerged, hopes dimmed that Port Angeles would become a major commercial port. The townspeople grieved in 1865, when the steamer *Brother Jonathon* collided with another vessel, killing Victor Smith and more than 160 others onboard. The following year, Port Townsend was restored as the port of entry, leaving Port Angeles separated once again from the flow of international commerce.

In the wake of these momentous events came a period of relative calm that was characterized by sharply diminished expecations. When the Northern Pacific Railroad reached Tacoma in 1883, however, the fervor returned. Over the next several years, growing numbers of travelers arrived in Port Angeles on steamships destined for Victoria, British Columbia.

Port Angeles once again seemed poised to become an important city when a lawyer with utopian visions, George V. Smith (no relation to Victor Smith) created a commune near town in 1887. Smith organized the Puget Sound Cooperative Colony in part because of misgivings he and others had about the region's growing Chinese population. Offering members the promise of a life free of taxes and unemployment, this commune's future appeared promising enough that its members set their sights on the construction of a large opera house.

As the colony recruited new members, worked on the opera house, and took steps to attract a railroad, Port Angeles gave every appearance of a community that would become an important port. The commercially minded Norman Smith (son of Victor Smith) was so optimistic about the prospects for rail service in 1890 that he built a 15-foot stretch of track at a strategic point west of the community and held out hope that he could sell this "railroad"—a strip of track touted by *Ripley's Believe It or Not* as "the shortest railroad in the world"—to an authentic transportation provider at a considerable profit.

Optimism abounded over the next several years, when Port Angeles incorporated as a city, wrested the seat of Clallam County from nearby New Dungeness, and dedicated both the opera house and the three-story City Hotel. As investment flowed to the community, it seemed inevitable that steam trains would soon reach its waterfront. According to one account, the townspeople learned of more than a dozen proposals for rail lines, including a high-profile effort by the Union Pacific Railroad to build onto the peninsula. Hope was especially high in 1903

Still water reflects an attractively painted F-7 locomotive as a Seattle & North Coast excursion train rolls through Port Angeles on 28 May 1983. The short line abandoned its entire route the following year. (Photo by John C. Illman.)

A deserted wooden trestle crossing an inlet along the Strait of Juan de Fuca west of Port Angeles keeps the memory of the Milwaukee Road alive. (Photo by author.)

when Norman Smith attracted eastern capital to build the Port Angeles Pacific Railroad on a route incorporating his railroad. This carrier began laying track through town but barely reached the city limits before suspending work. Neither this railroad nor any of the other railroads slated for construction at the time ever inaugurated service.

Port Angeles businesses made the best of their unfortunate situation. Although the commune struggled to attract new members, community leaders built many more attractive buildings and moved forward with plans for the construction of a streetcar line. They held out hope that the Chicago, Milwaukee & St. Paul Railway (St. Paul Road), which completed its transcontinental route to Tacoma in 1909, would soon build the so-called Olympic Belt Line around the southern edge of Puget Sound onto the peninsula.

Within a few years, however, it became evident that neither the streetcar line nor the Olympic Belt Line would materialize. Local officials were now desperate for rail service and offered generous financial support to the Seattle, Port Angeles & Lake Crescent Railroad, which began work in 1913 on a line to Port Ludlow, a location on Puget Sound southeast of Port Townsend. To their disappointment, the railroad remained unfinished two years later, when the Seattle, Port Angeles & Western Railroad (SPA&W), an entity controlled by the St. Paul Road, acquired it. SPA&W built along the strait in both

directions from Port Angeles and inaugurated passenger service on the route extending west into the peninsula's lumber-rich hinterland in 1914. It did not provide the community with an intercity rail connection, however, until late the following year, when it commenced service over a 30-mile route east to Discovery Junction. Beyond Discovery Junction, SPA&W used the tracks of the Port Townsend Southern Railway to reach the wharf in Port Townsend, where railcars were shipped on carfloats (barges) across Puget Sound to Seattle.

The new line generated extensive tonnage despite having only an indirect connection to the rest of the U.S. rail system. The reliance on carfloats, while cumbersome, proved suitable for hauling timber and other products to main-line railroads serving the region. West of Port Angeles, at a remote location called Disque, the carrier interchanged traffic with the newly constructed Port Angeles Western Railroad, a carrier built to haul spruce for the production of aircraft urgently needed on the battlefields of World War I.

As community leaders had anticipated, the synergy between railroads, lumber companies, and ocean-going vessels brought considerable prosperity to Port Angeles. Residents dedicated a magnificent new county courthouse in 1915 and the spacious Lincoln School in 1917. Three years later, a subsidiary of the Zellerbach Paper Company entered into a contract to build a pulp and paper mill in Port Angeles.

The railroad era was at its zenith when the St. Paul Road acquired the SPA&W in 1919. The St. Paul conveyed thousands of freight cars annually to the wharf in Port Townsend and operated a pair of daily passenger trains to the same wharf, where travelers made transfers to Puget Sound Navigation Company steamboats. Those arriving for extended stays often relaxed at the Olympic Hotel, a fine guesthouse with fifty rooms located near the Port Angeles depot, and at the Olympic Hot Springs Lodge, a resort situated several miles west of town.

By the early 1920s, Port Angeles had apparently triumphed over its long-standing transportation woes. Its population had risen to more than 10,000. A new Masonic Temple exemplified the optimism of its leaders as did the stately Olympus Hotel erected on the former site of the Opera House.

Changing Times

The St. Paul Road operated the local route, which it called the Olympic Branch, for only a few years before it began to make major changes. In the 1920s, it granted Port Angeles Western trackage rights over the portion of the branch west of the community and placed a gas-electric passenger car—a "doodlebug"—into service between Port Townsend and Port Angeles, allowing for faster and more economical service.

The financially troubled railway, which emerged from receivership as the Chicago, Milwaukee, St. Paul & Pacific Railroad (Milwaukee Road) in 1928, continued to generate large shipments of forestry products on the peninsula. The Great Depression, however, trimmed local industrial production and hampered the viability of the doodlebug operation. Increasingly, businesses and travelers opted for more flexible modes of transportation. In 1931, shortly after the completion of the Olympic Highway (U.S. Route 101), the Milwaukee Road bowed to the inevitable and ended its local passenger service.

Even as the scope of services diminished, the Olympic Branch remained vital to the peninsula's economy. During World War II, the Milwaukee Road used it to haul military personnel and large shipments of supplies destined for fortifications along the Strait of Juan de Fuca. The branch also provided crucial logistical support to Olympic Shipbuilders, a producer of large wooden barges. Rail service seemed indispensable as the dangers of waterborne transportation grew, an issue exemplified by the 1942 sinking of the U.S. freighter *Coast Trader,* a ship sailing from Port Angeles and torpedoed by a Japanese submarine near the mouth of the Strait.

After the war, the Olympic Branch surrendered much of its role. In 1953, the federal government dramatically expanded nearby Olympic National Park, thus reducing logging opportunities and laying the groundwork for a gradual shift in the area's orientation from forestry products to tourism. That same year, Port Angeles Western abandoned its entire route, and the Milwaukee Road eliminated the portion of the Olympic Branch west of Port Angeles. By the late 1960s, the Milwaukee Road was deferring maintenance on the remainder of the branch. After the boxboard mill closed in 1970, the company identified the route as a candidate for abandonment.

By the middle of the 1970s, the aging carfloat operation between Port Townsend and Seattle, which required between 5 and 9 hours for a 45-mile trip, had become a heavy financial burden. When the Milwaukee Road imposed restrictive weight limits on freight cars traveling over the deteriorating dock in Port Townsend, traffic plummeted from nearly 5,200 carloads in 1976 to fewer than 3,200 in 1978.

The Milwaukee Road ceased operating its entire system west of Miles City, Montana, in 1980, ending all rail service to Port Angeles and dozens of other towns. Despite the vigorous opposition of labor groups, the carrier leased the Olympic Branch to the Seattle & North Coast Railroad, a short line supported by funds from the Local Rail Service Assistance Program. Touted as a success story by proponents of federal assistance to lightly used railroads, the carrier served several customers in Port Angeles, including the Crown Zellerbach paper mill and the ITT Rayonier pulp mill.

The Seattle & North Coast, a favorite among railroad enthusiasts, operated an excursion train powered by an attractively painted pair of F-7 locomotives over its route in 1982. The short line also made significant repairs to the slip and transfer span along the Port Townsend wharf, thus allowing it to remove some of the existing weight restrictions. It could not afford, however, the cost of completely rebuilding the structure, an estimated $800,000 expense. The state warned that the line's abandonment would increase transportation costs

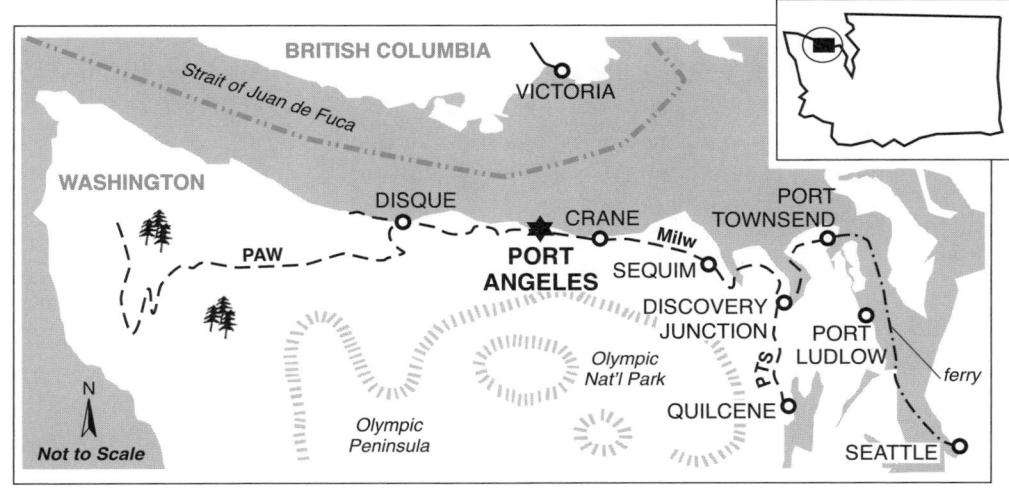

283

on the peninsula by nearly $1 million annually. Despite a state recommendation for funding to replace the dock, such financial support never materialized. In 1984, with little freight business remaining, the bankrupt short line discontinued its service and abandoned its route.

Abandonment's Legacy

Rumors that the dormant Olympic Branch would be saved circulated on the peninsula for several years. The Chicago Milwaukee Corporation, the successor to the Milwaukee Road, however, failed to find a buyer interested in restoring service.

Following the removal of the track in 1987, Port Angeles—a city of more than 17,000 residents—reclaimed its status as one the most populous western cities outside of a major metropolitan area that was bereft of a rail line. With the peninsula's economy rapidly shifting toward tourism, the state tried to purchase the former railroad property for the creation of a recreational trail in 1987. It quietly dropped this effort, however, due to ambiguity about Chicago Milwaukee's legal title to the land.

After much of the right-of-way reverted to local property owners, the municipal government began acquiring portions of the abandoned route on its own accord. By 1997, it had brought 8 miles of the route under its control. With assistance from the state, it rehabilitated several railroad bridges and converted 3 miles of the property into the Port Angeles Urban Waterfront Trail.

The decline of heavy industry on the peninsula reached another notable milepost when the Rayonier pulp mill closed in 1997, leaving hundreds of workers unemployed and pushing the local economy into a recession. Although this event cast a dark cloud over the community, it also presented an opportunity to extend the trail. The company donated the easements and property necessary to build the trail through to the mill site. Still, opposition from area property owners blocked subsequent efforts to extend the trail east of this location.

Epilogue

The investment made to preserve freight service to Port Angeles vividly illustrates the optimism that pervaded short-line railroading during the early 1980s. Many planners evidently still believed that light-density routes requiring rail-to-barge transfers could be operated without large-scale subsidies, which with few exceptions proved not to be the case.

The trains of the Olympic Branch and the car barges serving them nevertheless are fondly remembered in this part of Washington. A mural depicting the first train in Port Angeles is painted on a building on Railroad Avenue. Many motorists destined for the communities on the peninsula are ferried across Puget Sound today much like railroad passengers were years ago.

Contemporary visitors will find a dozen properties, including the county courthouse and the Lincoln School (envisioned to become the Clallam County Historical Society's museum), on the National Register of Historic Places. Although the passenger depot is gone, a wood-frame freight office and numerous trestles outside of town survive. At a local park, a steam locomotive donated by Rayonier is on display. In the Ediz Hook area of town, the strips of rail embedded in the pavement near a lumber mill seem vaguely reminiscent of the "shortest railroad in the world" that Norman Smith built more than a century ago.

For Further Study

SUGGESTED READINGS:

Dietrich, Don. "A Brief History of the Olympic Peninsula." *Milwaukee Railroader* (1986): 10–21.

Kornweibel, Theodore, Jr. "Is There Life after Milwaukee?" *Trains* 41, no. 12 (Oct. 1981): 26–30.

Martin, Paul J. *Port Angeles, Washington: A History.* Port Angeles, Wash.: Peninsula Publishing, 1983, 1:13–131.

OTHER PRINCIPAL REFERENCES:

Armbruster, Kurt E. *Orphan Road: The Railroad Comes to Seattle, 1853–1911.* Pullman: Washington State University Press, 1999, 159, 190, 246, 248.

Drury, George. *Historical Guide to North American Railroads.* Milwaukee, Wis.: Kalmbach Publications, 1995, 303–4.

Gary, Henry L. *Historic Railroads of Washington.* Seattle: Henry L. Gray, 1971, 12–17.

Lauridsen, G. M., and A. A. Smith. *The Story of Port Angeles.* Seattle: G. M. Lauridsen, 1937, 105–25.

Robertson, Donald B. *Encyclopedia of Western Railroad History.* Caldwell, Idaho: Caxton Printers, 1995, 3:134–35.

LAKE GENEVA, WISCONSIN (7,148)

Historic operator: Chicago & North Western Railway
Last route abandoned: 1982
Notable reuse of right-of-way: End of the Line motel and condominium complex

Chicago & North Western trains brought generations of travelers to Lake Geneva, a community widely known for its beautiful waterfront, luxurious mansions, and fine guesthouses. Despite mounting deficits and deteriorating track, these trains continued to operate long after other midwestern resorts had lost their rail service. When the last passenger train departed in 1975, a fondly remembered Wisconsin transportation tradition drew to a close.

Historical Perspective

For centuries the heavily forested land on the eastern bank of Geneva Lake was the dominion of the Potawatomi Indians. Where this Algonquin-speaking tribe once flourished, early European-American settlers found life to be extremely difficult. The community these settlers created in 1836 took its name from the nearby lake (which an early traveler had likened to its Swiss namesake). Geneva suffered greatly from its remote location and harsh climate; it consisted of little more than a modest cluster of log cabins when Wisconsin entered statehood in 1848.

The community became more accessible in the mid-1850s, when the Racine, Janesville & Mississippi Railway, a predecessor to the Milwaukee Road, built a rail line through nearby Elkhorn, just 6 miles away. Trains did not reach Geneva itself until the Wisconsin Central Railroad opened a line from Richmond, Illinois, its interchange with the Fox River Valley Railroad, in 1856.

Although the Wisconsin Central established direct passenger service to Elgin, Illinois, through its interchange, it did not simulate the economy as anticipated. The company never built north of Geneva as had been proposed and faced financial problems so severe that it suspended operations in 1860. For a brief period, a local resident operated a mule-car service over the derelict tracks. Within a few years, the rails and crossties had been removed, and Geneva was once again without a railroad.

Geneva remained little known to most prominent businessmen of Illinois and Wisconsin at the time, but this changed after Shelton Sturges, a Chicago industrialist, surveyed the shores of Geneva Lake to find an attractive site for a second home. Sturges completed his beloved Maple Lawn mansion in 1871—the same year the Lake Geneva & State Line Railroad reconstructed the line from Richmond. Within months of the first train's arrival, the Chicago Fire brought throngs of displaced Chicagoans to Geneva and pushed development to spectacular levels.

Shortly before dawn in 1971, a Chicago & North Western E-8 locomotive and several bi-level gallery cars await an early departure from Lake Geneva's classic brick-and-limestone depot. This train will make a 71-mile trip to the Windy City. (Collection of Mark L. Lanuza.)

Weekend and holiday train trips to the area became fashionable by 1880, when the local railroad became part of the Elgin & State Line Railroad, a Chicago & North Western (North Western) subsidiary. To avoid confusion in the delivery of mail with Geneva, Illinois, a city along the same rail line, the community that same year formally changed its name to Lake Geneva. Its economy thrived as business leaders followed Sturges's example by building second homes near the waterfront.

Lake Geneva was thriving when the North Western formally absorbed the Elgin & State Line into its system in 1883. Five years later, this railroad extended its tracks north and west of Lake Geneva to Williams Bay. Although hopes that the local route would become part of a new main line to Lake Superior eventually faded, the North Western opened a large new local station in 1890. Other steam railroads could promote their services to the area, but only the North Western reached Lake Geneva shores. However, the Chicago, Harvard & Geneva Lake Railway, a traction line, did initiate service in 1899 over an 11-mile route from Harvard, Illinois, to Fontana, a resort destination on the opposite side of the lake.

By the turn of the century, thousands of travelers congregated in Lake Geneva's hotels and restaurants each summer. Most visitors arrived and departed on North Western passenger trains operating directly between Lake Geneva and Chicago. All trains bound for the Windy City used the former Elgin & State Line route as far as Crystal Lake, Illinois. Some continued south (or east, in railroad terms) through Elgin to West Chicago (Turner Junction) before finishing their assigned run on the North Western's Chicago–Galena main line. Other trains—those on the fastest schedules—operated over the Chicago–Madison main line east of Crystal Lake via Barrington, Illinois.

As Lake Geneva's economy blossomed, senior North Western officials built fine homes in town and commuted to the company's headquarters in Chicago aboard the "Millionaires' Train"—an express run operating via Barrington that regularly conveyed private cars. Many graceful mansions, dozens of fine Victorian homes, and several resorts sprouted up on Lake Geneva's tree-lined streets. Beginning in 1912, arriving passengers could relax at the newly built Hotel Geneva, a guesthouse designed by the eminent architect Frank Lloyd Wright.

By the early 1920s, Lake Geneva was considered "the Newport of the Midwest" because of its aesthetic and social similarities to Newport, Rhode Island. To tap this lucrative market, the Chicago, North Shore & Milwaukee Railway, one of the nation's most prominent interurbans, established bus service (through a subsidiary) to the community from Kenosha in 1922.

Changing Times

The popularity of railroad travel faded as the creation of paved highways and the travails of the Great Depression weakened the demand for local service. The interurban operating to Fontana discontinued its passenger service in 1929 and ceased all operations the following year. In 1932, the North Western ended passenger service from Lake Geneva to points south of Crystal Lake on the route to Elgin and West Chicago. With people increasingly turning to hard-surface roads, the number of passengers using the remaining route via Barrington fell at an alarming rate.

The recovery in passenger business during World War II was particularly impressive, necessitating that trains occasionally be operated in multiple sections. After the war, however, this business lost much of its vigor. The North Western reduced passenger service in 1950 to two morning trips to Chicago and two evening return trips, a schedule continuing for the next quarter-century. The introduction of bi-level gallery-style commuter cars during the mid-1950s improved passenger comfort, but the railroad's market share continued to slip.

By the time the North Western terminated operations between Lake Geneva and Williams Bay in late 1965, its trains had surrendered much of their transportation role. In 1970, a developer announced plans to renovate the deteriorating Lake Geneva depot and bring several passenger cars to the depot site for a new restaurant. Not only did the depot restaurant never materialize, but the railroad petitioned the Interstate Commerce Commission in 1971 to close the station and relocate its Lake Geneva passenger stop to the outskirts of town. Although the carrier received approval, it never made the change—perhaps recognizing that the end of passenger service was, at most, only a few years away. Deteriorating track conditions required

the carrier to lengthen its schedules progressively. Making matters worse, in 1971 an individual boarded a parked locomotive in Crystal Lake and sent the unoccupied unit north toward Lake Geneva. The runaway locomotive crashed into a commuter train at the local depot, slightly injuring a crew member and destroying an E-8 locomotive as well as the stolen GP-7.

The status of the rail service diminished further in 1972 when the carrier (reorganized as the Chicago & North Western Transportation Company) lowered speed limits for passenger trains on the Lake Geneva Branch to a mere 30 mph. By 1974, the faster of the two trains took 2 hours and 40 minutes to reach Chicago, about an hour longer than scheduled service in the previous decade. Intent on drawing attention to the lengthening schedules, a Lake Geneva schoolteacher used his bicycle to race a commuter train from McHenry to Lake Geneva. Before a small audience of television and newspaper reporters, the cyclist reached the depot first, an embarrassing moment for both train advocates and company officials.

Following the 1974 creation of the Regional Transportation Authority (RTA), an Illinois public agency, North Western executive James Wolfe negotiated with public officials on a plan to subsidize the money-losing commuter rail system. The RTA considered the Lake Geneva route to be an unattractive candidate for such subsidies, not only because the resort was too far from Chicago to become a major commuting destination, but also because it was outside the RTA's jurisdictional boundaries.

The Lost Caboose, a lodging and condominium complex consisting of retired Chicago & North Western and Milwaukee Road cabooses, lines a portion of the abandoned Lake Geneva Branch. (Photo by author.)

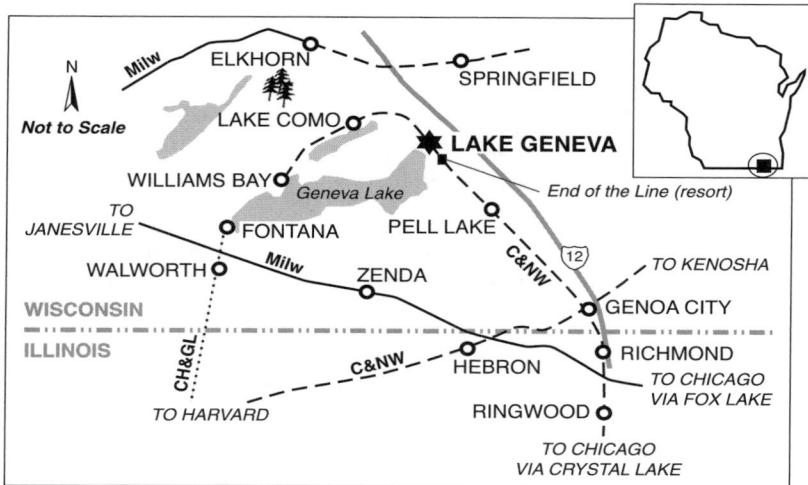

With subsidies unavailable, the North Western terminated its suburban service north of Richmond in August 1975, bringing local passenger service to a close.

The loss of service greatly concerned residents of the affected communities, who organized the Geneva Lake Area Joint Transit Commission to assess their options. The commission considered a plan to operate trains between Lake Geneva and the commuter station in Crystal Lake, possibly using a rail-diesel car. Without new sources of public funds, the futility of these efforts soon became evident.

The future of the North Western's local freight service also appeared grim. In 1978, the carrier reported that it had generated only seventeen carloads of freight (all lumber) in Lake Geneva over the past year. With losses reported to be $300,000 per year, observers understood that the North Western would not continue freight service unless either subsidized or compelled to do so by the ICC. In late 1980, however, the ICC granted permission to abandon the 17-mile stretch from Lake Geneva to Ringwood, Illinois, a small community south of Richmond.

Although the state opted neither to acquire the Lake Geveva segment nor to subsidize operations, freight trains continued operating as the transit coalition worked with the ICC on arrangements to purchase the track and other railroad property north of Ringwood. The organization received approval for a $400,000 loan from the state's Department of Transportation, but could not satisfy the need for additional financing, nor overcome ambiguities in the ownership of the land.

In the midst of this difficult period, the terminus for RTA commuter trains was further cut back from

Richmond to McHenry, Illinois. Some passengers affected by this change turned to commuter trains operating between Walworth, Wisconsin, and Chicago, a former Milwaukee Road corridor which vaulted over the Lake Geneva Branch on a high embankment south of Richmond. These passengers, however, were further inconvenienced in October 1982 when the RTA suspended service on the route west of Fox Lake, Illinois, leaving Lake Geneva even farther separated from the region's network of suburban passenger services. The following month, as commuters adjusted to this latest round of cutbacks, the North Western received permission once again to abandon freight service on its Lake Geneva–Ringwood segment, and Lake Geneva's railroad era quietly drew to a close.

Abandonment's Legacy

Starting in the summer of 1983, salvage workers began to remove the local tracks and to raze both the depot in Genoa City and the station in Richmond. Some of the right-of-way reverted to adjacent property owners, while other portions were sold. Before the first rail was lifted, however, an entrepreneur brought a large fleet of North Western and Milwaukee Road cabooses to the Lake Geneva vicinity. The developer transformed this surplus equipment into the End of the Line, a motel and condominium complex that opened in 1985. The herald of a past or present railroad company emblazoned on each caboose, as well as an old railroad semaphore modified to inform motorists about vacancies, added a decorative flair.

Public officials fashioned some of the abandoned right-of-way in Richmond into a recreational trail and created the Duck Lake Trail along a portion of the route near Williams Bay. Landscaping and real estate development soon altered other portions of the route beyond recognition. Near the center of Lake Geneva, a work crew removed the railroad bridge over Route 50, eliminating a landmark dating back many years.

The community launched a campaign to acquire and preserve its redbrick-and-limestone depot—an effort supported by the mother of North Western executive James Wolfe, who maintained her summer home in Lake Geneva. Mrs. Wolfe reportedly tried to persuade her son, who had risen to the company's presidency, to have the company donate the depot to the community.

Her effort, it is said, was hindered by the executive's unpleasant memories of the bicycle race years earlier. Despite interest in using the depot as a railway museum, it fell into the hands of a private owner who razed the landmark in the middle of the night in 1986, an act eliciting considerable outrage from the townspeople.

One nostalgic observer went so far as to write a song, "The Railroad Runs No More," to voice her sorrow about the closing of the railroad and the demolition of the depot. During the academic year beginning in 1988, Lake Geneva's Badger High School compiled an oral and pictorial history of the local North Western branch. Students gathered anecdotes and photographs for an illustrated volume, a project lauded by editor J. David Ingles in *Trains* magazine.

Over the years, the idea of bringing passenger service back to Lake Geneva periodically attracted attention, but few expected the community ever to be listed as a station stop for an Amtrak train. As it happened, railroading in southern Wisconsin took an unexpected turn in 2000, when Amtrak introduced the *Lake Country Limited*, a train operating over the ex-Milwaukee Road route between Chicago and Janesville via Fox Lake. Established with the goal of generating revenue from express cargo shipments, the train made a "Lake Geneva" stop in Zenda, Wisconsin, a small crossroad 8 miles south of the resort town. Revenues were so low, however, that the train—which on some trips had no paying customers—generated a deficit of several hundred dollars per passenger and attracted national notoriety as an example of wasteful government spending. Its service was canceled in the autumn of 2001.

The idea of serving Lake Geneva by rail again received attention in 2002. As part of an RTA study, a crew inspected the former North Western tracks (owned by Metra, the regional commuter-rail operator) north to their terminus in Ringwood and followed much of the abandoned portions of the route via truck. Although the RTA later dropped the idea for financial reasons, it moved ahead with a more modest plan to restore suburban service from McHenry to the vicinity of Ringwood.

Epilogue

Transportation in Lake Geneva is vastly different today from what it was years ago. The thunderous sounds of locomotives departing for Chicago are now just memories. The community's intercity buses have gone the way of the Millionaires' Train, leaving the town without regularly

scheduled passenger service. An office building, straightened street, and parking lot have altered the depot site beyond recognition. Direct evidence of Lake Geneva's railroad is limited mostly to grassy embankments and an arched concrete bridge over a small creek near the center of town.

The abandonment of the branch to Lake Geneva would likely have provoked a more vigorous state or regional response had it occurred ten years later, when the region began to feel the encroachment of metropolitan Chicago. Although few residents of Lake Geneva work in Chicago, the need for public transportation improvements in the region is becoming acute as the metropolitan area expands to the north.

Visitors to Lake Geneva will find its downtown district one of southern Wisconsin's premier tourist destinations. During the summer months, a bus resembling an old-time trolley carries many people through town in an effort to help relieve traffic congestion. Although the Frank Lloyd Wright hotel is gone, eight properties are listed on the National Register of Historic Places, and numerous mansions, including Maple Lawn, offer graceful reminders of the community's heritage as a place of wealth and refinement.

For Further Study

SUGGESTED READINGS:

Behrens, Paul L. *Steam Trains to Geneva Lake: C&NW's Elgin-Lake Geneva Branch.* Hebron, Ill.: Paul Behrens, 2002, 11–50.

OTHER PRINCIPAL REFERENCES:

Grant, H. Roger. *The North Western: A History of the Chicago & North Western Railway System.* DeKalb: Northern Illinois University Press, 1996, 66.

Lanz, Daniel J. *Railroads of Southern & Southwestern Wisconsin: Development to Decline.* Monroe, Wis.: Daniel J. Lanz. 1985, 138.

Porter, Russ. *Chicago & North Western-Milwaukee Road Pictorial.* Forest Park, Ill.: Heimburger House Publishing, 1994, 24.

Tracks Through Time: A Community Remembers. Lake Geneva, Wis.: Badger High School, 1989.

Wolfmeyer, Ann, and Mary Burns Gage. *Lake Geneva, Newport of the West: 1870–1920.* Lake Geneva, Wis.: Lake Geneva Historical Society, 1976.

PLATTEVILLE, WISCONSIN (9,989)

Historic operators: Chicago, Milwaukee, St. Paul & Pacific Railroad; Chicago & North Western Railway
Last route abandoned: 1980
Notable reuse of right-of-way: Pecatonica State Park Trail

Few parts of the Midwest have surrendered a greater share of their rail system than southwestern Wisconsin. At one time, the region's two largest railroads supported a vast lead- and zinc-mining industry and carried passengers to and from Platteville—the region's largest city—on a dozen weekday trains. Today, grassy embankments and old bridge abutments are nearly all that remain of this community's ore-hauling routes.

Historical Perspective

The beauty and commercial potential of the upper Mississippi River greatly impressed French explorers Jacques Marquette and Louis Joliet in 1673. Their expedition cleared the way for the expansion of fur trading in the area and the establishment of Prairie du Chein, a settlement along the river's eastern banks. For more than a century, Prairie du Chein prospered from growing commerce on the river.

Despite the expansion of Prairie du Chein, the rolling countryside east of the river attracted few settlers, even after the region came under British control in 1763. The situation did not markedly change until the mid-1820s, when prospectors discovered sizable deposits of lead in the area. As word of the discovery spread, a large number of English settlers entered the mineral-laden region, founded the village of Mineral Point, and cultivated the development of large lead mines.

Migration spread south after Emmanuel Metcalf, a trapper, discovered a deposit of lead in an animal den near the Platte River Diggings, a series of lead-mining excavations created by an Indian tribe many years before. The community that emerged near the discovery site (about 15 miles east of the river) was soon to benefit from the leadership of Major John H. Rountree and Major James B. Campbell, who, after arriving in 1827, purchased Metcalf's land and opened a general store. In 1829, the townspeople christened the settlement Platteville.

Platteville endured great hardship during the Black Hawk War, when the U.S. Army battled a determined band of Sauk and Fox led by Chief Black Hawk. After the chief surrendered at Prairie du Chein in 1832, however, the community was again poised to prosper. In 1835, Rountree hired a surveyor to lay out the town, who platted it to resemble his own birthplace, Yorkshire, England.

The townspeople had much to celebrate during these formative years. In 1836, officials named nearby Belmont, just 7 miles from Platteville, the capital of the newly created Wisconsin Territory. Platteville incorporated as a village in 1841 and saw its prestige grow with the opening of the Platteville Academy, an institution devoted to higher learning. By the time Wisconsin entered statehood in 1848, the community was one of the Midwest's premier lead-mining towns, albeit never as significant as Mineral Point.

Platteville also emerged as as a place of cultural enlightenment, a process underscored by its role as an important stop on the underground railroad—the so-called Abolition Hollow—before the Civil War and the creation of the State Normal School in 1866. General Ulysses S. Grant, a native of Galena, Illinois, and a military hero on his way to the U.S. presidency, dedicated a new wing at this teaching institution the following year.

For the community to reach its potential, however, it needed a railroad. The possibility had long existed that a major railroad would build from Milwaukee to the Mississippi River by way of Platteville. When the Dubuque, Platteville & Milwaukee Railroad (DP&M) completed a 17-mile line between Calamine and Platteville in 1870, this long-distance route appeared to be on its way to becoming a reality. Nevertheless, the DP&M never reached either Dubuque nor Milwaukee. In fact, it embarked on no further construction, much to the disappointment of the communities it served.

Platteville would never become a great railroad center, but its transportation connections did improve when a second carrier, the Galena & Southern Wisconsin Railroad, arrived in 1875. This narrow-gauge operator laid its tracks north from Galena to the booming mining town and anticipated extending the line to Montfort. It soon

commenced work on this extension from a rural location southeast of town interchangeably called Ipswich and Platteville Junction.

Businesses in Platteville derived substantial benefits from these railroads as well as from the expansion of mining and, to a lesser extent, from the country's first long-distance telephone line, which linked the community to Lancaster, the county seat, in 1877. Although operations on the financially troubled narrow gauge temporarily ended with the route to Montfort still unfinished in 1878, services resumed the following year under the auspices of a new carrier, the Galena & Wisconsin Railroad.

As in so many other Wisconsin cities, Platteville's rail lines were soon assimilated by larger and more powerful carriers, a process that occurred quickly but involved an unusually large number of corporate transactions. The DP&M became part of the Mineral Point Railroad in 1880, which was acquired that same year by the Chicago, Milwaukee & St. Paul Railway (St. Paul Road). Also in 1880, the Chicago & North Western Railway (North Western) purchased 92 miles of narrow-gauge routes in the area, including the Galena & Wisconsin. The carrier

The last Milwaukee Road train to depart Platteville heads east toward Calamine in November 1974. This event was photographed by a local college student who considered the occasion important enough to miss class. (Photo by Kameron A. Miller.)

Typical of abandoned routes in industrial towns of the Midwest, this former Milwaukee Road route (the dirt path at far right) in Platteville is lined with structures no longer used for their original purposes. (Photo by author.)

merged these lines into a subsidiary called the Milwaukee & Madison Railway and further improved its regional system in 1881 by building a standard-gauge line from Montfort to Madison. In 1882, it converted all of the other routes in the region to standard gauge, except for an undulating 16-mile segment between Fennimore and Woodman burdened with a horseshoe curve.

While oriented principally toward the excavation of ore, Platteville continued to exhibit unusually lofty cultural goals for a midwestern town of its size. In 1900, the community dedicated the first hospital in the state west of Madison. Six years later, its residents organized the Platteville Tourism Club to build awareness of the community's fine amenities. After the Normal School moved into a new campus, officials retrofitted the college's old building into the Wisconsin School of Mines.

The traditions of mining and railroading remained interwoven in the community for the next forty years. In 1910, a dozen trains with passenger accommodations

served its depots daily, except Sunday. The North Western operated two Galena–Madison trains in each direction through Platteville while the St. Paul Road operated four round-trips between the community and Calamine. Below the surface, small industrial railways operated within the cavernous expanses of the region's mines, including numerous tunnels within city limits, to support a new mining boom that revolved principally around zinc.

Changing Times

After the mining boom ended around 1918, the region's lead companies and railroads entered a long and excruciating period of decline. The rail passenger business ebbed due to rising competition from motor vehicles and a precipitous fall in population. In 1927, the North Western abandoned the Fennimore–Woodman segment—dooming the "Dinkey," its last narrow-gauge line in the state. Both carriers replaced their passenger trains to Platteville with self-propelled gas-electric cars, but the St. Paul quickly returned to steam after only a few months of operation in 1927. After plunging into bankruptcy, the carrier reorganized in 1928 as the Chicago, Milwaukee, St. Paul & Pacific Railroad (Milwaukee Road).

Unlike Platteville's railroads, the School of Mines fared comparatively well during the Great Depression. In 1936, the student body expressed their pride for the school by building an immense letter M on a mound outside of town. The concrete and stone letter measured more than 200 feet, making it the largest structure of its kind in the world. Unfortunately, however, the majestic image it projected belied the diminishing vitality of the mines working at great depths below. As production ebbed and highways improved, the North Western abandoned the portion of its line south of Hazel Green Junction in 1939, severing the route to Galena and leaving Madison as the only outlet for its local routes.

The industrial demands of World War II rejuvenated the county's railroads. Local Milwaukee Road and North Western trains handled many travelers on short-distance trips while the famed Zephyrs operating on the Chicago, Burlington & Quincy Railroad (Burlington Route) main line through East Dubuque, Iowa, shouldered a heavy burden of long-distance traffic. The Zephyrs between Minneapolis and Chicago remained popular after the war, but most of the region's other passenger trains soon passed into history. When the Milwaukee Road replaced its passenger train to Platteville with a mixed train around

1951 and the North Western ended local passenger service in 1952, the Burlington Route became the county's last operator of passenger trains.

As more mines closed and many small shippers turned their loyalties to trucks, the North Western razed nearly all of its stations in the area, including its wood-frame Platteville depot. The Milwaukee Road depot survived but no longer served travelers after the termination of mixed-train service in 1958. Nine years later, the North Western abandoned the remaining portions of its line to Galena south of Cuba City, pushing Platteville's railroad era ever closer to its demise.

The changes under way were not lost on a group of residents who joined the faculty at the university to support a municipal plan to create the Mining Museum. In 1968, they opened the museum in a former grade-school building directly above one of Platteville's abandoned mines. This institution acquired added significance the following year when the Elmo Mine closed, ending more than 130 years of lead and zinc mining in the county. These circumstance accelerated the need for Platteville to cultivate other forms of development, a process that took a notable step forward in 1971 when the former mining school (which twelve years before had become Wisconsin State College and Institute of Technology) became part of the University of Wisconsin system.

With the inception of Amtrak that year, the Zephyrs that had long graced the ex-Burlington Route main line (with stops in nearby Cassville) made their final runs, leaving the entire county without any rail passenger service. Although this route still hauled extensive tonnage, the routes serving Platteville gradually surrendered most of their freight-hauling roles. The Milwaukee Road razed its local depot and earned revenue in the community principally by delivering coal to the university's heating plant. It received approval to abandon its branch in 1974 and operated its last train to Platteville that same year.

To allow for the continued delivery of coal by rail to Platteville, university officials explored the possibility of building storage and unloading facilities along the North Western. The carrier, now reorganized as the Chicago & North Western Transportation Company, reportedly would not authorize such construction, possibly due to its interest in abandonment. Coal was instead barged to

Dubuque and trucked to the university campus.

Concerns about the future of rail freight service to Platteville were barely perceptible as carriers petitioned to eliminate vast amounts of track in Wisconsin. Over a twenty-year period beginning in 1976, carriers abandoned nearly 3,000 miles of routes in the state, putting Wisconsin near the top in total mileage eliminated during this period. By the late 1970s, the North Western was generating, on average, only a few carloads of freight each week in Platteville—mostly fertilizer and building materials. When the carrier petitioned to abandon its Platteville Branch and the rest of its lines in the region, it consequently encountered little opposition from municipal officials. In August 1980—only months after the railroad industry had been partially deregulated—it formally abandoned these routes.

Abandonment's Legacy

Soon a salvage crew removed the tracks, rendering Platteville one of the most populous municipalities in the state without a rail line. Recognizing the magnitude of its cultural and industrial heritage, the community took further steps to showcase the past. In 1981, the city opened the Rollo Jamison Museum in another former school building adjacent to the Mining Museum. The institution's collection grew to include hundreds of artifacts donated by Jamison, a native of Grant County, and other

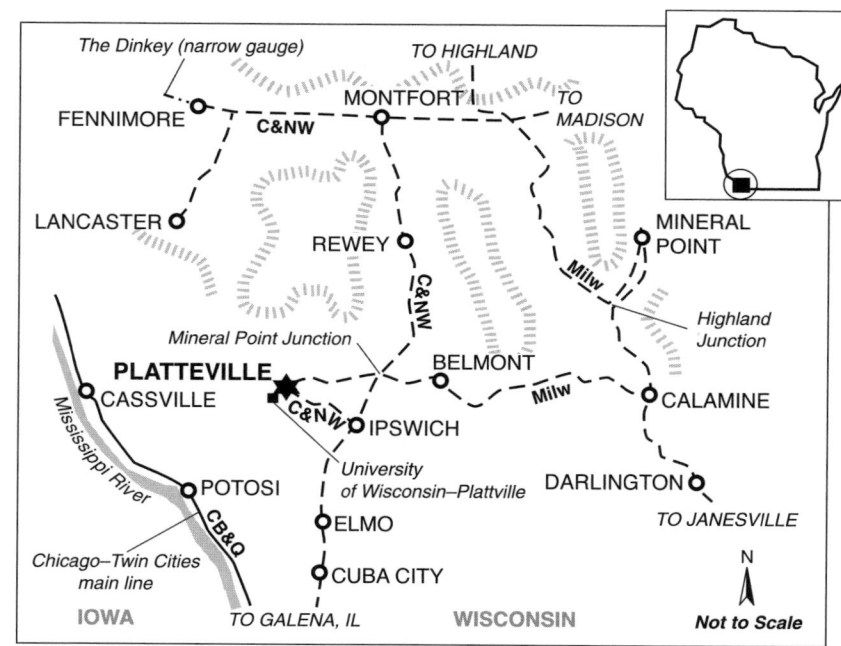

293

acquisitions of historical significance, including a former North Western switch stand, stove, and sign from the carrier's local depot. The Rountree Mansion was entered on the National Register of Historic Places in 1986, followed by the downtown district four years later.

The state government, meanwhile, acted upon citizen interest in converting abandoned rights-of-way into recreational trails. Having acquired most of the former Milwaukee Road branch to Platteville, the state fashioned the property into the Pecatonica State Park Trail. Several stretches west of Belmont, however, remained under private ownership, thwarting trail improvements and preventing the creation of a continuous rail-trail. Opposition from landowners also blocked an effort to convert the North Western route into a trail, although portions of this route were incorporated into the Ipswich Prairie State Natural Area.

Railroad enthusiasts in Platteville had a special fondness for an 11-acre entertainment complex with a nostalgic railroad theme that an entrepreneur opened in 1996 along the former North Western right-of-way. This complex, called Grizzly Flats, was decorated with a brightly painted caboose and a passenger car reportedly once used on the Twentieth Century Limited. It offered indoor amusements and railroad-related exhibits, including a mural depicting the community's former depots. The complex closed only a few years later, and the railcars were eventually moved away.

Today, travelers with an interest in railroad history will find that the depot in Belmont survives but is in poor condition. In Platteville, a rebuilt mining railway (equipped with a gasoline-powered locomotive dating back to the Great Depression) carries visitors across the Mining Museum's grounds. In Cuba City, a former North Western caboose is on display. The legacy of the North Western is more prominent in Fennimore, where the Fennimore Railroad Historical Society maintains a museum with a collection that includes a narrow-gauge locomotive built in 1907 and a replica of the local water tank that once served the Dinkey.

Epilogue

Platteville's example illustrates the extent to which heavy industry had declined in many midwestern towns by the mid-1970s, leaving many communities with negligible demand for rail service—a phenomenon felt more acutely in Wisconsin than in many states on the western

rail system. The absence of organized opposition to the abandonment of Platteville's rail lines exemplified how far this process had progressed by the time Congress approved the Staggers Act in 1980.

Today, downtown Platteville's resemblance to the central business districts of European communities clearly attests to the work of Rountree's surveyor many years ago. Although expanding enrollment at the University of Wisconsin–Platteville campus has been beneficial, and improvements to U.S. Route 151 bring the promise of improved mobility, the absence of high-quality transportation links remains a critical issue in the town's economic development. Platteville is more than 50 miles from an interstate highway or a commercial airport with jet service. The community's last regularly scheduled passenger service was a Greyhound bus that made its final run years ago between Milwaukee and the Mississippi— the route once envisioned for a railroad that would bring Platteville lasting transportation importance.

Unlike the rail systems in most midwestern towns, Platteville's routes skirted the community's periphery and crossed few streets. While historically minded travelers will see the immense letter M near the edge of town, they will encounter little more than concrete abutments from the North Western's bridge over Mineral Street to remind them of the railroad system that served the community for generations before slowly and quietly fading away.

For Further Study

SUGGESTED READINGS:

Condon, Gregg, Robert Felton, and James Nickoll. *The Dinkey: C&NW Narrow Gauge in Wisconsin.* Altoona, Wis.: Marsh Lake Publications, 1993.

Lanz, Daniel J. *Railroads of Southern & Southwestern Wisconsin: Development to Decline.* Monroe, Wis.: Daniel J. Lanz, 1985, 138.

OTHER PRINCIPAL REFERENCES:

Holford, Castello. N. *History of Grant County, Wisconsin.* Lancaster, Wis.: Teller Print, 1900, 557–58.

Hilton, George W. *American Narrow Gauge Railroads.* Stanford: Stanford University Press, 1990, 557– 58.

Interstate Commerce Commission. *Abandonment of Rail Service in Southwestern Wisconsin.* February 1976, 17, a-3.

Wisconsin Department of Transportation. *Wisconsin Railroad Plan.* February 1978, VII-46–VII-47.

STURGEON BAY, WISCONSIN (9,437)

Historic operator: Ahnapee & Western Railway
Last route abandoned: 1969
Notable reuses of right-of-way: Municipal park; Ahnapee State Park Trail

 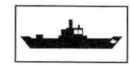 

For generations, shipbuilders and other industries in Sturgeon Bay depended on a short-line railway to haul passengers as well as coal and steel. Although their reliance on the railway eventually diminished, community leaders fought with great determination to prevent its abandonment, generating hundreds of pages of legal testimony in the process. Today, Sturgeon Bay's redbrick depot and earthen causeway, both bereft of their tracks, testify to the unwanted ending of this Great Lakes transportation saga.

Historical Perspective

Generations of the Potawatomi and Winnebago Indians traveled on foot across the Door Peninsula to avoid the treacherous waters at the tip of its rocky promontory. The trail they blazed was used later by notable seventeenth-century explorers, including the legendary Jacques Marquette, and eventually became an overland supply route between Lake Michigan and Green Bay.

Europeans did not permanently settle in this part of the Northwest Territories until Increase Claflin arrived in 1835. Claflin, a hardworking Englishman, established a trading post adjacent to Little Sturgeon Bay on land he had purchased from the federal government. More substantial forms of commerce came to the area after Captain Justin Bailey ordered his crew to make a desperate landing farther north on the peninsula during a fierce storm in 1848. The stranded sailors discovered marketable assets here, including large deposits of rock and tall stands of timber. After bringing their

discovery to the attention of Milwaukee financier Alanson Sweet, these men shipped extensive quantities of lumber and stone from Bailey's Harbor, an inlet north of Little Sturgeon Bay on the Lake Michigan side of the peninsula.

Migration to the more southerly parts of the area accelerated following the construction of a sawmill along the banks of Little Sturgeon Bay during the early 1850s. At this locale a community initially called Graham (later renamed Tehema) emerged, but its inhabitants found the harsh climate nearly intolerable, especially the Great Freeze of 1857, when they faced near starvation. They survived by the slimmest of margins and, in 1860, renamed their community Sturgeon Bay in honor of the plentiful fish in the adjacent body of water.

Sturgeon Bay prospered greatly from the rising quantities of cordwood shipped from its wharf after the Civil War. As logging companies felled the peninsula's tall stands of timber, arable land became available for growing apples, strawberries, peaches, cherries, and other fresh

An Ahnapee & Western freight train crosses the swing bridge and trestle over the ice-covered Sturgeon Bay Ship Canal, date unknown. The tank cars in this train probably carried fuel for lake-going vessels. (Photo by W. C. Schroader.)

fruit. By the time Sturgeon Bay became an incorporated community in 1876, it had a diverse economy supported by orchards, quarries, and commercial fishing.

Business leaders recognized that the community had the potential to become a prominent Great Lakes ship-building center and commercial port—provided they could persuade the U.S. Congress to appropriate funds for a canal between Lake Michigan and Little Sturgeon Bay. Consequently, there was great optimism when the federal government embarked on this massive earth-digging effort during the late 1870s. The completion of the canal in 1881—a milestone in Great Lakes commerce—gave vessels on Lake Michigan a safe and reliable route to the city of Green Bay.

The shipbuilding industry soon employed several thousand men and had a pressing need for rail service. On at least three occasions, though, efforts to attract a railroad to Sturgeon Bay ended in disappointment. The townspeople waited for more than a decade after the completion of the canal until the arrival of the first Ahnapee & Western Railway train in 1894, making Door County the last county in the state to gain access to a rail line. Sturgeon Bay greeted the moment with a celebration that attracted some 2,000 people.

The Ahnapee & Western originated at Casco Junction, an interchange point with the Kewaunee, Green Bay & Western Railroad near Luxemburg. It crossed the Kewaunee River and followed an inland route to the vicinity of Ahnapee (later renamed Algoma), where the line split into two branches. One branch terminated at the wharf in Ahnapee; the other extended north onto the Door Peninsula and crossed Sturgeon Bay on a wooden trestle and steel swing bridge. Trains on the second branch terminated on the west side of the city of Sturgeon Bay.

Within a few years of the line's completion, the county's railroad era rose to its zenith. Trains hauled extensive shipments of commodities and carload freight to shipbuilders and other businesses in Sturgeon Bay, as well as large outbound shipments of lumber and fresh fruit. Quarries also built their own private industrial railways for hauling rock to loading areas along the bay. By the early twentieth century, the Anhapee & Western hauled entire trainloads of cherries from town during harvest season.

Travelers also relied heavily on the Anhapee & Western. In 1914, the carrier greatly improved passenger service by introducing the Door County Special, a train operating between Green Bay and Sturgeon Bay and supported by an automobile service shuttling passengers to and from the peninsula's numerous resorts. Many travelers from Chicago and Milwaukee rode long-distance trains to Green Bay and then transferred to the Special, an arrangement that established rail service as a formidable competitor to steamships sailing along the western shore of Lake Michigan. Meanwhile, large vessels operated by the Ann Arbor Railroad between Frankfort and Menomonee, Michigan, added to the bustle of Sturgeon Bay life. These ships (called car ferries) carried both railcars and passengers through the canal, albeit without calling on the local port.

Sturgeon Bay rose in transportation prestige in 1923 by becoming the destination of a weekend Pullman sleeping-car service from Chicago, a service provided through the carrier's interchange in Green Bay with the Chicago & North Western Railway. By the decade's end, the community had grown to nearly 5,000 inhabitants and boasted one of the largest downtown districts in the northern part of the state. In 1931, it dedicated a new highway bridge over the bay that eliminated the need for motor vehicles and trains to share the swing bridge, which had been built principally for the railroad.

Changing Times

The decline of heavy industry brought considerable hardship to the Door Peninsula over the next several years. The Great Depression weakened the short line, its parent company (Green Bay & Western Railway), and the shippers that used its services. With shipbuilders and other companies scaling back production, and competition from buses and cars intensifying, the railroad ended regular passenger service in 1937 and razed its local engine house.

Even as Sturgeon Bay struggled, discontinuance of rail freight service remained an almost unthinkable concept. The railway brought fuel and other supplies to the massive Great Lakes vessels docking at the port, and handled a spectacular rise in tonnage during World War II. When the shipbuilding sector retooled to support the military effort, it produced boats desperately needed by the militaries of the United States and Great Britain to move troops and materials. Sturgeon Bay's shipyards expanded to employ more than 7,000 workers, many of whom lived in a pair of newly built residential complexes called Sunrise and Sunset. By the end of the war, the Sturgeon Bay Shipbuilding and Dry Dock Corporation—the community's leading employer—had produced eighty-five vessels for military use.

After the war, the railway continued to ship coal, petroleum, and steel, but traffic diminished by 1947 to the point that the Green Bay & Western expressed interest in abandoning the Algoma–Sturgeon Bay segment. That same year, the parent company sold the short line to V. M. Bushman of Green Bay, who was eager to interchange freight cars with the Ann Arbor Railroad. Bushman petitioned the Interstate Commerce Commission to require the company's ferries to call at the local port—an idea the Ann Arbor Railroad management strongly opposed. To the chagrin of both Bushman and the municipal government, the ICC ruled in favor of the

Only the causeway remains of the Ahnapee & Western near the former site of the Ship Canal bridge. A large vessel moored in the harbor attests to Sturgeon Bay's continuing maritime role. (Photo by author.)

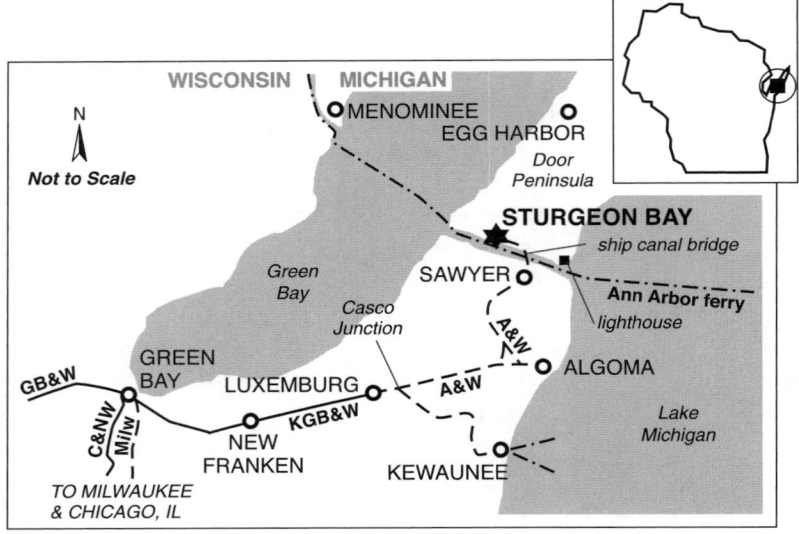

ferry operator in 1949. Bushman continued his push for a federal order requiring the vessels to serve Sturgeon Bay, but to no avail.

The short line usually ran three or four trains per week to Sturgeon Bay during the 1950s, but heightened competition from trucks, declining fruit shipments, and the 1964 closing of the Evangaline Milk Company (a producer of condensed milk) eventually diminished its commitment to the community. Adding to the railway's problems were its difficulties with the bridge over the bay—an aging span the company had sold to the city government for a nominal fee in 1966 but continued to use. After the lake vessel *Cherokee* struck and damaged the bridge in 1967, the railroad concluded that the span was no longer structurally safe and could not safely accommodate more than one loaded freight car at a time, rendering freight service woefully uneconomical.

Local shippers disputed the Ahnapee & Western's assessment of the bridge. Some dismissed it as a thinly veiled attempt to convince public officials to authorize the abandonment of the Algoma–Sturgeon Bay segment. The level of distrust escalated as the short line accused the municipal government of failing to meet its obligation to keep the bridge in good repair.

For those advocating the continuation of rail service, the timing of the alleged bridge failure could hardly have been worse. A severe recession buffeted the community's industry and precipitated a sharp drop in population. The outlook for the local railroad further deteriorated when the carrier removed the remainder of the Algoma–Sturgeon Bay segment from service in the summer of 1968 due to water damage that, it claimed,

further compromised the safety of train operations. The county's economic development agency and railroad customers, including the Door County Cooperative (which used rail service to receive feed and phosphate) questioned the carrier's motives and remained skeptical about the extent to which high water had damaged the route.

The debate entered its most contentious phase after the carrier received ICC approval to abandon the segment in June 1969. Assisted by an attorney, local shippers announced their intention to formally protest the decision before the commission, arguing that the cancellation of rail service the previous year had been illegal and had burdened shippers with more than $100,000 in additional costs.

Some alleged that this accusation was only a ploy to pressure the owner of the short line to sell the Algoma–Sturgeon Bay segment to local shippers or the city government at a favorable price. If this was indeed the motive, it failed to achieve its intended result.

Abandonment's Legacy

The route's abandonment rendered Door County the first county in Wisconsin to permanently lose rail service. Railroad companies distanced themselves farther from the peninsula in 1970, when the Ann Arbor Railroad's ferries made their final runs. The North Western published in its timetables the schedule of a bus operating from Green Bay to Sturgeon Bay, but this practice ended with the inception of Amtrak in 1971, when the last passenger trains departed Green Bay.

Over the next several years, travelers throughout the Midwest grew more interested in the serenity and scenic beauty of the peninsula. Eager to promote tourism, the state government created the Ahnapee State Park Trail on the abandoned right-of-way from Sturgeon Bay's southern periphery to Algoma. As part of a municipal beautification effort, the local government removed the movable bridge over the bay and transformed the adjoining causeway into Bayview Park—a civic amenity with a plaque commemorating the bygone short line. The city was also successful in having the downtown district listed on the National Register of Historic Places in 1983 and the canal's lighthouse added to the National Register the following year.

The Ahnapee & Western continued to operate between Algoma and Casco Junction and for several years even made its tracks available to a diesel-powered excursion operator called the Algoma Railroad. Problems with the Kewaunee River bridge in 1986, however, forced it to suspend all service.

By this time, the former Sturgeon Bay depot, which had not been included in the historic district, appeared headed for demolition. Many residents were grateful, therefore, when a private investor acquired this attractive masonry structure and converted it into the Cherryland Brewery and Del Santos Restaurant in 1987. To lend a nostalgic air to the property, the entrepreneur purchased for display a caboose reminiscent of those once used by Ahnapee & Western. After resolving problems related to the local zoning ordinance, he put the caboose in front of the station on tracks held together with spikes salvaged from the old railroad bridge. In the Sawyer neighborhood south of the bay, another former Ahnapee & Western station was transformed into an office for a water-softener supplier.

After the state equipped the trail with a crushed gravel surface in 1995, the 15-mile path emerged as one of the region's most heavily used tourist attractions. Real estate development and a sand quarry prevented the extension of the trail north into the center of Sturgeon Bay, but county planners eventually extended the trail southwest to Casco, creating a 31-mile amenity.

Epilogue

The Victorian facades of Sturgeon Bay's downtown district, together with the peninsula's natural charm, attract thousands of tourists during the summer season. Exhibits at the Door County Historical Museum showcase the community's industrial past, with an emphasis on ship-building and waterborne commerce. Farther east, the lighthouse on the canal is today one of Wisconsin's most widely photographed landmarks.

Along the northern banks of Sturgeon Bay, two commercial shipyards, each employing hundreds of workers, provide steady year-round employment. The county's flourishing tourism sector has contributed to the state government's interest in extending Amtrak service from Milwaukee to Green Bay with connecting bus service to Sturgeon Bay—an arrangement similar to the one promoted years ago by the North Western. Nevertheless, it seems significant that Sturgeon Bay, a community once having dedicated Pullman service, today has no scheduled passenger service at all.

Considering the Ahnapee & Western's enormous contributions to Sturgeon Bay's shipbuilding industry, it is a bitter irony that a wayward vessel ramming the railway bridge in this community precipitated the abandonment of service. Even so, the legacy of the railway can be felt in memories, memorabilia, and a variety of municipal landmarks, most notably in the causeway and depot. As recounted in many pages of ICC testimony, the town's struggle with rail service will remain an extraordinary part of its past.

For Further Study

SUGGESTED READINGS:

Mailer, Stan. *Green Bay & Western: The First 111 Years.* Edmonds, Wash.: Hundman Publishing, 1989, 124–47.

Specht, Ray, and Ellen Specht. "The Green Bay Route." *The Railway and Locomotive Historical Society Bulletin* 115 (1966): 53.

Zurawaski, Joseph W. *Door County.* Charleston, S.C.: Arcadia Press, 1998, 21–58.

_____. *Sturgeon Bay Shipbuilding.* Charleston, S.C.: Arcadia Press, 2001, 21–58.

OTHER PRINCIPAL REFERENCES:

Boque, Margaret Beattie. *Around the Shores of Lake Michigan: A Guide to Historic Sites.* Madison: University of Wisconsin Press, 1985, 212–17.

Forero, George A. *The Algoma Railroad Company.* Algoma, Wis.: Trans Northern, 1979, 1–8.

Hilton, George W. *The Great Lakes Car Ferries.* Berkeley, Calif.: Howell-North Books, 1962, 108–10.

Lewis, Edward A. *American Short Line Railway Guide.* Waukesha, Wis.: Kalmbach Publishing, 1996, 354.

RIVERTON, WYOMING (9,310)

Historic operators: Chicago & North Western Railway; Wyoming Tie & Timber Company
Last route abandoned: 1991
Notable reuse of right-of-way: Wyoming Heritage Trail

Riverton's livelihood for generations depended on the Wyoming Tie & Timber Company, which grew to become the nation's largest producer of railroad crossties. The company's entire output once supported the maintenance-of-way program of the Chicago & North Western Railway. Ironically, Riverton finally lost its rail service due to a local decision to withhold investment from a deteriorating route that needed thousands of new crossties and major repair of lengthy timber trestles.

Historical Perspective

Legendary mountain man Jedediah Smith led a small party of trappers along the Yellowstone and Bighorn rivers in late 1823. The contingent passed through the present-day Riverton area, reportedly filled their packs with pelts, and continued south through what is today central Wyoming. After reaching the Sweetwater River in early 1824, they turned west and came upon a relatively gentle route across the Continental Divide—the South Pass—which would become the principal route across the American West's rugged interior.

Another important chapter in western migration began when Captain Benjamin Bonneville led the first wagon train across this pass in 1832. Growing numbers of pioneers headed to the West soon made their way over this gentle route, which would become part of the famed Oregon Trail. Untold numbers took to the trail after the discovery of gold in the Sierra Nevada in 1848. Many paused along the

Sweetwater at Independence Rock to inscribe their names in stone.

The historic effort to build a railroad to California had profound and initially unfavorable implications for development in this part of the Wyoming Territory. When the Central Pacific and Union Pacific met in Promontory, Utah, in early 1869, attention shifted south to communities along the transcontinental line. Soon thereafter lengthy stretches of the Oregon Trail were obsolete.

Many years later, in 1888, the Wyoming Central Railway, an affiliate of the Fremont, Elkhorn & Missouri Valley Railroad, built west from Chadron, Nebraska, to Casper (formerly Fort Casper), bringing this outpost its most important transportation route since the glory days of the Oregon Trail. By the time Wyoming emerged as the nation's forty-fourth state in 1890, hundreds of settlers had created homesteads in the Casper area.

The presence of a Shoshone reservation along the Wind River prevented homesteading farther west on a large parcel of land near

300

present-day Riverton that was well suited for irrigation. An agreement with the Shoshone and Arapaho during the early twentieth century, however, gave the federal government the authority to distribute "surplus" parcels on the reservation north of the river to homesteaders, on the condition that all proceeds be given to the tribes. In 1906, this arable land was opened to settlers, and the Wyoming & North Western Railway, a Chicago & North Western (North Western) subsidiary, completed an extension of the rail line from Casper to a newly created town site along the Wind River. The carrier built a large combination freight and passenger depot in this emerging community—Riverton—that soon welcomed the arrival of scores of homesteaders eager to forge a new life on the frontier. These settlers produced bountiful crops by channeling the river's water into an elaborate system of irrigation ditches.

The North Western continued to build west and reached Lander that same year. Speculation arose that the granger road would extend this route more than 1,000 miles to the Pacific Coast. Although the carrier eventually scuttled the plan, it established Lander as its

principal gateway to Yellowstone Park and made it the destination of a Pullman sleeping car during the summer months, thus giving Riverton and other communities on the route direct service to places as far away as Chicago.

The booming economy of central Wyoming virtually guaranteed that other rail lines would arrive to market their services. In 1911, the Chicago, Burlington & Quincy Railroad (Burlington Route) began operating trains between Casper and southern Montana over a route that virtually paralleled the North Western for more than 80 miles. The Burlington's trains, however, reached no closer to Riverton than 20 miles, leaving the North Western as the sole source of rail transportation for many local businesses, including the Wyoming Timber Company. Only a few years after commencing wood-cutting operations in 1914, this company grew to

Only a few miles from the westernmost point on the entire railroad, a Chicago & North Western freight passes through the desolate terrain near Riverton in the early 1980s. The wires above the train allow the crew to determine whether the train's height exceeds clearances. (Photo by Rick Mills.)

A towering structure along the former Chicago & North Western route in River-ton (note the recreational trail at far left) brings to mind the railway's role in sugar-beet shipments. (Photo by author.)

more than 600,000 ties annually—for its maintenance of way program.

With its lumber and agricultural industries blossoming, Riverton became an important stop on the daily passenger train that made the 1,276-mile trip between Lander and Chicago—the longest passenger route on the carrier's system. Although the North Western replaced the passenger train with a gas-electric motorcar operating between Lander and Chadron in the early 1930s, the motorcar adhered to a schedule that allowed for well-timed connections to an Omaha-bound train at Chadron. A mixed train also worked the western end of the branch to Lander with a Riverton stop.

The gradual mechanization of the timber company's facilities helped Riverton maintain its status as one of the country's largest suppliers of railroad ties during the Great Depression. The opening of a new bank in 1934, the establishment of airmail service in 1938, and federal investments in rural electrification all suggested that prosperity would return. In 1939, residents gathered at the depot to greet the train carrying former President Herbert Hoover. By 1940, Riverton's population had grown to about 2,500—an increase of more than 33 percent in only ten years.

Changing Times

The profitable operation of a lengthy branch that served only a few communities, all of which had relatively small populations, became an increasingly tenuous proposition as economic circumstances changed. Although Riverton remained an important source of rail freight, the North Western severed its Lander Branch in 1941 by abandoning the 87-mile segment between Ilco (a junction near Casper) and Shoshoni (near Bonneville), a move made possible by an agreement allowing its trains to operate over the nearly parallel Burlington Route tracks.

After World War II pulled America into battle, the Lander Branch saw a dramatic rise in tonnage, as well as special trains bringing German prisoners of war to work at the timber company. While the gas-electric car stopped running in 1943, passengers could still travel on the mixed train to the Casper terminus or detrain in

become the community's principal source of livelihood

When U.S. presidential candidate William Jennings Bryan arrived by train in 1916 to give a speech, Riverton had every appearance of being a successful community. The timber company's expanding production provided stable employment for hundreds of men. The newly completed Wyoming Canal improved irrigation and allowed for record harvests of sugar beets. The Teton Hotel, a four-story masonry building opened in 1919 and reputed to be one of the finest guesthouses in the state, was the source of great community pride.

By the early 1920s, the timber company floated such large quantities of handsawn crossties down the river during the summer months that at times the waterway's surface could hardly be seen. Near Riverton, the lumber company's private narrow-gauge railway hauled ties from the river to a large yard for drying and preparation for outbound rail shipment. In 1917, the North Western hauled a 138-foot cylinder stretching across three flatcars—possibly the largest individual shipment in the history of the local branch—to be used by the lumber company to apply treatments of crude oil. Four years later, the carrier provided a loan to the lumber company, which changed its named to Wyoming Tie & Timber and grew to become the nation's largest producer of railroad ties. The company's documents suggest that the North Western purchased its entire output—

Bonneville and transfer to the Burlington Route's trains destined for southern Montana and Denver. As hard-surface roads improved, fewer and fewer travelers exercised these options. A commercial airline began flying from Riverton to Denver and Salt Lake City in 1947 as the mixed train faded into virtual irrelevance as a provider of passenger travel. The train made its last run four years later.

A slump in agricultural production raised difficult questions about the community's economy during the early 1950s, but both the discovery of large deposits of uranium in the Gas Hills east of town in 1953 and a resurgence in sugar beet production eventually ameliorated such concerns. As the economy boomed once again, the North Western tracks in Riverton bustled with activity for a final time, transporting large rigs on flatcars to support the uranium industry, as well as timber and beets.

Sagging lumber shipments and less sugar beet production, coupled with heightened competition from motor freight carriers, eventually ended the postwar renaissance. In 1960, the timber company came under new ownership and ended production of railroad ties. By 1968, the Burlington Route had operated its final Denver–Billings passenger train through Bonneville, limiting rail service in all of Fremont County to the conveyance of freight. In 1972, the North Western abandoned the segment from Riverton to Lander, rendering Riverton the westernmost point on its entire system. The employee-owned corporation, renamed the Chicago & North Western Transportation Company that year, then accelerated efforts to divest itself of unprofitable routes.

Adding to the North Western's interest in abandoning the branch to Riverton were cutbacks by the Louisiana–Pacific Corporation, the region's largest supplier of lumber. As traffic diminished, the carrier generally operated only one train per week over the deteriorating tracks west of Bonneville. Civic leaders, the municipal government, and the *Riverton Ranger* (a local newspaper whose newsprint was delivered by the railroad) felt strongly that preserving the route was an important community objective. In the 1980s, these officials enlisted the support of the governor and other elected officials to create a substantial amount of publicity in favor of saving the branch. The Wyoming legislature, however, upheld its policy of not providing funds for rail freight projects. (Over the twenty-year period beginning in 1976, Wyoming was one of only three states where no federal or state funds were directly appropriated for such projects.)

When the North Western operated its final train

from Riverton in September 1988, a small group of photographers recorded the event. The locomotive crew, accompanied by a reporter from the *Riverton Ranger* and several railroad enthusiasts, continued the unusual tradition of throwing candy to the children gathered alongside the tracks. The following month, the carrier sold the 26-mile segment between Shobon (near Bonneville) and Riverton to Bad Water Line, Inc., a unit of Bonneville Transloaders, Inc., a local shipper of soda ash. This newly created carrier evaluated but rejected the possibility of restoring service to Riverton, citing the deteriorating conditions of the tracks and of many of the line's twenty-two bridges and sixty-three culverts. The carrier considered the costs of rehabilitating the lengthy bridge over the river to be prohibitive and estimated the costs of repairing the entire line to be as high as $20 million.

The Bad Water Line's losses reportedly totaled $37,000 through January 1991. Thereafter, Fremont County, which once had been the nation's largest supplier of railroad ties, found itself in the ironic position of having to decide whether to take responsibility for the maintenance and operation of a route saddled with aging crossties and timber bridges. The county commissioners voted unanimously to refuse an offer to purchase and operate the line. That same year, the short line ended service west of Shoshoni and abandoned all but the first 3

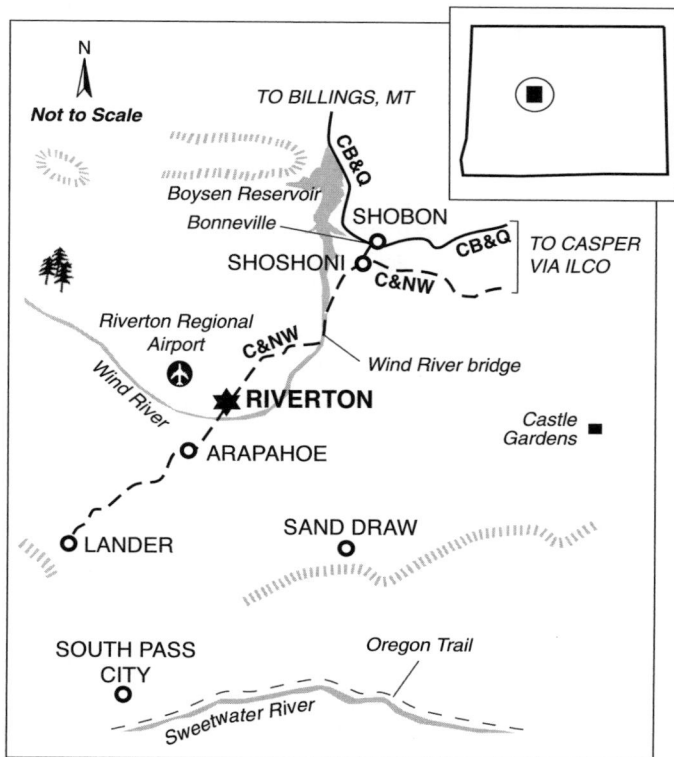

303

miles of this 25-mile segment, formally bringing River-ton's railroad era to an end. The removal of the tracks was soon under way.

Abandonment's Legacy

County and local officials identified the Riverton–Shoshoni segment as a potential recreational trail and found this idea supported by Bonneville Transloaders. The company donated the right-of-way to a nonprofit organization through the guidelines established by the National Trails System Act, and funded a government-mandated evaluation of the line. The Fremont County Farm Bureau and other groups maintained that the rail-trail initiative violated the rights of those holding title to the land, including members of the Arapaho and Shoshone tribes. After resolving these concerns, the county completed the Wyoming Heritage Trail—the first rail-trail in the state—with the support of private benefactors.

Distant echoes of the railroad era could be heard in 1997. That year, the Riverton Museum launched an unsuccessful effort to purchase a former Wyoming Tie & Timber steam locomotive for a historical display, and Bonneville Transloaders reopened 3 miles of dormant track west of Shoshoni for fertilizer shipments. Since then, memories of the railroad have fallen further from recollection.

Today, the storefronts on Main Street stand as reminders of Riverton's heritage as a frontier boomtown. The community's well-maintained depot remains a particular source of civic pride. The community used grant funding and volunteer labor to convert this wood-frame structure into a restaurant and Chamber of Commerce office during America's bicentennial year. The landmark has been listed on the National Register of Historic Places since 1978 and is today flanked with several hundred feet of track and a former North Western caboose. Although agriculture and lumber are major contributors to the local economy, all shipments are conveyed by truck. The uranium mines are now closed.

Epilogue

Many visitors pass through Riverton on their way to Independence Rock, the South Pass, and other storied locations on the Oregon Trail. The heritage of the community's railroad corridor is modest in comparison to the overland route to the south, but agricultural structures alongside the abandoned rail grade and its numerous bridges, especially the Wind River span, enhance its historical appeal.

Riverton today struggles to provide travelers with viable alternatives to the automobile. Despite the opening of a spacious new airport terminal in 1998, air service rests precariously on provisions of the federal Essential Air Service program. The community is near the geographic center of the largest state without a regularly scheduled passenger train. Riverton, consequently, is farther from an Amtrak station—more than 300 highway miles—than just about any other city of its size on the American mainland. Bus service to Lander, Rawlins, and Rock Springs has gone the way of the railroad, leaving only a motor coach operating twice daily to Shoshoni, a far cry from the Pullman-equipped trains operating to Chicago at the height of the North Western's glory.

For Further Study

SUGGESTED READINGS:

Grant, H. Roger. *The North Western: A History of the Chicago & North Western Railway System.* DeKalb: Northern Illinois University Press, 1996, 91–92, 174, 226.

Riverton: The Early Years. Riverton, Wy.: Riverton Historical Research Committee, 1991, 7–94.

OTHER PRINCIPAL REFERENCES:

Bartles, Mike, Bill Kratville, Rick Mills, and Jerry Penry. *The Chicago & North Western Cowboy Line: A History of the Longest Rail-to-Trail Project in America.* David City, Neb.: South Platte Press, 1998, 5–21.

Maiken, Peter T. *Night Trains: The Pullman System in the Golden Years of American Rail Travel.* Baltimore: Johns Hopkins University Press, 1989, 198.

Potter, Janet Greenstein. *Great American Railroad Stations.* New York: Wiley & Sons, 1996, 536.

CLOSING THOUGHTS

For residents of both large and small communities of the West, there can be little doubt that rail line abandonment holds implications well beyond a reduction in transportation alternatives. When the railroad leaves town, it alters the appearance and character of corridors that have been focal points of daily life for generations, routinely bringing forth controversial and unexpected developments. These events continue to affect communities for years following the departure of the last train.

The extraordinary experiences of communities featured in this book show how unpredictable the consequences of rail line abandonment can be. Government agencies monitoring the railroad divestment process can nonetheless glean several notable lessons from their examples. For rural towns separated by long distances from major cities, abandonment is frequently an impediment to the development of agribusiness and other forms of industry. In urbanized areas, on the other hand, abandonment often comes in the midst of robust expansion and, in some situations, actually facilitates growth by making land available for real estate development. In the largest metropolitan areas, the key issues surrounding rail line abandonment often center on the ability of towns to restore their links to regional rail-transit systems.

Abandonment takes its greatest toll on those railroad terminals and division points that lack other sources of jobs. In these locales, the outcome is often a gradual but largely unavoidable devolution to much smaller and less successful communities. For most communities, however, the negative consequences attached to the loss of the railroad are not as great as town leaders feared.

Former Oregon & Northwestern track withers away on desolate terrain near Burns, Oregon, a route that once generated extensive lumber shipments. (Photo by author.)

A streamlined passenger car glistens in the sun on an abandoned portion of the Peavine—the former Santa Fe route to Phoenix—in Prescott, Arizona, during 2002. (Photo by author.)

Arkansas, and Okemah, Oklahoma, experienced a discernable drop in population (and apparently employment as well) after the departure of their last train. Although it is arguable whether the availability of rail service would allow these towns today to attract a significant amount of new industry, the absence of service is clearly a component of their lingering economic development problems.

Nevertheless, large-scale governmental financial support to allow for the continuation of rail service in most of these communities would have been difficult to justify. As a general rule, if a rail freight line has little chance of becoming financially self-sufficient, merely subsidizing the operator for lengthy periods of time is not considered to be an effective regional transportation strategy. The experiences of Burns, Oregon, and Mineral Wells, Texas, clearly illustrate the risks of investments in rural lines with uncertain revenue potential.

A more compelling case can be made for supporting rural rail lines that are operated (or are sought to be operated) by companies who have the resources and management expertise for developing new sources of revenue. Unlike the years when businesses flocked to railroads, attracting new customers today often requires long planning horizons and significant marketing sophistication—and usually a high degree of coordination between private and public entities. The routes to Issaquah, Washington, and Ferriday, Louisiana, as well as the towns along the former Chicago & North Western Cowboy Line through northern Nebraska and central Wyoming would have been especially good candidates for long-term development through a public-private partnership.

The evidence is overwhelming that narrow-gauge lines could not have remained viable transportation corridors even with significant government financial support. The current market potential of these bygone corridors, however, merits consideration. Several communities in this volume, most notably Gunnison, Colorado, and Farmington,

Rural Towns versus Urban Towns

The absence of a railroad remains a sensitive topic in many rural towns of the Great Plains states. It is in these towns that abandonment has often fostered a sense of isolation. In this book, the profiles of Currie, Minnesota; Hot Springs, South Dakota; Long Pine, Nebraska; and Watford City, North Dakota, highlight the difficulty of cultivating new forms of economic development in such thinly populated areas. Each of these communities, as well as the more southerly towns of Booneville,

306

A Denver & Rio Grande Western flanger trains heads south out of Alamosa on March 20, 1963. Narrow-gauge service over this historic segment, which had dual-gauge track at the time, ended in 1969. (Photo by Tom Gildersleeve.)

New Mexico, might well have been able to support rail service today had their rail operators made the investment years ago to widen the tracks to standard gauge. In evaluating the legacy of rail service to these towns, George Hilton's observation that carriers could have recouped their investment from the conversion of more lines to the prevailing national standard seems particularly relevant.

Communities in urbanized areas have far less at stake from the loss of rail freight service than those in rural regions. Most of these towns no longer draw their livelihood from agriculture or heavy industry; many are today successful suburbs with diverse residential and commercial sectors. The absence of rail service in these places primarily affects a town's management of economic development that is already well under way. In many towns featured in this volume, including Carpentersville, Illinois; Issaquah, Washington; and Vacaville, California, there is a great deal of synergy between the local economy and that of other communities in their vicinity.

Regardless of a town's economic orientation, public officials usually expected that the economic effects of rail line abandonment would be far worse than they ultimately proved to be. Most towns, especially those in nonagricultural regions, found new sources of economic vitality, often in ways few expected when the last railroad departed. For example, in the West, the expansion of tourism allowed the local economies to overcome the decline of more traditional industry in Aspen and Gunnison, Colorado; Red Lodge, Montana; and Kerrville, Texas. Outdoor recreation has helped revitalize Ely, Minnesota; Sturgeon Bay, Wisconsin; and other declining industrial towns in the Great Lakes region. In Decorah, Iowa, and Platteville, Wisconsin, the expansion of colleges has helped offset the effects of a decline in industrial employment.

Communities with attractive climates or pleasing amenities, especially those in states experiencing rapid population growth, have fared particularly well in adjusting to the loss of railroad service. Today, officials in Prescott, Arizona, and Boulder City and Carson City, Nevada, for example, generally voice little concern over the absence of rail freight service. To help fuel local economic development, they instead look to the growth of small businesses and government agencies, which in most situations can be adequately served by motor carriers.

A less charitable fate awaited former railroad division points that had not previously attracted other forms of economic development. For the foreseeable future, Avery, Idaho; Harlowton, Montana; Laws, California; and Long Pine, Nebraska, have little chance of seeing population or employment returning to the levels achieved years ago. Even more striking, Glenwood, California, and Promontory, Utah, have ceased to be viable communities.

Although these communities saw little or no industrial development after the departure of their last train, the argument in favor of state or federal intervention solely to preserve railroad jobs was tenuous at best. Economists generally hold that the loss of transportation jobs in one location tends to be offset by job gains in others. State governments evaluating the impending abandonment of rail lines apparently share this view; none of the states evaluating rail service to the communities featured in this volume considered railroad jobs in its assessment of the benefits and costs of keeping trains running.

When viewed in their entirety, the experiences of the fifty-eight communities featured in this book suggest that the economic effects of abandonment depend heavily on circumstances unique to each town. Some of these circumstances are physical, such as the town's proximity to highways and population centers capable of providing support services. Others are less tangible and include the level of political leadership and the presence of stable institutions to anchor a community through turbulent times.

Physical Remnants

From the prairies of Illinois to the shores of Oahu, the transformation of old railroad corridors into retail areas, parks, and roads offers a poignant illustration of people's capacity to reshape environments to meet the demands of contemporary times. While research for this book was under way, commercial strip development in some towns erased nearly all trace of the notable railroad routes of the past. In other towns, the creation of recreational trails marked a new beginning for corridors that long ago saw the passage of their final trains. The pace of recreational-trail development in the West, however, lagged behind that taking place in the East. Staunch opposition from landowners, especially on the Great Plains, as well as low population densities doomed or delayed many initiatives to create trails.

Observant travelers following bygone rights-of-way will find stark contrasts between former railroad towns in various parts of the country. Many eastern towns emerged years before the arrival of their first trains and therefore had well-established economies by the time the railroad era began. In contrast, many western communities came into being only a few years before, or as a result of, the construction of a rail line. These towns reflect the influences of railroad companies in a more profound way, with railroad stations more likely to be located at the heart of town, former yards and rights-of-way tending to be more centralized and spacious, and the street grids more likely to possess features commonly associated with railroad towns. Harlowton, Montana, is perhaps the quintessential example of a community with such a development pattern.

Another notable difference between East and West is the sheer number of rail lines built to rural towns. Western communities tended to have fewer rail lines, rendering the abandonment of each line a matter of stronger municipal concern. Greater distances between towns also limited the frequency of local passenger service and made mixed trains (rather than conventional passenger trains) a more common part of each town's railroad history. The low population densities of the West, however, also impaired the construction of hard-surface roads and allowed passenger service to remain viable far longer than in many eastern towns of comparable size.

Compared to towns featured in the eastern volume of this set, fewer great passenger trains of the past—or even regularly scheduled Amtrak trains—have left their mark on the western communities that today lack railroads. It seems ironic, therefore, that passenger trains are poised to return in a greater number of towns highlighted in this volume than in the first volume. California, in particular, has taken an active role in preserving routes to allow for extensions to regional light-rail or commuter-rail systems. Today, the routes to Folsom, Monterey, Santa Monica, and San Rafael are poised to become modern passenger corridors. By choosing to let the abandonment of routes run its course, other communities have watched potential avenues for a rail-passenger-service renaissance slowly disappear.

Keeping Options Open

At this writing, the future of rail service in hundreds of towns rests precariously on the ability of local railroads to make improvements to support the movement of 286,000-pound freight cars, which are rapidly becoming the industry standard. Railroads also bear the burden of public policies that have the effect of subsidizing other modes of transportation. Unlike trucking companies, with which railroads compete and which operate over tax-exempt highways, or barge operators, which operate over taxpayer-supported waterways, private railroads must cover the costs of property taxes on their rights-of-way (except in instances where they operate over government-owned corridors). Although state property taxes account for a relatively small share of total railroad operating costs, such levies constitute a significant obstacle to providing service to small towns in states like Illinois and New York, where railroad property taxes are comparatively higher.

Distortions in the system of fees paid for using highways also threaten to derail rail service to many locales. Federal studies show that the heaviest trucks (that is, those weighing in excess of 70,000 pounds) generally pay only about 60 percent of their fully allocated highway costs. There is a virtual consensus among policy analysts that these vehicles do not pay their full share of the cost of maintaining and improving roads. The federal government's reliance on fuel taxes and vehicle registration fees is partially responsible for these implicit subsidies. Nevertheless, efforts to substitute a system of fees based on a truck's gross weight along with the number of miles it travels lack strong political support, due in part to concerns about the associated administrative costs.

Whether government institutions will adopt policies that significantly improve the outlook for lightly used railroad routes remains to be seen, but policies that keep our railroad options open are attracting greater political support now than in the past. Intensified efforts by a coalition of politicians to provide grants and loans for short-line railroads and Class I freight carriers suggest that some constituencies previously unreceptive to railroad issues are becoming more attentive to these concerns. As the problems of highway congestion and inadequate capacity on main-line railroads grow, policymakers will undoubtedly look to light-density routes to help solve a broad range of mobility issues.

Even as railroads respond to the challenge of handling rising freight and passenger volumes, the inexorable demands of the marketplace will push still more historic routes toward oblivion. Some of these corridors may eventually be called back into service while others will be left to quietly wither away. No matter their destiny, from the Atlantic to the Pacific, old railroad rights-of-way will continue to open a window to a community's past. With high embankments, historic stations, graceful viaducts, and gentle curves, these routes can bring us back, if only in our thoughts, to a colorful transportation era that millions so fondly remember. Though memories of trains may fade, the corridors left behind will remain forever woven into the fabric of community life.

APPENDIX
PRESERVING INTERCITY CORRIDORS

More than a dozen communities featured in the two volumes of *When the Railroad Leaves Town were along corridors whose abandonment ended the opportunity for direct rail service between metropolitan areas with populations of 100,000 or more. In these locales, abandonment had implications extending beyond the needs of local shippers and potentially altered the flow of commerce between much larger population centers.*

Before the Staggers Act was passed, few public agencies saw much need to intervene in the abandonment process with the explicit goal of preserving direct railroad routes between metropolitan areas. Governmental officials generally relied on market forces or the ICC abandonment process to foster the preservation of routes linking major cities. In some instances, the presence of multiple rail routes along most major corridors lulled officials into believing that rail service would always be available between cities.[1]

Analysis suggests that between 1940 and 1979 the railroad industry eliminated direct rail routes in only eleven corridors between major metropolitan areas. Among the most notable corridors losing their direct rail lines prior to Staggers were Santa Cruz–San Jose, Baltimore–Annapolis, Harrisburg–Baltimore, Fort Myers–Sarasota–Bradenton, and Indianapolis–South Bend. Direct rail routes are defined as those connecting metropolitan areas with populations of at least 100,000 and involving travel distances of at least 25 miles. Loss of direct rail service meant that rail distances were at least 15 percent (or 50 miles) longer due to closures or abandonments, and were at least 20 percent (or 70 miles) longer than associated highway distances.

As private railroads launched major initiatives to reduce their physical plant following the passage of the Staggers Act in 1980, abandonment began to have more significant effects on the structure of the intercity rail system. Public officials, in turn, adopted more ambitious policies to manage transportation capacity and service quality.[2]

Between 1979 and 1995, the number of intercity corridors that had experienced the partial abandonment or closure of all direct rail routes rose from eleven to at least forty. Three of those corridors—Indianapolis–Dayton–Columbus (part of the former Pennsylvania Railroad route between Pittsburgh and St. Louis), Raleigh–Richmond (part of the former Seaboard Air Line Railway main line between Virginia and Florida), and Cincinnati–Washington, D.C. (the former Baltimore & Ohio Railroad route via Parkersburg, West Virginia)—had been used by Amtrak trains only a few years before their abandonment. Readers of railroad history will recognize these corridors as the former routes of the Spirit of St. Louis, the Silver Star, and the National Limited, respectively. Amtrak still operates trains between Raleigh and Richmond and between Cincinnati and Washington but on indirect routes that were 44 and 60 miles longer, respectively, than other railroad routes that had once linked these cities.[3]

Abandonments also severed other notable long-distance routes in the south and south central regions, including Little Rock–Oklahoma City–Amarillo (Chicago, Rock Island & Pacific Railroad), Nashville–Knoxville (Tennessee Central Railway and Southern Railway), and Tampa–Tallahassee (Seaboard Coast Line via the Perry Cutoff), despite policymakers' interest in preserving them for long-distance freight service. These corridors, too, had once been along the route of notable passenger trains.

Numerous short-distance corridors that had been important passenger routes well into the post-World

War II era ceased having active rail lines capable of providing direct service. Notable among these corridors are San Francisco–Monterey (Southern Pacific), New York–Scranton (Delaware, Lackawanna & Western Railroad), and Philadelphia–Bethlehem/Allentown (Reading Railroad and Lehigh Valley Railroad or Central Railroad of New Jersey). These routes may be familiar as the former routes of the Del Monte Express, Phoebe Snow, and Scranton Flyer.

All of the aforementioned routes are discussed in the community profiles appearing in this volume or in the companion volume on the eastern United States. Portions of most routes are legally abandoned. Others are now under the stewardship of state and local governments and protected as future transportation corridors. Still others are preserved as rail-trails through the National Trails Act. Along a few corridors, only a short stretch of track is out of service, while along others much of the right-of-way is obstructed by residential and commercial development.

At this writing, more intercity corridors are also at risk of losing their most direct rail lines. The eastern end of the old Southern Pacific's Los Angeles–Phoenix route, used by Amtrak's Sunset Limited through 1996, has been of particular concern to many rail travel advocates in that region.[4] The most direct routes from Denver to Albuquerque and Phoenix also hang in the balance due to the uncertain future of the former Atchison, Topeka & Santa Fe main line through Raton Pass.[5]

Recognizing the implications of the loss of corridors, public agencies are today substantially more active in preserving intercity routes than years ago. They have gradually shifted attention away from more traditional concerns (such as fostering industrial development in small towns) toward more comprehensive corridor management objectives.[6] Increasingly, railroads are viewed as an integral component of planning efforts that aim to lessen the need for additional highway capacity within or between expanding metropolitan areas.

Evaluating Intercity Corridors

Using a simple forecasting tool, a general estimate was developed of the relative amount of passenger traffic (point-to-point travel on highways or via air carriers) in each of the corridors that had lost their direct rail links.[7] A summary of the findings appears in table 1. All of the corridors listed in the table are described in greater detail in this volume or the companion volume devoted to the eastern United States.

The information presented in the table suggests that government agencies responded to the effects of abandonment on intercity routes in understandable ways during the Staggers Act era, devoting their attention principally to preserving rights-of-way in corridors with the heaviest travel volume. In six of the eleven corridors with the heaviest travel volume but without a currently active direct rail line, public agencies have assumed stewardship of the rights-of-way or worked with railroads to preserve the integrity of the rights-of-way corridors.

On the basis of this method of analysis, one would expect that the Philadelphia–Bethlehem–Allentown and the New York–Scranton routes (having the highest traffic volumes) would be among those acquired by public agencies—and they are.[8] Also as expected, public agencies have preserved substantially fewer routes that ranked lower in travel demand. In ten of the fifteen most heavily traveled corridors, government agencies have studied scenarios for rebuilding or reopening the abandoned or out-of-service rail lines. In seven instances, there have been significant investments in right-of-way acquisitions or full-scale feasibility assessments for restoring freight or passenger service. In the Raleigh–Richmond/Washington corridor (partially abandoned), state governments are actively exploring the potential of establishing high-speed passenger service.

Of course, this particular analytical approach offers only a selective look at the investments made by public agencies to preserve or expand capacity in intercity corridors. With some notable exceptions, many short-haul routes appear to have little potential for freight development at present, while many long-haul routes apparently have minimal passenger carrying potential. Furthermore, it focuses only on the status of corridors currently linking metropolitan areas without direct rail lines in active service; this is only one small dimension of a much broader policy issue. The evaluation does not consider the mix of freight and passenger traffic, which is critical to any comprehensive evaluation of corridor preservation. None of the aforementioned city pairs, it should be emphasized, are among the nation's most heavily used freight or passenger corridors.[9] Nevertheless, the results show clearly that abandonment has done far more than eliminate either redundant routes or those routes serving only small communities.

Table 1: Intercity travel corridors losing all direct rail lines (Ranked by estimated total passenger-miles[a])

Route (Rail Corridor Served)	Year Lost[b]	Status	Discussion[c]	Funds[d]	Historic Operators[e]	*When the Railroad Leaves Town* (vol. and pg.)
New York–Scranton	1982	Partially abandoned[f]	Y	Y	DL&W	1:178
Philadelphia– Bethlehem & Allentown	1990s	Sold to public agency	Y	Y	RDG–CNJ+	1:253
Cincinnati– Washington & Baltimore	1988	Partially abandoned	N	N	B&O	1:312
Santa Cruz– San Jose & San Francisco	1940	Partially abandoned	Y	Y	SP	2:45
San Francisco–Santa Rosa[g]	1980	Sold to public agency	Y	Y	NWP	2:70
Monterey– San Jose & San Francisco	1989	Sold to public agency	Y	Y	SD&AE	2:55
San Diego– Phoenix & Tucson	1979	Sold to public agency[h]	Y	Y	SP	2:34
Indianapolis– Dayton & Columbus	1981	Partially abandoned	N	N	PRR+	1:79
Baltimore–York–Harrisburg	1975	Partially abandoned	N	N	PRR	1:119
Hartford–Providence	1967	Partially abandoned	Y	N	NH	1:273
Raleigh– Richmond & Washington	1986	Partially abandoned	Y	Y	SAL–RF&P	1:303
Tampa–Tallahassee	1989	Partially abandoned	Y	N	SAL–ACL	1:30
Des Moines–St. Louis	1991	Partially abandoned	Y	Y	Wabash	1:163
Indianapolis–South Bend	1973	Partially abandoned	N	N	PRR+	See note[i]
Nashville–Knoxville	1986	Partially abandoned	Y	Y	TC–SOU	1:283

a. Routes are ranked on the basis of total estimated passenger-miles (highway and air) from highest to lowest.
b. Indicates the year a portion of the corridor was abandoned, severed, or removed from service.
c. Indicates whether a public agency has formally issued a document indicating interest in restoring service in the corridor.
d. Indicates whether a public agency has invested in feasibility studies or property acquisition to facilitate restoring service in the corridor.
e. Lists railroads providing corridor service in 1940. In this table, the plus sign (+) indicates corridors also once served by an electric intraurban railway. See 1:xxiv and 2:xxxi for lists of carrier abbreviations.
f. The abandoned segment was acquired by New Jersey in the 1990s. DL&W operated from Hoboken, New Jersey.
g. Ferry transfers provided in Marin County.
h. Portions of this corridor remain out of service.
i. The southern end of the interurban railway route between these cities, operated by the Indiana Railroad, is mentioned in *When the Railroad Leaves Town,* 1:69–70.

ENDNOTES

1   In the years before the Staggers Act, public or quasi-public entities made few significant financial investments in intercity routes threatened with abandonment aside from the large federal investment in Conrail. Perhaps the most notable exception to governmental indifference was Amtrak's acquisition in 1976 of a portion of the former Michigan Central corridor between Chicago and Detroit following the recommendation by the United States Railway Administration (USRA) that this route be excluded from Conrail. Another noteworthy example involves Penn Central's decision to remove 12 miles of former Boston & Albany track near Rensselaer, New York. Although this required Amtrak to use a more circuitous route between Boston and Albany between 1975 and 1979, when the missing track was rebuilt, it did not constitute the loss of a direct route on the basis of the criteria used here.

2. The 1990 Intermodal Surface Transportation Efficiency Act in particular provided impetus for agencies to engage in long-range rail planning in response to growing congestion on highways and heightened environmental concerns.

3. The former C&O route between Cincinnati and Washington used by Amtrak, while having certain operational advantages over the severed B&O route, is about 56 miles longer.

4. The efforts of Union Pacific to eliminate a lengthy portion of this former passenger route east of Wellton, Arizona, have far-reaching implications for those interested in the resumption of Amtrak service to the Arizona capital. Due to the survival of the former AT&SF route between Phoenix and Los Angeles via Parker, Arizona, however, this would not result in the loss of direct rail service (on the basis of the criteria previously described).

5. Most transcontinental freight on the former Santa Fe now moves over the Belon Cutoff through Amarillo, Texas, leaving the Raton Pass route—a corridor used by the Southwest Chief—with only modest freight tonnage.

6. Although various government agencies have conducted demand forecasts to assess the amount of travel in several of these corridors, these forecasts do not lend themselves to inter-route comparisons. The most widely circulated numbers are those published in the Bureau of Transportation Statistics' American Travel Survey (ATS).

7. The gravity model forecasts are based on an exponential function of the populations located at the endpoints of the corridor and the distance between these endpoints. The model does not consider the trip-generating potential of intermediate cities. It also omits from consideration local economic conditions, political boundaries, demographic characteristics, quality of service, weather, and the price of travel, which can sharply affect demand. Nevertheless, the model reduces demand estimates to a few observable and quantifiable variables and appropriately recognizes that travel volume declines as travel distance increases.

8. This portion of the analysis was limited to corridors involving metropolitan areas separated by at least 25 miles. The model suggests that the Philadelphia–Bethlehem corridor generates the greatest number of daily travelers in corridors without an active rail line, while the New York–Scranton corridor generates the greatest number of passenger miles of travel.

9. The Bureau of Transportation Statistics' America Travel Survey shows that New York–Scranton has the highest travel volume of the corridors listed. During 1995, it ranked 54th in total travel volume. The ATS estimates, however, are subject to considerable measurement error.

ADDITIONAL REFERENCES

T*he following references, sorted alphabetically by community, are among the more significant government reports, company documents, newspaper articles, newsmagazine features, pamphlets, videos, and other ancillary sources used in this historical compilation.*

Aspen, Colorado: Paul Anderson, *Aspen: Portrait of a Rocky Mountain Town* (Aspen, Colo.: Who, 1992), 1–20; *Aspen Times,* 23 January 1969, 1-C, 6 February 1969, 7-C, 20 February 1969, 11-B; Citizens Transit Design Committee and Howard R. Ross Associates, *Light Rail Transit: Community Criteria for Final Design* (Aspen, Colo.: Pitkin County, 1975); Colorado Department of Transportation (CDOT), Federal Highway Administration, *Record of Decision: State Highway 82—Entrance to Aspen: Project STA 082A–008* (Denver: CDOT, 1998); Colorado Department of Transportation, *Colorado Passenger Rail Study,* January 1997, 2–24; *Railnews* 403 (June 1997): 82.

Astoria, Oregon: *Daily Astorian,* 16 January 1967; Oregon Department of Transportation, *Oregon Rail Plan: 1986 Update,* 4–17; D. C. Jesse Burkhardt, *Backwoods Railroad* (Pullman: Washington State University, 1994), 134–37; "Lewis & Clark Bicentennial Celebration," *Wheel Clicks.* Quarterly Publication of the Pacific Railroad Society, March 2003, 1; Oregon Department of Transportation, *2001 Oregon Rail Plan,* 1–20; Peter T. Maiken, *Night Trains: The Pullman System in the Golden Years of American Rail Travel* (Baltimore: Johns Hopkins University Press, 1989), 303; Rails-Trails Conservancy, *Trailblazer* (July–Sept. 1997): 5; Don Thomas, "Facelifting A-102-6 Youngs Bay Draw Span:" *The Dope Bucket: Magazine of the Spokane, Portland & Seattle Railway* 23, no. 1 (Spring 1961): 2–5.

Avery, Idaho: Mark Hemphill, "A Railroad Too Far: Remembering Milwaukee Road's Lines West." *CTC Board,* no. 157 (March 1988): 47; U.S. Forestry Service, "Route of the Hiawatha Rail-Trail Fact Sheet," January 1998, 1–2.

Beverly Hills, California: Electric Railway Historical Association of Southern California, "A Guide to the Electric Traction Heritage of the Los Angeles Region," accessed at http://www.erha.org on 15 April 2003; "Track Bulletin: Commuter/Transit," *Railnews,* no. 404 (July 1997): 70; *Los Angeles Times,* 2 April 2000.

Booneville, Arkansas: *Booneville Democrat,* 1 November 1979; Oklahoma Department of Transportation, *Oklahoma State Rail Plan Update: 1981,* V-37–V-42; *Oklahoma Journal,* 11 November 1967; *Southwest Times Record* (Fort Smith), 20 November 1981; "Toy Factory Comes to Booneville," *The Rocket: Publication of the Rock Island Lines* 39, no. 5 (Sept.–Oct. 1969): 2; Ed Wojtas, "When Rock Meant Rocket," *Passenger Train Journal* 10, no. 7 (Sept. 1973): 19–30.

Bothell, Washington: George Werkema, "The Sumas Connection: The Other Line to the Border," *CTC Board Railroads Illustrated,* no. 279 (Jan. 2002): 18–23; *Northshore Citizen,* 15 July 1982, A3; Seattle Department of Parks and Recreation, "Burke Gilman Trail," 1997; *Seattle Times,* 5 March 1992, 10 February 1999, 28 May 1999, 20 September 1999, 10 November 2001; *The Enterprise* (Bothell), 12 February 1997.

Boulder City, Nevada: "Union Pacific at Boulder City, Nevada," *The Railway & Locomotive Historical Society Newsletter* 18, no. 1 (Winter 1998): 11.

Burns, Oregon: *Burns Times-Herald,* 17 January 1990, 7 February 1990.

Carpentersville, Illinois: *Carunal Free Press,* 11 March 1981, 20 July 1981, 2 September 1981; Joe Piesen, "C&NW's Real Estate Department." *North Western Lines* 29, no. 1 (Summer 2001): 36–43; Illinois Department of Transportation, *Illinois Rail Plan: 1985 Update,* VI-10.

Carson City, Nevada: Janet Greenstein Potter, *Great American Railroad Stations* (New York: Wiley & Sons, 1996), 509; John Gruber, "V&T to be Rebuilt," *Trains* 62, no. 11 (Nov. 2002): 91–92.

Coronado, California: *Coronado Journal,* 2 January 1969; "News from San Diego," *SP Trainline* (Summer 2000): 6; Fred Wert, *Rail-Trail Guide to California* (Seattle: Infinity, 1995), 155; "Short Stuff," *Pacific News* 18, no. II (Nov. 1978): 26.

Cripple Creek, Colorado: Colorado Department of Transportation, *Colorado Passenger Rail Study,* January 1997, I-55–I-56.

Currie, Minnesota: Heather Taylor, *Where the Trains Are!* (Rocklin, Calif: Prima, 1996), 170–72.

Decorah, Iowa: *Cedar Rapids Gazette,* 13 August 1977; *Decorah Journal,* 25 August 1938; *Decorah Public Opinion,* 18 December 1946, 20 September 1979, 18 October 1979; "Rock Island: Farewell Decorah," document dated November 1963, collection of Gillmer Seegmiller, I–3; Iowa Department of Transportation, *Iowa Rail Plan,* March 1978, 52.

Ely, Minnesota: Edward A Lewis, *American Short Line Railway Guide* (Waukesha, Wis.: Kalmbach, 1996), 107; Minnesota Department of Transportation, *Minnesota State Rail Plan: 1981–1982,* 58.

Española, New Mexico: State of New Mexico Highway and Transportation Department, *Abandoned Railroad Rights-of-Way Analysis for New Mexico* (1996), 92–93; *Rio Grande Sun,* Commemorative Edition, 2 July 1998.

Eureka Springs, Arkansas: "Eureka Springs: Healing History and the Healing Arts." *The Flashlight Visitors Guide* (April 1997): 9–11; Clinton E. Hull, *Shortline Railroads of Arkansas* (Norman: University of Oklahoma Press, 1969), 49–52.

Farmington, New Mexico: Elinor M. McGinn, "Sixty Years on the Durango-Aztec-Farmington Branch Railroad (1905–1965)," Collection of the Farmington Public Library, I–14; George W. Hilton, *American Narrow Gauge Railroads* (Stanford: Stanford University Press, 1990), 344–53; State of New Mexico Highway and Transportation Department, *Abandoned Railroad Rights-of-Way Analysis for New Mexico* (1996), 101; Grace Barker Wilson, "The Denver and Rio Grange Railroad in the San Juan Basin: On the Occasion of the Transfer of the Denver & Rio Grande Railroad's Right of Way to Aztec, Farmington and San Juan County, June 2, 1971," collection of the Farmington Public Library, I–8.

Ferriday, Louisiana: Bob Karsen, "Mo-Pac's Navy-Part I," *Railfan & Railroad* 4, no. 7 (1982): 40–47; *Concordia Sentinel,* 6 June 1990; George Drury, *The Historical Guide to North American Railroads* (Milwaukee, Wis.: Kalmbach, 1995), 176–77; Louisiana Department of Transportation and Development, *Louisiana State Rail Plan Update 1988,* 19–20; "MoPac's Bayou Streamliner," *National Railway Bulletin* 61, no. 5/6 (1996): 34–40.

Folsom, California: Garth G. Groff, "The Folsom State Prison Railroad." *Narrow Gauge & North Line Gazette* (May/July 1991): 18–22; *Sacramento Bee,* 28 September 2001.

Fredericksburg, Texas: *Fredericksburg Standard,* 18 March 1998; *Hill Country Times,* October 1988, 16–17.

Glenwood, California: *Aptos Times,* 1 April 1996; Dick Houghton, "SP's Picnic Line," *Trains* 8, no. 9 (July 1948): 46–51; *Los Gatos Weekly Times,* 17 January 2001; Jon Pullman Porter, "60 Years Mark The Passing of Southern Pacific's Mountain Line," accessed at http://www5.pair.com/rattenne/nrhs/santacruz/ on 27 September 2003.

Gunnison, Colorado: John Krause, "The Last Roundup at Parlin," *Railfan* I, no. 8 (1976): 42–46; Mallory Hope Ferrell, *Colorado & Southern Narrow Gauge* (Boulder Colo.: Pruett, 2003), 11–18.

Harlowton, Montana: Michael P. Malone, *James J. Hill: Empire Builder of the Northwest* (Norman: University of Oklahoma Press, 1996), 232; Montana Department of Highways, *State of Montana Rail Plan,* August 1979, A-80–A-81.

Honolulu, Hawaii: *Honolulu Star Bulletin,* 21 September 1946; "Honolulu Rapid Transit System," Lee & Elliott Company, accessed at http://www.leaelliott.com/ on 12 April 2001.

Hot Springs, South Dakota: "Abandonments," *Pacific News* 260 (June 1994): 6; Ed Ripley, "Dakota, Minnesota & Wyoming," *Railnews* 423 (Feb. 1999): 78–79; *Casper Star-Tribune,* 21 March 1998; Frank Wilner, "STB's Tangible Test: Interest Grows in Third Alternative to BNSF, UP from Powder River Basin," *Traffic World* (19 July 2000): 31–35; "Gold in the Black Hills," *Rails to Trails* (Fall 1998): 8–13; *Hot Springs Star,* 16 March 1944; Jay Jorensen, with Rick Mills, "Passenger Service in the Black Hills," *North Western Lines* 20 (2): 22–34; *Rapid City Journal,* 26 September 1998; South Dakota Department of Transportation, *Railplan South Dakota,* 1978, 173.

Issaquah, Washington: "Issaquah Railway History Chronology," collection of the Issaquah Historical Society, 2000, I–2; Thomas Strand, "Snoqualmie Branch '45," *The Mainstreeter: The Official Publication of the Northern Pacific Railway Historical Association* 20, no. 4 (Fall 2001): 4–13; Warren Wing, *To Seattle by Trolley* (Edmonds, Wash.: Pacific Fast Mail, 1988), 78.

Kerrville, Texas: *Kerrville Daily Times,* 29 December 1991; *Mountain Sun,* 20 May 1970.

Lake Geneva, Wisconsin: George W. Hilton and John F. Due, *The Electric Interurban Railways in America* (Stanford: Stanford University Press, 1964), 342; J. David Ingles, "Remembering, and Learning," *Trains* 50, no. 4 (April 1991): 5–6; Wisconsin Department of Transportation (WDOT), *Wisconsin State Rail Plan, January 1981,* VII-11; WDOT, *Wisconsin State Rail Plan: 1982 Update,* VII-12–VII-13;

Lakewood, Colorado: *Rocky Mountain News,* 6 June 2001, 18 June 2001.

Laws, California: Bishop Museum & Historical Society, "Laws Railroad Museum" (document prepared for the Laws Railroad Museum and Historical Site), 3.

Long Pine, Nebraska: Hazel Schmidt, "Long Pine," document available from the Long Pine Heritage House Museum; Nebraska Game and Parks Commission, "The Cowboy Trail: Update September 1996," Lincoln, Nebr., 1–9.

Lynnwood, Washington: George W. Hilton and John F. Due, *The Electric Interurban Railways in America* (Stanford: Stanford University Press, 1964), 342; *Seattle Times,* 1 October 1999.

Mineral Wells, Texas: "Baker Hotel," documents of the Mineral Wells Chamber of Commerce; *Mineral Wells Index,* 30 September 1992, 16 October 16, 1992; Gene Fowler, "Mineral Wells: The Town That Crazy Built," *Texas Highways* 40, no. 6 (June 1993): 18–25.

Monterey, California: Bob McVay, "Streetcars in Monterey," *Pacific Rail News* 250 (June 1984): 5–6; *Monterey Peninsula Herald Weekend Magazine,* 30 April 1989, 10–13; Transportation Agency for Monterey County, *San Francisco–Monterey Train Service Implementation* (1994), 22–37; *Railnews* 401 (April 1997): 3–7; Kyle Wyatt, "Monterey & Salinas Valley," *Slim Rails: Southern Pacific Narrow Gauge Society* 2, no. 3 (Feb. 1982); "SP Monterey Branch," *The Ferroequinologist* (Jan. 1995): 3–9.

Newport Beach, California: Steve Donaldson, "The Ocean Wharf and Depot at Newport Beach," *Trainline: A Publication of the Southern Pacific Historical and Technical Society* 10 (June 1985): 3–9; *Railroad Right-of-Way Evaluation Project* (Los Angeles: Southern California Association of Governments, 1989).

Nome, Alaska: Howard Clifford, *Alaska Adventures, Wyatt Earp and Friends* (Seattle: Sourdough Enterprises, 2000), 55–68; Charles O. Cole, "Gold Rush Railroad," *Alaska Sportman* (Oct. 1953): 12–14, 33–34.

Okemah, Oklahoma: Edwin C. McReynolds, *Oklahoma: A History of the Sooner State* (Norman: University of Oklahoma Press, 1954), 266–69.

Park City, Utah: Utah Department of Transportation, *Utah State Rail Plan,* 1978, 100–102; Janet Greenstein Potter, *Great American Railroad Stations* (New York: Wiley & Sons, 1996), 522–23.

Placerville, California: *Mountain Democratic* (Placerville, Calif.), 22 April 1996, 25 May 1998, 2 March 2001.

Platteville, Wisconsin: Wisconsin Department of Transportation, *Wisconsin Railroad Plan,* January 1981, VI-6.

Port Angeles, Washington: American Association of State Highway and Transportation Officials, *803 Successes: National Conference of State Railway Officials,* April 1987, 6–10; "Historical Society: Past, Present, Future," *Strait History: Quarterly Publication of the Clallam County History Society and the Museum* 2 (1): 1–2; U.S. Army Corps of Engineers, *Ports of Port Angeles, Everett, Anacortes, and Bellingham, Washington,* 1987, 2–3, 28–29; Washington Department of Transportation, *Washington State Rail Plan: 1982 Update,* 83.

Prescott, Arizona: Arizona Department of Transportation, *Arizona State Rail Plan: 1985 Update,* 94–123; Bob P. R. Griswold, *Arizona's Railroads: Arizona Traveler Guidebooks* (Phoenix, Ariz.: Primer Publishers, 1992), 14.

Promontory, Utah: National Park Service. *Proposal to Construct a Tourist Rail Operation Between Ogden and Promontory Summit.* National Park Service Briefing Statement, 2 August 1996, 1–2.

Red Lodge, Montana: Montana Department of Highways, *State of Montana Railroad Plan,* August 1979, A-81.

Riverton, Wyoming: *Riverton Ranger,* 2 September 1988, 16 September 1988, 30 January 1991, 20 February 1991, 8 March 1991; Edward A. Lewis, *American Short Line Railway Guide* (Waukesah, Wis.: Kalmbach, 1996), 37; "Shortlines," *CTC Board Railroad Illustrated* 286 (Aug. 2002): 14; Wyoming State Highway Department, *Wyoming State Rail Plan: Technical Supplement,* July 1980.

San Rafael, California: Golden Gate Bridge, Highway and Transportation District, "Briefing Paper on Northwestern Pacific Railroad Right-of-Way Acquisition" (1997), 2–3; "Marinship: NWP's Major Wartime Customer," *The Northwesterner: Semi-Annual Publication of the Northwestern Pacific Railroad Historical Society* 15, no. 2 (Fall-Winter 2001): 15–20; *Sonoma-Marin Transportation and Land Use Study* (Berkeley, Calif.:

Calthorpe Associates, 1997), 4; *The Headlight: A Publication of the Northwestern Pacific Railroad Historical Society*, various issues, 1999–2003.

Santa Monica, California: "A Guide to the Electric Traction Heritage of the Los Angeles Region," 2003, accessed at http://www.erha.org on 1 May 2003; *Los Angeles Times*, 2 April 2000, 19 June 2001; Electric Railway Historical Association.

Sausalito, California: George Drury, *The Historical Guide to North American Railroads* (Milwaukee, Wis.: Kalmbach, 1995), 240–44; "Sausalito Tourist Railroad Approved," *The Western Railroader* 36, no. 396 (April 1973): 3–12; Fred Wert, *Rail-Trail Guide to California* (Seattle: Infinity, 1995), 40–51.

Seaside, Oregon: "Fantrip," *The Dope Bucket: Magazine of the Spokane, Portland & Seattle Railway* 19, no. 4 (Autumn 1957): 4; Oregon Department of Transportation, *Oregon Rail Plan: 1986 Update*, 4–17; *Seaside Signal*, 20 November 1969, 10 May 1979, 24 June 1999; "The Railroad To Seaside: A Chronological Listing of Notes," Collection of the Seaside Historical Museum, June 1995.

Sturgeon Bay, Wisconsin: *Door County Advocate*, 11 August, 1894, 10 June 1969, 26 June 1969; Interstate Commercial Commission, *Finance Docket No. 25126*, 7 January 1969, 1–22.

Tombstone, Arizona: James R. Doughty, "The San Pedro & Southwestern," *Railfan & Railroad* 16, no. 11 (Nov. 1997): 40–45; "Shortlines," *CTC Board*, no. 300 (Oct. 2003): 9; *Tombstone Epitaph*, 5 May 1996.

Vacaville, California: Caltrains, *California State Rail Plan: Map Supplement*, 1982, 14.

Valley Falls, Kansas: Atchison, Topeka and Scenic Railroad, Inc., *The Conductor: The Official Publication of the Atchison, Topeka and Scenic Railroad*, April 1993, 1–4; Kansas Department of Transportation, *Kansas State Rail Plan 1996*, 100; *Valley Falls Vindicator*, 16 August, 1992.

Virginia City, Nevada: Lucious Beebe and Charles Clegg, *The Trains We Rode* (New York: Promontory, 1965), 106, 766–67, 803.

Wallace, Idaho: *Gold Strikes and Silver Linings* (Wallace, Idaho: Silver Valley Economic Development Corporation, 1995), 1–11; Idaho Department of Transportation, *Idaho Rail Plan Update* (1981), G-15; Robert Darwin, "Wallace...footnote," *The Streamliner: The Official Publication of the Union Pacific Historical Society* 8, no. 4 (1993): 29.

Watford City, North Dakota: *McKenzie County Farmer*, 24 September 1981, 9 April 1997. "Line Sales," *Railnews* 420, (Nov. 1998); Frank N. Wilner, "Just the Way It Is: Retiring North Dakota PSC Commissioner Hagen has been Fighting Transport Monopolies for 40 Years," *Traffic World* (27 November 2000): 12–13.

West Branch, Iowa: "Annual Raccoon Valley Railway Museum Meeting Held," *West Branch Times*, 15 October 1981, 5; "Greater Iowa Railway and Museum," *West Branch Times*, 12 November 1981; Iowa Department of Transportation, *Iowa Rail Plan*, March 1982, 49–51.

SELECTED BIBLIOGRAPHY

Armbruster, Kurt E. *Orphan Road, The Railroad Comes to Seattle, 1853–1911.* Pullman: Washington State University Press, 1999.

Association of American Railroads. *Railroad Facts.* Washington, D.C.: Association of American Railroads, 1995.

————. *Statistics of Regional and Local Railroads.* Washington, D.C.: Association of American Railroads, 1988.

Best, Gerald M. *Railroads of Hawaii: Narrow and Standard Gauge Common Carriers.* San Marino, Calif.: Golden West Books, 1978.

Black, William R. *Railroads for Rent: The Local Rail Service Assistance Program.* Bloomington: Indiana University Press, 1986.

Bryant, Keith L., Jr., ed. *Railroads in the Age of Regulation, 1900–1980.* Encyclopedia of American Business History and Biography series. New York: Bruccoli Clark Layman, 1988.

Conant, Michael. *Railroad Mergers and Abandonments.* Los Angeles: University of California Press, 1964.

Crump, Spencer. *Ride the Big Red Cars: How Trolleys Helped Build Southern California.* Los Angeles: Crest Publications, 1962.

Demoro, Harry W., and Vernon J. Sappers. *Rails to San Francisco Bay.* New York: Quadrant Press, 1992.

Derleth, August, and H. Roger Grant, eds. *The Milwaukee Road: Its First Hundred Years.* Iowa City: University of Iowa Press, 2001.

Drury, George H. *The Historical Guide to North American Railroads.* Milwaukee, Wis.: Kalmbach Books, 1985.

Due, John F. *The National Experience with New Small Railroads Formed to Take Over Abandoned Rail Lines 1971–1984.* University of Illinois at Urbana–Champaign, 1984.

Due, John, and S. D. Leever. "The Post-1994 Experience with Small and Regional Railroads." *Transportation Journal* 33 (1993): 40–52.

Edson, W. D. *Railroad Names.* Potomac, Md.: William Edson, 1993.

Fickewirth, Alvin A. *California Railroads.* San Marino, Calif.: Golden West Books, 1992.

Fogel, Robert W. *Railroads and American Economic Growth: Essays in Econometric History.* New York: Johns Hopkins University Press, 1964.

Grant, H. Roger. *Getting Around: Exploring Transportation history.* Melbourne, Fla.: Krieger Publishing, 2002.

————. *The North Western: A History of the Chicago & North Western Railway System.* DeKalb: Northern Illinois University Press, 1996.

Gross, Joseph. *Railroads of North America.* Spencerport, N.Y.: Joseph Gross, 1986.

Hilton, George W. *American Narrow Gauge Railroads.* Stanford: Stanford University Press, 1990.

Hilton, George W., and John F. Due. *The Electric Interurban Railways in America.* Stanford: Stanford University Press, 1964.

Hofsommer, Donovan L. *The Southern Pacific: 1901–1985.* College Station: Texas A&M, 1986.

Jenson, Oliver. *American Heritage History of Railroads in America.* New York: Wings Book, 1993.

Keeler, Theodore E. *Railroads, Freight, and Public Policy.* Washington, D.C.: Brookings Institution, 1993.

Krieger, Michael. *Where Rails Meet the Sea.* New York: Metro Books, 1998.

LeMassena, Robert L. *Rio Grande. . . . To the Pacific!* Denver: Sundance Limited, 1974.

Lewis, Edward A. *American Shortline Railway Guide.* 5th ed. Waukesha, Wis.: Kalmbach Publishing, 1996.

Lewis, R. G. *Handbook of American Railroads.* New York: Simmons-Boardman, 1951.

Maiken, Peter T. *Night Trains: The Pullman System in the Golden Years of American Rail Travel.* Baltimore: Johns Hopkins University Press, 1989.

Martin, Albro. *Railroads Triumphant: The Growth, Rejection, and Rebirth of a Vital American Force.* Oxford: Oxford University Press, 1992.

McFarland, H. B. "Railroad Abandonment Policy in the 1990s." *Transportation Practitioners Journal* 58 (1991): 331–40.

Myrick, David F. *Railroads of Arizona.* Vol. 2, *Phoenix and the Central Roads.* Berkeley, Calif.: Howell-North Books, 1963.

————. *New Mexico's Railroads: A Historical Survey.* Albuquerque: University of New Mexico, 1990.

————. *Railroads of Nevada and Eastern California.* Vol. I,

The Northern Roads. Berkeley, Calif.: Howell-North Books, 1962.

Norwood, John B. *Rio Grande Narrow Gauge: From Birth to Abandonment.* River Forest, Ill.: Heimburger House, 1983.

Nielsen, Waldo. *Right-of-Way: A Guide to Abandoned Railroads in the United States.* Bend, Ore.: Maverick, 1992.

Overton, Richard C. *Burlington Route: A History of the Burlington Lines.* New York: Knopf, 1965.

Potter, Janet Greenstein. *Great American Railroad Stations.* New York: Wiley & Sons, 1996.

Renz, Louis Tuck. *The History of the Northern Pacific Railroad.* Fairfield, Wash.: Ye Galleon Press, 1980.

Sanders, Richard, Jr. *Merging Lines: American Railroads, 1900–1970.* DeKalb, Ill.: Northern Illinois University Press, 2001.

Schwieterman, Joseph P., and Elaine M. Crowley, "Keeping Track: An Inventory of Rail Service to U.S. Urban Areas." *Transportation Quarterly* 50 (1986): 65–78.

Stilgoe, John R. *Metropolitan Corridor: Railroads and the American Scene.* New Haven: Yale University Press, 1983.

Stindt, Fred A. *The Northwestern Pacific Railroad.* Redwood City, Calif.: Fred A. Stindt, 1964.

Stover, John F. *American Railroads.* Chicago: University of Chicago Press, 1961.

U.S. Bureau of the Census. *Historical Statistics of the United States, Colonial Times to 1970, Part 2.* Washington, D.C.: U.S. Goverment Printing Office, 1975.

Wilner, Frank N. *Railroad Mergers: History, Analysis, Insight.* Omaha, Neb.: Simmons-Boardman, 1997.

Wood, Charles R. *The Northern Pacific: Main Street of the Northwest.* Seattle: Superior Publishing, 1996.

Zlatkovich, Charles P. *Texas Railroads.* Austin: University of Texas, 1981.

ABOUT THE AUTHOR

Joseph P. Schwieterman, Ph.D., is professor of public services management and director of the Chaddick Institute at DePaul University. He has published extensively on air, rail, and urban-planning issues and is a long-standing contributor to the Transportation Research Board. Schwieterman holds a master's degree in transportation from Northwestern University and a doctoral degree in public policy studies from the University of Chicago. He is a member of the National Railway Historical Society and the Railway & Locomotive Historic Society (R&LHS). His article "Abandoned Corridors" was a finalist in the R&LHS's 2003 David P. Morgan Award for excellence in the interpretation of railroad history.

INDEX

Note: "m" following page numbers = "map"
"p" following page numbers = "photograph"